ENCYCLOPEDIA OF
WORLD CONSTITUTIONS

Volume II

ENCYCLOPEDIA OF
WORLD CONSTITUTIONS

Volume II

(Gabon to Norway)

EDITED BY GERHARD ROBBERS

An imprint of Infobase Publishing

Encyclopedia of World Constitutions

Facts On File, Inc.
An imprint of Infobase Publishing
132 West 31st Street
New York NY 10001

Library of Congress Cataloging-in-Publication Data
Encyclopedia of world constitutions / edited by Gerhard Robbers.
p. cm.
Includes index.
ISBN 0-8160-6078-9
1. Constitutions. 2. Constitutional law. 3. Comparative law. I. Robbers, Gerhard.
K3157.E5E53 2006
342.02—dc22   2005028923

Text design by Erika K. Arroyo
Cover design by Cathy Rincon

Printed in the United States of America

VB Hermitage 10 9 8 7 6 5 4 3 2 1

This book is printed on acid-free paper.

Contents

Entries G to N

GABON

At-a-Glance

OFFICIAL NAME
Gabonese Republic

CAPITAL
Libreville

POPULATION
1,389,201 (2005 est.)

SIZE
103,346 sq. mi. (267,667 sq. km)

LANGUAGES
French (official), Fang, Myene, Nzebi, Bapounou/Eschira, Bandjabi

RELIGIONS
Christian 55–75%, animist 4%, Islam less than 1%

NATIONAL OR ETHNIC COMPOSITION
Bantu tribes (including four major tribal groups: Fang 33%, Sira, Nzebi, and Mbete 50%), others 17%

DATE OF INDEPENDENCE OR CREATION
August 17, 1960 (from France)

TYPE OF GOVERNMENT
Semipresidential

TYPE OF STATE
Unitary state

TYPE OF LEGISLATURE
Bicameral parliament

DATE OF CONSTITUTION
March 26, 1991

DATE OF LAST AMENDMENT
August 19, 2003

The Gabonese regime is characterized by the dominant position of the president of the republic (the head of state). Gabon's current president, Albert Bernard Bongo, has been in office since 1967. The constitution of 1991 legalized opposition parties. Gabon is officially a representative democracy, a democratic and social republic that respects the principle of the separation of the powers. The Gabonese constitution includes a long list of fundamental rights and principles and refers to human rights declarations. The Parliament is bicameral, with the lawmaking process predominantly carried out in the National Assembly. The Constitutional Court plays an essential role.

CONSTITUTIONAL HISTORY

Interest in the lucrative slave trade attracted Europeans to Gabon from the 15th century. The French eventually won a dominant position, notably with the agreement of the Mpongwe ruler in 1839. From 1910 to 1957 Gabon was part of French Equatorial Africa. After World War II (1939–45) it became an overseas territory of France.

Gabon declared its independence from France on August 17, 1960, and Leon Mba became its first president. Albert Bernard Bongo succeeded him in 1967. The following year, Bongo declared Gabon a one-party state under his new party, the Gabonese Democratic Party. Bongo was returned to office in every subsequent presidential election.

The 1988 election was followed by a period of major political and civil discontent. A transitional constitution in May 1990 legalized opposition parties, and multiparty legislative elections were held for the first time in 22 years. The ruling Gabonese Democratic Party won the elections, but the opposition accused them of electoral fraud. The constitution of March 26, 1991, replaced the interim arrangements of 1990. The new constitution aimed to give more transparency to the electoral process and also to reform governmental institutions. Bongo won the first presidential election under the new constitution in 1993; he was again accused of fraud.

The constitutional reform of 1995 tried to reduce election fraud, while introducing major reforms, such as the creation of a bicameral parliament (the National Assembly and the newly created Senate). The constitutional reform of 1997 created the office of vice president of the republic and increased the presidential term of office from five to seven years. The last reform of the constitution in 2003 allowed the president to be reelected several times.

FORM AND IMPACT OF THE CONSTITUTION

The Republic of Gabon has a written constitution contained in one single document with 120 articles. The structure of the Gabonese constitutional text corresponds to the structure of the current French constitution.

The Gabonese constitution refers in its preamble to the 1789 French Declaration of the Rights of Man and the Citizen, the 1948 Universal Declaration of Human Rights, the 1981 African Charter of the Rights of Man and the Rights of Peoples, and the 1990 National Charter of Liberties. These texts have constitutional force.

BASIC ORGANIZATIONAL STRUCTURE

Gabon is a unitary state. The country is divided into nine provinces, which are subdivided into 36 prefectures and eight separate subprefectures. The president of the republic appoints the provincial governors, the prefects, and the subprefects.

LEADING CONSTITUTIONAL PRINCIPLES

The predominance of the president of the republic is characteristic of the Gabonese regime. The constitution proclaims Gabon to be a democratic and social republic. It affirms the principles of national sovereignty; separation of the executive, legislative, and judicial powers; and a state of laws.

The principle of republican government is delineated in the Gabonese constitution as an untouchable principle. It cannot be the object of any constitutional amendment.

Finally, Gabon is a representative democracy. The possibility of referendums does exist for the revision of the constitution, for the "referendum laws," and for any modifications of Gabonese territory.

CONSTITUTIONAL BODIES

The predominant constitutional body in Gabon is the president of the republic. The other important bodies are the administration, consisting of the prime minister and the Council of Ministers; the bicameral Parliament; and the judiciary, including the Constitutional Court. The constitution also provides a National Council of Communication and an Economic and Social Council, which is to be consulted in all economic, social, and cultural development issues.

The President of the Republic

The president of the republic is the head of state and the most powerful figure in Gabon. The president is elected by direct universal suffrage for a seven-year term and can be reelected many times. Since independence in 1960 only two autocratic presidents have ruled the country. Gabon's current president, Bongo, has dominated the country since 1967.

The president is the supreme holder of the executive power, which the president shares with the prime minister. A vice president of the republic, whom the president appoints, assists the president. The president appoints the prime minister and, upon the latter's advice, appoints or dismisses all the other members of the executive administration. The president also chairs the Council of Ministers. The president promulgates the adopted laws and may submit to referendum any bill of law touching certain topics.

The Gabonese constitution provides for the dissolution of the National Assembly by the president of the republic after consultation with the prime minister and the presidents of the two chambers of the Parliament.

The Executive Administration

The prime minister and the cabinet ministers compose the executive government, which administers the policy of the nation. The prime minister is responsible to the president of the republic and to the National Assembly. The prime minister heads the executive government, directing its actions and ensuring the execution of the laws. The executive government meets in the Council of Ministers, which is chaired by the president of the republic.

The Parliament

The Gabonese Republic has a bicameral legislature with a National Assembly and a Senate. The National Assembly is the central representative organ of the people on the national level. Its members are elected for five years by direct universal suffrage. Currently it has 116 members. The National Assembly can adopt a motion of censure or deny its confidence to the prime minister, who must then submit the cabinet's resignation to the president.

The Senate is the chamber of representation of the local communities It currently has 91 members. The senators are elected for six years by indirect universal suffrage.

The Parliament's main activity is making laws. It meets by right in the course of two sessions per year, and in extraordinary session by request of the president of the republic or the absolute majority of its own members.

The Lawmaking Process

The constitution distinguishes between laws and regulations. Parliament can pass laws only in the areas determined in Article 47—for example, the exercise of fundamental rights and duties of citizens or the organization of the civil state. Parliament and the administration can both initiate legislation. Any bill must be examined successively by the National Assembly and the Senate, which must adopt identical texts. In case of disagreement between the two chambers, the prime minister may summon a mixed commission composed of deputies and senators. If the disagreement persists, the administration presents the bill to the National Assembly for a final decision. Thereby, the administration has an active role during the lawmaking process.

Legislative matters that do not belong to the field of law have the character of regulation. These regulations are adopted by decree of the president of the republic.

The Judiciary

According to the constitution and the separation of powers, the judiciary is independent of the legislative and executive branches. The president of the republic guarantees this independence with the assistance of the Superior Council of the Magistrature.

The judicial system is composed of two high courts, the Judicial Court and the Administrative Court, each with tribunals and courts of appeal below it. The Judicial Court has jurisdiction in civil, commercial, social, and penal matters; the Administrative Court deals with administrative matters and is consulted during the lawmaking process.

There are also a Constitutional Court, a Court of Accounts (for the control of the public finances), a High Court of Justice (for violation of oath or high treason by the president of the republic), and other special jurisdictions.

The Constitutional Court

The Constitutional Court is the highest court of Gabon on constitutional issues. Its decisions are not susceptible to any review. The court judges the constitutionality of laws and international treaties and guarantees fundamental human rights and public liberties. It also guarantees the regular operation of public institutions.

The Constitutional Court must rule before certain laws are promulgated, for example, organic laws. Any law can be submitted to the court by the president of the republic or by any citizen or legal person aggrieved by the law or contested act. Further, any person subject to trial before an ordinary tribunal may raise an objection of unconstitutionality against a law or act on grounds of violation of fundamental rights.

THE ELECTION PROCESS

All Gabonese of both sexes over the age of 18 are electors if they are registered on the electoral roll.

POLITICAL PARTIES

President Bongo has been in office since 1967 and his Gabonese Democratic Party has always won the parliamentary elections. Some observers believe Gabon will again become a one-party state.

CITIZENSHIP

Gabonese citizenship is primarily acquired by birth, if either parent is a citizen of Gabon regardless of the country of birth. Birth within Gabon does not automatically confer citizenship except for a child of unknown parents. Naturalization is possible on condition of 10 years of residence and renunciation of former citizenship. Dual citizenship is not recognized in Gabon.

FUNDAMENTAL RIGHTS

The Gabonese constitution includes a long preliminary title concerning fundamental rights and principles. Furthermore, its preamble refers to various international human rights declarations as having constitutional force. Gabon has ratified most international human rights treaties.

Impact and Functions of Fundamental Rights

The Ministry of Justice and Human Rights is obliged to protect and promote human rights. In addition, a National Commission on Human Rights was created in 2000. Nevertheless, the government continues to restrict freedom of press and movement. In criminal procedures there are still torture of prisoners and detainees, arbitrary arrests or detentions, and harsh prison conditions. Violence and societal discrimination against women are still problems. Finally, forced labor and child labor still exist in Gabon.

Limitations to Fundamental Rights

Fundamental rights can be limited by law. For practical purposes, in many areas there remain problems and limitations to fundamental rights.

ECONOMY

The Gabonese constitution does not impose any particular economic system. It affirms the individual and collective right to property, the right to work and to obtain employment, and the right to form associations.

RELIGIOUS COMMUNITIES

According to the constitution, Gabon is a secular republic. It affirms the separation of state and religions, provides for freedom of religion, and recognizes all beliefs. For practical purposes, the government generally respects these principles.

MILITARY DEFENSE AND STATE OF EMERGENCY

The president of the republic appoints high civil and military offices, such as army generals. The president is the supreme chief of the armed forces and of security. The National Assembly by a two-thirds majority of its members authorizes the declaration of war by the president of the republic.

The president has full powers in cases of emergency. Before taking the necessary measures, the president must consult the prime minister and the presidents of the National Assembly, the Senate, and the Constitutional Court. During the emergency the president cannot dissolve the National Assembly, and the constitution cannot be amended.

AMENDMENTS TO THE CONSTITUTION

The president of the republic or the members of Parliament may take the initiative in constitutional amendment. The Constitutional Court must also be consulted. The amendment is adopted either by the citizens in a referendum or by the Parliament in a two-thirds majority of voting members.

PRIMARY SOURCES

Constitution in English (extracts). Available online. URL: http://www.chr.up.ac.za/hr_docs/constitutions/docs/GabonC%20(english%20summary)(rev).doc. Accessed on August 7, 2005.

Constitution in English: Gisbert H. Flanz, ed., *Constitutions of the Countries of the World*. New York: Oceana, 1998.

Constitution in French. Available online. URL: http://www.democratie.francophonie.org/article.php3?id_article=482&id_rubrique=95. Accessed on June 22, 2006.

SECONDARY SOURCES

Association des Cours Constitutionnelles ayant en Partage l'Usage du Français, "Gabon." Available online. URL: http://www.accpuf.org/gab/. Accessed on August 10, 2005.

Bureau of Public Affairs, U.S. Department of State, "Background Note and Country Reports on Human Rights Practices and International Religious Freedom Report 2004." Available online. URL: http://www.state.gov/. Accessed on July 18, 2005.

Christine Schmidt-König

THE GAMBIA

At-a-Glance

OFFICIAL NAME
Republic of The Gambia

CAPITAL
Banjul

POPULATION
1,641,564 (July 2006 est.)

SIZE
4,363 sq. mi. (11, 300 sq. km)

LANGUAGES
English (official), Mandinka, Wollof, Fula, Jola, Serahuleh

RELIGIONS
Muslim 90%, Christian 9%, indigenous beliefs 1%

NATIONAL OR ETHNIC COMPOSITION
African (Mandinka 42%, Fula 18%, Wolof 16%, Jola 10%, Serahuleh 9%, others 4%) 99%, non-African 1%

DATE OF INDEPENDENCE OR CREATION
February 18, 1965

TYPE OF GOVERNMENT
Republic under multiparty democratic rule

TYPE OF STATE
Unitary state

TYPE OF LEGISLATURE
Unicameral national assembly

DATE OF CONSTITUTION
January 16, 1997

DATE OF LAST AMENDMENT
June 4, 2001

The Gambia is a parliamentary democracy that has an executive president who is directly elected by the population for a term of five years. The constitution requires that governmental functions be carried out on the basis of a separation among the executive, legislative, and judicial powers subject to appropriate checks and balances. For administrative purposes, the country is divided into a capital city, one municipal area, and five administrative divisions.

The constitution guarantees fundamental human rights and freedoms and empowers the judiciary to hear and determine alleged violations of constitutional norms. However, since the military takeover in 1994, and despite the conversion of the military junta into a civilian democratic regime in 1997, there have been increasing incidents of human rights abuses including arbitrary arrest and detention without trial, torture, intimidation of journalists and political opponents, arson, and murder. In many cases, the lack of investigation by state authorities has resulted in speculation that some of these violations might have occurred with the active or tacit support of some quarters of the government.

The constitution guarantees freedom of conscience and religion. There is a large degree of religious tolerance, and the various religious groups (Muslims, Christians, and traditional believers) have lived together peacefully throughout the country's history.

CONSTITUTIONAL HISTORY

The territory that comprises present-day Gambia has, from about the fifth and eighth centuries to the arrival of the first Europeans in the 15th century, been inhabited by members of several ethnic groups, including the Serahuleh, Mandinka, Wollof, and Fula. At various times before colonialism, these people were subject to the influence of the great African empires, including Ghana, Mali, and Songhai. British rule was established over parts of the country in the 17th century, and by the middle of the 18th century, the rest of the country was declared a protectorate to be administered by Britain. The queen of England was represented by a colonial governor.

The Gambia attained full internal self-government in 1963 and won independence from Britain on February 18, 1965. Alhaji Sir Farimang Singhateh was appointed as the first indigenous governor-general to represent the queen as head of state. Sir Dawda Jawara was elected prime minister. The pioneers of The Gambia's struggle for self-determination included the trade unionist Edward Francis Small in the 1920s and J. C. Faye, Ebrahima Garba Jahumpa, and Pierre S. Njie in the 1950s. The first political parties were formed between 1951 and 1954, including the Democratic Party led by Faye, the Muslim Congress led by Jahumpa, and the United Party led by Njie. The Protectorate Peoples Party (PPP), to be called the People's Progressive Party after independence, was formed by Dawda Jawara in 1959. In 1970, The Gambia adopted its first republican constitution. This constitution was set aside in 1994 after a military takeover. In 1996, with the planned return of the country to civilian democratic rule, the population approved the constitution of the second republic by referendum, and it took force on January 16, 1997.

FORM AND IMPACT OF THE CONSTITUTION

The Gambia has a written constitution, codified in a single document called the Constitution of the Republic of the Gambia, 1997. The constitution is the supreme law of the land and any law that is found to be inconsistent with the constitution is to be considered void to the extent of the inconsistency. The constitution states that the laws of The Gambia include acts adopted by the National Assembly; orders, rules, and regulations adopted by other bodies under authority granted by the National Assembly; the laws existing in the country at the time the constitution entered into force; the common law and principles of equity; customary law; and Islamic law on marriage, divorce, and inheritance among Muslims. While the constitution is by and large respected by the majority of the population, there have been instances of human rights abuses by the government and security forces.

BASIC ORGANIZATIONAL STRUCTURE

The Gambia is a unitary state under an executive presidency. There is a national judiciary with power to administer law throughout the country.

The country is divided into Banjul, the capital city, which is administered by a mayor and an elected city council; Kanifing Municipal Area, which is headed by a chairperson and a municipal council elected by the popu-

lation; and five administrative divisions, each of which is headed by a divisional commissioner selected by the minister of local government. Each division is further divided into districts headed by elected chiefs, and villages headed by Alkalos or headmen, who are elected by local landowners.

LEADING CONSTITUTIONAL PRINCIPLES

The Gambia operates a liberal democratic style of government under a system of checks and balances. Lawmaking power is conferred on the National Assembly, whose bills have to be signed into law by the president. The president has the power to veto bills sent from the National Assembly. Judicial power is vested in the courts of law, and the Supreme Court has the power to interpret the constitution and can declare acts of the National Assembly and the actions of the executive inconsistent with the constitution.

The constitution guarantees equality before the law and equal protection of the law. It requires state action to be anchored on the rule of law and good governance.

CONSTITUTIONAL BODIES

The constitution establishes the offices of president of the republic, a cabinet of secretaries of state, a National Assembly, and the judiciary.

The President

The president of the republic is both head of state and head of the executive administration. The president holds executive power in the country and is also the commander in chief of the armed forces. The president is elected for a term of five years and is eligible for reelection. There is no limit on the number of terms that a person can seek reelection to the office of president.

The Cabinet

The constitution provides for a cabinet composed of the president, the vice president, and secretaries of state selected by the president. The role of the cabinet is to advise the president on government policy. The president selects the vice president and the cabinet, which is collectively responsible to the National Assembly for the advice they give the president.

The National Assembly

The National Assembly is made up of members elected by universal adult suffrage to represent electoral constituencies. Each member is elected for a term of five years and can run for reelection. The National Assembly holds the power to make law for the governance of the whole of the Gambia. This lawmaking power is exercised by adopting bills, which are then assented to (signed) by the president. A bill becomes law once it is signed by the president.

The Lawmaking Process

The constitution designates the president and National Assembly as the lawmaking organs of the country. The National Assembly has power to adopt bills on any subject of national interest. The bill becomes law upon its signing by the president. The constitution provides that the National Assembly cannot adopt a bill that introduces a one-party state, establishes any religion as a state religion, or alters the decision or judgment of a court.

The Judiciary

The constitution establishes a hierarchical court system with power to administer justice in the country. The highest court of the land is the Supreme Court. Between five and seven justices sit on each case, depending on the issue being judged. The Supreme Court has the power to interpret provisions of the constitution.

The Court of Appeals is made up of three judges, who hear appeals from judgments of the High Courts in criminal and civil cases. The High Courts are each composed of a single judge who decides both criminal and civil cases. In criminal cases, the constitution gives the accused the right to choose to be tried by jury instead of by a judge alone, but most accused persons do not choose this option because of the small size of the population and the difficulty of finding impartial juries in such a closely knit society.

The Judicial Service Commission is empowered by law to appoint judges and magistrates. In practice, they recommend candidates for appointment by the president. While the law provides that judicial officers should hold office during good behavior and can be removed from office only for good cause, the executive government has on several occasions summarily dismissed judges and magistrates. This state of affairs reflects poorly on the assertion of independence of the judiciary.

THE ELECTION PROCESS

Every citizen of The Gambia who is 18 years of age or older has the right to vote in national and local elections and referenda. The constitution creates an Independent Electoral Commission with the responsibility to register voters and conduct all elections in the country.

POLITICAL PARTIES

The Gambia is by law a multiparty state. The constitution prohibits the passing of any law that would limit the number of political parties and empowers every citizen of The Gambia to join a political party of his or her choice. The Independent Electoral Commission has responsibility to register or cancel the registration of political parties. Currently, the Alliance for Patriotic Reorientation and Construction (APRC) of President Yayha Jammeh holds power, since winning presidential and National Assembly elections in 2001. The main opposition party, the United Democratic Party (UDP), boycotted the 2001 National Assembly elections, claiming unfair voter registration processes. The other opposition parties are the National Reconciliation Party (NRP), the Peoples Democratic Organization for Independence and Socialism (PDOIS), the Gambia Peoples Party (GPP), the People's Progressive Party (PPP), and the National Convention Party (NCP). In January 2005, the UDP, NRP, PDOIS, GPP, and PPP formed a national coalition with a view to contesting the 2006 presidential and National Assembly elections on a single ticket. The new opposition coalition has been named the National Alliance for Democracy and Development (NADD).

CITIZENSHIP

Every person born in The Gambia becomes a citizen if either one or both of his or her parents are Gambian. Children born outside The Gambia to parents who are Gambian citizens become Gambian citizens by descent. It is also possible to acquire Gambian citizenship by marriage or by naturalization.

FUNDAMENTAL RIGHTS

Chapter IV of the constitution guarantees a number of fundamental rights and freedoms to every person in The Gambia. The notion that fundamental rights are applicable to all persons in the country, as opposed to merely citizens or Africans, derives from the belief that human rights relate to the human person as such, irrespective of race, nationality, ethnic origin, or sex. The constitution guarantees the right to life, to liberty (especially freedom of movement, assembly, and association), freedom of speech and publication, the right to secure the protection of the law, and equality before the law. In addition to these general rights, the constitution guarantees special rights for women, children, and the disabled.

Impact and Functions of Fundamental Rights

In theory, respect for fundamental rights and human dignity should form the cornerstone of all governmental action; in practice, there have been many problems. Despite the fundamental rights guaranteed under the constitution, there have been many instances of blatant violations of the rights of citizens by the government and security forces. There have been regular incidents of arrest and detention of political opponents, journalists, and students in breach of fundamental human rights provisions. Some media firms viewed as critical of the government have been either closed down, threatened with closure, or violently attacked and destroyed.

In 2003, unknown assailants attempted to assassinate a leading human rights lawyer by shooting him several times; he is now in self-imposed exile in the United States. In December 2004, the editor of one of the country's independent newspapers was shot to death as he drove home from his office. While the government has said it is investigating, many observers believe that these were incidents of state-sponsored violence and that they were politically motivated.

Limitations to Fundamental Rights

The only limitations on the enjoyment of fundamental rights under the constitution are respect for the rights and freedoms of other persons and the public interest.

ECONOMY

The constitution does not specifically provide for an economic system for The Gambia. In practice, however, the country operates a liberal, market-based economy, the main features of which are subsistence agriculture, reexport trade, low import duties, a fluctuating foreign exchange system, and a vibrant services sector, especially tourism and banking. There is a significant government stake in many public enterprises so as to balance market outcomes with the government's development and welfare objectives.

RELIGIOUS COMMUNITIES

The constitution guarantees freedom of thought, conscience, and belief and proscribes the imposition of any state religion. Muslims, Christians, and traditional believers have lived together in harmony throughout the country's history, and there is a marked absence of religious fanaticism. In a move criticized by many observers in the late 1990s, the current president, Yahya A. J. J. Jammeh, built a mosque on the premises of State House, the official residence of the president. This was viewed by many as a deliberate association of state and religion in violation of the spirit of the constitution.

MILITARY DEFENSE AND STATE OF EMERGENCY

The constitution provides for an armed force comprising the army, navy, and air force. These bodies are staffed entirely by volunteers, as there are no military draft and no requirement for compulsory military service. All persons above 16 years of age may volunteer to join the armed forces.

The armed forces have responsibility to secure the defense and territorial integrity of the state, to provide disaster relief and assistance to civil authorities, and to engage in such productive activities as the civil authorities determine are necessary for the development of the country. The armed forces operate under the overall command of the president as commander in chief and of the Armed Forces Council.

The president has power to declare a state of emergency in the country. That declaration must be approved by a resolution of the National Assembly.

AMENDMENTS TO THE CONSTITUTION

The constitution can be changed only by a bill supported by three-quarters of all the members of the National Assembly and signed by the president. Certain provisions, such as those relating to fundamental human rights, the judiciary, and some fiscal matters, cannot be changed except by referendum.

PRIMARY SOURCES
Constitution in English (extracts). Available online. URL: http://www.chr.up.ac.za/hr_docs/constitutions/docs/The%20GambiaC(english%20summary)(rev).doc. Accessed on August 15, 2005.
Constitution of the Republic of The Gambia 1997. Banjul, The Gambia: Government Printer, 1997.

SECONDARY SOURCES
U.S. Central Intelligence Agency, *World Factbook, 2003 (The Gambia).* Washington, D.C.
U.S. Department of State, Bureau of African Affairs, "Background Note: The Gambia." Available online. URL: http://www.state.gov/r/pa/ei/bgn/5459.htm. Accessed on August 22, 2005.

Alhagi Marong

GEORGIA

At-a-Glance

OFFICIAL NAME
Georgia

CAPITAL
Tbilisi

POPULATION
4,695,000 (2005 est.)

SIZE
26,911 sq. mi. (69,700 sq. km)

LANGUAGES
Georgian, Abkhaz

RELIGIONS
Georgian Orthodox Christian 70%, Muslim 11%,
Armenian Apostolic 8%, unaffiliated or other 11%

NATIONAL OR ETHNIC COMPOSITION
Georgian 73.1%, Armenian 8.1%, Azeri 6.7%, Russian
4.3%, Ossetian 3%, Abkhaz 1.8%, other (largely

Greek, Jewish, Kurdish, Ukrainian,
Chechen) 3%

DATE OF INDEPENDENCE OR CREATION
April 9, 1991

TYPE OF GOVERNMENT
Semipresidential democracy

TYPE OF STATE
Unitary state with autonomous regions

TYPE OF LEGISLATURE
Unicameral parliament

DATE OF CONSTITUTION
August 24, 1995

DATE OF LAST AMENDMENT
December 27, 2005

Georgia is a semipresidential democracy based on the division of executive, legislative, and judicial powers. Organized as a unitary state with a strong central government, Georgia is in the process of becoming an asymmetric decentralized state (different units at the same level have different degrees of power), with three autonomous entities and approximately 10 administrative regions.

The place of honor in the constitution is its second chapter, which provides far-reaching guarantees of fundamental rights and freedoms as directly applicable legal norms. In case of violations of these rights and freedoms, a citizen can directly apply to the constitutional court, which can overrule unconstitutional decisions of all government bodies.

The president is the head of state and has considerable power over the executive branch. The president is elected by direct popular voting and is the central political figure in the country. The parliament of the country is relatively weak vis-à-vis the executive branch.

Religious freedom is guaranteed and state and religious communities are separate. However, the Georgian Orthodox Christian Church enjoys exclusive constitutional guarantees.

The economic system can be described as a transitional market economy bearing the heavy burdens of the communist past.

Two breakaway regions at the border with Russia, Abkhazia and South Ossetia, are governed by separatist regimes; this condition imposes considerable difficulties for the political and economic development of the country.

CONSTITUTIONAL HISTORY

The Georgian Kingdom, which declared Christianity as state religion in the fourth century C.E., reached the highest level of its economic and cultural development during the 11th and 12th centuries. Georgia was absorbed into the Russian Empire in the 19th century. Independent for three years (1918–21) after the Russian revolution, it was forcibly incorporated in the Union of Soviet Socialist Republics (USSR) until the Soviet Union dissolved in 1991.

During the short period of the first independence, Georgia had a social-democratic government, which adopted the first constitution of the country in 1921. According to this constitution, Georgia was a parliamentary democracy, a unitary republic, and a social state. During the Soviet period, the Georgian Socialist Republic had several constitutions. The last one was adopted in 1978 and was based on principles of Marxism-Leninism: a one-party system and centrally planned economy.

The first government of independent Georgia removed all these principles from the constitution in 1991 but did not have enough time to produce a new constitution before its overthrow in early 1992. In January 1992, the military government abolished the 1978 constitution and reestablished the 1921 text. However, this was a political and symbolic move only; the law on state power played the role of supreme law until 1995.

The constitution of 1995 established a U.S.-style presidential democracy and, because of the de facto separated regions, left the question of the administrative territorial arrangement of the country open. The document underwent major changes after the Rose Revolution of November 2003. In February 2004 the legislative and executive powers were reorganized, to yield a much stronger president and a weaker parliament. Political debates about other important amendments to the constitution are permanent in the country, which is still far from constitutional stability.

FORM AND IMPACT OF THE CONSTITUTION

Georgia has a written constitution that takes precedence over all other national law. International law must be in accordance with the constitution to be applicable within Georgia. Human rights and freedoms guaranteed by international documents are applicable within the country even if the constitution does not directly mention such rights and freedoms. Constitutional laws defining the status of autonomous regions are adopted separately but become part of the constitution.

BASIC ORGANIZATIONAL STRUCTURE

Georgia is a unitary state in the process of decentralization. Governments of the two breakaway regions do not recognize the jurisdiction of the Georgian constitution and are seeking to be incorporated into neighboring Russia. One other politically separated region (Ajaria) was reincorporated into the Georgian state in 2004 with the status of an autonomous republic. The rest of the country is divided into several big cities and about 60 small regions, which are in the process of being consolidated into 10 to 12 larger regions.

LEADING CONSTITUTIONAL PRINCIPLES

Georgia is a democratic republic based on the rule of law. Its system of government is a semipresidential democracy. There is a division of the executive, legislative, and judicial branches, but the predominance of power is held by the executive.

CONSTITUTIONAL BODIES

The predominant bodies provided for in the constitution are the parliament; the president; the administration, made up of prime minister and cabinet of ministers; and the judiciary, including the constitutional court.

The Parliament

The parliament of Georgia exercises legislative power, determines the main directions of domestic and foreign policy, approves the prime minister and his or her cabinet, and monitors the administration and other executive agencies. Its period of office is four years. The 235 members of Parliament are elected in a direct, free, equal, and secret balloting process through a mixed proportional and majoritarian electoral system. In certain circumstances prescribed by the constitution, the president may dismiss the parliament.

The constitution envisions a division of parliament into two chambers—Council of the Republic and the Senate—after reintegration of the two de facto separated regions of the country.

The President

The president is the head of state and is at the same time responsible for and carries out the domestic and foreign policy of the country. The president is the supreme commander in chief of the armed forces. The president nominates the prime minister and other ministers and can dismiss the administration. The president can call and chair cabinet meetings. The constitutional powers of the president make the president the dominant figure in Georgian politics. The president is elected by the citizens of Georgia by direct voting for a five-year term and can be reelected only once.

The Administration

The administration is accountable to the president and to the parliament at the same time. The administration consists of the prime minister and ministers. The prime minister, under the leadership of the president, is responsible for setting and implementing the administration's policy.

The Lawmaking Process

Draft laws can be initiated by members of the parliament, by the president, by the administration, or by 30,000 voters. Adoption of organic laws, which regulate the most important issues, requires support of an absolute majority in parliament. The president may veto a law, which enters into force only if parliament overrules the veto by a three-fifths majority of the members of parliament.

The Judiciary

The judiciary consists of the constitutional court and general courts. The constitutional court, consisting of nine judges, deals exclusively with constitutional disputes. The system of general courts consists of the Supreme Court, four appellate courts, and about 70 lower courts. The Supreme Council of Judiciary led by the president of Georgia regulates the selection of judges, initiates disciplinary actions against judges, and deals with other administrative issues within the judiciary.

THE ELECTION PROCESS

All Georgian citizens over the age of 18 have the right to vote. Only citizens over the ages of 21 and 25 have the right to stand for local government and parliamentary elections, respectively.

POLITICAL PARTIES

Georgia has a pluralistic system of political parties; so far, at least two or three parties have always been represented in parliament. The multiparty system as a basic structure of the constitutional order is still in the process of formation; the ruling party still plays a dominant role in public life. Political parties can be banned only by a decision of the constitutional court.

CITIZENSHIP

A child of a Georgian citizen acquires Georgian citizenship. A citizen of another country can acquire Georgian citizenship after living in Georgia for at least 10 years. A citizen of Georgia may not be at the same time a citizen of another country. The president may grant citizenship of Georgia to a citizen of another country who has made a special contribution to Georgia.

FUNDAMENTAL RIGHTS

The constitution recognizes and defends universal human rights and freedoms as eternal and supreme values. These rights and freedoms, as directly applicable law, have binding force for the state and for the people. When relevant, the rights and freedoms provided in the constitution apply to corporate bodies as well. The protection of human rights and freedoms is supervised by the public defender, who is elected for five years by parliament.

Impact and Functions of Fundamental Rights

Constitutional rights and freedoms are essential tools for building a democracy in postcommunist Georgian society, which suffered from a totalitarian regime for decades. Many of these rights face frequent resistance from different elements of society. However, liberal democratic values are spreading in Georgian society, while the legal mechanisms and remedies for protecting fundamental rights are becoming more and more effective.

Limitations to Fundamental Rights

Fundamental rights may be limited only in specific circumstances precisely prescribed by the constitution and laws. Certain rights, such as the protection against torture and inhumane, brutal, or degrading treatment or punishment, are declared absolute rights and cannot be limited.

ECONOMY

Many principles included in the constitution are attempts to exorcise the fears of the Communist past. The constitution does not specify a specific economic system, but it does provide a set of individual rights and state obligations that must be met when structuring such a system. The state is obliged to foster conditions for the development of free enterprise and fair competition. The Georgian economic system is still in the process of transition with the clear tendency toward deregulation and limited involvement of the state in the economy.

RELIGIOUS COMMUNITIES

The constitution of Georgia declares complete freedom of religious beliefs and confessions, as well as independence of the church from the state, but simultaneously recognizes the special role of the Georgian Orthodox Church in Georgian history. This special recognition led to the conclusion of a constitutional agreement between the state and the Georgian Orthodox Church. This agreement does not give the church the status of a state church, but it does provide some exclusive tax and property privileges. Adoption of a special law on religious organizations is planned to guarantee independence and self-determination for all religious communities.

MILITARY DEFENSE AND STATE OF EMERGENCY

The constitution provides that Georgia has the right to wage a defensive war. General conscription requires all men over the age of 18 to perform basic military service of 18 months. Women can volunteer but are not required to serve. Conscientious objectors are obliged to perform service in social institutions.

Apart from defending the country against a military attack, the armed forces may be used only for emergencies such as natural disasters or civil unrest. Such use of armed force requires parliamentary approval, as does their dispatch abroad in fulfillment of international obligations. The president may declare a state of emergency by a spe-

cial decree, which loses its force if parliament does not approve it within three days.

AMENDMENTS TO THE CONSTITUTION

The constitution can be changed only by two-thirds of the members of parliament. The president, half of the members of parliament, or 200,000 voters can initiate amendments. Before parliament votes, the draft amendment must be published for public debate for a period of at least one month.

PRIMARY SOURCES

Constitution in Georgian. Available online. URL: http://www.parliament.ge/index.php?lang_id=ENG&sec_id=68. Accessed on June 21, 2006.
Constitution in English. Available online. URL: http://www.parliament.ge/index.php?lang_id=GEO&sec_id=68. Accessed on June 21, 2006.

David Usupashvili

GERMANY

At-a-Glance

OFFICIAL NAME
Federal Republic of Germany

CAPITAL
Berlin

POPULATION
82,536,700 (2005 est.)

SIZE
137,821 sq. mi. (357,021 sq. km)

LANGUAGES
German

RELIGIONS
Catholic 32%, Protestant 32%, Muslim 3.9%, Jewish 0.24%, Christian Orthodox 1.3%, unaffiliated or other 30.56%

NATIONAL OR ETHNIC COMPOSITION
German 91.5%, Turkish 2.4%, other (largely Serbo-Croatian, Italian, Russian Greek, Polish, Spanish, Wend, Danish, Sinti, and Roma) 6.1%

DATE OF INDEPENDENCE OR CREATION
January 18, 1871

TYPE OF GOVERNMENT
Parliamentary democracy

TYPE OF STATE
Federal state

TYPE OF LEGISLATURE
Bicameral parliament

DATE OF CONSTITUTION
May 23, 1949

DATE OF LAST AMENDMENT
July 26, 2002

Germany is a parliamentary democracy based on the rule of law with a clear division of executive, legislative, and judicial powers. Organized as a federation, Germany is made up of 16 federal states and a strong central government. The federal constitution provides for far-reaching guarantees of human rights. It is widely respected by the public authorities; if a violation of the constitution does occur in individual cases, there are effective remedies enforceable by an independent judiciary, which includes a strong and visible Federal Constitutional Court. The constitution also has become a centerpiece of German self-understanding.

The federal president is the head of state, but his or her function is mostly representative. The central political figure is the chancellor as head of the administration. The chancellor depends on the Parliament as the representative body of the people. Free, equal, general, and direct elections of the members of Parliament are guaranteed. A pluralistic system of political parties has intense political impact.

Religious freedom is guaranteed and state and religious communities are separated. The economic system can be described as a social market economy. The military is subject to the civil government in terms of law and fact. By constitutional law, Germany is obliged to contribute to world peace.

CONSTITUTIONAL HISTORY

Germany as a political entity emerged in central Europe in the 10th century C.E. It called itself the Holy Roman Empire, claiming continuity with the imperial and religious authority of ancient Christian Rome. It was an electoral monarchy; the ruler of the empire was chosen by a small number of nobles, called the prince electors, and then crowned as emperor. The emperor shared power with the Imperial Diet (Reichstag), in which the prince electors and the high nobility had seats and voting rights together with representatives from autonomous cities.

The Protestant Reformation, which began in the early 16th century, led to deep changes in the basic constitutional structure of the empire. Together with the power struggle between regional monarchs and the emperor, religious disputes caused devastating wars, culminating in the Thirty Years' War of 1618–48. The Peace of Westphalia of 1648 laid the basis for peaceful coexistence between Catholics and Protestants. The Jewish minority, after the Europe-wide pogroms in the Middle Ages, enjoyed some, often unstable autonomy.

The wars led by the French emperor Napoléon I (1769–1821) after the French Revolution of 1789 put an end to the German Empire in 1806. Austria, which had been a central part of Germany during the past several centuries, established itself as an independent empire. From 1815 onward, Austria, together with the sovereign kingdoms of Prussia, Bavaria, and Hanover and the 37 other now-independent German states and cities, formed the German Confederation (Deutscher Bund). Many of these German states had constitutions guaranteeing fundamental rights, providing for shared powers between the monarch and parliament, and creating an independent judiciary. Many cities kept their centuries-old republican system. Yet people's sovereignty was not generally recognized since sovereignty rested with the monarch.

During the Revolution of 1848, a constitution was drafted for a newly united Germany under the king of Prussia as the German emperor. This constitution provided for far-reaching and modern human rights, democratic parliamentary institutions, and a strong judiciary. Although the revolution failed, the draft constitution had strong influence on later German constitutions.

The German Confederation lasted until 1866, when Prussia, under its prime minister, Otto von Bismarck (1815–98), founded the North German Federation (Norddeutscher Bund), which was constituted as a strong empire with a centralist structure. After the Franco-German war of 1870–71, the South German States, with the exception of Austria, acceded to the North German Federation, thus creating the German Empire (Deutsches Reich) of 1870/71, the so-called Bismarck Empire. Its constitution was based in large part on that of the North German Federation. It was a federal state and had a relatively strong central government with the king of Prussia as hereditary German emperor. The emperor was the head of state and appointed the administration of the empire. Laws were enacted by parliament together with the Federal Council, in which the federal states were represented. Ordinary law provided for a strong judiciary and rights for citizens. Laws were also enacted to improve social security, in large part to counteract the rise of left-wing political parties and trade unions.

After World War I (1914–18), monarchy was abolished, and a democratic constitution was adopted in 1919 for the new Weimar Republic. Under the republic, equal voting rights were enjoyed by men and women, and extensive fundamental rights were guaranteed in the national constitution. The administration was led by the chancellor and was responsible to parliament. The president of the republic was head of state and commander in chief of the military. He was elected directly by the people for a seven-year period. The president chose and appointed the chancellor.

A number of provisions, however, were not favorable to political stability: The government could be removed by parliament even in the absence of a replacement majority. Furthermore, the president of the republic and the administration had far-reaching authority during a state of emergency, including the power to suspend fundamental rights. These shortcomings of the constitution later helped the National Socialists to overthrow the republic in 1933.

The complete moral breakdown of Germany under the Nazi terror regime led to the murder of millions of Jews and other people, the bloody suppression of opposition and resistance, and World War II (1939–45), during which tens of millions died. The shock over this suffering and this disruption of culture and history deeply influenced the drafters of the current constitution of the Federal Republic of Germany, which was enacted on May 23, 1949. The framers of the constitution tried to ensure that nothing like the Nazi regime would ever happen again. Referring to Germany's responsibility for the crimes committed under National Socialist rule, the Preamble to the Constitution also contains a promise for the future: "Conscious of their responsibility before God and man, inspired by the determination to promote world peace as an equal partner in a united Europe, the German people, in the exercise of their constituent power, have adopted this Basic Law."

The constitution of 1949 follows in the footsteps of the 1848 and 1919 constitutions and is rooted in old German constitutional traditions, such as the rule of law, people's sovereignty, and human rights. New measures were introduced to improve the stability of democratic institutions. Among them are the prohibition of constitutional amendments that adversely affect the protection of human dignity, basic constitutional structures such as the rule of law, and the principle of federalism.

After World War II, Germany was divided into the Federal Republic of Germany and the German Democratic Republic. The latter remained until 1990 under the influence of the Soviet Union and Communist rule. Its constitutions of 1949 and 1968 (substantially amended in 1974) contained human rights and democratic institutions. Yet these provisions were never particularly relevant, since the Communist Party always had final and arbitrary decision-making power. The German Democratic Republic ceased to exist after it joined the Federal Republic of Germany in 1990 after the breakdown of the Communist bloc. Reunified Germany amended its constitution to ensure that the unification process was complete and no territorial claims persisted.

The Federal Republic of Germany is a member of the United Nations and of the North Atlantic Treaty Organization (NATO), and a founding member of the European Union. As a member of the European Union, it participates in an increasingly intense integration process that seeks to ensure peace, stability, and prosperity across the continent. As have the other members, Germany has transferred extensive sovereign rights to the European Union. The law of the union has a tremendous and increasing impact on German law.

FORM AND IMPACT OF THE CONSTITUTION

Germany has a written constitution, codified in a single document called the Basic Law (Grundgesetz), which takes precedence over all other national law. International law must be in accordance with the constitution to be applicable within Germany. The law of the European Union generally has precedence over the German constitution, as long as it does not contradict the constitution's basic principles.

All laws must comply with the provisions of the Basic Law. The Federal Constitutional Court is strict and powerful in implementing constitutional law. However, the constitution is significant not only for the legal system of the country but also as a source of values. It has helped shape the way Germans think of themselves as a people.

BASIC ORGANIZATIONAL STRUCTURE

Germany is a federation made up of 16 federal states, called Länder. Each of the Länder has a state constitution modeled in part on the Basic Law while establishing an identity of its own. The Länder differ considerably in geographic area, population size, and economic strength. All have identical legislative, administrative, and judicial powers, making the federal states essentially equal from a constitutional point of view.

The historical origins of the federal structure reach back to the beginnings of the Holy Roman Empire. The central imperial authority and the individual territorial governments have coexisted throughout the history of Germany, sometimes in cooperation and sometimes in conflict.

The states of the Federal Republic of Germany have sovereign status, as does the federation itself. However, the Länder cannot leave the federation. The constitutional status of the Länder is strong, but the federal government has far greater political impact today.

The powers of the federation and the states are interrelated in many fields. Those powers reserved to the states are their sole responsibility, except as limited by the federal constitution, as is often the case. The starting assumption is that legislation is the task of the states.

However, numerous important issues are subjected to the legislative authority of the federation. In some fields, such as international relations, defense, citizenship, and the regulation of currency, the federation has exclusive authority. In others, such as civil law, criminal law, the structure and procedures of the courts, the law relating to foreigners, and commercial and labor law, the states have concurrent legislative authority only as long as the federation does not step in; for most of these fields, the federation has indeed enacted legislation. In the course of the history of the Federal Republic of Germany, many legislative powers have passed from the states to the federation by constitutional amendments.

The administration of the law is in principle the business of the states, even of laws passed by the federation. True, the Basic Law assigns significant administrative functions to the federal government regarding the armed forces, the foreign service, and numerous other areas, but in general the states provide the administrative apparatus. Thus, even in fields within the exclusive legislative competence of the federation, citizens generally deal with the administrative officials of the Länder.

Local government is strong in Germany. The local communities are incorporated into the state administrative structure, but they make their own decisions on many issues, including construction and development policies and local economic development. The citizens of the local communities elect mayors and other members of local political bodies.

LEADING CONSTITUTIONAL PRINCIPLES

Germany's system of government is a parliamentary democracy. There is a strong division of executive, legislative, and judicial powers, based on checks and balances. The judiciary is independent and includes a constitutional court.

The German constitutional system is defined by a number of leading principles: Germany is a democracy, a federation, a republic, and a social state, and it is based on the rule of law. Article 28 of the constitution extends these principles to the states: "The constitutional order in the Länder must conform to the principles of a republican, democratic, and social state governed by the rule of law, within the meaning of this Basic Law."

On the federal level, political participation is shaped as an indirect, representative democracy: The people elect delegates to Parliament, who then decide on the political questions. Direct democracy by means of a referendum is very limited on the federal level. The constitutional law of the states allows for more direct democracy, but it is rarely invoked.

According to the principle that the Federal Republic of Germany is a social state, government must take action to ensure a minimal standard of living to every resident of Germany. It binds public authority to the general welfare. Rule of law is of decisive impact. All state actions impairing the rights of the people must have a basis in parliamentary law, and the judiciary must be independent and effective.

Further structural principles are implicitly contained in the constitution, such as religious neutrality and the commitment of the state to the support of culture. The preamble of the constitution commits Germany to promoting world peace. Protection of the environment and of animals ranks as a constitutional principle as well. The constitution obliges Germany to take an active part in European integration.

CONSTITUTIONAL BODIES

The predominant bodies provided for in the constitution are the federal president; the chancellor and cabinet ministers; the Federal Diet, or Federal Assembly, called the Bundestag; and the Federal Council, called the Bundesrat, which functions as the representative organ of the states. Often, Bundestag and Bundesrat are seen as two chambers of Parliament, but the constitution sees them as separate bodies. The judiciary, which includes the Federal Constitutional Court, and the Joint Committee, which functions as a representative body when Parliament is unable to convene.

The Federal President

The federal president is the head of state. He or she formally appoints and dismisses the chancellor after the latter has been elected or deposed by Parliament. The federal president promulgates the laws, but before signing a law he or she must decide whether it is constitutional. This task frequently puts the president at the center of political issues; historically, the federal president has in a number of cases withheld his or her signature and thus prevented a bill from becoming law. The president also represents the federal republic in international affairs and formally appoints and dismisses the civil servants, soldiers, and judges of the federation. The federal president also has the right to pardon criminal offenders.

Still, the office consists largely of representative functions. The president is neither the commander in chief of the armed forces nor the head of government. In general, all official activities of the president must be countersigned by the chancellor. The president's political impact depends largely on personal charisma. Indeed, the relative lack of political power enables the president to be representative of the whole German nation and play an integrative role in society.

The president is elected for a five-year term and can be reelected only once. He or she must be at least 40 years old and may not hold any other office nor exercise any other profession. Electing the federal president is the sole and exclusive function of the Federal Convention. It is made up of all the members of the Bundestag and an equal number of representatives elected by the parliaments of the states. There is no election campaign; normally, the candidates are presented by the political parties and elected according to the existing majorities in the parliaments. The federal president can be deposed only by the Federal Constitutional Court, if it finds him or her guilty of a willful violation of the Basic Law or of any other federal law.

The Federal Administration

The federal administration is the political nerve center of Germany. It consists of the chancellor (*Bundeskanzler*)—its head—and the federal ministers. He or she is nominated by the federal president and elected by the Bundestag. The president usually nominates the leading politician of the strongest party in the Bundestag. The federal ministers, who make up the cabinet, are appointed and dismissed by the president on the advice of the chancellor. Each minister directs his or her department independently and is responsible for its actions. However, the chancellor has the authority to set government policy. All ministers are bound by his or her decisions on broad, fundamental issues of policy and, sometimes, specific questions of particular importance.

The federal administration has the authority to define each minister's responsibilities, with the exception of certain functions defined in the Basic Law. For example, the finance minister's consent is required for any extraordinary or additional expenditure; also, the defense minister is commander in chief of the armed forces in times of peace.

The goal is to assure a strong, stable administration responsible to the Bundestag. To that end, the Bundestag can dismiss a chancellor only by way of electing a new one with the votes of more than half of its members. The chancellor can also initiate a vote of confidence. If he or she does not win a majority, the chancellor can ask the president to dissolve the Bundestag. The Bundestag can, however, prevent its dissolution by electing a new chancellor.

The chancellor and the federal ministers serve for the legislative period of the Bundestag, unless dismissed early in a vote of confidence. Each newly elected Bundestag must go through the process of electing a chancellor.

The chancellor is generally the dominant figure in German politics, with the power to set policy guidelines and choose the ministers. Ministers cannot individually be dismissed by a vote of no confidence. The role of the Bundestag is thus somewhat weakened, and its independence is further limited by the dominant role of the political parties. In general, the majority in the Bundestag backs the administration.

The German Bundestag (Parliament)

The German Bundestag is the central representative organ of the people at the federal level. As a legislative body, it cooperates with a number of other constitutional organs, especially the Federal Council (Bundesrat), in which the states are represented. In terms of the legislative process but not in strictly legal terms, Bundestag and Bundesrat can be regarded as two chambers of parliament. The Bundestag also elects the chancellor and monitors the administration and civil service. Members of the Bundestag have the right to put questions to the administration, and any federal minister can be cited to appear before the body.

Decisions in the Bundestag are generally made by a simple majority of the members present, as long as a quorum is achieved. Some decisions, such as choice of a chancellor, require an absolute majority, that is, more than half of all members. Particularly important decisions, such as amendments to the constitution, require a two-thirds majority.

Members are not legally bound to follow instructions from their party leadership, as they all represent the whole nation and are bound only by their own consciences. In practice, members depend on the party in ways that often limit their independence. Delegates have a duty to disclose to the president of the Bundestag any activities they undertake on behalf of groups or organizations and any financial contributions they receive from such sources.

Members enjoy parliamentary privilege, which confers far-reaching protection against legal action arising from their vote or statements on the floor. Parliamentary privilege also serves to protect their personal freedom. Only with the permission of the Bundestag may a member of Parliament be subjected to any criminal prosecution, arrested, or restrained, unless the member is arrested in the course of committing a crime or on the following day.

The Bundestag consists of 598 delegates (slight variations are possible because of complicated electoral procedures). Its period of office, the legislative term, is four years, unless it is dissolved early. The legislative term ends when the newly elected Bundestag assembles for the first time. The delegates are elected in a general, direct, free, equal, and secret balloting process.

The Bundesrat (Federal Council)

The Bundesrat allows the states (*Länder*) to participate in legislation and administration at the federal level. It can play an important role, especially when a minority party in the Bundestag hold a Bundesrat majority.

The Bundesrat consists of members of the state administrations. Depending on the size of its population, each state has a minimum of three and a maximum of six votes. These must always be cast en bloc.

The members of the Bundesrat are appointed and dismissed by the administration of the state they represent, and they are bound to vote in accordance with the directions the administration gives them. There are some exceptions to this rule: For example, it does not apply to

votes in the Mediation Committee, which resolves differences in bills passed by both houses.

The main business of the Bundesrat is to participate in the federal legislative function. Certain important ordinances promulgated by the federal administration that are specifically listed in the Basic Law also need the consent of the Bundesrat, giving the body an administrative role as well. The Bundesrat also influences federal policy on the European Union.

The Lawmaking Process

A bill may be introduced by the federal administration, by a group of members representing not less than 5 percent of the Bundestag, or by the Bundesrat. If the Bundestag passes a bill, the bill then goes to the Bundesrat, whose assent is needed in the case of certain types of legislation enumerated in the Basic Law—mostly those laws that would have a significant impact on the states. In other cases, the Bundesrat may raise objections but cannot block passage.

In case the Bundestag and the Bundesrat disagree over a draft law, the Mediation Committee can negotiate a compromise. This body is made up of 16 members of each chamber. The committee's compromise wording is then once more put through the legislative process.

Once the bill has been passed by the Bundestag and, if necessary, by the Bundesrat, it must be countersigned by the chancellor and the responsible minister. For the law to take effect, the president needs to assent and promulgate it.

The Judiciary

The judiciary in Germany is independent of the executive and legislative branches and is a powerful factor in legal life. Its structure is somewhat complicated as a result of historical developments and the federal nature of Germany. Federal and state jurisdiction may overlap.

There are five different sets of courts, defined by the matters they adjudicate: civil and criminal courts, administrative courts, labor courts, revenue courts, and finally courts for social law. In general, the courts of first instance and appeal are on the *Länder* level. Each branch also has a supreme court, residing at the federal level.

The highest court in Germany is the Federal Constitutional Court. It ranks above the supreme courts of the five different branches and deals exclusively with constitutional disputes. It has often proved difficult to decide whether a question is of constitutional or of ordinary law nature.

The Federal Constitutional Court consists of two senates of eight judges each. Half of the candidates are chosen by the Bundesrat, and half are chosen by an electoral committee consisting of 12 members of the Bundestag. The candidates are presented by the political parties represented in Parliament. Since the candidates need a two-thirds majority of the votes in the respective electoral body to be elected, the judges of the federal constitutional court enjoy a broad basis of trust.

The importance of the court arises from the fact that all state actions must be in compliance with the constitution. Its decisions are binding not only in the particular case before it, but also for the future. The court has often declared acts of Parliament void on constitutional grounds. A constitutional complaint can be taken before the Federal Constitutional Court by any person who claims the state has infringed one of his or her fundamental rights. Before doing so, the plaintiff must have tried all other legal remedies without success.

The Federal Constitutional Court, as is any other court in Germany, is obliged to make a decision on any case before it. It has no discretion in accepting or rejecting cases on political grounds. The court's decisions have often managed to bridge deep political divisions; many decisions have had great legal and political impact. It enjoys a high level of public esteem.

For example, some of the many important, and highly controversial, decisions it has taken relate to the question of abortion. The basic ruling has been that in general abortion is illegal. However, neither the mother nor the medical personnel performing the abortion can be punished if the mother has undergone a formalized process of advice on the pros and cons of the intended abortion, and the abortion is performed within the first three months of pregnancy. The constitutional court decided that the unborn child should be protected by the state but that this protection can only be successful in full cooperation with the mother and in respect to her personal situation.

THE ELECTION PROCESS

All Germans above the age of 18 have both the right to stand for election and the right to vote. Only in very limited circumstances, for example, when someone has been convicted of certain criminal offenses, can these rights be taken away, and then only for a limited period.

Parliamentary Elections

Half of the number of members of the Bundestag are elected according to a winner-takes-all majority vote. The remaining delegates are elected on the basis of proportional representation. Every voter, therefore, has two votes.

Germany is divided into constituencies of approximately the same number of voters. In each constituency, candidates stand for election and each voter casts his or her first vote for the preferred candidate. The candidate who wins the most votes in the constituency wins a seat.

Each voter casts his or her second vote for a list of candidates. The lists of candidates are submitted by the political party of each state, who determine the candidates and their rank on the list by internal party elections. In each state the number of votes cast for a particular party's list are totaled. The proportion of the total votes won by each list determines the number of the candidates on a particular list who are elected.

Subject to certain exceptions (for example, to provide for national minorities) a party must win at least 5 percent of all second votes if it is to gain seats in the Bundestag by means of the state lists. The aim of this rule is to prevent splinter groups from obstructing the work of the Bundestag or gaining excessive influence when no single party wins a majority.

POLITICAL PARTIES

German democracy has always given rise to many different political parties. The multiparty system is a basic structure of the constitutional order.

The Basic Law covers the parties' roles and responsibilities in Article 21. The constitution acknowledges that the political parties play a role in forming the political will of the people. Their internal structure must be in accordance with democratic principles. They must be primarily self-financing, relying on membership fees and donations. Additional financing from public funds is possible to a limited extent.

Political parties can only be banned by a decision of the Federal Constitutional Court. This has happened only twice and in the very early days of the Federal Republic. The Socialist Imperial Party, a successor party to the National Socialist Party, which had been disbanded by the Allied forces immediately after the Second World War, was itself banned in 1953. In 1956 the Federal Constitutional Court also prohibited the Communist Party of Germany as unconstitutional. A political party is unconstitutional only when the party or its adherents aim to impair or do away with the free democratic basis of the country, or threaten the existence of the Federal Republic of Germany. The provision is rooted in the experience of the overthrow of the democracy of the Weimar Republic by the Nazi party. At the same time, such limits to political freedom are intended to be highly exceptional, and only the highest court can impose them.

CITIZENSHIP

German citizenship is primarily acquired by birth. The principle of *ius sanguinis* is applied; that is, a child acquires German citizenship if one of his or her parents is a German citizen, wherever the child is born.

A foreigner can also acquire German citizenship if he or she legally resides in Germany, has a clean criminal record, has been able to find a residence, and is in a position to support his or her dependents. It is easier for the spouse of a German citizen to acquire citizenship than for a person not attached to a German citizen. There are also more lenient rules for foreigners who have legally resided in Germany for longer periods. It is still German policy to prevent dual citizenship, although exceptions to this rule have been made in the past few years.

From a constitutional point of view, the decisive factor regarding fundamental rights is not citizenship but the concept of being a "German." A German, in terms of the Basic Law (Article 116), is any person who has German citizenship or who is of German origin and, as a refugee or expellee, has taken refuge in the area of the German Empire as defined by the borders of December 31, 1937, which is the territory that belonged to Germany before the Nazis began to occupy neighboring states. Certain rights that tend to be reserved for citizens in other countries, such as voting rights, are assigned to all "Germans" by the German constitution.

FUNDAMENTAL RIGHTS

The Basic Law defines fundamental rights in its first chapter. They are the foundation of the German state and constitution. They encompass both human rights and citizen or "German" rights.

The German constitution guarantees the full traditional set of human rights. Social human rights, such as the right to work or the right to an education, are somewhat underrepresented; they are explicitly guaranteed, however, in a number of state constitutions.

The starting point is the guarantee of human dignity. Article 1 says: "Human dignity shall be inviolable. To respect and protect it shall be the duty of all state authority. The German people therefore acknowledge inviolable and inalienable human rights as the basis of every community, of peace and of justice in the world."

Taking human dignity as its starting point, the Basic Law guarantees numerous specific rights. These rights have binding force for the legislature, the executive, and the judiciary as directly applicable law.

The rights guaranteed by the constitution can be classified either as freedom rights or as equality rights. Article 2 protects the free development of the personality. To some extent it is a catch-all right that operates whenever the numerous individual freedom rights do not apply.

The equal treatment clause is contained in Article 3, which guarantees that all persons are equal before the law. This fundamental right is fleshed out with a number of specific provisions such as equality for men and women and the equality of voting rights. Another special equality right is provided for in Article 3(3): "No person shall be favored or disfavored because of sex, parentage, race, language, homeland and origin, faith, or religious or political opinions. No person shall be disfavored because of disability."

The Basic Law distinguishes between human rights, which apply to every human being, and those reserved for Germans in the sense of Article 116, the so-called Germans' rights. Examples of general human rights are freedom of belief or opinion. Examples of Germans' rights are freedom of assembly and association, freedom to choose one's career, and the right to vote in national elections. Germans' rights tend to relate to the national political or social system. As part of the process of European integration, these rights are increasingly being applied to citizens of the European Union.

Foreigners living in Germany are protected by the human rights specified in the constitution, including the right to the free development of personality stated in Article 2. These rights can, however, be limited somewhat more easily than the more specific Germans' rights.

Impact and Functions of Fundamental Rights

According to German thought, human rights are the axis on which all legal thinking turns. The functions that are ascribed to them are correspondingly numerous. Fundamental rights are first of all defensive rights, as has been emphasized since the 19th century. The state may not interfere with the legal position of the individual unless there is special reason to do so. Unjustified infringements can be blocked by the individual, implying that every person has legal remedies against unjustified detention, against the confiscation of property, against the banning of a particular point of view, and against any other unconstitutional infringement on his or her rights by state authorities.

Fundamental rights also traditionally involve the right to participate in the democratic political process. Particularly important are freedom of assembly, freedom of the press and of opinion, and the right to vote.

To a limited extent, a certain individual entitlement to services from the state is also recognized. Insofar as this is practical, the state has a duty to ensure that circumstances are conducive to the exercise of fundamental rights. For example, the right to choose one's career obliges the state to make available a reasonable number of places in educational institutions that prepare people for the various careers.

The Basic Law creates a duty of the state to protect its residents from harm to their fundamental rights. As such, affirmative action for the equality of men and women is an explicit duty of the state, in Article 3(2). Similarly, the state is not only required to respect the right to life and physical integrity but also obliged by Article 2 to intervene to protect these rights against infringements by third parties or other sources of danger. Thus, the state must ensure a healthy, natural environment insofar as this is practical.

Finally, the fundamental rights are also a guarantee of due process. The state must provide appropriate organizational and procedural structures to ensure the prompt and effective protection of individual rights.

With only one exception, the constitution specifies rights for the individual and not duties. The only situation in which private persons are directly limited by fundamental rights is set out in Article 9, which guarantees the freedom to form coalitions. The right to form associations for the protection and promotion of working and economic conditions is guaranteed for every person and for all trades and professions. Agreements that attempt to limit or hamper the exercise of this right are void, and measures with such an object are illegal. Article 9 thus directly forbids an employer to make it a condition for employment that a worker belong to a particular union or that the worker not belong to a union.

Other than Article 9, the fundamental rights do not explicitly regulate relations between private individuals. However, the idea of an indirect horizontal application has gradually been accepted. The fundamental rights permeate all areas of the law because they represent a constitutional decision in favor of certain values. Thus, even in relations between individuals, human dignity may not be violated, and freedom and equality must be respected in any circumstances.

Limitations to Fundamental Rights

The fundamental rights specified in the constitution are not without limits. The German constitution establishes potential limits imposed by specific needs of the public and the rights of others. However, no fundamental right can be disregarded completely. Each limit faces limits itself.

One of the most important of the "limitation limits" is the principle of proportionality. This concept expresses the idea that all law must be reasonable, one of the central principles of German law. Any rights limit must be appropriate, and there must not be any alternative that is less impairing. As always, the advantages and disadvantages of any state action must be weighed against one another; all legal interests involved must be drawn into a reasonable balance.

Further limiting the limitations is the requirement of legal certainty. The limits must be sufficiently clear and certain that the affected persons can orient themselves and adapt to the new situation. A limitation may also not interfere with the essential content of a right.

Article 18 of the Basic Law provides that anyone who uses rights such as freedom of opinion, assembly, and association to undermine the free democratic constitutional order can be found to be abusing these rights. This provision is based on the experience of the Weimar Republic and National Socialist eras. Up to now, this provision has not had any practical significance.

ECONOMY

The German constitution does not specify a specific economic system. The legislature is thus free to structure the economy. On the other hand, certain basic decisions by the framers of the constitution provide for a set of conditions that have to be considered in making economic decisions.

Freedom of property and the right of inheritance must be protected. Confiscation by the government is legal only in the public interest and if adequate compensation is given. The fundamental rights also protect the freedom of occupation or profession, general personal freedom, as well as the right to form associations, partnerships, and corporations. The right to form associations in order to safeguard and improve working and economic conditions is guaranteed to every individual and all corporations and professions. This right guarantees autonomy for trade unions and employers' associations in labor bargaining.

Germany is also defined by the constitution as a social state, providing for minimal social standards. This guarantee is of high political and legal impact. The constitution allows the government to transfer land, natural resources, and means of production to public ownership, but this provision has never been applied.

Taken as a whole, the German economic system can be described as a social market economy. It combines aspects of social responsibility with market freedom. This idea has had considerable impact also on shaping the economic system of the European Union.

RELIGIOUS COMMUNITIES

Freedom of religion or belief, which is guaranteed as a human right, also involves rights for religious communities. In addition, the Basic Law recognizes their special status. The constitution incorporates provisions regulating the relations between state and religions that had previously been part of the constitution of the Weimar Republic.

There is no established state church. All public authorities must remain strictly neutral in their relations with religious communities. Religions must be treated equally. Nonreligious philosophies of life, such as those of the Humanist Association, are accorded the same status as religious views.

The Catholic Church, the Protestant churches, and a series of smaller religious communities, such as the Jewish faith communities, the Adventist church, or the Church of Jesus Christ of Latter-Day Saints, are corporations under public law and enjoy a number of specific powers. The administrative authorities grant this status to communities if they show a minimal number of adherents and adequate internal statutes. As any other administrative act, the decision can be challenged in court.

Despite the essential separation of religions and the state, there are many areas of cooperation. Religious communities incorporated under public law are empowered to collect taxes from their adherents. The church tax can be collected by the state tax authorities on behalf of the community in exchange for a fee. Every taxpayer can opt out of this church tax by formally leaving the religious community in question.

Religious education is part of the curriculum in public schools and is taught in accordance with the principles of the religious community involved. Currently there are classes for Catholic, Protestant, Christian Orthodox, Jewish, and Hindu pupils as well as for some other beliefs, whenever there are a minimum of six to eight pupils of any of these religions at a school and the religious community requests that instruction. If the pupil does not want to participate in religious instruction, he or she can opt out, usually by taking classes in ethics instead. Classes that target Turkish or Iranian pupils that offer education on their home culture usually encompass teaching on Islam.

The independence and self-determination of the religious communities are of central importance. Religious communities regulate and administer their affairs independently within the limits of the laws that apply to all.

MILITARY DEFENSE AND STATE OF EMERGENCY

Creation and maintenance of armed forces for defense are responsibilities of the federal government. Apart from defending the country against an external or internal military attack, the armed forces may be used only for purposes specifically listed in the constitution, such as assistance during a natural disaster or a major accident, when police forces are insufficient.

General conscription requires all men above the age of 18 to perform basic military service for nine months. In addition there are professional soldiers who serve for fixed periods or for life. Women can volunteer. Conscientious objectors can file a petition to be excluded from military service, and these petitions are usually accepted. They then are obliged to perform service in social institutions for nine months.

The military always remains subject to civil government. During times of peace, the commander in chief is the minister of defense. Only in a state of defense does the chancellor assume that role. A special resolution of the Bundestag is required before the military can undertake any mission abroad.

Most units of the federal defense force are under the supreme command of NATO. Increasingly, multinational units oriented toward Europe are being organized. The Federal Republic of Germany has obliged itself in international treaties not to produce atomic, biological, or chemical weapons.

Federal defense forces may be committed to operations under United Nations auspices, whether as peacekeeping forces or in armed conflicts aimed at restoring peace and order. The constitution permits the integration of the armed forces into organizations for mutual collective security.

The Basic Law defines the state of defense in great detail. A state of defense exists only if the Federal Republic of Germany is attacked with armed military force. At that point, a series of laws aimed at ensuring the ability to mount an effective defense are operative. The powers of the civil authorities remain essentially intact; those of the military do not significantly increase, and there is no martial law. Fundamental rights may not be limited, with a few minor exceptions. The main impact of a state of defense relates to the redistribution of powers between state bodies.

AMENDMENTS TO THE CONSTITUTION

The Basic Law was designed so as to be difficult to change. Amendments require support from two-thirds of the members of the Bundestag and the Bundersat. A change can be made only by express alteration of the text. The aims are to ensure that there is a broad consensus supporting any change and to remove the constitution from the influence of short-term political trends. Nevertheless, the 1949 constitution has been amended more than 50 times.

Certain fundamental provisions are not subject to change at all. Article 79(3) says: "Amendments to this Basic Law affecting the division of the Federation into Länder, their participation on principle in the legislative process, or the principles laid down in Articles 1 and 20 shall be inadmissible." This so-called guarantee of eternity applies to the federal structure of Germany and the protection of and respect for human dignity. It also applies to certain central principles such as constitutional government under the rule of law, democracy and the sovereignty of the people, the social state, and the principle of republican form. In sum, the essential identity of the constitution may not be changed. This does not prevent the replacement of the constitution by a new one, but it does prevent the deformation of its fundamental structures by a process of creeping subversion.

PRIMARY SOURCES

Constitution in German: *Grundgesetz für die Bundesrepublik Deutschland.* Bonn: Bundeszentrale für politische Bildung, 2002. Available online. URL: http://www. bundesregierung.de/Gesetze/-,4222/Grundgesetz. htm. Accessed on August 14, 2005.

Constitution in English. Available online. URL: http:// www.bundesregierung.de/en/Federal-Government/ Function-and-constitutional-ba-,10206/Basic-Law. htm. Accessed on August 12, 2005.

SECONDARY SOURCES

David P. Currie, *The Constitution of the Federal Republic of Germany.* Chicago: University of Chicago Press, 1994.

Mathias Reimann and Joachim Zekoll, *Introduction to German Law.* München: Beck, 2005.

Gerhard Robbers, *An Introduction to German Law.* 4d ed. Baden-Baden: Nomos Verlagsgesellschaft, 2006.

Axel Tschentscher, *The Basic Law (Grundgesetz).* Würzburg: Jurisprudentia Verlag, 2002.

Gerhard Robbers

GHANA

At-a-Glance

OFFICIAL NAME
Republic of Ghana

CAPITAL
Accra

POPULATION
20,757,032 (2005 est.)

SIZE
92,456 sq. mi. (239,460 sq. km)

LANGUAGES
English (official), African languages (including Akan, Moshi-Dagomba, Ewe, and Ga)

RELIGIONS
Christianity 63%, Islam 16%, traditional beliefs 21%

NATIONAL OR ETHNIC COMPOSITION
African tribes (major tribes—Akan 44%, MoshiDagomba 16%, Ewe 13%, Ga 3%, Gurma 3%, Yoruba 1%) 98.5%, European and other 1.5%

DATE OF INDEPENDENCE OR CREATION
March 6, 1957

TYPE OF GOVERNMENT
Mixed presidential-parliamentary system

TYPE OF STATE
Unitary state

TYPE OF LEGISLATURE
Unicameral parliament

DATE OF CONSTITUTION
January 7, 1993

DATE OF LAST AMENDMENT
December 16, 1996

Ghana is a democratic state, founded on the sovereign and free will of its people to establish for themselves a nation built on freedom, justice, probity, accountability, the rule of law, and the respect for and protection of fundamental human rights. It is a unitary state, governed by an executive branch headed by the president; a 230-member Parliament headed by the speaker; and a judiciary headed by the chief justice. The powers and functions of these three institutions are distinctly separate under the constitution.

CONSTITUTIONAL HISTORY

Ghana, formerly known as the Gold Coast, was the subject of Portuguese, Danish, Dutch, and British influence between 1470 and 1957, but it officially became a British Colony in 1874. The country became an independent and sovereign state on March 6, 1957, governed under the 1956 constitution, which provided for a parliamentary system similar to the Westminster model of Britain.

On July 1, 1960, a new constitution, changing Ghana from a parliamentary to a presidential system and declaring the nation a republic, was adopted. The constitution had no bill of rights and gave the president wide executive powers. In 1964, a referendum officially made Ghana a one-party state.

On February 24, 1966, the army and the police overthrew the Nkrumah regime and formed the government of the National Liberation Council. The council suspended the 1960 constitution, but the judiciary and civil service were allowed to continue to operate.

A new constitution was promulgated in October 1969, ushering in the Second Republic. This constitution established a mixed parliamentary-presidential system. It provided for a 140-member Parliament, a prime minister, and a presidential commission to exercise executive powers.

Between 1972 and 1979, three more military governments, namely, the National Redemption Council, the Supreme Military Council, and the Armed Forces Revolutionary Council, ruled Ghana. In 1979, the last council instituted a program to restore constitutional rule. The third republican constitution entered into force on September 24, 1979. This constitution departed extensively from the Westminster model. The constitution advocated separation of powers and had a bill of rights. However, it granted indemnity from prosecution to members of the Armed Forces Revolutionary Council for any executive, legislative, or judicial action it had taken or omitted to take.

On December 31, 1981, there was another coup d'état, led by Flight Lieutenant Jerry John Rawlings. Rawlings became chairman of the Provisional National Defence Council.

In 1991, with pressure from the international community and Ghanaians to restore democracy, the Provisional National Defence Council established a 258-member Consultative Assembly. Representing all sections of the Ghanaian community, it was mandated to consider proposals for a new constitution drafted by a seven-member committee of experts.

The final draft constitution was put to a national referendum on April 28, 1992, and was accepted by a 92 percent majority. The constitution entered into force on January 7, 1993, and established the Fourth Republic.

FORM AND IMPACT OF THE CONSTITUTION

The 1992 constitution is embodied in a single document. The constitution is the supreme law of the republic and forms the standard against which all other law is measured. To prevent a repeat of past history, the constitution prohibits Parliament from enacting a law to make Ghana a one-party state.

BASIC ORGANIZATIONAL STRUCTURE

Ghana is divided into 10 administrative regions, which are further divided into 138 districts. The president appoints regional ministers and district chief executives to exercise executive authority in the name of the president and in accordance with the constitution. The district assembly is the highest body at the local government level and exercises deliberative, legislative, and executive powers. In addition, the constitution mandates Parliament to enact laws to coordinate the relationship between the central government and the district assemblies.

LEADING CONSTITUTIONAL PRINCIPLES

The constitution upholds democracy, freedom, justice, supremacy of the constitution, popular sovereignty, probity, accountability, rule of law, and separation of powers.

CONSTITUTIONAL BODIES

The main constitutional bodies under the constitution are the president, Parliament, the House of Chiefs, and the judiciary. Others are the Council of State, the Commission for Human Rights and Administrative Justice, and the National Commission for Civic Education.

The President

The president is the head of state, head of the executive administration, and commander in chief of the armed forces. The executive authority of Ghana vests in the president. A candidate for the presidency must nominate a vice president before running. Any presidential candidate must be a citizen of Ghana and at least 40 years old. The election of the president is by universal adult suffrage for a term of four years. No one may hold the presidency for more than two terms. There is a cabinet consisting of the president, the vice president, and no fewer than 10 and no more than 19 ministers of state assisting the president in the determination of general policy.

The Parliament

Parliament consists of no fewer than 140 elected members. The legislative power of Ghana is vested in Parliament.

The Lawmaking Process

Parliament exercises its legislative authority by passing bills, which must be approved by the president. In the ordinary lawmaking process, a bill is published in the *Gazette,* accompanied by an explanatory memorandum. After 14 days, the bill is laid before Parliament, which deliberates extensively on it through the appropriate parliamentary committee and the whole house. The president assents to bills to make them law. A bill affecting the institution of chieftaincy, however, cannot be introduced unless it has first been referred to the National House of Chiefs.

The House of Chiefs

The constitution guarantees the institution of chieftaincy, together with its traditional councils, as established by customary law and usage. Parliament has no power to enact any law that confers on any person or authority the right to accord or withdraw recognition to or from a chief for any purpose whatsoever or in any way that detracts from or derogates the honor and dignity of the institution of chieftaincy.

There is a National House of Chiefs. The House of Chiefs for each region elects a member to the National House of Chiefs. The National House of Chiefs advises any person or authority charged with any responsibility under the constitution concerning any matter related to chieftaincy. The house also is charged with the development of customary law and exercises jurisdiction over matters affecting chieftaincy through a Judicial Committee.

The Judiciary

Article 125 vests judicial power in the judiciary and declares its independence. The judiciary is made up of the superior courts, namely, the Supreme Court, the Court of Appeals, the High Court, and the Regional Tribunals, and the lower courts and tribunals established by Parliament, currently the Circuit, Magistrate, and District Courts. The chief justice is the head of the judiciary.

The Supreme Court is made up of the chief justice and no fewer than nine other justices. The court has original jurisdiction in the interpretation and enforcement of the constitution and is the final court of appeal in all matters. The court also has supervisory jurisdiction over all courts and adjudicating authorities in the country.

The Court of Appeals is composed of a chief justice and no fewer than 10 justices. It has jurisdiction to hear appeals from any judgment, decree, or order of the High Court, as well as from regional tribunals and the lower courts.

The High Court is composed of a chief justice and no fewer than 20 justices. It has original jurisdiction in all civil and criminal matters, including treason and high treason, and appellate jurisdiction over the lower courts. It also has exclusive original jurisdiction to enforce fundamental human rights.

The regional tribunals are made up of a chief justice, a chair and other members, who may or may not be lawyers, designated by the chief justice to sit as panel members for specified periods. The regional tribunal has jurisdiction to try such offenses as Parliament may prescribe by law.

Since the inception of the Fourth Republic, the judiciary has ensured that both private and public persons, including the government, act in a manner consistent with the constitution. Landmark decisions of the Supreme Court in this regard include the "31st December" case, in which the Court ruled that the celebration of 31st December, the anniversary of a coup d'état, was contrary to the spirit and letter of the constitution in the light of the nation's painful history of military interventions.

The Council of State

Article 89 establishes a 25-member Council of State to counsel the president, ministers of state, and Parliament in the performance of their duties. The council also re-

views bills, particularly those dealing with constitutional amendments. The council is akin to a council of elders in Ghanaian tradition. The president appoints the members of the council in consultation with Parliament. Members of the council serve a four-year term, coterminous with the president, unless a member resigns, becomes permanently incapacitated, dies, or is removed from office by the president, in consultation with Parliament.

The Commission for Human Rights and Administrative Justice

The Commission for Human Rights and Administrative Justice is an independent body established under Article 216 of the constitution. This commission is made up of a commissioner and two deputy commissioners, appointed by the president in consultation with the Council of State. The commissioner and the two deputies cease to hold office upon attaining 70 and 65 years of age, respectively. The president may also remove them from office.

The commission investigates complaints of human rights abuses, corruption, injustice, abuse of power, and unfair treatment by public officers or private persons, and those against the Public Services Commission concerning unequal access to recruitment into the security services of Ghana. The commission has quasi-judicial powers and can adopt a number of remedial measures, including alternative dispute resolution mechanisms and institution of proceedings in a competent court.

National Commission for Civic Education

The National Commission for Civic Education is established under Article 231 and is composed of a chair, two deputy chair, and four other members, all appointed by the president in consultation with the Council of State. Members of the commission cannot be members of any political party and must be eligible to be elected members of Parliament. The commission's functions include the education of the general public on the principles and objectives of the constitution and assistance to the government in inculcating civic responsibility and awareness in Ghanaians.

The commission, in conjunction with the electoral commission, has played an important role in voter education, helping to ensure four successful national elections and three local government elections.

THE ELECTION PROCESS AND POLITICAL PARTICIPATION

Every citizen of Ghana who is at least 18 years of age and of sound mind has the right to vote and be registered as a voter for any public election and referenda.

Presidential and parliamentary elections are held every four years. The president appoints the seven-member electoral commission, which is responsible for the compilation and periodic review of a register of voters, the demarcation of electoral boundaries for national and local government elections, the conduct and supervision of all public elections and referenda, the education of voters on the electoral process, and any other functions prescribed by law.

POLITICAL PARTIES

Ghana is a multiparty democracy. Every citizen of Ghana has the right to form and join a political party of his or her choice and to participate in political activity. Political parties are, subject to the constitution, free to participate in political discourse in the state and disseminate information on political, social, and economic issues of a national character. The constitution prohibits formation of political parties along ethnic, religious, regional, or other sectional lines. The state is required to provide fair opportunities to all political parties to present their programs to the electorate by ensuring equal access to state-owned media. Given this opportunity, political parties have been the main instruments for shaping political opinion since the birth of the Fourth Republic.

CITIZENSHIP

Citizenship of Ghana is primarily by birth. Citizenship may, however, also be acquired by marriage to a Ghanaian citizen, by registration, and through any other means prescribed by Parliament. Dual citizenship is also permitted.

FUNDAMENTAL RIGHTS

Fundamental rights and freedoms are enshrined in Chapter 5 of the constitution. The executive, legislative, and judicial authorities, as well as private individuals and corporate bodies, are obliged to respect and uphold the enumerated rights and freedoms. The courts are responsible for enforcement.

Chapter 5 captures the primary human rights and freedoms, categorized as civil, political, economic, social, and cultural rights. It forms the clearest definition of rights in Ghanaian constitutional history.

Article 18 safeguards the right to enjoy property without unjustifiable interference. Article 20 goes further to prohibit compulsory acquisition of private property by the state, except for the public good, with prompt, fair, and adequate compensation. Article 22 gives a surviving spouse a right to a fair share of the estate of a deceased intestate spouse and requires Parliament to enact legislation regulating the property rights of spouses.

Impact and Functions of Fundamental Rights

The bill of rights in the 1992 constitution draws on the lessons learned from the nation's past, when both civilian and military regimes showed no regard for human rights. On the other hand, the transitional provisions in the constitution, which prohibit any inquiry into the acts and omissions of past military regimes, present a debatable limitation on the right to justice.

Limitations to Fundamental Rights

Most of the rights in the constitution require that such rights must be exercised with due regard to the rights of others and the public interest. When rights are limited by the state, the constitution requires that such limitation be justifiable according to law and the constitution.

ECONOMY

The constitution does not specify a particular economic system. However, the directive principles of state policy in Chapter 6 of the constitution enjoin the state to take all necessary steps to maximize the rate of economic development and to ensure a sound and healthy economy. The constitution also encourages private sector and foreign investment.

RELIGIOUS COMMUNITIES

The freedom of thought, conscience, and belief, as well as the freedom to practice any religion publicly, are guaranteed by the constitution. There is no state religion and no religion may receive preferential treatment by state institutions.

MILITARY DEFENSE AND STATE OF EMERGENCY

Parliament is the only institution authorized to raise an armed force. The president is the commander in chief of the Ghana armed forces and chair of the Armed Forces Council.

Only the president has the power to declare a state of emergency, by a proclamation published in the *Gazette,* acting in accordance with the advice of the Council of State. The proclamation must also be approved by Parliament. The military may be engaged in a state of emergency only on the authority of the president. There is no compulsory military service in Ghana.

AMENDMENTS TO THE CONSTITUTION

The ease or difficulty in amending the constitution depends on whether a provision is "entrenched." The constitution lists the entrenched provisions in Article 290. A provision that is not entrenched may be amended by an act of Parliament, with prior consideration of the bill by the Council of State.

An entrenched provision requires consideration by the Council of State and a majority vote in a referendum on the bill. At the referendum, at least 40 percent of registered voters must vote and at least 75 percent of the persons who voted must vote in favor of the bill.

PRIMARY SOURCES

Constitution of the Republic of Ghana, 1992. Available online. URL: http://www.parliament.gh/const_constitution.php. Accessed on August 19, 2005.

The Constitution of the Republic of Ghana. Accra: Ghana Publishing, 1992.

SECONDARY SOURCES

S. K. B. Asante, *Reflections on the Constitution, Law and Development.* J. B. Danquah Memorial Lectures 35th Series, 2002. Available online. URL: http://ghana.fes-international.de/pages/03_publications/02_key_institutions.htm. Accessed on June 21, 2006.

F. A. R. Bennion, *The Constitutional Law of Ghana.* African Law Series No. 5. London: Butterworths, 1962.

T. O. Elias, *Ghana and Sierra Leone.* London: Stevens and Sons, 1962.

S. O. Gyandoh Jr. and J. A. Griffiths, *Sourcebook of the Constitutional Law of Ghana.* Accra: Catholic Press, 1972.

Kwadwo Afari-Gyan, *The Making of the Fourth Republican Constitution of Ghana.* Accra: Friedrich Ebert Stiftung, 1998.

Edmund Amarkwei Foley

GREECE

At-a-Glance

OFFICIAL NAME
Hellenic Republic

CAPITAL
Athens

POPULATION
10,934,097 (2005 est.)

SIZE
50,942 sq. mi. (131,940 sq. km)

LANGUAGES
Greek

RELIGIONS
Christian Orthodox 97%, Muslim 1.3%, Catholic 0.4%, Protestant 0.1%, unaffiliated or other 1.2%

NATIONAL OR ETHNIC COMPOSITION
Greek 93%, Albanian 4%, other (Bulgarian, Russian, Romanian, American, Cypriot, Georgian) 3%

DATE OF INDEPENDENCE
February 3, 1830

TYPE OF GOVERNMENT
Parliamentary republic

TYPE OF STATE
Unitary state

TYPE OF LEGISLATURE
Unicameral parliament

DATE OF CONSTITUTION
June 11, 1975

DATE OF LAST AMENDMENT
April 6, 2001

Greece is a parliamentary republic, based on the rule of law and on the principle of the separation of powers. It is a unitary state with a unicameral legislature. The strongest political body is the cabinet. The role of the prime minister is central. The cabinet depends on Parliament's confidence. The head of state is the president of the republic. The role of the president is symbolic. Political parties are free. Elections take place every four years.

Human rights are constitutionally guaranteed and protected by independent courts of justice. Religious freedom is guaranteed, though the Orthodox Church enjoys some privileges, dictated by tradition and by the fact that 97 percent of the population is Orthodox. The economic system is a social market economy. The military is controlled by the government.

CONSTITUTIONAL HISTORY

After the successful revolt against the Ottoman Empire (1821–27), the independence of Greece was internationally recognized by the London Protocol of 1830. During the first year of the revolution, three local constitutions were voted, all of them to be superseded by the first national constitution of 1822. In 1823, the constitution was amended and in 1827 a new constitution was approved. All these constitutions were democratic and liberal, influenced by French and American political thought of the late 18th century.

The foundations of the Greek state were built under the leadership of Ioannis Kapodistrias, a statesman of international prestige who became the first governor of the republic. The republic fell with his assassination in 1831.

Greece then became a monarchy. The first king was Otho, son of King Ludwig I of Bavaria. He did not assume his duties until 1835, when he became of age, and a three-man regency exercised absolute royal power in the interim. A new constitution was voted in 1832, the so-called Hegemonic Constitution, which was actually never applied. This constitution was monarchic, but it included provisions guaranteeing fundamental rights and freedoms.

King Otho maintained the absolutism of the regency. In 1843, a one-day revolt, pervaded by the spirit of constitutionalism, forced Otho to proclaim elections. The resulting Parliament issued the constitution of 1844. This constitution remained monarchic, with the king as the supreme organ of the state and having major political power. However, fundamental rights were also protected, and Parliament passed an electoral law that actually introduced universal suffrage.

Otho's absolutism continued. The dynasty was dethroned after a revolt by the people and the army in 1862. Parliament elected Prince George of Denmark as the new king of the Greeks. A year later, the constitution of 1864, the first democratic constitution of the independent state, was written. Royal power was limited, the list of fundamental rights was enlarged, and the principles of separation of powers and judicial independence were emphasized.

Continued royal interference in political matters, especially in choice of the cabinet and in provocation of the breakup of political parties, stirred up political resistance. The leading political personality of this period, Harilaos Trikoupis, managed to introduce an authentic parliamentary system of government in 1875, in which the cabinet would depend only on Parliament's confidence, and not on the king's approval.

A long crisis in Greek politics and in the Greek economy put in power, in the beginning of the 20th century, Eleftherios Venizelos, who dominated Greek political life for a quarter of a century. An amendment of the constitution of 1864 was passed under his guidance in 1911. During its implementation, the country suffered a major constitutional crisis, known as the national split. The main issue was the extent of royal power in foreign policy, in the appointment and the dismissal of the cabinet, and in the dissolution of Parliament. During 1916–17, Greece was governed by two cabinets, one in Athens and one in Thessaloniki. The national split had consequences that affected the country for decades.

Antiroyalist movements succeeded in dethroning the dynasty in 1924. A republican constitution was created the following year and amended in 1926 and in 1927. The last amendment remained in force until 1935, when a coup d'etat restored the Crown and restored the constitution of 1911.

A military dictatorship in 1936 suspended the constitution. It lasted until the occupation of the country by German forces, after successful resistance of the Greek people to the Italian invasion. Greece was liberated in 1944. A civil war immediately after liberation delayed the normalization of political and constitutional life. In 1952, the constitution of 1864/1911 was revised. A major constitutional issue arose in 1965, when King Constantine II claimed the right to appoint ministers. This action led Prime Minister George Papandreou to resign. The crisis that followed culminated in a military coup in 1967. A military dictatorship lasted until 1974. The dictatorship abolished the constitution of 1952 and imposed the "constitution" of 1968, and later the "constitution" of 1973, which replaced the democracy monarchy with a republic. The military regime fell in 1974 after ineptly provoking the Turkish invasion of Cyprus.

Constantine Karamanlis, a conservative politician with an international profile, now formed a government of national unity. A referendum chose a republican form of government, and a new constitution was written in 1975. It is based on the principles of popular sovereignty, parliamentarianism, separation of powers, political pluralism, and the rule of law. It is a modern constitution with respect to human rights.

The 1975 constitution strengthened the political role of the president of the republic, thus creating a bipolar parliamentarianism. An amendment was voted in 1986, under the socialists, which limited the powers of the president to those of a merely symbolic head of state. The last constitutional amendment was passed in 2001. It enlarged the list of fundamental rights, simplified legislative procedure, and gave constitutional backing to independent regulatory authorities.

With the constitution of 1975, Greece's political life has been fully normalized. Institutions of democracy and parliamentarianism function without turbulence. Greece is a member of the European Union and the North Atlantic Treaty Organization (NATO), and has accepted the most important European and international conventions. Its legal system has absorbed all the principles of modern European legal culture.

FORM AND IMPACT OF THE CONSTITUTION

Greece has a written constitution that is placed at the top of the hierarchy of legal norms. The constitution is a single document consisting of 120 articles.

Both statutory law and the normative acts of the administration must comply with the constitution. Conflicts between the constitution and all other legal norms are resolved in favor of the former.

European law constitutes an exception to this rule. It has priority over internal statutory law, but its priority over the Greek constitution is not yet explicitly recognized. Actual conflicts between European law and the Greek constitution are very rare, but in case they arise, they will probably be resolved in favor of the primacy of European law.

The constitution is the most important law; since law reflects the values of the society, it is also a guarantor of such values. The Greek constitution has adopted all the significant values of modern legal culture. It is nevertheless an open constitution, leaving large margins of appreciation (leeway) to the government in the formation of general policy, as well as in balancing conflicting values and private interests with the public interest.

BASIC ORGANIZATIONAL STRUCTURE

Greece is a unitary state, not a federation. There is only one policymaking administration, that of the central government. Yet administrative authority is decentralized. The central government guides, coordinates, and reviews the work of the decentralized authorities (regions), which wield decisive powers on local matters. Decentralization is actually a constitutional ideal not yet fully achieved, and the central government still possesses serious decisive powers. This system does not necessarily contradict the constitution, which permits a slow transition to full decentralization.

Apart from regions, that is, decentralized state authorities, the constitution provides for local self-governed authorities of the first and second levels, which are entities of public law, separate from the state (i.e., separate from central government and decentralized authorities). To the first level belong the municipalities and communities, and to the second the prefectures. Local self-governed authorities administer local affairs. Their basic organs (prefect, mayor, and councils) are elected by universal and secret ballot. State control over local agencies is confined to the review of the legality of their actions.

While decentralized and local authorities are all confined within specific geographical areas, there are other public corporate bodies, functionally decentralized, whose authority covers the whole country. They are legal entities of public or private law. Examples are the regulatory authorities (for competition, telecommunications, energy, data protection, etc.), social security organizations, and public enterprises (for electricity, water supply, transport, etc.). Central state supervision varies from case to case, according to the law.

LEADING CONSTITUTIONAL PRINCIPLES

Greece is a parliamentary republic. The main principles of the form of government are democracy, representative government, parliamentarism, separation of powers, the rule of law, and the welfare state.

Greece is a democracy based on popular sovereignty; this means that Parliament, which represents the people and the nation, is elected through free, universal, and secret ballot. The cabinet is formally chosen by the president of the republic, but it must enjoy the confidence of Parliament or resign. Through Parliament's confidence, the cabinet represents the people, too.

Parliament legislates and exercises control over the administration. This is made possible by the cabinet's supervision over government bodies, local authorities, and so on.

Parliament and the administration are separate, but the separation of powers is not absolute. Thus, the president of the republic is an organ of both the legislative and the executive power. The cabinet initiates legislation and issues normative acts and regulations of its own. Cabinet ministers are usually members of Parliament.

A strict and absolute separation of powers obtains, however, for the judiciary. Judges are subject only to the constitution and the law. Because of the hierarchy of legal norms, courts of justice are bound not to apply laws whose content is contrary to the constitution, to European law, or to any other superior law.

The principle of the rule of law is expressly guaranteed by the constitution. Therefore, the executive may not act without a law (principle of legality of administrative action). It further means that fundamental rights and freedoms are guaranteed and that access to independent courts of justice is free.

The principle of the welfare state is also expressly guaranteed by the constitution. Furthermore, the constitution contains a list of social rights and obligations of the state, for health, social security, and the environment.

CONSTITUTIONAL BODIES

The constitution provides for the main organs of the state. These are the president of the republic, the cabinet, Parliament, and the courts of justice.

The President of the Republic

The president of the republic is elected by Parliament for a tenure of five years. Any person who has Greek citizenship for at least five years and is a descendant of a Greek parent is eligible to be elected president after having attained the age of 40. Reelection of the same person is permitted only once.

The institution of the vice president is unknown in Greece. The constitution provides instead for the replacement of the president, in case of incapacity to perform his or her duties lasting more than 30 days. The incapacity has to be ascertained by Parliament, in which case the election of a new president must follow. In any case, during the period of incapacity the president of the republic is replaced by the president of Parliament.

The president of the republic is the head of state. The constitution characterizes the president as a "mediator" or "arbitrator"; this attribute underlines the prestige of the office rather than its powers. Since the constitutional amendment of 1986, the president is a symbolic organ of the state deprived of any real political power.

Many state acts require the signature of the president. Examples of such acts are the promulgation of bills voted by Parliament, the issuance of administrative acts, the appointment of the prime minister, and, at the latter's advice, of the members of the cabinet. In all these functions, the president has little or no margin of appreciation (leeway).

The president does not have criminal and civil liability for acts related to the duties of the office, except for high treason or intentional violation of the constitution. Criminal proceedings against the president are initiated by Parliament. The trial is performed by a special court. For acts not related to presidential duties the president is fully responsible, before ordinary criminal courts, but prosecution may not start until the expiration of his or her term. For such acts the president also bears full civil liability.

The Cabinet

The cabinet determines and exercises internal and foreign policy, according to the law. Having the right of legislative initiative, and enjoying the majority in Parliament, the cabinet often proposes laws that are approved by the legislature. It can thus determine the policy of the land, making it the strongest political body.

The cabinet comprises the prime minister and the ministers. In order to become a member of the cabinet one has to be Greek, at least 25 years old, and legally entitled to vote. Ministers may not engage in any other professional activities while serving in the cabinet.

The cabinet is governed by the principle of collegiality, though the prime minister has a predominant role. The prime minister's decision to appoint and dismiss ministers is binding on the president of the republic.

The president appoints as prime minister the leader of the political party that enjoys the absolute majority of seats in Parliament. If no party attains such a majority, the president gives a mandate to the leader of the largest party to explore the possibility of forming a cabinet that could enjoy the confidence of Parliament. If this seems possible, the president proceeds to the appointment. If not, the president addresses the leader of the second largest party with a similar mandate, and in case of failure the leader of the third largest party. If all the exploratory mandates are unsuccessful, the president proclaims new elections.

The cabinet, after its appointment, has to appear before Parliament for a vote of confidence. During its term, a vote of confidence or of censure may be initiated by the cabinet or by the opposition, respectively. The loss of Parliament's confidence results to the resignation of the cabinet. If no new cabinet enjoying Parliament's confidence can be formed, the president proclaims new elections.

The members of the cabinet have criminal responsibility for acts related to their duties. Prosecution is entrusted to Parliament and trial to a special court. For other acts, ordinary laws are applicable and ordinary courts of justice are competent. Members of the cabinet have full civil liability as well.

The Parliament

The Parliament is the representative body of the people. It legislates and exercises control over the executive. It also chooses the president of the republic and has the power to press charges against him or her or against cabinet members.

Parliament consists of 300 delegates. It is elected for a term of four years through free, direct, universal, equal, and secret elections, held simultaneously throughout the country. Parliament does not function under the principle of continuity; when its term is over, or when it is dissolved, there is no Parliament; elections must be held within one month of termination or dissolution, and the next Parliament must convene within the next month.

Parliament works in plenum during its annual sessions, which last at least five months, but some members carry on during the period between two sessions in a smaller version of Parliament. The body is organized into committees, the most important those responsible for drafting bills.

Members of Parliament enjoy parliamentary privilege, which safeguards their independence. They may not be prosecuted for opinions or votes in the discharge of their duties, except for libel, if Parliament gives its permission. They may be neither arrested nor prosecuted for acts not relating to their duties, without Parliament's permission, except in cases of flagrant felonies.

The Lawmaking Process

Legislative initiative belongs to each member of Parliament and to each cabinet minister. In practice, however, only bills proposed by the cabinet are voted by Parliament.

Bills are discussed and elaborated in parliamentary committees and in the plenum or in the smaller version of Parliament that operates between sessions. They are voted up or down by the plenum and by the section. Bills of major importance are voted only by the plenum.

Once Parliament passes a bill, the president of the republic proceeds to promulgate it and publish it in the official gazette. The president may choose to send the bill back to Parliament, in case of a serious violation of the legislative procedure. If the bill is passed again, the president is obliged to promulgate it.

The Judiciary

Justice is administered by two types of court: one for civil and criminal cases, the other for administrative cases. At the top of civil and criminal justice (which is composed of courts of first instance and appeal courts) is the Areios Pagos (a Supreme Court); at the top of administrative justice (which is also composed of first instance and appeal courts) is the Council of State. Both are supreme courts. There is also a third supreme court, the Court of Accounts.

A Special Highest Court is provided to settle matters of constitutionality, conflicting interpretation of laws by two supreme courts, and conflicts between different jurisdictions. The Special Highest Court also judges cases concerning parliamentary elections.

Since the end of the 19th century, judicial review of the constitutionality of laws has been diffuse—that is, it can take place in any court. If a lower court concludes that a law is unconstitutional, it simply does not apply it to the case before it; it does not have the power to derogate (invalidate) the law. This power belongs only to the Special Highest Court.

The judiciary is independent of the legislative and the executive power. Judges enjoy constitutional guarantees that safeguard their independence. No change of their status is permitted without a decision by the Judicial Council.

THE ELECTION PROCESS

All Greeks have the right to vote at the age of 18 and the right to be elected at the age of 25.

Of the 300 members of Parliament, 288 are elected in electoral districts as candidates of political parties or, in very rare cases, as independents. The other 12 are elected as state deputies under the flag of political parties. The election is by proportional representation. No candidate of a political party and no independent candidate is elected if the party or the independent candidate does not win 3 percent of the electorate.

POLITICAL PARTIES

Greece has a multiparty system. Every Greek is free to found and join a political party. Parties are entitled to receive financial support from the state, but they are obliged to have transparent financial management. Banning of political parties is not provided for in the Greek legal system.

CITIZENSHIP

Greek citizenship is acquired by birth and after birth. A child born to a Greek father or a Greek mother is Greek, irrespective of the place of birth. Furthermore, a child born in Greece is also Greek, if he or she does not acquire any other citizenship. A person obtains Greek citizenship after birth if he or she is recognized or adopted by a Greek parent before the age of 18, if he or she voluntarily renders military service, if he or she is admitted to Mount Athos as a monk, or if he or she is naturalized by a decision of the minister of the interior. No person acquires or loses Greek citizenship through marriage. Loss of citizenship (which is very rare) may be decided by the minister of the interior upon application of the interested person, or if a Greek citizen acts to the detriment of the country.

FUNDAMENTAL RIGHTS

The Greek constitution protects fundamental rights and freedoms, civil as well as political and social.

Civil rights and freedoms establish a claim of the individual against the state and against public power in general not to intervene in certain spheres of action. They set limitations to the state and to public power. Examples of such rights in the Greek constitution are the dignity of the person, personal freedom, freedom of movement, privacy, habeas corpus, the right to freely develop one's own personality and to participate in the economic and social life of the country; property rights; freedom of thought, of art, of science, of the press; religious liberty, freedom of correspondence, free access to courts of justice, and fair trial. The current Greek catalogue of civil rights and freedoms contains new 21st-century rights as well, such as the right to be informed and to participate in the information society, protection of personal data and genetic identity, and protection against biomedical interventions.

Greek political rights are rights of participation: Participation in the legislative power is exercised with the right to vote and the right to be elected; participation in the executive power is guaranteed with the right to be appointed as a civil servant; participation in the judicial power is expressed with the right to be appointed as a member of a jury and as a judge. Establishment of political parties and free participation therein are also guaranteed by the constitution.

Greek social rights establish claims for certain services to be provided by the state, guaranteeing a decent standard of living. These claims are not enforceable directly on the basis of the constitution but only when a law concretizes them as legal. What the constitution actually guarantees are the responsibility of the state to advance health and social security; to protect homeless and disabled persons; to provide special care for family, maternity, and childhood; to establish good working conditions for the population; and to protect the environment. Social rights are guaranteed for both Greeks and aliens. The extent of the guarantee is specified by law.

The constitution expressly guarantees equality as a general principle of law. Special mention is made of the equality of men and women.

Civil rights and freedoms are recognized for every person, independently of Greek nationality. An exception is made for the right of assembly and association, which is endowed only to Greeks. Aliens enjoy this right, too, on the basis of the European Convention of Human Rights, but not for political purposes. While political rights are guaranteed only for Greeks, European citizens may vote and be elected in local self-government bodies, in accordance with European law.

Apart from civil rights and freedoms, and political and social rights, the Greek constitution contains institutional guarantees in matters such as ownership and competition; marriage; press, radio, and television; universities; and local self-government. These guarantees, though closely connected to the rights of individuals pertaining to them, protect the institutions as such and not the individuals.

Impact and Functions of Fundamental Rights

The constitution contains fundamental rights in a legal text at the top of the hierarchy of all legal norms, in recognition that rights are the basis of the relationship between the state and the individual. Fundamental rights incorporate the highest values of society and state; they must be respected in every aspect and in every dimension of state action.

Greek constitutional theory and jurisprudence have gradually proceeded to further recognition of the importance of fundamental rights. They are considered to be applicable not only vis-à-vis the state and public power but also vis-à-vis individuals. The most recent constitutional amendment (2001) expressly adopted this "horizontal effect."

In brief, fundamental rights are defensive rights of individuals and groups of individuals, rights of participation in state affairs, and rights of the population for a decent living. These rights are not isolated one from another but are in fact complementary.

Limitations to Fundamental Rights

Fundamental rights are concretized and limited in the constitution itself and in the law. Ordinary laws may restrict fundamental rights only if they are based on a concrete reservation within the constitution. This rule is a consequence of the supreme hierarchical status of the constitution. It applies, however, only to fundamental rights and not to institutional guarantees.

There are a few rights that are privileged and can never be restricted by law. These are basically human dignity and freedom of religious conscience (not of religious practice).

The general right of free development of the personality may not infringe upon the rights of others. The infringement clause of the constitution applies to all fundamental rights. It relies on a balancing test of conflicting rights, using logical, systematic, and teleological interpretation of the constitutional and legal provisions that guarantee these rights. No right may be surrendered completely in favor of another; all conflicting rights must be implemented at least partially, and to the greatest possible extent.

The main principles controlling limitations of fundamental rights are proportionality (the limit cannot be greater than the need), respect for the *core* of the rights, and the principle of equal treatment.

While the constitution prohibits the abuse of fundamental rights, it does not provide for sanctions. The prohibition is still legally binding, as the abusive exercise of rights is not protected.

ECONOMY

The constitution does not mandate a specific economic system. Nevertheless, a free market economy is guaranteed by freedom of contracts, professional freedom, and economic and property rights. It is, however, balanced by explicit provisions for state planning and coordination of economic activities. State intervention in the free market economy aims to consolidate social peace, protect the general interest, and safeguard the economic development of all sectors of the national economy.

The Greek state is defined as a welfare state under the rule of law. This means that it is both liberal and social. Its liberal character is manifested in the guarantee of fundamental civil rights and liberties, its social character in the guarantee of social rights of the members of society. The Greek economic system is, in other words, a social market economy.

RELIGIOUS COMMUNITIES

Parallel to the guarantee of individual and collective religious freedom, which includes the freedom of religious communities, the Greek constitution reserves a special status for the Orthodox Church. The Orthodox Church of Greece is dogmatically united with the Patriarchate of Constantinople and the other Orthodox Churches, but administratively it is autocephalous (rules itself). It is recognized by the constitution as the prevailing religion.

The attribute "prevailing" does not mean that the Church of Greece prevails over other religious communities. It means, according to the traditional doctrine, that the great majority of Greeks are Orthodox. The Church of Greece enjoys several privileges: It is a legal person of public law, whereas other religious communities are normally legal persons of private law. Important Orthodox holidays are recognized as state holidays. The Orthodox clergy is paid by the Greek state; the state undertook this obligation after major donations by the church in periods of economic crisis.

The constitution of 1975 dropped certain other privileges of the Church of Greece, included in former constitutions. Thus, the head of state does not have to be Orthodox, and his or her oath, while Christian, does not pledge protection of Orthodoxy. Proselytism is now forbidden in general, not just when aimed at Orthodox believers as in the past. Finally, education retains a religious orientation but is more detached from the so-called Hellenic and Christian ideals.

A special constitutional provision refers to Mount Athos, a monastic area in the northern part of Greece. The 20 monasteries collectively enjoy a special self-governing status, under the spiritual jurisdiction of the Patriarchate of Constantinople. No person may dwell as a monk in Mount Athos if he is not Orthodox, and no woman may be admitted even for a visit. These exceptions to the principle of equality of sexes and to religious freedom are justified by an Orthodox tradition of more than 1,000 years. They are recognized in the constitution and in international treaties.

MILITARY DEFENSE AND STATE OF EMERGENCY

The army is politically responsible to the cabinet. Its main objective is the defense of the country, though it also assists in cases of natural disasters, for example, if other public forces cannot cope. All Greek men at the age of 18 are obliged to contribute to the defense of the country by 12 months of military service. Women can volunteer but are not required to serve. Conscientious objection is recognized, but men exempted on that basis must serve in social institutions for twice the normal period.

In case of war, mobilization, or an armed coup d'état the Law on the State of Emergency may be put in effect. All powers concerning the protection of the security of the state and of public order are then transferred to the military authorities. Provisions on fundamental rights may be suspended and military tribunals acquire jurisdiction over civilians. The law takes effect after a three-fifths vote of all the members of Parliament, upon recommendation of the cabinet.

AMENDMENTS TO THE CONSTITUTION

The Greek constitution is relatively rigid. The most fundamental constitutional principles and provisions cannot be changed at all. These are the form of government as a parliamentary republic, the separation of powers, the dignity of the person, the freedom of movement and of the development of the personality, equality, and religious freedom. All other provisions may be amended but only under a complicated two-phase procedure. Parliament, upon proposal of at least 50 of its members, decides by a three-fifths majority of its members' vote on the need to revise the constitution and specifies the provisions to be amended. The next elected Parliament proceeds to the revision, which now requires only the support of an absolute majority of all members. If the first Parliament only achieved an absolute majority to the proposal, then the second Parliament needs the three-fifths vote to pass the change. Revision of the constitution is not permitted before a lapse of five years from the previous revision.

PRIMARY SOURCES

Constitution in Greek. Available online. URL: http://www.ministryofjustice.gr/files/Syntagma.pdf. Accessed on September 22, 2005.

Constitution in English. Available online. URLs: http://www.ministryofjustice.gr/; http://www.ministryofjustice.gr/eu2003/constitution.pdf. Accessed on September 18, 2005.

SECONDARY SOURCES

Philippos C. Spyropoulos, *Constitutional Law in Hellas*. The Hague: Kluwer Law International, 1995.

Philippos Spyropoulos

GRENADA

At-a-Glance

OFFICIAL NAME
Grenada

CAPITAL
Saint George's

POPULATION
100,800 (2005 est.)

SIZE
133 sq. mi. (344 sq. km)

LANGUAGES
English (official), French patois

RELIGIONS
Roman Catholic 53%, Anglican 13.8%, other
Protestant 33.2%

NATIONAL OR ETHNIC COMPOSITION
African descent 82%, European 13%, European and
East Indian 5%, trace of Arawak or Carib Indian

DATE OF INDEPENDENCE OR CREATION
February 7, 1974

TYPE OF GOVERNMENT
Constitutional monarchy with British Westminster
style Parliament

TYPE OF STATE
Unitary state

TYPE OF LEGISLATURE
Bicameral parliament

DATE OF CONSTITUTION
December 19, 1973 (in force February 7, 1974)

DATE OF LAST AMENDMENT
July 19, 1992

Grenada is a constitutional monarchy, divided into executive, legislative, and judicial branches of government, all of which are independent of each other.

As a member state of the British Commonwealth, Grenada is headed by the British monarch, currently her majesty the queen of England, who appoints the governor-general as her representative in Grenada. The executive is formed by the prime minister as the head of the executive branch and the cabinet. As a result of Grenada's character as a Commonwealth state and a part of the Eastern Caribbean legal system, the country maintains only local magistrates' courts. Grenada's legal system subordinates itself under the jurisdiction of the Eastern Caribbean Supreme Court, which was established by the West Indies Associated States, as well as the jurisdiction of the Privy Council of the United Kingdom.

The constitution of Grenada protects a wide range of fundamental freedoms, the enforcement of which lies in the original jurisdiction of the High Court as one branch of the Eastern Caribbean Supreme Court. In accordance with Grenada's common law tradition, religious freedom is protected under the umbrella of freedom of conscience and guaranteed to the individual and to religious communities. There is a separation between the state and religious communities.

The economic system of Grenada can be characterized as a free market system with a few social elements. Grenada does not maintain separate military forces but integrates them into its police forces.

CONSTITUTIONAL HISTORY

The island of Grenada, originally inhabited by Arawak and later by Carib, was discovered in 1498 by Columbus. After more than 100 years without colonization, Grenada was under French rule in 1650. In 1762 the island was captured by the British. Pursuant to the Treaty of Versailles between France and Great Britain, Grenada became a British colony, to which African slaves were taken.

After constituting a part of the British Windward Islands Administration from 1833 until 1958, under which slavery was outlawed in 1834, Grenada joined the Federation of the West Indies until the collapse of this union in 1962. Afterward Grenada gained the status of a state associated with Great Britain. Under the Associated Statehood Act in 1967, Grenada attained full autonomy in internal affairs.

On February 7, 1974, Grenada achieved full independence and adopted a constitution, framed by Great Britain, which established a modified British Westminster parliamentary system. As a result of a coup d'état in 1979, this constitution was suspended and a Marxist-Leninist government, which established strong ties with the Communist bloc countries, was installed. During a power struggle in Grenada in 1983, U.S.-Caribbean forces landed in Grenada and restored the power of the pre-1979 government until general elections could be held the following year. As a result of these elections, the 1974 constitution was restored. In 2003, the Grenada Constitutional Review Commission was established in order to examine the necessity of fundamental changes of the constitution.

FORM AND IMPACT OF THE CONSTITUTION

Grenada has a written constitution, codified in a single document, called the Grenada Constitution Order 1973. This constitution forms the supreme law of Grenada. Every law contradicting it is void.

BASIC ORGANIZATIONAL STRUCTURE

Grenada is a unitary state structured in six parishes and one dependency, which comprises Carriacou and Petit Martinique Islands. Each of the latter two has a local government.

LEADING CONSTITUTIONAL PRINCIPLES

The constitution of Grenada establishes as guiding concepts the principle of the democratic society and the values of peace, order, and good government.

CONSTITUTIONAL BODIES

Under Grenada's constitution, the British monarch, represented by a governor-general, is head of state; the prime minister is the central figure of the executive, while the House of Representatives constitutes the predominant force in the legislature, which also includes the Senate.

In matters of judicial solution of constitutional questions, the High Court tends to be the most active part of the judiciary in Grenada.

Her Majesty

The executive powers of the state are vested in the monarch, currently her majesty the queen of England, who exercises them through the governor-general.

The Governor-General

The governor-general, who according to convention is chosen by the prime minister, is appointed by her majesty as her representative in Grenada. The governor-general is a constitutional member of Parliament and has the power to dissolve Parliament at any time. In accordance with the advice of the prime minister, the governor-general assigns responsibilities to the prime minister and other cabinet ministers and plays an active role in the government of Grenada.

The Prime Minister

The prime minister must be a member of the House of Representatives. The governor-general appoints to the post whoever he or she believes is likely to gain the support of the majority of the House of Representatives.

The Cabinet

The cabinet is composed of the prime minister, the other cabinet ministers, and the attorney-general. The cabinet ministers, all members of the Senate or the House of Representatives, are appointed by the governor-general in accordance with the advice of the prime minister.

The Parliament

The Parliament of Grenada is formed by her majesty, the Senate, and the House of Representatives.

The Senate

The Senate consists of 13 members, all appointed by the governor-general, 10 of them on the advice of the prime minister and three on the advice of the leader of the opposition. Given this influence, the Senate does not actually function as an effective and independent balance to the House of Representatives.

The House of Representatives

The House of Representatives represents the 15 constituencies of Grenada. They are elected in general, direct, and secret elections for a term of five years. Each of the members represents the constituency in which he or she has won the majority of the votes ("first-past-the-post").

The Lawmaking Process

Generally speaking, a bill must be first passed by the Senate and the House of Representatives and then assented to by the governor-general on behalf of her majesty. The house plays the major role, in part because it is the house speaker who monitors the constitutionality of the process; in some cases the consent of the Senate to a bill is not obligatory.

The Judiciary

The constitution determines the supreme, independent courts for Grenada to be the High Court and the Court of Appeal that together form the Eastern Caribbean Supreme Court of the West Indies Associated States, and the Privy Council of the United Kingdom. The original jurisdiction of constitutional questions, including those concerning possible infringements on fundamental freedoms, is vested in the High Court. Three of its 13 members are resident judges in Grenada. The Court of Appeal handles only appeals against the High Court's decisions that relate to the interpretation of the constitution or the violation of fundamental rights. The Privy Council's jurisdiction is not restricted to constitutional matters.

THE ELECTION PROCESS

Every Commonwealth citizen who has reached the age of 18, is domiciled in Grenada, and is registered to vote has the right to vote for the House of Representatives. In order to stand for election, a person must, in addition to the aforesaid, have held his or her residence in Grenada for 12 months immediately before the date of the nomination for election or be domiciled in the state and resident in Grenada at that date. The prospective candidate must also have a sufficient knowledge of the English language to take an active part in the proceedings.

POLITICAL PARTIES

Grenada can be described as a multiparty democracy. However, the role of political parties is not established by the constitution.

CITIZENSHIP

In general, every person born in Grenada is a citizen of Grenada, as are those born outside Grenada if one of their parents is a citizen of Grenada. A person who is married to a state citizen is, under certain circumstances, entitled to citizenship.

FUNDAMENTAL RIGHTS

In its preamble, the constitution of Grenada bases itself on inalienable rights. The first article of the document anchors the equal right of every person to a range of fundamental rights and freedoms, as long as their exercise does not conflict with the freedom of others.

Impact and Functions of Fundamental Rights

Although the constitution ascribes a high status to fundamental rights, their impact is rather small. Not all of the rights enshrined in the first article are legally enforceable. The constitution describes, for each fundamental right, the permissible legislation that should not be regarded as limitations of that right. For example, according to the constitution the execution of a court's death sentence shall not be regarded as an intentional deprivation of a person's right to life. Also, the right to life shall not be regarded as implicated when someone dies as the result of the use of force for the defense of property, as long as this result is reasonably justifiable and its extent and circumstances permitted by law.

Limitations to Fundamental Rights

Each fundamental right is, according to the constitution of Grenada, subject to the limits of other individuals' rights and of public values (e.g., public morality). Only in a few cases must these limits be balanced with the values of a democratic society.

ECONOMY

The constitution of Grenada does not establish a specific economic system. However, the text does protect the right to own property, freedom of association, and the right to work (which is not judicially enforceable). The economy is in fact a free market system, while the government fosters social values by setting a 40-hour workweek as a binding standard for the state and by subsidizing the umbrella labor federation.

RELIGIOUS COMMUNITIES

State and religious communities in Grenada are separated. Religious communities have the right to provide their respective members with religious instruction, as long as they do so at the communities' own expense and at sites they fully maintain.

MILITARY DEFENSE AND STATE OF EMERGENCY

Grenada does not have a military, but a paramilitary force (the coast guard) is integrated into the police forces, the latter of which is partly governed by the constitution. There are no constitutional provisions concerning service in the paramilitary force or detailing its powers.

AMENDMENTS TO THE CONSTITUTION

The constitution, as well as the Courts Order and Section 3 of the 1967 West Indies Associated States (Appeals to Privy Council) Order, can be amended by a majority of at least two-thirds of all the members of the House of Representatives. Any changes to the amendment subsequently adopted by the Senate must be approved by the House of Representatives with the same two-thirds majority.

PRIMARY SOURCES
Grenada Constitution Order 1973 in English. Available online. URL: http://www.georgetown.edu/pdba/Constitutions/Grenada/gren73eng.html. Accessed on July 23, 2005.

SECONDARY SOURCES
Francis R. Alexis, *Grenada: The Legal Question.* Cave Hill, Barbados: Faculty of Law, University of the West Indies, 1991.
Scott Davidson, *Grenada: A Study on Politics and the Limits of International Law.* Avebury, England: Aldershot, 1989.
Ian Ramsay, *The Legal Crisis in Grenada.* Kingston: Jamaica Bar Association, 1988.

Angelika Günzel

GUATEMALA

At-a-Glance

OFFICIAL NAME
Republic of Guatemala

CAPITAL
Guatemala City

POPULATION
14,280,596 (July 2004 est.)

SIZE
42,043 sq. mi. (108,890 sq. km)

LANGUAGES
Spanish 60%, Amerindian (23 officially recognized languages, e.g., Quiche, Cakchiquel, Kekchi, Mam, Garifuna, and Xinca) 40%

RELIGIONS
Roman Catholic 55%, Protestant 40%, indigenous Mayan beliefs and other 5%

NATIONAL OR ETHNIC COMPOSITION
Mestizo (mixed Amerindian-Spanish or assimilated Amerindian) approximately 55%, Amerindian or predominantly Amerindian approximately 43%, whites and others 2%

DATE OF INDEPENDENCE OR CREATION
September 15, 1821

TYPE OF GOVERNMENT
Presidential democracy

TYPE OF STATE
Unitary state

TYPE OF LEGISLATURE
Unicameral congress

DATE OF CONSTITUTION
May 31, 1985 (in force January 14, 1986)

DATE OF LAST AMENDMENT
November 17, 1993

Guatemala's 1985 constitution provides for a presidential democracy with a separation of powers among the executive, legislative, and judicial branches. Guatemala is organized as a unitary state.

The classical presidential system is modified. There is a strong vice president and there are elements of parliamentarism, such as the congressional power to vote no confidence against ministers of state.

Free, equal, general, and direct elections of the members of parliament are guaranteed. Guatemala has a pluralistic system of political parties. Referendums can be held.

The constitution provides a number of far-reaching guarantees of human rights, including freedom of religion or belief. The economic system can be described as a social market economy. The constitution provides that the military is subject to the civil government. Guatemala is obligated to conduct its international relations with the purpose of contributing to the maintenance of peace and freedom.

CONSTITUTIONAL HISTORY

From the fourth to the 11th century C.E., the lowlands area of the Peten region of Guatemala was the center of the flourishing Maya civilization. After the decline of the lowland states, the Maya states of the central highlands continued to exist until the Spanish conquest.

The colonial period began on July 25, 1524, when the Spanish conqueror Pedro de Alvarado founded the first permanent conquistador settlement in the capital city of Iximché. The *encomienda*, a system of tributes to be paid by the native people introduced to all the Spanish colonies by the Laws of Burgos 1512, was applied to Guatemala as well. Most of Central America (including San Salvador, Honduras, Nicaragua, Costa Rica, and Chiapas) was under the control of the Captaincy General of Guatemala.

Spanish royal authority in the New World weakened during the European wars of the Napoleonic era. Guatemala had the opportunity to participate in the first Spanish constituent congress of Cadiz (1811), but creoles (the locally born descendents of Spaniards) were still in practice excluded from participation in the government of the colonies, and local opposition to the colonial system grew. Influenced by the Plan de Iguala in Mexico (which called for the unification of all the colonies from California to Panama under the rule of a European king), a group of nobles convened in the capital city (present-day Guatemala City) on September 15, 1821, to declare independence.

After a short period as part of the first Mexican Empire of Agustín de Iturbide, Guatemala (except the province of Chiapas) joined El Salvador, Honduras, Nicaragua, and Costa Rica in a united federal state and adopted the Constitution of the Federal Republic of Central America (Provincias Unidas del Centro de América) on November 22, 1824. The federation, independent of both Spain and Mexico, fell apart in a civil war between liberals and conservatives (1838–40). Guatemala had already withdrawn from the federation in 1839, under a conservative counterrevolution led by José Rafael Carrera. Carrera heavily revised the 1824 constitution of Guatemala and also signed a treaty with the United Kingdom in 1859 that defined the borders with Belize, then known as British Honduras.

The 1879 constitution introduced habeas corpus rights. The document was amended nine times and lasted until 1945.

Despite the liberal constitution, presidents became increasingly dictatorial. The country passed through a series of dictatorships, insurgencies, and periods of military rule with only occasional periods of representative government. These dictators, known as *caudillos,* all had the strong support of the armed forces. The last was overthrown in the "October Revolution" (1945) and a new constitution was proclaimed. In addition to civil liberties, it included social rights, the possibility of expropriation of landowners, and the neutrality of the armed forces. A successful United States–backed invasion from the territory of Honduras in 1954 led to the constitutions of 1956 and 1965. In the meantime, guerrilla groups emerged to conduct armed insurrections against the government that lasted for the next 36 years.

After a series of insurgencies and another coup d'état in 1982, a Statute of Government was promulgated, but it was supplanted by emergency measures on several occasions. The 1985 constitution was an attempt to start a process of democratization. It included many provisions of the 1965 constitution and was similar to other Latin American constitutions.

Guatemala, Costa Rica, Honduras, Nicaragua, and El Salvador signed a peace treaty for Central America in 1987, and in 1996, the Guatemalan government and rebels finally signed peace accords that ended the 36-year conflict. However, a referendum on a constitutional amendment that permitted the appointment of a civilian minister of defense failed in 1999.

Guatemala is a member state of the Organization of American States (OAS).

FORM AND IMPACT OF THE CONSTITUTION

The written constitution comprises 307 articles (280 articles in the main constitution and 27 transitory and final provisions) and four constitutional laws (*leyes constitucionales*): on elections and political parties, on constitutional remedies, on public order and the state of emergency, and on freedom of expression. These make up the Political Constitution (Constitución Política de la República de Guatemala), which takes precedence over all other national law.

Ratified international human rights treaties and agreements have precedence over national law.

BASIC ORGANIZATIONAL STRUCTURE

Organized as a unitary state, Guatemala is made up of 22 departments administered by governors appointed by the president. Local autonomy is constitutionally protected. In practice, in some instances there is a parallel administration for indigenous people.

LEADING CONSTITUTIONAL PRINCIPLES

The constitution defines the state of Guatemala as free, independent and sovereign, organized to guarantee its inhabitants the enjoyment of their rights and liberties. Its system of government is republican, democratic, and representative.

It is also a social state, based on the rule of law. It is a duty of the state to guarantee the inhabitants of the republic life, liberty, justice, security, peace, and the integral development of the person. Furthermore, Article 1 reads: "It is the duty of the state to protect the person and the family; its supreme goal is the realization of the public good."

CONSTITUTIONAL BODIES

The predominant bodies are the president and the vice president, the Congress of the Republic, the judiciary including the Constitutional Court, and the human rights ombudsman.

The President and the Vice President

The president of the republic is both the chief of state and head of the executive. The president appoints and dismisses the cabinet ministers, in accordance with the law.

In view of negative experiences with past leadership, the constitution limits the president to one four-year term. Reelection or extension of the term can be punished in accordance with the law. Furthermore, no one who has served in the armed forces in the previous five years or has taken part in a coup d'état or armed movement may run for president.

The vice president also has a strong position. The vice president coordinates the ministers of state, assists the president in implementing general policy, and participates jointly with the president in foreign policy.

The president, the vice president, and the ministers of state, meeting in session, constitute the Council of Ministers (Consejo de Ministros). The ministers have the obligation to appear before the Congress of the Republic if called.

The Congress of the Republic (Congreso de la República)

The legislative power is vested in the Congress of the Republic. Its period of office is four years.

If congress is dissatisfied with the performance of a cabinet minister, the deputies can so indicate with a vote of no confidence. If the president does not accept the subsequent resignation of a cabinet minister, congress can dismiss the cabinet minister with a two-thirds majority.

The Lawmaking Process

Laws may be proposed not only by the president and the congress, but also by the Supreme Court, the Supreme Electoral Tribunal, and the University of San Carlos, in their respective areas of authority.

The president may veto acts of congress, but congress may override the veto by a vote of two-thirds of its members.

The Judiciary

According to the constitution, the judiciary is independent. The Supreme Court of Justice (Corte Suprema de Justicia) consists of 13 justices or *magistrados,* who serve for five-year terms. The justices are proposed by an expert commission and are elected by the Congress of the Republic.

Rulings on the constitutionality of laws are reserved for the Constitutional Court (Corte de Constitucionalidad), which consists of five justices, who serve for five-year terms. The following institutions appoint one justice each: the Supreme Court Plenary, the Congress of the Republic, the president, the Superior University Council of the University of San Carlos of Guatemala, and the Assembly of the Guatemala Bar Association.

Human Rights Ombudsperson (Procurador de Derechos Humanos)

Any citizen may submit a complaint to the office of the human rights ombudsperson. The ombudsperson, pro-

posed by a Human Rights Commission and elected by the Congress of the Republic, investigates complaints and makes recommendations.

THE ELECTION PROCESS

All Guatemalans over the age of 18 have the right to vote in elections except active members of the armed forces, who are restricted to their barracks on election day. Deputies to the Congress of the Republic are elected directly by the people in universal and secret suffrage for a period of four years. There is a system of proportional representation with 75 percent of the members of congress elected in multimember districts and the remainder chosen from a single national district.

Active members of the armed service may not stand for elections as deputies, president, or vice president; they must wait for five years after their retirement or resignation. This provision has been tested several times: In 1993, when Vice President Espina unsuccessfully tried to succeed Serrano, and in 1995, when the retired general Efraín Ríos Montt, who had led the coup d'état in 1982, tried to run for president, the Constitutional Court decided that they could not run.

POLITICAL PARTIES

Guatemala has a pluralistic system of political parties; however, the party system lacks stability.

CITIZENSHIP

Those born in the territory of Guatemala and children of a Guatemalan father or mother born abroad are considered native Guatemalans. Nationals of the republics that make up the Central American Federation may also acquire citizenship.

FUNDAMENTAL RIGHTS

Fundamental rights are defined at the beginning of the constitution, after the definition of the overall duty of the state. There are the classic individual rights, such as the right to life and equality, as well as social rights, such as the right to food.

Impact and Functions of Fundamental Rights

Human rights in the constitution are regarded as natural rights. The procedure of *amparo* entitles a person to sue for "protection" by the courts, if constitutional rights are threatened. According to international organizations, the respect for human rights and the implementation of the rule of law by the Guatemalan administration of justice still face serious challenges.

Limitations to Fundamental Rights

Many rights can be limited by law, such as the inviolability of home, correspondence, and private documents. The state can also suspend some rights during a state of emergency.

ECONOMY

The constitution does not specify any type of economic system. It acknowledges private property as well as expropriation, provides for state economic planning, and obliges the state to provide electricity and certain other goods. Taken as a whole, the economic system can be described as a social market economy.

RELIGIOUS COMMUNITIES

Freedom of religion or belief is guaranteed as a fundamental right. The legal status of the Catholic Church is recognized; other associations of a religious character can apply for recognition by law.

MILITARY DEFENSE AND STATE OF EMERGENCY

It is the constitutional duty of citizens to serve and defend the country and to perform military and social service in accordance with the law. Citizens at the age of 18 and 24 must serve either in the armed forces or in social service projects, respectively. The length of service in the army is 30 months.

The army is still authorized to maintain both internal and external security. According to the constitution, it must be "apolitical." The constitution emphasizes that the president is commander in chief of the armed forces. Should a president refuse to leave office after the term has expired, the army automatically falls under the authority of Congress of the Republic.

The law of public order knows five different states of emergency. The president may suspend some fundamental rights in a state of emergency but must submit the decree to the Congress of the Republic within three days for review.

AMENDMENTS TO THE CONSTITUTION

The constitution, as well as constitutional laws such as the electoral law, can generally be amended by a two-thirds vote of the total number of deputies. Amendments must then be ratified through a referendum.

The human rights provisions of Chapter 1 of Title 2 of the constitution, and the amendment provisions themselves, can be changed only by a National Constituent Assembly. Such an assembly can be called by a two-thirds majority vote of the members of congress.

Some provisions are not subject to change at all: "In no case can Articles 140, 141, 165g, 186 and 187 be amended, nor can any question relating to the republican form of government, to the principle of the non-re-electability for the exercise of the presidency of the republic be raised in any form, neither may the effectiveness or application of the articles that provide alternating the tenure of the presidency of the republic be suspended or their content changed or modified in any other way." In other words, the essential identity of the constitution may not be changed.

PRIMARY SOURCES
Constitution in English: Albert P. Blaustein and Gisbert H Flanz, eds., "Political Constitution of the Republic of Guatemala." In *Constitutions of the Countries of the World.* Vol. 6. New York: Oceana, 1986–.
Constitution in Spanish: Luis Emilio Barrios Pérez, *Constitución Política de la Republica de Guatemala.* Guatemala: Ediciones Legales Comercio e Industria, 1996. Available online. URL: http://www.guatemala.gob.gt/index.php/cms/content/download/272/1392/file/Constitucion.PDF. Accessed on July 22, 2005.

SECONDARY SOURCES
Maria Luisa Beltranena de Padilla, "Guatemala Constitutional Court." *Florida Journal of International Law* 13 (2000) 1: 26–32.
Justice Studies Center of the Americas, *Report on Judicial Systems in the Americas 2002–2003.* Santiago: Justice Studies Center of the Americas JSCA, 2003 in English and Spanish.
Richard F. Nyrop, ed., *Guatemala—a Country Study,* Area Handbook Series. Washington, D.C.: The American University, 1983.
Andrew Reding, *Democracy and Human Rights in Guatemala.* New York: World Policy Institute, 1997.
United Nations, "Core Document Forming Part of the Reports of States Parties: Guatemala" (HRI/CORE/1/Add.47), 5 October 1994. Available online. URL: http://www.unhchr.ch/tbs/doc.nsf;
United Nations Verification Mission in Guatemala (MINUGUA), "Various Documents." Available online. URL:http://www.un.org/Depts/dpko/dpko/co_mission/minugua.htm. Accessed on June 21, 2006.

Michael Rahe

GUINEA

OFFICIAL NAME
Republic of Guinea

CAPITAL
Conakry

POPULATION
9,246,462 (2005 est.)

SIZE
94,926 sq. mi. (245,857 sq. km)

LANGUAGES
French (official), ethnic group languages

RELIGIONS
Muslim 85%, Christian 8%, indigenous belief 7%

NATIONAL OR ETHNIC COMPOSITION
Peuhl 40%, Malinke 30%, Soussou 20%, smaller
ethnic groups 10%

DATE OF INDEPENDENCE OR CREATION
October 2, 1958

TYPE OF GOVERNMENT
Constitutional democracy

TYPE OF STATE
Centralist state

TYPE OF LEGISLATURE
Unicameral parliament

DATE OF CONSTITUTION
December 23, 1990

DATE OF LAST AMENDMENT
June 12, 2003

Guinea is a centralist democratic state with a unicameral parliament. The constitution provides for separation of executive, legislative, and judicial powers. The fundamental set of human rights is guaranteed. The Supreme Court of Guinea has the jurisdiction over certain constitutional disputes as specified in the constitution.

The president of the republic is the head of state, the central political figure, and the head of the executive administration. The prime minister holds responsibility for the execution of government policy. The legislative power lies with the unicameral parliament as the representative body of the people. Elections for parliament and president are secret, equal, general, and direct. The pluralistic system of political parties has major political impact.

The Guinean constitution establishes the principle of secularity, under which religious freedom is assured for the individual as well as for religious communities. The economic system outlined in the constitution is that of a market economy with social responsibility.

CONSTITUTIONAL HISTORY

Since gaining independence from France in 1958, Guinea has had only two presidents. After the death of the first president in 1984, the military seized power and General Lansana Conté became head of the military government.

In the period of the transition to a civil government, the constitution was enacted in 1990. In 1993, the general became the civil president in Guinea's first democratic election, and he was reelected in 1998. He was reelected for a third time in 2003 after the constitution was altered to allow him to run for another term.

In the 2003 election, Mamadou Bhoye Barry, the only other presidential candidate and a member of the Union for National Progress, gained less than 5 percent of the votes and contested the results. Other opposition parties boycotted the elections, saying they would not be free or fair. The Guinean Human Rights Organization accused the election organizers of substantial and severe violations of the law.

The stability of the Republic of Guinea has been threatened on numerous occasions when humanitarian crises and unrest in neighboring countries spilled over into Guinea.

FORM AND IMPACT OF THE CONSTITUTION

Guinea has a written constitution, codified in a single document that takes precedence over all other laws in the country. Thus, the wide range of customary law may have to be modified to put it into conformity with the constitution.

Recent history shows a lack of attachment to the constitution; in some situations the constitution was amended to meet specific political needs. The last amendment, for example, was passed to allow the president to be reelected for a third term.

BASIC ORGANIZATIONAL STRUCTURE

Guinea is a centralist state with a primarily presidential organizational structure. For administrative reasons, the country is divided into 33 prefectures and one special zone.

LEADING CONSTITUTIONAL PRINCIPLES

Guinea is a secular state with a legal system based on the French civil law and influenced by indigenous customary law. The governmental system provided by the constitution is that of a presidential democracy with a unicameral parliament. Executive, legislative, and judicial powers are separated and bound by the rule of law. The judiciary is independent.

CONSTITUTIONAL BODIES

The predominant organs provided for in the constitution are the president of the republic; the prime minister, who bears chief responsibility for the executive administration; the president's cabinet; the National Assembly, Guinea's unicameral parliament; and the judiciary, including the Supreme Court of Guinea, which has jurisdiction over specific constitutional disputes.

The President of the Republic

The president of the republic is the head of state and the dominant figure in politics. The president serves a five-year term and can be reelected. The election is direct, by means of a general, public, and secret vote. The president appoints the cabinet of ministers, including the prime minister, who supports the executive functions of the president.

The Cabinet

The cabinet determines the general policy of the executive administration. The main responsibility lies with the prime minister. This position is not specifically regulated in the constitution; the prime minister is selected out of the group of cabinet ministers as the first minister. As are all the other cabinet ministers, the prime minister is appointed by and responsible only to the president.

The National Assembly (Assemblée Nationale)

The parliament, as the main representative organ of the people, is the supreme legislative power. The members of parliament are elected for a term of five years in a general and secret balloting process; reelection is possible.

Article 59 of the Guinean constitution contains a detailed enumeration of topics in which the parliament has the right and the duty to exercise its legislative powers.

The Lawmaking Process

Parliament passes laws in the form of acts of parliament, which are then signed by the president. The president has the right to refuse to sign, in which case the president must return the unsigned bill to parliament for a second reading. To overcome the veto, the bill must win approval from no less than two-thirds of the members of parliament. If the president still is opposed, he or she can ask the Supreme Court to review whether the bill is in conformity with the constitution.

The Judiciary

The independence of the judiciary is guaranteed by the constitution. The highest court is the Supreme Court of Guinea, which has two functions. It is the final court of appeal for all inferior courts (High Court of Justice and lower local courts). In addition, the constitution gives the Supreme Court exclusive jurisdiction to decide whether a new law is in conformity with the constitution. The Supreme Court also decides other constitutional disputes, especially those between state organs.

THE ELECTION PROCESS

Guinea has universal suffrage for all citizens over the age of 18. The minimal age of eligibility to run for parliament is 21 years. A presidential candidate must be between 40 and 70 years old.

POLITICAL PARTIES

Guinea has a pluralistic system of political parties. The constitution provides several instruments to regulate the involvement of political parties in public life. Such topics as the maximal number of political parties, the conditions under which they can act, and the procedure to ban a party are left to be regulated by law. Political parties play an important role in political life. The constitution requires that presidential candidates and candidates for deputy be proposed by a political party.

CITIZENSHIP

A child of a Guinean father acquires citizenship regardless of the child's country of birth. Citizenship can also be obtained by descent through the maternal line, provided that the mother was a Guinean citizen and the father is unknown or stateless. A foreign woman who marries a citizen of Guinea is entitled to citizenship.

FUNDAMENTAL RIGHTS

Fundamental rights are described specifically in the first part of the constitution. The traditional basic set of human rights and civil liberties is guaranteed. The constitution not only guarantees protection against the violation of fundamental rights but even requires the state to become active in their support. Workers' rights are outlined very clearly.

Impact and Functions of Fundamental Rights

All public organs are bound by fundamental rights, but there is no special court or procedure to guarantee their enforcement. As a result of the long history of human rights abuses, the impact of fundamental rights in Guinean political life must be considered limited.

Limitations to Fundamental Rights

The exercise of the fundamental rights guaranteed in the constitution can be limited by law. The constitution stipulates that any such limitation is justifiable only as long as it is essential to the upholding of public order and democracy.

ECONOMY

No specific economic system is required by the constitution; however, certain principles can be derived from the list of fundamental rights, including the right to work and freedom of property. These provisions in effect oblige the state to create conditions in which the right to work can be exercised. Hence the constitution favors a system that recognizes social responsibility in the context of a relatively free market.

RELIGIOUS COMMUNITIES

Freedom of thought and religion is guaranteed as a human right. Religious communities have an explicit right to organize and administer themselves without interference from the state. The constitution follows the principle of secularity.

MILITARY DEFENSE AND STATE OF EMERGENCY

In Guinea, all men over the age of 18 are obligated to serve in the military for two years. In addition to this, professional soldiers can enter military service at the age of 18.

The purposes of the armed forces are not specifically outlined in the constitution. The president has responsibility for the national defense, the administration of the military, and the appointment of military personnel.

A state of emergency can be decreed by the president after consultation with the president of the parliament and the president of the Supreme Court. The president can take every measure necessary to reestablish public order or to defend the territorial integrity, but he or she cannot dissolve the National Assembly.

AMENDMENTS TO THE CONSTITUTION

The initiative to amend the existing constitution can originate with the president or National Assembly deputies. If the bill is a presidential proposal, it can be approved if a two-thirds majority of the members of parliament vote in favor. Otherwise, it requires a popular referendum. The type of government, the principle of secularity, and separation of powers are not open to amendment.

PRIMARY SOURCES
Constitution in English (extracts). Available online. URL: http://www.chr.up.ac.za/hr_docs/constitutions/docs/Guinea(english%2Osummary)(rev).doc. Accessed on August 6, 2005.
Constitution in French. Available online. URL: http://www.droit.francophonie.org/doc/html/gq/con/fr/1995/1995dfgqcofr1.html. Accessed on June 21, 2006.

SECONDARY SOURCES
Christof Heyns, ed., *Human Rights Law in Africa*. Vol. 2 Leiden: Martinus Nijhoff, 2004.

Anja-Isabel Bohnen

GUINEA-BISSAU

At-a-Glance

OFFICIAL NAME
Republic of Guinea-Bissau

CAPITAL
Bissau

POPULATION
1,388,363 (2005 est.)

SIZE
13,946 sq. mi. (36,120 sq. km)

LANGUAGES
Portuguese (official), Crioul, African languages

RELIGIONS
Indigenous beliefs 50%, Muslim 45%, Christian 5%

NATIONAL OR ETHNIC COMPOSITION
Balanta 30%, Fula 20%, Manjaca 14%, Mandinga 13%, Papel 7%, European and Mulatto 1%, other 15%

DATE OF INDEPENDENCE OR CREATION
September 24, 1973 (unilaterally declared by Guinea-Bissau); September 10, 1974 (recognized by Portugal)

TYPE OF GOVERNMENT
Mixed presidential-parliamentary system

TYPE OF STATE
Unitary state

TYPE OF LEGISLATURE
Unicameral parliament

DATE OF CONSTITUTION
May 16, 1984

DATE OF LAST AMENDMENT
June 9, 1996

The Republic of Guinea-Bissau is a centralist democracy with a unicameral legislature. The constitution provides a separation of executive, legislative, and judicial powers. The fundamental set of human rights is guaranteed. A claim of violation of fundamental rights can be taken before the regular courts. Parliament has the right to resolve constitutional disputes.

The president of the republic is the head of state; he or she is assisted in the executive functions by the Council of State. The prime minister is responsible for the execution of the administration's policy. The legislative power lies with the unicameral parliament as the representative body of the people. Elections for parliament and the office of the president are secret, equal, general, and direct. In recent years, a pluralistic system of political parties has had an increasing impact on political life.

The constitution of Guinea-Bissau establishes the principle of secularity, in which religious freedom is assured for the individual as well as for legally recognized religious communities. The economic system outlined in the constitution is that of a market economy with social responsibility.

CONSTITUTIONAL HISTORY

Since Guinea-Bissau gained independence from Portugal in 1974, the country has suffered from extensive turmoil. The founding constitution implemented a single-party system and a state-regulated economy. The ruling party, Partido Africano da Independência (PAIGC), connected the country closely to Cape Verde. Fearing an increasing influence of Cape Verde in Guinea-Bissau's politics, the military seized power in 1980. Joao Vieira became president, and a multiparty system as well as a market economy were established.

Several attempts to overthrow the government during the 1980s and early 1990s failed. Vieira became the country's first freely elected president in 1994. In 1998, a civil war broke out, and in 2004, Kumba Yala took the office of the president after a transparent election process.

In September 2003, Henrique Rosa followed him after a bloodless coup.

The stability of the Republic of Guinea-Bissau is threatened by its crippled economy and the consequences of prolonged civil war.

FORM AND IMPACT OF THE CONSTITUTION

Guinea-Bissau has a written constitution, codified in a single document, that takes precedence over all other national law. However, political practice shows increasing disrespect for the constitution. A number of changes of the constitution have occurred according to day-to-day political preference.

Therefore, the impact of the constitution is highly dependent on actual political situations.

BASIC ORGANIZATIONAL STRUCTURE

Guinea-Bissau is a centralist state with nine administrative divisions. The regional authorities have little political influence.

LEADING CONSTITUTIONAL PRINCIPLES

Guinea-Bissau is a secular state. The government system established by the constitution is that of a constitutional democracy. Executive, legislative, and judicial powers are separated and bound by the rule of law. The judiciary is independent.

CONSTITUTIONAL BODIES

The predominant organs provided for in the constitution are the president of the republic, assisted by the Council of State; the executive administration, with its prime minister; the National People's Assembly, Guinea-Bissau's unicameral parliament; and the judiciary, including the Supreme Court of Justice, which does not have special constitutional jurisdiction but is named expressly by the constitution as an independent constitutional organ.

The President of the Republic

The president of the republic is the head of state and represents the republic. The president serves a five-year term and is elected in a general, public, and secret vote.

The constitution provides a political organ called the Council of State to advise and assist the president. The 15 members of the Council of State are elected from among the members of parliament. In times when the legislature is not in session, the Council of State executes the functions of the National People's Assembly.

The Executive Administration

The executive administration comprises the prime minister, its head; the cabinet ministers; and the secretaries of state. It sets its own program, which must be approved by the parliament. The administration conducts the affairs of the state in accordance with this program.

The prime minister is appointed by the president after consultation of the political parties represented in parliament. It is the prime minister's duty to inform the president about important political issues.

The National People's Assembly

The parliament, as the main representative organ of the people, is the supreme legislative power. The members of parliament are elected for a term of four years in a general and secret balloting process. Reelection is allowed.

The Lawmaking Process

The constitution of Guinea-Bissau does not give a detailed description of the procedure to pass a law. In the articles dealing with the National People's Assembly, the constitution establishes that parliament has the right to create law, and that the right to initiate bills belongs to members of the Council of State, the parliament, the executive government, and the president. The president of the National People's Assembly must sign each new bill and order its publication in the *Official Bulletin*.

The Judiciary

The independence of the judiciary is guaranteed by the constitution. The highest court is the Supreme Court or Supremo Tribunal da Justica. It is the final court of appeals for all inferior courts. The first courts of appeal are the Regional Courts. The 24 Sectoral Courts are inferior courts in which the judges are not necessarily trained lawyers.

The National People's Assembly has the right to resolve constitutional disputes, rather than the Supreme Court.

THE ELECTION PROCESS

Guinea-Bissau has universal suffrage for all citizens over the age of 18. The minimal age to be eligible to run for office is 21 years.

POLITICAL PARTIES

The constitution of Guinea-Bissau guarantees the existence of political parties as an instrument for promoting political pluralism.

The constitution leaves the following matters to regulation by law: the role of the parties in public life, the conditions under which they can act, and the procedure for banning them. To ensure the unity of the country, a party is not allowed to use a name that can be identified with a person, a region, or a religion.

Political parties play an important role in public life, not only in elections for parliament, but also in designation of the prime minister, who is appointed by the president only after consultation of the main political parties.

CITIZENSHIP

Birth within the territory of Guinea-Bissau automatically confers citizenship on the newborn regardless of the nationality of the parents. A child born abroad acquires citizenship if at least one of the parents is a citizen of Guinea-Bissau. A foreign person who marries a citizen of Guinea-Bissau is eligible for citizenship, as are foreign persons whose grandparents were citizens of Guinea-Bissau.

FUNDAMENTAL RIGHTS

Fundamental rights are enumerated in the first part of the constitution. The traditional set of liberal human rights and civil liberties are included.

The constitution in particular clearly outlines the rights of the workforce and the rights of an accused person. The constitution guarantees protection against the violation of fundamental rights through the regular judicial organs.

Impact and Functions of Fundamental Rights

All public authorities are bound by the fundamental rights, but there is no special court or procedure to guarantee their enforcement. The jurisdiction lies with the regular courts, which are often overloaded and generally do not consist of trained lawyers.

As a result of the long history of human rights abuses, the impact of fundamental rights in Guinea-Bissau's political life has its limits. The full realization of civil and political rights also suffers from an underresourced administration of justice and the generally insecure economic situation.

Limitations to Fundamental Rights

The exercise of the fundamental rights guaranteed in the constitution can be limited by law. The constitution states that any such limitation is justifiable as long as it is necessary to uphold other constitutionally protected rights and interests. Such a limitation is valid only on condition that it is not retroactive and the limited right is not diminished so far as to endanger its essence.

ECONOMY

No specific economic system is mandated by the constitution. However, the 1984 constitution was created after the era of state-regulated markets, and it appears to provide the basis for a liberal economy, in fundamental rights provisions dealing with the workplace and property rights. In sum, the constitution favors a system that provides a system of social responsibility in a relatively free market.

RELIGIOUS COMMUNITIES

Freedom of religion is guaranteed as a human right. In addition, the constitution declares a separation between state and religion, except that legally recognized religious communities are respected and protected. The conditions for legal recognition are not stated in the constitution, but any exercise of religion, as well as any activity of a religious community, can be made subject to regulation by law.

MILITARY DEFENSE AND STATE OF EMERGENCY

The military of Guinea-Bissau consists only of professional soldiers, as general conscription does not exist. All men over the age of 18 are allowed to volunteer.

The purposes of the armed forces are not specifically outlined in the constitution. The president bears responsibility for national defense, the administration of the military, and the appointment of military personnel.

A state of emergency can be declared by the Council of State, which then takes over the functions of the parliament. The constitution spells out the measures that can be taken in a state of emergency; fundamental rights can be suspended, but only in part.

AMENDMENTS TO THE CONSTITUTION

The initiative to alter the existing constitution can originate with the president, the Council of State, the administration, or one-third of the members of parliament. To be adopted, such a proposal needs a two-thirds majority of all deputies in the National People's Assembly. The republican form of the state, the unitary structure, the principles of secularity, and the integrity of national territory are not open to amendment.

PRIMARY SOURCES
Constitution in English (excerpts). Available online. URL: http://www.chr.up.ac.za/hr_docs/constitutions/docs/

Guinea-BissauC(english%20summary)(rev).doc. Accessed on August 24, 2005.

SECONDARY SOURCES
Bureau of Public Affairs, U.S. Department of State, "Background Note and Country Reports on Human Rights Practices and International Religious Freedom Report 2004." Available online. URL: http://www.state.gov/. Accessed on July 24, 2005.

Christof Heyns, ed., *Human Rights Law in Africa*. Vol. 2. Leiden: Martinus Nijhoff, 2004.

Anja-Isabel Bohnen

GUYANA

At-a-Glance

OFFICIAL NAME
The Co-operative Republic of Guyana

CAPITAL
Georgetown

POPULATION
772,200 (2005 est.)

SIZE
83,000 sq. mi. (214,970 sq. km)

LANGUAGES
English (official), Amerindian dialects, Creole, Hindi, Urdu

RELIGIONS
Christian 50%, Hindu 35%, Muslim 10%, other 5%

NATIONAL OR ETHNIC COMPOSITION
Indo-Guyanese 49.5%, Afro-Guyanese 35.6%, Amerindian 6.8%, Chinese, European, and other 8.1%

DATE OF INDEPENDENCE OR CREATION
May 26, 1966

DATE OF CREATION
February 23, 1970

TYPE OF GOVERNMENT
Presidential democracy, cooperative republic within the Commonwealth

TYPE OF STATE
Centralist state divided into 10 administrative regions

TYPE OF LEGISLATURE
Unicameral parliament

DATE OF CONSTITUTION
October 6, 1980

DATE OF LAST AMENDMENT
August 12, 2003

After achieving independence from the United Kingdom in 1966, the former British Crown Colony of Guyana has embarked on a slow but steady route to representative democracy. Ruled by a series of authoritarian and socialist-oriented governments, it held its first genuinely free and fair elections in 1992.

The Co-operative Republic of Guyana is a secular, democratic, and sovereign state, with socialist economic tendencies. Its constitution provides for a division of executive, legislative, and judicial powers. The constitution, based on the principle of participatory democracy, enshrines certain fundamental civil and political rights, as well as economic, social, and cultural rights, mainly in the field of employment and work. As a result of its colonial past, Guyana forms part of the British Commonwealth. The great ethnic diversity of population, with the Indo-Guyanese and Afro-Guyanese representing the two largest antagonistic groups, marks the political reality of Guyana's past, present, and future.

CONSTITUTIONAL HISTORY

A former British colony, the Co-operative Republic of Guyana was founded in 1970, four years after achieving independence. Its initial constitution was replaced by the constitution of the Co-operative Republic of Guyana Act in 1980, which enshrined socialist values and concentrated executive power in the hands of the president.

This constitution was amended in 1996. Further initiatives to strengthen the role of parliament, create constitutional commissions under a human rights umbrella commission, and reform the electoral system were stifled by opposing forces. Territorial disputes with Venezuela and Suriname have led to the inclusion of various enemy-related provisions in the constitution.

FORM AND IMPACT OF THE CONSTITUTION

The constitution of Guyana is codified in a single written and detailed document, constituting the supreme law of the country. Any national legal provision inconsistent with its provisions shall be null and void. Provisions guaranteeing fundamental rights and freedoms may be directly invoked in any court of law; invocation of such provisions automatically leads to the jurisdiction of the High Court.

BASIC ORGANIZATIONAL STRUCTURE

Guyana is a centralist state, organized as a presidential democracy and consisting of 10 regional administrative districts. A certain level of decentralization grants administrative powers to lower government bodies at the regional and local levels.

LEADING CONSTITUTIONAL PRINCIPLES

Guyana's constitution subscribes to a clear division of powers, people's participation, and secularism. The principal objective of its constitution is the establishment of a socialist democracy with an emphasis on national economic planning, national development through cooperation, and the rights and duties of all citizens to achieve the highest possible levels of production and productivity.

CONSTITUTIONAL BODIES

Constitutional bodies provided for by the constitution are the president; the administration or cabinet; the National Assembly; the regional administration, including the National Congress of Local Democratic Organs; the Supreme Congress of the People; and the judiciary.

The President

The executive power is vested in the president, who serves simultaneously as head of state, supreme executive authority, and commander in chief of the armed forces. Elected for a term of up to five years, the president may dissolve all representative bodies, such as the National Assembly and Local Democratic Councils, at any time by proclamation; he or she can veto any bills, grant pardons, and repeal Guyanese citizenship. The president may also appoint the prime minister as his or her principal assistant and as leader of executive business in the National Assembly. Although extremely powerful, the president must answer to the National Assembly, which is granted power to investigate any allegations of misconduct or violation of constitutional provisions.

The Administration

The government of Guyana consists of the president, the vice president, the prime minister, and the cabinet of ministers.

The National Assembly

The National Assembly, consisting of 65 members elected by a system of proportional representation for a term of five years, constitutes the central representative organ of the people of Guyana. It exercises legislative powers by drafting and passing bills with the approval of the president.

All members of the National Assembly are granted immunity from civil and criminal proceedings while in office. The High Court exercises full judicial review of all National Assembly actions.

Regional Administration

Local Democratic Councils are the elected regional administrative bodies, charged with ensuring the development of their areas. As the lowest level of government, they have as their primary tasks maintenance of law and order, protection of public property, safeguarding of fundamental rights and freedoms, and improvement of living and working conditions. Parliament may assign more extensive powers.

The National Congress of Local Democratic Organs represents the interests of local government in Guyana and serves the central government in an advisory function.

Supreme Congress of The People

Consisting of all members of the National Assembly and the National Congress of Local Democratic Organs, the Supreme Congress of the People may discuss issues and make recommendations concerning matters of public interest and advise the president on all matters the president may refer to it.

The Lawmaking Process

Any member of the National Assembly may introduce a bill. After parliamentary debate and passage, the bill is presented to the president for approval. The president may either approve or veto it; in the latter case, he or she returns the bill to the speaker of the National Assembly. If the assembly overrides the veto by two-thirds majority, the president must either approve the bill or dissolve parliament. The latter option has been used in the past to stifle parliamentary opposition. The National Assembly has no authority over fiscal matters, unless the cabinet recommends or consents to fiscal legislative changes.

The Judiciary

The judiciary is made up of a magistrate's court for each of the 10 regions as well as the Supreme Court of Judicature, consisting of a Court of Appeal and a High Court. It is granted full independence in reviewing legislative and executive acts.

The legal system of Guyana is based on British common law. A heavy backlog of cases, lengthy court proceedings, increasingly long periods of pretrial detention, as well as alleged violations of fundamental rights of indigenous peoples render the judiciary's effectiveness questionable.

In addition to the judiciary, an ombudsperson is granted investigative powers into government and administrative acts, with exceptions extending to actions taken with regard to foreign relations, national security, official appointments to office, presidential pardons, and the opening and conduct of civil or criminal court proceedings.

THE ELECTION PROCESS

The right to vote is granted to all Guyanese citizens and Commonwealth citizens resident in Guyana above the age of 18. The right to run for parliamentary elections is granted Guyanese citizens above 18 with English proficiency, unless they have allegiance to a foreign power, are declared mentally unsound, or are under a death or other prison sentence of more than six months. Elections are held by secret ballot, organized and supervised by the Central Elections Commission.

POLITICAL PARTIES

The constitution explicitly guarantees the right to form political parties and their freedom of action, subject only to respect for national sovereignty and democratic principles. Consequently, a pluralistic party landscape has developed. However, as political parties are mainly formulated along ethnic lines, the People's Progressive Party/Civic (PPP/Civic), representing the Indo-Guyanese population as the largest single ethnic group, has been able to win all free elections in the past. Guyana's ethnic division renders any change in the current distribution of political power unlikely.

CITIZENSHIP

The constitution makes detailed provisions for the acquisition and deprivation of Guyanese citizenship, linking citizenship to both Guyanese descent (*ius sanguinis*) and place of birth (*ius soli*). Every person born in Guyana, or to Guyanese citizens abroad, is accorded citizenship, with exceptions applying only to offspring of diplomats rightfully accredited to Guyana or of an enemy alien. Citizenship may also be acquired by marriage, subject to exceptions prescribed in the interests of national security or public policy. Dual citizenship is prohibited.

FUNDAMENTAL RIGHTS

The constitution of Guyana guarantees, in detail, a wide range of fundamental civil and political rights, as well as economic, social, and cultural rights. Among these are the right to life, liberty, and security of the person; the protection of the law including fair trial; freedom from forced labor and torture; and freedom of opinion, assembly, and association. Bound by socialist values, economic, social, and cultural rights include the right and duty to work and workers' rights and needs; the right to property of private enterprises as well as personal belongings and assets; free education and health care; and the right to adequate housing.

Impact and Functions of Fundamental Rights

Allegations of human rights violations are subject to judicial review of the High Court. All fundamental rights and freedoms may only be invoked in disputes governing the relationship between individual and government. Although respect for human rights in practice has improved considerably over the years, human rights groups claim counterterrorism measures have had deleterious effects on the protection of human rights.

Limitations to Fundamental Rights

The constitution contains several limitations on fundamental rights and freedoms and includes a broad derogation (suspension) clause. Fundamental rights and freedoms may be restricted in the interest of defense, public safety, public order, public morality, public health, as well as town or country planning. Private property may be expropriated in a wide range of cases, for example, for public benefit or the protection of Amerindian communities. Enemy property may be expropriated at all times.

ECONOMY

The constitution envisages a socialist economic system of national economic planning, based on the principle of social ownership of the means of production and eradication of the exploitation of human by human. While recognizing privately owned enterprises and property, the constitution envisages cooperation as the underlying principle of socialist transformation and national development, supposedly to reflect the historical experience of the people of Guyana. The economy's supreme goal, according to the constitution, is the fullest possible satisfaction of the people's growing material, cultural, and intellectual requirements, as well as the development of their personality and their socialist relations in society.

RELIGIOUS COMMUNITIES

The constitution of Guyana respects freedom of religion and belief. With a view to the wide ethnic and religious diversity among its population, freedom of religion may be limited by law for the purpose of protecting the rights and freedoms of other persons, including the right to practice any religion without unsolicited intervention of members of any other religion. There is no state religion, as the constitution aspires to complete secularism.

MILITARY DEFENSE AND STATE OF EMERGENCY

Guyana's military, the Guyana Defense Force, is a non-conscription army, consisting mostly of Afro-Guyanese. Women are allowed to enlist, but rarely do so. The force's main tasks include protection from external threats, mainly border disputes with neighboring Venezuela and Suriname, as well as civilian work. Although it has acquired a reputation of being a heavily politicized army, it is no longer obedient to either of the political forces in the country.

The president may declare a state of emergency only for a period of up to 14 days. Unless the National Assembly makes use of its power to extend it up to six months, the state of emergency expires after the initial period of 14 days.

AMENDMENTS TO THE CONSTITUTION

The power to amend the constitution is vested in the National Assembly, which may amend any provision by passing a bill, by an absolute majority. In most cases the president's approval is required. The constitution explicitly allows itself to be suspended and repealed through amendment.

PRIMARY SOURCES

Constitution in English. Available online. URL: http://pdba.georgetown.edu/Constitutions/Guyana/guyana96.html. Accessed on June 21, 2006.

SECONDARY SOURCES

Concluding Observations of the United Nations Human Rights Committee: Guyana. 25/04/2000, CCPR/C/79/Add.121.

Joan R. Mars, *Deadly Force, Colonialism and the Rule of Law.* Westport, Conn: Greenwood Press, 2002.

Brian Moore, *Race, Power and Social Segmentation in Colonial Society—Guyana after Slavery 1838–1891.* Philadelphia: Gordon and Breach Science, 1987.

Thomas J. Spinner Jr., *A Political and Social History of Guyana 1945–1983.* Boulder, Colo.: Westwood Press, 1984.

Johanna Nelles

HAITI

At-a-Glance

OFFICIAL NAME
Republic of Haiti

CAPITAL
Port-au-Prince

POPULATION
8,100,000 (2001 est.)

SIZE
10,714 sq. mi. (27,750 sq. km)

LANGUAGES
French, Creole (both official)

RELIGIONS
Roman Catholic 80%, Protestant 16%, other or none 4%

NATIONAL OR ETHNIC COMPOSITION
Black Haitians 95%, white and mulatto Haitians 5%

DATE OF INDEPENDENCE OR CREATION
January 1, 1804 (from France)

TYPE OF GOVERNMENT
Presidential republic

TYPE OF STATE
Unitary state

TYPE OF LEGISLATURE
Bicameral parliament

DATE OF CONSTITUTION
March 29, 1987

DATE OF LAST AMENDMENT
No amendment

The Republic of Haiti was one of the first countries in the Western Hemisphere to become independent. It now has a progressive constitution that provides a presidential democracy, with safeguards against an overly strong presidency and against military rule. The executive, legislative, and judicial powers are divided, enforced by checks and balances. The constitution provides for liberal and social rights, but there is no mechanism for individuals to enforce these rights.

Haiti is organized as a unitary state. It is made up of nine departments, run by officials elected by universal suffrage on all levels.

The president is the head of state. The constitution provides for a strong bicameral parliament. Free and fair multiparty elections are guaranteed. Religious freedom is also guaranteed. No specific economic system is favored by the constitution. After being ratified, international treaties become part of the national legislation and take precedence over any law in conflict with them.

CONSTITUTIONAL HISTORY

Haiti comprises the western part of the island of Hispaniola as well as several smaller islands in the Caribbean. The Spaniards were the first Europeans to land and settle on Hispaniola, as early as the late 15th century. As people from France started to settle in the western part of the island, about a third of its territory was ceded to them by Spain in 1697. More and more African slaves were imported to the county. At the end of the 18th century, a huge slave revolt took place. After first seizing the northern part of the colony, the rebels won complete independence from France in 1804. After a brief period when the northern, western, and southern regions each had their own regimes, the sectors were united in 1820. Haiti even ruled the eastern part of Hispaniola (today's Dominican Republic) for some 20 years until 1844.

The country faced turbulent times with many different governments, until in 1915 the United States began a military intervention that lasted until 1934.

For almost three decades, the Duvalier family ruled Haiti. The 1983 constitution implemented by the family granted vast powers to the president. In January 1986, François Duvalier was forced to resign after months of political unrest and growing demonstrations against his leadership. The Duvalier constitution was suspended and the National Assembly was dissolved. In the following months, a Constituent Assembly drafted a new constitution. On March 29, 1987, this constitution was approved in a national referendum.

In 1990, Jean-Bertrand Aristide was elected president. Only a few months later, in September 1991, he was overthrown in a coup and had to flee to the United States. A military regime took control of Haiti. Several articles of the 1987 constitution were temporarily suspended. In 1994, a Human Rights monitoring mission (called MICIVIH), set up by the United Nations (UN) and the Organization of American States, was expelled. As a reaction, the United Nations Security Council passed Resolution 940 authorizing member states to "use all necessary means" to restore Haiti's government. A multinational force led by the United States intervened. In the 1995 presidential election, René Préval became president. Aristide's subsequent split with the ruling party led to more politically difficult times with disputed elections.

In 2000 new elections returned Aristide to office, but the political stalemate did not end. Most international troops had gone by 2000, but the situation did not improve. Political strikes and fighting between opposition and progovernment followers grew violent. Rebels gained effective control over major cities. In February 2004, Aristide resigned as president of Haiti and the president of the Supreme Court took over as interim president. During all those troubled years, the constitution was not changed. Since 2004, the UN Stability Mission in Haiti (MINUSTAH) has deployed some 7,500 peacekeeping troops to Haiti. New elections were to be held in 2006. Préval was declared the victor, despite allegations of electoral fraud.

FORM AND IMPACT OF THE CONSTITUTION

The 1987 constitution is a relatively long document with 298 articles plus several more that were inserted in the final stage, but not renumbered. Despite the political crises the country has faced in the past two decades, the constitution can be called relatively stable. After the resignation of the elected president of the republic in 2004, the president of the Supreme Court became interim president, as provided for in the constitution.

BASIC ORGANIZATIONAL STRUCTURE

Haiti is a centralist state and a parliamentary republic. It consists of (currently) nine departments, which are further subdivided into communes and communal sections. Each administrative level is run by a council of three, its members elected by universal suffrage for four years. Representatives of these councils form an Interdepartmental Council, which works together with the national executive on decentralization programs.

LEADING CONSTITUTIONAL PRINCIPLES

Haiti has a strict separation of the three powers: the executive, legislative, and judicial. According to the constitution, Haiti is a social state, a democracy, and a republic. Furthermore, it is indivisible, sovereign, independent, cooperatist, and free.

CONSTITUTIONAL BODIES

The predominant bodies provided for in the constitution are the president of the republic; the administration, headed by the prime minister; the parliament, consisting of two houses; and the judiciary, including the Supreme Court.

The President of the Republic

The president of the republic is the head of state. He or she chooses the prime minister from the party that has a majority in parliament. The president is also the nominal head of the armed forces.

Compared to those in previous Haitian constitutions, presidential powers are reduced. The president cannot serve consecutive terms and must wait five years to be reelected.

The Executive Administration

The administration is headed by a prime minister. As must the president of the republic, the prime minister must be a native-born Haitian. The prime minister is responsible for enforcing the law.

The members of the cabinet of ministers are chosen by the prime minister. While serving in the administration, they may not be members of parliament.

The Parliament

The two chambers of the Haitian parliament are the House of Deputies and the Senate, both of them elected by direct, universal suffrage. Delegates to the House of Deputies represent municipalities. Every department is represented by three senators. Both chambers are legislative bodies.

Together, the House of Deputies and the Senate compose the National Assembly. The joint body has limited, but important functions, such as declaring war or amending the constitution.

Neither of the chambers can be dissolved or adjourned at any time; nor can the term of their mandate be extended. These rules must be seen as safeguards developed after bitter experiences with dictators who ruled in Haiti in the past.

The Lawmaking Process
Either chamber of parliament can initiate legislation, as can the executive. However, only the administration may initiate legislation in certain areas, such as budget laws. After a bill has been passed by the legislature, it is forwarded to the president of the republic. The president has the right to make objections. These objections may in turn be rejected by either house of parliament. In that case, the president must promulgate the law.

The Judiciary
The judiciary is independent. The legal system is based on Roman civil law. At the top of the Haitian court system is the Supreme Court (Cour de Cassation). Other courts are the courts of appeal, courts of first instance, and various special courts. Under certain circumstances, the Senate constitutes itself as the High Court of Justice, responsible for the indictment of elected state officials.

Other Bodies
In addition to these primary organs of state, the constitution enumerates many others as well, such as the permanent electoral council, the superior court of auditors and administrative disputes, the conciliation commission, and the office of citizen's protection. There is also a Haitian Academy, which standardizes the Creole language.

THE ELECTION PROCESS AND POLITICAL PARTICIPATION

Suffrage is universal for Haitians aged 18 and older. Both chambers of the bicameral parliament as well as the president of the republic are directly elected by the people. The term of office of the 83 members of the House of Deputies is four years, while the 27 senators serve for six. The president may serve up to two nonconsecutive terms of five years. He or she must be Haitian by birth, be at least 35 years old, own at least one real property in Haiti, and have resided in the country not less than five years before the election.

The constitution provides for public elections on many administrative levels.

POLITICAL PARTIES

After a ban on opposition parties under the Duvaliers' rule, many new parties have emerged in recent years. Their political appeal is usually based on personalities rather than policies. There is no threshold for parties to win seats in the elections, but only parties who win at least 10 percent of the votes nationwide, with a minimum of 5 percent in each department, are reimbursed with government funds.

CITIZENSHIP

Haitian nationality is primarily acquired by birth to a native-born Haitian parent. Foreigners may acquire nationality after having lived continuously for five years in Haiti. Dual citizenship is not allowed. Under special circumstances, a person can lose Haitian nationality, for example, when serving in a foreign government.

FUNDAMENTAL RIGHTS

The constitution of Haiti specifies a large number of both liberal and social rights, found in Title III, Chapter II. Duties of the citizens are listed in Chapter III. Freedom and its protection by the state are formulated as the starting point.

The constitution makes much mention of education—for example, that it is the state's first responsibility and must be free of charge. The same is true of the "right to security" (Articles 41–51). The right to work is guaranteed, combined with the obligation to engage in work.

Impact and Functions of Fundamental Rights
The constitution of Haiti does not provide for clear mechanisms to enable individuals to enforce their enumerated basic rights.

Limitations to Fundamental Rights
Fundamental rights are not without limits. The constitution provides some specific limits, such as provisions limiting the right to strike, the right to own private property, or the practice of religion. The practical human rights situation in the country is rather problematic.

ECONOMY

The constitution does not favor a special economic system. Owning private property is recognized and guaranteed. Nationalization for political reasons is forbidden. However, according to the constitution, ownership entails obligations. Failure to comply can result in a penalty; for example, landowners have the duty to cultivate their land.

RELIGIOUS COMMUNITIES

The constitution recognizes freedom of conscience as well as freedom of assembly. The right not to belong to a religious community is also accepted. A vast majority of Haitians are of the Roman Catholic faith, though many practice Voodoo at the same time. The government officially recognized Voodoo as a religion in 2003. Roman Catholicism was the official state religion until the enactment of the 1987 constitution.

MILITARY DEFENSE AND STATE OF EMERGENCY

The "Public Forces" of Haiti are composed of the regular Haitian armed forces, which have been demobilized since 2005, and the police force. According to Article 268, military service is compulsory.

A state of siege is declared by the president of the republic. However, the state is lifted if it is not renewed by a vote of the National Assembly every 15 days.

AMENDMENTS TO THE CONSTITUTION

Only the legislature may propose amendments to the constitution, and a majority of two-thirds in both chambers is needed for passage. The constitution strictly forbids holding referendums to amend the constitution. No amendment that would impact the democratic and republican nature of the state is allowed.

PRIMARY SOURCES

Constitution in English. Available online. URL: http://www.haiti.org/constitu/constabl.htm. Accessed on August 2, 2005.

Constitution in French. Available online. URL: http://www.haiti-reference.com/politique/legislatif/constitution_87.html. Accessed on July 16, 2005.

SECONDARY SOURCES

Robert Fatton Jr., "The Impairments of Democratization: Haiti in Comparative Perspective." *Comparative Politics* (1998/1999): 209–229.

Yasmine Shamsie, "Building 'Low-Intensity' Democracy in Haiti: The OAS Contribution." *Third World Quarterly* 25 (2004): 1097–1115.

Hartmut Rank

HONDURAS

At-a-Glance

OFFICIAL NAME
Republic of Honduras

CAPITAL
Tegucigalpa

POPULATION
6,975,204 (July 2005 est.)

SIZE
43,433 sq. mi. (112,492 sq. km)

LANGUAGES
Spanish and indigenous dialects

RELIGIONS
Roman Catholic 97%, Protestant 3%

NATIONAL OR ETHNIC COMPOSITION
Mixed 90%, indigenous 7%, African descent 2%, white 1%

DATE OF INDEPENDENCE OR CREATION
September 15, 1821 (from Spain)

TYPE OF GOVERNMENT
Parliamentary democracy

TYPE OF STATE
Federal state

TYPE OF LEGISLATURE
Unicameral congress

DATE OF CONSTITUTION
January 11, 1982

DATE OF LAST AMENDMENT
May 4, 2005

Honduras is a state of law, sovereign, constituted as a free republic, democratic, and independent. It has a unitary government under a president and a vice president and a unicameral congress of deputies. Both congress and the president are elected for four-year terms. Reelection of the president is prohibited, but it is allowed for the deputies.

The Supreme Court of Justice is composed of 15 magistrates, elected by the National Congress but nominated by a committee in which representatives of civil society participate. Magistrates' terms last seven years, and they can be reelected.

The constitution establishes respect for the human person as a fundamental principle and as the supreme aim of society and the state. It details an ample catalogue of human rights, emphasizing the economic, social, and cultural rights, and in particular, the rights of workers. In order to guarantee the supremacy of the constitution, a Constitutional Chamber was recently created within the Supreme Court of Justice.

The president of the republic commands the armed forces. Military service, during periods of peace, is voluntary.

National education is secular. Basic education is obligatory and paid for by the state. Religious freedom is guaranteed, and the state is separated from any religious creed. The economic system established in the constitution has a strong orientation toward a social market economy, but neoliberal measures have been implemented in recent years.

CONSTITUTIONAL HISTORY

Honduras became independent of Spain on September 15, 1821, along with its fellow Central American republics Guatemala, El Salvador, Nicaragua, and Costa Rica. Together they had formed the old Captaincy General of Guatemala. Once they reached independence, after a short period of Mexican rule, they decided to establish a federal system, adopting the Constitution of the Federal Republic of Central America on November 22, 1824.

Honduras, as a state member of the federation, issued its first constitution in 1825. But in spite of the struggles of General Francisco Morazán to maintain the union, the federation was soon dissolved.

Honduras underwent numerous revolutions in the 19th century. The most important constitutions of the era were implemented in 1880 and 1894. Both adopted liberal principles. The same is true of the 1957 constitution, which initiated the modern political era. President Ramón Villeda Morales, who governed under the 1957 constitution, was overthrown by a military takeover in 1963. The new constitution issued in 1965 was almost identical to the 1957 text. In 1972 President Ramón E. Cruz was overthrown by another military takeover. The armed forces held power for an entire decade. In April 1980 a Constitutional National Assembly was elected; after almost two years of discussions, the current constitution was adopted on January 11, 1982. It has by now achieved the longest duration of any constitution in the history of Honduras.

Honduras supports the union of Central America and participates in the efforts for its economic integration.

FORM AND IMPACT OF THE CONSTITUTION

Honduras, following the Latin American tradition, has a written constitution that has generous and detailed content, with a total of 379 articles. The constitution represents a unifying point for all Hondurans, and it serves as a warranty of the enjoyment and exercise of their rights.

BASIC ORGANIZATIONAL STRUCTURE

Honduras is a unitary state, with a central government administratively divided into 18 departments, which are in turn divided into 298 municipalities. These autonomous municipalities are each administered by a mayor and a vice mayor and a number of advisers according to the number of inhabitants. Municipalities are becoming more and more important, as they develop their own projects in close contact with the needs of the region. However, most of them depend on subsidies from the central government.

LEADING CONSTITUTIONAL PRINCIPLES

Honduras is a law-abiding state, the sovereignty of which belongs to the people, from whom the powers of the state emanate by representation. The constitution nobly aims to strengthen and perpetuate the rule of law through representative democracy, in order to assure all inhabitants respect for the dignity of the human person, justice, peace, and the common good.

The Honduran government is a republican democracy. The three powers, legislative, judicial, and executive, are complementary and independent and are not subordinate to one another, as a result of checks and balances. For example, the reelection of the president of the republic is prohibited.

The government is to be founded on participatory democracy, leading to national integration; this implies the participation of all political sectors in public administration. Recently, the constitution was amended to add the referendum as an instrument of participatory democracy.

In international matters, the constitution upholds the principles and practices of international law that promote human solidarity, self-determination of nations, nonintervention, reinforcement of peace, and universal democracy. Also, it proclaims an inescapable obligation to arbitration and international courts.

CONSTITUTIONAL BODIES

The Honduran system is largely presidentialist. Nevertheless, the influence of the president of the republic has diminished through electoral law reform; citizens now cast votes for deputies on a separate sheet. As a result, the party of the president does not have the majority in congress.

Consequently, congress has recently played an important role in controlling the president and the administration. It has even used its power to question ministers.

The President

Executive authority is exercised by the president and vice president of the republic, who in theory represent and work for the benefit of the people. They are elected by direct popular vote by a simple majority. They serve for a period of four years and cannot be reelected.

The president is in charge of the general administration of the state. The main duties of the president are to direct the general administration of the state and to represent it; to name and remove freely the cabinet ministers and vice ministers; to participate in the formation of laws, presenting bills through the cabinet ministers; to issue agreements, decrees, regulations, and resolutions in accordance with the law; to direct foreign policy and international relations; to conclude treaties and international conventions and ratify them after congressional approval; to name the heads of diplomatic missions; to administer the public finances; to direct the economic and financial policy of the state; and to formulate the National Plan of Development, discuss it in the cabinet, deposit it for approval by the National Congress, and direct its implementation.

The president of the republic summons the ministers into cabinet sessions. The ministers collaborate with the president in directing, coordinating, and supervising the components of the national public administration. In their respective fields, they are responsible alongside the president for the acts that they authorize.

The ministers must annually present to the National Congress a report of their activities. They can be questioned by the congress on issues related to public administration.

The National Congress

Legislative power is exercised by the Congress of Deputies of 128 members, chosen by direct suffrage for a period of four years, with the potential to be reelected. The deputies represent the people.

The chief function of the National Congress is to create, decree, interpret, reform, and countermand the laws. As a unique characteristic of the Honduran constitutional system, congress is the power that interprets the constitution for the given legislative period. It votes on specific interpretations by a two-thirds majority of all its members. Congress chooses the high civil officers of the state: magistrates of the Supreme Court of Justice, members of the Superior Court of Accounts, the attorney-general and assistant attorney-general of the republic, magistrates of the Electoral Supreme Court, the general prosecutor and subgeneral prosecutor of the republic, the attorney-general of the environment and his or her assistant, the national commissioner for human rights, the superintendent of concessions, and the director of the national civil registry and his or her assistant. Congress also approves the national budget and international treaties, establishes taxes, declares war and calls for peace, and fixes the number of permanent members of the armed forces.

The Lawmaking Process

The most important task of the National Congress is to discuss and approve laws. Once a bill is presented, it is passed to a standing committee, and later discussed in a plenary session of congress. Once approved, the bill is sent to the president of the republic for approval and promulgation as law. If the president rejects the law, it is returned to the National Congress, which can now adopt the law only with a majority of two-thirds of those voting. At this point, it is passed to the president, who must publish it without delay. If the president's rejection is based on constitutionality issues, it must undergo a hearing before the Supreme Court of Justice. The Supreme Court of Justice issues its final ruling within the time that the National Congress indicates.

The Judiciary

The judicial power is composed of a Supreme Court of Justice, courts of appeal, courts of first instance, and other branches as designated by the law.

The Supreme Court of Justice has jurisdiction over the entire state. It is composed of 15 magistrates elected for a period of seven years, eligible to be reelected thereafter.

A recent reform to the constitution, effective in 2001, established a new procedure for the election of magistrates to the Supreme Court of Justice. The National Congress, with a two-thirds majority of all its members, elects 15 magistrates from a list of no fewer than three potential magistrates for every open position. The Joint Appointment Committee, which proposes to congress its candidates for magistrates of the Supreme Court, is composed of seven members who represent these different sectors of society: the Supreme Court of Justice, the Bar Association of Lawyers of Honduras, the National Commission of Human Rights, the Honduran Council of Private Business, the universities of the country, the organizations of the civil society, and the worker's unions.

This same reform created a Constitutional Court within the Supreme Court, to guarantee the supremacy of constitutional standards.

THE ELECTION PROCESS

Every Honduran over the age of 18 has the right to stand for election and to vote. Voting is universal, obligatory, egalitarian, direct, free, and secret.

All issues related to electoral procedures fall under the jurisdiction of the Electoral Supreme Court. This court is independent. It is made up of three magistrates and a substitute. Members are elected by a vote of two-thirds of all the members of the National Congress for a term of five years, with the ability to be reelected.

POLITICAL PARTIES

The political party system in Honduras is very dynamic. Five parties exist, two of which—the Liberal and the National Parties represent together more than 90 percent of the voters. Both parties have existed for over a century. The Liberal Party is Left center, while the National Party is oriented Right of center. The other parties are the Party of Innovation and Unity, the ideology of which is social democrat; the Christian Democratic Party; and the Democratic Unification Party, which is oriented to the Left.

CITIZENSHIP

People born in the national territory of Honduras, with the exception of diplomats' children, and those born abroad of a Honduran father or mother are Honduran. Naturalization is possible in certain cases such as marriage to a Honduran citizen by birth.

FUNDAMENTAL RIGHTS

The constitution establishes and guarantees a long list of human rights starting with the recognition of the dignity of human life. It protects human life, prohibits the death penalty, and protects the unborn child. It recognizes specifically individual rights, social rights, the rights of children, worker's rights, social security rights, health rights, education and cultural rights, and the right to life.

Impact and Functions of Fundamental Rights

Human rights represent, for the society and the state of Honduras, the principles that govern their life. In order to guarantee respect for these rights, a constitutional reform that went into effect in 1995 created the institution of the National Commission of Human Rights, which additionally carries out the functions of the ombudsperson.

Limitations to Fundamental Rights

The rights of everyone are limited by the rights of others, by the need to protect the security of all, and by the requirements of general well-being and of developing democracy.

ECONOMY

The economic system of Honduras is founded on principles of efficiency in production and social justice in the distribution of wealth and national income. The state promotes economic and social development, which are subject to national economic planning. The national economy is sustained through the harmony of diverse forms of business and property and coexists with the democratic political system.

Despite these principles, Honduras is one of the poorest countries in Latin America.

RELIGIOUS COMMUNITIES

The constitution guarantees the free exercise of all religions and forms of worship without preference and ensures the separation of laws and religion. Clergy of the diverse religions are not permitted to proclaim public positions, participate in any form of political propaganda, or invoke the religious beliefs of the community as a tool for such aims.

The state is separated from the church, and public education is secular. The majority of the Honduran population is Catholic, although in the last few years the number of evangelical Christian churches has increased.

MILITARY DEFENSE AND STATE OF EMERGENCY

The armed forces have played an important role in the life of Honduras, seizing power on various occasions.

The 1957 constitution gave the army internal autonomy, which was retained in both the 1965 and current 1982 constitutions. In 1998, an amendment to the constitution put the armed forces under the control of the president of the republic, who became its commander in chief. The secretary of national defense is appointed and can be removed freely by the president, who serves as chief of combined state headquarters.

Another important reform affirming the supremacy of the civil power was the constitutional amendment that entered into effect in 1997, which separated the national police from the armed forces.

The armed forces participate in international peace-keeping missions, in the fight against drug traffic, in assistance during natural disasters, and in environmental conservation programs. Military service is voluntary.

The suspension of fundamental rights can be declared by the president of the republic, in the Council of Ministers. In this case, the suspended rights must be specified and the National Congress must be informed within 30 days. If the congress is in session, the president must inform it immediately. The suspension cannot last more than 45 days.

AMENDMENTS TO THE CONSTITUTION

The National Congress, in ordinary session, can amend the constitution with two-thirds of the votes of all members. The measure must indicate the article or articles that have been reformed. To enter into effect it must be ratified by the next ordinary session of congress, with at least an equal number of members voting for ratification.

An ordinary session of congress runs from January through October every year, and on occasion is prolonged through December. Thus, constitutional reforms can be approved in very little time, as long as the two major parties are in agreement to supply the needed two-thirds vote. Political pacts are often made for this purpose.

Consequently, the constitution of Honduras has been reformed 24 times since its inception in 1982, affecting some 100 of its articles. Some critics have criticized the frequency of these reforms and have even suggested that a new constitution should be adopted; others have argued that the process has encouraged a gradual and peaceful transformation of Honduran society and has solidified the rule of law.

PRIMARY SOURCES

Constitution in Spanish: Mariñas Otero Luis, *Las Constituciones de Honduras*. Madrid: Ediciones Cultura Hispánica, 1962. Available online. URL: http://www.georgetown.edu/pdba/Constitutions/Honduras/hond82.html. Accessed on August 17, 2005.

SECONDARY SOURCES

Jorge A. Coello, *Digesto Constitucional de Honduras.* Tegucigalpa: Imprenta Soto, 1978.

Honduras—a Country Study. Washington, D.C.: U.S. Government Printing Office. Available online. URL: http://countrystudies.us/honduras/. Accessed on July 28, 2005.

Otto Martínez Velásquez and María T. Flores, *Constitución de la República: Edición actualizada y aumentada 2004.* Tegucigalpa, Honduras.

Moncada Silva, *Efraín Temas Constitucionales.* Tegucigalpa, Honduras; Edigrafic, 2001.

United Nations, "Core Document Forming Part of the Reports of States Parties: Honduras" (HRI/CORE/1/Add.96), 15 September 1998. Available online. URL: http://www.unhchr.ch/tbs/doc.nsf. Accessed on July 27, 2005.

Leo Valladares Lanza

HUNGARY

At-a-Glance

OFFICIAL NAME
Republic of Hungary

CAPITAL
Budapest

POPULATION
10,117,000 (2005 est.)

SIZE
35,919 sq. mi. (93,030 sq. km)

LANGUAGES
Hungarian

RELIGIONS
Catholic (Roman Catholic 52%, Greek Catholic 3%) 55%, Protestant (Calvinist 16%, Lutheran 3%) 19%, smaller religious communities: Jewish, Orthodox, Evangelical 1%, unaffiliated 15%, no data 10%

NATIONAL OR ETHNIC COMPOSITION
Hungarian, Roma (approximately 5%), German (approximately 2%), Slovak, Croat, Romanian, Serb (under 1%)

DATE OF INDEPENDENCE OR CREATION
1000 C.E.

TYPE OF GOVERNMENT
Parliamentary democracy

TYPE OF STATE
Unitary state

TYPE OF LEGISLATURE
Unicameral parliament

DATE OF CONSTITUTION
August 20, 1949 (revised October 23, 1989)

DATE OF LAST AMENDMENT
January 1, 2005

Hungary is a parliamentary democracy based on the rule of law with a clear division of executive, legislative, and judicial powers. The country is organized as a unitary state, with a central government counterbalanced by local self-government. The constitution provides for guarantees of human rights. Remedies include a strong constitutional court.

The president of the republic is the head of state, but the functions of the office are mostly representative or symbolic. The central political figure is the prime minister as head of the administration, depending on parliament as the representative body of the people. Free, equal, general, and direct elections of the members of parliament are guaranteed. A pluralistic system of political parties has intense political impact.

Religious freedom is guaranteed and religious communities are separated from the state. The economic system can be described as a market economy. The military is subject to the civil government in terms of law and in fact. By constitutional law, Hungary is obliged to support international cooperation, European integration, and responsibility for ethnic Hungarians living abroad.

CONSTITUTIONAL HISTORY

Hungary emerged as a state a century after Magyar tribes arrived in central Europe in 896 C.E. In the year 1000, the pope acknowledged Hungarian statehood by sending a crown to its Christian king, the founder of the monarchy later known as Saint Steven (977–1038). By the 15th century—despite a devastating Tatar invasion in 1241—Hungary emerged as a significant feudal kingdom in central Europe. The nobility gained important rights that were embodied in a Magna Carta in 1222, seen as a fundament of the Hungarian constitution. The privileged status of the nobility was a source of later parliamentary powers: The king could make laws only with the consent of the peers.

The expanding Ottoman Turks occupied the central part of the country for 150 years in the 16th and 17th centuries. In the east, the Principality of Transylvania emerged as a safe haven for religious freedom and Hungarian national culture. The Kingdom of Hungary was reduced to its northwestern lands, maintaining statehood and its traditional legal system even as it was absorbed into the emerging Habsburg Empire. As the Turks were driven out by the end of the 17th century, ethnic Hungarians in Hungary were outnumbered by ethnic minorities (Germans, Romanians, Slovaks, Serbs).

The following centuries were characterized by the fight for independence, Protestant emancipation, and a drive to catch up with the economic and cultural progress that had occurred in western Europe. The revolutionary legislation of 1848 created a new constitutional settlement: Parliament (the House of Representatives) became a representative, elected body while the king lost nearly all his executive powers, as these were now to be exercised by an administration responsible to parliament. Although it was not until 1867 that Austria and Hungary reached a new compromise (Austro-Hungarian Empire) that consolidated the constitutional structure, the era saw economic progress and rapid modernization. With the breakup of the Austro-Hungarian Empire after World War I (1914–18), the Kingdom of Hungary lost about two-thirds of its territory, most of its ethnic minorities, and a large part of its ethnic Hungarian population. Hungary became a small country surrounded by former territories, all populated with large ethnic Hungarian minorities.

Despite the influence of Continental legal traditions and some efforts at codification after 1867, Hungarian law remained to a large extent customary: There was neither a written constitution, nor a civil code. In matters of civil law, the law book (*Corpus Iuris Hungarici*) collected and published by the judge Werbőczy in 1514 remained authoritative for centuries. A peculiar cornerstone of Hungarian public law was the theory of the Holy Crown. According to this, the nobility (the "nation") was to be regarded as member of the Crown, as an expression of shared sovereignty.

The country became involved in World War II (1939–45) as a German ally. In 1944 three-fourths of all Hungarian Jews became victims of the Holocaust. After the war, in 1946, Hungary became a republic. A short democratic period was undermined by massive Soviet influence and ended with the outright Communist takeover in 1948. A written constitution was adopted in 1949, breaking away from centuries of constitutional tradition and neglecting all established values of constitutionality: eliminating human rights, democracy, the rule of law, and the separation of powers. The revolution against communism in 1956 was crushed by a Soviet invasion, but the regime had to grant some concessions that made Hungary a relatively open place behind the iron curtain.

With the collapse of European communism in the late 1980s, Hungary won a new chance to establish itself as an independent country. After revision of the constitution as a result of negotiations between the Communist Party and the democratic opposition in 1989, free elections were held in 1990. Since then Hungary has had a multiparty system, a parliamentarian form of government, an independent court system, and judicial review, with a Constitutional Court as the ultimate warrant of the constitution. The country joined the North Atlantic Treaty Organization (NATO) in 1998 and the European Union in 2004.

FORM AND IMPACT OF THE CONSTITUTION

Hungary has a written constitution, codified in a single document, that takes precedence over all other national law. The principle of the hierarchy of norms requires that regulations of local self-government conform to central norms and that regulations of the administration conform to acts of parliament. The constitution provides for the harmony of international and domestic law. The question of precedence of the law of the European Union is a current issue: An eventual collision between directly applicable European law and the constitution of Hungary would confront the Constitutional Court with a delicate legal issue.

The preamble of the constitution calls for a new replacement constitution, but the political consensus needed to achieve that end has not existed since the collapse of communism. However, considering the revisions introduced during the transition of 1989 and 1990, the constitution has become a new constitution in fact. Since then, it has also become "real law," whereas before it had a merely declarative-political character.

The Constitutional Court has proved to be a powerful instrument in safeguarding the letter and the spirit of the constitution.

BASIC ORGANIZATIONAL STRUCTURE

Hungary is a unitary state with a central government.

Local self-government has a strong position in Hungary. There is a long historical tradition of territorial self-government (counties), dating back to the founder king, Saint Steven. Local communities enjoy significant autonomy in many fields: They provide public services in both villages and cities, such as education, health care, and public transport; they pursue their own economic development programs; and they enjoy limited taxation powers. The residents of the communities elect mayors and members of local political bodies.

LEADING CONSTITUTIONAL PRINCIPLES

Hungary's system of government is a parliamentary democracy. There is strong division among the executive, legislative, and judicial powers, based on checks and balances. The judiciary is independent; apart from the regular court system there is an independent Constitutional Court.

The Hungarian constitutional system is based on a number of leading principles. Article 2, Section (1), provides the following definition: "The Republic of Hungary shall be an independent, democratic state under the rule of law."

Indirect, representative democracy has precedence over direct democracy. Direct democracy, whereby voters can voice their choice directly, has a more practical role on the local than on the national level. However, even parliament may be bound by a referendum, although no referenda are allowed in certain matters enumerated by the constitution and the law, including modification of the constitution itself, the budget, taxes, duties and fees, and international obligations. A national referendum must be held if requested by at least 200,000 voters—and if the question complies with the constitution.

The principle of republican government has rather limited meaning in Hungary today. It simply means that there shall be no monarchy, although some understand the republican principle to include the participatory nature of decision making as well.

Rule of law is of decisive impact. All state actions impairing the rights of the people must have a basis in parliamentary law, and the judiciary must be independent and effective. The principle of legal certainty is inherent in the rule of law: Legal certainty requires the law to be stable, foreseeable, and accessible, so that those obligated by the law can learn of the obligations they are supposed to observe.

Further structural principles are implicitly contained in the constitution, such as ideological-religious neutrality. The constitution commits Hungary to respect international law and renounces war as a means of solving disputes between nations. The constitution contains a comprehensive bill of rights, including not only civil and political rights and freedoms, but also "second-generation" economic, social, and cultural rights. The environment is protected by the acknowledgment of a right of everybody to a healthy environment.

The constitution declares that Hungary exercises certain public powers jointly with other European countries, and that these actions may also be exercised by the organs of the European Union itself.

CONSTITUTIONAL BODIES

The predominant bodies provided for in the constitution are the president of the republic and the administration, headed by the prime minister; the parliament; and the judiciary. The court system has four levels: local courts, county courts, courts of appeal, and the Supreme Court. Constitutional jurisdiction (primarily the control of the constitutionality of laws) is held exclusively by the Constitutional Court. A number of other entities complete the list of constitutional bodies, such as the National Bank, the chief public prosecutor, and the Defense Council, which functions as a representative body in a state of defense if parliament cannot convene.

The President of the Republic

The president is the head of state of the Republic of Hungary, expressing the unity of the nation and guarding over the democratic operation of the state. The prime minister is elected by parliament upon nomination by the president. The president appoints the ministers upon the presentation of the prime minister and appoints ambassadors, generals, and university professors. However, as the president carries no political responsibilities, a member of the government countersigns all his or her appointments and presents the candidate. The president can refuse such a recommendation only if legal preconditions have not been met or if the president holds that the appointment may endanger the democratic operation of the state. The president also appoints all judges, upon the recommendation of the judiciary, and no countersignature is necessary in this case. Finally, the president nominates candidates to some important posts such as the chief public prosecutor, the president of the Supreme Court, and the ombudsperson, although in these cases parliament makes the final choice.

The president promulgates the laws, with the right to veto a law adopted by parliament once. If parliament passes the law again, the president has to promulgate it. If the president considers a law passed by parliament to be unconstitutional, he or she must refer it to the Constitutional Court. The president can dissolve parliament and call for new elections in strictly defined cases. This can happen if parliament is unable to elect a prime minister within 40 days of the first nomination, or if within a year there are at least four successful votes of no confidence against the prime minister.

The president also represents the republic in international affairs and has the right to pardon individual criminal offenders. The president is the commander in chief of the armed forces; this role does not imply the power to give any commands; it is the responsibility of the administration to direct the armed forces.

The political position of the president is limited, as the office consists largely of representative functions, but under critical circumstances the president may help the state overcome a crisis. The political impact of the president depends largely on personal charisma. On the other hand, this relative lack of political power enables the president to be representative of the whole of the nation, above everyday politics.

The president of the republic is elected by parliament for a five-year term and can be reelected only once. A majority of two-thirds of the members of parliament is needed, but if this is not achieved in two rounds, a simple majority is sufficient. The president must be at least 35 years of age. An impeachment procedure is possible only if the president intentionally violates the law while exercising the functions of the office. The procedure has to be initiated by 20 percent of the members of parliament, followed by a positive impeachment vote of two-thirds of the members. It is the Constitutional Court that decides on the actual removal from office.

The Administration

The administration is the central policymaker and the head of the entire government. It consists of the prime minister and the ministers. The prime minister is elected by the majority of all members of parliament upon the proposal of the president of the republic.

The administration serves for the legislative period of the parliament, unless dismissed early in a vote of non-confidence by a majority of members of parliament; the no-confidence motion must include the name of a new prime minister, who takes office if the motion passes. Each newly elected parliament must go through the process of electing a prime minister and adopting the program of the new administration.

The prime minister is generally the dominant figure in Hungarian politics. The administration depends on the prime minister; it loses office if he or she dies or resigns. The administration bears responsibility for the implementation of law and the administration of the state.

The Parliament

The parliament is the supreme body of state authority and popular representation. It is the legislative body, and it adopts and modifies the constitution itself. For the latter a qualified majority is needed. Parliament elects the prime minister and monitors the administration. The members of parliament have the right to put questions to ministers, to the chief public prosecutor, to the chair of the national bank, to the president of the state audit office, and to the ombudsperson. Any minister can be cited to appear before parliament.

An important right of members of parliament that helps to ensure their independence is parliamentary privilege. This gives them far-reaching protection against legal action or other negative consequences arising from their voting or statements in parliament. Parliamentary privilege also serves to protect the personal freedom of the members of parliament. Only with the permission of the parliament may a member be subjected to any criminal prosecution, be arrested, or have his or her personal freedom limited. The only exception to this privilege occurs if the member of parliament is arrested in the course of committing a crime.

The parliament consists of 386 members. Its period of office, the legislative term, is four years. Parliament can dissolve itself, except during a state of defense; the president of the republic also has the power, under politically extreme conditions, of dissolving parliament. The mem-

bers are elected in a general, direct, free, equal, and secret balloting process, partly in winner-takes-all constituencies, partly on party lists.

Parliament has two independent controlling agencies: the State Audit Office, which monitors the use of public moneys, and the ombudsperson, the public watchdog for the protection of fundamental rights. Their power lies in the influence they may have on the public: They cannot impose penalties, but they submit reports on their findings to parliament and to the general public. The president of the State Audit Office is elected for a term of 12 years, the ombudsperson for six years, both by two-thirds of the votes of all members of parliament upon the nomination of the president of the republic.

The Lawmaking Process

One of the main functions of parliament is to pass legislation. This is done in cooperation with various other constitutional bodies. The right to introduce a bill is enjoyed by the president of the republic, the administration, and any member of parliament. In fact, it is mostly the administration that submits the bills, as drafted by the ministries. Bills are first debated at the committee level in parliament. Then, the plenum generally holds two readings: the first a discussion of the general principles of the proposed legislation, the second a section-by-section debate. To pass a bill, the majority of the members of parliament have to be present, and their majority has to vote in favor.

The constitution enumerates a list of laws that can be passed and modified only by two-thirds of the votes of those members present. These include human rights issues, such as the media law or the law on religious freedom, and some sensitive issues of state organization such as the law on courts or the law on local self-government. These statutes do not constitute a separate level in the hierarchy of legal norms: They are below the constitution, at the same level with any other statute. However, a collision of a statute passed by a two-thirds majority with one passed by a simple majority may lead to legal uncertainty (as may the collision of any other laws) and be unconstitutional for this reason, but not because of the violation of the hierarchy of norms.

For the law to take effect, the president needs to assent and promulgate the law in the official gazette. The president has a limited right of political veto (which can be overridden) as well as the right to submit the bill to the Constitutional Court for review if he or she holds it to be unconstitutional. The president must exercise these rights within 15 days, in urgent cases within five days.

The Judiciary

The judiciary in Hungary is independent of the executive and legislative branches and is a powerful factor in legal life. The court system has four levels—local courts, county courts, courts of appeal, and the Supreme Court. The courts are uniform; that is, the same courts (though different panels) deal with civil, criminal, and administrative cases. The only exception is the labor court on the county level, but appeal against a labor court judgment is decided by the county court.

The administration of the judiciary is performed by an independent body presided over by the president of the Supreme Court. The majority of its members are judges elected from among the judiciary. One of its important powers is the nomination of judges, who are then appointed by the president of the republic. The president of the Supreme Court is elected by parliament with the vote of two-thirds of all members of parliament, on the nomination of the president of the republic.

The Constitutional Court deals exclusively with constitutional disputes. It consists of 11 judges elected by two-thirds of all the members of parliament for a nine-year term. A special commission, in which all parties represented in parliament have one member, nominates the candidates, who shall be university professors or outstanding practitioners. The members of the Constitutional Court elect a president from among their number. The court can declare void any act of parliament, administration decree, or decision by local self-government, on grounds of its being unconstitutional. A constitutional complaint can be taken before the Constitutional Court by any person. The claim can be abstract; that is, no specific case or individual controversy is needed.

The Constitutional Court has proved to be a powerful instrument in safeguarding the constitution; it has gained a high level of public esteem. In many sensitive cases of high political impact, it was the court that resolved the issue. Significant cases have included the abolition of capital punishment, the regulation of abortion, media issues, and borderline cases concerning freedom of expression.

In addition to these human rights cases, the court has resolved a number of delicate political issues such as the relationship between the president of the republic and the prime minister, the role of referenda and their effect on representative democracy, the independence of the judiciary, and the autonomy of local self-government. The Constitutional Court also played an outstanding role in making fundamental choices during the transition from communism to democracy: how to handle criminal acts committed by former rulers, how to compensate for expropriations and the denial of liberty, and what kind of consequences should ensue for collaboration with the communist secret services.

THE ELECTION PROCESS

All citizens who reside in the territory of Hungary and are over the age of 18 have both the right to stand for elections and the right to vote, to initiate a referendum, and to take part in one. Election procedures are guarded by independent electoral committees that supervise and ensure due process.

Parliamentary Elections

Parliamentary elections follow a complex process. Of the 386 members of parliament, 176 are elected in single-member constituencies by an absolute majority of votes. One-half of all voters have to participate in the elections as a condition of validity. The rest of the deputies are elected on party lists. Every voter, therefore, has two votes. As the party lists do not fully compensate the disproportion arising from the constituencies where the winner takes the mandate, the results of the elections are not always entirely proportionate. A party must win at least 5 percent of the party list votes to gain any seat in parliament on party lists. The aim of this rule is to prevent splinter groups from obstructing the work of the legislature. Between four and six parties cleared this hurdle in each of the four elections conducted under the present law between 1990 and 2002.

Local Elections

Residents who are not Hungarian citizens have the right to vote in local election and to stand for municipal councils if they are citizens of any member state of the European Union. Mayors, however, have to be Hungarian citizens.

There is no minimal turnout for local elections. Mayors are chosen by a winner-takes-all plurality vote. The election system for local councils varies; municipalities with fewer than 10,000 choose council members by name from a list of candidates; these members are usually independent. In larger localities, where the parties dominate local politics, 60 percent of the council members are elected in constituencies by plurality, while 40 percent of the mandates are distributed on a compensatory basis among the participating parties.

European Elections

The Hungarian members of the European Parliament are elected on party lists, by proportional representation. All European Union citizens have the right to vote. If they decide to vote in Hungary, they cannot do so in their country of citizenship. There is no minimal turnout, but the 5 percent party list hurdle applies.

POLITICAL PARTIES

Hungary has a pluralistic system of political parties. The multiparty system is a basic structure of the constitutional order. According to the constitution, political parties play a role not only in expressing, but also in forming the political will of the people. They cannot exercise direct political power as the Communist Party used to do, and they must respect the pluralistic system. Parties are to a large extent financed from the state budget, according to the proportions of votes gained at the last two general elections. Political parties are registered with courts and can be deleted from the registry as a consequence of a court procedure.

CITIZENSHIP

Hungarian citizenship is primarily acquired by birth. The principle of *ius sanguinis* applies: That is, a child acquires Hungarian citizenship if one of his or her parents is a Hungarian citizen. It is of no relevance where a child is born. Dual citizenship is not excluded.

The law on citizenship strives to prevent statelessness and to ensure that family members have the same citizenship. Ethnic Hungarians who move to Hungary acquire citizenship more easily. Ethnic Hungarians who live as national minorities in neighboring countries who are citizens of those countries may apply for a "Hungarian certificate" that provides certain benefits for them in their kin state, Hungary. This status, however, does not qualify as citizenship.

FUNDAMENTAL RIGHTS

The Hungarian constitution guarantees the traditional classic set of human rights, as well as a list of economic, social, and cultural rights, such as the right to work, the right to social security, and the right to free education. As a third-generation human right, the right to a healthy environment appears in the constitution, too.

The starting point for human rights in the constitution is the guarantee of life and human dignity. The constitution guarantees numerous specific rights as well. The basic rights set out in the constitution have binding force for the legislature, the executive, and the judiciary, as directly applicable law. This applies to all acts of public authority in all circumstances. The constitution's equal treatment clause is worded generally, but it is open to the possibility of affirmative action or "positive discrimination" as a means to eliminate "inequality in opportunities."

Some rights apply only to citizens, such as the right to vote in national elections and rights to certain social benefits.

Impact and Functions of Fundamental Rights

Fundamental rights are first of all defensive rights. This means that the state may not interfere with the legal position of the individual unless there is special reason to do so. This is the subjective aspect of the right. On the other hand, the state has a duty to ensure that circumstances conducive to the exercise of the fundamental rights are created. This is the objective aspect of the right.

For example, to ensure the freedom of press it is not sufficient not to violate this right: The state has to maintain the public media, providing space to all relevant social and cultural sectors in a balanced way. Respecting the right to life makes it a duty of the state to protect the fetus, who has no rights but deserves protection. The right to a healthy environment has no subjective content, but mere objective aspects: A setback in the level of protection of the environment may be allowed only if another, competing constitutional right or value compels it.

Human rights apply not only in the relation of the individual to the state, but to some extent also to the relations of private persons. One significant area in which this concept plays an important role is equal treatment.

Limitations to Fundamental Rights

The fundamental rights specified in the constitution are not without limits. However, the constitution states that no limits are allowed, even if by law, that would compromise the *essential content* of these rights. This means that one can never be totally deprived of his or her rights. Furthermore, fundamental rights can be limited only by law, that is, by acts of parliament, and not by regulations passed by the administration or a local self-government.

According to the approach of the Hungarian constitutional court, by its very nature the right to life (in dignity) cannot be limited, since life can be wholly taken, or wholly respected, but never taken or respected in part. Other fundamental rights can be limited by law, if this is necessary to ensure another fundamental right or a value recognized by the constitution itself. A mere claim of public order, public safety, public health, or morals is not a sufficient reason to limit a fundamental right. The limitation has to be proportionate with the aim of limitation; that means that the least restrictive limitation has to be applied.

Constitutional, but not fundamental, rights can be limited more easily, on the basis of a commonsense test. An unreasonable limitation would be regarded as arbitrary, and hence unconstitutional.

The right to property is a special case. On the one hand, expropriation is permissible as an extraordinary measure for the public interest; on the other hand, immediate, unconditional, and full compensation has to be provided.

ECONOMY

The constitution defines the economy of Hungary as a "market economy." This general statement leaves the government a broad margin to form economic policy.

Enumerated fundamental rights protect freedom, property, and the right of inheritance. They also protect freedom of occupation or profession, general personal freedom, as well as the right to form associations, partnerships, and corporations. The right to form associations to safeguard and improve working and economic conditions is guaranteed to every individual and all corporations and

392   Hungary

professions. This right guarantees the autonomy of trade unions and employer's associations in labor bargaining.

RELIGIOUS COMMUNITIES

Freedom of religion or belief, which is guaranteed as a human right, also involves rights for the religious communities. As church and state are separate, there is no established church. All public authorities must remain strictly neutral in their relations with religious communities. Religious communities cannot exercise public power, on the one hand, but, on the other hand, the state cannot interfere with their internal affairs.

Religions must be treated equally; however, relevant social differences between religious communities, such as number of adherents, can be taken into consideration. A religious community can register with a county court to gain legal personality as a church. Neutrality does not mean indifference: Despite the essential separation of religions and the state, there are many areas in which they cooperate, for example, in education, health, and social care.

MILITARY DEFENSE AND STATE OF EMERGENCY

The creation and maintenance of armed forces are responsibilities of the administration. The fundamental duty of the armed forces is the military defense of the country. The domestic use of the armed forces is permitted only under extreme conditions such as in a state of emergency, when police forces have proved to be insufficient. This might be the case in the event of armed actions that aim to subvert the constitutional order or to gain exclusive control over public power, or in the case of grave acts of violence committed by armed groups that endanger the lives and property of citizens on a mass scale. With the exception of military maneuvers carried out through a decision of NATO, the army may cross the country's borders only with the prior consent of parliament.

Prior to 2005 the law required all men to perform military service for six months. Conscientious objection is allowed. According to a constitutional amendment, which entered into force on January 1, 2005, national service can only be required in the state of defense. As conscription was abandoned, the armed forces became a professional force consisting of soldiers who voluntarily serve for fixed periods or for life.

Hungary has obligated itself by international treaties not to produce nuclear, biological, or chemical weapons.

The military always remains subject to civil government. The president of the republic is the official commander in chief, but the army is administered through the minister of defense. In case of a state of defense, a special defense council exercises the powers of the administration, and to a limited extent those of parliament as well.

The constitution describes the state of defense in great detail. Such a state exists only if the country is attacked with armed military force. There are some fundamental rights that may not be limited, even in a state of defense.

A state of emergency could exist in the case of an internal armed conflict endangering the constitutional order. In a state of emergency the president of the republic has special powers, in order to help the constitutional system overcome the crisis.

AMENDMENTS TO THE CONSTITUTION

Changing the constitution is relatively easy, requiring only the votes of two-thirds of the members of the parliament. Only the proportion of required votes makes a constitutional amendment different from any other law. In case of an amendment of the constitution, the president of the republic has no right to refer the amendment to the Constitutional Court for preliminary review, as the Constitutional Court itself had no jurisdiction over the constitution itself.

Only the lack of political consensus, on the one hand, and the moral respect of the constitution as a value, on the other, prevent overly frequent changes. If one day a new constitution were to be passed, the general presumption is that a referendum would be required for adoption.

PRIMARY SOURCES
Constitution in English. Available online. URL: http://www.mkab.hu/en/enpage5.htm. Accessed on July 26, 2005.
Constitution in Hungarian. Available online. URL: http://www.mkab.hu/hu/alkotm.htm. Accessed on June 21, 2006.

SECONDARY SOURCES
László Sólyom and Georg Brunner, eds., with a Foreword by Justice Stephen G. Breyer, *Constitutional Judiciary in a New Democracy: The Hungarian Constitutional Court.* Ann Arbor: University of Michigan Press, 2000.

Balázs Schanda

ICELAND

At-a-Glance

OFFICIAL NAME
Republic of Iceland

CAPITAL
Reykjavík

POPULATION
290,054 (2005 est.)

SIZE
39,756 sq. mi. (103,021 sq. km)

LANGUAGES
Icelandic, English, Nordic languages, German widely spoken

RELIGIONS
Protestant 91.5%, Catholic 2%, Asatruar 0.26%, Buddhist 0.17%, Muslim 0.09%, unaffiliated or other 5.98%

NATIONAL OR ETHNIC COMPOSITION
Icelandic 93.4%, other Nordic 1.9%, other European 2.7%, American 0.5%, Asian 1.1%, other 0.4%

DATE OF INDEPENDENCE OR CREATION
June 17, 1944

TYPE OF GOVERNMENT
Parliamentary democracy

TYPE OF STATE
Centralist

TYPE OF LEGISLATURE
Unicameral parliament

DATE OF CONSTITUTION
June 17, 1944

DATE OF LAST AMENDMENT
July 1, 1999

Iceland is a parliamentary democracy based on the rule of law and separation of powers. Organized as a centralized state, Iceland is made up of 105 municipalities, towns, and rural districts. In addition to these, there are 23 regional districts or counties. The constitution of the republic provides for guarantees of classical rights and freedoms as well as some social and economic rights. It is generally well respected by the public authorities; if a violation of the constitution does occur in individual cases, there are effective remedies enforceable by an independent judiciary. Since the review of its Human Rights Chapter in 1995, the constitution has become a centerpiece of Icelandic self-understanding.

The president is the head of state. Although the president is a part of the legislative as well as the executive branch, the office remains mostly representative or symbolic.

The central political figure is the prime minister, as head of the administration. The prime minister depends on parliament as the representative body of the people. Free, equal, general, and direct elections of the members of parliament are guaranteed. Iceland has a pluralistic system of political parties. Religious freedom is guaranteed by the constitution. According to the constitution, the Evangelical Lutheran Church is the national church of Iceland. The country's economic system can be described as a social market economy. Iceland has no military of its own.

CONSTITUTIONAL HISTORY

During the settlement period, 874–930 C.E., no formal system of central government existed in Iceland. With the foundation of the parliament, the Althing (Alþingi), in 930, Iceland emerged as political entity. The period from 930 to 1262 has often been referred to as the time of the Icelandic Free State.

In 1262, Iceland was under the rule of the Norwegian king. It followed Norway in 1380 to become a part of the Danish kingdom. This monarchy became absolutist in Iceland from 1662 until 1845, the same year the Althing was reestablished (it had been formally abolished in 1800).

In 1874, Iceland implemented its first modern constitution. However, the constitution covered only certain domestic matters, and the king of Denmark reserved the veto even there. An amendment to the constitution in 1904 created home rule. Through the Union Act with Denmark, Iceland became a sovereign state in 1918 with the king of Denmark as its king. The Constitution of the Kingdom of Iceland entered into force in 1921. The Union Act was an international treaty as well as domestic law in both Denmark and Iceland; it lasted 25 years.

As a result of German occupation of Denmark in World War II (1939–45), the Danish government was unable to take care of Iceland's foreign affairs. A referendum, held in May 1944, showed that over 90 percent of Icelanders favored the dissolution of the Danish-Icelandic Union. This led to the Declaration of the Republic of Iceland on June 17, 1944, based on a new constitution, which the Icelanders approved in the May referendum.

Although some major amendments have been made to the 1944 constitution, such as the change from a bicameral to a unicameral parliament in 1991 and revisions to the Human Rights Chapter in 1995, no changes have been made to its structure or basic concepts.

FORM AND IMPACT OF THE CONSTITUTION

Iceland has a written constitution, codified in a single document, called the Constitution of the Republic of Iceland (Stjórnarskrá lýðveldisins Íslands). The constitution takes precedence over all other domestic law. International law must be implemented explicitly into national law to have direct application within Iceland. In general, the law in Iceland in fact complies with the constitution.

BASIC ORGANIZATIONAL STRUCTURE

Iceland is a unitary, centralized state made up of 105 municipalities, towns, and rural districts. According to the constitution, the municipalities govern their own affairs as provided by law. The municipalities differ considerably in geographical area, population size, and economic strength. In addition to the municipalities, there are 23 regional districts, or counties. All have equal rights and administrative and judicial competencies.

LEADING CONSTITUTIONAL PRINCIPLES

Iceland's system of government is a parliamentary democracy. There is a division of the executive, legislative, and judicial powers, and an independent judiciary.

The Icelandic constitutional system is defined by a number of leading principles: Iceland is a democracy, a republic, and a social state, and it is based on the rule of law. On the national level, political participation is for the most part shaped as an indirect, representative democracy. Should the president refuse to sign a piece of legislation into law, the people have the opportunity to vote on it in a referendum. The president is chosen by the people. Rule of law is respected. All state actions restricting the rights of the people must have a basis in parliamentary law. Religious freedom is implicit in the constitution. According to the constitution, the death penalty may never be required by law. The constitution does not allow Iceland to become a member of the European Union or any other supranational organization.

CONSTITUTIONAL BODIES

The predominant bodies provided for in the constitution are the president; the prime minister and cabinet ministers; the parliament, called the Althing; and the judiciary, including the Supreme Court.

The President

The president is the head of state. The president appoints and dismisses the prime minister. As the formal head of the administration, the president can have a significant political role in launching coalition negotiations after parliament elections.

The president is elected by the people in a free, equal, general, and direct election for a four-year term. The candidate who receives the most votes becomes president. There are no limits to the number of times a president can be reelected. The constitution requires the signature of the president on all new laws, and the countersignature of the relevant cabinet minister. The constitution gives the president the power to call a referendum on a proposed law, simply by refusing to sign it.

Draft legislation prepared under the auspices of the administration must also receive the president's sanction before it can be placed before the Althing. The president agrees to administrative acts by adding his or her signature, which is also countersigned by a cabinet minister, who thereby becomes legally responsible for the act.

The Council of State consists of the president as chair and the cabinet ministers including the prime minister. The president is the head of state and carries such status under international law, with the power to conclude treaties with other states.

The Administration

According to the constitution, formal executive power is jointly vested in the president and the administration. The cabinet of ministers is the political center of Iceland. The ministers are the heads of executive authority, each in his or her own field. At district levels the central executive authority is represented by the magistrates (*sýslu-menn,* singular *sýslumadur*).

The Althing (Parliament)

The Icelandic Althing is the central representative organ of the people at the state level. Together with the president, the Althing is the legislative body. Its term of office is four years. The delegates are elected in a general, direct, free, equal, and secret balloting process.

The Lawmaking Process

One of the main duties of the Althing is to pass legislation. It debates draft legislation and approves it when appropriate. Althing legislation consists of constitutional amendments as well as ordinary acts or statutes. Provisional laws are enacted by the administration.

The Judiciary

The judiciary is independent of the administration and a powerful factor in legal life. There are only two levels of courts in Iceland, district courts and the Supreme Court. In contrast to some European states, Iceland has very few specialized courts. The Supreme Court consists of a single chamber of nine justices.

Supreme Court cases may be heard by panels of three or five justices, which are sufficient for a ruling. In the most important cases seven judges take part in the judgment. For judgments determined by five or seven justices, participation is determined by seniority.

The Court has issued many legally and politically significant decisions; for example, decisions regarding pensions for the disabled have been highly controversial.

THE ELECTION PROCESS

All Icelanders over the age of 18 have both the right to stand for election and the right to vote in all elections, except that presidential candidates must be at least 35 years of age. Members of the Althing are chosen by direct, proportional suffrage in eight multimember constituencies.

POLITICAL PARTIES

Iceland has traditionally had a pluralistic system of political parties. The multiparty system is a basic structure of the political order without any reference to the constitution or other laws. The political parties are a fundamental element of public life.

CITIZENSHIP

Icelandic citizenship is primarily acquired by birth. A child born in Iceland acquires Icelandic citizenship automatically if one of his or her parents is an Icelandic citizen.

FUNDAMENTAL RIGHTS

The constitution defines freedom of religion and belief in Chapter 6 and other fundamental rights in its seventh chapter. Fundamental rights are of foundational importance for the state and constitution in Iceland. The constitution guarantees the traditional set of liberal human rights, civil liberties, and some social and economic rights. The human rights provisions of the constitution were reviewed and amended in 1995.

A "memorandum" attached to the amendments presented three main reasons for the amendments. First, the changes were proposed to make the articles more sound, in certain matters. Second, most of the articles, unchanged since the 1874 constitution, needed to be modernized to increase their clarity. Third, the articles needed to be reevaluated in light of Iceland's international commitments concerning human rights, such as the International Covenant on Civil and Political Rights and the European Convention on Human Rights and Fundamental Freedoms, which were both made a part of Icelandic domestic law in 1994.

The constitution guarantees numerous specific rights. The basic rights set out in the constitution have binding force on the legislature, the executive, and the judiciary as directly applicable law. Thus, they are binding for all public authorities in any circumstances in which they act.

The general equal treatment clause, contained in Article 65, guarantees that all persons are equal before the law, and that men and women shall enjoy equal rights in all respects.

Impact and Functions of Fundamental Rights

In Iceland, human rights are the axis on which all legal thinking turns. Fundamental rights relate to all areas of the law because they represent a constitutional decision in favor of certain values. In the interpretation and application of all law, the value judgments contained in the fundamental rights must be given effect.

Limitations to Fundamental Rights

The fundamental rights are not without limits, but no fundamental right may be disregarded completely. Each limit to a fundamental right faces limits itself. One of the most important of the "limitation limits" is the principle of proportionality—the limitation must be proportional to the need, and no greater. It gives expression to the idea that all law must be reasonable.

ECONOMY

The Icelandic constitution does not specify a specific economic system. However, certain basic decisions by the framers of the constitution provide for a set of conditions that have to be met in laws or acts impacting the economic system. Among them are the right to property, freedom of occupation or profession, and the right to form associations. The constitution also defines Iceland as a social state. Taken as a whole, the Icelandic economic system can be described as a social market economy. It combines aspects of social responsibility with market freedom.

RELIGIOUS COMMUNITIES

Freedom of religion or belief, which is guaranteed as a human right, also involves rights for religious communities. According to the constitution, the Evangelical Lutheran Church is the established national church of Iceland. When amending the human rights provisions of the constitution in 1995, changes were made to two of Chapter VI's three articles concerning the national church and other societies of religion and belief. The intention was to give new emphasis to the wording of the provisions and to specify the right to be unaffiliated with a religious group. According to Article 64, "Anyone who is not a member of a religious group [is obliged to] pay to the University of Iceland the dues he would otherwise have been required to pay to his congregation."

MILITARY DEFENSE AND STATE OF EMERGENCY

Iceland has no armed forces of its own but is a member of NATO. When amending the human rights provisions of the constitution in 1995, the previous Article 75, concerning the obligation to take part in the defense of the country, was deleted without any form of substitute.

AMENDMENTS TO THE CONSTITUTION

The constitution can be changed only if an amendment is passed by the Althing twice, with elections held in between.

PRIMARY SOURCES
Constitution in English. Available online. URL: http://www.government.is/constitution/. Accessed on July 25, 2005.
Constitution in Icelandic. Available online. URL: http://www.althingi.is/lagasofn/nuna/1944033.html. Accessed on August 1, 2005.

SECONDARY SOURCES
Constitution of the Republic of Iceland. Reykjavik: Office of the Prime Minister, 1992.
The Supreme Court of Iceland. Reykjavik: Supreme Court of Iceland, 1999.

Agúst Thor Árnason

INDIA

At-a-Glance

OFFICIAL NAME
Republic of India

CAPITAL
New Delhi

POPULATION
1,028,700,000 (2005 est.)

SIZE
1,269,219 sq. mi. (3,287,263 sq. km)

LANGUAGES
Hindi (official language), English (also used for all official purposes); states may, by law, adopt any one or more of the languages in use in the state or Hindi for official purposes; constitution recognizes 18 languages as national: Assamese, Bengali, Gujrati, Hindi, Kanada, Kashmiri, Konkani, Malayalam, Manipuri, Marathi, Nepali, Oriya, Punjab, Sanskrit, Sindhi, Tamil, Telugu, and Urdu

RELIGIONS
Hindu 80.5%, Muslim 13.4%, Christian 2.33%, Sikh 1.84%, Buddhist 0.76%, Jain 0.40%, other (including unclassified) 0.77%

NATIONAL OR ETHNIC COMPOSITION
The peoples of India are largely the mixed product of successive invasions. Language, rather than ethnicity, is the main distinction between India's peoples.

DATE OF INDEPENDENCE OR CREATION
August 15, 1947

TYPE OF GOVERNMENT
Parliamentary democracy

TYPE OF STATE
Federal state

TYPE OF LEGISLATURE
Bicameral parliament

DATE OF CONSTITUTION
January 26, 1950

DATE OF LAST AMENDMENT
January 20, 2006

India, a union of states, is a sovereign socialist secular democratic republic with a parliamentary system of government. The constitution envisages a federal state with unitary features. It distributes legislative powers between the union parliament and state legislatures and vests residual powers in parliament. Power to amend the constitution also vests in parliament.

The president of India is the constitutional head of the executive of the union. The real executive power vests in the Council of Ministers, with the prime minister as the head; the council is collectively responsible to the House of the People (lower house of parliament). Similarly, in the states, the governor is head of the executive, but real executive power is vested in the Council of Ministers, with the prime minister as its head.

The constitution offers all citizens, individually and collectively, some basic freedoms in the shape of fundamental rights that are justiciable. These include freedom of conscience and freedom to profess, practice, and propagate religion; the right of any section of citizens to conserve their culture, language, or script; and the right of minorities to establish and administer educational institutions of their choice. By the 42nd amendment of the constitution, adopted in 1976, fundamental duties of citizens have also been enumerated.

The constitution also specifies certain directive principles of state policy that although not justiciable, are fundamental in the governance of the country. Apart from various provisions for the welfare of citizens, these principles also stipulate that the state shall endeavor to promote international peace and security, maintain just and honorable relations between nations, foster respect for international law, and encourage settlement of international disputes by arbitration.

The constitution provides for universal adult suffrage. Free and direct elections are provided for the union and for the state and local levels of government. A multiparty system prevails throughout the country. The constitution also provides for the independence of the judiciary, the comptroller, the auditor general, the public service commission, and the special commissioners for scheduled castes and tribes, minorities, and languages.

The framework of the constitution is based on ideals of participatory democracy, guaranteed rights of citizens, secularism, egalitarianism, cooperative federalism, rule of law, and independent judiciary.

CONSTITUTIONAL HISTORY

India is known to be the largest functioning democracy in the world. It is also known as an ancient society and a new state. India joined the community of sovereign nation-states on August 15, 1947. The process of state formation and the establishment of a constitutional polity were guided not only by the nature, influence, and governmental structures of British colonial rule, but also by the long struggle for independence against that very rule by the peoples of India.

British colonial rule had two faces: from 1757 to 1858 that of the British East India Company and from 1858 to 1947 that of the British Crown. The British, of course, were not the first invaders of India. From Alexander of Macedon to Nadir Shah of Persia, many invaders crossed the Indian frontiers. Although most of these invaders were tempted by the wealth of Hindustan, their invasions were transient. The difference of British colonialism lay in its sustained exploitation of India through what the British called "trade" and "administration."

What is historically significant is that British colonialism was a product of an economic system that originated in England and gradually spread over the rest of the world. The traditional political system of India was exposed to the impersonal coercive machine of the modern state. In other words, the British Empire destroyed much of traditional India, its self-sufficient village economy, its traditional structure of authority, and its system of hereditary division of labor. It shook Indian civilization to the roots. Yet in that very destructive process was sown the seed of regeneration and modernization.

In the context of two phases of colonialism, the freedom struggle also had two distinct phases. In the meantime, a new system of governance had been growing in India—the Regulation Act of 1773 can be taken as its starting point. This was the first statute that recognized the British East India Company as fulfilling functions other than those of trade. It applied chiefly to the presidency of Bengal, where it imposed a governor-general and a council with four members. The governor-general was given the power to control the presidencies of Madras and Bombay and all events relating to war and peace.

In 1784, Pitt's India Act was passed. It established a board of control with six members called commissioners. The six commissioners were the secretary of state, the chancellor of the exchequer, and four privy councilors appointed by the Crown.

Pitt's India Act remained the basis of British government in India until 1857. In 1813 the company's charter was renewed, but under terms that destroyed its trading monopoly. The 1833 Charter Act, while once more renewing the charter, extended the authority of the governor-general to all of British India. All civil and military powers came to be vested in him.

Opposition to British rule emerged parallel to the imperial expansion of governance. The disastrous effect of British rule was apparent almost immediately. India ceased to be a manufacturing country. Old manufacturing centers were ruined. India developed into a supplier of minerals, food, and plantation products such as rubber, tea, and coffee and became a purchaser of finished industrial products. After 1833, the surplus of export over import from India to England came to be called "tribute." In 1848 alone this amounted to 3.5 million pounds a year.

Resentment grew among the established ruling classes of India, now deprived of their economic, political, and social status. As a result, from the day of the British occupation, the people of India resisted. There were uprisings and rebellions in various regions by different sectors of the population.

These revolts climaxed in 1857. The revolt began with an uprising of Indian soldiers at Meerut, whose religious sentiments were offended when they were given new cartridges greased with cow and pig fat, whose covering had to be stripped out by lifting with the mouth. Soon the revolt spread to a wider area, and there were uprisings in almost all parts of the country. The rebel forces marched toward Delhi and proclaimed Bahadur Shah Zafar, the last Mughal ruler, as the emperor of India. The British succeeded in crushing the revolt within a year, but the Indian rulers, masses, and militia participated so enthusiastically that it came to be regarded as the First War of Indian Independence. British historians traditionally called it "the Sepoy Mutiny."

The revolt of 1857 forced many important changes in the British government's policy toward India. Queen Victoria's proclamation of November 1, 1858, declared that India would thenceforth be governed by and in the name of the British monarch through a secretary of state in London. The governor-general was given the title of viceroy.

Some administrative and constitutional reforms were introduced by the 1861 Indian Councils Act. This added one more ordinary member to the Executive Council, which already consisted of the governor-general, four ordinary members, and the commander in chief of the army as extraordinary member. The Legislative Council, which comprised six members in addition to the members of the Executive Council, was also expanded by another six to 12 members, half of whom were to be nonofficials. The 1861 act also initiated a process of decentralization. It restored to the Legislative Councils of Bombay and Madras some of their lost powers and provided for new, similar councils in other provinces as well. However, most of the legislation enacted by the provincial legislatures still had to receive the consent of the governor-general.

Whatever the reforms, it became clear to the Indian intelligentsia that India was administered for the interest of England alone. Some among them began to document, by hard statistics, the depth of Indian poverty and to hint that colonialism was its cause. The liberal dream of the empire was shattered by the discrepancy between the profession and the practice of British rule. At the same time, the spread of English education increased the strength of that class of Indians who were influenced by Western political thought and likely to criticize that discrepancy.

Thus, in the post-1857 period the more politically conscious people in the country took to agitating public opinion against the evil effects of the British administration. Although they did not go so far as questioning British control, they wanted the Indian government to be guided more in the economic interest of India. Various associations and organizations were formed in several parts of the country for that purpose. The birth of the Indian National Congress in 1885 was the culminating point of India's political awakening. It was the first all-India association of a permanent nature, and it signaled a new era in the political life of India.

The early rebellions and agitations had been more militant, but they were ineffective as a result of geographical isolation, poor communication, and the local character of the grievances. The new political leadership was aware of the strength of the British colonial power, its all-India scope, its technological superiority, and its economic resources. In light of these realities, the Indian National Congress was formed on an all-India basis and took a more moderate tone. Among its important demands were the abolition of the Council of India, reform and expansion of the national and provincial legislative councils, holding of Indian civil service examinations simultaneously in India and Britain, appointment of Indians to higher posts, a reduction in military expenditure, training of Indians for commissioned posts in the army, separation of the judiciary from the executive, repeal of various repressive laws, and removal of restrictions on the Indian press.

The popular agitation bore some fruit. Lord Ripon introduced reforms in the field of local self-government, although the measures were halfhearted. The British government, however, was reluctant to accept expansion of legislative councils by the addition of elected members. However, some concessions were made in 1892, when the Indian Councils Act enlarged the functions of the Legislative Councils. Although direct elections were not approved, the government was obliged to consult municipalities, landholders, and others, before nominating council members. The government could, however, reject their recommendations.

After the turn of the century, nationalism became an ever greater factor in India's freedom movement, while the stabilization of parliamentary institutions cast its lengthening shadow over the fortunes of the British rule in India. Extreme nationalism and a wave of religious revivalism grew throughout this period. Although the moderates held a majority in the congress, they were losing ground because of lack of adequate response from the government. In 1907, the conflict between the moderates and the extremists split congress in two.

In 1909 the British government, to keep moderates on its side, announced the Morley-Minto Reforms. The number of additional members in the Central Legislative Council was raised from 16 to 60, of whom 27 were to be elected by organizations of landlords and industrialists. Separate representation was given to Muslims. The number of provincial councils was also increased. In spite of their defects and shortcomings, the Morley-Minto Reforms constituted an important stage in the evolution of representative institutions in India.

The reforms received a mixed reaction, and they did not much satisfy the nationalist aspirations of self-rule. Extremists and revolutionaries stepped up their activities. Nevertheless, India fully cooperated with the British in World War I (1914–18) in the hope that they would grant at least "Dominion status" to India after the war. The government's response was the 1919 Montague-Chelmsford Reforms, embodied in the 1919 Government of India Act. The act called for popular control of local government, the responsibility of provincial administrations to the popular representatives, and a relaxation of control by the British Parliament and the secretary of state.

The act basically dealt with the structure and authority of provincial governments and imposed a system called diarchy. Under this scheme, the responsibilities of government were divided into two categories: reserved and transferred. The administration of the reserved subjects was entrusted to members of each provincial governor's Executive Council, who were appointed by the Crown for a period of five years at fixed pay. They were not responsible to the provincial legislature. The transferred subjects were entrusted to ministers, who were chosen by the governor from among the elected members of the Provincial Council and who were to hold office during his pleasure. The transferred list included those departments that required local knowledge, and social services such as medicine, health, and education.

At least 70 percent of the members of provincial councils (whose power varied from one province to another) were to be elected. No more than 20 percent could be officials. The act also provided for communal representation (as for Muslims), as had its predecessor. Detailed qualifications for voters were also specified. The pattern of the central government did not undergo much change; the government of India was still responsible to the British Parliament through the secretary of state.

The experiment of diarchy was a glaring failure. In any case, the reforms did not satisfy the aspirations of the Indian people, who had hoped to achieve self-rule after the end of the war. Mohan Das Karam Chand Gandhi (known as Mahatma) soon became the undisputed leader of congress, and the organization adopted a new form of struggle against the British—the noncooperation movement—which was a great success. New leaders such as Jawaharlal Nehru and Subhash Chandra Bose also emerged; they advocated the goal of complete independence.

In 1927 the British government sent the Simon Commission to India to suggest further reforms in the structure of Indian government. The commission did not include any Indian member, and the government showed no intention of accepting self-rule. Therefore, the congress as well as the Muslim League boycotted the commission. The congress annual session of 1929 adopted a resolution demanding complete independence and launched a civil disobedience movement, which spread throughout the country. In response, the British organized roundtable conferences. Gandhi attended the second of these in London, but with no results forthcoming, the civil disobedience movement was revived.

The 1935 Government of India Act reflected Parliament's decision to seek eventual Dominion status for India. For the first time provincial ministers were entrusted with responsibility for specific domains of government. However, the governors retained control of certain special responsibilities and reserved functions. If the constitutional machinery failed, the governor could assume the functions of any provincial body or authority and suspend any provision of the act.

In the 1937 spring elections for the provincial Legislative Assemblies, congress made further gains. The elections and the process of building ministries, however, widened the gulf between the congress and the Muslim League, and communal tensions increased. In 1940, the Muslim League's Pakistan Resolution called for the independence of Muslim-majority areas from India.

When World War II (1939–45) broke out, congress offered moral support to the British war effort. However, it wanted assurances about India's position after the war. The clarifications provided by the British government were found unsatisfactory. There also were differences between congress and the Muslim League. Congress, therefore, decided not to cooperate and resigned from ministries.

The right of Indians to determine their form of government was finally conceded in March 1942, when Sir Stafford Cripps took to India the reform proposals of the war cabinet. The Cripps proposals were rejected, but the right of Indians to frame their own constitution through a Constituent Assembly was now established.

Britain's war with Germany was over in May 1945. On June 15, 1945, Viceroy Wavell called the Shimla Conference with Indians to frame a new executive council. The conference collapsed as a result of ideological differences between the congress and the Muslim League. The biparty division became clearer in the 1945–46 voting, particularly in elections for the Central Legislative Assembly. When a British commission reached India in March 1946, it quickly realized that the constitutional problem of India boiled down to the communal problem. After another failed conference at Shimla, the cabinet decided that immediate arrangements should be made for Indians to draft a future Constitution of India.

Elections (based on limited franchise) for the Constituent Assembly were held in July 1946. The Muslim League won all but seven of the seats reserved for Muslims, and congress secured the large majority of the general seats. Congress had also captured one Sikh and four Muslim seats. The autonomous Indian princely states were to have 93 seats.

The Constituent Assembly met as scheduled on December 9, 1946. The Muslim League boycotted its deliberations. The assembly was adjourned until January 20, 1947, but the Muslim League continued its boycott when it met after the adjournment. On February 20, 1947, the Labor prime minister, Attlee, announced in the Parliament the intention to transfer power to Indian hands by June 1948. If no agreement was reached among the Indian parties, the government would have to consider whether to transfer power to a single central government or to some other system of governance (i.e., partition). Lord Louis Mountbatten was appointed in place of Lord Wavell to arrange the transfer of power. Mountbatten reached India, held a series of conferences with the Indian leaders, and, finding no agreement, announced on June 3, 1947, the plan to partition India.

On July 4, 1947, the Indian Independence Bill was introduced in the British Parliament to create the two independent dominions of India and Pakistan. The Constituent Assembly of British India was split into two, one for each of the new states.

The members of the Constituent Assembly had been indirectly elected by a system of proportional representation from the provincial legislatures, which had themselves been elected on a restricted franchise consisting of about 20 to 24 percent of the adult population. Of course, these voters constituted, as a rule, the most politically conscious section of the population and the leaders of public opinion. The assembly completed its work on November 26, 1949, with the formal adoption of the Constitution of India. It entered into force on January 26, 1950. That day is celebrated as Republic Day every year.

FORM AND IMPACT OF THE CONSTITUTION

The Constituent Assembly of India produced a comprehensive written constitution that is considered to be one of the lengthiest constitutions in the world. It contains 395 articles and eight schedules detailing almost all aspects of governance. The constitution is the basic law of

India and takes precedence over all other national laws. India is one of the founding members of the United Nations and a signatory to various international conventions and treaties, which it is bound to implement while keeping in view the national interest.

Aware of the conditions of the people and the consequence of colonial rule, and because of their training and orientation, almost all the members of the assembly favored a social revolution. This revolution could fulfill the needs of the common people, and, it was hoped, would produce fundamental changes in the structure of the Indian society.

Rivaling the social revolution in importance were the goals of national unity and stability. At the outset, the modern elite was much attracted to the idea of a centralized national state, through which their authority would be consolidated and which could be a bulwark against the divisiveness and centrifugal tendencies inherent in the Indian situation. Partition of the subcontinent had created mutual insecurity and suspicion between India and Pakistan, which made political order and territorial integration the most important problems on the agenda. The assembly also believed that the goal of economic progress could be fulfilled only by a strong centralized authority. Other aims such as the protection of minority interests, creation of efficient government and administration, and national security also played roles in shaping the constitution.

The distinctive features of the constitution reflect the political culture of postcolonial nationalism that was shared in different degrees by a heterogeneous elite cutting across class and identities. This is especially true concerning the explicit goals of the state and the fundamental rights with which the goals were to be pursued. The constitution of India has been framed on a philosophy of liberalism. Democracy is its functional manifestation and the concept of the welfare state is its socioeconomic basis. The document paved the way for an active state designed to achieve simultaneous development on many fronts. Commentators have observed that the Indian constitution is more than an instrument of governance and the basic law of the country: It is also an instrument for socioeconomic transformation and change.

BASIC ORGANIZATIONAL STRUCTURE

India comprises 28 states and seven union territories. Although it is a federal system, the constitution does not use that term. Rather, its first article declares that India is a union of states. It is not the product of an agreement among the units, who have no freedom to secede. The very existence and boundaries of the states are at the discretion of the union government. Although the opinion of the states must be consulted in the matter, Parliament is not obliged to accept their opinions.

Not only does the union government have greater and more significant powers than the states, it can intervene in state matters as well, and any residual powers automatically belong to the union. Furthermore, when the union Parliament and a state legislature pass laws on subjects in the list of concurrent powers, in case of differences union law prevails. Finally, a state governor can reserve any bill passed by the state legislature for the consideration of the president of India.

Article 355 of the constitution vests a duty and a corresponding power with the union government to protect the states against internal disturbances and to ensure that the governance of every state is carried out in accordance with the provisions of the constitution. In case a state is considered remiss in that regard, the union government can take over its administration through a proclamation by the president. This is popularly known as president's rule. Proclamation can be issued either on receiving a report from the governor of the state or on the president's will.

Taxation powers under the constitution are included in both the union and the state lists. These tax lists are both exhaustive and mutually exclusive. Various taxes levied and collected by the union government are divided with the states. The union may also give grants-in-aid to states from its consolidated fund as Parliament may by law provide.

States in India do not have constitutions of their own; the Constitution of India itself contains provisions for their governance. Thus, the system of government in all states is the same. It resembles the parliamentary form of the union level, with crucial differences. Unlike the elected union president, the state governors are unelected. In fact, each governor is appointed by the union president, who may remove him or her at any time. Furthermore, the governor enjoys certain discretionary powers independent of the Council of Ministers.

Thus, while India is a federal state, the constitution contains significant unitary features, leading jurists and commentators to describe India with such labels as "quasi-federal." Nevertheless, a degree of federalism, with occasional trends of centralization and decentralization, has been accepted from the start as an essential principle of India's constitution. If anything, federalism has strengthened since the 1980s, as opposition parties established administrations in different states, and regional parties played an important role in forming administrations even at the union level.

LEADING CONSTITUTIONAL PRINCIPLES

The framers of the constitution of India provided for a parliamentary democratic system of government, a federal and secular polity, recognizing the worth of the individual by guaranteeing fundamental rights, while aiming at a welfare state based on mildly socialist principles. The preamble of the constitution describes India as a sovereign, socialist, secular, and democratic republic.

The constitution provides for universal adult suffrage and elections at every level of the government. The 14 general elections that India has had since 1950 have demonstrated that in spite of their poverty, widespread illiteracy, and difficulties in communication, the people, in general, have been able to exercise robust common sense in electing candidates of their choice.

The idea of secularism as it emerges from the provisions on fundamental rights means freedom of worship, religious tolerance, and communal harmony, crucial provisions in a pluralist society such as India. Similarly, the provisions on federalism help promote fraternity among citizens, assure the dignity of the individual, and encourage the unity and integrity of the nation within a multilingual, multicultural, and multiethnic society.

The framers provided an independent judiciary, to help safeguard individual rights, protect minorities, and monitor the federal distribution of powers and functions. The judiciary in India has been framed more on the United States' model of a federal state than the British model of a parliamentary system. Thus, it has been kept free of executive or legislative control and has been assigned the roles of keeping every wing of state within its legitimate bounds and interpreting the meaning of law.

The constitution's concept of social justice has not been rigidly defined, in order to maintain the constitution as a living organ and keep pace with changing needs.

CONSTITUTIONAL BODIES

The constitution provides for a well-defined executive, legislature, judiciary, and other statutory bodies both for the union and for the state governments. The union executive consists of the president, the vice president, and the Council of Ministers, which is headed by the prime minister and is mandated to aid and advise the president. The legislature of the union, the Parliament, consists of the president and two houses, known as the Council of States (Rajya Sabha) and the House of the People (Lok Sabha).

At the state level, the executive consists of the governor and the Council of Ministers with a chief minister as its head. For every state, there is a legislature, which consists of a governor and one or two houses as the case may be. The lower house is called the Legislative Assembly and the upper house, where it exists, is called the Legislative Council. Parliament, by law, can abolish an existing legislative council or create one where it does not exist, if the proposal is supported by a resolution of the corresponding Legislative Assembly.

Unlike many federations, India has a single, integrated judicial system. It is in the shape of a hierarchy, with the Supreme Court at the apex. The constitution also establishes independent statutory bodies to perform and supervise important functions. These include the Union Public Service Commission, the Election Commission, the comptroller and the auditor general of India, the attorney general, and the National Commission for Scheduled Castes and Scheduled Tribes.

The President

The president is elected by members of an electoral college consisting of elected members of both houses of Parliament and legislative assemblies of the states in accordance with the system of proportional representation by means of single transferable vote. To secure equality among the states as well as between the states and the union, suitable weight is given to each vote. The president must be a citizen of India, not less than 35 years of age, and qualified for election as a member of the Lok Sabha. The term of office is five years, and the president is eligible for reelection. The president's removal from office by impeachment is defined in Article 61 of the constitution.

The executive power of the union is vested in the president, as is the supreme command of the union defense forces. The president summons, prorogues, addresses, and sends messages to Parliament and dissolves the Lok Sabha. The president promulgates ordinances whenever either house of Parliament is not in session, initiates financial and money bills, and gives assent to bills in general. The president also grants pardons, reprieves, respites, or remission of punishment or suspends, remits, or commutes sentences in certain cases. When there is a failure of the constitutional machinery in a state, the president can assume all or any of the functions of the administration of that state. The president can proclaim an emergency in the country if satisfied that a grave emergency exists whereby the security of India or any part of its territory is threatened, whether by war, external aggression, or armed rebellion.

Vice President

The vice president is elected by members of an electoral college in a similar fashion to the president. The candidate must be a citizen of India, not less than 35 years of age, and eligible for election as a member of the Rajya Sabha. The term of office is five years, and the vice president is eligible for reelection. The vice president's removal from office is defined in Article 67b.

The vice president is chairperson of the Rajya Sabha. He or she acts as union president when the latter is unable to discharge the functions of office because of absence, illness, or any other cause. The vice president remains in power until the election of a new president; during that period, he or she ceases to chair the Rajya Sabha.

Council of Ministers

The Council of Ministers, headed by the prime minister, aids and advises the president in the exercise of presidential functions. The prime minister is appointed by the president, who also appoints other ministers on the advice of the prime minister. The Council of Ministers comprises ministers who are members of the cabinet, ministers of state, and deputy ministers. The council is collectively responsible to the Lok Sabha.

It is the duty of the prime minister to communicate to the president all decisions of the Council of Ministers relating to the administration of affairs of the union, and all proposals for legislation as well as information relating to them. The president is bound by the advice of the Council of Ministers.

Legislature

The legislature of the Union, called Parliament, consists of the president and two houses, known as the Council of States (Rajya Sabha) and House of the People or House of Commons (Lok Sabha). Each house of parliament has to meet within six months of its previous sitting. A joint sitting of the two houses can be held in certain cases.

The constitution provides that the Rajya Sabha (Council of States) shall consist of 250 members, of whom 12 are nominated by the president from among persons who have special knowledge or practical experience in such matters as literature, science, art, and social service. The other 238 representatives are from the states and union territories.

Elections to the Rajya Sabha are indirect; members representing states are elected by the elected members of legislative assemblies in accordance with proportional representation by means of the single transferable vote, and those representing union territories are chosen in such manner as Parliament may by law prescribe. The Rajya Sabha is not subject to dissolution; one-third of its members retire every second year.

The Lok Sabha is composed of representatives of the people chosen by direct election on the basis of adult suffrage. The maximal strength of the house envisaged by the constitution is now 552 (530 members to represent the states, 20 to represent the union territories, and not more than two members of the Anglo-Indian community to be nominated by the president, if, in the president's opinion, that community is not adequately represented in the house). The total elective membership of the Lok Sabha is distributed among the states in proportion to their population. The Lok Sabha at present consists of 545 members.

The term of the Lok Sabha, unless dissolved, is five years from the date appointed for its first meeting. In order to be chosen a member of Parliament, a person must be a citizen of India and not less than 30 years of age in the case of Rajya Sabha and not less than 25 years of age in the case of Lok Sabha.

Functions and Powers of Parliament

As in other parliamentary democracies, the Parliament of India has the cardinal functions of legislating, overseeing the administration, passing the budget, ventilating public grievances, and discussing various matters such as development plans, international relations, and national policies. The Parliament can, under certain circumstances, assume legislative power even over matters falling within the sphere exclusively reserved for the states. The Parliament is also vested with powers to impeach the president and to remove the judges of the Supreme Court and High Courts, the chief election commissioner, and the comptroller and auditor general.

All legislation requires consent of both houses of Parliament. In the case of money bills, however, the will of the Lok Sabha prevails. Delegated legislation is also subject to review and control by parliament.

The Lawmaking Process

Legislation is dealt with in three stages: introduction, consideration, and passing, which roughly correspond with (1) the first reading in the House of Commons; (2) the second reading, committee, and report stages; and (3) the third reading. At the second stage, the bill may be referred to a select committee. One of the differences between the Lok Sabha and the British House of Commons is the absence in the former of standing committees and committees of the whole house. Instead, the Indian Parliament uses ad hoc select committees of 20 to 25 members, chosen by the administration's chief whip and the speaker and reflecting the balance between the parties. The minister in charge of the bill may not participate. After the completion of its third stage, a bill is passed on to the other house and goes through an identical procedure. In case of unresolved disagreement between the two houses, the president in consultation with the speaker may call a joint session.

Each Friday about two hours is reserved for nonofficial business, when private members can move their own resolutions and bills. Additional time for private members may be allotted on any other day after consultations between the speaker and the leader of the house.

The Judiciary

The judiciary in India has been kept independent of the executive and the legislature of both the union government and state governments. Unlike many federations, India has a single judicial system. At the apex of the judicial system is the Supreme Court of India with a High Court for each state or group of states and a hierarchy of subordinate courts in each.

The judiciary in India performs four important functions: (1) It is the protector and guarantor of fundamental rights, (2) it maintains federal equilibrium, (3) it acts to check the executive and legislature and enforce the rule of law, and (4) it interprets the constitution.

The Supreme Court of India consists of 26 judges (including the chief justice of India), who hold office until the age of 65. The court has original jurisdiction in any dispute arising between the states, or between them and the union government. The Supreme Court also hears appeals from any judgment, decree, or final order of a High Court, whether in a civil, criminal, or other proceeding.

The High Court stands at the head of the state's judicial administration. There are 21 High Courts in the country, three of which have jurisdiction over more than one state. Each High Court comprises a chief justice and such other judges as the president may, from time to time, appoint. The chief justice of a High Court is appointed by the president in consultation with the chief justice of India and the governor of the state. The procedure for appointing the other High Courts judges is the same except that the initiative lies with the chief justice of the High Court concerned. The justices hold office up to the age of 62.

The structure and functions of subordinate courts are more or less uniform throughout the country. These courts deal with all disputes of civil or criminal nature according to the powers conferred on them.

THE ELECTION PROCESS

Elections to various offices and bodies are held on the basis of universal adult suffrage. Every adult 18 years of age or older has the right to vote, apart from those who have unsound mind or have been punished for election-related offenses.

An Indian citizen who is registered as a voter and is above 35 years of age is allowed to stand for the Lok Sabha or State Legislative Assembly. For the Rajya Sabha the age threshold is 30 years. A candidate for the Rajya Sabha should be a resident of the state that he or she wishes to represent. A person who has been convicted of an electoral offense or certain criminal offenses cannot contest an election for a period of six years from the date of conviction.

Elections in India are events involving political mobilization and organizational complexity of an amazing scale. Happily, the record of free, fair, and peaceful elections has so far been remarkable.

POLITICAL PARTIES

Political parties are an established part of the political process in India. As a liberal democracy, India has a pluralistic system of political parties.

The list of recognized parties is revised by the Election Commission after every general election in the light of written criteria. A political party enjoys the status of a national party if it is recognized in four or more states; otherwise, it is deemed a state party. Among the major national parties, the Indian National Congress and the Bharatiya Janta Party (Hindu nationalist) enjoy almost all-India political support in recent times. Among the other important national parties are the Communist Party of India (Marxist) and the Bahujan Samaj Party (alliance of Dalits and low castes) at the national level.

CITIZENSHIP

The constitution of India provides for a single citizenship for the entire country. Every person who was domiciled in the territory of India at the inception of the constitution and who was born in India or who had been ordinarily resident in India for not less than five years became a citizen of India. No person may be a citizen of India if he or she has voluntarily acquired the citizenship of any foreign state.

There are four ways to become an Indian citizen: by birth, descent, registration, and naturalization. A newborn child is a citizen if either parent is an Indian citizen at the time of birth, irrespective of whether the child is born in India. Registration is for people of Indian origin or spouses or children of Indian citizens. Naturalization applies to all other people, who can acquire citizenship by residing in India for 10 years.

FUNDAMENTAL RIGHTS AND DIRECTIVE PRINCIPLES

The constitution of India contains, in Chapters III and IV, two sets of fundamental rights and directive principles of state policy; the first set of rights are justiciable and the latter nonjusticiable.

In the chapter on fundamental rights, the constitution affirms the basic principle that every individual is entitled to enjoy certain rights as a human being. They include all the basic liberties such as freedom of speech, movement, and association; equality before the law and equal protection of the law; freedom of belief; and cultural and educational freedoms. There is also a right to constitutional remedies that entitle every aggrieved person to approach the highest judicial organ to restore to him or her any fundamental right that may have been violated. Subject to specific exceptions under the constitution, the state cannot make any law that abridges or takes away fundamental rights. These rights, however, can be amended by the process of constitutional amendments.

There are five articles dealing with the right to equality. Article 14 deals with equality before the law and equal protection of the law. Article 15 prohibits discrimination on grounds of religion, race, caste, sex, or place of birth. It explicitly declares that no citizen shall on ground only of religion, race, sex, or place of birth be subject to any disability or restriction with regard to access to public places, such as shops, or the use of public facilities, such as wells. However, the state is empowered to make special provisions for women and children. Equality of opportunity is guaranteed under Article 16. The commitment of the constitution to eradicate untouchability (of people of lowest social standing in the caste system traditionally regarded as unclean) finds emphasis in Article 17, which abolishes untouchability and makes its practice in any form an offense punishable by law. Article 18 specifies that no title, other than military or academic distinction, shall be conferred by the state.

The framers of the constitution wanted to balance the general right of citizens to equality of opportunity in public employment with social justice for the disadvantaged castes and tribes. Therefore, though Clauses (1) and (2) of Article 15 prevent discrimination, Clauses (3) and (4) provide for protective discrimination in favor of women and children, and for the advancement of any socially and educationally disadvantaged classes of citizens. Similarly Articles 16 (1) and (2), which guarantee equality of opportunity in matters of public employment and nondiscrimination, provide for similar exceptions.

The constitution therefore permits the reservation of jobs and of seats in educational institutions for women and "socially and educationally backward classes of citizens" or for the scheduled castes and scheduled tribes. It may be pointed out here that what constitutes a "socially and educationally backward class of citizens" has nowhere been defined in the constitution; therefore, by implication the legislatures have to interpret these words.

Article 20 forbids retrospective criminal legislation and double punishment for the same offense and protects the right of an accused person not to be a witness against himself or herself. Article 21 provides that no person shall be deprived of life or liberty without legal authority and without the procedure stated in the law.

Related to this are provisions of Article 22, which stipulate that no person can be detained without being informed of the grounds of such arrest. The constitution, in Articles 23 and 24, also guarantees rights against exploitation by prohibiting traffic in human beings.

The constitution in Articles 29 and 30 protects the cultural and educational rights of minorities. Any group that has a distinct language, script, or culture has the right to conserve them. It also has the right to establish and administer educational institutions of its choice.

Article 300A in Part XII of the constitution provides that no person can be deprived of private property save by authority of law. This provision gives protection against executive orders depriving a person of property, but not against legislative deprivation.

Impact and Functions of Fundamental Rights

The constitution offers judicial protection and sanctity in the enforcement of enumerated rights, by granting every person the right to appeal to the High Court or the Supreme Court (at the person's choice). The right to move the Supreme Court to issue orders or directions for the enforcement of fundamental rights is guaranteed and cannot be suspended except when a proclamation of emergency is in force.

Thus, the fundamental rights under the constitution have been made effective by the right to explicit constitutional remedies. Citizens as well as noncitizens can exercise and enjoy these rights to the fullest extent with an assurance of judicial protection.

Limitations to Fundamental Rights

The fundamental rights guaranteed by the constitution are not absolute. Such rights, however basic, cannot override national security and collective welfare. The constitution contains express provisions for limitations on fundamental rights. Equality is subject to restrictions in favor of special provisions for women, children, scheduled castes and tribes, and other backward classes.

The state can impose reasonable restrictions on most freedoms in the interests of the sovereignty and integrity of India, the security of the state, friendly relations with foreign states, public order, and decency or morality, or in relation to contempt of court, defamation, or incitement to an offense. The phrase *public order* does not have a definite accepted connotation, raising the danger of illegitimate use. The right of assembly is subject to two special limitations: It must be exercised peaceably and without arms.

The operation of fundamental rights can be partly suspended during a state of national emergency. These can also be modified or restricted by constitutional amendments.

Directive Principles of State Policy

Fundamental rights can make room for social justice by asking the state not to deny equality and liberty of individuals. In addition, in the constitution of India the idea of positive socioeconomic justice is explicitly addressed through directive principles of state policy contained in Part IV. Through these principles, the state is instructed to direct its policy toward securing a wide range of measures essential to the achievement of social justice. The inclusion of these principles, which can be called nonjusticiable rights, can be described as a "novel feature" of the constitution of India. The ideas in the directive principles are borrowed from the Irish constitution of 1937.

Directive principles of state policy are not legally enforceable by courts. Nevertheless, the constitution makes it clear that these principles are fundamental in the governance of the country and that it must be the duty of the state to apply these principles in making laws. It has been said that these directives are aimed at furthering the goals of social revolution, and that by establishing these positive obligations of the state, the members of the Constituent Assembly made it the responsibility of future Indian governments to find a middle ground between individual liberty and the public good, between protection of the privileges of the few and bestowing of benefits on the many, with the aim of liberating the powers of all citizens equally and building the common good. The directive principles, thus, state ideals for the country's administration and expectations for its people, which require India to establish social and economic democracy.

Though directive principles are not justiciable, and no one can go to a court of law for their violation, the judiciary in India has taken due notice of them. It has tried to strike a proper balance between fundamental rights and directive principles of state policy.

Fundamental Duties

The 1950 constitution originally did not contain any list of duties of citizens. Once it was in operation, many observers felt that there had been rather disproportionate emphasis on the rights of citizens as against their duties. They complained that the text failed to impregnate the social and political process with the inspiration of patriotic citizenship and ignored the most basic concepts of reciprocity and responsibility.

To overcome this criticism, fundamental duties of citizens were introduced into the constitution. It is the express duty of every citizen of India to abide by the constitution and respect the national flag and national anthem, as well as to cherish and observe the noble ideas that inspired India's national struggle for freedom. It is also a fundamental duty to protect the sovereignty, unity, and integrity of India and to defend the country. Every citizen has the duty to promote the spirit of common brotherhood among all the people of India, to preserve the rich heritage of India's composite culture, and to protect and improve the natural environment. Finally, the constitution makes it a fundamental duty to develop the scientific temper and spirit of enquiry, to safeguard public policy, and to strive towards excellence in all spheres of individual and collective activity.

The very fact that these fundamental duties have been inserted alongside the directive principles of state policy suggests that these are not justiciable.

ECONOMY

Having obtained political independence in 1947, India had to cope with the monumental task of implementing far-reaching socioeconomic and cultural changes, aimed to reorganize the country's feudal and colonial social structure, to put an end to economic and cultural backwardness, and to create a modern diversified economy as the foundation of its own independent development.

Although the constitution does not mention any specific economic model for the country, the directive principles of state policy establish a social welfare state. They do so by proclaiming the right of all citizens to an adequate means of livelihood. In addition, ownership and control of material resources are to be distributed so as best to serve the common good, and the operation of the economic system is not to be allowed to result in the concentration of wealth and means of production to the common detriment.

In the context of these needs and guidelines, India adopted what came to be known as a mixed economy model. The methods and instruments stipulated to meet these needs were political democracy, governmental planning, and regulation and control of the economy. The creation of a public sector and of a system of tax relief and state financial aid to the private sector in priority areas was also meant to serve these aims.

In December 1954, the Parliament declared that the objective of the country's economic policy should be a socialistic pattern of society. The process, however, remained as described. In 1976 the word *socialist* was included in the preamble of the constitution itself. From the 1980s onward, a reorientation toward liberal policy took place. This process emphasized the relaxation or removal of controls, greater competition, a larger role for the private sector, and reforms in the public sector. A major goal was the modernization of industries, especially in technical fields.

The process of liberalization and privatization has been further strengthened since the early 1990s through structured adjustments and economic reforms. India now is a member of the World Trade Organization and a partner in the process of globalization—but an advocate of a humane implementation of that process.

RELIGIOUS COMMUNITIES

India is perhaps one of the most complex countries in terms of religious-cultural plurality. Its geopolitical and historical characteristics have hardly any parallels. Its size and population, and its geographical, linguistic, religious, social, and other diversity, give it the character of a subcontinent. Eight major religious communities coexist in India, comprising four originating in southern Asia—Hindus, Sikhs, Buddhists, and Jains—and four in West Asia—Muslims, Christians, Zoroastrians, and Jews. The same multiplicity marks the linguistic scene. One linguistic survey of India identified 179 languages and 554 dialects; other studies discern more than 200 languages and about 700 dialects. These languages belong to the Indo-Aryan, Tibeto-Burman, Dravidian, and Austro-Asiatic families. Eighteen languages have been scheduled in the constitution as national languages. In this context, it has been suggested that there are four types of minorities in India: linguistic, religious, caste, and tribal.

In the context of plurality, the framers of the constitution considered a secular society and secular state as indispensable for social harmony and social peace. Various provisions in the chapter on fundamental rights clearly reveal the secular perspective. The idea of secularism emphasizes freedom of religious worship, religious tolerance, and communal harmony. It also implies allowing all the existing and even new religions to flourish, with the role of the state that of neutrality.

Religious freedom as envisaged in the constitution has two aspects. Positively, it safeguards the free exercise of religion by all persons, subject to public order, morality, and health. Negatively, it prohibits compulsion by law to accept any particular religious practice as an essential part of religion.

The constitution also recognizes the right of every religious denomination to manage its own affairs and to own, acquire, and administer properties for religious or charitable purposes. Compulsory religious instruction in educational institutions maintained or assisted by the state is prohibited, and so is the payment of tax to benefit any particular religion.

Through provision of these rights, the constitution guarantees equality in the matter of religion to all individuals and groups irrespective of their faith, emphasizing that there is no religion of the state itself.

MILITARY DEFENSE AND STATE OF EMERGENCY

The military is kept out of politics and is formally subordinate to civilian leaders. The supreme command of the armed forces is vested in the president of India. The responsibility for national defense rests with the cabinet. The defense minister is responsible to Parliament for all defense matters.

Following the directive principles of state policy, the government is expected to promote international peace and security and encourage settlement of international disputes by arbitration. India's defense policy aims at promoting and sustaining durable peace in the subcontinent and equipping the defense forces adequately to safeguard against aggression.

The Indian constitution also makes provisions for proclamation of emergency in specific situations. This power is vested in the president. Three types of emergency situations are specified. The first is the proclamation of emergency, either for the whole of India or for a part thereof, on the grounds of a threat to the security of India or of a part thereof, either from external aggression or armed rebellion from within. The second refers to the proclamation that the government of a state cannot be continued in accordance with the provisions of the constitution; this is called the president's rule. Finally, there can be a financial emergency on the grounds that the financial stability or credit of India, or of any part of the territory thereof, is threatened.

Any proclamation of emergency by the executive must be ratified by the Parliament to remain in force. During the period of national emergency, the union government can give directions to any state, make laws on any subject, extend the normal life of the House of the People, and restrict the fundamental freedoms mentioned in Article 19. During the president's rule in a state, the functions of the state are under the powers of the union administration. During a financial emergency, the union government may direct any state to observe canons of financial propriety.

AMENDMENTS TO THE CONSTITUTION

The framers of the Indian constitution were aware that a constitution, to be more than a mere manifesto, must provide the legal instruments for change and be flexible enough to facilitate the process of development and transformation of society. At the same time, it was necessary to keep the constitution rigid enough to protect the rights of the constituent states and to assure various minority groups that no future majority would be able to use its numerical strength to negate their rights and equal position.

The Indian scheme of formal amendment of the constitution is a combination of flexibility and rigidity. The provisions of the constitution fall under three broad headings. The first category consists of those articles in which change can be effected by a simple majority of the members of the Parliament. The second category consists of those articles in which amendment requires a clear majority of the total members of Parliament and two-thirds of members present and voting. The third category consists of those basic or entrenched articles with additional safeguards, which require, in addition to special majority of Parliament, ratification by resolution passed by not less than one-half of the state legislatures. This concurrence of state legislatures is required for any vital change that affects the interest of the states.

PRIMARY SOURCES

Constitution in English. Available online. URL: http://indiacode.nic.in/coiweb/welcome.html. Accessed on September 1, 2005.
Constitution in Hindi. Available online. URL: http://lawmin.nic.in/olwing/coi/coimain.htm. Accessed on September 3, 2005.

SECONDARY SOURCES

S. V. Desika Char, *Readings in the Constitutional History of India, 1757–1947*. New Delhi: Oxford University Press, 1983.
B. Shiva Rao, *The Framing of India's Constitution, Selected Documents*. New Delhi: Indian Institute of Public Administration, 1968.
Arthur Berriedale Keith, *A Constitutional History of India, 1600–1935*. Reprint. New Delhi: Low Price Publications, 1990.
Amarjit S. Narang, *Indian Government and Politics*. 6th ed. New Delhi: Gitanjali, 2000.
Burt Neuborne, "The Supreme Court of India." *International Journal of Constitutional Law* 1 (2003): 476–510.

Amarjit Narang

INDONESIA

At-a-Glance

OFFICIAL NAME
Republic of Indonesia

CAPITAL
Jakarta

POPULATION
238,452,950 (2004 est.)

SIZE
735,310 sq. mi. (1,904,444 sq. km)

LANGUAGES
Bahasa Indonesia (official), many local languages and dialects spoken

RELIGIONS
Muslim (mostly Sunni, some Shiites, a few Sufi and Amadhiyah) 87%, Protestant 6%, Roman Catholic 3%, Hindu 2%, Buddhist 1%, other 1%

NATIONAL OR ETHNIC COMPOSITION
Javanese 45%, Sundanese 14%, Madurese 8%, Coastal Malay 7%, other (350 distinct ethnic groups) 26%

DATE OF INDEPENDENCE OR CREATION
August 17, 1945

TYPE OF GOVERNMENT
Presidential democracy

TYPE OF STATE
Unitary state

TYPE OF LEGISLATURE
Bicameral parliament

DATE OF CONSTITUTION
August 18, 1945 (reinstated July 5, 1959)

DATE OF LAST AMENDMENT
August 10, 2003

Indonesia, the largest state that has a predominantly Muslim population in the world, is in many respects a wonder of heterogeneity and plurality. Countless ethnic, cultural, religious, and linguistic groups live in a state that is composed of thousands of islands. The legal system is also not homogeneous, but characterized by a blend of traditional, colonial, and modern influences.

Politically, Indonesia is a presidential democracy, which has undergone fundamental constitutional changes and reform in recent years. In regard to the constitution, after a long history of authoritarian leadership based on the power of military and security forces, redemocratization began in 1998. The process of *reformasi* is formally documented in four constitutional amendments so far, but further constitutional reform steps are being discussed by a recently established constitutional commission.

CONSTITUTIONAL HISTORY

Indonesia displays some of the oldest remains of human settlement, with evidence for human ancestors dating back about 2 million years. There is archaeological evidence that early kingdoms emerged from the fifth century C.E. Subsequently, two types of kingdoms established themselves: seafaring trading states along the coasts and territorial kingdoms based on rice production inland. After a period of domination by Hinduism and Buddhism, major social changes followed the arrival of Islam in the region beginning in the 13th century.

Portuguese traders established the first European presence in the 16th century. Starting from the early 17th century, Dutch influence in the area was established. The consolidation of the territory of Indonesia gradually took place during the time of Dutch control, at the expense of the earlier Portuguese presence and later French and British imperial probes at the start of the 19th century. Legally, the Dutch implemented a highly complex system of "legal pluralism" in Indonesia, combining *adat* (traditional), *sharia* (Islamic), and Western elements.

During World War II (1939–45) Indonesia was under Japanese control for about three years. After the defeat of Japan the leader of the Indonesian Nationalist Party, Sukarno, together with other local leaders, declared the country to be independent on August 17, 1945. A temporary constitution (Undang Undang Dasar 1945), consisting of only 37 articles, was enacted the following day. It emphasized the office of the president, whereas parliament remained weak. Human rights were reflected in only a few short provisions, as they were seen as an inappropriate restriction of the state.

In any case, the constitution soon lost its relevance, as the former colonial power tried to restore its position through military force. Four years of intense fighting led the Dutch in the end to recognize Indonesia's independence on December 27, 1949. The first independent government ignored the 1945 constitution in favor of a short-lived federation. On August 17, 1950, another provisional constitution entered into force, making Indonesia a unitary state. This constitution provided for a parliamentary democracy with a largely symbolic presidency, and it paid substantial attention to human rights.

This constitution was still in force on July 5, 1959, when the then-president, Sukarno, reinstated the 1945 constitution by decree, after dissolving the constituent assembly that was debating a new constitution. Under the formal framework of the 1945 constitution, Sukarno followed the policy of "guided democracy" (the phrase was coined in 1957), allegedly more suited to the national character of Indonesia than any Western-style democracy.

Sukarno's regime did not survive the crises of the 1960s, when violence escalated between the military and Muslims, on the one hand, and the communists on the other. After an alleged coup attempt in 1965, Lieutenant Colonel Suharto seized control of the army and then of the state. On March 11, 1966, Sukarno was urged to sign a document giving Suharto full authority to restore order. Subsequently Suharto became the second president of independent Indonesia and established a "new order."

Under Suharto, Indonesia opened economically to the West and positioned itself on the side of the West in the geopolitical power struggle, but internally he consolidated an authoritarian regime that abolished genuine democratic structures and violated human rights on a large scale. During his rise to power between the end of 1965 and early 1966 a purge of communists left at least 500,000 people dead, according to most estimates.

In 1975, with reported backing from the United States, Indonesia invaded East Timor, a Christian country that had become independent of Portuguese rule under a radical regime. Gross human rights violations continuously occurred in annexed East Timor until Indonesia withdrew in consequence of the Timorese independence referendum in August 1999. Without ever changing the constitution of 1945, Suharto was able to control political life, including the work of parliament, courts, and the media, for more than three decades. His power eroded in the second half of the 1990s for several reasons. The Asian economic crisis of 1997, which hit Indonesia most heavily, may be seen as the final straw. Suharto resigned on March 21, 1988, and Vice President B. J. Habibie became his successor in office.

Although Habibie had been a long-term confidant of Suharto, political reforms started immediately. In regard to the constitution itself, *reformasi* began in 1999, when the next president was already in office. The 1945 constitution, which had without any explicit amendments been the formal framework for the different authoritarian regimes of Sukarno and Suharto, was substantially reshaped during this process. Technically, it was decided not to enact a new constitution (as was done in Thailand at that time), but to go the path of piecemeal reform of the existing constitution, which is still widely regarded as a symbol of Indonesia's struggle for independence. Four constitutional amendments in 1999, 2000, 2001, and 2002 attempted to redefine Indonesia as a constitutional state based on the principles of pluralistic democracy and human rights. On the institutional level the significant empowerment of parliament and the corresponding limitation of the president's authority as well as the establishment of a constitutional court are most remarkable.

FORM AND IMPACT OF THE CONSTITUTION

Indonesia's constitution is codified in a single document. The impact of the constitution was limited in postindependence Indonesia until 1998, but the recent constitutional reforms seem to suggest that its relevance is increasing. As exhaustive provisions on human rights have been included, the constitution is now also a source of substantial values; a Constitutional Court has been established to guarantee its effectiveness.

However, the constitution remains sparse, with few details about the functioning of the constitutional bodies, the lawmaking process, the judiciary, or the criteria for restricting fundamental rights. Important questions in all these fields are therefore left to the discretion of ordinary legislation. Furthermore, critics have bemoaned the lack of consistency in the constitution, a weakness that becomes more relevant as the country tries to constitutionalize the legal order and political life.

BASIC ORGANIZATIONAL STRUCTURE

Despite being an archipelago with nearly 13,700 islands (about half of which are inhabited) and despite having a substantial cultural heterogeneity, Indonesia is a unitary state (Article 1 [1]). However, since the end of the highly centralized politics of the Suharto era, decentralization has become a major topic on the reform agenda. An analyst recently suggested that Indonesia has undergone "one of the most radical decentralizations of power in the world." Chapter VI (Articles 18, 18 A, 18 B) is the constitutional outcome of this process.

The state comprises 32 provinces (including two special regions and the Jakarta special metropolitan district). The provinces themselves comprise regencies (*kabupaten*) and municipalities (*kota*). The administrative heads of the decentralized levels (governors, regents, and mayors) are now to be elected, as are the provincial and local assemblies (Article 18). A "wide-ranging autonomy" is explicitly guaranteed to all these levels. Autonomy is especially strong on the level of the 349 regencies and 91 municipalities. "Traditional communities" also must be respected (Article 18 B). On the national level, the Council of Representatives of the Regions has the exclusive function of safeguarding the interests of the decentralized levels of administration within the legislature.

LEADING CONSTITUTIONAL PRINCIPLES

Indonesia is a presidential democracy. The philosophy of *Pancasila* (Sanskrit, five principles), as stated in the preamble of the 1945 constitution, is traditionally regarded as the underlying idea of the Indonesian constitution and the philosophical basis of the Indonesian state. The five principles are "the belief in the One and Only God, a just and civilized humanity, the unity of Indonesia, democratic life directed by the wisdom of thoughts in deliberation amongst representatives of the people, and achieving justice for all the people of Indonesia."

Article 1 of the constitution may also be seen as a description of fundamental principles. According to this provision, Indonesia is a "unity in the form of a republic"; "sovereignty is in the hands of the people and is implemented according to the constitution" and is "based on the rule of law." These fundamental proclamations, together with respect for human rights stipulated in an extensive body of human rights provisions, can be regarded as a description of the leading constitutional principles of the "postreform" version of the constitution.

Indonesia has been a member of Association of South-East Asian Nations (ASEAN) since its formation in 1967, hosting the headquarters of this regional organization in Jakarta.

CONSTITUTIONAL BODIES

The set of constitutional bodies provided by the Indonesian constitution is in some respects unique. Whereas the executive branch is headed by the president, the representative organs consist of the People's Consultative Assembly (MPR), the House of People's Representatives (DPR), and the Council of Representatives of the Regions (DPD). In addition, the Constitutional Council must be mentioned as a newly established constitutional body.

The President

The president is the head of state with power to represent Indonesia internationally; he or she is also the head of the Indonesian executive branch of government. The office has undergone fundamental political and constitutional change in recent years.

According to the constitution, the candidates for presidency and vice presidency have to be citizens of Indonesia by birth. According to the new procedure the president and vice president are elected as a "single ticket" directly by the people. The candidates need an absolute majority of more than 50 percent of the votes. If no ticket wins this majority in the first round, the two tickets that receive most votes run in a second round. The new procedure was first practiced in 2004; the retired general Susilo Bambang Yudhoyono became the first directly elected president of Indonesia. The regular term is five years, and only one reelection is allowed (a restriction clearly reflecting recent history). An impeachment procedure that involves the Constitutional Court allows the early dismissal of the president and/or vice president under narrowly defined circumstances.

The Executive Branch of Government

As the head of government, the president appoints and dismisses the ministers of state. Apart from stipulating that each minister of state shall be responsible for a particular area of government, the constitution gives no details on the organization of the administration. However, it does provide that the formation, change, and dissolution of ministries must be regulated by law; this in itself limits the organizational power of the president.

The House of People's Representatives

The House of People's Representatives (Dewan Perwakilan Rakyat [DPR]) is the central body of democratic representation. Its current 550 members are elected by the people for a five-year term from 69 electoral districts. The participants in the elections are not individual candidates, but the political parties (Article 22 E [23]). The House of People's Representatives has legislative, budgeting, and oversight functions (Article 20 A). The elected representatives individually have the right to propose laws, and they enjoy immunity.

The Council of Representatives of the Regions

The 128 members of the Council of the Representatives of the Regions (Dewan Perwakilan Daerah [DPD]), sometimes also called the Regional Senate, are elected as individual candidates (Article 22 E [4]) in the provinces; all provinces have the same number of members in the Council of Representatives of the Regions. The Council of Representatives of the Regions has no full legislative power, but it proposes laws relating to the decentralized structure of the state in areas such as taxation, religion, and education. It also participates in the deliberation of bills. Some analysts have argued that the role of the Council of Representatives of the Regions is too limited to call the Indonesian system bicameral, but considering the often restricted roles of second chambers in constitutions around the world this position seems unconvincing. The DPD also has a role in amending the constitution, as part of the People's Consultative Assembly.

The People's Consultative Assembly

In the 1946 constitution, the People's Consultative Assembly (Majelis Permusyawaratan Rakyat [MPR]) was usually seen as the highest representative organ and the centerpiece of an "integralistic" state, reflecting the "principles of unity between leaders and people and unity in the entire nation." It consisted of the members of the People's Representative Council plus some 200 additional members (regional party representatives, appointed members, some nonparty regional representatives). In theory, the assembly had wide discretionary power to appoint and dismiss the president and to give binding guidelines for policies.

The structure and role of the People's Consultative Assembly have significantly changed during the recent reform process. It now consists of the members of the House of People's Representatives and the Council of Representatives of the Regions. It therefore has 678 members, all democratically legitimized through elections. Constitutionally it is still only required to assemble once every five years, but by amending its standing orders it began to meet annually in 2000.

The functions of the assembly have also changed. It no longer selects or dismisses the president, although it still inaugurates the president and plays an important role in the impeachment procedure. It can no longer issue broad guidelines of state policy. Its most important remaining power is to amend the constitution.

The Lawmaking Process

The authority to make laws rests mainly with the House of People's Representatives and the president. Proposals for laws can be made by them or by the Council of Representatives of the Regions in matters of decentralization. Laws are discussed by the House of People's Representatives and the president with the goal of reaching joint approval. Jointly approved drafts have to be signed by the president within 30 days; otherwise they become law automatically.

In urgent cases the president can enact a government regulation instead of a law, but this has to be confirmed by the House of People's Representatives in its next session. The details of the lawmaking process are determined by law (Article 22 A). Laws are typically accompanied by official explanations called "Elucidations," which are not formally part of the law but play an important role in the work of interpretation. Legislation is published in the *State Gazette of the Republic of Indonesia,* the Elucidations in a supplement thereto.

The Judiciary

The Indonesian judiciary must be independent (Article 24). There is a Supreme Court (Mahkamah Agung) with a system of courts underneath (district courts and appeal courts). There are special courts for religious affairs, military tribunals, an administrative court, and a commercial court. Criminal law is codified, but in civil law the courts apply a range of sources including traditional law (adapt law). An independent Judicial Commission has been established to improve judicial ethics and appointment procedures and strengthen the independence of the traditionally weak judiciary.

A Constitutional Court was established by the third amendment to the constitution in 2001. Judicial review of laws, forbidden under the Suharto regime (with the consequence that numerous unconstitutional laws were enacted), is now part of the formal constitutional framework. The jurisdiction of the Constitutional Court encompasses rulings of the constitutionality of laws, disputes between state institutions, dissolution of political parties, and the results of general elections. Individual human rights complaints cannot be taken to the court for the time being. In its brief tenure since its startup in 2003, the court has already played an important role in constitutional life; it has already declared a number of laws unconstitutional.

THE ELECTION PROCESS

General elections shall take place every five years to elect the House of People's Representatives, the Council of Representatives of the Regions, the president and vice president, as well as the Regional People's Representative Council (Dewan Perwakilan Rakyat Daerah [DPRD]). Participants in the elections to the House of People's Representatives and the Regional People's Representative Council are political parties, whereas individual candidates are elected to the Council of Representatives of the Regions. The elections must be conducted in a "direct, general, free, secret, honest, and fair manner" (Article 22 E). The constitution does not provide any details regarding the election but stipulates that a law shall regulate further provisions. An independent general election commission is responsible for organizing the elections.

POLITICAL PARTIES

Under President Suharto, the multiparty system was basically abolished. A Joint Secretariat of Functional Groups, known by the acronym Golkar, consistently held the majority of seats in parliament. Opposition groups were merged into two parties, which were tightly controlled and weakened by internal conflicts. After the ban on political parties had been repealed in the aftermath of Suharto's resignation, more than 100 national political parties were founded. There are also regional parties with an agenda of independence or autonomy for the regions. The dissolution of parties is within the jurisdiction of the Constitutional Court.

CITIZENSHIP

The constitution does not provide details for citizenship, except stipulating that citizens shall consist of "indigenous Indonesian peoples and persons of foreign origin who have been legalized as citizens in accordance with law" (Article 26 [1]). Citizenship is a guarantee of equal rights and opportunities under Indonesian law. Interestingly, a provision in the human rights chapter stipulates that "every person shall have the right to citizenship status" (Article 28 E).

FUNDAMENTAL RIGHTS

The original version of the 1945 constitution lacked a catalogue of fundamental rights. Article 27 stipulated the equal status of all citizens and the right to work and to live in human dignity. Freedom of association, assembly, and expression (Article 28) was to be regulated by law. Professor Raden Soepormo, chief author of the constitution, explained: "There will be no need for any guarantee of *Grund- und Freiheitsrechte* (Basic and Liberal Rights) of individuals against the state, for the individuals are nothing else than organic parts of the state, having specific positions and duties to realize the grandeur of the state."

Even less did constitutional practice reflect any respect for the idea of human rights. Sukarno's "guided democracy" and Suharto's "new order" were both conceptually in tension with a modern fundamental rights approach. To justify the nonacceptance of the allegedly "Western" concept of human rights, President Suharto, together with the leaders of Singapore and Malaysia, promoted a concept of "Asian values" in the early 1990s. In practice, extrajudicial killings were in some cases official state policy, political parties and associations could not be freely founded, and the media were tightly controlled, to give only a few important examples of "Asian values" in action.

After the resignation of President Suharto, the era of human rights reached the Republic of Indonesia. The Second Amendment of 2000 introduced a long catalogue of fundamental rights (Article 28 A to 28 J) into the text of the constitution, which now stands clearly in the tradition of the Universal Declaration of Human Rights of 1984. The importance of this amendment cannot be exaggerated. As one analyst wrote: "This is a radical reinvention of the basic assumptions on which the Indonesian state was founded."

This catalogue consists of liberal rights, a wide range of social rights, and modern provisions such as a right to a "good and healthy environment." Some controversy arose over the prohibition of retroactive punishment (Article 28 I), which was criticized by some nongovernmental organizations as a barrier to punishing the human rights violations of the Suharto era.

Impact and Functions of Fundamental Rights

The impact of Indonesian fundamental rights in "real life" has improved during the constitutional reform process since 1998. Political, communicative, and academic freedoms have been established in practice. However, gross violations of human rights, including extrajudicial killings by security forces, continue to be reported, and the situation is particularly troublesome in areas where independence movements are strong (such as Aceh and Papua).

The mass killings in East Timor in the year 1999, which occurred when that former Portuguese colony refused to join Indonesia, were not prevented by the authorities; in fact, elements of the armed forces were involved in these atrocities. Indonesian policies to prosecute those responsible have been denounced as insufficient and "lip service" by most international observers. A leading general widely regarded as a major culprit was later a major contestant in the 2004 elections for presidency. Apart from the special case of East Timor, the accountability of authorities for rights violations seems to have increased in recent years but is still limited in consequence of a weak judiciary. In Aceh, a peace agreement between the government and the rebels negotiated in the aftermath of the devastating tsunami catastrophe of December 2004 and signed in August 2005 may pave the way for a future in which human rights are respected there.

Limitations to Fundamental Rights

The option to limit and restrict fundamental rights has its constitutional basis in one general provision, which stipulates that "in exercising his/her freedoms, every person shall have the duty to accept the restrictions established by law for the sole purposes of guaranteeing the recognition and respect of the rights and freedoms of others and of satisfying just demands based upon considerations of morality, religious values, security and public order in a democratic society" (Article 28 J [2]).

ECONOMY

The Indonesian constitution has traditionally been silent in regard to the economic system. Under the framework of the constitution of 1945, socialist as well as capitalist models have been pursued. A 1967 investment law contained substantial guarantees for foreign investors. In principle, the country currently follows the model of a liberal market economy.

RELIGIOUS COMMUNITIES

The overwhelming majority of Indonesians are Muslims, making the country the largest Islamic country in the world. However, there are significant religious minorities of Christians, Hindus, and Buddhists. The belief in "one god" is mentioned in the Preamble as one of the basic principles of the state, but religious freedom is explicitly guaranteed in the constitution. The legal system has traditionally embraced religious law to a certain extent, but the recently discussed introduction of a reference to the Sharia as the relevant law for Muslims (so-called Jakarta Charter) into the preamble of the constitution has been rejected so far. However, some small but violent extremist religious groups pose a significant security threat to the country.

MILITARY DEFENSE AND STATE OF EMERGENCY

The military forces traditionally have had a strong position in Indonesian politics. The role of the military was especially strong during the Suharto years. With the collapse of his "new order" regime, it became possible to discuss the wide-scale involvement of the military in illegal activities including terrorism and corruption. The reform process has included intensive deliberations on the role of the military in political and government life. Significant results have been achieved: the abolition of the reserved seats for members of the armed forces in the House of People's Representatives and the People's Consultative Assembly, and an explicit constitutional provision separating military and police responsibilities.

The military forces are currently around 300,000 strong. Legally there is a compulsory military service of two years, but in practice the military consists mainly of volunteers.

The president with the approval of the House of People's Representatives has the authority to declare war and make peace. The president may also declare a state of emergency. Preconditions and consequences of a state of emergency are not detailed in the constitution but must be determined by law.

AMENDMENTS TO THE CONSTITUTION

The Indonesian constitution of 1945 was not amended until 1999. Since then four substantial amendments have been adopted in order to democratize the Indonesian political system and to strengthen the rule of law and respect for the constitution itself.

Responsibility for amending the constitution lies with the People's Consultative Assembly. The preamble and the provisions relating to the form of the unitary state of the Republic of Indonesia are not amendable.

PRIMARY SOURCES
1945 Constitution in English as amended 2002. Available online. URL: http://www.indonesia.nl/articles.php?rank=2&art_cat_id=22. Accessed on August 23, 2005.

SECONDARY SOURCES
Andrew Ellis, "The Indonesian Constitutional Transition: Conservatism or Fundamental Change?" *Singapore Journal of International and Comparative Law* 6 (2002): 116.

Tim Lindsey, "Indonesia: Devaluing Asian Values, Rewriting Rule of Law." In *Asian Discourses of Rule of Law,* edited by Randall Peerenboom, 286. London/New York: Routledge 2004.

Tim Lindsey, "Indonesian Constitutional Reform: Muddling towards Democracy." *Singapore Journal of International and Comparative Law* 6 (2002): 244.

Jörg Menzel

IRAN

At-a-Glance

OFFICIAL NAME
Islamic Republic of Iran

CAPITAL
Tehran

POPULATION
69,018,924 (July 2004 est.)

SIZE
636,296 sq. mi. (1,648,000 sq. km)

LANGUAGES
Persian and Persian dialects 58%, Turkic and Turkic dialects 26%, Kurdish 9%, Luri 2%, Balochi 1%, Arabic 1%, Turkish 1%, other 2%

RELIGIONS
Shiite Muslim 89%, Sunni Muslim 9%, Zoroastrian, Jewish, Christian, and Bahai 2%

NATIONAL OR ETHNIC COMPOSITION
Persian 51%, Azeri 24%, Gilaki and Mazandarani 8%, Kurd 7%, Arab 3%, Lur 2%, Baloch 2%, Turkmen 2%, other 1%

DATE OF INDEPENDENCE OR CREATION
April 1, 1979 (Islamic Republic of Iran proclaimed)

TYPE OF GOVERNMENT
Theocratic republic

TYPE OF STATE
Unitary state

TYPE OF LEGISLATURE
Unicameral Islamic Consultative Assembly (Majles-e-Shura-ye-Eslami)

DATE OF CONSTITUTION
December 2–3, 1979; revised June 31, 1989

DATE OF LAST AMENDMENT
No amendment

The regime of the Islamic Republic of Iran is considered by some to be democratic and progressive and by others to be absolutist, terrorist, and reactionary. These views, however, do not lead to an objective knowledge of this regime, whose power arises from very diverse sources.

A short presentation of the principles and basic mechanisms of the constitution can improve understanding of the present and future questions at stake. It must include the design of the principal institutions—the leader (*vali-ye faqih*), the president of the republic, the Council of Ministers, the Islamic Consultative Assembly, and auxiliary institutions—their powers, and their interrelations.

According to the constitution, the state of Iran is a republic, which finds its legitimacy in the authority of the nation. It is based on national sovereignty, pluralism, term limits, separation of powers, and the supremacy of the constitution. In this presidential regime, the leader is elected by indirect suffrage, the president and the members of parliament by universal and direct suffrage. The executive power is placed under the control of the legislature.

In its structure, this regime shares certain similarities with the Western democracies while departing from their liberal and secular character. The Iranian state is a republic in which Islam as the official religion provides the basic source of legitimacy for the supreme organs of the state. In spite of this essential difference, Iranian political theory claims that the people can find ways to reconcile Islam and democracy, because according to the Quran belief is not incompatible with the free will of the believers. On the contrary, the submission to the word of God does not have any value if it is not based on a free and conscious choice.

Political participation and free choice constitute the quintessence of all democracy. In the secular societies, this participation is based on reflection of reason, whereas in the religious societies it is based on belief. However, from the moment when freedom of choice is guaranteed by law, one can talk of a similarity between the two kinds of democracy.

CONSTITUTIONAL HISTORY

The long history of Iran is full of the rise and fall of many dynasties. Indo-European tribes first entered Iran about the second millennium B.C.E. and established several kingdoms. About 728–550 B.C.E., the Medes flourished. The Persian Empire was established in 550 B.C.E. by Cyrus II the Great; it was soon to become the major power of the time. The invasion by the Macedonian king Alexander the Great put an end to the Persian Empire. Several dynasties followed, including the Sassanians, who ruled from about 226 C.E.

Arab Muslims accomplished their conquest of the region by 640. For the following 850 years the country was ruled by non-Iranian Muslim princes. Under the Iranian Safavids, who gained ascendancy in 1502, Shiite Islam became Iran's official religion. The Safavids ruled until 1736 and were followed by the Qajars dynasty.

The first constitution was promulgated in 1906.

In 1979, the Islamic Revolution led by Imam Khomeyni overthrew the Pahlavi dynasty, which had taken power after World War I (1914–18) and had alienated large parts of the people and many religious leaders. On April 1, 1979, a plebiscite was held by which 98.2 percent of the people chose an Islamic republic as the system of government.

The constitution of the Islamic Republic was passed by an assembly of experts (khobregan) and ratified by the voters in December 1979. It was revised by the Revision Council and again ratified by the voters in July 1989, a month after the death of Imam Khomeyni.

FORM AND IMPACT OF THE CONSTITUTION

Iran has a written constitution contained in a single document. Article 56 states that "absolute sovereignty over the world belongs to God, and it is He who has made man master of his own social destiny. No one can deprive man of this divine right, nor subordinate it to the vested interests of a particular individual or group. The people are to exercise this divine right in the manner specified in the following articles." No laws contrary to the official religion of the country or to the constitution may be enacted.

The Islamic revolution has led to the emergence of two contradictory political approaches. The first, a liberal and democratic approach, stresses the compatibility between belief and freedom. It is shared by intellectuals, academics, officials, young people, and some of the ulemas,

the learned theologians, who are opposed to absolutism. The other, traditionalist, approach rejects the principle of human freedom and demands total submission to and implementation of Islamic commandments and prescriptions. This approach is primarily shared by the merchants of the basar and the majority of the ulema. It adheres to the absolute authority of the leader (velayat-e motlaqeh-ye faqih), who is the representative of the Prophet and whose word is that of God. By attributing an absolute power to the leader this approach tends to weaken the supremacy of the constitution and national sovereignty.

The presidential elections of 1997 represented a contest between these two approaches. Despite the partiality of the media, especially national radio and television, and despite the recommendations of the majority of the ulema, who were in favor of the "absolutist" candidate, the overwhelming majority of the voters voted for Khâtami, the democratic and liberal candidate, thus confirming the victory of the partisans of Islamic democracy. This choice was confirmed in the elections for parliament in 2000 and for the president in 2001. Antidemocratic repression by the leader caused a continuous political crisis, which has exacted a high price for the internal and international social political life of the country. The 2005 presidential elections again strengthened the conservative forces.

BASIC ORGANIZATIONAL STRUCTURE

Iran is a unitary state, structured in provinces, municipalities, cities, divisions, and villages. In each of these entities, a council is elected by the local people. Article 101 provides for a Supreme Council of the Provinces composed of representatives of the provincial councils. This council has the right within its jurisdiction to draft bills and to submit them to parliament for consideration.

LEADING CONSTITUTIONAL PRINCIPLES

Islam is the official religion of the state (Article 4). The constitution explains the divine and human origins of sovereignty and provides for the division of political power in its fifth chapter.

Article 56 states that "absolute sovereignty over the world and man belongs to God, and it is He Who has made man master of his own social destiny." Thus, all regulations and laws adopted by the public authorities must be in conformity with Islam. The Council of the Guardians of the Constitution (Shora-ye Negahban), or Guardian Council, serves to ensure that they are (Article 4). Until Imam Mahdi reappears (the 12th imam, the hidden imam of Shiite teaching), it is the task of the vali-ye faqih, the leader, to lead the people (Article 5).

Individual and national sovereignty is guaranteed by Article 56, which states that "no one can deprive man of this divine right nor subordinate it to the vested interests of a particular individual or group." The people exercise their legal sovereignty over the state by elections and by referenda. In the political field, freedom of association ensures the organized participation of the people, thus recognizing human sovereignty. In the social field, it is equally up to the people to make sure that the activities of the authorities conform to the law.

Political power is divided into legislative, executive, and judiciary authorities. Political powers are placed under the control of the leader, the source of whose authority is divine sovereignty. The mechanisms of this control are stipulated by the constitution, which limits the leader's power.

According to the law, the leader and other officials have no privilege whatsoever before the rest of the people. The leader is responsible before the Assembly of Experts; the president before the people, the leader, and parliament; the cabinet ministers and the Council of Ministers are responsible before the president and parliament.

The law recognizes the supremacy of the legislative to the executive. The law also gives the legislative supremacy over the judiciary. The national general inspector has power to supervise the proper conduct of affairs by the executive and to take appropriate actions. It should be noted that no member of the executive enjoys any immunity before the criminal courts, which have the power to judge the president of the republic, the cabinet ministers, and their staff. The Supreme Court has the power to find the president of the republic guilty of violating his constitutional duties.

CONSTITUTIONAL BODIES

The main constitutional organs are the leader, the Islamic Consultative Assembly (parliament), the president, the Council of Guardians of the Constitution, and the judiciary. Also of high importance are the Nation's Exigency Council, the Supreme Council for National Security, and the Assembly of Experts.

The Leader

Until the reappearance of the 12th imam the leadership of the *ummah* (the people or the nation) is vested in the leader.

Opinions vary among Iranian Shiites as to the succession of leadership in the absence of the 12th imam. One camp believes that the successors of the imam must not intervene in the political and social affairs of Muslims and must care for only their personal affairs. The other camp combines religion and politics, underlining that the Quran has given laws concerning courts, taxes, war, public order, and social justice. In other words, it provides laws to guide public life. The idea of the leader in the constitution of Iran (Article 5) is based on that opinion, and his qualifications for office reflect that view. He must be a *mojtahed* (doctor in Islamic jurisprudence), virtuous and just, possessed of political and social perspicacity, prudent, and capable of leadership.

According to the 1979 constitution, the leader must have the status of an example to follow (*marja' -e taqUf*). Only a minority of religious authorities succeed in acquiring this status, and most of them refuse to intervene in the political domain. Imam Khomeyni was the exception; two months before his death on April 29, 1989, he recommended that the Council for Revision of the Constitution suppress this qualification.

According to the 1979 constitution, the leader is either recognized and accepted by the absolute majority of the people or appointed by the Assembly of Experts (Articles 5 and 107). Since only Imam Khomeyni succeeded in obtaining the near-unanimous support of the population, the 1989 revision of the constitution reserved the power to appoint or remove the leader to the majority in the Assembly of Experts, itself elected by direct and universal suffrage. The head of the judicial power controls the assets of the leader, his spouse, and his children. The law does not give any legal privilege to the leader. As any other citizen, he has to respect the law, and in case of violation, he would have to appear before ordinary tribunals. While the constitution attributes absolute authority to the leader, it nevertheless limits his powers.

In comparison to the 1979 constitution, the revised 1989 version has fewer restrictions on the powers of the leader. A number of social and political problems, especially those created by the Iraq-Iran War (1980–88), evoked interventions by Imam Khomeyni that were not provided for by the constitution. This led to the idea of expanding the powers of the leader. The Declaration of July 23, 1987, confirmed his absolute authority (*velayat-e motlaqeh-ye frqih*). The revised constitution confirmed this authority. Nevertheless, his new powers did not give him absolute power, which would imply despotism by enlarging the range of powers of the public authorities in general.

In fact, Imam Khomeyni understood "absolute authority" to refer to the state rather than any one person, in this case, the leader. Similarly, the constitution is based on the principle of the inalienable sovereignty of the people. No other authority, not even the authority of the leader, which is called "absolute," can contradict that sovereignty of the people.

The powers of the leader can be divided into two categories. As head of state, he can decide on the general policies of the state after consultation with the Nation's Exigency Council (*majma' -e tashkis-e maslahat-e nezarn*). The policies approved by the leader must be executed, and he supervises their proper execution. The leader also issues decrees for national referenda, a necessary step for all constitutional amendments and optional for important laws concerning economic, social, political, or cultural affairs.

The leader can suggest amendments or additions to the constitution, but he has to consult the Nation's Exigency Council before submitting them to the Council for the Revision of the Constitution. If the latter approves the amendments, the leader signs them and calls the referendum. He has authority to resolve differences among the legislative, executive, and judicial powers that cannot be resolved by conventional methods. In this task, he is assisted by the Nations' Exigency Council. He has supreme command of the armed forces; he appoints and dismisses the religious members of the Guardian Council, the supreme judicial authority of the country, and he appoints the head of the national radio and television network.

The leader's other major group of powers derive from his control of the legislature through the Guardian Council, which has broad responsibilities in supervising the elections to the legislature and is vested with the authority to rule on the constitutionality of laws.

Half the members of the council are clerics appointed by the leader. The council also ratifies the appointment of the president of the republic, who is elected by universal suffrage, and dismisses the president after the Supreme Court finds him guilty of violating his constitutional duties, or after the parliament votes him incompetent.

The leader also wields power over the judiciary, since he appoints its head. He can also pardon convicted prisoners, on the recommendation of the head of the judiciary.

The Islamic Consultative Assembly (Parliament)

The Islamic Consultative Assembly (parliament) is composed of 270 members, five of whom are elected by the religious minorities (Zoroastrians, Jews, and Christians). The deputies are elected by universal and direct suffrage; voters choose one representative from each local constituency. The legislative power is unicameral, but it does not hold any legal status if there is no Guardian Council in existence.

The deputies must be Iranian nationals, Muslims (except for the minority religions), loyal to the regime of the Islamic Republic, educated, between 30 and 75 years of age, and of good physical and mental health.

The elections are supervised by the Guardian Council as well as by parliament. Parliament verifies the regularity of the elections at its opening session. Members of the assembly cannot hold any executive office. Parliament has the power to pass and to interpret laws, and to control the executive. Cabinet ministers are appointed by the president but need a vote of confidence by the majority of the deputies.

Through parliament, the citizens can inform themselves about the functioning of the executive, and they can complain. Each deputy can ask for information or explanation by a cabinet minister. In order to question the president of the republic, one-quarter of the deputies must file their question before the president of the assembly, who passes on the question to the relevant cabinet minister or to the president.

The legislature uses the following means to exercise its authority over the executive: the vote of confidence; questions and inquiries; financial control (adoption of the budget and control of expenses); censure of the president, the cabinet, and cabinet ministers; and prior approval of important decisions of the executive.

After a question from a deputy, a cabinet minister must appear before parliament within 10 days, and the president within one month. The assembly has the right to investigate and to examine all affairs of the country; it can appoint an Inquiry Commission to accomplish this task.

A motion of censure against the president or cabinet ministers can be tabled by a minimum of 10 members of parliament and needs the approval of the majority of the deputies present. If censured, either the entire Council of Ministers or a particular minister subject to censure is dismissed.

The president of the republic can be censured by one-third of the deputies. The president then must appear before the assembly within one month. If two-thirds of the members declare a vote of no confidence, the leader is informed in order to make a final decision. All important governmental decisions (international treaties, bilateral changing of the borders of the country, etc.) are submitted for previous approval to the assembly. The assembly also approves the budget and supervises the expenses and income of the state.

The Lawmaking Process

The Islamic Consultative Assembly can establish laws on all matters within the limits of its competence as specified in the constitution. Bills can be initiated by a minimum of 15 deputies as well as by the Council of Ministers. The Guardian Council has the authority to veto legislation it regards as inconsistent with the constitution or Islamic law.

The President

The 1979 constitution established a threefold executive (the leader, the president of the republic, and the prime minister). The 1989 revision abolished the office of prime minister; the president of the republic now presides over the Council of Ministers. The president must be a well-recognized religious and political figure of Iranian origin and nationality. The president must also have a good record and be trustworthy, pious, and a convinced believer in the fundamental principles of the Islamic Republic.

All candidates must be approved by the Guardian Council. The presidential elections are supervised by the council and must be ratified by the leader. The president must take the oath of office before the assembly in the presence of the head of the judicial power and the members of the council. The second person in the state, after the leader, the president is head of the executive power and directs international relations. The president receives foreign ambassadors and their credentials and signs international conventions and treaties after their approval by the assembly.

The president is the guardian of the official religion of the Islamic Republic and of the constitution and defends the independence of the nation and its territorial integrity. The president, and not the leader, is responsible for implementing the constitution.

The Judiciary

According to the 1979 constitution, the judicial power was supervised by a collective directory called the Superior Council of the Magistrature. It was composed by five magistrates of whom two were appointed by the leader after consultation with the members of the Supreme Court. Three other members were elected by the magistrates of the country. The minister of justice, nominated by the president of the republic, had the exclusive responsibility for the relationship between the judiciary and the other powers.

The 1989 revisions suppressed the collective directorate of the judiciary and put the judiciary under the supervision of a single individual, the head of the judiciary. This official is responsible for maintaining the organizational structure for the administration of justice, drafting judiciary bills, and recruiting judges. The head of the judiciary may delegate authority over financial and administrative matters to the minister of justice.

The constitution does not specify the qualifications for judges. By law, they must be of Iranian nationality, Muslims, just, of good health, and of legitimate birth and must have a degree *(ejtehad)* in law or theology. Originally, only men were allowed to exercise this function. However, thanks to changes to the law in recent years, the head of the judiciary may appoint women to some auxiliary functions in the judiciary. It, therefore, does not seem impossible that in the near future women will once again be appointed as judges.

The constitution guarantees immunity to judges, stipulating that "a judge cannot be removed from the post he occupies except by trial and proof of his guilt." However, the process does not inspire confidence. A decree of the Nation's Exigency Council is enough to authorize the removal of judges by the head of the judiciary. The head of the judiciary conveys the council's report to a commission of experts and then to a Supreme Disciplinary Commission, composed of him and four magistrates of his choice.

In fact, this body is merely an administrative filter commission; no provision exists for the judge to defend himself. The constitutionally guaranteed immunity of judges is thus endangered.

Although the judiciary is supposed to be independent of the other powers, the supremacy attributed by the law to the legislature somewhat diminishes this independence. The legislature may pursue petitions against the judiciary. On the other hand, the judiciary enjoys a privileged relation to the executive: The Administrative Court of Justice receives complaints by citizens against the administration and its officials.

Only the Supreme Court, the military courts, and the administrative courts are expressly created by the constitution. The Supreme Court supervises the correct implementation of the laws by the courts and ensures uniformity of judicial procedure. It is the only court with power to judge the president of the republic.

The special courts include the revolutionary courts, which according to the law of July 6, 1994, have authority to judge crimes against national security, conspiracy against the Islamic Republic, and espionage. The special courts of the ulema, which exclusively judge crimes committed by religious persons, were initiated by Imam Khomeyni and confirmed by his successor as leader, Ayatollah Khamenehyi.

Political and press offenses are to be tried openly and in the presence of a jury.

The Council of the Guardians of the Constitution

The Council of the Guardians of the Constitution (Guardian Council) resembles the model specified in the constitutional law of 1906. It seems also to have been inspired by the 1958 French constitution. It is made up of 12 members. Six are appointed by the leader from among clerics trained in Islamic law; the other six are jurists specializing in different areas of law, nominated by the head of the judiciary and elected by parliament. They all serve six-year terms, with half the members chosen every three years.

The council's main function is to determine the compatibility of legislation with the laws of Islam and with the constitution. The Islamic component is determined exclusively by the clerics, while the constitutionality of laws is determined by all the members. All laws passed by the assembly must obtain the approval of the council, which must examine them within 10 days. If the Guardian Council finds the legislation incompatible, it returns it to the assembly for review.

The control of the constitutionality of laws has retroactive force, but their conformity with Islam can be examined at any moment. The clerical members of the Guardian Council can abrogate laws or provisions at their will and invalidate norms established by society. The council also has the power to decide on the admissibility of candidates in elections for the legislature and the presidency, to the Assembly of Experts, and to other posts. They also supervise the elections and referenda and have the power to invalidate them.

The Nation's Exigency Council

The Nation's Exigency Council was established by a decree of Imam Khomeyni on February 6, 1988, to arbitrate between the Guardian Council and the Islamic Consultative Assembly. The new institution was legalized by a constitutional amendment. The members of the council are appointed by the leader. In general, it is composed of the six clerical members of the Guardian Council; the heads of the legislature, judiciary, and executive branches; the responsible cabinet minister; the president of the relevant assembly committee; and a dozen other personalities. The period of mandate of the members varies at the discretion of the leader.

In the past, the president of the republic has typically presided over the Exigency Council as well. When Hachemi-Rafsanjani's term as president was ending, Khomeyni in March 1997 named him to a separate five-year term as president of the council.

The constitution now allows the council to intervene only in exceptional circumstances, to protect the higher interest of the state. It also denies the council any legislative powers, but this restriction is not respected. For example, when the Guardian Council and parliament differed over labor legislation, the Exigency Council added new provisions to the law.

The term *solution of insurmountable difficulties of the regime (hall-e mo'zalât-e nezâm)*, the original mission of the Nation's Exigency Council, was used during the Iraq-Iran War to justify unconstitutional actions in the face of disagreements among the authorities. When the constitution was revised, the term was given legal status. Thus, problems that cannot be solved by conventional methods are passed to the leader, who passes them to the Nation's Exigency Council. Because of its ambiguity, the term can be used as an excuse to bypass the rule of law. On several occasions, the Nation's Exigency Council has made decisions and passed laws that had no emergency character whatsoever.

The Nation's Exigency Council also has the authority to give advisory opinions on questions posed by the leader. The constitution provides two examples of such consultation: the delineation of the general policies of the state and the revision of the constitution.

The term *general policies* is open to wide interpretation. When the president of the council is personally powerful, this function allows its power to expand at the expense of the legal power of the other authorities.

The Supreme Council for National Security

The Supreme Council for National Security is presided over by the president of the republic and consists of the heads of the legislature, the executive, and the judiciary; the Supreme Command Council of the armed forces and the highest-ranking officials from the armed forces and the Islamic Revolution Guard Corps; the officer in charge of planning and budget affairs; two representatives nominated by the leader; the ministers of foreign affairs, interior, and information, and other appropriate cabinet ministers as needed.

The Supreme Council for National Security determines defense and national security policy within the framework of general policies determined by the leader; coordinates defense-related matters in political, intelligence, social, cultural, and economic life; and mobilizes the material and intellectual resources of the country to face internal and external threats. Observers warn that concentrating such power in the hands of a few politicians is not prudent.

THE ELECTION PROCESS AND POLITICAL PARTICIPATION

Every citizen 16 years of age and older is entitled to vote. The president of the republic, the members of parliament, the members of the Assembly of Experts, and the local Islamic councils are elected by direct and universal suffrage. The president is elected for a period of four years and is eligible only for a second consecutive mandate. The election period for members of parliament and the members of the local councils is four years; they can be reelected. The members of the Guardian Council are elected to serve for a period of six years. Only the leader of the revolution is elected for an undetermined period by the Assembly of Experts and can be removed by this assembly.

There are referenda on certain important matters such as the revision of the constitution.

POLITICAL PARTIES

The constitution states in Article 26 that political parties can be freely organized, provided that they do not violate the principles of independence, liberty, national unity, and Islamic standards. A variety of political parties exist in Iran. Political influence is also exercised by a number of informal political pressure groups.

CITIZENSHIP

Iranian citizenship is primarily obtained by birth to an Iranian father regardless of the child's country of birth. Dual citizenship is not recognized. A foreign woman who marries an Iranian man is entitled to citizenship. Foreign citizens can apply for Iranian citizenship, provided they have reached 18 years of age, have been legal residents in Iran for five years, have not evaded military service in their respective country of origin, and have not been convicted of any significant felony or nonpolitical crime in any country.

Those who have been of outstanding service and assistance to public welfare in Iran can be granted Iranian citizenship without any need to satisfy the residency requirement, provided that the government of Iran considers such citizenship as expedient. The same applies to those who have an Iranian wife along with a child born to her or have distinguished scientific standing.

FUNDAMENTAL RIGHTS

The Iranian constitution guarantees the rights of the people in its third chapter. This chapter opens with the provision that all people of Iran, whatever their ethnic group or tribe, enjoy equal rights; color, race, language, and the like, do not bestow any privilege. All citizens of the country, both men and women, equally enjoy the protection of the law and enjoy all human, political, economic, social, and cultural rights, in conformity with Islamic criteria. The dignity, life, property, rights, residence, and occupation of the individual are inviolable, except in cases sanctioned by law. All forms of torture for the purpose of extracting confession or acquiring information are forbidden by the constitution.

Numerous other rights are specified in the constitution. Thus, the investigation of individuals' beliefs is forbidden, and no one may be molested or taken to task simply for holding a certain belief. Also, publications and the press have freedom of expression according to the constitution, except when it is detrimental to the fundamental principles of Islam or the rights of the public.

Special attention is paid in the constitution to the rights of women. The government must ensure the rights of women in all respects, in conformity with Islamic criteria, and accomplish the following goals: to create a favorable environment for the growth of woman's personality and the restoration of her rights, both material and intellectual; to protect mothers, particularly during pregnancy and childbearing, and protect children without guardians; to establish competent courts to protect and preserve the family; to provide special insurance for widows, aged women, and women without support; and to award guardianship of children to worthy mothers, in order to protect the interests of the children, in the absence of a legal guardian.

Government must provide all citizens with free education up to secondary school and must expand free higher education to the extent required by the country for attaining self-sufficiency.

Impact and Functions of Fundamental Rights

The Iranian constitution explicitly gives a wide interpretation to fundamental rights. It does not only contain rights against government abuses, such as the inviolability of life, property, or residence. It also protects the instruments of political participation. It thus guarantees the right to form parties and freedom of the press. Other rights are in effect economic, social, and cultural guarantees. Thus, government has to respect property and occupation, it has to provide social security and housing, and it must provide a level of free education.

The constitution also guarantees judicial protection. Every citizen may seek justice by recourse to competent courts.

The constitution recognizes the concept of human rights and thus extends many rights to all people. However, many constitutional rights are limited to Iranian citizens, such as the right to judicial remedy.

Limitations to Fundamental Rights

Most fundamental rights such as dignity, life, property, residence, or occupation have limits in the law. In addition, fundamental rights are guaranteed only "in conformity with Islamic criteria" (Article 20); however, these criteria are not detailed. Freedom of expression and the right to disseminate ideas over the radio and television of the Islamic Republic of Iran must also be in the best interest of the country.

ECONOMY

The constitution of Iran includes numerous provisions relevant to the economic system. It states that the Islamic Republic of Iran has as its objectives economic independence, an end to poverty and deprivation, and fulfillment of human needs while preserving human liberty. The government is expected to ensure the basic necessities for all citizens, including housing, food, medical treatment, education, and the necessary facilities for the establishment of a family. Concentration of wealth in the hands of a few individuals or groups is to be prevented, but the government must not itself become a major employer. Individuals may not inflict harm or loss upon others, through monopoly, hoarding, usury, and other "illegitimate and evil practices."

According to the constitution, the economy of the Islamic Republic of Iran is to consist of three sectors: state, cooperative, and private. The state sector is to include all large-scale industries and sectors, foreign trade, major minerals, banking, insurance, power generation, radio and television, aviation, and shipping. All these are to be publicly owned and administered by the state. The cooperative sector includes companies concerned with production and distribution in accordance with Islamic criteria. The private sector consists of activities such as agriculture, industry or trade, and services that supplement the economic activities of the state and the cooperative sector. Ownership in each of these three sectors is protected by law insofar as it is in conformity with the constitution and does not exceed the bounds of Islamic law, contributes to the economic growth and progress of the country, and does not harm society.

The right to choose one's occupation freely and to acquire private ownership legitimately is protected by the constitution.

RELIGIOUS COMMUNITIES

Islam is the official religion of the state. According to Article 26 of the constitution, religious associations may be freely established, whether Islamic or of the minority religions, provided they do not violate the principles of independence, liberty, national unity, and Islamic standards. No one may be prevented from participating in such an organization or forced to participate in one.

As far as religious minorities are concerned, the constitution distinguishes between their individual rights and their political rights. The constitution recognizes the individual rights and liberties of all inhabitants without distinctions as of race or religion. However, all high offices of the state (leader, president, cabinet ministers, magistrates, etc.) are reserved for Muslims. The officially recognized religious minorities (Zoroastrians, Jews, and Christians) are represented by five deputies in parliament and can obtain positions in the administration, in teaching, in universities, and as technicians.

MILITARY DEFENSE AND STATE OF EMERGENCY

The leader is the supreme commander of the armed forces. His powers include declaration of war and peace and mobilization of the armed forces, as well as the appointment and dismissal of the commanders of the armed forces. He also directs the Supreme Council for National Security, which has considerable political impact.

The army of the Islamic Republic of Iran must be committed to Islamic ideology and the people. It must recruit into its service individuals who have faith in the objectives of the Islamic revolution and are devoted to the cause of realizing its goals. The army is responsible for guarding the independence and territorial integrity of the country. No foreigner can be accepted into the army or security forces of the country.

The Islamic Revolution Guard Corps has played an important political role. The proclamation of martial law is forbidden. In case of war or emergency conditions akin to war, the executive has the right to impose necessary restrictions with the agreement of parliament.

AMENDMENTS TO THE CONSTITUTION

Amendments to the constitution are initiated by the leader after consultation with the Nation's Exigency Council. The amendments are then passed to the Council for Revision of the Constitution, which refines the wording and makes the final decision on approval. The council consists of members of the Council of the Guardians of the Constitution and the Nation's Exigency Council and five members from among the Assembly of Experts; 10 representatives selected by the leader; the heads of the three branches of government; three each from the Council of Ministers, the judiciary, and university professors; and 10 members of parliament. Amendments adopted by the council must be confirmed by the leader and must be approved by the absolute majority in a national referendum.

According to Article 177 no amendments relating to basic principles of the constitution such as the Islamic character of the system and the democratic character of the government can be made.

PRIMARY SOURCES
Constitution in English (Embassy of The Islamic Republic of Iran, Ottawa, Canada). Available online. URL: http://www.salamiran.org/IranInfo/State/Constitution/; http://www.iranonline.com/iran/iran-info/Government/constitution.html. Accessed on August 16, 2005.

SECONDARY SOURCES
S. H. Amin, *Middle East Legal Systems*. Glasgow: Royston, 1985.
K. Iftikhar, K. Eftikhar, and S. H. Amin, *Basic Documents in Iranian Law*. Glasgow: Royston, 1987.
Lawyers Committee for Human Rights, *Report of the Justice System of the Islamic Republic of Iran*. Washington D.C.: 1993.
Kenneth Robert Redden, "Iran." In *Modern Legal Systems Cyclopedia*. Vol. 5. Buffalo, N.Y.: Hein, 1990.

Seyed Mohammad Hashemi

IRAQ

At-a-Glance

OFFICIAL NAME
Republic of Iraq

CAPITAL
Baghdad

POPULATION
26,074,906 (2005 est.)

SIZE
168,754 sq. mi. (437,072 sq. km)

LANGUAGES
Arabic, Kurdish (official); Turkoman, Assyrian (official in some areas)

RELIGIONS
Muslim (Shiite 60–65%, Sunni 32–37%) 97%, Christian and other 3%

NATIONAL OR ETHNIC COMPOSITION
Arab 75–80%, Kurdish 15–20%, Turkoman, Assyrian, or other 5%

DATE OF INDEPENDENCE OR CREATION
October 3, 1932

TYPE OF GOVERNMENT
Parliamentary democracy

TYPE OF STATE
Federal state

TYPE OF LEGISLATURE
Bicameral legislation

DATE OF CONSTITUTION
Approved by referendum October 15, 2005, in force with the seating of the government pursuant to the constitution. Government sworn in on May 20, 2006

DATE OF LAST AMENDMENT
No amendment

Iraq's constitution establishes a new form of democratic government respecting fundamental rights after the deposition of a dictatorial regime. It sets up a federal republic with a clear division of powers among the legislative, the executive, and the judiciary. Islam is the official religion of the state and is a fundamental source of legislation. Time will tell whether the new constitution can contribute to stabilizing the country.

CONSTITUTIONAL HISTORY

Iraq was called Mesopotamia in the classical world. It is the homeland of famous ancient cultures such as Sumer, Babylon, and Assyria. The Codex Hammurabi, established by the ruler of that name (1728–1686 B.C.E.), is one of the oldest known comprehensive codified written laws in the world. In 634 C.E. the country began to be ruled by Muslim conquerors. Ali, son-in-law of the Prophet Muham-

mad, was killed in the country in 661. Since then Iraq has been the center of Shiite Islam. From 750, the caliphs of the Abbasid Empire ruled from Baghdad. Their rule was ended by the Mongolians, who devastated the country in 1258.

Iraq was a part of the Turkish Ottoman Empire from 1534 until 1916, when it was captured by British forces. From 1920 onward Britain ruled the country under a mandate of the League of Nations. Amir Faisal Ibn Hussain of the Hashemite dynasty was crowned King Faisal I in 1921. Iraq gained independence on October 3, 1932. A military coup d'état overthrew the Hashemite dynasty in 1958, establishing a republic with General Qassim as head of a military-led Council of Sovereignty. General Abdul Salam Aref overthrew Qassim in 1963 and partially restored a civilian government. The 1968 coup d'état by the Ba'ath Party gave General Ahmed Al Bakr power, which was peacefully transferred to Saddam Hussein in 1979.

Iraq invaded Iran in 1980, opening a war that lasted until 1990 and produced huge loss of life. Iraqi forces overran Kuwait in 1990. Under the authorization of the United Nations (UN) Security Council, United States–led forces defeated the Iraqi army and reestablished Kuwaiti sovereignty.

Accusing Iraq of illegally possessing weapons of mass destruction, supporting terrorism, and threatening world peace, the United States, supported by the United Kingdom and in coalition with a number of other supporting states, launched attacks on Iraq in 2003. They soon occupied the entire country, ending Saddam Hussein's rule.

The coalition provisional authority enacted a Law of Administration for the State of Iraq for the Transitional Period as an interim constitution on March 8, 2004. Despite ongoing intensive terrorist attacks, general elections were held for the National Assembly. The National Assembly drafted the permanent constitution approved by referendum on October 15, 2005, which came into force with the seating of the government pursuant to the constitution.

FORM AND IMPACT OF THE CONSTITUTION

The Iraqi constitution is codified in a single document. It sets out principles of democracy, rule of law, and human rights after a long period of dictatorship. It tries to provide a constitutional basis for holding together a country divided into often conflicting national and religious groups such as Sunni Arabs, Shiite Arabs, and Kurds. Time will tell whether this challenge can be met.

The constitution is the supreme and highest law in Iraq. No law that contradicts the constitution may be passed, and any law that contradicts the constitution is considered null.

The constitution entails a number of transitional guidelines that take into account some of the special challenges of transition, such as guarantees for the welfare of political prisoners of the former dictatorial regime. It also guarantees compensation to the families of martyrs and those wounded by terrorist acts. The constitution itself is open for intense amendment during the current transition period.

BASIC ORGANIZATIONAL STRUCTURE

The constitution establishes Iraq as a federal republic. The federal system is made up of the capital, regions, decentralized provinces (governorates), and local administrations. The authorities of each region include legislative, executive, and judicial bodies, which exercise their powers except in matters listed by the constitution as the exclusive preserve of the federal authorities. A fair share of the revenues collected federally are to be designated to regions and governorates, sufficient to fulfill their duties

and obligations, taking into consideration the regions' resources and needs.

Provinces that are not organized into regions are granted extensive administrative and financial authority to enable them to manage their affairs according to the law.

The constitution states explicitly the powers of the federal authorities such as drawing up foreign policy, national defense policy, or financial and customs' policy. Oil and gas are the property of all the Iraqi people in all the regions and governorates. The federal government is to administer oil and gas extracted from current fields in cooperation with the governments of the producing regions and governorates on condition that the revenues will be distributed fairly in a manner compatible with the demographic distribution all over the country. A quota is to be defined for a specified time for regions that were deprived in an unfair way by the former regime or since its demise, in a way to ensure balanced development in different parts of the country.

LEADING CONSTITUTIONAL PRINCIPLES

The Republic of Iraq is an independent, sovereign state. The system of rule is a democratic, federal, representative republic. The constitution calls itself a guarantor of the unity of Iraq.

Islam is the official religion of the state and is a fundamental source of legislation. No law can be passed that contradicts the established provisions of Islam, and no law can be passed that contradicts the principles of democracy or the rights and basic freedoms outlined in the constitution. The constitution guarantees the Islamic identity of the majority of the Iraqi people, the full religious rights of all individuals, and freedom of creed and religious practices. Called by its constitution a country of multiple nationalities, religions and sects, it is part of the Islamic world.

No entity or program may adopt racism, terrorism, *takfir* (declaring someone an infidel), or ethnic cleansing; or incite, facilitate, glorify, promote, or justify thereto, especially the Saddamist Ba'ath Party in Iraq. The state is committed to fighting terrorism in all its forms and to working to protect its territory from being a base or pathway or field for terrorist activities.

CONSTITUTIONAL BODIES

The main constitutional institutions are the legislative authority, made up of the Council of Representatives and the Federation Council; the executive authority, consisting of the president of the republic and the Council of Ministers (cabinet); and the judiciary. There also are independent commissions such as the High Commission for Human Rights and the Independent Electoral High Commission. They are subject to monitoring by the Council of Representatives.

The Legislative Authority

The Council of Representatives is the parliament. It legislates federal laws, after the future creation of the Federation Council together with that council. It also oversees the performance of the executive authority, and certifies treaties or international agreements. It approves the appointments of high officials such as the head and members of the Federal Cassation (final appeals) Court, ambassadors, the army chief of staff, and the head of the intelligence service, on the basis of the recommendation of the cabinet. The Council of Representatives can relieve the president of the republic of his or her duties by an absolute majority of its members, if the president is convicted by the Supreme Federal Court of high treason or violation of the constitution or of the constitutional oath.

The Council of Representatives may withdraw confidence from the prime minister and from an individual minister by an absolute majority, removing him or her from office.

The Council of Representatives is made up of enough members to provide one seat for every 100,000 Iraqi persons. The members represent the entire Iraqi people. They are elected by general, direct, and secret ballot. The term of office of the Council of Representatives is four years.

The Council of Representatives can be dissolved by the absolute majority of its members, on the basis of a request from one-third of its members or from the prime minister and with the approval of the president of the republic.

The legislative Federation Council includes representatives of regions and governorates. The makeup of the council, the conditions for membership, and all matters related to it will be organized by law. The application of all the provisions related to the Federation Council is postponed until the Council of Representatives issues a decision by a two-thirds majority vote in its second electoral term that is held after the constitution has come into force.

The Lawmaking Process

Federal laws are legislated by the Council of Representatives. Bills can be presented by the president and the prime minister, and proposed laws can be presented by ten members of the Council of Representatives or by one of its specialised committees. Laws are in general passed by a majority of the members present. The president of the republic endorses and issues laws enacted by the Council of Representatives. They are considered validated 15 days after being sent to the president.

THE EXECUTIVE AUTHORITY

The federal executive authority consists of the president of the republic and the Council of Ministers, the cabinet. For a transitional period of one term there is a Presidency Council made up of the president of the republic and two vice presidents who together exercise the powers of the president of the republic; these powers are subject to special provisions during the transitional period. The president of the republic is the symbol of the country's unity and represents the sovereignty of the country. The president safeguards the commitment to the constitution, the preservation of Iraq's independence, sovereignty, and unity, and the security of its territory, in accordance with the constitution.

The candidate for the president's post must be Iraqi by birth of Iraqi parents, be legally competent, and have reached the age of 40. The candidate must have a good reputation and political experience and must be known for his or her integrity, righteousness, fairness, and loyalty to the homeland; he or she must not have been convicted of a crime that involves moral turpitude.

The Council of Representatives selects the president of the republic from among the candidates by a two-thirds majority. The term of president of the republic is limited to four years. The president has the power of amnesty and pardon, upon the recommendation of the prime minister.

The president assigns the candidate of the parliamentary majority to form a cabinet. The prime minister chooses members of his or her cabinet and presents the names and the cabinet's platform to the Council of Representatives. They are considered to have won confidence when the ministers and the platform are approved by an absolute majority.

The prime minister must meet the conditions set for the president of the republic, must be no younger than 35 years of age, and must have a university degree or the equivalent.

The cabinet plans and implements the general policy of the state. It also proposes draft laws and issues regulations, instructions, and decisions to implement the laws.

The president of the republic becomes the acting prime minister when the position is empty for any reason. The president of the republic must then name another prime minister within no more than 15 days.

The Judiciary

The judiciary is independent, as are individual judges, with no authority over them in their rulings except the law. No authority can interfere in the judiciary or in the affairs of justice. The federal judiciary includes the Higher Juridical Council, the Federal Supreme Court, the Federal Court of Cassation (final appeals court), the Public Prosecution Department, the Judiciary Oversight Commission, and other federal courts that are organized by law.

The Higher Juridical Council administers judicial affairs. It also nominates the head of the Federal Court of Cassation and other high-ranking officers of the judiciary.

The Federal Supreme Court is made up of a number of judges and experts in Sharia (Islamic law) and law. Their number and method of selection are to be defined by law. The Federal Supreme Court has far reaching powers such as overseeing the constitutionality of laws and regulations. It rules also in accusations against the president of the republic, the prime minister, and the ministers. Furthermore, it endorses the final results of parliamentary general elections. Resolutions of the Supreme Federal Court are binding for all authorities.

THE ELECTION PROCESS

Citizens, male and female, have the right to participate in public matters and enjoy political rights, including the right to vote and to run as candidates. The Iraqi armed forces and its personnel are not allowed to run as candidates in elections for public office. They also must not engage in election campaigning for candidates.

POLITICAL PARTIES

The constitution guarantees a multiparty political system in Iraq as defined by law. However, the Saddamist Ba'ath Party in Iraq and its symbols are banned. A national De-Baathification Commission works as an independent body in coordination with the judiciary and the executive authorities, linked to parliament.

CITIZENSHIP

An Iraqi is anyone who has been born to an Iraqi father or an Iraqi mother. It is forbidden to withdraw Iraqi citizenship from anyone who is an Iraqi by birth for any reason. Every Iraqi has the right to carry more than one citizenship. Those who take a leading or high-level security position must give up any other citizenship. Iraqi citizenship may not be granted for the purposes of a policy of population settlement that causes an imbalance in the population composition of Iraq. An Iraqi shall not be handed over to foreign bodies and authorities.

FUNDAMENTAL RIGHTS

The Iraqi constitution guarantees extensive rights and freedoms. No law that contradicts the rights and basic freedoms outlined in the constitution can be passed.

The constitution starts its list of rights and freedoms by guaranteeing that Iraqis are equal before the law without discrimination based on gender, race, ethnicity, origin, color, religion, sect, belief, opinion, or social or economic status. Classic human rights are guaranteed such as personal privacy, sanctity of home and the right to life in security, and protection against arbitrary detention. The constitution also guarantees economic, social, and cultural rights such as the right to work and to form syndicates or professional unions. Private property is pro-

tected. However, ownership with the purpose of population change is forbidden.

Family is declared as the foundation of society. Children have the right to upbringing, education, and care from their parents. Parents have the right to respect and care from their children. Economic exploitation of children in any form is banned.

Every Iraqi has the right to health service, and every individual has the right to live in a healthy environment. Free education at all levels is a right for Iraqis.

Freedom of opinion, press, assembly, and communication is guaranteed. Freedom of religion or belief, thought, and conscience is also guaranteed.

The state is keen to advance Iraqi tribes and clans, in conformity with religion, law, and noble human values and in a way that contributes to developing society. It forbids tribal customs that run contrary to human rights.

The constitution guarantees administrative, political, cultural, and educational rights for the various ethnicities such as Turkomen, Chaldeans, Assyrians, and others.

Impact and Functions of Fundamental Rights

The Iraqi constitution guarantees the whole range of fundamental rights, including social and cultural rights as well as the interests of tribes and clans, although the latter are guaranteed as constitutional directives and not as individual rights.

All individuals have the right to enjoy the rights enumerated in international human rights agreements and treaties endorsed by Iraq, as long as they are not contrary to the principles and rules of the constitution. Since Islam is a fundamental source of legislation and no law can be passed that contradicts the established provisions of Islam, it can probably be said that human rights must comply with Islamic principles.

Limitations to Fundamental Rights

The freedoms and liberties guaranteed by the constitution may be limited only by or according to law. The restriction or limitation must not undermine the essence of the right or freedom. A number of fundamental rights are explicitly subjected to further regulation by law, such as the free use of private property or the right to form or join syndicates or professional unions. The right to personal privacy is guaranteed as long as it does not violate the rights of others or public morals. The exercise of freedom of opinion, press, or assembly and of peaceful protest must not violate public order and morality.

ECONOMY

The state guarantees to reform the Iraqi economy on a modern economic basis, in a way that ensures the best use of Iraqi resources, by diversifying its sources of income and encouraging and developing the private sector. The country must encourage investments in the different sectors. Public property is sacrosanct, and its protection is the duty of every citizen.

RELIGIOUS COMMUNITIES

Islam is the official religion of the state and is a fundamental source of legislation. At the same time, the constitution states that Iraq is a country of multiple religions. Discrimination based on religion is prohibited, and freedom of religion is guaranteed by the constitution.

MILITARY DEFENSE AND STATE OF EMERGENCY

The Iraqi military forces are subject to the civil authorities. They consist of the components of the Iraqi people, keeping in consideration their balance and representation without discrimination or exclusion. They may not intervene in political affairs. The prime minister is the commander in chief of the armed forces.

The Council of Representatives has the right to approve by a two-thirds majority a declaration of war or a state of emergency when jointly requested by the president of the republic and the prime minister. The state of emergency may be declared for a period of 30 days, which may be extended by approving it each time. The prime minister is given the powers necessary to run the administration during a war or a state of emergency.

Military service is to be regulated by law.

AMENDMENTS TO THE CONSTITUTION

A constitutional amendment may be proposed by the president of the republic and the cabinet acting jointly, or by one-fifth of the members of the Council of Representatives. Amendments require a vote of two-thirds of the members of the Council of Representatives, the consent of the people in a general referendum, and the endorsement of the president.

The basic principles cited in the first chapter of the constitution can be amended as well, by the same procedure, but in that case the Council of Representatives must reiterate its support in two consecutive parliament cycles. No amendment that lessens the powers of the regions is allowed, except with the agreement of the legislative council of the concerned region and the consent of a majority of its population in a general referendum.

PRIMARY SOURCES

Text of Iraqi Constitution in English. Available online. URL: http://msnbc.msn.com/id/9719734/print/1/displaymode/1098/. Accessed on February 6, 2006.
The Coalition Provisional Authority. Available online. URL: http://www.cpa-iraq.org/government/TAL.html. Accessed on September 7, 2005.

SECONDARY SOURCES

B. Turner, *The Stateman's Yearbook 2004*. New Zealand: Macmillan, 2004.

Gerhard Robbers

IRELAND

At-a-Glance

OFFICIAL NAME
Ireland

CAPITAL
Dublin

POPULATION
3,917,203 (2002)

SIZE
27,135 sq. mi. (70,280 sq. km)

LANGUAGES
Irish, English

RELIGIONS
Catholic 88.39%, Protestant (Anglican, Methodist, or Presbyterian) 3.73%, Muslim 0.49%, Orthodox 0.48%, Jewish 0.05%, other stated religion 1.32%, no religion or not stated 5.54%

NATIONAL OR ETHNIC COMPOSITION
Ethnicity not recorded in Irish census, except travelers 0.6%; foreign nationals (European 4%,

African 0.6%, Asian 0.6%, United States 0.3%, multiple nationality 0.1%, other or unspecified nationality 1.6%) 7.2% (2002 census)

DATE OF INDEPENDENCE OR CREATION
December 6, 1922

TYPE OF GOVERNMENT
Parliamentary democracy

TYPE OF STATE
Centralist state

TYPE OF LEGISLATURE
Bicameral parliament

DATE OF CONSTITUTION
December 29, 1937

DATE OF LAST AMENDMENT
June 24, 2004

The republic of Ireland is a parliamentary democracy based on the rule of law and the doctrine of separation of powers among the executive, legislature, and judiciary. Bunreacht na hÉireann, the constitution of Ireland, is the basic law of the country; it states that all political and judicial power is derived from the people. No law that does not agree with the constitution can be passed. Furthermore, under the system of judicial review, the Irish High Court can strike down any preexisting law that is found to be unconstitutional.

The constitution guarantees a number of fundamental rights, mainly of a civil nature. Ireland has been a member of the European Union and its predecessors since 1973. Therefore, European law has supremacy over domestic Irish law in the areas of competence of the European Union.

The president as the head of state is independent of Parliament, although she or he is formally part of the Oireachtas by virtue of the president's role as promulga-

tor of legislation. The president's functions are primarily symbolic and ceremonial, although they include some responsibilities relating to legislation and appointments. The central political figure is the taoiseach (prime minister) as head of the administration. The taoiseach is appointed by a majority of the Dáil (lower house of Parliament) and nominates members of the administration.

Ireland operates a liberal economic system, with a mixture of state- and privately owned utilities. Throughout its history, Ireland has maintained a relatively small military force and is militarily neutral. However, it has made significant contributions to United Nations peacekeeping, monitoring, and inspection operations.

CONSTITUTIONAL HISTORY

An independent island nation that was never conquered by the Roman Empire, Ireland became increasingly dominated by Britain between the 12th and 18th centuries and was formally subsumed within the United Kingdom of Great Britain and Ireland in 1801. A number of military rebellions against British rule broke out across the 19th century, accompanied by political efforts in Ireland and in Britain to attain some form of autonomy or devolved power (home rule) for Ireland. These efforts were frustrated, particularly by the British House of Lords; however, they finally culminated in the passing of the Home Rule Act in 1914. At the outbreak of World War I (1914–18), implementation of this act was suspended until 1918.

Frustration at the delay in granting home rule was one of a number of factors that led to an unsuccessful rebellion in 1916, during which an Irish Republic was declared. By 1918, popular opinion had turned in favor of independence rather than devolution, and a war of independence ensued between January 1919 and July 1921. The war led to negotiations with the British government and the signing of the Anglo-Irish Treaty in December 1921. The treaty granted extensive home rule to two separate Irish parliaments: one in Dublin governing 26 southern counties and one in Belfast governing six northeastern counties, which had a Protestant as opposed to Roman Catholic majority. The new Irish Free State in the south was to have dominion status similar to that of other former British dependencies such as Canada.

The Irish Free State came into being in December 1922 and with it the constitution of the Irish Free State. The new constitution was subordinate to the terms of the Anglo-Irish Treaty. Some of its key elements were an oath of allegiance to the British Crown and the inclusion of a constitutional position for the British king and the governor-general, the king's representative in Ireland. These provisions and the partition of the island led to bitter disputes between rival factions of the national independence movement, leading to a civil war between 1922 and 1923 at the end of which the protreaty side triumphed.

Many of the contentious elements of the Free State constitution were removed over the following 15 years, particularly after a government led by Eamon de Valera, the antitreaty leader during the civil war, rose to power in 1932. The oath of allegiance to the Crown was removed in 1933. The role of the governor-general had already become largely formal in nature, and it was abolished formally in 1936 along with any reference to the British Crown.

In 1935, de Valera indicated to the Dáil that he had been working on a revised constitution, called Bunreacht na hEireann, which he introduced in 1937. A decision of the Supreme Court had cast doubt on the legitimacy of some of the constitutional changes that de Valera had introduced since gaining power. Besides, the extensive amendments of the Free State constitution had made it an unwieldy and patchwork document by that point. The 1937 constitution was introduced as a new document independent of the Free State constitution. The Dáil ap-

proved a draft, and the text was put before the people in a plebiscite in July 1937. It was approved by a small majority and entered into force on December 29, 1937.

One of the main weaknesses of the 1922 constitution was that it was subject to change via ordinary legislation, which deprived it of the status of "basic law" in the sense generally understood. The 1937 constitution, however, is amendable only by referendum and has proved to be remarkably robust. A key feature of the constitution is that it relies on the declaratory language of natural law. A further notable feature is the inclusion of a juridically suspended territorial claim to the six northeastern counties that compose Northern Ireland in Articles 2 and 3. These two articles were amended by popular referendum in 1998 as a preliminary requirement of the British-Irish Agreement, which attempted a political resolution of the conflict in Northern Ireland that had dominated the previous 30 years.

FORM AND IMPACT OF THE CONSTITUTION

The Irish constitution is the basic law of the state and takes precedence over all other sources of law. It cannot be amended by legislation but only by popular referendum. After Ireland's accession to the European Community, now the European Union, the constitution was amended to state that no provision of the constitution would invalidate European legislation, which is binding on the state. The various European Union treaties, however, are referenced in the text of the constitution and are subject to popular referendum as a result of a Supreme Court challenge in the 1980s.

The constitution provides a foundation for the political institutions of the state. It includes an explicit system of judicial review in which the High Court and Supreme Court can review laws and administrative practices and strike down those that are in conflict with the constitution. In general, however, the courts exercise a presumption of constitutionality, interpreting legislation as being compatible with the constitution where it is reasonably possible to do so.

BASIC ORGANIZATIONAL STRUCTURE

Ireland is a heavily centralized state and, while reference to the role of local authorities was appended to the constitution by referendum in 1999, the main administrative and economic activities of the state are exercised through an independent national civil service. There have been efforts in recent years to relocate some state agencies and some functions of the civil service from Dublin to other locations. At present, about one-quarter of the state's population lives in the Dublin metropolitan area.

LEADING CONSTITUTIONAL PRINCIPLES

Ireland is a sovereign independent parliamentary democracy, and the state is characterized by strong adherence to the separation of powers among Parliament, the executive, and the judiciary. In reality, the executive and Parliament are fused and the appointment of the judiciary is within the control of the executive.

The constitution sets out the values of a liberal republic rooted in a strong commitment to individual civil rights. The constitution is also influenced by Roman Catholic social values, as can be seen most clearly in the provisions dealing with the position of the family and in the Directive Principles of Social Policy contained as nonjusticiable principles in Article 45.

CONSTITUTIONAL BODIES

The constitution sets out the political institutions of the state, namely, the president, the administration, the Oireachtas or national Parliament, and the judiciary. It provides for other secondary institutions such as the attorney general as legal adviser to government; the Council of State, appointed by the president to assist and advise her or him in the exercise of the presidential functions; and the comptroller and auditor general, who oversees the expenditures of the Oireachtas. Important new offices of state, such as the office of ombudsperson and the Human Rights Commission, are not yet referenced in the constitution.

The President

The president is the head of state elected for a seven-year term by all adult citizens, if there is more than one candidate. The president is charged with a number of important constitutional functions including the signing of legislation, the dissolution of the Dáil, and the formal appointment of the administration. Generally, however, the president must act on the advice and authority of the administration and does not exercise executive power. The president's role is largely symbolic and ceremonial, and she or he carries out important representative duties on behalf of the state.

The Administration

The constitution provides for an administration as the executive to be formally appointed by the president on the nomination of the taoiseach or prime minister. In practice, a party, or more usually a coalition of parties, commands a majority in the Dáil, and the taoiseach generally chooses the cabinet ministers from among the Dáil members of the controlling party or coalition, although the constitution states that members of the Seanad (Senate or upper house of Parliament) are also eligible to be members of the administration. The prime minister is appointed by the president on the nomination by the Dáil.

The Oireachtas (Parliament)

The Oireachtas comprises two houses: the Dáil and the Seanad. The president is also referred to in the constitution as being part of the Oireachtas by virtue of the largely formal role of signing legislation. The Dáil consists of 165 members and is the primary legislative body.

The Seanad consists of 60 members. Of these, 43 are elected through a complex system of vocational panels nominated by specialist bodies and elected by outgoing members of the Oireachtas and members of local authorities. Eleven senators are nominated by the taoiseach and a further six are elected by university graduates. Elections take place at the same time as elections to the Dáil. The system of election generally ensures that the government commands a majority in the Seanad. The Seanad has limited legislative powers complementary to the powers of the Dáil.

Parliamentary committees play an important role, presenting reports on legislation and other matters to the two houses of the Oireachtas. The committees have powers to compel attendance before them and to request official papers from the administration. The overall administration of the Oireachtas was formerly controlled by the Department of Finance, but since January 1, 2004, it has been vested in an independent commission of the houses of the Oireachtas.

The Lawmaking Process

Legislation can generally be introduced in either house of the Oireachtas by the government, by a group of seven or more deputies in the Dáil, by the leader of the Seanad, or by a group of seven senators in the Seanad. There are five stages in the legislative process, including a first reading, a substantive debate on the bill, a committee stage, a report stage, and a final stage in both houses. The president must sign all legislation within a fixed time frame but may refer legislation to the Supreme Court when she or he believes there is a legitimate concern that the legislation may be unconstitutional.

As of August 2005, this procedure had been exercised 15 times. When the Supreme Court finds that any section of the bill is repugnant to the constitution, the president is prohibited from signing.

The Judiciary

There are four levels of courts in Ireland. The District Court, divided geographically into 24 districts, has jurisdiction in minor civil and criminal matters and in licensing matters. Appeals lie in all cases from the District to the Circuit Court, which has jurisdiction in more significant civil and criminal cases. The High Court hears appeals from the Circuit Court and has full jurisdiction in all civil and criminal matters, including for serious crimes such as murder and rape, for which it sits with a jury as the Central Criminal Court. The High Court is the only court charged with examining whether a law enacted after 1937 is unconstitutional. Finally, the Supreme Court acts as an appeals court; it has no original jurisdiction except where proposed legislation is referred to it by the president to test its constitutionality.

THE ELECTION PROCESS

All citizens over the age of 18 have both the right to stand for election and the right to vote in any election. For local elections, a wider electorate that comprises all those legally resident in the state can vote. There is a considerable body of legislation dealing with the regulation of elections, addressing the funding of political parties and of campaigns and the recouping of certain election expenses. The primary regulatory bodies overseeing the electoral process are the Public Offices Commission and the Department of Environment and Local Government.

Parliamentary elections must take place at least every five years. Ireland operates a system of proportional representation by means of a single transferable vote in multiseat constituencies of three, four, or five seats.

POLITICAL PARTIES

There is no prescribed system of political parties set out in the constitution, but in practice parliamentary politics has always been dominated by a number of organized political parties. The rules of procedure of the Oireachtas grant privileges to groups of seven or more members in each house, and there have always been at least two major parties in the Dáil with a number of smaller parties. Governments are formed by either a majority party or, more commonly, by a coalition of two or more parties, which may include a party or parties supported by a group of independent deputies.

Generally, the right to form and join political parties is assumed as a normal product of the right to association and of the older common law. The Electoral Act of 1992 makes provision for a register of political parties. The main restriction on freedom of association in relation to political parties is contained in the Offences Against the State Act, which allows the government to declare as unlawful and suppress organizations that are engaged in "treason or treasonable activity" or that advocate violence as a means to constitutional change.

CITIZENSHIP

After independence Ireland operated a system of citizenship whereby all persons born on the island of Ireland were entitled to Irish citizenship (*ius soli*). Certain descendants of Irish citizens were also so entitled, and procedures existed for naturalization of noncitizens who lived in the state for extended periods. After the British-Irish Agreement of 1998, Article 2 of the constitution was amended to state that all persons born on the island of Ireland were entitled to be "part of the Irish Nation." This was generally considered to elevate to the constitutional level the existing statutory system of *ius soli*.

In June 2004, the administration introduced a constitutional amendment empowering the Oireachtas to regulate the citizenship rights of children born on the island of Ireland. This does not apply to the children of Irish or British citizens, who continue to have a constitutional right to citizenship. The administration also plans to introduce legislation to restrict the citizenship rights of certain categories of children born in the state to non-Irish parents.

FUNDAMENTAL RIGHTS

Articles 40–44 of the constitution set out a large number of rights and freedoms, including 21 rights specified in the text of the constitution. The Irish courts have also identified a number of rights that, although not expressly referred to in the constitution, are nevertheless protected by it. These rights are generally civil in nature, although Article 42 does provide for a right to free primary education. The rights contained in the constitution include equality before the law, the right to life, the right to protection of one's person, the right to a good name, the right to private property, personal liberty, inviolability of the dwelling, freedom of expression, freedom of assembly and association, family rights, the right to vote, the right to a fair trial, and the right to trial by jury.

In relation to international human rights norms, Ireland has a dualist legal order. International treaties to which the state is a party, including international human rights treaties, do not have the force of law in Ireland unless given legal effect by legislation or by constitutional amendment. Ireland ratified the European Convention on Human Rights and Fundamental Freedoms in 1960; it was given further legal effect by the European Convention on Human Rights Act of 2003. Ireland is also party to the main United Nations human rights covenants and conventions, but to date they have not been incorporated into domestic law.

Impact and Functions of Fundamental Rights

Under the constitution, Ireland has a strong tradition of protecting citizens' civil and political rights. The constitution is a living document and, particularly from the 1960s, the Supreme Court has taken an activist role in expanding on the rights contained in the 1937 text and applying the principles contained in the constitution to contemporary situations, and in such a way as to reflect contemporary social and moral values.

Recent years have seen a more conservative approach by the Supreme Court, and the doctrine of unenumerated rights has received some criticism. The debate around the European Convention of Human Rights Act of 2003 has also prompted a review of the relationship between the provisions of the convention and the fundamental rights listed in the constitution.

In recent years the Supreme Court has been reluctant to impose positive duties on public bodies to vindicate the rights of citizens, particularly in the area of economic and social rights. The constitution is largely silent on this issue, and the Report Constitution Review Group of 1996 recommended against any amendment of the constitution to make economic and social rights judiciable.

Limitations to Fundamental Rights

Few, if any, of the rights contained in the constitution are unlimited or absolute. In respect of many of the rights contained in Articles 40–44, limitations are specified in the text itself. There are also many situations in which the courts must draw a balance between competing rights, and in such cases the courts generally apply the principle of proportionality, in which the limitation must be no more severe than the need.

ECONOMY

Ireland operates a successful market economy, and, in recent years, its growth rate has dramatically exceeded the average rate of both the European Union and the Organisation for Economic Co-operation and Development. The state retains a role in providing utilities, but recent years have seen moves to privatize a number of state companies in the fields of telecommunications, fuel, and transport.

Economic policy has been strongly influenced in recent years by a system of social partnership among labor, business, the state, and other interests. Under this influence, a succession of national development plans have been issued. They have included agreements on wage growth in the public and private sectors and provisions covering a wide range of social and economic policy matters. The currency of Ireland is the euro; formerly it was the Irish pound or *punt*.

RELIGIOUS COMMUNITIES

Ireland is a predominantly Roman Catholic country, with a small Protestant minority, mainly composed of the Anglican (Church of Ireland), Methodist, and Presbyterian denominations. There is also a small but well-established Jewish population. In recent years, as a consequence of increased immigration, there have been a significant increase in the previously very small Muslim population and a similar dramatic increase in the number of Orthodox Christians living in the state. Many other religious communities can also now be found, such as organized groupings of the Hindu, Buddhist, and Ba'hai faiths as well as small numbers of minority Protestant churches such as Jehovah's Witnesses, Quakers, and Mormons.

In the early years of the state, the Roman Catholic Church enjoyed considerable influence over the political organs of the state, and its role was recognized in the constitution. In 1973, the special position of the Catholic Church and the recognition of other named religious denominations were removed from the constitution. Today, the state is avowedly secular in nature, although religious, mainly Roman Catholic, organizations retain a significant role in state-funded education and, to a lesser extent, in state-funded health care.

MILITARY DEFENSE AND STATE OF EMERGENCY

Ireland has historically adopted a policy of military neutrality and has not been part of any military alliance, although in recent years the increasing activity of the European Union in the area of peacekeeping and security has been the source of some controversy in Ireland. Throughout its short history, Ireland has made a significant contribution to United Nations peacekeeping, monitoring, and inspection operations, including assignment of military forces to missions in all five countries of Central America, Lebanon, Congo, West New Guinea, Cyprus, India and Pakistan, Somalia, Kosovo, South Africa, Western Sahara, East Timor, Liberia, and Eritrea.

AMENDMENTS TO THE CONSTITUTION

Proposed amendments must be approved by a simple majority of both houses of the Oireachtas, and subsequently by a majority of those voting in a popular referendum. The constitution has been amended 27 times since 1937.

PRIMARY SOURCES

Constitution of Ireland: *Bunreacht na hÉireann* (available from Government Publications Sales Office, Sun Alliance House, Molesworth Street, Dublin 2, Ireland).

Constitution in English. Available online. URL: http://www.taoiseach.gov.ie/upload/static/256.pdf. Accessed on August 5, 2005.

Report of the Constitution Review Group, 1996 (also available from Government Publications). Dublin: Stationary

Office, 1996. Available online. URL: http://www. constitution.ie/constitutional-reviews/crg.asp. Accessed on June 21, 2006.

SECONDARY SOURCES

James P. Casey, *Constitutional Law in Ireland.* 3d ed. Dublin: Round Hall, 2000.

Michael Forde, *Constitutional Law.* 2d ed. Dublin: First Law, 2004.

John Kelly, *The Irish Constitution,* edited by G. Hogan and G. Whyte. 4th ed. Dublin: Butterworth's, 2004.

Liam Herrick

ISRAEL

At-a-Glance

OFFICIAL NAME
State of Israel

CAPITAL
Jerusalem

POPULATION
6,780,000 (2005 est.)

SIZE
8,019 sq. mi. (20,770 sq. km) within the 1967 borders and 2,884 sq. mi. (7,470 sq. km) of the occupied territories

LANGUAGES
Hebrew and Arabic (official languages)

RELIGIONS
Jewish 79%, Muslim 17.3%, Christian 2.1%, Druze 1.6%

NATIONAL OR ETHNIC COMPOSITION
Jewish 79%, Arab 19%, other 2%

DATE OF INDEPENDENCE OR CREATION
May 14, 1948

TYPE OF GOVERNMENT
Parliamentary democracy

TYPE OF STATE
Unitary state

TYPE OF LEGISLATURE
Unicameral parliament

DATE OF CONSTITUTION
No single date

DATE OF LAST AMENDMENT
July 26, 2005

The State of Israel defines itself as a "Jewish and Democratic State" and has a parliamentary system of government. The president is the head of state, but his or her function is primarily representative. The prime minister is Israel's political leader and depends on the support and confidence of the majority of parliament (Knesset) members.

Israel has not yet adopted a complete formal constitution. However, many constitutional matters have in fact been settled and are incorporated in 11 basic laws. This partial constitution has three main limitations: No legislation exists as to how a full constitution might be established, and how it would then be amended; most existing constitutional laws are not entrenched or protected from amendment by a simple majority of Knesset members; and not all recognized human rights are protected by the existing constitutional provisions.

The institutional part of the Israeli constitution is established in basic laws that define the authority of the various state bodies that make up the legislature, the government as the executive authority of the state, and the judiciary. The substantive part of the constitution is established mainly in two basic laws concerning human

rights enacted in 1992. In addition to the written parts of the Israeli constitution, the Israeli Supreme Court has developed a judicial bill of rights, which affords considerable protection of human rights.

The State of Israel was established after the Holocaust of the Jewish people in Europe during World War II (1939–45), when some 6 million Jews were murdered. Immigration to the country began as a Jewish nationalist movement of return to the perceived ancient homeland, which arose outside the country and stimulated Jewish immigration into the British Palestine Mandate in the decades before World War II.

Israel is an immigrant state in the midst of a vigorous process of nation building. At the same time, it suffers social tensions between the Jewish majority and the Arab minority, between secular and religious Jews, and between Jewish immigrants of European descent and those from the Muslim world. Since the 1967 war, Israel has occupied territories conquered from Jordan, Syria, and Egypt. The majority of the Palestinian Arab population, about 3 million people, have since lived under Israeli rule in conditions of belligerent occupation.

433

CONSTITUTIONAL HISTORY

After Britain conquered the land of Israel (then called Palestine) from Turkey during World War I (1914–18), the Council of the League of Nations approved a mandate that allowed Britain to exercise its rule there. The mandate required Britain to act to establish a national home for the Jewish people without harming the civil and religious rights of non-Jews. The Palestine Order-in-Council of 1922 authorized the high commissioner to legislate those laws he found necessary to maintain peace, order, and government within the bounds of the mandate. This Order-in-Council was sometimes called "The Land of Israel Constitution," and it determined the rules of government and the sources of mandatory law. It included, inter alia, a slightly modified version of the British system of judicial review. Accordingly, while there was no judicial review of laws, the Supreme Court, in its function as High Court of Justice, was authorized to review the actions of administrative authorities.

On November 29, 1947, the General Assembly of the United Nations voted to end the British Mandate in Palestine and approved the "Partition Plan." According to this plan, the country was to be divided into two states: a Jewish state and an Arab state. Jerusalem was to be placed under international control maintained by the United Nations.

On May 14, 1948, the date British rule ended, the People's Council, which represented the various political segments of the Jewish settlement in Palestine, convened and proclaimed the foundation of the State of Israel. This Proclamation of Independence shaped the founding principles of the state, establishing the following central concerns:

The State of Israel will be open for Jewish immigration and for the Ingathering of the Exiles; it will foster the development of the country for the benefit of all its inhabitants; it will be based on freedom, justice and peace as envisaged by the prophets of Israel; it will ensure complete equality of social and political rights to all its inhabitants irrespective of religion, race or sex; it will guarantee freedom of religion, conscience, language, education and culture; it will safeguard the Holy Places of all religions; and it will be faithful to the principles of the Charter of the United Nations.

The Proclamation of Independence was not intended to serve as a constitution. The proclamation did, however, detail the state's basic values and objectives, as well as establish its primary institutions. This included the People's Council as the legislature and the executive branch as the provisional government. The proclamation also determined that a Constituent Assembly should be elected no later than October 1, 1948, to adopt a constitution for the state.

Shortly after British departure and the Proclamation of Independence, the newly founded State of Israel was attacked by Palestinian Arabs and neighboring Arab nations, who challenged Israel's right to independence, and

Israel's War of Independence began. The war caused a delay in the election of the Constituent Assembly. The elections for the Constituent Assembly, which also functioned as the first legislature (the first Knesset), were eventually held in January 1949.

During the assembly's deliberations, some members raised arguments against the immediate adoption of a constitution. They were concerned that any constitution formulated during the then-existing state of emergency would provide insufficient guarantees for the long-term protection of human rights. Also, after the foundation of the state many Jewish immigrants were expected to settle in Israel. Hence, it was argued that it would be wrong for the few citizens of the state in its first years to establish principles for the many who would later arrive. Furthermore, in the spirit of British parliamentarianism, it was argued that parliament should not limit itself by any entrenched constitution. Finally, the representatives of the religious parties argued that the true constitution already existed in the form of the Hebrew Bible interpreted as a book of laws, and that there was therefore no need for a secular one.

For these reasons and others, the Knesset reached a compromise known as the Harari Resolution on June 15, 1950, forgoing an immediate decision and authorizing the Knesset's Constitution Law and Justice Committee to draft a constitution for the state. The constitution was to be created chapter by chapter, each constituting a separate basic law.

To date, the Knesset has approved 11 basic laws. Nine of these deal with the status of state authorities: The Knesset; The Government (administration); The President; Israel Lands; The State Economy; The Army; Jerusalem, The Capital of Israel; The Judiciary; and The State Comptroller. Two, enacted in 1992, deal with human rights: Human Dignity and Liberty and Freedom of Occupation. These two basic laws have had significant impacts on public debate and on the legislative process.

Nevertheless, the endeavor to create a constitution remains incomplete. Constitutional protection of human rights remains limited since there is not yet explicit constitutional protection of such basic rights as equality, freedom of expression, freedom of religion, and freedom of movement. Moreover, the basic law Human Dignity and Liberty does not permit judicial review of laws made prior to its enactment in 1992. Furthermore, the Basic Law *Legislation,* which is supposed to set the provisions for the legislation and amendment of the constitution, has not yet been enacted.

FORM AND IMPACT OF THE CONSTITUTION

The written constitution of the state of Israel is not codified in a single document. Instead, a series of basic laws regulate many but not all constitutional matters.

The Israeli Supreme Court has played an important role in extending and completing the constitutional enterprise. First, it established an extensive judicial constitutional bill of rights. Thus, for example, the Supreme Court deduced a rule of interpretation from the Proclamation of Independence, whereby laws should be interpreted in a manner consistent with human rights. In one important decision in 1953, the court invalidated the minister of interior's decision to close a communist newspaper that the minister found harmful to public peace. The court ruled that the law authorizing the closure should be interpreted so as to authorize action only in the face of "near certain" harm. In this affair, and in many subsequent cases, the Supreme Court created an unwritten bill of rights. However, while the court could overrule secondary legislation and administrative action, it was ineffectual when faced with explicit legislation harming human rights. In other words, until the enactment of the relevant basic laws protecting human rights, explicit legislation could overpower human rights.

The Supreme Court's second contribution was to recognize the Knesset's power to create a constitution. Although the Harari Resolution implies that the basic laws would constitute a binding constitution only upon completion of the enterprise, the Supreme Court ruled that the provisions contained within the basic laws have superiority vis-à-vis contradictory provisions contained in other Knesset legislation. In a landmark decision from 1995, the court determined that the constitutive authority was passed on from the first Knesset to succeeding ones and that the Knesset "wears two hats." When it creates or amends a basic law it is exercising its authority under the hat of Constituent Assembly, and when it creates or amends regular laws it is exercising its authority under the hat of legislative authority. On the basis of these assertions, it appears that an ordinary law cannot contradict a constitutional norm in a basic law. The court further claimed the power to review the validity of ordinary laws contradicting basic laws, despite the fact that the basic laws do not explicitly grant the court such authority.

The Supreme Court's rulings on constitutional matters have had substantial political repercussions. The court is known for its judicial activism and does not hesitate to address delicate political issues.

BASIC ORGANIZATIONAL STRUCTURE

The central government is the highest executive authority of the state and decides on all major issues, including security affairs, government policy, and economics. Local authorities have the power to collect taxes for the provision of local services only. When a local authority transgresses against a human right, it must point to explicit authorization in a Knesset statute. For example, a local authority may not prohibit the opening of a cinema on the sabbath if the only motivation behind it was religious, unless Knesset legislation explicitly authorizes it to do so.

During the 1967 war, Israel conquered territories of Syria (the Golan Heights), Jordan (the West Bank and East Jerusalem), and Egypt (Sinai and the Gaza Strip). Sinai was later returned to Egypt after a peace treaty in 1979; Israeli law was applied to the territories of East Jerusalem and the Golan Heights; and parts of Gaza and the West Bank were placed under the administration of the Palestinian Authority after 1993. In 2005, Israel fully retreated from the Gaza Strip.

According to international law, these territories are under the belligerent occupation of the State of Israel. The sovereign is the military commander who is subject to the laws of war. Under Israeli internal law, the military commander is not bound by the 1949 Fourth Geneva Convention Relative to the Protection of Civilian Persons in Time of War. However, Israel is committed by internal law to uphold the humanitarian stipulations of this convention. The military commander is fully bound by the Hague Convention on Laws and Customs of War on Land of 1907.

In addition, the military commander is bound by the principles of Israeli administrative law, including the obligation to act fairly and proportionately. Soon after the 1967 war, the Supreme Court ruled that the inhabitants of the occupied territories had the right to petition the court against decisions of the military commander. The Supreme Court often handles such petitions in matters such as the destruction of houses, the expulsion of terrorist activists, and the placing of curfews. In practice, most petitions are denied. However, the mere right of petition serves to curb offenses by the military.

LEADING CONSTITUTIONAL PRINCIPLES

The State of Israel is defined in the basic laws as a Jewish and democratic state. After widespread persecution of Jews and especially after the Holocaust of the Jewish people during World War II, the creation of a home for the Jewish people was perceived as essential to its survival. The Jewish nature of the state has both national and religious significance. In the national sense, Israel is a state that asserts its continuity with the historic Jewish people, whose primary language is Hebrew, and that offers refuge and citizenship to Jewish immigrants from all over the world. In the religious sense, Israel is a state where the sabbath, Jewish religious holidays, and kosher food laws are observed by all agencies of the government; where the official rabbinate has authority over personal and family law among Jews; and where the past and future ties between Jews and the Land of Israel, a key tenet of the Jewish religion since its inception, find expression.

Israel is a representative democracy; the people elect their representatives to the Knesset, and these representatives determine political issues. The direct democracy of referenda is not practiced. Israel is also a democracy in the sense that both its written and its unwritten constitution evidence a commitment to protecting human rights.

Two other Israeli constitutional principles are the rule of law and the separation of powers. Government authorities have no power beyond that established in law. There is a prohibition on vague legislation and on legislation that gives officials pervasive discretion, if that would impact constitutionally protected rights. Separation of powers is apparent in the system of checks and balances among the various government authorities, especially the Knesset, the government, and the judiciary. The Israeli judiciary is independent and the Supreme Court functions as a powerful restraint on governmental power.

CONSTITUTIONAL BODIES

The president is the head of state, whose tasks are principally representational. The prime minister as head of the government is the state's political leader and depends on the confidence of the majority of parliament members, who are elected in general, national, direct, equal, secret, and proportional elections. The parliament, called Knesset, fulfills a dual task: It is authorized to create a constitution and to pass regular laws. The judiciary includes the Supreme Court, which as High Court of Justice performs an important role in the supervision of government authorities.

The President

Section 1 of the Basic Law, The President of the State, stipulates that "a President shall stand at the head of the State." The president is elected by the Knesset by secret ballot for only one term of seven years. The president's authorities are principally representational and include signing laws and international treaties approved by the Knesset and receiving the credentials of foreign ambassadors. The president generally represents values of social morality that are not under political dispute.

The president's two primary powers relate to the formation of a government and the pardon of offenders on the recommendation of the minister of justice. In exceptional circumstances, the president can pardon people even before conviction. The Basic Law The Government grants the president authority to assign the task of forming a government to a member of Knesset willing to undertake the task, after consulting the Knesset parties' representatives. The president customarily assigns the task to the candidate who has the best chance of succeeding.

The Government

The government is the principal executive body in Israel, and it serves by virtue of the confidence of the Knesset. The government is led by a Knesset member nominated by the state president to become prime minister and to whom the state president assigns the task of forming a government, which then has to obtain the Knesset's confidence.

The prime minister is the predominant figure in Israeli political life and guides the policy of the government. The prime minister has the authority to appoint ministers and to remove them from office. In rare circumstances the removal becomes obligatory. For example, it was ruled that the then-prime minister Yitzhak Rabin must remove from office a minister and a deputy minister whom the attorney general had decided to indict.

Should the prime minister decide to resign, the president is authorized to approach another candidate, who will try to win support by a majority of Knesset members. The Knesset may express its lack of confidence in the government, without dissolving itself, only by proposing a new prime minister supported by the votes of more than half of its members. This action is called "constructive lack of confidence."

The Basic Law The Government was amended in time for the 1996 elections, so that each voter would cast two ballots: one for Knesset members, the other for the prime minister. This was designed to strengthen the prime minister's status vis-à-vis the Knesset and the small political parties, and thus to increase political stability. However, the amendment failed to stabilize Israel's political system, and the law was amended again at the time of the 2003 elections; the old voting was reinstated with some alterations, including the requirement for a constructive lack of confidence.

The prime minister directs the work of the government, whose decisions are made by majority vote without need of quorum. With the Knesset's approval, the government may alter the division of labor among ministers, except with regard to the prime minister. Not only is the government accountable before the Knesset, but most ministers are also Knesset members. Members of the government have both ministerial and collective accountability.

The government has extensive powers, not limited to those explicitly granted by law, and it enjoys prerogative powers in various areas such as foreign affairs. This notwithstanding, the Supreme Court has ruled that the government may not utilize its prerogative powers to limit human rights. Ministers have the right to promulgate regulations, and the government in its entirety is authorized to establish emergency regulations that can even override explicit Knesset legislation for a period of up to three months.

The Knesset

The Knesset, Israel's parliament, consists of 120 members elected in general, secret, national, equal, and proportional elections for a period of four years. Knesset members enjoy substantive parliamentary immunity from indictment for acts or utterances related to the fulfillment of their tasks. Knesset members further enjoy procedural immunity from criminal indictment for other acts, although the Knesset may revoke a member's procedural immunity, usually at the request of the attorney general, by a simple majority of the plenum.

Knesset decisions are made in the plenum by simple majority, with no quorum required. Elections for state president and no confidence votes require an absolute majority of Knesset members. The Knesset's parliamentary supervision of the government is implemented by means of written and verbal interpellations and motions for the agenda. The Knesset is entitled to form parliamentary investigation committees, and it supervises the government's financing and the state budget. The Knesset presidency, which comprises the Knesset speaker and deputies, presides over sessions and determines the urgency of the motions for agenda.

Working procedures are established in the Knesset rules and not in primary legislation. Despite being a type of secondary legislation, the rules of procedure have elevated status. Interpretation of these rules is the purview of the Knesset Committee; the Supreme Court tends not to intervene except in exceptional cases when the Supreme Court believes it necessary to prevent severe damage to the fabric of parliamentary life.

The Knesset is composed of factions based on the parties' election lists. The Basic Law The Knesset disciplines members who change factions and refuse to resign, by denying financing and barring him or her from running for subsequent Knesset. Such limitations do not apply when faction members leave to form a new Knesset faction.

The Lawmaking Process

When the Knesset passes a Basic Law it is fulfilling its role as a constitutive authority; when it passes ordinary laws it is fulfilling its role as a legislative authority. There is no significant difference between the procedures in the two cases. Legislation procedures are established in the Knesset's rules of procedure and not in basic laws or in legislation.

Except ministers and deputy ministers, every Knesset member may submit a private bill, although the procedure for passing such bills is complex. The member must first obtain the permission of the Knesset presidency, which will not move a bill that, in its opinion, is "racist in its essence, or rejects the existence of the State of Israel as the State of the Jewish People." If the budgetary cost of the private bill is high, it must win at least 50 votes at every stage of the legislation process. Finally, if the private bill passes a preliminary reading in the plenum it is referred to the relevant Knesset committee, in which it is prepared before being placed on the Knesset table for a first reading.

Administration bills, approved by the ministers' Legislation Committee, are placed directly on the Knesset table for first reading. From this point on, the procedure for private and governmental bills is identical. At the first reading stage, the Knesset votes on the proposal in general; if it is passed, the Knesset refers it to the appropriate committee, in which the bulk of legislative work is performed. At this stage, representatives of the attorney general advise as to the proposal's compliance with constitutional requirements. If approved by the committee, the proposal is passed on for second and third readings in the plenum. During the second reading, each section is voted upon separately; during the third, the proposal in its entirety is voted upon. Legislation passed by the Knesset is signed by the Knesset speaker, the prime minister, and the president.

The Supreme Court tends to avoid intervention in legislative procedures. Judicial review of a law is usually conducted only after the law has been passed in the Knesset.

The Judiciary

The Israeli judiciary enjoys institutional independence. The Basic Law The Judiciary stipulates that Israeli judges are subject to no authority save that of the law. A judge may not obey instructions from any individual or institute other than higher courts acting within their authority. The manner in which judges are appointed helps protect their independence from political influence. The Judges' Election Committee consists of three Supreme Court judges, two representatives of the Israeli bar, and only four representatives of the political system—two cabinet ministers and two Knesset members.

Israel's principal court system consists of three levels: magistrate courts, district courts, and the Supreme Court. The Supreme Court functions as the final court of appeals for matters of civil and criminal law and as the High Court of Justice. In this latter function, it hears petitions of a public or constitutional nature against state authorities. There are also a number of court branches that adjudicate matters of specific legal nature, including labor courts, family courts, religious courts, and courts for administrative affairs, which operate as part of the district courts. The decisions of all these courts can be appealed before the Supreme Court.

Although the basic laws do not grant courts specific rights to strike down laws, the Supreme Court has determined that courts are authorized to do so in cases in which laws contradict basic laws. Any court may annul a provision of law that contradicts a basic law, if necessary for resolving the legal dispute before the court. However, most rulings on constitutionality are made by the High Court of Justice. Thus far, the High Court of Justice has demonstrated restraint and has annulled few provisions of law.

Everyone has standing to submit a petition to the High Court of Justice on public matters, and almost every issue is justiciable, including issues of a distinct political or military nature. The court enjoys widespread public faith in comparison with the Knesset and the government. However, its judicial activism has in recent years caused a certain decline of its public support. The religious public within the Jewish majority group reveals the lowest degree of faith in the Supreme Court.

One of the most noticeable examples of judicial activism is the High Court of Justice's rulings on torture. In a landmark decision from 1999, the Supreme Court invalidated the Israel Security Service's torture policy toward those suspected of terrorist acts. The Supreme Court determined that Israeli law nowhere explicitly authorizes such practices. This decision received severe public criticism for damaging the state's ability to defend against acts of terror. However, the Knesset has, thus far, elected not to amend the law so as to grant explicit authority to torture people who are being interrogated.

THE ELECTION PROCESS

The Basic Law The Knesset stipulates that "the Knesset shall be elected by general, national, direct, equal, secret and proportional elections." Every Israeli citizen 18 years or older has the right to vote for the Knesset. There are no limitations, as prisoners are entitled to vote.

The Parliamentary Elections

In Knesset elections the entire territory of the state is considered one jurisdiction. Seats in the newly elected Knesset are divided in accordance with the votes each party list of candidates wins. Elections for the Knesset are held on an earlier date when a law to that effect is passed by an absolute majority of Knesset members, or when an absolute majority of Knesset members express lack of confidence in the government. Between 1948 and 2005, there were only 16 general election campaigns for the Knesset, a fact that reflects the relative stability of the Israeli political system, although this stability has somewhat diminished in recent years. In order to obtain representation in the Knesset, a party must win at least 2 percent of all votes cast.

Any Israeli citizen of the age of 21 or older may be elected to the Knesset, except those who have been sentenced to at least five years' imprisonment for an offense against state security. Also, anyone who has held a high-ranking position in the state service or the military must observe a six-month interval between resigning the post and running for the Knesset. Dual citizenship does not preclude candidacy for the Knesset; however, an elected candidate must do everything in his or her power to be released from foreign citizenship.

In the 1960s, the Supreme Court upheld the disqualification of an Arab candidates' list that negated the existence of the State of Israel as the Jewish state, even though the Central Elections Committee had never been granted explicit legal authority to disqualify a list on such grounds. The Basic Law The Knesset was amended in 1985

and 2002 so as to allow disqualification of a candidates' list or candidate found to negate the Jewish or democratic character of the state, incite racism, or support armed struggle and terrorist acts against the state. The Central Elections Committee's decision can be appealed before the Supreme Court. In fact, this provision has thus far been used only to disqualify an extreme right-wing Jewish party and its offshoots.

POLITICAL PARTIES

In Israel, party pluralism is practiced and a large number of parties have representation in the Knesset. Israeli parties are usually perceived by law as public entities. Accordingly, in addition to the provisions of private law, party structures and procedures are subject to public law, including the obligation of equal and fair treatment. Most Israeli parties are now run in a democratic manner, and they conduct primaries for the nomination of the party's candidates for Knesset elections.

The Parties' Law of 1992 requires the registration of every party with the parties' registrar, who may refuse to register parties on the grounds that they negate the Jewish and democratic nature of the state or act to promote illegal objectives. The courts have applied a narrow interpretation to this power.

Parties elected to the Knesset obtain public funding, in proportion to the number of their Knesset members. The purpose of the public funding is to allow parties to function efficiently without becoming dependent on wealthy contributors. Parties are permitted to raise funds independently, but the law restricts a party's income from donations.

CITIZENSHIP

The central principle for acquiring citizenship in Israel is *ius sanguinis*. The adoption of this principle in Israel is based on the desire to facilitate the Jewish people's return to its land after millennia of exile. The Law of Return of 1950 affords all Jews and their non-Jewish next of kin who wish to return to the homeland a near-automatic right to acquire Israeli citizenship. This right can be limited only on those rare occasions when the visa applicant has acted against the Jewish people or represents a threat to public health or state security. The Knesset restricted the principle of *ius sanguinis* with regard to Jews in those cases in which the child of Israeli citizens was not born in Israel and does not live in Israel.

Non-Jews who were subjects of the British mandate on Palestine prior to the formation of the State of Israel and who did not leave the state during its War of Independence in 1948 became Israeli citizens, and Israeli citizenship was also granted to their children by birth. For non-Jewish foreigners, citizenship can be acquired only by virtue of residence in Israel. To be nationalized one must (1) be in Israel, (2) remain in the state for at least three of five years, (3) be entitled to permanent residence, (4) know the Hebrew language, and (5) give up prior citizenship. Although these are not exceptionally stringent requirements, the ministry of internal affairs' traditional policy is to curtail the grant of citizenship by virtue of residency in Israel.

Citizens enjoy the right to participate in elections, to work in state service, and to carry an Israeli passport. Along with these rights, Israeli citizenship entails an obligation of allegiance to the state and obligatory military service.

FUNDAMENTAL RIGHTS

The protection of human rights is an important part of Israeli constitutional law. The bulk of constitutional protection is granted in the areas of civil and political rights. The Basic Law Human Dignity and Liberty and the Basic Law Freedom of Occupation explicitly grant that the rights to life, body, dignity, personal freedom, property, privacy, entry and exit into Israel, and occupation will be protected from violation. The main significance of the constitutional status of these rights is their supremacy over regular Knesset legislation. Complementarily, the Supreme Court's unwritten bill of rights ensures the antidiscrimination principle; the freedoms of expression, religion, conscience, movement, and association; and other liberties. This judiciary bill of rights is limited in the sense that a regular Knesset law can negate it. In addition to the constitutional and the judicial protection of rights, the Knesset has passed laws ensuring the realization of the principle of equality and the rights to privacy and reputation.

The State of Israel has not yet enacted the Basic Law Social Rights, and, for the time being, the Supreme Court provides sparse protection of these rights. The common legal opinion is that only an attack against a person's right to "minimal conditions of subsistence" constitutes a prohibited offense against the constitutional right to human dignity. Israeli law further recognizes to some extent certain group rights, in particular with regard to the Arab minority: Arabic is recognized as an official language, Islamic and Christian religious communities enjoy autonomy in affairs of matrimonial law, and lessons in schools attended by Arab pupils are taught in Arabic.

The supreme value governing Israeli constitutional law is the value of human dignity. This value is based on the proviso developed by the philosopher Immanuel Kant whereby all rational beings must be treated as ends unto themselves and not merely as means to an end. In the year 2000, the Supreme Court ruled that holding Lebanese captives as bargaining chips to obtain the release of Israeli prisoners of war and persons missing in action was unconstitutional. The court found the action a violation of the principle of personal liability, and therefore an illicit offense against human dignity.

Despite widespread agreement that human dignity ought to be protected, the meaning of this value is disputed in Israel. Some judges believe that the value of human dignity is meant to protect people's autonomy and may therefore be broadly interpreted to encompass unenumerated rights such as equality, freedom of expression, and freedom of religion. Other judges believe that the value of human dignity should be interpreted more narrowly, to bar only offenses against unenumerated rights that entail humiliation. According to the second view, since discrimination based on group identity such as sex or nationality offends human dignity, the Knesset is prohibited from doing so.

Impact and Functions of Fundamental Rights

Human rights in Israel are based on a liberal conception, which traditionally perceives such rights as negative, in that they prohibit the state from limiting human liberty. However, in recent years there is a growing tendency in Israeli constitutional law to grant rights positive meaning, namely, to require the state to act to ensure the realization of rights. For example, with regard to antidiscrimination it has been ruled that the Israeli army must bear the costs necessary to ensure the integration of women into an air pilot training course. Moreover, the state has a general obligation to practice affirmative action to remedy discrimination against women, Arabs, and disabled persons within state service.

In the past, Israeli law upheld the liberal distinction between the private and the public spheres; courts refrained, for example, from applying the antidiscrimination principle to private entities. In recent years, however, Israeli courts have tended to interpret the principles of private law in a way consistent with constitutional rights. For example, provisions established in a collective agreement that discriminated against women were annulled on the grounds that they conflicted with the private law doctrine of "public policy." Furthermore, private entities are required by legislation to uphold such rights as equality and privacy.

The human rights section of constitutional law has a tangible effect on Israeli public discourse. Constitutional protection of the freedom of expression ensures vibrant political discussion. The Supreme Court contributes significantly to the fortification of freedom of expression, in particular, and of human rights in general.

Limitations of Fundamental Rights

The prevalent assumption in Israeli constitutional law is that there are no absolute rights. The basic laws concerning human rights enacted in 1992 establish a general formula for evaluating rights limitation clauses. The Basic Law Human Dignity and Liberty stipulates: "There shall be no limitation of rights under this Basic Law except by a law befitting the values of the State of Israel, enacted for a proper purpose, and to an extent no greater than is required, or by regulation enacted by virtue of express authorization in such law."

This provision places three principle restrictions on the state's power to limit rights: Any limitation of a fundamental right must be based upon an explicit and clear provision of law, which establishes criteria under which rights may be limited. This requirement illustrates the principle of the rule of law and is meant to function as a safeguard against abuse of governmental power by the executive. The Supreme Court ruling that disallowed torture on the grounds that it was not authorized by an explicit provision of law is an example of this approach.

Second, the limitation must serve a worthy purpose. The courts tend not to permit limitations based on administrative or monetary considerations. The Supreme Court has emphasized that respecting human rights costs money. The validity of the justifying purpose is also related to the values of the State of Israel. Limitation of human rights for the purpose of preserving the Jewish character of the state may be considered legitimate.

Finally, limitations of rights must be proportional; that requirement has been interpreted in Israel as entailing three subtests: (1) The means of limitation must be rationally connected to the purpose of limitation; (2) preference must be given to those means that least drastically impair the right; and (3) the benefit derived from the limiting arrangement must be balanced against its negative consequences. The least drastic means requirement is the heart of proportionality, and most judicial intervention in governmental rights limitations is based on the existence of less drastic means to obtain the same goal.

ECONOMY

The Basic Law The State Economy contains formal elements that establish checks on the economic authorities in the executive branch. Taxes can be imposed only by law, that is, by the Knesset. The Knesset must approve the state budget and thus has final say on the distribution of state resources. If the government fails to win approval for the budget within three months of the beginning of the tax year, the Knesset is considered dissolved and new general elections will take place.

The Israeli constitution does not give substantial preference to any particular economic system. The state is nevertheless restricted by a system of economic rights. The basic laws on human rights enacted in 1992 explicitly protect two such rights: the right to own property and freedom of occupation. Social rights are not explicitly protected; however, the Supreme Court tends to require the state to act, within existing resources, to ensure that people will not live below the minimal standard of dignified subsistence. In general, though, the courts rarely challenge legislation limiting economic and social rights

because, inter alia, they lack the tools to address complex economic questions.

RELIGIOUS COMMUNITIES

The State of Israel practices religious pluralism. Religious communities enjoy autonomy in managing their internal affairs, as well as authority over personal status issues including marriage and divorce. This practice derives from the Milet system that flourished under Turkish rule (up to 1917). The system is tolerant of religious minorities and allows multiculturalism. However, it permits the enforcement of religious law in matrimonial affairs on secular people who were born to a given religious community and did not change their religion. Hence, there is no legal option of civil marriage; those seeking civil marriage, for example, interreligious couples, are forced to marry abroad.

Israel is not a theocracy; Israeli law is secular and the sovereign is the Knesset, which represents the will of the people. However, there is no separation of state and religion. Thus, laws passed by the Knesset endorse some limitations originating in religious law, such as a ban on raising and selling pork (with exceptions for Christians), the import of nonkosher meat, and the display of leavened bread during the Jewish holiday of Passover. Additionally, the state establishes or supports religious institutions such as the Chief Rabbinate as well as the Jewish, Muslim, Druze, and Christian religious courts. The state also funds many religious practices including worship services.

The relationship between religion and state is based on a communitarian concept that emphasizes the importance of the connection between people and their religious communities. Alongside the advantages of this attitude, there is a concern that personal liberties might be impaired. The Israeli Supreme Court endeavors to curb the state's power to impair personal liberties while advancing religious causes. It has ruled that a governmental decision based solely on religious considerations must be supported by an explicit provision of law. The court intervenes to ensure that the allocation of resources for religious services is as equal as possible. Moreover, the Supreme Court exercises judicial review over the decisions of religious institutions and is willing to intervene if they impair citizens' fundamental rights.

Private religious schools enjoy a large degree of autonomy. In practice the state exercises little supervision over nonstate religious educational institutes even when they receive substantial state funding. The State of Israel has established state-run religious schools for the Jewish religious community. These schools are fully funded by the state and subject to its supervision. On the other hand, private schools established by the *haredi* (ultraorthodox) Jewish communities, which also enjoy state funding, are in fact subject to almost no state supervision.

MILITARY DEFENSE AND STATE OF EMERGENCY

The Israel Defense Force is subject to government control through the minister of defense. The chief of staff is appointed by the government on the recommendation of the minister of defense. The government has the authority to control even tactical acts of the armed forces. The heads of the Mosad—the central covert intelligence agency—and the General Security Service—which collects intelligence within state borders and the occupied territories—are direct subordinates of the prime minister.

Under the Security Service Law, every Israeli citizen is obligated to serve in the army. Men serve for three years and women for two. In practice, because it was thought unreasonable to expect Arab citizens to fight against their brethren in Arab nations, compulsory recruiting has been applied only to Jewish and Druze citizens and not to Muslim and Christian Arab citizens. Students of *haredi yeshivas* (institutes of religious studies) have, since the first years of the state's existence, been exempted from military service out of consideration for this community's unique cultural characteristics. However, as the number of such students has soared, the High Court of Justice has ruled that the exemption policy must be established in explicit Knesset legislation so as to ensure democratic supervision of deviations from the principle of equal division of burden.

Israeli authorities differentiate between pacifist conscientious objectors, who are entitled to an exemption from military service, and selective conscientious objectors, who are not entitled to exemption. A selective objector is someone who does not morally object to military service in itself but refuses to perform certain actions that military service entails; an example can be the objection to serving in the occupied territories out of moral objection to the occupation. The security authorities strongly oppose selective objection, and the Supreme Court has backed their position.

From a legal perspective, the State of Israel has been in a state of emergency ever since it was founded. The Knesset is the organ authorized to declare a state of emergency and such declaration is valid for one year. In practice, the Knesset annually redeclares a state of emergency. This declaration has allowed the enactment of legal arrangements that permit the taking of acute measures such as administrative detention. Furthermore, the government is authorized to enact Emergency Regulations that can override laws for a period of up to three months. The government is required to demonstrate why the enactment of the regulations directly derives from the state of emergency.

AMENDMENTS TO THE CONSTITUTION

Most of the provisions established in the Israeli basic laws can be altered by a simple majority of Knesset members, despite their constitutional status. However, an absolute majority of Knesset members is needed to amend the Basic Laws Government and Freedom of Occupation, and some provisions of Knesset, Jerusalem, the capital of Israel, and State Economy.

Since it is so easy to amend the constitution, it has been amended to excess, according to critics, at times merely to satisfy day-to-day political needs. For example, the constitutional limit of 18 ministers was dropped in order to include additional parties in a new government. The frequent changes in the election system constitute another example.

In a further twist, the Knesset added a clause to the Basic Law The Freedom of Occupation that allows it to pass ordinary laws contradicting that basic law (a Notwithstanding Clause). Each such law must explicitly state that it is being enacted notwithstanding the provisions of the basic law, and that it is valid for only four years.

As all the basic laws, Human Dignity and Liberty, the focal point of the Israeli bill of rights, is not formally entrenched. In this case, however, the basic law enjoys relative stability, even though the Supreme Court's interpretations often raise objections in the political system. Since 1992 it has been amended only once, and then only to generally extend its reach. The relative stability of this basic law results, inter alia, from the fact that it expresses the nucleus of Israel's existence as a Jewish and democratic state protecting human dignity.

PRIMARY SOURCES

Constitution in English. Available online. URL: http://www.knesset.gov.il/description/eng/eng_mimshal_yesod1.htm. Accessed on August 11, 2005.

SECONDARY SOURCES

Daphne Barak-Erez, "From an Unwritten to a Written Constitution: The Israeli Challenge in American Perspective." *Columbia Human Rights Law Review* 26 (1995): 309.

Amnon Rubinstein and Barak Medina, *Constitutional Law of the State of Israel*. 5th ed. Tel-Aviv: Shocken, 1997 (in Hebrew).

Amos Shapira, "Why Israel Has No Constitution." *Saint Louis University Law Journal* 37 (1993): 283.

Itzhak Zamir and Allen Zysblat, eds., *Public Law in Israel*. Oxford: Clarendon Press, 1996.

Itzhak Zamir and Sylviane Colombo, eds., *The Law of Israel: General Surveys*. Jerusalem: Hebrew University, 1995.

Yaacov S. Zemach, *The Judiciary in Israel*. Jerusalem: The Institute of Judicial Training for Judges, 1998.

Moshe Cohen-Eliya

ITALY

At-a-Glance

OFFICIAL NAME
Italian Republic

CAPITAL
Rome

POPULATION
56,995,744 (2005 est.)

SIZE
116,347 sq. mi. (301,338 sq. km)

LANGUAGES
Official languages Italian, German (South Tyrol), Ladin (South Tyrol), French (Val d'Aosta), Slovene (Friuli-Venezia Giulia)

RELIGIONS
Catholic majority, Protestant 0.7%, Christian Orthodox 0.17%, Jewish 0.05%, Waldenses 0.04%, Muslim and other 1.7%

NATIONAL OR ETHNIC COMPOSITION
National composition: Italian majority; other (mainly Moroccan, Albanian, Filipino, Romanian, Tunisian, Yugoslav, Chinese) 2.7%; linguistic and ethnic minorities: German, Ladin, Albanian, Catalan, Croat, French, Greek, Provençal, Sardinian, and Slovene

DATE OF INDEPENDENCE OR CREATION
March 17, 1861

TYPE OF GOVERNMENT
Parliamentary democracy

TYPE OF STATE
Unitary state with wide regional autonomy

TYPE OF LEGISLATURE
Bicameral parliament

DATE OF CONSTITUTION
January 1, 1948

DATE OF LAST AMENDMENT
May 30, 2003

The present Italian constitution was enacted in 1947 after the fall of the fascist regime during World War II (1939–45). The Italian state is a democratic parliamentary republic and a unitary state but with wide guaranteed regional autonomies.

The constitution prevails over any other law. In case of conflict, a Constitutional Court can be called upon to ensure its superiority.

Individual and collective fundamental rights—civil, political, and social—are guaranteed, as is the equal protection of law. The state is neutral vis-à-vis the different religions, although special relations exist with the Catholic Church and some other religious communities. A free market economy is guaranteed, but public authorities have the right and the duty to regulate it to safeguard human dignity and rights, social justice, and the public interest.

The division of powers and the independence of the judiciary are ensured, as well as pluralism of political parties. Political power is mainly entrusted to the bicameral parliament, elected by the people, and to the administration, on the basis of its parliamentary majority. The head of state has a coordinating and balancing role.

The constitution allows limitations of the state sovereignty in favor of international and supranational authorities such as the United Nations and the European Union. It bans war as a means of settling international controversies.

CONSTITUTIONAL HISTORY

Italy is a young state. For many centuries after the fall of the ancient Roman Empire "Italy" was only a "geographical expression," its territory divided into kingdoms, duchies, grand duchies, lordships, free communes, the Papal States in the center of the country, and areas ruled by foreign powers, such as France, Spain, or the Austrian Empire.

After the French Revolution of 1789 and the Napoleonic wars, a movement started for the political unification of Italy. Unification was eventually realized during the 19th century through the annexation of the various territories to the Kingdom of Piedmont and Sardinia, ruled by the Savoia dynasty and renamed the Kingdom of Italy in 1861. The capital was first Turin, then Florence, and eventually Rome, after Italian troops occupied what remained of the ancient Papal States in 1870.

The conquest of Rome left the so-called Roman question open, because the Holy See refused for a long time to accept the loss of its secular powers. In 1929, the Vatican agreements recognized Italian sovereignty, creating an independent state, the City of Vatican, with a very small territory inside Rome, in order to ensure the full freedom and independence of the pope. The agreement also regulated the rights and the obligations of the Catholic Church in Italy.

The first constitution of Italy was simply the "statute" that the king of Piedmont and Sardinia, Carlo Alberto, had issued in 1848. That explains the centralized structure of the new state, divided into provinces ruled by governmental officials, the *prefetti* (prefects), according to the French model. The main administrative powers were entrusted to the central government, while the autonomy of the communes was limited.

The kingdom was governed by a parliamentary monarchy according to the British traditional pattern. The king was formally the head of the executive power, exercising mainly through the ministers and the prime minister, who were based in the parliamentary majority. The Parliament was composed of two houses, formally with equal powers: the Chamber of Deputies, elected by very limited suffrage (at the beginning only 2 percent of the citizens), and the Senate, whose members were appointed by the king from among various categories of officers and other personalities.

The legislative power was entrusted to the Parliament and the king, but in fact the king enacted all the statutes that the Parliament approved. The judiciary power enjoyed a certain, although not complete, independence from the executive. The constitution provided for the main civil liberties (not including freedom of association) but left wide space to the law for regulating their exercise. No control on the legislation was contemplated from the constitutional point of view so that although the constitution has never been formally amended, ordinary laws could substantially change and even nullify its provisions, as happened under the fascist regime.

With the end of World War I (1914–18), the unification of the country was completed, and even the South Tyrol area, where a German-speaking population lives, was annexed. In the following years a process of intensified democratization started but was soon interrupted.

The Fascist Party of Benito Mussolini took over power in a formally legal way in 1922 and changed the constitutional framework of the state. The head of the administration became the only strong power. The elected house was first dominated and weakened, then abolished; in its place was created an assembly ruled by the head of the administration. Political liberties and freedom of speech were suppressed; the Fascist Party became a state institution.

Italy entered World War II (1939–45) in 1940 at the side of Germany. However, in 1943, with military defeat looming, the fascist regime was overthrown and Italy signed an armistice with the Allies. For one and a half years, the country was divided, the southern part occupied by the Allies and the northern part occupied by German troops, and ravaged by the struggle between antifascist partisans and a new fascist republican regime.

Antifascist parties, assembled in a National Liberation Committee, took power in the south and made an agreement with the king to delay any decisions about the form of the new state (through a Constitutional Assembly to be elected by the people) until the end of the war. On June 2, 1946, the election of the assembly, in which women had the right to vote for the first time in a national scale, and a referendum chose a republican form of government with a majority of 51 percent of voters (54 percent of valid ballots).

For one and a half years, the assembly prepared the new constitution of the Italian Republic. It was approved with an 87 percent majority; was enacted on December 27, 1947; and took force on January 1, 1948.

The almost unanimous goal of the assembly was to build a democratic state where it would not be possible for an authoritarian regime such as fascism to take power and suppress the people's liberties. A large majority wanted the Italian Republic to be open to the interests and the participation of the poorer classes, especially the workers. Some of the parties represented in the assembly favored a socialist system; more were in favor of the "Western" democratic pattern. In fact, the structure and the principles of the constitution reflect the ideals and the fundamental rules of Western contemporary constitutionalism.

The constitution became for decades a factor of unity and consensus among the people, although the process of implementation was slow and even controversial. In these decades Italy became part of the North Atlantic Treaty Organization (NATO) (1949) and of the United Nations (1955). Italy was among the founding states of the European Communities (1951, 1957), then of the European Union (1992). The increasing transfer of powers to the European institutions took place without substantial controversy on the basis of the constitution, which did not need to be amended.

In recent years, since the old parties disappeared or were transformed and a new political system took shape, a trend toward substantive constitutional changes has gathered force. In particular, the relationship of Parliament, the prime minister, and the head of state has been challenged, and a new framework of regional autonomy has been proposed. The structure of citizens' rights and duties has remained mainly unchallenged.

Far-reaching reforms of the constitution relating to regional and local authorities were enacted in 1999 and in 2001. At present, a major bill to amend the constitution's political provisions is being debated by Parliament in a climate of strong disagreement between the current center-Right majority and the center-Left opposition.

FORM AND IMPACT OF THE CONSTITUTION

The Italian constitution is a single written document. It binds all individuals and public authorities as the strongest statutory law. It can be amended only by a special procedure.

By the same procedure, other "constitutional laws" that have the same value in the hierarchy of norms as does the constitution can be enacted. In some cases the constitution itself states that a matter must be regulated by a constitutional law; this applies, for example, to the special statutes of five regions as stated in Article 116.

Any other law must be consistent with the constitution and must be interpreted and applied, whenever possible, in a way consistent with the constitution. The Constitutional Court can declare a law unconstitutional; such a declaration has general effect, binding all judges and public authorities not to apply the law.

According to the constitution, general international law is automatically recognized as internal law in Italy and therefore has the same rank as constitutional laws. Ordinary legislation must respect the international obligations of the state. Moreover, European law is recognized not only as being directly applicable but also as having precedence over internal laws, and even over the constitution, unless it contradicts the constitution's fundamental principles.

The constitution not only is a legal document and the strongest source of the law but also expresses the fundamental political values underlying Italian society. It links the country to the constitutional tradition of modern Europe.

BASIC ORGANIZATIONAL STRUCTURE

Italy was created as a unitary centralized state on the model of Napoleonic France. Article 5 of the constitution declares the Italian Republic "one and indivisible." Immediately after World War I, however, before the fascist regime took over, the "People Party" under the Catholic priest Luigi Sturzo proposed the creation of political regions with legislative and administrative powers. After World War II, the Constitutional Assembly accepted the idea of a "regional" state, intermediate between centralist and federal patterns, and created 20 regions corresponding to the traditional partitions of the country used for statistical purposes. Five regions have special autonomy: the two main islands, Sicily and Sardinia, and three ethnically varied border regions: Valle d'Aosta, with a French-speaking population; Trentino-Alto Adige, including the German-speaking southern Tyrol; and Friuli-Venezia Giulia, with its Slovenian minority.

In fact, governmental structures were not established for the 15 "ordinary" regions until 1970. Thus, it had taken a century to give legal expression to the profound economic, cultural, and even linguistic differences among the various areas of the country. These differences have somewhat eased under the influence of the national school system and television, but they have not disappeared.

The constitutional reforms of 1999 and 2001 have deeply changed the former constitutional framework. The regions have built their own constitutional structures; each has its own council and executive board president directly elected by universal suffrage.

The central state's legislative powers are now limited to specified matters, such as foreign policy, defense, and the police. All other legislation is in the purview of the regions, although regional laws relating to such fields as town and country planning, health care, and education must be consistent with the fundamental rules established by national framework laws. Administrative functions, whether in national or regional matters, are usually carried out by local communities, except when the law specifically gives the job to the provinces, the regions, or the central government to ensure uniform implementation. Regions still lack any powers in civil and criminal law, court procedure, and constitutional matters, which all depend on centralized organization.

As a matter of fact, local government is deeply rooted in the Italian administrative tradition. A strong sense of local identity characterizes Italian communities, due in part to the long history of many large and small cities. Italy has more than 8,000 local communities.

The new text of the constitution provides for far-reaching financial autonomy and tax power for regions, provinces, and local communities, within the framework of national legislation. However, regional and local authorities still largely depend on the state budget.

LEADING CONSTITUTIONAL PRINCIPLES

Article 1 of the constitution defines Italy as "a democratic republic founded on labor." The sovereignty "belongs to the people, who exercise it in the forms and within the limits of the constitution." This means that the highest political authority resides in institutions that are elected, directly or indirectly, by the citizens. However, these institutions are not unlimited in their authority—they must respect the constitution. The constitution not only determines the decision-making processes but also guarantees the fundamental rights of individuals and groups, asks all citizens to observe the unbreakable duties of solidarity, and ensures the equal protection of law. The constitution obliges public authorities to pursue justice in social and economic relations in order to make freedom and equality effective for all and to allow the development of each person's personality.

The republic was the system of government chosen over monarchy in the constitutional referendum of 1946, and it cannot be legally changed. The phrase *founded on labor* is a recognition of the value of labor, instead of origin or wealth, as the basis of the social role of the individual.

The government is founded on the division of legislative, executive, and judicial powers, and on the rule of law. Rule of law means that any act of public authorities that impairs the rights of individuals or groups must find its basis in a law enacted by Parliament or, when provided for by the constitution, by the cabinet, and must be consistent with the law. Further, everyone has the fundamental right to defend any specific rights claim before an independent and impartial court, constituted according to the law.

Political participation mainly takes the form of indirect, representative democracy. Nevertheless the constitution provides for some possibilities of direct democracy, that is, of referendum, both to abrogate existing laws and to accept or reject constitutional amendments and other constitutional laws approved by Parliament. The abrogative referendum has been used on many issues. For example, a law on divorce was challenged but confirmed in a referendum in 1974. More possibilities for direct democracy are provided at the regional and local levels.

Among other fundamental principles in the constitution are mutual independence of state and church, although cooperation between the two is allowed; protection of the environment; promotion of culture and science; and a ban of war as a means to solve international controversies. The constitution also favors supranational institutions that limit national sovereignty in order to promote peace and justice among people. It is on that basis that Italy has entered the European Union.

CONSTITUTIONAL BODIES

The structural bodies named in the constitution are the president of the republic; Parliament; the administration or cabinet (Council of Ministers), which includes the prime minister (president of the Council of Ministers) and other ministers; the judiciary; and the Constitutional Court.

A number of other bodies complete this list, including administrative organs with consultative and control functions. Examples of these are the Council of State, the Court of Accounts, and the National Council of the Economy and Labor.

The President of the Republic

The president of the republic is the head of state and represents national unity. He or she coordinates and guarantees the correct functioning of the constitutional system. Any citizen who is at least 50 years of age and enjoys civil and political rights is eligible to become president of the republic.

The two houses of Parliament in joint session, with the participation of regional delegates, elect the president of the republic by secret ballot for a seven-year term; reelection is permitted. A majority of two-thirds of the assembly, or after the third ballot an absolute majority of all the members, is required. This provision gives the president a wider base of parliamentary support than the cabinet, which can be backed by a simple majority.

If the president is temporarily unable to fulfill his or her duties, they are performed by the president of the Senate, as the constitution does not provide for a vice president. The president cannot hold any other office.

The president of the republic plays an important role in forming a new administration, by nominating a prime minister and appointing the ministers on the latter's advice. The president also accepts their resignation.

The president has the authority to send messages to Parliament or to dissolve the houses and call elections. He or she authorizes the submission of bills to Parliament drafted by the Council of Ministers and promulgates laws once they are approved; issues decrees that have the force of law and regulations; calls popular referenda as provided for by the constitution; nominates important state officials; confers state honors; accredits and receives foreign diplomats; and ratifies international treaties approved, when it is required, by Parliament. The president also serves as high commander of the armed forces, presides over the Supreme Council of Defense, and makes declarations of war approved by Parliament. The president also presides over the High Council of the Judiciary, grants pardons, and commutes punishments.

The president is not legally accountable for acts performed in the exercise of official functions, except high treason or fraudulent violations of the constitution. Therefore, no act of the president is valid until countersigned by the ministers, who assume responsibility for it.

Parliament

Parliament is made up of two houses—the Chamber of Deputies, which consists of 630 members, and the Senate, which consists of 315 regular members plus five members appointed by the head of state from among outstanding citizens and the former presidents of the republic. Both houses are elected by the voters for a period of five years by a general, direct, free, equal, and secret balloting process. One or both houses can be dissolved by the president of the republic before the end of its regular term. The two houses exercise identical functions in a perfect bicameral system of legislative power and political control over the executive.

Parliament meets in joint session when electing or impeaching the president of the republic and nominating members of the panel that will try the president, when electing one-third of the members of the High Council of the Judiciary, and when electing one-third of the justices of the Constitutional Court.

Both houses generally make decisions by a simple majority of the members present, as long as there is a quorum. Particularly important decisions can be made only by a qualified majority; for example, amendments to the constitutions require an absolute or a two-thirds majority, and amnesty laws require a two-thirds majority.

Each chamber drafts its own procedural rules by absolute majority. They each enjoy accounting autonomy, which allows them to draw up and approve their own budget and to determine expenses free of any audit by external bodies. Each house acts as a judicial body in such matters as challenges to the qualifications of members and legal appeals by its public officers.

Members of Parliament enjoy privileges that guarantee their independence. As representatives of the whole nation, they are not legally bound to follow the instructions of their party or their constituents. They may not be prosecuted for opinions expressed or votes given in the exercise of their duties. The consent of the chamber is necessary to arrest or restrain a member or search his or her person or domicile, except when caught in the act of committing a crime for which arrest is mandatory.

The internal structure of each chamber is complex. Each house elects its president, by secret ballot and qualified majorities, to represent the chamber and supervise its work. Each member of Parliament must belong to a parliamentary group, with at least 20 members in the Chamber of Deputies and 10 in the Senate, or to the "mixed" group. These groups elect their own presidents, who jointly meet to schedule the activities of the chambers. Other important permanent bodies include the Committee on Election and the Committee on Privileges, as well as Standing Committees dealing with specific matters, partly coinciding with those dealt with by the ministers. There are 14 such Standing Committees in the Chamber of Deputies and 13 in the Senate. The Standing Committees must reflect the party alignment within the chamber; they are elected every two years. Each committee elects its own president, who organizes the work in coordination with the rest of the chamber.

Bicameral committees, made up of an equal number of members of the two houses, are sometimes set up, particularly to conduct parliamentary inquiries. The Parliamentary Committee for Regional Matters is the only one specifically required by the constitution.

The Lawmaking Process

Bills may be initiated by the Council of Ministers (with formal authorization by the president of the republic), by every member of Parliament, by Regional Councils, by the National Council of the Economy and Labor, and by groups of at least 50,000 voters. In practice, the Council of Ministers is the most important source of bills.

The committees in each chamber must examine each bill and refer it to the plenum; they also can be empowered to approve bills on their own, unless a qualified minority asks for plenary debate. Some kinds of laws require approval by the plenum.

A law is considered approved only when an identical bill is adopted by both chambers. If a chamber makes amendments to the text approved by the other, the latter has to reexamine the bill with regard to the amended parts.

The law is promulgated by the president of the republic, who can also send it back to the houses for one more deliberation, giving the reasons in a message. If they remain firm, the president must promulgate the law, which enters into force after being published in the official journal.

The Administration

The bodies of the administration explicitly defined in the constitution are the Council of Ministers; its president, who is the prime minister; and the other ministers. In practice, by custom or by law, there are additional organs such as one or more vice presidents of the council, vice ministers, under-secretaries of state, high commissioners, committees of ministers, and the Cabinet Council, composed of the most authoritative members of the administration.

The powers of the Council of Ministers are stated by law. Most importantly, it establishes the general lines of administration policy, which must win the confidence of Parliament, and approves the most important acts necessary to implement this policy. It is responsible for settling conflicts among ministers.

The prime minister leads the general policy of the administration and is responsible for it, by promoting and coordinating the activities of the ministers and ensuring their coherence. He or she convenes the council and determines its agenda and superintends the government. The prime minister can provide political and administrative guidelines to the ministers. They are not legally obliged to conform, as relations between the prime minister and the ministers are not hierarchical; however, the prime minister can submit the issues at any time to the Council of Ministers and thus force a dissenting minister to resign. The prime minister can also (although this is open to debate) ask the president of the republic to replace a minister.

There are two kinds of ministers: those with portfolio and those without. Ministers with portfolio head up the 14 ministries mandated by law; they are personally liable for the actions performed by their ministry, as well as, in a collegiate way, for the resolutions of the council. Ministers without portfolio take part in the council's activities with the same rank of their colleagues; they are charged with special functions, often in support of the prime minister's activity.

The government must enjoy the confidence of Parliament at all times. The president of the republic must appoint as prime minister a person who seems likely to win the support of both houses. The person charged with forming the cabinet conducts consultations and submits the list of ministers to the head of the state, who formally appoints the prime minister and the ministers. The president may exercise an informal veto on proposed ministers. Within 10 days of its formation, the government must present its program to Parliament for an open vote of confidence, which requires a simple majority in each house.

Only if a no confidence motion, setting out its reasons, is approved by an open vote and a simple majority must the Council of Ministers resign. In practice, the stability of the administration depends on the continued unity of the ruling party or coalition. In recent years, the dominance of the two major coalitions has made for longer-lasting administrations than in the past, when the multiplicity of independent parties made sustaining governing coalitions difficult.

The Judiciary

In accordance with the continental European tradition, judicial functions are, in general, performed by professional magistrates selected by competitive examination designed to test their technical skills. They are independent of any other authority and subject only to the law.

The members of the "ordinary" judicial bodies, which deal with civil and criminal matters, have a centralized system of self-government, headed by the High Council (Consiglio superiore della magistratura), composed mainly of representatives elected from among the magistrates themselves, with other members elected by Parliament. The independence of the special courts that deal with administrative, accounting, and military matters is protected by law.

The trial system is divided into various jurisdictions, which culminate in the Court of Cassation (Court of Appeals), which guarantees the uniform enforcement of the law.

The Constitutional Court

A special feature of the 1947 constitution was the creation of an organ of constitutional justice separate from the three state powers. It was based on the model first established in Europe by the Austrian Republic.

The Constitutional Court is composed of 15 legal experts, five elected by the higher judiciary courts, five elected by Parliament, and five appointed by the president of the republic. All of them are fully independent. Their method of election reflects the dual nature of their function: the impartial interpretation of constitutional provisions and the politically charged judicial review of legislation.

The court exercises judicial review whenever a common court decides that the law it is supposed to apply in the case before it may be not consistent with the constitution. The Constitutional Court often strikes down or corrects only a part of a law; it even sometimes upholds the law only on condition that it is interpreted and applied in a certain way.

The court is also called upon to settle constitutional disputes between the central and regional powers or between the different branches of the state. It also tries the president of the republic in case of impeachment and decides whether to allow a referendum to repeal a law.

THE ELECTION PROCESS AND POLITICAL PARTICIPATION

All Italians above the age of 18 have the right to vote in the election of the Chamber of Deputies and, at the age of 25, to stand for this same election. Those aged 25 may also vote for senators, but they must be over 40 to stand for the Senate. These rights can be taken away only in closely defined circumstances, such as when a person has been convicted of certain criminal offenses.

Local election laws provide different rules for choosing regional, provincial, and communal councils. However, these councils, as well as most of the regional presidents, province presidents, and local mayors, are elected by direct and universal suffrage.

Parliamentary Elections

The constitution does not specify the procedures for parliamentary elections, which are left to the law. In the past, a proportional voting system led to the remarkable fragmentation of the Italian political system.

In 1993, a reform providing for a mixed electoral system for both chambers was passed. A plurality first-past-the-post system in single-member districts allocates 75 percent of the seats, and a proportional method allocates the remaining 25 percent in larger districts. In the Chamber of Deputies, the 25 percent proportional seats are allocated to party lists of candidates; the Senate allocates these seats among the losing candidates in the single-member districts.

Political Participation

In addition to representative democracy, the constitution provides some forms of direct democracy. The most important of these is abrogative referendum to repeal national laws. It can be proposed by 500,000 voters or five regional councils. Some laws, such as fiscal legislation, are not subject to referendum.

Referenda can also be held on constitutional amendments, and on regional laws and other regional acts. Consultative referenda can be held to redraw regional, provincial, and communal boundaries. Apart from referenda, any group of 50,000 voters can propose a bill to Parliament.

POLITICAL PARTIES

Italy has a pluralistic system of political parties as a basic structure of the constitutional order. The constitution guarantees the right to form and join political parties freely, as an expression of the general freedom of association. *Parties* are defined as groups of citizens who "contribute by democratic means to determine national politics."

The only general limitation in the constitution is that party activities must be democratic. So-called antisystem parties are allowed, but the former Fascist Party is permanently banned. To guarantee impartiality in the exercise of public or institutional functions, members of the judiciary, the armed forces, and the police, and diplomatic and consular representatives abroad, can be prevented from joining any political party.

Political parties are reimbursed by law for electoral expenses. The funds are allocated in proportion to the electoral results.

CITIZENSHIP

The rules to acquire or lose citizenship are fixed in ordinary laws. The constitution guarantees only that no one be deprived of citizenship for political reasons.

Citizenship is obtained according to the *ius sanguinis*. This means that a child is born as an Italian citizen when one of his or her parents is an Italian citizen, regardless of birthplace.

Anyone born within Italian territory acquires citizenship by birth if both parents are unknown or stateless or, according to the law of the parents' state, the citizenship of that state is not transmitted by birth (*ius soli*).

Citizenship can also be obtained when a foreign child is adopted by an Italian citizen, and when a foreign or stateless person whose parent or grandparent was a citizen by birth performs military or civil service in Italy or has been living for at least two years in Italy when he or she comes of age. Citizenship can also be obtained by a foreign or stateless person who has a clean criminal record three years after marrying an Italian citizen or even after six months if he or she has been living in Italy once married. Finally, the president of the republic may accord citizenship, on request, to any foreign or stateless person after he or she has been living in Italy for a certain number of years.

Italian citizens may renounce their citizenship if they take up residence abroad, but the acquisition of the citizenship of another country does not automatically cause the loss of Italian citizenship.

FUNDAMENTAL RIGHTS

The underlying idea of the constitution is the central importance of the human being. Article 2 states that "the republic recognizes and guarantees the inviolable rights of man, as an individual and in the social groups where he expresses his personality, and demands the fulfillment of the unavoidable duties of political, economic and social solidarity." The starting point is thus the preeminent value of the human person, conceived as preexistent to the political community. Human dignity must never be violated; rights are qualified as "inviolable:" Not even a constitutional amendment can abrogate them.

Parallel to the rights guaranteed in Article 2 is the equality clause of Article 3: "All citizens have equal social dignity and are equal before the law, without distinction of sex, race, language, religion, political opinions, [or] personal and social conditions. It is the duty of the republic to remove those obstacles of an economic and social nature which, by limiting in fact the freedom and equality of citizens, impede the full development of the human person and the effective participation of all workers in the political, economic and social organization of the country."

The constitution thus includes both formal equality—the prohibition of different treatment of equal situations or equal treatment of different situations—and substantial equality—the requirement to take measures, even affirmative actions, to compensate for social disadvantages. Even though discrimination on the ground of certain factors such as sex, race, or religion is in principle always prohibited, affirmative action, for example, for women or national and linguistic minorities may be allowed or even necessary. It is eventually up to the courts, particularly the Constitutional Court, to decide whether a difference in treatment may be reasonably justified by the difference of situations. "Reasonableness" is indeed a catch-all criterion used in constitutional jurisprudence.

Certain political rights are expressly attributed only to Italian citizens. The right to vote in parliamentary elections or the right to enter the state territory is restricted to Italian citizens, as are the rights of assembly and of association. However, such rights are provided for all persons in international charters such as the 1950 European Convention for the Protection of Human Rights and of Fundamental Freedoms legally enforceable in Italy.

Impact and Functions of Fundamental Rights

Articles 13–54 of the constitution enumerate rights and duties and often regulate them in detail. They are divided into four parts.

1. *Civil relations* include the traditional liberal rights such as habeas corpus and freedom of domicile, communication, assembly, association, religion, and expression. They also include access to courts and specific guarantees in the realm of criminal law such as the right to defense, nonretroactivity of criminal law, and the ban on capital punishment.
2. *Ethical-social relations* are rights and duties involving family and health, freedom of teaching, the right to create schools, and the right to an education.
3. *Economic relations* provisions include the rights of any form of work, and social protection in old age, illness, unemployment, or invalidism. This section covers the guarantee of property and its social function, the rights and limits of economic enterprises, and the duties of the state to the national economy.
4. *Political relations* cover the right to vote, the role of political parties, and the right to petition Parliament. All citizens are to have equal access to public charges and offices. They also have the duty to defend the fatherland, interpreted as military defense as well as civil forms of service; the duty to contribute to the public expenditure in proportion to one's wealth; and the duty to be faithful to the republic.

Some of the rights have "negative" content: They prohibit any act that illegally impairs the freedom of the citizen. For example, the constitution prohibits detention or arrest unless required by a law consistent with the conditions stated by the constitution. Other rights have "positive" content: The public authorities must allow individuals to take part in a legal procedure, for example, to take part in the election of Parliament. As for "social" rights, the practical content must be defined by law. For example, the law has to define the sums granted as unemployment compensation.

The constitution ensures that citizens may protect all their enumerated rights in court. That protection must be effective.

The constitutional protections on individual rights are essentially aimed at public authorities. However, they can also affect relations between individuals. Actions that violate human rights are prohibited and can be punished, and victims can be awarded damages in court.

Limitations to Fundamental Rights

Any right has limits, which are due to the necessity to ensure other subjects' rights of the same or another kind and to ensure the protection of public interests. In some cases the constitution defines precise limits, for example, when it specifies the reasons why printed matter may be seized. Otherwise the constitution allows limits to be defined by law, but they must be specific and within a framework and under conditions fixed by the constitution itself. The application of these limits is often reserved to judicial authorities, who must verify that the legal conditions are fulfilled.

Moreover, limitations may never affect the essential contents of the constitutionally granted rights, must not be introduced unless necessary to protect other rights or interests founded on the constitution, and must be proportional to that necessity. The problem of defining the limits is often an exercise by legislators and judges in balancing conflicting interests. It is the duty of the Constitutional Court to check that a correct and reasonable balance has been achieved by the law.

ECONOMY

The task facing the Constitutional Assembly regarding the economic system was very difficult. In the end, the constitution consents to different possibilities of economic development and defines only some fundamental principles: freedom of economic enterprise and property, on the one hand, and the need to ensure social interests and fair social relations on the other.

The constitution states that the government is responsible for correcting the market in order to direct free economic activity toward the end of social justice. The coexistence of public and private economic activities and the limitations on the rights of private companies aimed at guaranteeing the social function of the economy characterize the Italian "mixed" model as a social market economy.

Expropriation of private properties must be prescribed by law and must be in the general interest. It must be compensated, but not necessarily with the property's market value.

RELIGIOUS COMMUNITIES

The Italian constitution guarantees freedom of religion and protects its collective expressions. Religious communities enjoy "equal freedom" treatment by the law and freedom of self-organization, and they can enter into agreements with the state. The religious character or aims of an institution must not be taken by the state as the basis of any special legal limitations or special fiscal burdens for its constitution, legal status, or any of its activities.

Italy is not a confessional state—the Catholic Church is no longer established. For historical reasons, however, that church is the only religious community expressly mentioned in the constitution. The relationship between the state and religious groups is based on the principle of separation and regulated on the basis of agreements with the representatives of those groups. There are a concordat with the Catholic Church and covenants with non-Catholic communities, including the Waldensian and Methodist communities, the Jewish community, the Assemblies of God in Italy, the Seventh Day Adventist Church, the Baptist Church, and the Evangelical Lutheran Church. Agreements with Jehovah's Witnesses and the Buddhist have been signed but not yet enacted as laws.

Those religious communities that have such agreements enjoy special treatment relating to education in state schools and spiritual assistance in military institutions, hospitals, nursing homes, rest homes, and prisons. They receive financial contributions from a state fund equivalent to eight per 1,000 of the personal income tax; taxpayers decide by their signature which part of this amount is contributed to each community or to the state. Those who donate to the communities are given tax relief.

In 1989, the Constitutional Court affirmed the laicity or secular character of the state as a supreme and inviolable principle, implying impartiality of the state toward religions. Equal treatment of all religious communities has been enforced by recent judgments of the same court, especially regarding criminal treatment and financial subventions.

MILITARY DEFENSE

The constitutional provisions relating to participation in supranational organizations are inspired by the general principle that Italy condemns war as an instrument of aggression against the freedom of other peoples and as a means for settling international controversies. Thus, beyond the national territory the armed forces may be organized and deployed for the sole purpose of external defense or collaboration within the context of supranational institutions, for peacekeeping operations, and for humanitarian duties. Italy's membership in NATO in 1949 has led to strict integration of the Italian armed forces within the military system of the Atlantic organization and to the establishment of NATO bases within Italian territory.

From a strictly national perspective, the constitution's principal concern with respect to the armed forces is that the defense of the fatherland is the sacred duty of citizens and that military service is compulsory within the limits and in the manner established by law. Conscientious objection is guaranteed, with an option of alternative civil service. Compulsory military service was suspended on January 1, 2005; since then the armed forces are made up of professional or voluntary soldiers, both men and women. Compulsory recruitment can take place only in times of war or international crisis in order to supplement the professional and voluntary forces.

The constitution requires that armed forces organization be based on the democratic principles of the republic. This statement aims at preventing the armed forces from becoming a separate body within the state or adopting principles in conflict with those governing the civil society.

The president of the republic is the commander of the armed forces and presides over the Supreme Defense Council, a cocoordinating organ that comprises specific members of the government and the head of the general defense staff. The president's command is not the effective command, which is exclusively that of the organs of the executive authority, but it is a "high command," expressing the political neutrality of the armed forces and their loyalty to the Italian state and its institutions. The constitution establishes that a state of war must be deliberated by both houses, which must assign the necessary powers to the administration, and be declared by the president of the republic.

AMENDMENTS TO THE CONSTITUTION

Article 138 specifies amendment procedures more burdensome than those for amending ordinary laws. This provision guarantees the stability of the constitution.

Proposed amendments or other constitutional laws must be debated twice in each house at intervals of no less than three months. They require an absolute majority of the members of each house in the second voting.

These laws can be submitted to a popular referendum within three months of their publication, at the request of one-fifth of the members of a house, 500,000 electors, or five regional councils. The amendment is promulgated only if approved by a majority of valid votes. A referendum is not held if the law has been approved in the second reading in each house by a majority of two-thirds of the members.

Not all constitutional rules are subject to amendment. The form of republic shall not be modified, according to Article 139. The republican structure should be understood not only in the limited sense of periodical election of the head of state but in the broader context of a government structure that implements a pluralist democracy. Furthermore, judicial rulings have established that no amendment can impair the essential contents of the "inviolable" rights guaranteed by the constitution or the "supreme principles of the constitutional order," such as the laicity of the state.

PRIMARY SOURCES
Constitution in English. Available online. URL: http://www.cortecostituzionale.it/eng/testinormativi/costituzionedellarepubblica/costituzione.asp. Accessed on September 21, 2005.
Constitution in Italian: *La Costituzione della Repubblica italiana*. Available online. URL: http://www.governo.it/Governo/Costituzione/principi.html. Accessed on June 21, 2006.

SECONDARY SOURCES
Andre Alen, ed., *International Encyclopaedia of Laws: Constitutional Law*. The Hague: Kluwer Law International, 2003.
Valerio Onida, *La Costituzione*. Bologna: Il Mulino, 2004.

Valerio Onida and Barbara Randazzo

JAMAICA

At-a-Glance

OFFICIAL NAME
Jamaica

CAPITAL
Kingston

POPULATION
2,731,832 (2005 est.)

SIZE
4,181 sq. mi. (10,830 sq. km)

LANGUAGES
English and Patois

RELIGIONS
Protestant (Church of God 21.2%, Seventh Day Adventist 9%, Baptist 8.8%, Pentecostal 7.6%, Anglican 5.5%, Presbyterian 5%, Methodist 2.7%, United Church 2.7%, Brethren 1.1%, Jehovah's Witnesses 1.6%, Moravian 1.1%), 66.3%, Roman Catholic 4%, Rastafarianism 3.5%, other (including spiritual cults, e.g., Pocomania and Kumina) 26.2%

NATIONAL OR ETHNIC COMPOSITION
Black 90.9%, East Indian 1.3%, white 0.2%, Chinese 0.2%, mixed 7.3%, other 0.1%

DATE OF INDEPENDENCE OR CREATION
August 6, 1962

TYPE OF GOVERNMENT
Parliamentary democracy

TYPE OF STATE
Unitary state

TYPE OF LEGISLATURE
Bicameral parliament

DATE OF CONSTITUTION
August 6, 1962

DATE OF LAST AMENDMENT
1999

Jamaica is an independent unitary state and a parliamentary democracy with the queen of England as head of state. The legislative, executive, and judicial powers are separated.

Jamaica's long history is mostly unrecorded. The inhabitants who lived there longest died off over 300 years ago. The overwhelming majority of the population today has its roots in the forced migration of slaves from western Africa. Thus Jamaica's modern history is rooted in the exploitation of slavery and colonialism.

Jamaica began to emerge from colonial rule after World War II (1939–45). Arguably, with the British queen as head of state and the British Privy Council as final court of appeal, the country has still not achieved full independence. Nevertheless, it is gaining confidence in its ability to govern itself, while it seeks closer ties with its island neighbors in an effort to compete economically in the global market.

The founding story of Jamaica is quite different from those of former colonies that fought wars of independence. Jamaica's independence was achieved through convergence, not divergence, of Jamaican and British interests. Jamaica sought political independence as an assertion of national identity. Britain sought Jamaica's independence as part of its effort to unload its duties and responsibilities and shed the stigma of colonial empire. The Jamaican constitution was preceded by a political process in which Britain cooperated.

That Jamaica has a written and codified constitution demonstrates its participation in modern constitutionalism. That it was adopted by Parliament in Britain reveals a degree of ambiguity in the process of independence. Drafting a list of fundamental rights and freedoms showed an openness to non-British models. Keeping the British Privy Council as the highest court of appeal perhaps reveals a lack of self-confidence.

Both of the dominant political parties in Jamaica have discussed constitutional reform over the past 20 years. The current effort to become part of the Caribbean Court of Justice shows a willingness to take those steps. Jamaica plays a leadership role in the Caribbean on a number of fronts, particularly with the Caribbean Community (CARICOM), as it also seeks to discern how to pursue its national interests in geographical proximity to a political and economic hegemonic superpower.

CONSTITUTIONAL HISTORY

The earliest inhabitants of the island of Jamaica for whom records exist were the Arawak, also called Taino. They migrated from Venezuela and Guyana, working their way up through the Lesser Antilles to the Greater Antilles and reaching Jamaica around 650 C.E. Later on, the Carib tribe entered the region, also from the direction of South America. Fierce fighters and cannibals, they conquered their way north through the Lesser Antilles, enslaving the Arawak, who reportedly had no weapons and had not experienced war. The Carib had not reached Jamaica when Christopher Columbus arrived on May 3, 1494, during his second voyage to the New World.

Arawak villages were each composed of several family clans headed by a chief, called *cacique,* whose hereditary yet largely ceremonial title was passed down by primogeniture. Society was communal, and materialism seems to have been an alien concept—they gladly gave what gold they had to the gold-hungry Spaniards. Columbus described the Arawak as "honest and content with what they have ... peaceful and generous people."

Over 20 governors administered Jamaica for Spain over the next 150 years from the capital of Spanish Town. The duke of Veragua appointed the governors who ruled with the assistance of the *cabildo,* a council of nominated members, and the Catholic Church. Spain never developed Jamaica, considering it a provisioning station for the lucrative shipping trade between Spain and Central America. The Spaniards killed off the substantial Arawak population (some historians estimate it as high as 100,000) through hard labor, ill treatment, and European diseases. Realizing that Arawak slave labor was disappearing, the Spaniards began importing slaves from Africa in 1517.

In 1654 Oliver Cromwell devised the ill-fated "Grand Western Design" to destroy the Spanish trade monopoly in the Caribbean and sent Admiral William Penn (father of the founder of the U.S. state of Pennsylvania) and General Robert Venables to conquer the Caribbean. After the Spanish repulsed their efforts to take Hispaniola (present-day Haiti and Dominican Republic), the British settled for the weakly defended Jamaica. Before escaping to Cuba, the Spanish released their slaves and encouraged them to fight guerrilla warfare from the mountains. These Maroons (derived from the Spanish word *cimarrones,* meaning wild or untamed) fought fiercely to retain their newly found freedom. Eventually they signed a peace treaty in 1738 with the British in which, in return for peace and land, they agreed to return runaway slaves to their owners. To this day many Jamaicans think the Maroons sold out to the British instead of remaining a force for liberation.

Jamaica was caught in the middle of the European wars for the Caribbean, involving Britain, France, Spain, Portugal, and the Netherlands. Britain, because it was overextended and because the cost was low, encouraged and sponsored pirates to attack the Spanish. The British governor of Jamaica asked these buccaneers, who had formed the Confederacy of the Brethren of the Coast, to protect Jamaica. Based in Port Royal on Kingston Harbor, the pirates soon turned Port Royal into Jamaica's largest and wealthiest city with reportedly more brothels and ale houses than any other city on Earth. A massive earthquake in 1692 sent half of the city into the ocean, killing over 2,000 people.

Slavery and the plantation economy it supported reached their pinnacle around 1800, when about 21,000 whites ruled over 300,000 black slaves. The slaves were taken from many tribes on Africa's west coast, a majority of them Coromantee, Ibo, and Mandigo. Jamaica also served as a large slave market, as it supplied slaves to many of the Spanish islands after the English made peace with Spain. Jamaica experienced a number of slave revolts; the largest and last occurred in 1831 and was led by Sam Sharpe, an educated slave and lay preacher.

Slaves were set free unconditionally in 1838, toppling the plantation economy. However, the white plantocracy's political power remained, as free blacks had no political voice. By law, only titled property owners could vote, and blacks were routinely denied land claims by courts still run by white magistrates schooled in a plantation mentality.

Jamaican nationalism grew in the 20th century under leaders such as Marcus Garvey, who called for black self-reliance. However, independence was gained politically, not militarily. Britain's realization that it could no longer economically support its colonies was perhaps as important as Jamaica's pull for independence. After all, Norman Manley, the founder of the People's National Party, had stated in 1945 that he did not believe any island in the region could be an independent modern state.

In 1947, as a prelude to full independence, Britain granted much autonomy to Jamaica, even as a British colony under the jurisdiction of Parliament and the Crown. When Manley took power in 1955, he steered Jamaica into a Caribbean Federation, but Alexander Bustamante, founder of the Jamaican Labor Party, pressed for secession. In 1961, the voters supported Bustamante's position, and Jamaica withdrew from the federation, which promptly collapsed. A new constitution was drafted.

The new constitution was part of a law adopted by the British Parliament, not by a defiant group of founders breaking away from the mother country. The country remained in the Commonwealth and retained many legal, economic, cultural, and social ties with Britain.

FORM AND IMPACT OF THE CONSTITUTION

Jamaica's constitution is an act, taken before Parliament in England on July 24, 1962, and signed by the queen of England, which entered into force on August 6, 1962. It takes precedence over all other Jamaican laws. It addresses issues of citizenship, fundamental rights, the governor-general (appointed by the queen of England), Parliament, executive powers, the judiciary, finance, a public service commission and police service commission, and pension law.

BASIC ORGANIZATIONAL STRUCTURE

Jamaica is divided into three counties: Cornwall, Middlesex, and Surrey. The counties are subdivided into 12 parishes: Clarendon, Hanover, Manchester, Portland, Saint Ann, Saint Catherine, Saint Elizabeth, Saint James, Saint Mary, Saint Thomas, Trelawny, and Westmoreland. The latter subdivision also includes two contiguous corporate areas, Kingston and Saint Andrew.

Local government is administered by two bodies: elected members of parish councils and elected members of city or municipal councils presided over by an elected mayor.

LEADING CONSTITUTIONAL PRINCIPLES

Jamaica's system of government is a parliamentary democracy with a few colonial and monarchical components. The legislative, executive, and judicial powers are divided, in keeping with the principle of separation of powers and checks and balances. Government is based on the rule of law with the constitution, as interpreted by the British Privy Council, serving as the supreme law of the land. The prime minister and the cabinet effectively hold executive powers, although the British monarchy, through an appointed governor-general, carries a number of ceremonial duties. The constitution, through mechanisms such as a Judicial Services Commission, seeks to create an independent judiciary.

CONSTITUTIONAL BODIES

Jamaica's constitution creates a parliamentary democracy modeled on the British system. Jamaica remains within the British Commonwealth and reflects its English bias in that its titular head of state remains the British monarch, its highest court of appeal is the Privy Council in London, and its black speaker of Parliament wears a white wig and holds a gold scepter. The chief local bodies are the governor-general, the cabinet, Parliament, and the judiciary.

The Governor-General

The head of state for Jamaica, Queen Elizabeth II of England, is represented in Jamaica by a Jamaican-born governor-general appointed by the queen on the advice of the prime minister of Jamaica and a six-member Jamaican Privy Council. The governor-general's duties are largely ceremonial and include appointing the prime minister, who is always the leader of the majority party after each national election.

The Cabinet

Executive power resides with a cabinet appointed and led by the prime minister and responsible to Parliament. The cabinet is the principal instrument of government policy. Besides the prime minister, it consists of a minimum of 13 other ministers of government, who must be members of one of the two houses of Parliament. No more than four members of the cabinet may be members of the Senate; the minister of finance must be an elected member of the House of Representatives.

Parliament

Parliament consists of a bicameral legislature. A 60-member elected House of Representatives serves as the deliberative body for national legislation. The Senate is a nominated body of 21 members, of whom 13 are appointed by the prime minister and eight by the leader of the opposition.

The Lawmaking Process

The Senate's main function is to review legislation forwarded by the elected House of Representatives, which may override a Senate veto.

The Judiciary

The judiciary begins with specialized courts dealing with such matters as revenues, gun crime, traffic offenses, industrial disputes, and family law. The next higher level is the Resident Magistrates Courts, which exist in each parish. The next court, primarily of appeal, is the Supreme Court, followed by the Court of Appeal, which is the highest court on the island. However, the final court of appeal is the Privy Council in England—a controversial matter in Jamaica for many years. Jamaica participates in the efforts of the Caribbean Community (CARICOM) to create a Caribbean Court of Justice (CCJ) as a court of final appeal for the member countries. The Privy Council struck down as unconstitutional Jamaica's first attempt to make the CCJ the final court of appeal. It remains to be seen whether Jamaica can meet the Privy Council's requirements.

THE ELECTION PROCESS AND POLITICAL PARTICIPATION

All Jamaicans aged 18 and over are eligible to vote. Although a full parliamentary term is five years, the governor-general may call a national election at any time the prime minister requests; that usually occurs when timing seems propitious for the ruling party.

POLITICAL PARTIES

Jamaica has a multiparty system dominated by two political parties, the People's National Party (PNP), which was in power in 2005, and the Jamaica Labor Party (JLP). There are several minor parties including the National Democratic Movement and the communist Worker's Party of Jamaica.

The People's National Party was formed in 1938 under the leadership of Norman Manley, a barrister who headed the party for 31 years before his son, Michael, a journalist and trade unionist, took the reins. The PNP is a social democratic party, and when Michael Manley became prime minister in 1972 he tried to turn Jamaica into a democratic socialist nation. He initiated greater state control over the economy and developed closer ties to Cuba and other leftist third world states. The Reagan administration responded by cutting aid to Jamaica, encouraging foreign companies to withdraw investment, discouraging tourists from traveling there, and developing strategies to topple the Manley government. Michael Manley was considered a hero by the poorer classes, who benefited from his literacy campaign and socialist health care, and despised by the upper class, who took much of their capital out of Jamaica. Inflation went above 50 percent, foreign investors fled, unemployment and crime skyrocketed, and Jamaican society became increasingly polarized. These conditions laid the groundwork for a change in power.

The Jamaica Labor Party (JLP) was founded in 1943 by the labor leader Sir Alexander Bustamante, who, upon Jamaica's independence in 1962, was elected prime minister. Despite its name, the JLP is a conservative party with ties to the Bustamante Industrial Trade Union. In 1981, the Boston-born and Harvard-educated Edward Seaga of the JLP was elected prime minister. He inherited a country on the verge of bankruptcy and embroiled in domestic unrest. He initiated a privatization scheme, devaluation of the Jamaican dollar, and an austerity program. He severed ties with Cuba and restored close links with the United States, which in turn restored aid to Jamaica. However, his austerity program, particularly cuts in education and health care, and his association with gangs caused his popularity to wane.

In 1989 the voters returned Michael Manley, who had converted to free market economics, to the prime minister's office. He maintained Seaga's policies of deregulation and cooperation with the U.S. government until he stepped down for health-related reasons in 1992. He handed over control to his deputy, Percival James Patterson, who has since been elected in his own right three times.

CITIZENSHIP

Articles 3 to 12 of the Jamaican Constitution address Jamaican and Commonwealth citizenship. The three primary ways of acquiring Jamaican citizenship are being born in Jamaica, having a parent or spouse who is Jamaican, and proceeding through a process of naturalization.

FUNDAMENTAL RIGHTS

Chapter 3 of the Jamaican Constitution (Articles 13–26) delineates the fundamental rights and freedoms. The constitution grants every person in Jamaica the right to life, liberty, security of person, enjoyment of property, and protection of law; freedom of conscience, thought, and religion; freedom of expression, freedom of peaceful assembly and association, and respect for private and family life. In the criminal procedure area, the constitution prohibits deprivation of life or liberty absent criminal charges defined in law and guarantees a fair, speedy, and public trial before an independent and impartial court, with a presumption of innocence, legal representation, and reasonable time and facilities to prepare a defense. The constitution prohibits any laws from discriminating on the basis of race, place of origin, political opinion, color or creed.

According to the U.S. State Department, the government generally respects the human rights of its citizens. The problem areas include unlawful killings by security forces, mob violence and vigilante killings of those suspected of breaking the law, and abuse by police and prison guards of detainees and prisoners.

ECONOMY

Compared to that of most Caribbean islands, Jamaica's economy is highly developed. It has a vital financial sector with many international banks, a large skilled workforce, and a relatively broad-based economy. Nevertheless, it still struggles with poverty. The market economy is based largely on tourism, production of primary products (bauxite, aluminum, sugar, bananas, and coffee), and remittances. Other industries include textiles, agroprocessing, cement, and rum.

RELIGIOUS COMMUNITIES

The Jamaica constitution defines freedom of religion in greater detail than most constitutions. Freedom of religion includes the right to change one's religion or belief either alone or in community with others; the freedom to manifest and propagate one's religion in public or private, in worship, teaching, practice, and observance; freedom from being required to receive religious instruction or take part in any religious ceremony or observance at any place of education; freedom of any religious body from being required to change its constitution without the consent of its governing body; freedom of religious bodies to provide religious instruction for persons of that denomination whether or not they receive government subsidies; and freedom from being compelled to take an oath that is contrary to one's belief.

Jamaica claims to have the greatest number of churches per square mile of any country, a record to which the *Guinness Book of World Records* attests. In this deeply religious country, churches are more than places of worship—they serve as important social centers in Jamaica communities. Although the country is over 80 percent Christian, there are also revivalist cults such as Pocomania and Kumina as well as Rastafarianism.

MILITARY DEFENSE AND STATE OF EMERGENCY

Although Jamaica has no official army, navy or air force, the Jamaica Defense Force includes Ground Forces, a Coast Guard, and an Air Wing, all under the control of the executive branch of government. The Jamaica Defense Force is a well-armed, efficient military unit of some 2,500 service personnel. It was modeled after the West Indian Regiment of the British Army and now works closely with the U.S. Drug Enforcement Agency.

AMENDMENTS TO THE CONSTITUTION

Article 49 of the Jamaican constitution provides for two processes for amending the constitution depending on whether the provision(s) to be amended is entrenched or not. Entrenched provisions require a two-thirds vote in both houses of Parliament; unentrenched provisions require only a simple majority of both houses. The article lists the entrenched provisions, and all other provisions are considered unentrenched.

Perhaps the most controversial decision of the last 10 years was the Privy Council's ruling that the amendment of unentrenched provisions without a supermajority was unconstitutional because it affected rights established by entrenched provisions. At issue was the replacement of the Privy Council (an unentrenched provision) by the Caribbean Court of Justice as the final court of appeal for Jamaica.

PRIMARY SOURCES

Constitution in English: The Jamaican (Constitution) Order in Council 1962. Available online. URL: http://pbda.georgetown.edu/Constitutions/Jamaica/jam62.html. Accessed on August 29, 2005.

SECONDARY SOURCES

Clinton V. Black, *History of Jamaica.* Essex: Longman Group, 1999.

"The CIA World Factbook—Jamaica." Available online. URL: http://www.cia.gov/cia/publications/factbook/print/jm.html. Accessed on July 31, 2005.

Frank Cundall and Joseph L. Pietersz, *Jamaica under the Spaniards.* Kingston: Institute of Jamaica, 1919.

Harold A. McDougall, "Constitutional Form and Civil Society: The Case of Jamaica." *St. Thomas Law Review* 16 (2004): 423.

Simeon C. R. McIntosh, *Caribbean Constitutional Reform.* Kingston: Caribbean Law, 2002.

Fred Phillips, *Commonwealth Caribbean Constitutional Law.* London: Cavendish, 2002.

Selwyn Ryan, *The Judiciary and Governance in the Caribbean.* St. Augustine, Trinidad and Tobago: Multimedia Production Centre, School of Education, University of West Indies, 2001.

Stephen Vasciannie, *International Law and Selected Human Rights in Jamaica.* Kingston: Council of Legal Education, Norman Manley Law School, 2002.

U.S. Department of State, "Jamaica Country Report on Human Rights Practices—2004." Available online. URL: http://www.state.gov/g/drl/rls/hrrpt/2004/41766.htm. Accessed on August 11, 2005.

John C. Knechtle

JAPAN

At-a-Glance

OFFICIAL NAME
Japan

CAPITAL
Tokyo

POPULATION
127,333,002 (July 2004 est.)

SIZE
145,883 sq. mi. (377,835 sq. km)

LANGUAGES
Japanese

RELIGIONS
Observance of both Shinto and Buddhism 84%, other (including Christian 0.7%) 16%

NATIONAL OR ETHNIC COMPOSITION
Japanese 99%, other (Korean 511,262, Chinese 244,241, Brazilian 182,232, Filipino 89,851, other 237,914) 1%

DATE OF INDEPENDENCE OR CREATION
Uncertain (cohesive fifth-century kingdom suggested by ancient Chinese records)

TYPE OF GOVERNMENT
Constitutional monarchy with a parliamentary government

TYPE OF STATE
Centralist state

TYPE OF LEGISLATURE
Bicameral parliament

DATE OF CONSTITUTION
May 3, 1947

DATE OF LAST AMENDMENT
No amendment

The Japanese constitution was drafted under strong influence from the American occupation army immediately after World War II (1938–45). This constitution establishes the status of *tenno* (the reigning emperor of Japan), the principle of popular sovereignty, the renunciation of war, the bill of rights, the rule of law, and the separation of powers. Since the constitution authorizes the Supreme Court's judicial review of laws for constitutionality, which lower courts also exercise, courts may invalidate laws and government actions that contradict the constitution.

The *tenno*, or emperor, is today the symbol of the Japanese people; he had sovereign power before World War II. The constitution offers him no substantial political power, although he plays an important role in enacting laws. The prime minister is the head of the executive branch and is the central political figure. The prime minister must be a member of the Diet, the bicameral legislature. Legislators are elected by free, equal, general, direct, and secret votes of the people.

The Japanese constitution guarantees religious freedom, among other rights. Separation of state and religion is prescribed. The constitution provides for a free market economy, securing property rights. It renounces war and explicitly proscribes formal armed forces. However, the Japanese government maintains a self-defense force (Jieitai) to protect the Japanese people, property, and lands. The self-defense forces have assisted United Nations peacekeeping operations in Cambodia, Mozambique, Rwanda, the Golan Heights, East Timor, Angola, and El Salvador.

CONSTITUTIONAL HISTORY

Few authentic records exist to document the beginnings of Japanese history. Legendary nonverified accounts suggest that in 660 B.C.E. Japan was founded by a descendant of the gods. Ancient Chinese records show there were several kingdoms in Japan as early as the first century.

A strong and cohesive kingdom, ruled by the great king (*daioh*), governed the main part of the land around the fifth century.

The power and sophistication of Chinese civilization at that time naturally drew Japan under its influence, and the great king asked the Chinese court to confirm his royal title. The Chinese acknowledged his status as legitimate ruler over Japan and its representative in its relationship with China. Over the centuries, Chinese and Koreans fleeing to Japan from revolutions and invasions introduced the Chinese character, thought, and legal system to their adopted country. The emergence of a strong and unified state in China (Sui dynasty) stimulated the creation of a unified Japanese state ruled by the *tenno,* a descendant of the great king, in the late sixth century.

The first written law was issued in 604; it prescribed the basic organization of the government. A complete legal system, including administrative law, criminal law, military law, family law, and tax law, was established in 701. Modeled on the Chinese legal and government system, it made provisions for local government, roads connecting the capital and other cities, and a governing system that relied on the written word. The law decreed that all land and people belonged to the *tenno;* private property was denied. A class system placed *tenno* and his family at the top, with nobles, commoners, and slaves underneath. Although the sovereign power belonged to the *tenno,* in practice he had to consult noblemen to make political decisions.

This political system broke down in the ninth century, as noblemen lessened the gap between the classes by giving their daughters in marriage to *tenno.* Exploiting struggles within the *tenno* family, noblemen exercised their power to choose a new *tenno,* who ascended the throne in his childhood. The young age of the *tenno* allowed his grandfather to grasp power easily.

The denial of private landownership began to break down, partly in order to populate and cultivate newly opened land. By the 10th century, both the *tenno* and noblemen began to possess land of their own. Despite government efforts, the number of private estates grew fast, and thanks to powerful noblemen these estates became exempt from tax. Those who cultivated previously uncultivated land remained free of taxes and government control, although they were required to donate gifts to the noblemen. In order to protect their land, owners of private estates armed themselves. These armed landowners were probably the ancestors of the warrior class, the samurai.

In 1192, the samurai began to rule Japan under their head, the shogun, who used The *tenno* as a figurehead. The imperial family and the noblemen retained their status without political power, under the tight supervision of the new government, the Bakufu or shogunate.

The government system was based on feudalism. Although the shogun was the leader of the samurai, he did not have exclusive power to rule the country. Feudal lords retained strong autonomy in their territories. In the 14th century, the authority of the Bakufu was limited to arbitrating succession disputes within samurai families. Strong leaders arose in the 16th century and tried to build a centralist military state over the whole country. The strongest, the famous Oda Nobunaga, was assassinated before he could succeed, but after his death the Tokugawa Bakufu managed to implement his goals.

Samurai-controlled government continued through the middle of the 19th century. The last ruling shogun, Tokugawa Yoshinobu, gave up sovereign power in 1867. In that era, Western countries with colonialist goals and impressive military support forced Japan to open up to international trade via one-sided treaties that denied Japan authority to set tariffs and jurisdiction over foreign criminals. The shock caused by Western, especially American, warships, with their overwhelming power, made the Japanese people aware of the many defects of the Tokugawa government. They believed a more centralist state could respond better to the military emergency. The shogunate gave way to the Meiji Restoration of a centralized state, restoring the sovereign power to *tenno.* The new government, controlled in fact by former low-ranked samurai, had to negotiate with Western countries to amend the unfair trade treaties. They realized that Japan would have to establish a Western-type legal system, to include constitutionalism, human rights guarantees, and administration by law, for that purpose. This was the chief purpose behind the Meiji constitution of 1889.

The Meiji constitution was modeled on the era's German constitutional monarchy. The *tenno* possessed sovereign power, which the cabinet ministers were obliged to support. Human rights, such as freedom of speech, religious liberty, and freedom of assembly and association, were protected, but their exercise was limited by law. The independence of the judiciary was guaranteed, and there was a special court for administrative disputes. The *tenno* was the commander in chief, with no input from the legislature and cabinet ministers except for military budget. The *tenno* also had the power to issue imperial ordinances in an emergency and to proclaim martial law. A more democratic system was established at the beginning of the 20th century, but the continued political power of the *tenno* helps explain how the Japanese army escaped political and civil control before World War II (1939–45). Militarism in Japan produced total defeat in that war.

Surrendering to the Allied powers in 1945, after they dropped nuclear bombs at Hiroshima and Nagasaki, Japan accepted the Potsdam Declaration, which provided conditions for ending the war. The declaration authorized the Allied powers, predominantly the Americans, to occupy Japan until it had created a peaceful and responsible government that obeyed the freely expressed will of the Japanese people. Led by General Douglas MacArthur, the General Headquarters of the Allied Powers was given the task of establishing such a government. It abolished the Japanese military, reformed the system of landownership, and dissolved huge business conglomerates.

The Japanese government began to work on amending the constitution in line with the declaration. Its draft, which retained *tenno* as sovereign, was considered by MacArthur too conservative to make Japan a part of the free world. He ordered his staff to prepare a more democratic and liberal draft to establish a peaceful and responsible government. This version limited the status of *tenno,* renounced war, and ended all official class privileges. The Japanese government accepted these provisions and presented the draft to the legislature, which had in the meantime been elected (by women as well as men, for the first time). After a few minor changes, the Japanese constitution was promulgated in the name of *tenno* on November 3, 1946, and went into effect on May 3, 1947. The American occupation ended in 1952. Even though Japan had recovered its sovereignty, it decided not to change the constitution. In fact, not a single amendment has been made to it.

FORM AND IMPACT OF THE CONSTITUTION

The Japanese constitution is a written constitution, codified in a single document. It is "the supreme law of the nation and no law, ordinance, imperial prescript or other Act of government, or part thereof, contrary to the provisions hereof, shall have legal force or validity." The constitution does not make any statement on the validity of international law; international law must be in accordance with the constitution to be applicable within Japan.

The constitution of Japan can be seen as a product of the revolutionary changes in Japanese society immediately after World War II, helping the Japanese people shape a new sense of human rights and democratic society. This can be seen especially in Article 9, "the renunciation of war" clause.

BASIC ORGANIZATIONAL STRUCTURE

Japan is a centralist state with 47 prefectures and some 3,000 cities. The constitution provides for local government autonomy, and each prefecture and city has its own legislature and administration. While the central state has adopted a parliamentary system, the political system in the localities is more like a presidential system: Governor and mayor are elected directly by the citizens; however, they too must either resign or dissolve the local legislature when it passes a no confidence resolution. The local legislatures are unicameral assemblies. Elections are held to choose local legislators, governors, and mayors every four years.

Although local governments enjoy some autonomy, the central state has certain powers over local governments defined by law. There is often no clear line separating the two jurisdictions, except that the judicial, diplomatic, and military powers belong to the national state. A local legislature may levy taxes for its own budget and impose special criminal provisions that apply only to its region. Some local governments, most of which are cities, allow referenda on special and general issues.

LEADING CONSTITUTIONAL PRINCIPLES

The system of government in Japan is a constitutional monarchy with a parliamentary government. There is a strong division of the executive, legislative, and judicial powers, based on checks and balances. The judiciary is independent of political parties, and courts have judicial review of statutes.

There are several leading principles in the Japanese constitution. First, the sovereign power belongs to the people of Japan, who alone determine the nation's political decision. This emphasis contrasts sharply with the Meiji constitution, which gave *tenno* sovereign power.

The *tenno* system is the second principle. Under the constitution, *tenno* has no political power or authority. However, he participates in the lawmaking process. He appoints the prime minister as designated by parliament, the Diet, and the chief justice of the Supreme Court as designated by the cabinet. *Tenno* performs the following acts with the advice and approval of the cabinet: He promulgates amendments of the constitution, laws, cabinet orders, and treaties; convenes the Diet; dissolves the House of Representatives; proclaims the general elections of members of the Diet; certifies the appointment and dismissal of ministers of state and other officials as provided for by law; attests general and special amnesties, commutation of punishment, reprieve, and restoration of rights; awards honors; attests instruments of ratification and other diplomatic documents as provided for by law; receives foreign ambassadors and ministers; and performs ceremonial functions. All property of the *tenno* and his family, the imperial household, belongs to the state. All expenses of the *tenno* and his family are appropriated by the Diet in the budget. No property can be given to or received by *tenno* and his family; nor can any gifts be made therefrom, without the authorization of the Diet. With few exceptions, the emperors have been male, but an amendment to the Imperial House Law makes inheritance now hereditary, regardless of gender.

The constitution provides for the renunciation of war and the abandonment of military forces. Because of the hardship Japan caused to other countries and underwent itself during World War II, the constitution announces the determination that Japan will not invade or attack neighboring countries and will maintain world peace forever. As the cold war continued, however, Japan allied itself with the United States and enjoyed America's protection. Japan has also gradually built up a defensive armed force.

The Japanese constitution adopts an indirect, representative democracy, with no provision for national referendum. Some local governments allow referenda to decide local issues. Every person may sue for redress, as provided for by law, from the national or a local government, in a case when he or she has suffered damage through an illegal act of any public official.

The government is required by the constitution to guarantee a minimal standard of living to the people in a healthy and decent environment. The government and religious bodies must be definitively separated. The constitution includes provisions that guarantee the rule of law.

CONSTITUTIONAL BODIES

Apart from *tenno,* discussed previously, the political bodies described in the Japanese constitution are the parliament, called the Diet; the prime minister; and the cabinet ministers. The Supreme Court and its lower courts also play an important role in the constitutional system.

The Diet (Parliament)

The Diet is composed of the House of Councillors (Sangiin) and the House of Representatives (Shugi-in). The House of Councillors has 242 seats. The members are elected for six-year terms, half reelected every three years. The House of Representatives has 480 seats. The members are elected for four-year terms.

The Japanese constitution defines the Diet as "the highest organ of state power," with sole lawmaking power and the authority to designate the prime minister. The Diet also has the power to approve international treaties, to determine the budget, to conduct investigations of the government, and to set up an impeachment court from among the members of both houses for the purpose of trying judges against whom removal proceedings have been instituted.

If the House of Councillors disagrees with the House of Representatives on treaty or budget issues, and a joint committee fails to reach agreement, the House of Representatives prevails.

The House of Representatives may pass a no confidence resolution against the cabinet. In such a case, the cabinet must either resign en masse or dissolve the House of Representatives within 10 days. In the latter case, the general election for the House of Representatives must be held within 40 days of the date of dissolution. The House of Councillors suspends its session while its counterpart is dissolved. However, the cabinet may in times of national emergency convene the House of Councillors for an emergency session.

An ordinary session of the Diet is convened once every year, usually starting in January and lasting 150 days. The cabinet, by its own demand or the request of a quarter or more of the total members of either house, may convene extraordinary sessions of the Diet.

Members of both houses receive appropriate annual payment from the national treasury; the amount in 2002 amounted to 21 million yen (approximately $190,000). Members of both houses are exempt from arrest while the Diet is in session, except in a case of flagrante delicto outside the house; any members arrested before the session are freed during the term of the session upon demand of the house. A member of either house may be arrested if the house so allows on the demand of the cabinet, on the basis of a court request. Members of either house may not be held liable outside the house for speeches, debates, or votes cast within.

The Cabinet

The cabinet consists of the prime minister and the ministers of state, who are appointed by the prime minister. The total number of cabinet members must be less than 17, and a majority of them must be chosen from among the members of the Diet. The prime minister and other ministers of state must be civilians.

Executive power belongs to the cabinet, although it is collectively responsible to the Diet. The cabinet, therefore, must either resign en masse or dissolve the House of Representatives when the House of Representatives passes a no confidence resolution.

The authority of the cabinet is as follows: to provide advice and approval for the official acts of *tenno,* to administer the law faithfully, to conduct affairs of state, to manage foreign affairs, to conclude treaties (prior, or in some cases subsequent, approval of the Diet is required), to administer the civil service in accordance with standards established by law, to prepare the budget and present it to the Diet, to enact cabinet orders in order to execute the provisions of this constitution and of the law (although the orders cannot prevent penal provisions authorized by the law from being applied), and to decide on general amnesty, special amnesty, commutation of punishment, reprieve, and restoration of rights. In addition, the cabinet designates the chief justice of the Supreme Court and has the power to appoint the justices of the Supreme Court and the judges of the lower courts, to convene extraordinary sessions of the Diet, to convene the House of Councillors in an emergency session in times of national emergency, to submit bills and reports on general national affairs or foreign relations to the Diet, to exercise control and supervision over various administrative branches, to expand a reserve fund for the budget, and to submit final accounts of state expenditures and revenues to the Diet.

The cabinet exercises its power through cabinet meetings, which are regularly held on Tuesday and Friday mornings. An extraordinary meeting is held occasionally.

The Prime Minister

As the head of cabinet, the prime minister organizes it. He or she appoints or removes the ministers. Representing the cabinet, the prime minister submits bills, reports on general national affairs and foreign relations to the Diet, and exercises control and supervision over various administrative branches. All laws and cabinet orders are signed by the prime minister and countersigned by the relevant minister. Without the consent of the prime minister, a minister is not subject to legal action during his or her tenure of office.

The Lawmaking Process

As noted, the constitution of Japan confers lawmaking power on the Diet. However, local governments also have the power to enact their own ordinances within the limit of the law.

The authority to submit a bill to the Diet belongs to members of the Diet and the cabinet. At least 20 members must join to submit a bill to the House of Representatives (50 if it entails expenditure). The corresponding minimums for the House of Councillors are 10 and 20. When legislators draw up a draft bill, the legislative bureau of the initiating house checks conformity with existing laws and correctness of words and letters. Legislators then hand a draft to a political party represented in the Diet. Without a party's support, the bill goes no further; with party support, it is submitted for consideration.

A bill to be introduced by the cabinet is drafted by the ministry in charge, after consultations with other ministries and with the ruling political party(ies). In addition, the ministry may seek the opinion of advisory councils or hold public hearings. The draft is examined by the cabinet legislation bureau, which checks conformity with the constitution and other laws, its appropriateness, and correctness of words and letters. Afterward, the cabinet decides whether or not to authorize the prime minister to submit the bill to the Diet.

When a bill is submitted to either house, the Speaker of the House of Representatives or the president of the House of Councillors refers it to an appropriate committee, which conducts its own examination and decides whether or not to send the bill to a plenary session of the house.

A plenary session cannot conduct business unless one-third or more of the total membership is present. Once a quorum is present, a majority is enough to pass the bill and send it to the other house, where it undergoes the same procedures in committee and plenary sessions.

A bill becomes a law on passage by both houses. Even if it is rejected by the House of Councillors, the bill can be reapproved by the House of Representatives, by a majority of two-thirds or more of the members present. Failure by the House of Councillors to take final action within 60 days after receipt of a bill passed by the House of Representatives, time in recess excepted, may constitute a rejection of the bill and trigger a revote by the representatives.

The leader of the house that finally approves the bill then submits it via the cabinet to *tenno,* who formally promulgates a law. Promulgation must be done within 30 days by publication in an official gazette. The publication is necessary for enforcement of a law.

The Judiciary

Thanks to the adoption of French and German law at the beginning of the Meiji era, it is not surprising to find a civil law system embedded in the Japanese courts. During the U.S. occupation after World War II, the General Headquarters of the Allied Forces managed to Americanize some aspects of the legal system, especially in the constitution, criminal procedures, labor law, and family law.

The judiciary is independent of political power. As the constitution prescribes: "All judges shall be independent in the exercise of their conscience and shall be bound only by this constitution and the laws." Therefore, "judges shall not be removed except by public impeachment unless judicially declared mentally or physically incompetent to perform official duties." An impeachment court for removing judges may be set up in the Diet, formed by members of both houses. In theory, a Supreme Court justice may also be removed by referendum at the first general election after the justice's appointment, and every 10 years thereafter, but no justice of the Supreme Court has ever been removed by this method. Retirement age is 65 for ordinary judges and 70 for justices of the Supreme Court.

The Supreme Court, composed of a chief justice and 14 justices, is the final court of appeals in all cases, including administrative cases. Executive agencies may make decisions on administrative cases, but the decisions can be reviewed by courts. The Supreme Court also exercises judicial review to determine the constitutionality of any law, order, regulation, or government act. The court considers only questions of law.

The Supreme Court is responsible for nominating judges to lower courts, who are then appointed by the cabinet. The Supreme Court also has some power to set judicial procedures, although most procedures are legislated. The court also decides matters relating to attorneys, the internal discipline of the courts, and the administration of judicial affairs.

The Supreme Court is divided into two benches: the Grand Bench and the Petty Benches. The Grand Bench, with all 15 justices attending, is required when the court reviews for the first time the constitutionality of law, order, regulation, or government act; when the court recognizes a law, order, regulation, or government act as unconstitutional; or when the court overrides its own precedence in a similar case.

Each of the three Petty Benches is composed of five justices. The Supreme Court selects law clerks from among judges of lower courts; they work for the entire court, rather than for an individual justice.

The judicial system is unitary. Below the Supreme Court are eight high courts, which have appellate jurisdiction in both civil cases, in which they review questions of law and fact, and criminal cases, in which they mainly review questions of law. Fifty district courts provide the venues for most trials in general cases. In addition, 50 family courts handle family problems and juvenile delinquency cases. At the lowest level, 438 summary courts in cities, towns, and villages throughout the country (as of August 2000) have original jurisdiction over minor civil claims (not exceeding 1.4 million yen [approximately $12,700]), criminal offenses punishable by fines or other light penalties, minor theft and embezzlement, and conciliation proceedings for everyday disputes among citizens.

THE ELECTION PROCESS

Japanese above the age of 20 have the right to vote. They must be over 25 to run for a seat in the Diet or the office of local legislator or mayor. To be a councillor or governor of a prefecture, a candidate should be above the age of 30. *Tenno* and his family do not have these rights; nor do adult wards or those convicted of serious crimes. For certain criminals who have committed bribery, there is a five-year waiting period before electoral rights are restored.

The Japanese election system is based on five principles: popular election, direct election, one person one vote, free election, and secret voting. Therefore, there are no voting limits based on race, sex, economic status, or education. As of 2005, voters had to write the name of the candidate or party by hand. An electronic voting system caused serious problems at a local election in 2003, and thus it is unlikely to be introduced in national elections.

Parliamentary Elections

A general election for all members of the House of Representatives is held every four years, unless the house is dissolved earlier. Half the members of the House of Councillors are up for election every three years.

Of the 480 seats in the House of Representatives, 300 are filled in single-seat constituencies, and 180 seats are chosen by proportional representation from party lists in 11 regional blocs. To contest the regional seats, a political party must have five or more members in the Diet or must have won 2 percent or more of the votes in the most recent Diet election. Thus, each voter casts two ballots. A candidate can run for both a single-seat constituency and a regional party list in the same election.

Of the 121 seats available in each election to the House of Councillors, 73 seats are in single-seat constituency and 48 in proportional representation. For this house, a candidate may run in both categories.

POLITICAL PARTIES

The Japanese constitution does not explicitly provide for political parties, but a vigorous multiparty system has been in effect since the start of constitutional government in the middle of the Meiji era, with an interruption during World War II.

From the perspective of the constitution, a political party is simply a private association that enjoys the freedom of association clause. There is not even a comprehensive law governing the parties, though some laws have acknowledged them. The Supreme Court has recognized political parties as "important organs of parliamentary democracy."

Parties that have five or more members in the Diet or have won 2 percent or more of the votes at the most recent Diet election are financially supported by the government. Each party's subsidy is proportionate to its number of Diet members and the number of votes it won. The annual subsidy is more than 30 trillion yen (approximately $272 million). The parties can also receive contributions from individuals, companies, and interest groups, which cannot exceed 30 million yen (approximately $272,000) per party per year.

CITIZENSHIP

Anyone born to a Japanese parent or parents, no matter where, is a Japanese citizen. In addition, any minor whose parent has married a Japanese citizen or of whom the parent admits paternity acquires citizenship automatically.

A foreigner residing legally in Japan for five years or more who has no criminal record and is legally competent in his or her homeland may be naturalized with official approval. Those who marry Japanese citizens or Japanese-born Koreans or Chinese may be naturalized under more indulgent rules. Since dual citizenship is denied, a person who becomes Japanese must abandon his or her previous citizenship. A Japanese citizen who has foreign citizenship must choose between the two at the age of 22.

The constitution of Japan guarantees the freedom to give up citizenship. Those who seek to renounce Japanese nationality must first acquire the nationality of another nation.

FUNDAMENTAL RIGHTS

The Japanese constitution guarantees various kinds of fundamental rights. Traditional rights, such as free speech or religious freedom, as well as so-called social rights, are protected, including the right to education and the right to work. The constitution also guarantees labor unions the right to organize, collectively bargain with an employer, and strike.

As a first principle, the Japanese constitution states that the right to life, liberty, and the pursuit of happiness must be considered paramount in legislation and all other governmental actions. Under this provision, people have a general right to decide matters themselves to develop human dignity. Personal liberty, freedom of thought and conscience, freedom of assembly and association, academic freedom, freedom to choose and change one's residence and to choose one's occupation, freedom to move to a foreign country and to abandon one's nationality, and property rights are also protected.

The constitution contains an equal protection clause. It bars discrimination in political, economic, or social relations based on race, creed, sex, social status, or family origin. It also provides that both wife and husband have equal rights to maintain their marriage with mutual cooperation. The constitution emphasizes individual dignity and the essential equality of the sexes on issues concerning choice of spouse, property rights, inheritance, choice of domicile, divorce, and other matters pertaining to marriage and the family.

The right to petition and access to the courts are also protected. The constitution allows every person to sue the government at any level in the case when he or she has suffered damage through an illegal act of any official. A procedural due process clause is included, as well as precise provisions concerning the rights of criminal defendants.

The constitution also addresses the duties of the Japanese nation: to work, to send one's children to school until they complete compulsory education, and to pay taxes. The duty to work carries no sanction, since obligatory labor conflicts with the prohibition of involuntary servitude.

The Supreme Court has held that many of the fundamental human rights contained in the constitution apply equally to aliens living in Japan. The rights that are thought not to apply to foreigners are the freedom to enter Japan, the right to vote, the freedom to engage in political activities, and social rights generally. The freedom to enter Japan, however, does apply to some people born in Japan, mainly to Chinese and Korean parents or grandparents who were formerly Japanese until 1945 and have remained in Japan since.

The rights guaranteed by the constitution are not fully applied to the *tenno* and his family. Since the *tenno* has no political authority, he and his family may not engage in political activities or even vote. Nor may they receive or give property or money without the authorization of the Diet, to preserve the *tenno*'s neutrality on all matters. The *tenno* and his family are not free to seek any other occupation or to divest themselves of Japanese nationality.

A corporation as a legal person is allowed to enjoy certain applicable constitutional rights. Even the freedom to engage in political activities is recognized as a right of corporations.

Impact and Functions of Fundamental Rights

For Japanese citizens, the guarantee of human rights is one of the fundamental principles of the constitution. These rights are conferred as eternal and inviolable, to be maintained through the constant endeavors of the people, who must refrain from any abuse of these freedoms. The Japanese nation should also be respected as are individuals.

With respect to equal protection, the Japanese constitution does not provide for affirmative action to achieve substantial equality between men and women. Many commentators interpret the equal protection clause as requiring equal opportunity and conditions, *not* equal results.

Some commentators have called for constitutional recognition of a right to a good natural environment. However, the courts have not recognized constitutional protection for this value.

The liberal freedoms prescribed in the constitution are regarded as concrete—citizens may sue the government if it infringes these rights. Social rights, by contrast, are understood as abstract. They are not actualized unless the government has established a system to embody them, and even then, they cannot be used to sue the state. For example, the constitution recognizes the right to a minimal standard of living in healthy and decent circumstances. This right is embodied by government programs. The government defines the minimal standards. Thus, citizens cannot sue to compel the government to make their living accord with this standard.

Constitutional rights are defined mainly as protections against government abuses. They do not generally apply to instances in which a private person infringes upon another person's right. However, there are some exceptions. Labor unions, for example, have explicit rights in the constitution to organize, collectively bargain with employers, and go on strike; private employers are not allowed to deny those rights. Although most of the constitutional rights are not applied to private relations, the constitutional values are taken into account when a civil law is applied to a civil case.

Limitations to Fundamental Rights

The constitution makes clear that human rights are not fully protected in every circumstance. It explicitly calls on citizens to refrain from abusing their rights; the rights are guaranteed only if they are exercised within the bounds of the "public interest." Public interest includes the following: the "self-limitation of human rights," in which people must refrain from exercising their rights when they infringe on the rights of others; the state's obligation to protect the nation's life, health, and safety and eliminate social harms; and an affirmative state policy such as protecting social minorities and providing economic safeguards for the poor.

Many commentators have called on Japanese courts to apply a test that was elaborated by the United States Supreme Court, to judge whether laws or state actions impair a plaintiff's human rights. A similar test has indeed been applied in a few cases in Japanese courts. However, Japanese courts prefer to impose a "balancing test," weighing the interest advanced by the law or government action against an interest advanced if the law or action is *not* applied.

ECONOMY

The Japanese constitution guarantees the right to own or to hold property. It is understood that this implies a system of private ownership. Therefore, Japan cannot be a communist or socialist state under the constitution.

Property rights are defined by laws to conform to the public interest. Governments may take private property for public use upon just compensation. It is controversial whether "just" implies total or reasonable compensation. The Japanese Supreme Court has held that compensation must be total if a government taking is for an ordinary purpose such as expanding a road or building an airport; it need only be reasonable if the taking is based on a broad policy purpose such as land reform.

In addition to the right to work, the Japanese constitution provides a right to engage in business, as well as a right to establish a company or a corporation, which is part of freedom of association. The freedom to choose and change one's residence, to choose one's occupation, and to move to a foreign country is also constitutionally protected.

The constitution is silent as to the government's authority to control land, natural resources, and the means of production. The national government used to run the national railroad corporation and the tobacco company and still operates postal services, including retail banking. The government also may take over a company in bankruptcy to prevent large economic losses.

RELIGIOUS COMMUNITIES

The Japanese constitution guarantees religious liberty, including the freedom to form religious bodies. Religious bodies have the right to exercise and propagate their religious beliefs. Religious bodies that meet the requirements to be a corporation under general law can be incorporated. Religious bodies are allowed to possess property, especially land.

The constitution provides separation of religion and the state. The state and its organs must refrain from religious education or any other religious activity. No religious body receives any privileges from the state or exercises any political authority. There must be no established state religion in Japan. No public money or other property can be expended for the use, benefit, or maintenance of any religious body.

Despite the constitutional separation of religion and the state, some relations between the two are allowed. Government offices or facilities may display symbols that have minor religious significance such as a Christmas tree or Kadomatsu, a Japanese traditional decoration usually set up on New Year's Day. In one case, the Supreme Court ruled that it is constitutional for a local government to perform a religious ceremony at the groundbreaking of a city gymnasium.

The autonomy, independence, and self-determination of religious bodies are guaranteed. The courts may not interfere in the internal affairs of a religious body unless they concern individual liberties or the public interest.

MILITARY DEFENSE AND STATE OF EMERGENCY

A unique feature of the Japanese constitution is its provision renouncing war. To protect this renunciation, the constitution states that Japan must never maintain armed forces.

The clause has been the source of controversy over decades: Does Japan, as a nation, have the right of self-defense? A strict reading of the clause might find that it does not; however, the government has long considered it does. Using a more lenient interpretation, reinforced by U.S. pressure during the cold war, the government decided to establish the self-defense forces in 1950, organized as Jiei-tai in 1954. In short, the Japanese government has decided that the constitution does not deprive Japan, as a nation, of the right of self-defense.

The prime minister is in practice the commander in chief, although the constitution remains silent on this point. The minister of defense has jurisdiction over the administration of the self-defense forces. As the constitution expressly states, the prime minister and the minister of defense must be civilians to assure civilian control over the self-defense forces.

The self-defense forces would be sent into action against military attack by order of the prime minister with the permission of the Diet. In addition, the self-defense forces may act when the police force cannot maintain internal order or when a natural disaster has occurred. In those cases, the self-defense forces are sent into action by the order of the prime minister or at the request of the governors.

There is no compulsory draft in Japan. Furthermore, the government has suggested that conscription would constitute unconstitutional involuntary service under the personal liberty clause of the constitution.

Japan has concluded a treaty for mutual cooperation and security with the United States. Under this treaty, the United States must defend Japan when Japan is attacked militarily by another country. On the basis of the treaty, the United States has placed military bases in Japan.

As the only nation bombed with nuclear weapons, Japan has rigidly maintained a policy that the country shall not hold, produce, or import nuclear weapons. Japan has joined international treaties to prevent nuclear, chemical, and biological weapon proliferation and to ban landmines.

The self-defense forces may take part in the peacekeeping operations formed by the United Nations and has done so in Cambodia, Mozambique, Rwanda, the Golan Heights, East Timor, Angola, and El Salvador since 1992, despite arguments that such peacekeeping operations go beyond the definition of "self-defense" and may be unconstitutional. The administration, in response, points to the constitution's stress on international cooperation as justification for joining United Nations operations. In 2001, the government explicitly amended the law to allow the self-defense forces to join peacekeeping forces.

The Japanese constitution is silent with respect to the state of national emergency, and Japan has not passed any laws on the issue until recently. In 2003 and 2004, the Diet enacted a series of laws that define the role of the government in the state of national emergency. The laws do not authorize a military administration. The people are asked to cooperate with the government in a state of emergency, but the extent to which human rights might be limited is not clear.

AMENDMENTS TO THE CONSTITUTION

In the 60 years since adoption of the Japanese constitution, not a single amendment has been approved. The prescribed process is fairly difficult: Any amendment must first be approved by the Diet by two-thirds votes of all members of each house. It is then submitted to a national referendum, in which it must receive a majority. *Tenno* then promulgates the amendment in the name of the Japanese people.

The constitution does not specify any clause as unchangeable. Nevertheless, there is a strong argument that certain fundamental principles that constitute the essential identity of the constitution cannot be amended. The argument is that the constitution only authorizes amendments, not a new constitution, which would result if fundamental principles were substantially changed. These principles would include popular sovereignty, the renunciation of war, guarantees of human rights, the rule of law, and the separation of powers.

Recently, however, several major political parties have proposed an amendment draft that targets the re-nunciation of war clause. The draft would allow Japan to maintain armed forces more openly.

PRIMARY SOURCES

Constitution in English. Available online. URL: http://www.kantei.go.jp/foreign/constitution_and_government/the_constitution_of_japan.html. Accessed on September 12, 2005.

Constitution in Japanese: *Nihonkoku Kenpo.* Available online. URL: http://www.ndl.go.jp/constitution/etc/j01.html. Accessed on September 26, 2005.

SECONDARY SOURCES

Lawrence W. Beer and John M. Maki, *From Imperial Myth to Democracy: Japan's Two Constitutions, 1889–2002.* Boulder: University Press of Colorado, 2002.

The Constitutional Case Law of Japan, 1970 through 1990. Seattle: University of Washington Press, 1996.

Kyoko Inoue, *MacArthur's Japanese Constitution.* Chicago: University of Chicago Press, 1991.

Japan—a Country Study. Washington, D.C.: United States Government Printing Office.

Percy R. Luney Jr. and Kazuyuki Takahashi, eds., *Japanese Constitutional Law.* Tokyo: University of Tokyo Press, 1993.

United Nations, "Core Document Forming Part of the Reports of States Parties: Japan" (HRI/CORE/1/Add.111), 11 December 2000. Available online. URL: http://www.unhchr.ch/tbs/doc.nsf. Accessed on August 15, 2005.

Asaho Mizushima and Toshiaki Fukushima, "Constitutional Law." *Waseda Bulletin of Comparative Law* 21 (2001): 68–78.

Eiichiro Takahata

JORDAN

At-a-Glance

OFFICIAL NAME
Hashemite Kingdom of Jordan

CAPITAL
Amman

POPULATION
5,906,760 (2006)

SIZE
35,637 sq. mi. (92,300 sq. km)

LANGUAGES
Arabic (official), English widely understood

RELIGIONS
Sunni Muslim 92%, Christian (majority Greek Orthodox, but some Greek and Roman Catholics, Syrian Orthodox, Coptic Orthodox, Armenian Orthodox, and Protestant denominations) 6%, other (several small Shia Muslim and Druze populations) 2%

NATIONAL OR ETHNIC COMPOSITION
Arab 98%, Circassian 1%, Armenian 1%

DATE OF INDEPENDENCE OR CREATION
May 25, 1946 (from League of Nations mandate under British administration)

TYPE OF GOVERNMENT
Constitutional monarchy

TYPE OF STATE
Unitary state

TYPE OF LEGISLATURE
Bicameral parliament

DATE OF CONSTITUTION
January 8, 1952

DATE OF LAST AMENDMENT
January 9, 1984

Jordan's system of government is "parliamentary, with a hereditary constitutional monarchy." The written constitution of 1952 states that the nation is the source of all powers. It is complemented by the 1990 National Charter, which represents a political agreement between the king and the leaders of the main political groups. The king is vested with broad executive and legislative powers; however, there is a system of checks and balances. Jordan is a centralist state, divided into 12 governorates.

The king is both head of state and chief executive. He appoints the prime minister and the cabinet. The National Assembly, consisting of a Senate and a House of Representatives, has the power to override the monarch's veto, and cabinet ministers are responsible to the House of Representatives.

Judges are constitutionally independent in the exercise of their functions. Although the National Charter calls for a constitutional court, this has not yet materialized. Legislative acts may undergo judicial review by the High Tribunal and a Special Tribunal consisting of the highest civil court judges and an administrative official.

The National Charter established a multiparty system in exchange for the parties' acceptance of the constitution and the monarchy. The constitution provides for guarantees of both first- and second-generation human rights. The constitutional economic system can be characterized as a social market economy. Islam is the religion of the state. Emergency regulations that had preserved the status quo for more than 20 years were formally erased in 1992. No constitutional amendment may affect the rights of the king.

CONSTITUTIONAL HISTORY

Jordan today is part of what is broadly called the Middle East. Because of the territory's centralized location, it changed hands many times throughout antiquity, until it fell under the control of the Ottoman Turks in 1516.

When World War I (1914–18) broke out, the Ottoman Empire (centered in today's Turkey) took the side of the German Empire and Austria-Hungary. The Allies, such as the United States, France, the United Kingdom, and Russia, held out to the Arabs the hope of postwar independence in order to gain support against the Ottoman Empire. At the same time, Britain, France, and Russia secretly agreed in the 1916 Sikes-Picot Agreement to divide the Middle East among them. Furthermore, the 1917 British Balfour Declaration promised the establishment of a national home to the Jewish people in the region.

The Ottoman Empire was defeated in World War I (1914–18). After the war, the newly formed League of Nations awarded Britain a "mandate" that included today's Jordan. A mandate was a treaty between the league's council and the mandatory power, which became accountable for establishing an independent administration at some time in the future. According to the mandates, the areas roughly comprising today's Syria and Lebanon were assigned to France. Those now comprising Israel (plus the territories of the Palestinian Authority) and Jordan were assigned to the United Kingdom.

In 1922, the British divided the Palestine mandate by establishing the semiautonomous Emirate of Transjordan east of the Jordan River, ruled by the Hashemite prince Abdullah (whose brother, King Faysal, was made king of Syria, and then king of Iraq). They continued to administer Palestine under a British high commissioner. The Transjordan draft constitution provided for a unicameral legislative council with some elected members. The cabinet members (the executive council) also sat in the legislative council but were not responsible to it.

In 1936, the British proposed a partition between the Jewish and Arab areas of Palestine. It was rejected by both the Arabs and the Jewish Zionist Congress. The British mandate over Transjordan ended on May 22, 1946. On May 25 the country became the independent Hashemite Kingdom of Transjordan under King Abdullah. The constitution was amended and a Senate was introduced.

With the proclamation of an independent state of Israel in 1948, a series of Arab-Israeli wars began. In the 1948 war Transjordan, together with Egypt, Iraq, Syria, Lebanon, and other Arab states, who had all rejected the 1947 United Nations Partition Plan creating Israel, attacked the new country. After the fighting was over, separate cease-fire agreements were signed by the various belligerents. As a result, even more of the territory of mandatory Palestine wound up on Israel's side of the armistice line (Green Line) than had been foreseen in the partition plan. The Gaza Strip and the West Bank of the Jordan were annexed by Egypt and Transjordan, respectively. Palestine ceased to exist as a political and administrative entity.

In 1950, Transjordan was renamed the Hashemite Kingdom of Jordan to include those portions of Palestine annexed by King Abdullah. Abdullah was assassinated in 1951, and his grandson, Hussein I, became king the following year. In order to obtain support on both sides of the Jordan, a constitutional revision was promised. That constitution was ratified in 1952 and is still in force today. Jordan did not play a role in the 1956 war between Israel and Egypt.

After the remilitarization of the Sinai by Egypt and the closure of the Straits of Tiran, Israel attacked Egypt in 1967. In this Arab-Israeli war, Israel faced Egypt, Jordan, and Syria while additional Arab states began to mobilize their armed forces. As a result of the war, which lasted only six days (the Six-Day War), Israel annexed East Jerusalem (annexed previously by Transjordan) and gained control of the Sinai Peninsula (Egypt), the Gaza Strip (annexed by Egypt), the West Bank (annexed by Transjordan), and the Golan Heights (Syria).

The 1967 war led to a dramatic increase in the number of Palestinians living in Jordan. Martial law was declared and parliamentary elections were postponed. In 1970, a brief civil war broke out accompanied by a conflict with Syria, which supported Palestine Liberation Army activities against Jordan. The war resulted in the elimination of the Palestinian armed presence. The 1973 Arab-Israeli War, between a coalition led by Egypt and Syria and Israel, was a war to win back territory. It resulted in another cease-fire.

In 1978, King Hussein decreed that a National Consultative Council be created to replace parliament temporarily. This council consisted of representatives appointed by King Hussein from various sectors of Jordanian society. This was justified as "a temporary measure in view of the fact that one-half of parliament's seats remained under Israeli occupation." In 1984, the deputies elected to the Ninth Parliament of 1967 voted on new members to replace those who had died since 1967 or were otherwise unable to attend because of the Israeli occupation of the West Bank.

In 1988, Jordan renounced its claims to the West Bank in order to allow the Palestinians eventually to organize a state in the territory. According to other sources, claims were already renounced in 1974, when the League of Arab States (except Jordan) recognized the Palestinians' claim to the West Bank territory. The king formally dissolved parliament, ending West Bank representation. General parliamentary elections were held the following year. The formulation of a National Charter in 1990 established the framework for organized political activity in the country. Emergency regulations that had preserved the status quo for more than 20 years were frozen and formally erased in 1992. In 1994, a peace treaty was concluded with Israel.

Jordan is a founding member of the League of Arab States (LAS).

FORM AND IMPACT OF THE CONSTITUTION

Jordan's 1952 constitution is codified in a single document consisting of 131 articles. It is supplemented by the 1990 National Charter, which represents a political agreement between the king and the leaders of the main political groups.

The constitution tops the hierarchy of domestic norms. International conventions that Jordan has ratified have the force of law and take precedence over all local legislation, with the exception of the constitution.

The Sharia Courts apply the provisions of the Islamic Sharia law.

BASIC ORGANIZATIONAL STRUCTURE

Jordan is a centralist state. It is divided administratively into 12 governorates that are headed by appointed commissioners. The country is further divided into 99 municipalities for purposes of local governance. The constitution underscores the concepts that the people of Jordan form a part of the Arab Nation and that the Kingdom of Jordan is an independent and indivisible Arab state.

LEADING CONSTITUTIONAL PRINCIPLES

The constitution does not contain as many abstract fundamental principles as do other Arab constitutions, yet it contains some "general provisions." First, Jordan's system of government is "parliamentary, with a hereditary constitutional monarchy." Article 30 states that the king is immune from any liability and responsibility; however, the fact that Jordan is a constitutional monarchy limits the king's powers. The source of authority is the nation, specifically the people of Jordan. A system of checks and balances is provided. While the principles of the rule of law and of social justice are only implicitly included in the constitution (such as Articles 24 and 111), they are more explicitly outlined in the National Charter. According to the charter there are some "basic pillars of a state of law," such as adherence to the letter and spirit of the constitution, to the principle of the supremacy of the law, and, in the exercise of democracy, to the principles and requisites of social justice.

CONSTITUTIONAL BODIES

The predominant bodies provided for in the constitution are the king; the bicameral National Assembly consisting of the Senate and the Chamber of Deputies; and the prime minister and cabinet. There is no constitutional court to review the constitutionality of laws.

The King

The king is both the head of state and the head of the administration. He exercises his executive powers through his ministers. The king is immune from any liability or responsibility.

The king plays the key role in the political life of Jordan. He appoints the cabinet ministers and may dismiss them or accept their resignations upon the recommendation of the prime minister. The king exercises the powers vested in him by royal decree. Every decree must be countersigned by the prime minister and the relevant cabinet minister. The king expresses his concurrence by placing his signature above those of the ministers.

The king may dissolve the Chamber of Deputies and the Senate or relieve any senator of his or her membership.

Royal succession is generally organized by a system of male primogeniture within the Hashemite dynasty. This means that the royal mandate is passed to the eldest son of the reigning king. Should there be no suitable direct heir, the National Assembly selects a successor from among "the descendants of the founder of the Arab Revolt, the late King Hussein Ibn Ali."

According to a 1965 constitutional amendment, which was made after the Crown had been threatened several times, the king may also designate one of his brothers as heir apparent. Accordingly, the brother would succeed the king. However, this was not applied in practice: Prince Hassan and the brother of the present king, Prince Hamzah, both were designated as crown prince and then deposed as successor to the throne. In the absence of a crown prince, the present king's eldest son is automatically heir to the throne.

The Parliament

Technically, the legislative power of the Hashemite Kingdom of Jordan is vested in the king and the two houses of parliament, collectively referred to as the National Assembly. Parliament consists of the House of Notables or Senate, and a lower house called the Chamber of Deputies. Each parliament is formed after a general election to the Chamber of Deputies. Its maximal life is four years, but it is usually dissolved at an earlier time selected by the king.

Both houses meet simultaneously. The king summons the National Assembly to an ordinary session on the first day of October of each year. An ordinary session lasts four months, if the king does not prolong it, adjourn it, or dissolve the Chamber of Deputies.

The Senate

The Senate consists of the senators and their speaker, who are all appointed by the king for four-year terms. It is thus viewed as an extension of the king's legislative powers. The Senate members must number no more than half the number of deputies.

In 2003, the Senate consisted of 55 members, including their speaker. In law and fact, many of the senators are chosen from designated categories of public figures, such as present and past prime ministers, former deputies, former senior judges and diplomats, and retired military generals.

The Chamber of Deputies

The number of deputies is not fixed by the constitution. In 2003, it consisted of 110 members, elected by secret ballot in a general and direct election. Prior to 1988, both houses had an equal number of representatives from each bank of the Jordan River.

The real influence of both chambers in the legislative process is small. Decisions by each house are made by a majority of votes of the members present, excluding the speaker, who has a deciding vote in the case of a tie. Any senator or deputy may address questions or interpellations to the cabinet ministers concerning any public matter.

The Council of Ministers

The Council of Ministers consists of the presiding prime minister and an unspecified number of ministers. They are collectively responsible before the Chamber of Deputies with respect to the public policy of the state. In addition, each minister is responsible for the specific affairs of his or her ministry.

Should the Chamber of Deputies pass a vote of no confidence, either on individual ministers or the Council of Ministers as a whole, the responsible ministers must resign. However, this requires an absolute majority of all members of the house; the vote may be held only at the request of the prime minister or by no fewer than 10 deputies.

The Lawmaking Process

In theory, 10 or more senators or deputies may propose any law. In practice, most laws are government-sponsored proposals. The prime minister refers any governmental proposals to the Chamber of Deputies and the chamber is entitled to accept, amend, or reject the proposal. Each proposal is referred to a special committee of the lower house for consideration. If the deputies accept the proposal, they refer it to the executive administration to draft it in the form of a bill and resubmit it to the house for approval. A bill approved by the Chamber of Deputies is then passed on by the speaker of the Senate. No law is promulgated unless passed by both the Senate and the Chamber of Deputies and ratified by the king.

Should either house twice reject any draft law and the other accept it, the two houses hold a joint meeting chaired by the speaker of the Senate to discuss the matters in dispute. The draft law is acceptable if backed by a two-thirds majority of the members of both houses present. If the draft law is rejected, it cannot be resubmitted during the same session of parliament. Every draft law passed by the Senate and the Chamber of Deputies is submitted to the king for ratification.

The king either grants consent by royal decree or returns the bill unapproved with justification for his refusal. Should both houses, meeting jointly, pass the bill by a two-thirds majority, it becomes an act of parliament without the consent of the king. This majority constitutionally overrides the monarch's veto. A law generally enters into force after its promulgation by the king and 30 days after the date of its publication in the *Official Gazette*.

The Judiciary

The constitution provides for an independent judiciary. In practice, some political pressure and interference by the executive remains.

The Jordanian judicial system comprises three branches: civil, religious, and special courts. Religious courts' jurisdiction extends to all matters of personal status, including marriage, divorce, and inheritance. Civil courts hear all civil and criminal matters not reserved for the religious courts. They have a four-tiered hierarchy. At the top of their judicial hierarchy is the Court of Cassation (final appeals), which is composed of seven judges.

The special State Security Court is composed of both military and civilian judges. It has jurisdiction over offenses against the state and drug-related crimes.

Although the National Charter called for a Constitutional Court, it has not yet materialized. Legislative acts may instead be judicially reviewed by the Special Tribunal (Diwan Khass) consisting of the president of the highest civil court, two of its judges and one senior administrative official, who are appointed by the Council of Ministers. It also includes a member delegated by the ministry that is involved in the needed interpretation. The Special Tribunal may interpret the constitution at the request of the prime minister or the leader of either house. The High Tribunal is competent to try members of parliament accused of penal code violations. It is composed of the president of the Senate, three Senate members who are elected by that body, and five judges who are selected from among the highest courts in order of seniority.

THE ELECTION PROCESS

According to the Law of Election to the Chamber of Deputies, voters must be at least 19 years of age. Suffrage has been universal since 1973, when women were enfranchised.

Parliamentary Elections

Deputies are elected in 20 different constituencies. Voters used to have as many votes as there were seats to be filled within the district, but not all voters made use of all their votes. In 1993, Jordan's Law of Election was adjusted to the principle of "one person, one vote"; every voter is restricted to only one vote, no matter how many seats are allocated in his or her particular constituency. Those candidates who receive the highest vote totals fill these seats (single nontransferable vote). A number of seats were later reserved for certain minority candidates—Christians, Circassians, a few tribal seats, and six for women.

In general, the king may prolong the term of the Chamber of Deputies for a maximal period of two years.

POLITICAL PARTIES

Jordan now has a pluralistic system of political parties. Jordanians are constitutionally entitled to establish societies and political parties provided that their goals are lawful, their methods peaceful, and their by-laws not contrary to the provisions of the constitution.

Political parties had been allowed in the past, but were not allowed to run as such in the 1989 elections. However, they were formally included in the 1991 National Charter, and the 1992 Political Parties Law made political party pluralism legal once more. The number of political parties has increased. In practice, however, the parties remain marginal. Tribal interests, which have traditionally dominated Jordan society, are also represented in the current parliament.

CITIZENSHIP

Jordanian nationality is defined by law. Citizenship is primarily acquired by descent. A child acquires Jordan citizenship if he or she is born of a Jordanian father, regardless of the child's country of birth. Preference is given to certain groups of Arab descent, including West Bank Palestinian refugees. Dual citizenship is recognized. The Palestinian community is estimated at more than half of the total citizen population (although not according to official sources).

FUNDAMENTAL RIGHTS

Chapter 2 of the constitution deals with the Rights and Duties of Jordanians. The constitution distinguishes between rights that apply to every person as a human being and those fundamental rights that apply to Jordanians only. Personal freedom is guaranteed for everyone. Jordanians are assured equality before the law. Their rights and duties are equal regardless of race, language, or religion. Jordanians have the right to hold meetings and to express opinions. The constitution also guarantees some economic, social, and cultural rights. The government undertakes to ensure work and education within the limits of its capacity and to ensure a state of tranquility and equal opportunity to all Jordanians.

The National Charter further confirms these rights and addresses some matters, such as human rights, to which no direct reference is made in the constitution.

Impact and Functions of the Fundamental Rights

Observers have noted a general improvement in human rights in Jordan. The state of emergency, which had a negative impact on the exercise of fundamental human rights, was formally erased in 1992. Limited censorship is constitutionally provided for by martial law or a state of emergency. The 1993 Press and Publications Law removed restrictions on the publication of information about the military and security forces, although some restrictions still exist in other laws. Antiterrorism laws further restricted freedom of expression in 2001.

The constitution prohibits unlawful and arbitrary arrest and detention. However, in practice, allegations of arbitrary arrest and detention, of a lack of transparent investigations, and even of torture within the security services continue.

Jordan has ratified the 1966 International Covenant on Civil and Political Rights (ICCPR) and the International Covenant on Economic, Social, and Cultural Rights (ICESCR). Both have precedence over national legislation.

Limitations to Fundamental Rights

The fundamental rights specified in the constitution are not without limits. Some rights are guaranteed within the limits of the law, while others are assured only as long as they are exercised consistently with public order or morality. The free exercise of all forms of worship and religious rites is in a sense limited in two ways: It must be "in accordance with the customs observed" and must not be "inconsistent with public order or morality."

ECONOMY

The Jordanian constitution does not specify an economic system. However, certain provisions must be considered as legislative guidelines. No property of any person may be expropriated except for the purposes of public utility and in consideration of a just compensation. Work is the right of every citizen; the state is obliged to provide work opportunities for all citizens by directing and improving the national economy. Taken as a whole, the Jordanian economic system can be described as a social market economy. In fact, the government has made substantial progress in implementing market-based reforms in a mixed economy.

RELIGIOUS COMMUNITIES

Freedom of religion is guaranteed by the constitution, which provides for free exercise of all forms of worship and religious rites and forbids discrimination on the basis of religion. However, the constitutional text also declares that the king must be a Muslim and that Islam is the state religion of Jordan. Islamic Sharia norms influence the personal status law.

Muslims who convert to other religions often face threats from their family, Muslim religious leaders, and society. Under Sharia law, converts may legally be denied their property; however, in practice this principle is not applied.

MILITARY DEFENSE AND STATE OF EMERGENCY

The government suspended universal male conscription in the 1990s; however, the 1986 Compulsory Military Service Act, which required all male adults to perform military service for two years, was not formally repealed. Exemptions were available for only sons or those whose family members had died in service, or on health grounds. Voluntary recruitment is open to men and women.

The king is the supreme commander of land, naval, and air forces. The king declares war, concludes peace, and ratifies treaties and agreements, such as the peace treaty concluded with Israel in 1994.

The constitution provides that in the event of an emergency necessitating the defense of the kingdom, a Defense Law shall be enacted giving power to the person specified therein to take such actions and measures "as may be necessary," including the suspension of the operation of the ordinary laws of the state.

In the event of an emergency of such a serious nature that normal emergency action may be insufficient for the defense of the kingdom, the king may by a royal decree, based on a decision of the Council of Ministers, declare martial law in the whole or any part of the kingdom. When martial law is declared, the king may by decree issue such orders "as may be necessary" for the defense of the kingdom, notwithstanding the provisions of any law in force.

The emergency regulations authorized the Jordanian government to censor the press and other publications, ban political parties, and restrict the rights of citizens to assemble for political meetings and peaceful demonstration. These regulations, which had preserved the status quo for more than 20 years, were frozen and formally erased in 1992.

AMENDMENTS TO THE CONSTITUTION

The process of amending the constitution is not different from the general lawmaking process, except that bills must pass by a two-thirds majority of the members of each house. In the event of a joint meeting of the Senate and the Chamber of Deputies in accordance with Article 92, the amendment bill shall be passed by a two-thirds majority of the members of both houses. In both cases the amendment does not enter into force unless ratified by the king.

PRIMARY SOURCES

1952 Constitution in English. *Constitution of the Hashemite Kingdom of Jordan.* Available online. URLs: http://www.kinghussein.gov.jo/constitution.html; http://www.idlo.int/texts/leg5550.pdf. Accessed on August 26, 2005.

1991 Jordanian National Charter. Available online. URL: http://www.kinghussein.gov.jo/charter_national.html. Accessed on August 26, 2005.

SECONDARY SOURCES

Nathan J. Brown, *Constitutions in a Nonconstitutional World—Arab Basic laws and the Prospects for Accountable Government.* New York: State University of New York Press, 2002.

Bureau of Public Affairs, U.S. Department of State, "Background Note and Country Reports on Human Rights Practices and International Religious Freedom Report 2004." Available online. URL: http://www.state.gov/g/drl/rls/hrrpt/2004/41724.htm. Accessed on June 21, 2006.

"The League of Arab States." Available online. URL: http://www.arableagueonline.org/. Accessed on September 6, 2005.

United Nations, "Core Document Forming Part of the Reports of States Parties: Jordan" (HRI/CORE/1/Add.18/Rev.1), 3 January 1994.

United Nations Development Programme, "Constitutions of the Arab Region." Available online. URL: http://www.pogar.org/themes/constitution.asp. Accessed on September 3, 2005.

Michael Rahe

KAZAKHSTAN

At-a-Glance

OFFICIAL NAME
Republic of Kazakhstan

CAPITAL
Astana

POPULATION
15,074,200 (2005 est.)

SIZE
1,052,089 sq. mi. (2,724,900 sq. km)

LANGUAGES
Kazakh (official), Russian

RELIGIONS
Muslim 9.6%, Protestant 5.6%, Russian Orthodox 4%, Catholic 0.4%, other 0.4%, unaffiliated 80%

NATIONAL OR ETHNIC COMPOSITION
Kazakh 57.2%, Russian 27.2%, other (made up largely of Ukrainian, Uzbek, German, Tatar, and Uigur) 15.6%

DATE OF INDEPENDENCE OR CREATION
December 16, 1991

TYPE OF GOVERNMENT
Presidential republic

TYPE OF STATE
Unitary state

TYPE OF LEGISLATURE
Bicameral parliament

DATE OF CONSTITUTION
August 30, 1995

DATE OF LAST AMENDMENT
October 7, 1998

Kazakhstan is a presidential republic with a division of executive, legislative, and judicial powers. The constitution of the country provides for guarantees of human rights, and it is generally respected by the public authorities.

The president of the Republic of Kazakhstan is the head of state and its highest official. The president, who determines the main directions of domestic and foreign policy, is a very strong political figure with a huge influence on all state bodies.

The bicameral Parliament is the main legislative body. Some members of the Parliament represent political parties. The Supreme Court is the highest judiciary body. Among state bodies that are not included in the legislative, executive, and judicial branches are the Constitutional Council and the procurator general. Religious freedom is respected, and state and religious communities are separated. The economic system can be described as a developing market economy. The military is subject to the civil government in terms of law and fact.

The current constitution was adopted in 1995. It determines the basic principles of state organization, state-citizen relations, and fundamental individual rights and freedoms in the new political, economic, and cultural situation since the collapse of the Soviet Union and the first years of independence.

CONSTITUTIONAL HISTORY

Kazakhstan does not have a long constitutional history, although various political-state unities existed on the modern territory of the country, including the Turkic kaganat, Kipchak khanat, Mogulistan, and Ak-Horde. The Kazakh khanate of the 15th–18th centuries is considered to be the beginning of Kazakh statehood. The nomadic style of life explains peculiarities in the organization of political power in that system: concentration of power in the hands of the khan or ruler, especially in land, military, and judicial issues; seasonal mutability of the khan's actual power; dominance of customary law; and absence of developed institutions of political power such as a tax system or a regular army.

The annexation of the Kazakh lands into the Russian Empire was a long and complicated process that began in the 18th century. Eventually, all Kazakh lands were under the state-political protectorate of Russia. Russian authorities introduced their own system of state administration and legislation in the Kazakhstan territory.

The October Revolution (1917) in Russia brought about a new stage in political development. In 1920, under Soviet decree, Kazakhstan for the first time received its own formal state system. The country was included as an autonomous republic in the Union of Soviet Socialist Republics (USSR). In 1926, the Constitution of the Kazakh Autonomous Soviet Republic was adopted. In 1936, the Kazakh autonomous republic was reorganized into the Kazakh Soviet Socialist Republic, one of the highest-level components of the USSR. In 1937, the constitution of the new republic entered into force. All these constitutions had formal democratic provisions, but in practice many of them were not realized. The Communist Party leadership and rules were much more important than any other political-legal institution. Communist ideology permeated all state-legal systems.

Modern constitutional development began in 1990 when Kazakhstan adopted the Declaration on State Sovereignty. The next step was the adoption of the constitutional law On State Independence of December 16, 1991, as the Soviet Union collapsed and communist ideology imploded. The newly independent country needed a new organization of state power and a new legal system, as the old party-state system could not meet the requirements of political and legal development.

The first constitution of independent Kazakhstan, in 1993, was the legal act that accomplished this task. For the first time in the country's constitutional history, provisions were included on the separation of powers, the priority of the individual in relation to the state, and the equality of state and private property. Kazakhstan took on the appearance of a parliamentary republic, as compared with the acting constitution at the time, in which Kazakhstan was proclaimed a republic with a presidential form of government. During the preparation of the constitution, the framers paid special attention to the constitutional experience of the United States and France.

The constitution of 1993 existed for only two years. In 1995, a new constitution was adopted by a national referendum. The main change was the strengthening of presidential power. Some democratic practices were curbed; this alteration was justified by the problems of the reform period and the need for a strong power to effect a smooth transition to a new society.

FORM AND IMPACT OF THE CONSTITUTION

Kazakhstan has a written constitution, codified in a single document. The constitution takes precedence over all other national law. International law must be in accordance with the constitution to be applicable within Kazakhstan. The first and only amendments were adopted in 1998.

The chief importance of the constitution lies in its laying the legal grounds for independence and its commitment to new principles of organizing society, with the goal of a democratic, secular, social state based on the rule of law.

In reality, many constitutional provisions remain declarative only. The presidential orders and regulatory acts of high officials count for much more than the constitution for other state officials, despite the constitution's formal legal superiority on the entire territory of the republic. Many administrative regulations have revised constitutional norms or limited them with very complicated procedures. However, in legal terms, all laws must comply with the provisions of the constitution.

BASIC ORGANIZATIONAL STRUCTURE

Kazakhstan is a unitary state and a presidential republic, with a very strong presidential power. The president has influence on all branches of state powers, especially on executive bodies.

The main territorial division is the *oblast*. There are 14 *oblasts* and two cities with separate status—Astana, the current capital, and the former capital, Almaty. There is also a city with a special status under the jurisdiction of both Kazakhstan and Russia—the space center Baykonyr.

There is no real system of self-government on the local level. All local bodies are state bodies. The local legislative body is elected by the people, but the main power is in the hands of the local executive. All higher local officials are appointed by the president.

LEADING CONSTITUTIONAL PRINCIPLES

Under Article 2 of the constitution, the Republic of Kazakhstan proclaims itself a democratic, secular, legal, and social state whose highest values are the individual and his or her life, rights, and freedoms. The word *proclaims* means that the country is in the process of establishing such principles. Taking into account deep political and social changes, it may take a long time for democracy and the social welfare orientation of the state to prevail.

Kazakhstan's system of government does have some of the features of a democracy: The people elect the president, Parliament, and local legislative bodies; they can petition state bodies; they have access to the civil service; they can create political parties and other public associations in order to participate in political life; and finally, the constitution of the country was adopted by a national referendum.

That Kazakhstan is a secular state means that religious organizations are separate from the state. Under the Kazakhstan approach, religion is a private matter. Religious organizations have no governmental functions and no right to interfere in the affairs of the state. There is no state religion or state religious organization.

The phrase *social state* means that the state ensures a minimal standard of living and gives social guaranties in employment, health, education, and other areas. A *legal state* follows the rule of law, meaning the supremacy of the constitution and the leading role of law. The principle of rule of law also refers to limitation of the state by law. It entails mutual responsibility between state and individual, an independent court system, and human rights and freedoms.

One of the key constitutional principles is the separation of powers. There is a division of the executive, legislative, and judicial power, based on checks and balances.

Some other fundamental principles in the constitution are public concord and political stability, economic development for the benefit of all of the nation, Kazakhstani patriotism, recognition of ideological and political diversity, the right to public associations, equality before the law, equal protection of state and private property, respect for the principles and norms of international law, a policy of cooperation and good-neighborly relations between states, noninterference in the internal affairs of other countries, peaceful settlement of international disputes, and renunciation of the first use of military force.

CONSTITUTIONAL BODIES

The predominant bodies provided for in the constitution are the president, Parliament, the administration (cabinet), the Constitutional Council, and the Supreme Court. The constitution also mentions the National Bank, the procurator general, and some other bodies.

The President

The president is the head of state, its highest official, who determines the main directions of domestic and foreign policy and represents Kazakhstan within the country and abroad. The president of the republic ensures the coordinated functioning of all branches of state power and the responsibility of the institutions of power before the people.

The president appoints and dismisses the prime minister, who is the head of the administration; ministers; and other higher executive officials. The president also appoints judges (except Supreme Court judges), seven members of the Senate, and the heads of the local state authorities.

The president determines the structure of the administration and creates and abolishes ministries and other administrative agencies. The president may annul or suspend the administration's acts in whole or in part.

The president signs laws. In fact, the president has the right to issue laws if parliament so decides, for a term not exceeding one year. The president may issue decrees having the force of laws (if Parliament failed to consider the draft of a law that the president declared urgent or priority-driven, one month from the day of its submission). The president calls for regular and extraordinary elections to the Parliament of the republic, convenes the first session of Parliament, and calls extraordinary joint sessions of the chambers of Parliament.

The president conducts foreign negotiations and signs international treaties, signs ratification instruments, and receives letters of credentials and recalls from diplomatic and other representatives of foreign states.

The president acts as the commander in chief of the armed forces of the republic and appoints and replaces their highest commanders. In the case of aggression against the republic or immediate external threat to its security, the president may impose martial law on the entire territory of the republic or in particular areas.

The president also resolves issues of citizenship and political asylum and issues pardons.

The president of the republic is elected for a seven-year term by the citizens of the republic. No one may be elected as president more than twice in a row. The president can be prematurely released from office in case of continued incapacity due to illness. The president can also be discharged from office for high treason. In both cases, Parliament makes the final decision.

The Parliament

The Parliament of the Republic of Kazakhstan is the highest representative body of the republic performing legislative functions. Parliament also establishes state awards; issues honorary, military, and other titles; appoints high-ranked positions and diplomats; and defines state symbols. Parliament decides on issues of state loans and other international economic and other assistance. It issues amnesties, ratifies international treaties, and approves the appointment of some higher officials by the president.

Parliament consists of two chambers acting on a permanent basis: the Senate and the Majilis. The Senate is the higher chamber. It is composed of two deputies elected from each *oblast* and major city and from the capital of the republic. Elections are conducted at a joint session of the members of all representative bodies of the respective *oblast* or city. Seven members of the Senate are appointed by the president.

The Majilis is the lower chamber; it consists of 77 members, who are elected by citizens. The term of office is six years for Senate members and five years for Majilis members.

The president may dissolve Parliament for certain reasons: a vote of no confidence in the administration, the repeated refusal of Parliament to give consent to the appointment of the prime minister, and political crisis resulting from insurmountable differences between the chambers of Parliament or between Parliament and the other branches of state power.

The Administration

The administration (cabinet) has the executive power, leads the system of executive bodies, and exercises supervision of their activity. Members of the cabinet are the prime minister and deputies, ministers, and other officials appointed at the president's discretion.

The cabinet resigns when a newly elected president takes office. At all times, the president has the right to terminate the powers of the administration and release any of its members from their offices. The release of the prime minister from office denotes the termination of the powers of the entire cabinet.

The Constitutional Council

The Constitutional Council is a body of constitutional supervision. It reviews and considers the laws adopted by Parliament with respect to their compliance with the constitution before they are signed by the president. Similarly, it reviews the international treaties with respect to their compliance with the constitution before they are ratified. It is the official interpreter of the constitution, and it can declare existing laws unconstitutional in case of court appeals. The Constitutional Council also reviews the fairness of presidential and parliamentary elections and of national referendum.

The Constitutional Council consists of seven members whose powers last for six years. In addition, the former presidents of the republic have the right to be lifelong members of the Constitutional Council.

The chairperson and two other members of the Constitutional Council are appointed by the president. Two members are chosen by the chairperson of the Senate, and two by the chairperson of the Majilis. Half of the members of the Constitutional Council are elected every three years.

The Lawmaking Process

The right of legislative initiative belongs to the members of Parliament and to the administration. It is exercised exclusively through the Majilis.

A draft law, if considered and approved by the majority of all members of the Majilis, is transmitted to the Senate, which has 60 days to consider it. If the majority of all members of the Senate approve the draft, it is submitted to the president; if not, it is returned to the Majilis. If the Majilis approves the draft by a majority of two-thirds of all members, it is transferred once more to the Senate for a second discussion and voting. A twice-rejected draft may not be submitted again during the same session.

The president signs laws submitted by the Senate within 15 working days and promulgates them. He may also return it or its separate articles to Parliament for a second discussion and vote.

The Judiciary

The judiciary in Kazakhstan is formally independent of the executive and legislative branches. Judicial power is exercised through the constitutional, civil, administrative, criminal, and other forms of judicial procedure as established by law. In cases stipulated by law, criminal procedure requires the participation of a jury.

The only courts of the republic under the constitution are the Supreme Court and local courts. However, specialized courts that handle military, economic, administrative, and juvenile matters can be created by law. Currently, military, economic, and administrative courts do exist in Kazakhstan.

The Supreme Court and higher local courts consist of three collegiums: Criminal Collegium, Civil Collegium, and Supervising Collegium. These courts as a rule are not involved in political life. They do, however, sometimes make decisions based on political expediency and official government opinion.

The courts have no special constitutional jurisdiction, and judges cannot declare acts unconstitutional. However, if a court finds that a law or other regulatory legal act infringes on the constitutional rights and liberties of an individual, it can suspend legal proceedings in the case and ask the Constitutional Council to declare that law unconstitutional.

THE ELECTION PROCESS

All Kazakhstan citizens over the age of 18 have the right to vote in the elections.

Presidential Elections

The president of the republic is elected by universal, equal, and direct suffrage by secret ballot. A citizen of the republic is eligible for the office of president if he or she is over 40 years of age, has a perfect command of the Kazakh language, and has lived in Kazakhstan for not less than 15 years.

The candidate who receives more than 50 percent of the votes is deemed elected. If no candidate receives that percentage, a second round of elections is held between the two candidates who obtained the largest number of votes. The winner of the second round is deemed elected.

Parliamentary Elections

Sixty-seven members of the Majilis are elected in single-member constituencies, which are based on the administrative-territorial division of the republic with approximately equal numbers of voters. Ten members are elected from party lists according to a system of proportional representation, with a unified national constituency. Any citizen of the Republic of Kazakhstan who has reached the age of 25 can be elected a member of the Majilis.

A candidate is deemed elected if he or she receives more than 50 percent of the votes cast in a single-member constituency. If none of the candidates receives the necessary number of votes, a second round of voting is held between the two candidates who obtained the highest number of votes. The winner of the second round is deemed elected. A party must receive at least 7 percent of the votes to be eligible to receive any of the 10 party list mandates.

The Senate is elected on the basis of indirect electoral right. The majority of its members are chosen by the members of local representative bodies, and seven are appointed by the president. To be a member of the Senate, one must be a citizen of the Republic of Kazakhstan for not less than five years and be at least 30 years of age. He or she must also have a higher education, must have at least five years' work experience, and must have been a permanent resident for not less than three years in the constituent territory—*oblast* or city.

Local Elections

Local representative bodies—*maslikhats*—are elected by the population on the basis of universal, equal suffrage by secret ballot for a four-year term. Any citizen of the Republic of Kazakhstan who has reached 20 years of age can be elected as member of a *maslikhat*.

POLITICAL PARTIES

Kazakhstan has a pluralistic system of political parties. This is one of the new phenomena in political life after years of Communist Party domination.

Article 5 of the constitution states that the Republic of Kazakhstan shall recognize ideological and political diversity. Currently, there are 11 political parties registered by the Ministry of Justice. A political party must have at least 50,000 members in order to be registered.

Some political parties are progovernment and others are in the opposition. A pluralistic political system has only begun to develop, and the parties so far lack any strong impact in political life. Because many citizens are apolitical, potential parties may lack a serious social base.

Political parties that are based in other states or receive funds from foreign legal entities, foreign citizens, foreign states, or international organizations are not permitted in Kazakhstan. Religious parties are also banned.

Political parties, as may any other public associations, may be liquidated by courts if they violate the law. There are no special rules regarding banning of political parties.

CITIZENSHIP

Citizenship of Kazakhstan is acquired mainly by birth, although special procedures exist for acquiring citizenship. For birth, there is a combination of the "right of the blood" (*ius sanguinis*) and "right of the soil" *(ius soli),* with descent playing the greater role.

Noncitizens are not eligible to vote or to stand for office. They cannot create political parties or any other public association or be members of political parties. They also have no access to civil service.

FUNDAMENTAL RIGHTS

In Article 1, the constitution declares that the highest values of Kazakhstan are the life, rights, and freedoms of the individual. The majority of human rights and fundamental freedoms relate to both individuals and citizens, including the right to life, to personal freedom, to freedom of conscience, and to freedom of speech. However, there are some exceptions; for example, only citizens of Kazakhstan have the right to form associations.

There are constitutional provisions regarding social rights as well; in this case, too, some rights apply to everyone and others only to citizens of Kazakhstan. For instance, everyone has the right to freedom of labor, but only citizens have the right to protection of health.

There is also a group of political rights for citizens of Kazakhstan: the right to participate in running the affairs of the state, to address public bodies personally, to vote and stand for election, and to participate in national referenda.

In contrast to Soviet times, the modern constitution is very attentive to the protection and assurance of personal rights. Kazakhstan does not want to repeat the experience of Soviet constitutions, when the state formally ensured many rights and freedoms, but those rights remained mere declarations. One of the reasons Kazakhstan has hesitated to sign international covenants on human rights is the state's incapacity to provide these rights to the fullest degree. Only in 2003 did Kazakhstan sign two major human rights documents: the International Covenant on Civil and Political Rights and the International Covenant on Economic, Social and Cultural Rights.

Today, people actively defend the rights and freedoms described in the constitution. People have started to believe that these are not mere words on paper but real legal possibilities.

Under the constitution, rights and freedoms of individuals and citizens may be limited only by law, and only to the extent necessary for the protection of the constitutional system and the defense of the public order, the human rights and freedoms of others, or the health and morality of the population. Any restrictions to the rights and freedoms of citizens on political grounds are not permitted.

Fundamental rights do not only apply to the relations of the individual and the government; they also have effects among private persons.

ECONOMY

The constitution contains some provisions that can be seen to characterize the economic system. The Republic of Kazakhstan recognizes and protects both state and private property. This is an absolutely new condition in comparison with Soviet times, when state property dominated to an enormous degree.

One constitutional provision that still arouses much public opposition and many disputes is private landownership. Under the constitution, land may be privately owned on terms, conditions, and limits established by law. Other natural resources such as mines, oil, water, and wildlife are owned by the state.

Article 26 of the constitution guarantees freedom of enterprise and free use of one's property for any legal activity. Monopolistic activity is to be regulated and limited by law, as is unfair competition. The article explicitly provides that property, including the right of inheritance, shall be guaranteed by law.

The constitution also provides that everyone has the right to work and to a free choice of occupation and profession. Involuntary labor is permitted only after court sentencing or under conditions of a state of emergency or martial law. Everyone also has the right to safe and hygienic working conditions, to just remuneration for labor without discrimination, and to social protection against unemployment. The constitution also recognizes the right to pursue individual and collective labor disputes, using methods stipulated by law, and guarantees the right to strike.

Some civil constitutional freedoms have an economic aspect. For instance, freedom to form associations includes the right to organize trade unions or other professional communities. Taken as a whole, Kazakhstan's economic system can be described as a transitional economy from a state to a social market economy.

RELIGIOUS COMMUNITIES

Everyone has the right to freedom of conscience, exercised either individually or jointly through religious communities. Freedom of conscience is traditionally associated with freedom of religion in political and legal terminology. The constitution does not define a particular status of *religious community*. Activities of foreign religious associations within the territory of the republic, including the appointment of heads of religious associations by foreign religious centers, can be carried out only in coordination with the respective state institutions.

There is no established state church. All religious organizations, including the two main ones—Islam and Russian Orthodoxy—are equal from a legal point of view. Religious communities have the legal status of civil law corporations. There is a requirement for mandatory registration of religious communities.

The principle of separation of religious organizations and the state is not explicit in the constitution, but it has been included in special legislation regarding religious organization. Despite the principle of separation, the state and religious communities have begun to cooperate in certain areas, a striking new phenomenon after many years of suppression of religious freedom under communism.

MILITARY DEFENSE AND STATE OF EMERGENCY

The constitution contains only a few provisions regarding military defense and state of emergency, just enough to determine that the civil government dominates the military. The president is commander in chief of the armed forces. The president also imposes martial law and the state of emergency and decides on the use of the armed forces.

Parliament declares war and peace. On the president's proposal, it also decides about deploying the armed forces of the republic abroad, to fulfill international obligations in support of peace and security. The administration is responsible for developing the defense capability of the state.

In case of martial law, the military authorities can assume all police and security powers in the republic. In case of a state of emergency, the president can create special bodies within the state administration that are not subject to military command. The president can also use armed forces to help guard special objects and territories, suppress illegal military activity, and rescue people.

The defense of the Republic of Kazakhstan is, according to the constitution, a sacred duty and responsibility of every citizen. Citizens of the republic perform compulsory military service and can also enlist on contract. The term for compulsory military service is 12 months (24 months for officers). Kazakhstan does not provide for alternative service by conscientious objectors.

AMENDMENTS TO THE CONSTITUTION

The process of amending the constitution is complicated in comparison with changing other laws. Amendments may be passed by a national referendum called by the president, either on the president's own initiative or at the recommendation of Parliament or the cabinet. The proposal is passed if at least half of those voting approve.

If the president rejects a referendum request from Parliament, that body can still adopt the amendment by a majority of four-fifths of all the members of each chamber. In such a case the president can either sign the amendment or submit it to a referendum. In such a referendum, at least half of all citizens who have the right to vote must approve.

Certain constitutional provisions are not subject to change. Article 91 says, "The unitary status and territorial integrity of the republic, and the forms of government may not be changed."

PRIMARY SOURCES

Constitution in English: *The Constitution of the Republic of Kazakhstan.* Almaty: Zheti Zhargy, 2000. Available online. URL: http://www.kazakhstanembassy. org.uk/cgi-bin/index/225. Accessed on June 21, 2006.

Constitution in Kazakh: *Қазақстан Республикасының Қонституциясы.* Алматы: Жеті Жарғы, 2000.

Constitution in Russian: *Қонституция Республики Қазахстан.* Алматы: Жеті Жарғы, 2000. Available online. URL: http://www.kazakhstan_constitution. shtml. Accessed on June 21, 2006.

SECONDARY SOURCES

Bureau of Public Affairs, U.S. Department of State, "Background Notes and Country Reports on Human Rights Practices and International Religious Freedom Report 2004." Available online. URL: http://www.state.gov/g/ drl/rls/hrrpt/2004/41689.htm. Accessed on June 21, 2006.

Glenn E. Curtis, ed. *Kazakhstan—a Country Study.* Washington, D.C.: Library of Congress, 1996. Available online. URL: http://lcweb2.loc.gov/frd/cs/kztoc.html. Accessed on September 12, 2005.

Roman Podoprigora

KENYA

At-a-Glance

OFFICIAL NAME
Republic of Kenya

CAPITAL
Nairobi

POPULATION
34,707,817 (July 2006 est.)

SIZE
224,961 sq. mi. (582,646 sq. km)

LANGUAGES
English and Swahili (both official), local languages (e.g., Gikuyu, Kalenjin, Kamba, Luhya, Luo, Meru, Taita, Giryama, and Gusii)

RELIGIONS
Catholic, Protestant (unofficial combined estimate) 80%; Muslim, Jewish

NATIONAL OR ETHNIC COMPOSITION
Kikuyu, Luhya, Luo, Kamba, Meru, Taita, Giryama, Gusii, other Kenyan ethnic groups, European, Asian, and Arab

DATE OF INDEPENDENCE OR CREATION
December 12, 1963

TYPE OF GOVERNMENT
Parliamentary democracy

TYPE OF STATE
Unitary state

TYPE OF LEGISLATURE
Single-chamber parliament

DATE OF CONSTITUTION
December 12, 1963

DATE OF LAST AMENDMENT
July 2001

Kenya became independent on December 12, 1963, and was established as a parliamentary democracy based on the rule of law with a clear separation of powers among the executive, legislature, and judiciary. The founding fathers wrote a constitution that was based on liberal democratic values and followed the Westminster model.

The country was first organized as a federal state, but after only one year, constitutional changes turned the country into a strong unitary state with a strong presidency and weak local governments. According to the constitution, the president is the head of state, head of government, and commander in chief of the armed forces of the republic. Presidential and parliamentary elections are held simultaneously every five years.

The status of fundamental rights in Kenya has been problematic. The country is a secular state, and freedom of religion is guaranteed. Kenya supports a free market economy.

CONSTITUTIONAL HISTORY

What is today known as Kenya was founded as a British colony in 1920. Before then, European settlers, explorers, missionaries, and traders had been involved in farming, adventure, Christian evangelism, and trade, especially after 1895, when Kenya became a British "protectorate." Through a variety of methods (including treaty making with native chiefs and sheer use of force), the colonial establishment disenfranchised African natives and seized their land, relegating them to the "native reserves." During this period, the vast African majority had no role in political processes, structures, or decisions.

The 1920s saw the birth of African nationalism and protests against colonial rule. Agitation for the political and economic emancipation of Africans intensified in the late 1940s and reached its crest in 1952, when the Mau Mau war began. The outbreak of the war precipitated a serious legitimacy crisis of the colonial state.

The war achieved two things: First, it convinced both local colonial officials and the imperial authorities in London of the need to embark on far-reaching constitutional reforms to contain African discontent and lay the basis for eventual independence. Second, it involved the imperial government more intricately in the management of local affairs, and as a result the process of constitutional change was taken over and supervised directly from Britain, which gave the process new impetus. Despite this, the Mau Mau was quashed, and eight leaders associated with or sympathetic to it were arrested and detained after a state of emergency was declared on October 20, 1952. Among these was Jomo Kenyatta, who would later become the first president of the independent Republic of Kenya.

The Mau Mau war resulted in two constitutional dispensations fundamental to Kenya's history: the Lyttleton (1954) and Lennox-Boyd (1958) constitutions. The first, named after the colonial secretary of the British government at the time, produced two remarkable constitutional changes: First, it increased African representation in the Legislative Council (LEGCO). Second, it provided for separate racial representation as a way of controlling African political participation. The Lennox-Boyd constitution sought to achieve two conditions required for the establishment of a truly multiracial society in Kenya—to end racialism and to secure protection for migrant minorities. Protection of minority interests would become a significant issue in Kenya's constitutional development in the years ahead.

In spite of its significant innovations, African leaders in the LEGCO rejected the Lennox-Boyd constitution and demanded total control of the government based on African majority representation. They also wanted Jomo Kenyatta and others released and called for a combined nonracial electoral roll based on universal adult suffrage.

After these protests, the first constitutional conference was convened at Lancaster House, London, in January 1960. By this time, Britain had softened its stance as a result of increasing international pressure to decolonize from both the United States and the Soviet Union, and from the growing bloc of non-Western states. The twilight of the colonial state had arrived, and bargaining for the independence constitution had begun in earnest.

A constitution for Kenya, referred to as the Macleod constitution in honor of the then colonial secretary, was crafted on the Westminster parliamentary system (the so-called decolonization export model). It also sought protection for minorities. While the former caused little controversy, the latter was subject of serious disagreement insofar as it sought to guarantee European settlers' interests in an independent Kenya.

Under the Macleod constitution, significant progress toward independence under African majority rule was made. Specifically, the ban on political parties was lifted. In April 1960, the Kenya African National Union (KANU) was formed. Its leaders were James Gichuru (acting president), Oginga Odinga (vice president), and Tom Mboya

(secretary-general). Ronald Ngala and Daniel arap Moi, who had been elected to party office, declined to take up their positions, arguing that KANU was a party for the major ethnic communities such as the Kikuyu and Luo, and that the "smaller tribes" needed a voice of their own. Ngala and Moi teamed up with Masinde Muliro and others to found the Kenya African Democratic Union (KADU) in the same year. Kenyatta was released in 1961 and took the presidency of KANU.

Meanwhile, political pressure continued to mount in favor of an independence conference that would hammer out a final constitution leading to self-government. The pressure resulted in the Second Lancaster Constitutional Conference, held between February 15 and April 6, 1962. The conference, attended by 37 Africans, 14 Europeans, 11 Asians, and three Arabs, resulted in the "Self-government Constitution." Under it, the prime minister was to be appointed by the governor from among members of the House of Representatives most likely to command majority support. The legislature was renamed Central Legislature and was bicameral, consisting of the lower house (House of Representatives) and the upper house (Senate). Under this constitution, Kenyatta was named prime minister.

The Third Lancaster Constitutional Conference was held in September/October 1963. The conference was now between governments: the Kenyan government and the British government. This conference led to the adoption of the Independence Constitution in 1963. It was strongly federalist. Kenya became a republic in 1964 with Jomo Kenyatta as the first president of a largely unitary parliamentary democracy. A series of amendments led to the adoption of the current constitution, enacted as Act No. 5 of 1969. Jomo Kenyatta's presidency ended on August 22, 1978, when he died, and Daniel Arap Moi succeeded him.

Agitation began in the late 1980s and early 1990s for the reintroduction of multiparty politics, which had been banned in 1969 as a matter of fact and in 1982 by law. The clamor led to a constitutional amendment in 1991 to legalize multiparty democracy. The first two multiparty elections, held in 1992 and 1997, respectively, were won by KANU, but conditions were to change in the 2002 elections, which swept into power the National Rainbow Coalition (NARC) with Mwai Kibaki as the third president of the Republic of Kenya.

In the twilight years of Moi's rule, civil society and opposition politicians began to put pressure on the government to overhaul the constitution. In 2000, the Constitution of Kenya Review Commission (CKRC) was established under an act of parliament to review the constitution. In 2003, the commission adopted a draft constitution for parliament to promulgate. However, political differences (notably over the establishment of the prime minister's office and Islamic courts) have led to a stalemate. Yash Pal Ghai, an internationally acclaimed Kenyan-born professor who chaired the commission, resigned on June 29, 2004, throwing the process into further crisis.

Kenya is a member of the East African Community (EAC); the Common Market for Eastern and Southern Africa (COMESA); the African Union (AU), formerly known as the Organization of African Unity (OAU); and the United Nations (UN).

FORM AND IMPACT OF THE CONSTITUTION

Kenya has a written constitution, contained in a single document, the Constitution of Kenya, Act No. 5 of 1969. It is the supreme source of law in Kenya, and all other laws inconsistent with it are void to the extent of the inconsistency. The constitution symbolizes the aspirations of the people of Kenya and is, in addition to the flag, the national anthem, and the coat of arms, a symbol of national unity. There is no permanent constitutional court. However, where a question as to the interpretation of the constitution arises in proceedings in a subordinate court, such matters are referred to the High Court of Kenya, whose decision on the constitutional issue is binding and final.

Apart from the constitution, the other sources of law in Kenya are, in order of hierarchy, acts of parliament including delegated legislation; principles of the common law and equity; and African customary law insofar as it is not repugnant to justice or inconsistent with any written law. Courts can overturn these sources of law if they contradict the constitution. Although Kenya actively participates in regional and global affairs, the constitution is silent on the relationship between domestic and international law.

BASIC ORGANIZATIONAL STRUCTURE

Kenya is a unitary state with a strong central government and relatively weak local authorities. For administrative purposes, the country is divided into eight provinces, which in turn are divided into 70 districts. The provinces and districts differ considerably in geographical area, population, size, and economic strength. The administration of the country is highly centralized, with all legislative, executive, and judicial administration headquartered in Nairobi, the capital city. The local authorities (city, municipal, and county councils) make by-laws only for their areas of influence, in addition to collecting rates (property taxes) and providing services such as water and garbage collection.

LEADING CONSTITUTIONAL PRINCIPLES

The present constitution of Kenya does not have a preamble from which the country's constitutional principles may be distilled. In addition, the constitutional text does not contain any general principles upon which the state is established, except the statements that "Kenya is a sovereign Republic" (Article 1) and that "The Republic of Kenya shall be a multiparty democratic state" (Article 1A). Immediately after these two provisions, the constitution describes the organs of state, their powers, and functions.

However, the two provisions mentioned indicate that Kenya is based on three constitutional principles: The country is a democracy and a republic and is based on multiparty politics. Democracy in Kenya is exercised through general presidential, parliamentary, and local government elections held every five years. The constitution does not provide for ways of exercising direct democracy through, for instance, a referendum. While the statement that Kenya is a republic may be taken to mean that Kenya is not a monarchy, the provision that Kenya is a multiparty state enshrines in the constitution the norm that political pluralism is legitimate in the country.

Besides the above explicitly stated principles, one can note from the constitution two implied principles: the doctrine of separation of powers and that of the rule of law. The constitution sets up the three organs of state (executive, legislature, and judiciary) in separate chapters (Chapters 2, 3, and 4, respectively), which detail the powers and functions of each, suggesting that these organs were designed to function separately so as to act as checks and balances against one another.

The principle of the rule of law may be inferred from the supremacy clause (Article 3), which raises the constitution over all other laws and norms. The clause may imply not only that there is a hierarchy of laws, but also that the law is the basis for running the affairs of the country. The Bill of Rights in Chapter 5 of the constitution (Articles 70 to 84) also presupposes that the country is to be run on the basis of the rule of law as opposed to arbitrariness and abuse of fundamental rights and freedoms. That all persons are protected against unlawful deprivation of property (Article 75) or unlawful arrest and detention (Article 72) supports the view that the constitution establishes a system based on the rule of law.

Kenya is a secular state, with no formal, expressed relationship between state and religion. However, freedom of conscience, including the freedom of thought and of religion, is guaranteed in Article 78 of the constitution.

CONSTITUTIONAL BODIES

The predominant constitutional organs are the president, the executive or cabinet, and the parliament.

The President

The president, as the head of the executive arm, is vested with inordinately powerful functions, when compared with those of the other constitutional organs of state. The president is the head of state and commander in chief of the armed forces of the republic (Article 3). The president appoints and dismisses the cabinet. Although the attorney general, the auditor and comptroller general, and judges enjoy security of tenure, they are appointed by the president without requirement for parliamentary approval.

Many have viewed two constitutional provisions as vesting too much power in the presidency. First is Section 24, by which the president is empowered to constitute or abolish any office in Kenya and to hire or fire any person into/from those offices. Abuse of this power in the past has led to the establishment of numerous largely unnecessary offices, commissions, and task forces at the taxpayers' expense.

Then there is Section 25 of the constitution, which states that "every person who holds office in the Republic of Kenya shall hold that office during the pleasure of the president." Literally, this means that the president can dismiss any officer (including lower-cadre personnel) directly and without any procedure or reason for such dismissal. A senior civil servant was in this manner fired in the early 1980s, and the High Court of Kenya endorsed the dismissal. The president may pardon criminal offenders on the basis of the doctrine of prerogative of mercy.

The president is elected for a term of five years and can be reelected only once. To be elected president, one must be a citizen of Kenya, be at least 35 years old, and be registered in some constituency as a voter for parliamentary elections. The president is elected on the basis of simple majority. The office of the president may fall vacant in four ways: death of the incumbent, resignation, removal on the basis of incapacity, or nullification of the incumbent's election by an election court.

The Executive

According to the constitution, the executive authority of the government of Kenya vests in the president. In practice, the president runs the government with the support of the cabinet, which consists of the president, the vice president, and ministers.

The president selects the vice president from among the ministers, who are elected members of parliament. The vice president is the principal assistant of the president. This office may become vacant if the president so directs, if the holder of the office ceases to be an elected member of parliament otherwise than by dissolution of parliament, or if a new president is elected.

The number of ministers is not limited by the constitution. Although there is a provision empowering parliament to regulate the number of ministries (Article 16), this power has never been utilized. The president appoints ministers from among members of parliament (elected or nominated) and allocates their responsibilities.

There are four ways through which a vacancy may occur in the office of minister: (1) by the direction of the president, (2) if the holder of the office ceases to be a member of parliament otherwise than by reason of dis-

solution of parliament, (3) if a minister who before the dissolution of parliament was a member of parliament is not reelected into parliament in the ensuing general election, (4) immediately when a new term of the presidency begins, even if it is a reelection of the same president.

Parliament

According to Article 30 of the constitution, the legislative power of the Republic of Kenya vests in the parliament, referred to in the constitution as the National Assembly. Parliament is composed of 210 elected members, each representing a constituency and elected on the basis of simple majority; 12 members appointed by the president on the recommendation of political parties represented in parliament; and two ex officio members, the attorney general and the Speaker. The ex officio members have no voting rights in parliamentary debates.

Any person is qualified to be elected to parliament who is a citizen of Kenya and is at least 21 years old. This person must be a registered voter and be able to speak and, unless prevented from doing so by blindness or other incapacity, read the official languages of Swahili and English. He or she must be nominated by a political party, be of sound mind, and not be a public servant or judge or member of the armed forces of the Republic of Kenya, nor an undischarged bankrupt, nor under the death sentence or serving a prison term exceeding six months. To be a nominated member of parliament, one has to have the same qualifications as those of the elected members. The 12 positions for nomination are shared by the ruling party and opposition parties, depending on the strength (in terms of numbers) of parties in parliament.

A member of parliament vacates the seat if he or she ceases to be a citizen of Kenya or misses eight consecutive days of parliamentary sitting without the Speaker's permission, although the president may exempt a member from this requirement. Also, the elected Speaker, or any member, ceases to be member of parliament if he or she changes allegiance from the party that sponsored him or her to parliament while the party is still represented in parliament.

The Lawmaking Process

All legislative power in Kenya vests in parliament. Other entities, especially local authorities and ministers, can make delegated legislation, but the ultimate lawmaking responsibility is with parliament. The legislative power of parliament is exercisable by bills passed. The administration or any individual member of parliament can sponsor bills.

According to the standing orders of parliament, bills must undergo a number of stages. There is the first reading, in which only the title of the bill is read as a way of notifying members of parliament of the intended legislation. In the second reading, the bill and a memorandum of reasons for the bill are introduced to the house. Voting takes place, and if the bill receives the support of a simple majority, then it advances to the committee stage. Here, the whole house can transform itself into a committee, or it may form a committee that will report its recommendation to the whole house.

In the committee stage, the bill is given a clause-by-clause consideration, after which the matter is taken back to the whole house for voting. If a simple majority passes the bill, then the attorney general publishes it as an act and presents it to the president for assent. A two-thirds majority must support bills that amend or alter the constitution.

Within 21 days of receiving the bill, the president must inform the Speaker if it has been accepted or refused. In case of refusal, the president must specify which provisions of the bill are considered inappropriate and must recommend amendments. Parliament can either accept the president's recommendation(s) and resubmit the bill for presidential assent or refuse the recommendations of the president by a two-thirds majority resolution and then resubmit the bill as it was. In this case, the president is compelled to assent to the bill within 14 days of passing the resolution. A law passed by parliament cannot go into effect until it is published in the official *Kenya Gazette,* but parliament may postpone implementation; it may also make laws with retrospective effect, with the exception of laws pertaining to criminal matters.

The Judiciary

The judiciary in Kenya is independent of the legislature and the executive. The highest court in Kenya is the Court of Appeal, consisting of the chief justice and 11 judges (the number is set by an act of parliament). All 12 enjoy security of tenure, meaning that they can be removed from office only by special procedures and for special reasons set out in the constitution. While the president appoints the chief justice at his or her discretion, the judges of appeal are appointed by the president with the advice of the Judicial Service Commission, established under Article 67 of the constitution.

The jurisdiction of this court is purely appellate and relates to criminal or civil matters, on questions of law or mixed law and facts. It cannot entertain appeals against findings of facts only. Under the doctrine of judicial precedent followed in Kenya, the decisions of the Court of Appeal are themselves a source of law and are binding on all other courts in cases in which the facts and legal issues are similar. The Court of Appeal, can, however overturn its own decision, for instance, if it finds that the decision was wrong. A bench of three, five, or seven judges hears the cases.

Below the Court of Appeal is the High Court, which enjoys unlimited original (first instance) jurisdiction in all civil and criminal matters. It is also empowered to hear election petitions and to determine all constitutional matters. Its decisions in constitutional matters are final, and decisions of this court are binding on all subordinate courts. The High Court comprises judges, whose number is decided from time to time by an act of parliament. High Court judges also enjoy security of tenure. They are appointed by the president with the advice of the Judicial Service Commission. The chief justice of the Court of Appeal is also a member of the High Court. One or more judges can constitute a High Court Bench. At the same level with the High Court is the Industrial Court, which deals with labor disputes.

Below the High Court are subordinate or magistrate courts, which deal with both criminal and civil matters. Within the subordinate courts there are specialized courts and tribunals, such as the Kadhi courts, which deal with civil matters of personal law involving Muslim disputants. There is a Court Martial that handles cases involving members of the armed forces with a provision of appeals to the High Court only. Finally there are a number of quasi-judicial tribunals such as the Insurance Tribunal or the Rent Tribunals.

THE ELECTION PROCESS AND POLITICAL PARTICIPATION

All Kenyan citizens over the age of 18 have the right to vote in presidential, parliamentary, and local government elections. Kenyan citizens can stand for election if they have attained the age of 21 years (parliamentary and local elections) or 35 years (presidential elections).

Parliamentary Elections

The Kenyan parliament consists of one chamber. General parliamentary elections are held once every five years, but a by-election may be occasioned by death, resignation, or defection of a member of parliament to a political party other than the one that sponsored the member. Candidates are elected through direct popular vote in single-member districts.

POLITICAL PARTIES

Kenya has a pluralistic system of political parties, as provided in Article 1A of the constitution. Political parties, therefore, play an important role in Kenya's constitutional order. One cannot be elected to a local governmental authority, parliament, or the presidency without being supported by a particular political party.

Political parties are the vehicle for the people of Kenya to express their will, since they typically vote not only on the basis of individual competence, but also, perhaps largely, for the philosophy or ideals of the candidate's party, as expressed in its manifesto. The parties rely on membership fees and donations, although bills have been advanced for full government funding of all political parties.

CITIZENSHIP

Kenyan citizenship is primarily acquired by birth. Children whose parents are Kenyan automatically become Kenyans. Further, the constitution states that a child born outside Kenya will be a citizen of Kenya if his or her father is a citizen of Kenya. A woman who marries a citizen of Kenya can become a citizen, but only if she applies for citizenship. Thus, while men automatically pass Kenyan citizenship to their children wherever born, the same right does not accrue to women. Many have argued that this amounts to discrimination on the basis of sex, contrary to Section 82(3) of the constitution, but courts have yet to endorse that view.

Kenyan citizenship can also be attained by registration. A person who has been ordinarily resident in Kenya for a period determined in the relevant act of parliament can apply to be registered as a citizen of Kenya, provided the applicant is a citizen of another Commonwealth or African country that reciprocates this opportunity to Kenyan citizens resident in those countries. Applicants must be at least 21 years old, or an application can be made on their behalf by their parent or guardian.

Finally, Kenyan citizenship may be acquired by naturalization. To be naturalized, an applicant must be at least 21 years old, have ordinarily and lawfully resided in Kenya for a period of 12 months immediately preceding the application, must be of good character, must prove adequate knowledge of the Swahili language, and must show that if naturalized, he or she intends to continue residing in Kenya.

Citizenship acquired by registration or naturalization can be revoked. Grounds for revocation are set out in the constitution and include disloyalty or disaffection toward Kenya or assistance in any form of Kenya's enemies at war.

FUNDAMENTAL RIGHTS

Chapter 5 of the constitution of Kenya deals with fundamental rights and freedoms. The rights and freedoms protected are all of a civil and political nature except, perhaps, the right to property under Article 75, which can be categorized as a socioeconomic right. Conspicuously missing from Kenya's Bill of Rights are the other socioeconomic rights such as those related to health, education, or housing, but also the more controversial "group" or "people's" rights such as the right to a clean and healthy environment, the right to development, and the right to peace.

Impact and Functions of Fundamental Rights

Kenya, as do most African states, lacks a long history of constitutionalism and respect for human rights. The co-lonial administration oversaw a government with blithe disregard for the equal rights of all as envisaged in the 1948 Universal Declaration of Human Rights and other international agreements.

The postcolonial governments, however, have not fared any better in the area of human rights. Although the postindependence constitution has a Bill of Rights for the benefit of all, respecting and protecting these rights have been among the most serious challenges that have faced the governments of Jomo Kenyatta, Daniel arap Moi, and now Mwai Kibaki.

Despite constitutional guarantees, many people were detained without trial and others fled to exile in Western countries for fear of persecution, simply for holding views contrary to those of the governing elite. The period between 1982 and 1991 especially saw the outlawing of publications, the closure or censure of perceived antiestablishment media houses, and a major deterioration of the economy leading to tremendous abuse of internationally recognized socioeconomic rights.

Despite the freedom of association and assembly, the formation of parties other than the then-ruling KANU was prohibited in practice between 1969 and 1991. It was only allowed again after much pressure from donor countries and civil society–sponsored agitation with attendant arrests, detentions, and police shootings of demonstrators. The gains made since 1991 have been threatened, especially since 2004, when Mwai Kibaki co-opted members of the opposition into his government, threatening to restore single-party (or no-party) rule. The constitutionally protected right to freedom of association was greatly abused on July 3, 2004, when the police forcibly prevented opposition and civil society groups from holding a meeting of the constitutional review commission after almost 10 years of pressure.

Limitations to Fundamental Rights

Article 70 of the constitution contains a general limitation clause. It provides that while every person in Kenya is entitled to fundamental rights and freedoms without distinction, these are subject to the rights and freedoms of others and to the public interest.

Apart from this general limitation, various rights have their own "internal" limitations. For instance, the right to life is not violated when a death sentence imposed by a court of law is carried out, or if death arises as a result of lawful use of force to effect a lawful arrest or to defend any person or property from violence. Similarly, freedom of expression is subject to the interests of defense, public safety, public order, public morality, or public health, among other limitations.

ECONOMY

The Kenyan constitution does not specify the country's economic system. However, certain constitutional provisions, especially in the chapter on fundamental rights and freedoms, may shed light on the economic system envisaged by the drafters. For instance, Section 75 protects the right to property. No person may have his or her property or interest therein deprived without compensation. This presupposes a free market economy. Similarly, the right to form and join trade unions or other associations in order to pursue one's interests is protected.

RELIGIOUS COMMUNITIES

The constitution enshrines the right to freedom of conscience, and this includes freedom of thought, freedom of religion, and freedom to change one's religion or belief, either alone or in community with others. This right also incorporates the right to manifest and propagate, both in public and in private, one's religion or belief in worship, teaching, practice, and observance.

There is no state religion, presupposing that all religions, including atheism, are to be treated equally. Every religious community is entitled, at its own expense, to establish and maintain schools.

Unofficial figures estimate that 80 percent of the Kenyan population are Christians. Of these, the majority are Roman Catholics. Mainstream Protestant churches include Anglicans, Presbyterians, and Methodists. There are Pentecostal churches, Jehovah's Witnesses, and the Seventh Day Adventists as well. The remaining 20 percent of the population are Muslims, Hindus, and "new age" faiths such as the Theosophical Society. There are also traditionalists and atheists.

MILITARY DEFENSE AND STATE OF EMERGENCY

Interestingly, the constitution does not contain provisions relating to the establishment, administration, and discipline of the armed forces, leaving this to an act of parliament—the Armed Forces Act. However, under Article 4 of the constitution, the president is commander in chief of the armed forces of the republic.

Article 85 of the constitution authorizes the president to put in operation the provisions of the Preservation of Public Security Act. Under this act, a state of emergency may be declared in exceptional circumstances when the life of the nation is threatened. The effect of a state of emergency is that fundamental rights and freedoms except those specified as nonderogable are suspended in order to enable the government to deal with the emergency in question.

A state of emergency must last only for a specified period. In emergency situations when Kenya is at war, parliament can extend the state for up to 12 months at a time, for a maximum of five years (Article 59).

AMENDMENTS TO THE CONSTITUTION

Amendment of the Kenyan constitution is relatively difficult. Whereas passage of ordinary legislation requires a simple majority of members of parliament actually present and voting, any bill to amend the constitution must be supported by at least two-thirds of all the members of parliament excluding ex officio members.

PRIMARY SOURCES

The Constitution of Kenya. Rev. ed. Nairobi: Government Printer, 2001. Available online. URL: http://kenya. rcbowen.com/constitution/. Accessed on August 9, 2005.

SECONDARY SOURCES

Yash Pal Ghai, "Constitutions and Political Order in East Africa." *International and Comparative Law Quarterly* 21 (1972): 403.
Yash Pal Ghai and JPWB McAuslan, *Public Law and Political Change in Kenya.* 2d ed. Nairobi: Oxford University Press, 2001.
J. B. Ojwang, *Constitutional Development in Kenya: Institutional Adaptation and Social Change.* Nairobi: ACTS Press, 1990.

Kithure Kindiki

KIRIBATI

At-a-Glance

OFFICIAL NAME
Republic of Kiribati

CAPITAL
Tarawa

POPULATION
100,798 (2005 est.)

SIZE
Land area: 313 sq. mi. (811 sq. km)
Sea area: 1,371 sq. mi. (3,550 sq. km)

RELIGIONS
Roman Catholic 52%, Protestant (Congregational)
40%, some Seventh-Day Adventist, Muslim, Bahá'i,
Latter-Day Saints, and Church of God

LANGUAGES
I-Kiribati, English (official)

NATIONAL OR ETHNIC COMPOSITION
Predominantly Micronesian, minority Polynesian

DATE OF INDEPENDENCE OR CREATION
July 12, 1979

TYPE OF GOVERNMENT
Republican

TYPE OF STATE
Unitary state

TYPE OF LEGISLATURE
Unicameral parliament

DATE OF CONSTITUTION
July 12, 1979

DATE OF LAST AMENDMENT
No amendment

Kiribati is an island nation of 33 atolls located in the Pacific Ocean near the equator. Formerly the Gilbert Islands Colony of the United Kingdom, Kiribati was granted self-rule in 1971 and independence in 1979.

Kiribati has a written constitution. Its system of government is that of a democratic republic. The government has three branches, following the principle of the separation of powers: The executive is led by a president or Beretitenti, who is the head of state and chief of the administration; the legislature or Maneaba ni Maungatabu has a single chamber; and the judiciary is independent.

Kiribati has a small and isolated economy. As a consequence of internal migration approximately half of the population now resides on the main island of Tarawara.

CONSTITUTIONAL HISTORY

Kiribati was inhabited by people from Micronesia about 3,000 years ago. Polynesian people subsequently invaded Kiribati; frequent intermarriage between the two ethnic groups produced strong Polynesian influence on Kiribati's Micronesian culture. Europeans arrived in the 16th century, and the British established a protectorate in Kiribati in 1892. In 1900, Banaba island became part of the British protectorate after the discovery of phosphate. In 1916, the Ellice Islands and the islands of Kiribati became a British colony—the Gilbert and Ellice Islands Colony.

From 1941 to 1943, the Japanese occupied Kiribati. Tarawa was the site of a major battle of the Pacific war in 1943.

Moves toward self-government began in 1963 with the appointment of a local executive council and an advisory council. This council was replaced by a house of representatives that had powers of recommendation, which was in turn replaced by a legislative council of 23 elected members in 1971.

In 1975, the Ellice Islands separated from the colony to form the state of Tuvalu. Kiribati acquired independence as a republic within the Commonwealth on July 12, 1979.

FORM AND IMPACT OF THE CONSTITUTION

Kiribati has a written constitution, which is the supreme law of the country. Any act of the legislature that is inconsistent with the constitution is void to the extent of the inconsistency. The High Court has jurisdiction to enforce the constitution.

BASIC ORGANIZATIONAL STRUCTURE

Kiribati has a unitary state system, but it is administratively divided into three units; the Gilbert Islands, the Line Islands, and the Phoenix Islands. There are six districts and 21 island councils.

LEADING CONSTITUTIONAL PRINCIPLES

The constitution states, "Kiribati is a sovereign democratic republic." The preamble of the constitution sets out some guiding principles for implementation as follows: "(1) the will of the people shall ultimately be paramount in the conduct of the government of Kiribati; (2) the principles of equality and justice shall be upheld; (3) the natural resources of Kiribati are vested in the people and their Government; and (4) we shall continue to cherish and uphold the customs and traditions of Kiribati."

CONSTITUTIONAL BODIES

The predominant constitutional organs are the president; the cabinet; the Maneaba ni Maungatabu (House of Assembly); the judiciary, including the High Court; and the Public Service Commission.

The President

The president or Beretitenti is both the head of state and chief of the administration. The president is elected by popular vote for a four-year term. The legislature nominates presidential candidates from among its members, and those candidates compete in a general election. The president appoints a vice president from the ministers of the cabinet.

The Cabinet

The constitution states, "The executive authority of Kiribati shall vest in the cabinet, which shall be collectively responsible to the Maneaba ni Maungatabu for the executive functions of the Government." The cabinet consists of the president, the vice president, not more than eight other ministers, and the attorney general. The president appoints the ministers from among the members of the legislature.

The Parliament

The House of Assembly or Maneaba ni Maungatabu consists of a unicameral chamber with members elected by popular vote plus one ex officio member—the attorney general—and one member appointed to represent Banabans who live on Rabi Island (Fiji).

The Lawmaking Process

The Maneaba ni Maungatabu has power to make laws consistent with the constitution. A bill needs the assent of the Beretitenti to become law; the Beretitenti may withhold assent only on the grounds that the bill is inconsistent with the constitution.

The Judiciary

The High Court is the guardian of the constitution. It interprets and applies the law according to constitutional principles. Judges are appointed by the Beretitenti acting on the advice of cabinet given after consultation with the Public Service Commission. The system of courts is, in descending order, the Court of Appeal, the High Court, and the magistrates' courts.

Public Service Commission

The Public Service Commission is responsible for advising the Beretitenti on the appointment, removal, and disciplinary control of persons working in offices paid by public money.

THE ELECTION PROCESS

The constitution divides Kiribati into electoral districts, with boundaries and number of candidates to be provided by legislation. It expressly reserves one seat of the legislature for the Banaban community.

Article 64 of the constitution provides that people entitled to register to vote must be citizens of Kiribati over the age of 18, resident within an electoral district. A person is qualified to stand for election to Maneaba ni Maungatabu if he or she is a citizen of Kiribati and is over the age of 21.

POLITICAL PARTIES

There are no organized political parties in Kiribati. Candidates and voters tend to group themselves informally.

CITIZENSHIP

Every person born in Kiribati is a citizen by birth. The constitution also states that "Every person of I-Kiribati descent . . . has the right to become a citizen of Kiribati."

FUNDAMENTAL RIGHTS

The constitution provides for the protection of the fundamental rights and freedoms of individuals. For example, privacy of home and property, freedom of expression, and property rights are protected.

Limitations to Fundamental Rights

The rights and freedoms are not absolute. They are subject to limitations based on public interest and restrictions in a period of public emergency.

Impact and Functions of Fundamental Rights

The entrenched rights and freedoms, in the form presented by the constitution, are alien to the culture of Kiribati. That culture operated without courts or written laws and depended for its survival on a strong sense of community and cooperation. The emphasis was therefore on duties to the group rather than on the rights of individuals. Dispute resolution within the community was by reference to acceptance and respect for the local social norms and ultimately a respect for the expression of those norms by those more senior in the social hierarchy.

Christianity entered this environment in the 19th century. It was rapidly and comprehensively accepted to the point that it superseded traditional rules in the areas it addressed.

In the late 20th century, the notion of universal human rights was introduced into the formal legal system. At most points, the content of those human rights is consistent with the Christian views of the people of Kiribati. However, there remains a cultural resistance to the introduced human rights system, not least because of its emphasis on individualism and the notion of rights. There is a strong residual sense in the community of social duties and a respect for the interest of others before self-interest.

There is little litigation on human rights matters; however, in the judicial context the system operates in a manner not very dissimilar to that in Europe or North America. The most active part of the judicial system relates to criminal law, and the rules of due process are fully operative.

ECONOMY

There are no constitutional provisions regarding the economy. Copra, fish, remittances from workers abroad, and tourism (principally to Kiritimati and Tarawa) are the main sources of locally generated income. Some of the problems are Kiribati's remoteness from international markets, the shortage of skilled workers, and inadequate infrastructure (e.g., power supply, water supply, waste disposal). However, Kiribati has successfully managed its financial resources through the Revenue Equalization Reserve Fund (RERF), which was established in 1956 by the colonial administration with royalties from mining of the Banaba phosphate deposits. The Revenue Equalization Reserve Fund now operates as a special fund under Article 107 of the constitution.

RELIGIOUS COMMUNITIES

Freedom of thought, conscience, and religion is protected by Article 11 of the constitution. The population is almost exclusively Christian, as 52 percent are Roman Catholic and 40 percent are Congregationalist Protestant.

MILITARY DEFENSE AND STATE OF EMERGENCY

The constitution provides in Article 126 that no disciplined force shall be established other than the Kiribati Police, the Prison Service, the Marine Protection Service, and the Marine Training School.

AMENDMENTS TO THE CONSTITUTION

The constitution can be altered by an act of parliament passed with the special majority of two-thirds of the total membership of parliament. Amendments regarding fundamental rights and freedoms of individuals additionally require a referendum within the national electorate, and a two-thirds majority is needed to support change. Any amendment relating to Banaba island can be made only if the Banaban representative in the legislature does not vote against it.

PRIMARY SOURCES
Constitution in English. Available online. URL: http://www.paclii.org/. Accessed on August 25, 2005.

SECONDARY SOURCES
Ron Crocombe, *The South Pacific*. Fiji: University of the South Pacific, 2001.
Norman Douglas and Ngaire Douglas, *Pacific Islands Yearbook*. 17th ed. Suva: Fiji Times, 1994.

Anthony Angelo

KOREA, NORTH

At-a-Glance

OFFICIAL NAME
Democratic People's Republic of Korea

CAPITAL
Pyongyang

POPULATION
22,800,000 (2004)

SIZE
47,000 sq. mi. (120,410 sq. km)

LANGUAGE
Korean

RELIGIONS
Generally atheism

NATIONAL OR ETHNIC COMPOSITION
Korean; small Chinese and Japanese populations

DATE OF INDEPENDENCE OR CREATION
September 9, 1948

TYPE OF GOVERNMENT
Communist state

TYPE OF STATE
Extremely centralized state

TYPE OF LEGISLATURE
Unicameral Supreme People's Assembly

DATE OF CONSTITUTION
September 9, 1948

DATE OF LAST AMENDMENT
September 5, 1998

North Korea is one of the rare states that do not assemble their legal codes in the form of a single book. Furthermore, it is a state strongly closed to the outside world; information is fragmentary and hard to get. As a result, knowledge of its statutory laws is limited, and its judicial decisions are not accessible at all. The following overview of North Korea's constitutional history and constitutional law is as full and accurate as can be obtained given these obstacles.

CONSTITUTIONAL HISTORY

From 1910 to 1945, the old Korean Kingdom had been governed by Japan. The first constitution of the Democratic People's Republic of Korea was adopted on September 9, 1948, three years after the Russian occupation of the northern half of the Korean peninsula after World War II (1939–45); in the south the American military government ended the same year. The 1948 constitution consisted of 104 articles in 10 chapters. Since then North Korea has revised its constitution eight times, twice in

1954 and once each in 1955, 1956, 1962, 1972, 1992, and 1998. Each time, articles of the constitution were revised and administrative districts adjusted; one revision lowered the voting age.

The 1972 revision instituted a president-centered state system. In both structure and content the new so-called Socialist Constitution was entirely different from the former constitution; it focused solely on socialism and *juche* (self-reliance) ideology. It declared that North Korean society had completely embraced socialism, thereby institutionalizing Kim Il Sung's despotic rule. The document created a Central People's Committee and the Government Affairs Committee.

With the collapse of world communism in the 1990s, North Korea amended its constitution for the seventh time in April 1992. Juche was now the sole guiding ideology, replacing Marxism-Leninism. In structural terms, the defense committee of the Central People's Committee was upgraded to a state organ called the National Defense Commission. The commission became the most powerful body in the country, and North Korea became a military dictatorship.

In September 1998, the North Korean constitution was amended for the eighth time, on the occasion of Kim Jong-Il's official succession to power. The amended constitution was entitled the Kim Il Sung Constitution in an effort to perpetuate the late Kim Il Sung's legacy and lend credibility to the government. The power of Kim Jong-Il, the chairman of the National Defense Commission, was greatly reinforced by his new position as general secretary of the Korean Workers' Party, the ruling party. He now commands both the party and the military, giving him absolute power. At the same time, the constitutional amendment reduced Kim Jong-Il's state management responsibilities by creating a Supreme People's Assembly Executive Committee Chairmanship to handle foreign affairs and by authorizing the prime minister to take care of administrative affairs, including economic matters.

FORM AND IMPACT OF THE CONSTITUTION

The North Korean constitution is a single document that contains 166 articles. The document, in its most recent form, concentrates political power in the person of the chairperson of the National Defense Commission, allows private property ownership on a limited scale, and aims at economic autonomy, while opening a wider window for foreign investment. North Korea adopted a Civil Code on September 9, 1990. The Criminal Code, last revised on February 5, 1987, still serves as a tool for enforcing the socialist state ideology. Although the North Korean constitution contains some mention of international law, its ties to such law remain weak.

BASIC ORGANIZATIONAL STRUCTURE

The state is administratively divided into eight local principal authorities and four special cities.

LEADING CONSTITUTIONAL PRINCIPLES

North Korea is a Communist state, ruled by a one-man dictatorship. It does not embrace the ideas of separation of power or checks and balances among political powers. The name for communism as practiced in North Korea is *juche,* Kim Il Sung's interpretation of Marxism-Leninism that emphasizes nationalism and human beings as the prime mover to nature.

The current constitution is equipped with a new preamble, which describes the socialist principles of the state: The Democratic People's Republic of Korea is a socialist fatherland of Juche which embodies the ideas of and guid-

ance by the great leader Comrade Kim Il Sung. The great leader Comrade Kim Il Sung is the founder of the DPRK and socialist Korea. . . . The DPRK and the entire Korean people will uphold the great leader Comrade Kim Il Sung as the eternal President of the Republic, defend and carry forward his ideas and accomplishments and complete the Juche revolution under the leadership of the Korean Workers' Party of Korea. The DPRK Socialist Constitution is a Kim Il Sung Constitution which legally embodies Comrade Kim Il Sung's Juche state construction ideology and achievements.

However, it is interesting to note some striking "Confucian" expressions, which could hardly be understood from the viewpoint of socialist ideology. The preamble of the constitution puts it as follows: Comrade Kim Il Sung regarded "believing in the people as in heaven" (*Iminwichon*) as his motto, was always with the people, devoted his whole life to them, took care of and guided them with a noble politics of benevolence (*Indokjongchi*), and turned the whole society into one big and united family. . . . Comrade Kim Il Sung was a genius ideological theoretician and a genius art leader, an ever-victorious, iron-willed brilliant commander, a great revolutionary and politician, and a great human being.

The North Korean constitution thus shows a tension or perhaps a harmony between socialist and Confucian language in describing the official ideology.

CONSTITUTIONAL BODIES

The structure of the state is composed of the Supreme People's Assembly, the National Defense Commission, the Presidium of the Supreme People's Assembly, the Administration Council or cabinet, the Public Prosecutor's Office, and the judiciary. All of these institutions ultimately serve to support the one-man dictatorship. The Korean Workers' Party dominates all organs of government.

The Supreme People's Assembly

The highest organ of state power is the Supreme People's Assembly, which exercises the legislative power. The constitution stipulates that other constitutional bodies are accountable to the Supreme People's Assembly; they are controlled by the assembly's decisions. The assembly is composed of deputies elected on the principle of universal, equal, and direct suffrage by secret ballot for a term of five years.

The assembly has supreme sovereign power, including the authority to amend and supplement the constitution; adopt, amend, and supplement laws; and establish the basic principles of the state's domestic and foreign policies. The assembly also elects or removes members of various other constitutional bodies, examines and approves the state plan for the development of the national economy and the report on its progress, and examines and approves the report on the state budget and on its implementation.

Furthermore, the assembly receives reports on the work of the cabinet and other national institutions. Finally, it decides on the ratification or abrogation of treaties.

The Supreme People's Assembly holds regular sessions. The laws and decisions of the assembly are adopted when more than half of the deputies attending signify approval by a show of hands. The assembly also works through committees such as the legislation committee and the budget committee.

The National Defense Commission

The highest military organ of state power is the National Defense Commission. The chair of the commission directs and commands all the armed forces and guides defense affairs as a whole. Kim Jong-Il is the current chair of the National Defense Commission, as well as the secretary general of the Korean Workers' Party. The National Defense Commission has the responsibility and power to guide the armed forces and guide the state in defense matters as a whole. It creates or dissolves other institutions in the defense sector and has the power to proclaim a state of war and order mobilization.

The Presidium of the Supreme People's Assembly

During the intervals between sessions of the Supreme People's Assembly, its Presidium is the highest organ of power. The term of the Presidium is the same as that of the assembly itself. It has the power to convene sessions of the assembly and to examine and adopt bills, regulations, and various state plans for the national economy. It interprets the constitution, laws, and regulations in force; supervises state organs; works with deputies of the assembly; and elects or removes judges of the Central Court. The Presidium can also create or reorganize administrative units and districts.

The Cabinet

The cabinet is the administrative and executive body of the assembly and the general state management body. The 1998 constitution designated the cabinet responsible for oversight of the national policy implementation. The cabinet is staffed with loyal Korean Workers' Party officials who have some administrative and technical expertise. There are one premier, two deputy premiers, 27 ministers, and four directors of key state institutions. The eight provincial governors and heads of special administrative districts also are members of the cabinet. The cabinet's term is the same as that of the Supreme People's Assembly. Its main responsibilities are to adopt measures to execute state policy and to institute, amend, and supplement regulations concerning state management on the basis of the constitution and the laws. The cabinet is also charged with maintaining social order, protecting state and social cooperation, and guaranteeing citizens' rights. Furthermore, the cabinet concludes treaties with foreign countries and conducts external activities. Article 120 of the constitution states that the premier of the cabinet represents the government of the Democratic People's Republic of Korea.

The Lawmaking Process

Laws are enacted by the Supreme People's Assembly when more than half of the deputies present approve. However, when the assembly is not in session it is up to the Presidium of the Supreme People's Assembly to adopt bills.

The Judiciary

The judicial system consists of two elements: courts and prosecutors. The judicial system's primary role is to protect "the state and socialist system."

The constitution states that the North Korean judiciary is independently administered through the Central Court, the Courts of the Provinces (or of the municipalities directly under central authority), municipal and county courts, the separate military courts, and traffic and transportation courts. The Central Court is the supreme court of the Democratic People's Republic of Korea and supervises trial activities of all lower courts. However, Article 162 of the constitution stipulates that the Central Court is accountable to the Supreme People's Assembly.

Concerning the mechanism of dispute resolution in North Korea, the government relies heavily on the socialist law-abiding lifestyle of the North Korean people. Even though they have no written legal code, the people learn the laws through regular village meetings, which prevent them from violating laws. Regardless of the statistics, North Korea seems to be a rather stable and self-regulating society.

THE ELECTION PROCESS

All citizens who have reached the age of 17 have the right to vote in elections and to be elected, irrespective of sex, race, occupation, length of residence, property status, education, party affiliation, political views, or religion. Citizens serving in the armed forces also have the right to vote in elections and to be elected. However, a person who has been disenfranchised by a court decision or legally certified to be insane does not have the right to vote in elections or to be elected.

POLITICAL PARTIES

The constitution states that the government shall guarantee conditions for the free activity of democratic political parties and social organizations. However, the constitution also declares that the Democratic People's Republic of Korea shall conduct all activities under the leadership of the Workers' Party of Korea. In reality, the North Korean government is under the rigid control of the Korean Workers' Party, to which all government officials belong, and only a few minor parties are allowed to exist in name only. Kim Il Sung has spelled out ten rules that govern the conduct of those who wish to become and remain members of the Korean Workers' Party.

CITIZENSHIP

The terms for becoming a citizen of the Democratic People's Republic of Korea are defined by the Law on Nationality. A citizen is under the protection of the Democratic People's Republic of Korea regardless of his or her domicile.

FUNDAMENTAL RIGHTS AND DUTIES

Chapter 5 of the constitution lists the fundamental rights and duties of citizens, which are based on the collectivist principle "One for all and all for one." Article 64 proclaims that the state shall effectively guarantee genuine democratic rights and liberties as well as the material and cultural welfare of its citizens. The subsequent articles spell out specific rights such as freedom of speech, of the press, of assembly, of demonstration, and of association. Citizens have the right to work, to relaxation, to free medical care, and to education.

The constitution also provides for specified duties of citizens. The constitution demands political and ideological unity and solidarity. Highest value is accorded to organizations and collectives. Individual citizens are called upon to observe the laws of the state and the socialist standards of life strictly, thus ultimately defending their honor and dignity as citizens of the Democratic People's Republic of Korea. Work is considered not only as the fundamental right, but also as the fundamental duty of citizens. Finally, national defense is defined as the supreme duty and honor of citizens. Therefore, citizens must defend the country and serve in the army as required by law.

Impact and Functions of Fundamental Rights

The constitution outlines a wide range of rights, but in reality, with the government totally controlled by the Korean Workers' Party and dominated by Kim Il Sung, the state can freely control its citizens. Punishment of any "political crime," for example, is severe. Free speech and freedom of press may be guaranteed in one section of the constitution, but elsewhere in the same document North Koreans are required to observe "socialist norms of life."

Limitations to Fundamental Rights

The people are required to follow the collectivist principle of "one for all and all for one." This orientation constitutes a basic and general limitation to all individual human rights in Korea. North Korea's huge army and weapons of mass destruction impose enormous burdens on the people. The Western idea of human and individual political rights are alien to the North Korean people. Individuals who assert their personal desires and claim "rights" vis-à-vis the state and ruler are perceived as disloyal and subversive. They are easily categorized as the "enemy of the state" and purged, either through execution or banishment to the labor camp. Many North Korean people follow the outward flow of refugees such as to China and Mongolia. In 2004 the United States enacted the "2004 North Korean Human Rights Act" and the United Nations has passed resolutions three times since 2003 for the improvement of the human rights in North Korea.

THE ECONOMY

The Democratic People's Republic of Korea relies on a socialist system of production and on the principle of a national economy totally independent from other countries. Consequently, the means of production are owned only by the state and social cooperative organizations. In theory, the property of the state belongs to the entire people. Because there is no limit to the property that the state can own, the North Korean government basically owns all natural resources, railways, airports, transportation, communication organs, major factories, enterprises, ports, and banks. The constitution also allows social cooperative organizations to possess such property as land, agricultural machinery, ships, and medium or small factories and businesses. The state aims to replace all cooperative ownership with state ownership to "enhance the ideological consciousness and the technical and cultural level of the peasants, and increase the role of the property of the entire people in leading the cooperative property so as to combine the two forms of property systematically, shall consolidate and develop the socialist cooperative economic system by improving the guidance and management of the cooperative economy and gradually transform the property of cooperative organizations into the property of the people as a whole based on the voluntary will of all their members."

People may own some private property or savings. This may include the "socialist distribution of the results of labor" (wages), additional benefits from the state and society, and the products of personal sideline activities such as the kitchen gardens of cooperative farmers. Article 25 claims that the Democratic People's Republic of Korea considers the material and cultural well-being of its people as the supreme principle of its activities; therefore, the wealth of society is used entirely for the benefit of the working people. Taxes have been abolished.

The constitution stresses the importance of holding onto the *juche* ideology and strengthening self-sufficiency, so as to maintain a national economy independent from other countries within a completely socialist society. Since the technical revolution is deemed vital to the development of the socialist economy, the state asserts that it shall give top priority to solving the problems of technical development and accelerating scientific and technical development. This is meant ultimately to free the working masses from backbreaking labor, to narrow the differences between physical and mental labor, and to eliminate differences between urban and rural areas and class distinctions between the working class and the peasantry. Furthermore, Article 29 states that the working masses are freed from exploitation and suppression and that they do not have to worry about unemployment. The working day for most people is set at eight hours, although that can vary, depending on difficulty and conditions of work. The minimal working age is 16.

According to the constitution, the Democratic People's Republic of Korea has a planned economy. The national economy is managed according to the "Taean Work System," a form of socialist management in which the economy is purportedly operated and managed in a scientific and rational way, with reliance on the collective power of the producing masses, and in which agriculture is managed by using industrial methods.

Regarding foreign trade, the Democratic People's Republic of Korea emphasizes the principles of complete equality and mutual benefit. The state alleges that it will promote the establishment of equity and contractual joint venture enterprises with foreign corporations or individuals within "a special economic zone." Nevertheless, the state also pursues a tariff policy in order to protect and maintain the national economy independent from other countries. North Korea's future economic development remains tied to the question whether the regime will conform to international norms and win support of international financial institutions.

RELIGIOUS COMMUNITIES

Article 68 guarantees freedom of religion as follows: "Citizens have freedom of religious beliefs. This right is granted by approving the construction of religious buildings and the holding of religious ceremonies. No one may use religion as a pretext for drawing in foreign forces or for harming the state and social order."

In reality, however, North Korea has severely persecuted various religious communities in line with Communist ideology. The Christian churches in particular have suffered severe persecution, because they were thought to be agents of the "imperialistic Americans." Most Buddhist temples and Confucian shrines were also destroyed.

From 1945 to 1953, when the Korean War ended, several million North Koreans fled to the South for religious reasons. Christian churches have flourished and attracted millions of adherents in South Korea. To compete, the North Korean government quietly supports a new nationalistic religion, the Chondogyo (Eastern Learning). It is very hard to know how many religious communities are surviving and acting underground in the North. Since the 1990s, North Korean government propaganda has claimed that North Koreans fully enjoy freedom of religion. Although some Catholic and Protestant churches have been established in Pyongyang, it is highly likely that these churches were built solely for propaganda purposes.

MILITARY DEFENSE

National defense is proclaimed as the supreme duty and honor of citizens. Citizens are required to defend the country and serve in the army as regulated by law. North Korea strains to maintain a decisive advantage over the South and to be ready for full mobilization at a moment's notice. The North Korean military has the motto "National defense by self-defense." Article 60 of the constitution states: "The State shall implement the line of self-reliant defense, the import of which is to arm the entire people, fortify the country, train the army into a cadre army and modernize the army on the basis of equipping the army and the people politically and ideologically."

National defense seems to be the ultimate goal of the nation; Article 34 suggests that even the national economic development plans are formulated and implemented ultimately "in order to strengthen the national defense capability."

AMENDMENTS TO THE CONSTITUTION

The constitution is amended and supplemented with the approval of more than two-thirds of the total number of deputies to the Supreme People's Assembly.

PRIMARY SOURCES
Constitution in English. Available online. URL: http://www.novexcn.com/dprk_constitution_98.html. Accessed on August 31, 2005.
The Socialist Constitution of the Democratic People's Republic of Korea (1998). In Chongko Choi, *Law and Justice in Korea: South and North*. Seoul: Seoul National University Press, 2005: 469–493.

SECONDARY SOURCES
Sung-Yoon Cho, ed., *Law and Legal Literature of North Korea*. Washington, D.C.: Library of Congress, 1988.
Chongko Choi, *Introduction to Korean Law*. Seoul: Seoul National University Press, 2003.
Chongko Choi, *Law and Justice in Korea: South and North*. Seoul: Seoul National University Press, 2004.

Chongko Choi, *North Korean Law: Introduction and Text.* (Forthcoming).

"The Constitution of People's Republic of Korea" in *The Constitutions of the Communist World,* edited by William B. Simons, p. 640. Alphen aan den Rijin: Sijthoff & Noordhoff, 1980.

C. Kenneth Quinones and Joseph Tragert, *Understanding North Korea.* New York: Alpha Books, 2002.

Sung Chul Yang, *The North and South Korean Political Systems—A Comparative Analysis.* Seoul: Hollym, 1999.

Chongko Choi

KOREA, SOUTH

At-a-Glance

OFFICIAL NAME
Republic of Korea

CAPITAL
Seoul

POPULATION
47,900,000 (2005 est.)

SIZE
85,774 sq. mi. (222,154 sq. km)

LANGUAGES
Korean

RELIGIONS
Buddhist 25.3%, Protestant 20%, Catholic 7%,
Confucianist 0.6%, unaffiliated or other 47.1%

NATIONAL OR ETHNIC COMPOSITION
Korean (one ethnic family)

DATE OF INDEPENDENCE OR CREATION
August 15, 1945

TYPE OF GOVERNMENT
Parliamentary democracy

TYPE OF STATE
Unitary state

TYPE OF LEGISLATURE
Unicameral parliament

DATE OF CONSTITUTION
July 17, 1948

DATE OF LAST AMENDMENT
October 29, 1987

The Republic of Korea is a democratic republic based on the rule of law, a separation of powers, and a system of checks and balances. Sovereignty resides in the people, from whom all state authority derives. In order to protect freedoms and rights to the maximal extent, the constitution also provides for the independence of the three branches of government: the executive, the legislature, and the judiciary.

The constitution of Korea was adopted on July 17, 1948, and has been amended nine times. The Constitution of the Republic prescribes a presidential system for the executive branch of the government. The presidential system was designed to achieve strong and stable leadership based on a popular mandate.

The traditions of a royal regime and a Confucian hierarchical system, the historical experiences of Japanese invasion and colonial rule, and an autocratic period of rule by military authorities made it difficult to achieve democratic ideals and the rule of law and to realize the ideals and spirit of the constitution.

However, economic development and the advent of civilian government opened a new era in Korean democracy and constitutionalism. The Constitutional Court, established in 1988, has also contributed to the constitutional ideal and played an important role in protecting the people's concrete constitutional rights.

CONSTITUTIONAL HISTORY

The Constitution of the Republic of Korea was first promulgated on July 17, 1948, after independence from Japanese colonial rule. It has been amended nine times. The original constitution entailed detailed constitutional provisions for the protection of fundamental rights, as well as separation of powers, influenced by Western constitutions. However, there were numerous difficulties in adapting constitutionalism in South Korea. Frequent amendments of the constitution and the extension of the tenure of presidents were both meant to provide an aura of legitimacy to a regime that gained power by a coup d'état.

The original 1948 constitution underwent its first revision in 1952, when President Syngman Rhee tried to extend his term by instituting martial law. He altered the constitution to allow a direct popular vote for the presidency and additionally to provide for a bicameral legislature. Under the original constitution, the president was elected by a unicameral National Assembly.

In 1952, the assembly was controlled by political parties opposed to Rhee. Despite this opposition, Rhee succeeded in revising the constitution. It was the height of the Korean War (1950–53), and the assembly met in the temporary capital of Pusan, where the administration had taken refuge. Rhee declared and enforced martial law to repress all political activity. The assembly's vote for the constitutional revision was taken in the middle of the night with all 166 members standing in an atmosphere of fear. The amendment bill passed, as expected, without a dissenting vote. As a result, Rhee was reelected president by a popular vote.

The second constitutional revision, pushed through in 1954, enabled Rhee to enjoy an unlimited term as president. In this case, an egregious irregularity allowed the revision to pass with one vote less than the constitutionally mandated two-thirds majority of the National Assembly. Ultimately, however, Rhee's constitutional manipulations failed to guarantee him the presidency once he lost popular support in 1960.

The fall of Rhee's government by a popular revolt entailed another constitutional change. The rush in drafting a new constitution, however, failed to accommodate differing views or to provide procedural justice. This third revision adopted a parliamentary system to replace the presidential system. This change so drastically altered the constitution that the new government was dubbed the Second Republic. A fourth revision, also in 1960, accommodated legislation for the retroactive punishment of those found guilty of election irregularities, corruption, and misappropriation of public property. This amendment was a result of popular pressure and provided a constitutional exception to the principle prohibiting retroactive penalties.

The fifth amendment, in fact a full rewrite, was imposed in 1962 by the military government that followed the coup d'état of 1961. This amendment restored the presidential system and the unicameral legislature. The sixth amendment, written in 1969, raised the presidential term limit to three, thus enabling Park Chung Hee to seek a third consecutive term. The seventh amendment in 1972, a second rewrite, effectively allowed President Park Chung Hee to rule for life, by removing term limits and introducing indirect elections of the president through an electoral college. Under this constitution, the president was truly all-powerful, with the authority to fill one-third of the seats in the National Assembly, to dissolve the National Assembly, and to issue emergency decrees that could easily be used as means to oppress opposition groups or individuals.

The eighth amendment, the third rewrite, was passed in October 1980 by the military government of Chun Doo Hwan, who took power after the assassination of President Park Chung Hee in October 1979. The amendment provided for a single seven-year term for the president, while maintaining the system of indirect elections and thus shielding Chun Doo Hwan from the risk of defeat in a popular election.

In the latter part of the 1980s, public protests against the authoritarian military government intensified. The political authorities faced a dilemma—whether to extend their rule by extraordinary means, such as martial law, or whether to accommodate popular sentiments. Unlike previous regimes, those in power took the latter option. The 1987 constitutional revision represents a dramatic departure from previous changes in both its political process and its meaning.

The 1987 rewrite was the last amendment to date. It restored popular elections for president and limited the president to a single five-year term. The same year, South Korea experienced its first peaceful transfer of power since independence.

The 1987 constitution, which became effective on February 25, 1988, strengthened the power of the National Assembly, considerably reduced the power of the executive, and provided for stronger protection for basic rights. In particular, a European-style Constitutional Court was established as a venue for citizens to seek redress when basic rights are infringed. The Constitutional Court has played a decisive role in firmly establishing constitutionalism in Korea.

FORM AND IMPACT OF THE CONSTITUTION

South Korea has a written constitution codified in a single document that takes precedence over all other national laws. Article 6(1) states: "Treaties duly concluded and promulgated under the Constitution and the generally recognized rules of international law shall have the same effect as the domestic laws of the Republic of Korea." Therefore, international law is generally regarded as domestic law, and as must domestic law it must be in accordance with the constitution to be applicable within Korea. The constitution of Korea is the supreme law; all other must comply with its provisions.

The Constitutional Court has played an important role by reviewing the constitutionality of laws and controlling the exercise of governmental power. Today, the constitution is firmly rooted in the mind of the people as a supreme law of the state and a source of fundamental values for society.

BASIC ORGANIZATIONAL STRUCTURE

Korea is not a federal system. The Korean constitution foresees the decentralization of the nation, but Korea has a tradition of a highly centralized government.

Local governments, in the words of Article 117 of the constitution, "shall deal with matters pertaining to the well-being of local residents, shall manage properties, and may establish their own rules and regulations regarding local autonomy as delegated by national laws and decrees." This constitutional provision, however, remained largely unfulfilled until July 1995, when the nation elected governors and mayors for provincial and local governments for the first time in more than 30 years. Before, local governments were no more than administrative districts of the central government. The heads of local governments were appointed by the central government, and their capacity for autonomous decision making was virtually nonexistent.

Currently, there are 16 provincial-level governments and 235 municipal governments, including 72 *si* (city) governments, 94 *gun* (county) governments, and 69 *gu* (autonomous district) governments. Provincial governments, although they have some functions of their own, basically serve as intermediaries between the central and municipal governments.

LEADING CONSTITUTIONAL PRINCIPLES

Korea's system of government is a parliamentary democracy. There is strong division among the executive, legislative, and judicial powers based on checks and balances.

The Korean constitutional system is defined by a number of leading principles. Sovereignty in Korea is held by the people, and all governmental authority is derived from the people. Korea is a democratic republic, a social and cultural state, based on the rule of law. In Article 1(1), the constitution states: "The Republic of Korea shall be a democratic republic." This means that Korea is a nation based on freedom and democracy and there shall be no monarchy. Article 1(2) states: "The sovereignty of the Republic of Korea shall reside in the people, and all state authority shall emanate from the people."

Sovereignty held by the people is generally realized by indirect, representative democracy. However, Article 72 says: "The President may submit important policies relating to diplomacy, national defense, unification and other matters relating to the national destiny to a national referendum if the president deems it necessary." The constitution, therefore, provides for the possibility of direct democracy, which can prevent distortion of the people's true opinions.

The principle that Korea shall be a social state means that the government must take action to ensure a minimal standard of living for every citizen. This principle does not imply any denial of private property. According to Article 34 of the constitution: "(1) All citizens shall be entitled to a life worthy of human beings. (2) The State shall have the duty to endeavor to promote social security and welfare." This principle is also realized by Article

23(2), which states: "The exercise of property rights shall conform to the public welfare."

The rule of law is also a fundamental principle. All state actions impairing the rights of the people must have a basis in parliamentary law and must respect the priority of human rights and substantial equality.

The idea that the state must support culture in order for it to flourish and promote world peace is a constitutional principle in Korea. Article 9 of the constitution provides: "The state shall strive to sustain and develop cultural heritage and to enhance national culture." Article 5(1) further provides: "The Republic of Korea shall endeavor to maintain international peace and shall renounce all aggressive wars."

CONSTITUTIONAL BODIES

The constitution provides for a three-branch governing system, whereby administrative functions are under the executive branch, headed by the president, lawmaking functions are the preserve of the National Assembly, and judicial functions belong to the courts. Structurally, these three branches are highly independent of each other.

The members of the National Assembly are elected by the people, and the National Assembly's leaders and officers are chosen by the members themselves. As for the president, he or she is not required to obtain the approval of the National Assembly in appointing top executive officials, except the prime minister and the director of the Board of Inspection and Audit. The head of the Supreme Court, the chief justice, although appointed by the president with the consent of the National Assembly, has the power to recommend to the president the appointment of other Supreme Court justices and has the power to appoint all other judges.

It is not the Supreme Court but the Constitutional Court that has the authority to render judgments regarding the constitutionality of laws, impeachments, and the dissolution of political parties. The Constitutional Court also adjudicates jurisdictional disputes between government agencies, between national and local governments, and between different local governments.

The Executive (The President)

The president is the head of state and represents the state in international affairs. He or she is also the head of the executive branch, and the commander in chief of the armed forces. In case of the president's death or disability, the prime minister temporarily acts as president according to an order of succession provided by law. The Korean constitution gives many powers to the president, in order to maintain the functional effectiveness of the state and unify various administrative opinions.

The power and duties of the president are defined in the following six areas: First, the president, as head of state, symbolizes and represents the whole nation in both the governmental system and foreign relations. The president receives foreign diplomats; presents awards, decorations, and other honors; and performs pardoning functions. Upon inauguration, the president takes an oath to safeguard the independence, territorial integrity, and continuity of the state, as well as to protect the constitution. In addition, the president is entrusted with the unique duty to pursue the peaceful unification of the Korean Peninsula.

Second, the president, in the capacity of chief executive, enforces all laws passed by the legislature and issues orders and decrees for the enforcement of these laws. The president has the full power to direct the State Council and oversee a varying number of advisory organs and executive agencies. The president is authorized to appoint public officials, including the prime minister and the heads of executive agencies.

Third, the president, in the capacity of commander in chief of the armed forces, has extensive authority over military policy, including the power to declare war.

Fourth, the president is the chief policymaker and chief lawmaker. The president may propose legislative bills to the National Assembly or express views to the legislature, in person or in writing. The president cannot dissolve the National Assembly; rather, it is the National Assembly that may hold the president accountable under the constitution by means of the impeachment process.

Fifth, the president is vested with extensive emergency powers. In case of internal turmoil, external menace, natural disaster, or severe financial or economic crisis, the president can take emergency financial and economic action or issue orders that have the effect of law. The president can exercise these powers only when there is insufficient time to convene the National Assembly and the actions or orders are absolutely essential to maintaining national security or public order. The president must subsequently notify and obtain the concurrence of the National Assembly. If the National Assembly declines to do so, the measures are nullified.

Sixth, the president is empowered to declare a state of martial law in accordance with the provisions of law in time of war, armed rebellion, or similar national emergency. The exercise of such emergency power is, however, subject to subsequent approval of the National Assembly.

The president is elected for a single five-year term by popular vote through universal, equal, direct, secret balloting and cannot be reelected. The president must be at least 40 years of age and have been resident in Korea for over five years.

The Legislature (The National Assembly)

Legislative power is vested in the unicameral National Assembly. The assembly is composed of 273 members, each serving a four-year term. Assembly members elected by popular vote compose five-sixths of the membership, with the remaining seats distributed proportionately among parties winning five seats or more in the direct election. The proportional representation system is aimed at appointing assembly members who will represent national interests rather than local interests.

To be eligible for election, a candidate must be at least 25 years of age. One candidate from each electoral district is selected by a plurality of votes. An assembly member is not held responsible outside the assembly for any opinions expressed or votes cast in the legislative chamber. During a session of the assembly, no assembly member may be arrested or detained without consent of the assembly except in the case of a flagrant criminal act.

Except as otherwise provided in the constitution or law, the attendance of more than one-half of the entire assembly members and the concurrent vote of more than one-half of the assembly members present are necessary to make decisions of the National Assembly binding.

The National Assembly is vested with a number of functions under the constitution, the foremost of which is making laws. Other functions of the assembly include approval of the national budget; matters related to foreign policy, declaration of war, the dispatch of armed forces abroad, or the stationing of foreign forces within the country; inspection or investigation of specific matters of state affairs; and impeachment of the president.

The Lawmaking Process

Bills may be introduced by members of the National Assembly or by the executive. A bill passed by the National Assembly is sent to the executive, and the president promulgates it within 15 days.

The president can object to a bill and request that it be reconsidered. The president gives a written explanation for this request; however, he or she may not request the National Assembly to reconsider the bill in part, or with proposed amendments.

If the National Assembly repasses the bill in the original form with the attendance of more than one-half of the total members and with a concurrent vote of two-thirds or more of the members present, it becomes law.

The Judiciary

The judicial power is vested in courts composed of judges who are independent of the executive and legislative branches. There are three tiers of courts in Korea: the district courts, which include the specialized family courts and the administrative courts. The high courts and the district courts are divided into geographic districts. The Court Organization Act grants the courts general jurisdiction to preside over civil, criminal, administrative, electoral, and other litigious cases.

The act also allows for decisions in noncontentious cases and other matters that fall under their jurisdiction, in accordance with the relevant provisions. In addition, military courts may be established under the constitution as special courts to exercise jurisdiction over criminal cases in the military. Nonetheless, even in these cases the Supreme Court retains final appellate jurisdiction.

The most important issue in the judiciary is the independence of the courts—of the judiciary as an organization, and the justices as individuals. Article 103 of the constitution provides: "Judges shall rule independently according to their conscience and in conformity with the Constitution and Law." According to Article 105, the term of office of the justices of the Supreme Court is six years, and they may be reappointed. The term of office of other judges is 10 years, and they may be reappointed as well. Also in Article 106(1), the constitution guarantees that except by impeachment, or by a serious criminal sentence, no judge can be removed or suspended from office or suffer a reduction in salary or any other unfavorable treatment except by disciplinary action.

Constitutional Court

The Constitutional Court was established in September 1988, as provided in the Constitution of 1987, as a key component of the constitutional system. It was founded on the lessons of past constitutional history and with the clear goal of protecting basic rights and restraining the abuse of state power.

The court is empowered to interpret the constitution and to review the constitutionality of all statutes, to make judicial decisions on impeachment or on dissolution of a political party, and to pass judgment in disputes over authority or constitutional complaints. The court is composed of nine justices. The term of office for the justices is six years and is renewable.

Despite its relatively short history, the Constitutional Court has succeeded in firmly establishing both the constitutional adjudication system and itself as a constitutional institution. The mature awareness of the people and the favorable political environment also contributed to the increasing activity of the court. The high volume of cases demonstrates the court's present and future significance in implementing its goals, safeguarding the constitution, and protecting basic rights. Now the constitution is firmly rooted in the life of the people as the supreme law of the state.

THE ELECTION PROCESS

Any Korean national who is at least 20 years old as of the date of an election has the right to vote and the obligation to exercise his or her right in a sincere manner by participating in an election. Any Korean national of at least 40 years of age may declare himself or herself a candidate for the presidency, and anyone at least 25 years old, except those barred by law, may run for the National Assembly, a local government post, or a local council seat.

The National Election Commission is an independent constitutional agency established for the purpose of managing fair elections and referenda and administering affairs related to political parties and political funds. Political parties or candidates found to be violating election laws receive a fine and a warning or are ordered either to halt or to correct their activities. If the warning or injunction is not heeded, the party in violation is prosecuted, or the case is turned over to an investigative agency.

POLITICAL PARTIES

Political parties in Korea have developed in conjunction with the democratization process and the diversification of society. They are an essential ingredient of the modern democratic political system. The constitution guarantees the multiparty system and the freedom to establish political parties. Article 8 defines the important role and function that political parties play in the republic: "Political parties may be organized freely and multiple parties shall be allowed. The objectives, organization and activities of a political party shall be democratic. Political parties shall have an organization conducive to participating in the process of forming the people's political opinions." The constitution also declares that the purpose, organization, and activities of all political parties shall be in line with democratic principles. If the purposes or activities of a political party are contrary to the fundamental democratic order, the government may bring an action against it to the Constitutional Court for its dissolution, and the political party shall be dissolved in accordance with the decision of the Constitutional Court.

CITIZENSHIP

Korean citizenship is primarily acquired by birth. A child acquires Korean citizenship if one of his or her parents is a Korean citizen. It is of no relevance where a child is born.

FUNDAMENTAL RIGHTS

Korean constitutional law defines fundamental rights in its second chapter, Rights and Duties of Citizens. This chapter guarantees civil rights and human rights. The starting point for fundamental rights in the constitution is the guarantee of human dignity and the pursuit of happiness. Article 10 says: "All citizens shall be assured of human dignity and worth and have the right to pursue happiness. It shall be the duty of the State to confirm and guarantee the fundamental and inviolable human rights of individuals." After this provision, the constitution guarantees numerous specific fundamental rights. The rights guaranteed by the constitution can be classified as rights to freedom and equality, as well as social rights, among others.

Article 12 states that all citizens shall enjoy personal liberty and includes detailed provisions for the protection against unlawful imprisonment. Individuals may not be punished, placed under preventive restrictions, or subjected to involuntary labor "except as provided by law and through lawful procedures."

The constitution also provides for other freedoms such as the freedom of residence, occupation, privacy, conscience, religion, speech, press, and assembly. The constitution also guarantees the right to property, the right to vote, and the right to a public trial.

An equal treatment clause is contained in Article 11(1), which provides that "all citizens shall be equal before the law, and there shall be no discrimination in political, economic, social or cultural life on account of sex, religion or social status." The principle of equality stipulated by Article 11(1) of the constitution does not imply imposition of absolute equality without any differential treatment. Rather, it stipulates a relative equality prohibiting differential treatment without reasonable basis in legislation and enforcement of the law. Therefore, differential treatment or inequality with a reasonable basis does not violate the principle of equality.

The constitution guarantees basic social rights and thereby imposes on the state a duty to shape substantive conditions for everyone to exercise his or her basic rights by his or her own means. Article 34(1) of the constitution states: "All citizens shall be entitled to a life worthy of human beings." Also there are specific provisions including protection of working women from unjust discrimination; state protection for citizens incapacitated by disease, old age, or youth; environmental protection measures; housing development policies; and "protection for mothers."

Also the constitution guarantees people's inherent, but unlisted, rights. Article 37(1) provides that "freedoms and rights of citizens shall not be neglected on the grounds that they are not enumerated in the Constitution."

Impact and Function of Fundamental Rights

The Korean constitution provides for many basic freedoms that guarantee people's rights and liberties. These basic freedoms have distinct essences and functions, and their values are not uniform. For example, the protection of freedom of speech is stronger than that of the right to a healthy environment.

It is a leading opinion that the impact of fundamental rights applies only to the government, not to private citizens. There is no specific constitutional provision addressing this issue. Article 68(1) of the Constitutional Court Act provides that "any person who claims that his or her basic rights, guaranteed by the Constitution, have been violated by an exercise or non-exercise of governmental power may file a constitutional complaint."

Limitations to Fundamental Rights

The fundamental rights specified in the constitution are not without limitation. The Korean constitution states the specific requirements for possible limitation of fundamental rights. Article 37(2) states that "the freedoms and rights of citizens may be restricted by Law only when necessary for national security, the maintenance of law and order or for public welfare. Even when such restriction is imposed, no essential aspect of the freedom or right shall be violated."

The most important principle regarding the limitation of fundamental rights is the principle of proportionality. Laws restricting a fundamental right must not use excessive means to accomplish and facilitate the legislative purpose; this is called the appropriateness of means. Also, the means must be that which is the least restrictive of basic rights, among other equally appropriate means that could accomplish the legislative purpose; this is referred to as the minimal restriction. Finally, there must be an appropriate relationship of proportionality between the extent of restrictions on basic rights and the weight of the public interest accomplished; this is the idea of balancing of interests. Additionally, restrictive laws must not deny the essential content of the right to property.

ECONOMY

The Korean constitution espouses the principle of the free market as a basis for the Korean economy. Article 119(1) of the constitution states that "the economic order of the Republic of Korea shall be based on a respect for the freedom and creative initiative of enterprises and individuals in economic affairs," thereby declaring the adoption of a free market economy based on the right to private property, the principle of private autonomy, and the principle that the liabilities for general torts are allocated according to fault.

The constitution, however, also adopts the principle of a social state. Article 119(2) provides that "the State may regulate and coordinate economic affairs in order to maintain balanced growth and stability of the national economy, to ensure proper distribution of income, to prevent the domination of the market and the abuse of economic power, and to democratize the economy through harmony among the economic agents." Furthermore, Article 34(1) stipulates that "all citizens shall be entitled to a life worthy of human beings," and Article 34(5) pronounces that "citizens who are incapable of earning a livelihood due to a physical disability, disease, old age or other reasons shall be protected by the State under the conditions as prescribed by law."

In sum, while the economic order adopted by the constitution can be classified as a free market economy based on the protection of the right to private property and respect for free competition, it also has characteristics of a social market economy in that the state is expected to regulate and coordinate the economy to prevent the possible adverse effects of a free market economy, to promote social welfare, and to achieve social justice.

RELIGIOUS COMMUNITIES

Freedom of religion is guaranteed by the Korean constitution. Article 20(1) states that "all citizens shall enjoy the freedom of religion," and Article 20(2) stipulates that "no state religion shall be recognized, and church and state shall be separated."

Freedom of religion may include the freedom of belief in religion, religious activity, religious assembly, missionary work, or others. The freedom of belief and religion is regarded as an absolute one, but others can be restricted for the maintenance of law and order, or for public welfare.

There is no state religion, all public authority must remain strictly neutral in its relations with the religious communities, and all religions must be treated equally. In a case arguing that administering the judicial examination on a Sunday violated the freedom of religion and the right of equality, the Constitutional Court held that, unlike in numerous Western countries, where the Christian culture forms the basis of society, in Korea, Sunday is merely a holiday, not a day set out for specific religious service. Therefore, the state's decision to administer the judiciary examination on Sunday does not unreasonably discriminate against the complainant's religion in relation to other religions.

MILITARY DEFENSE AND STATE OF EMERGENCY

The armed forces are charged with the "sacred" mission of national security and defense. The Republic of Korea endeavors to maintain international peace and renounces all aggressive wars. Korea is seeking unification and follows a policy of peaceful unification based on the principles of freedom and democracy in the presence of a divided nation. This goal is specifically mentioned in Article 4 of the constitution and underlined by several other articles.

In Korea, all citizens have the duty of national defense, and general conscription requires all men above the age of 18 to perform basic military service for more than two years. Woman can volunteer. In addition, there are professional soldiers who serve for fixed periods or who pursue military careers.

The president is commander in chief of the armed forces. However, to declare war, dispatch the armed forces to foreign states, or station alien forces in the territory of the Republic of Korea, the consent of the National Assembly is required.

The president may proclaim martial law under the conditions prescribed by law, to cope with a military necessity, or to maintain public safety and order during a mobilization of the armed forces in time of war, armed conflict, or similar national emergency. Under martial law, limits may be put on the need for warrants or on freedom of speech, the press, assembly, and association, and special measures may be taken on the powers of the executive and the judiciary by law.

The president must notify the National Assembly on the proclamation of martial law without delay. When the National Assembly asks that martial law be lifted, by the concurrent vote of a majority of all its members, the president must comply.

AMENDMENTS TO THE CONSTITUTION

The Korean constitution has been designed to make amendment difficult. A proposal to amend the constitution can be introduced only by a majority of all the members of the National Assembly or by the president. The National Assembly must decide upon the proposed amendments within 60 days of the public announcement; adoption requires the concurrent vote of two-thirds of all the members. The proposed amendments must be submitted to a national referendum not later than 30 days after adoption by the National Assembly.

For the amendment to pass, more than half of eligible voters must participate, and more than half of the votes cast must be in favor. Furthermore, the constitution states in Article 128(2): "Amendments to the Constitution for the extension of the term of office of the President or for a change allowing for the reelection of the President shall not be effective for the President in office at the time of the proposal for such amendments to the Constitution."

PRIMARY SOURCES
Constitution in English. Available online. URLs: http://korea.assembly.go.kr/res/low_01_read.jsp?boardid=1000000035. Accessed on June 21, 2006.
Constitution in English: Government Legislative Administration Agency of the Republic of Korea, ed., *Current Laws of the Republic of Korea,* 4 vols. Seoul: Statutes Compilation & Dissimination Foundation of Korea, 1983–1997.
Han'guk Pophagwon, *Laws of the Republic of Korea,* 3 vols. Seoul: Korean Legal Center, 1983–1997.
Constitution in Korean. Available online. URLs: http://www.moleg.go.kr/; http://www.ccourt.go.kr/. Accessed on August 28, 2005.

SECONDARY SOURCES
The First Ten Years of the Korean Constitutional Court. Seoul: The Constitutional Court of Korea, 2001.
Sang Hyun Song, ed., *Introduction to the Law and Legal System of Korea.* Seoul: Kyung Mun Sa, 1983.

Un Jong Pak

KUWAIT

At-a-Glance

OFFICIAL NAME
State of Kuwait

CAPITAL
Kuwait

POPULATION
2,257,549 including 1,291,354 nonnationals (July 2004 est.)

SIZE
6,854 sq. mi. (17,820 sq. km)

LANGUAGES
Arabic

RELIGIONS
Muslim (Sunni 70%, Shia 30%), 85% Christian, Hindu, Parsi, and other 15%

NATIONAL OR ETHNIC COMPOSITION
Kuwaiti 45%, other Arab 35%, South Asian 9%, Iranian 4%, other 7%

DATE OF INDEPENDENCE OR CREATION
June 19, 1961 (from United Kingdom)

TYPE OF GOVERNMENT
Constitutional hereditary monarchy

TYPE OF STATE
Unitary state

TYPE OF LEGISLATURE
Unicameral parliament

DATE OF CONSTITUTION
November 11, 1962

DATE OF LAST AMENDMENT
May 16, 2005

In June 1961, after independence and under a possible Iraqi threat, the then-ruler (*amir*) of Kuwait announced his plan to establish constitutional rule. Drafted by a partially elected Constituent Assembly, the constitution was promulgated the following year. While Kuwait has experienced partial suspensions of the constitution (in 1967, 1976, 1986, and during the Iraqi occupation), the document has eventually been reenforced.

The constitution defines Kuwait as "a hereditary emirate" but does not define the precise line of succession. While granting the ruler substantial powers, the constitution also guarantees political participation to Kuwaiti full citizens. The system of government is defined as democratic with sovereignty residing in the people. Citizens participate, via the unicameral National Assembly, in making laws and in supervising the government.

The constitution protects civil rights as "specified by law." It also guarantees the judiciary's independence. Islamic Sharia is *a* (not *the*) main source of legislation.

The constitution grants citizens a number of social rights, which form the basis for Kuwait's extensive welfare system. It provides for state involvement in the national economy while also protecting private property. Non-Kuwaitis, however, enjoy only restricted access to the welfare system.

CONSTITUTIONAL HISTORY

Kuwait's ruling family, the Al Sabah, established themselves in the area early in the 18th century, along with allied tribes and leading merchant families. The family was never able to govern as a complete autocracy; it had to take the merchant families into account. By the end of the century the British had the country under their domination.

In the early 20th century the governing balance was disrupted, not least as a result of British intervention.

Discontent among the merchant elite led to the creation of a first National Legislative Council in 1938. The experiment lasted only six months.

Kuwait's present constitution was drafted after its independence by a Constituent Assembly. It consisted of 20 elected members and 11 appointed cabinet ministers. On November 1, 1962, the draft constitution was approved by the then-*amir*, Sheikh Abdallah al-Salim Al Sabah, and went into force on January 29, 1963, when the first National Assembly convened.

Parliament was dissolved temporarily in 1967 and again in 1976; this was accompanied by the suspension of some constitutional protections of political and civil rights. In 1980, the suspended articles were reinstated along with the National Assembly. In 1986, the constitution and the National Assembly were suspended again, prompting popular opposition as a constitutional movement was formed.

The opposition grew stronger after the Iraqi occupation in 1990, during which all constitutional rights were abrogated. During the Iraqi invasion, the exiled ruler, Sheikh Jabir al-Ahmad Al Sabah, met with members of the opposition in Saudi Arabia; he agreed to restore parliament and allow greater freedom once the Iraqis had been driven out. Accordingly, after Kuwait's recovery of sovereignty in 1991, most press restrictions were lifted and elections to a new National Assembly took place.

Atypically for its region, the Kuwaiti parliament has succeeded in forcing cabinet ministers to resign. It has also imposed legislation against the objections of the royal family.

FORM AND IMPACT OF THE CONSTITUTION

The constitution is contained in a written document. International law has to be transformed into national law to become applicable within the country.

BASIC ORGANIZATIONAL STRUCTURE

Kuwait is divided into five governorates (*muhafazat*).

LEADING CONSTITUTIONAL PRINCIPLES

Kuwait is a hereditary principality (emirate); succession is within the ruling family but can move laterally (along brothers). The Islamic Sharia is a (not the) principal source of law. The constitution states that the system of government is democratic, with sovereignty vested in the people. Separation of powers is established, but the executive is dominant. The legislative power is vested in the amir (emir) and the National Assembly. The executive power is vested in the amir, the cabinet, and the ministers (Articles 51 and 52).

CONSTITUTIONAL BODIES

The constitutional bodies are the *amir,* the cabinet, and the National Assembly. An audit commission is stipulated for budgetary control. The constitution makes no mention of a Constitutional Court, yet one has been established.

The Amir

The *amir* is the head of state. He appoints and dismisses the prime minister "after the traditional consultations" as well as the ministers. The *amir* designates the heir apparent, who has to be accepted by the majority of the National Assembly. The *amir* has the right to initiate laws and to send back laws passed by the National Assembly with an explanatory note. His rejection can be overridden by two-thirds of the assembly. The *amir* is supreme commander of the armed forces.

The Executive Administration

The executive branch of government consists of the prime minister and the Council of Ministers or cabinet. While no reference to that effect is made in the constitution, the ruling family is well represented in the Council of Ministers. Cabinet ministers are subject to votes of no confidence.

If the majority of elected members of the National Assembly (that is, excluding the ex officio members) decide to remove a minister, that minister is considered to have resigned. The prime minister is privileged; if the National Assembly decides that cooperation with him is impossible, the *amir* can either dismiss the prime minister and the cabinet or dissolve the National Assembly.

The National Assembly

Fifty members of the National Assembly are elected directly by secret ballot; 25 members are appointed by the *amir*. The assembly term is four years. The National Assembly makes legislation and supervises the government. The assembly has actually exercised its right to questioning, interpellation, and voting no confidence in ministers.

The Lawmaking Process

Any member of the National Assembly can initiate a bill. If it is accepted by a majority, it is presented to the *amir,* who can reject it. His rejection can be overridden by a two-thirds majority.

The Judiciary

Kuwait's legal system is a mix of British common law, Egyptian civil law, and Islamic legal principles. Sunni and Shii Muslims have separate Sharia courts for cases of personal status and inheritance. The constitution provides for an independent judiciary.

The judiciary is structured in three levels: the courts of first instance, the courts of appeal, and a Court of Cassation (final appeal), which was added in 1990. In 1973 a Constitutional Court was established as well. Its five members are chosen by the Judicial Council by secret ballot; one reserve member is appointed by decree. Judges of the Constitutional Court must be Kuwaiti nationals.

THE ELECTION PROCESS

Males who have reached the age of 21 and are Kuwaiti citizens by birth or have been naturalized for at least 30 years can vote. In 2005 the National Assembly approved a constitutional amendment that granted women full political rights, including the right to vote and run for political office. The amendment requires women voters and candidates to abide by Islamic law. Only a minority of residents are citizens. Hence only a small minority of the population are eligible to vote.

POLITICAL PARTIES

Political parties are formally illegal, but organizations that have similar functions are tolerated. Candidates run as independents, but the government allows parliamentary blocs. A wide spectrum of political groupings exists, respectively, representing merchants, liberals, leftists, nationalists, or Sunni or Shii Islamic groups.

CITIZENSHIP

The Kuwaiti citizenship law is constantly contested, debated, and amended. It distinguishes between Kuwaitis of first, second, or third class. Kuwaiti first-class citizenship is normally acquired by birth to a Kuwaiti father. Other nationals can apply for Kuwaiti citizenship after longtime residence. Apart from a huge population of foreign nationals, there are also many stateless long-term tribal residents (*bedoon*), whose status is still largely unresolved.

FUNDAMENTAL RIGHTS

Civil liberties are guaranteed in the constitution. There are safeguards against illegal searches and arrests, and protections for the privacy of homes. The constitution guarantees the right to a fair trial and protects freedom of opinion and the press and academic freedom. Freedom of religion is guaranteed "provided it does not conflict with public policy or morals." The freedom to form associations is guaranteed; private assemblies are permitted without prior permission, and public assembly with such permission. Social rights for Kuwaiti nationals are prominently stated in the constitution: The state aims to eliminate illiteracy and provide education and health care. Work, and the freedom to choose an occupation, are guaranteed rights for Kuwaiti nationals.

Impact and Functions of Fundamental Rights

While Kuwaiti history has experienced stages in which fundamental rights have been suspended, they have nonetheless become ingrained in Kuwaiti society. Their permanent abrogation now seems unlikely.

Limitations to Fundamental Rights

Civil and political rights, though guaranteed in the constitution, are limited by law. For example, several laws empower the government to jail or fine journalists for a variety of offenses. In fact, however, convictions are extremely rare. While media criticize the government, self-censorship is applied with regard to criticism of the *amir*.

Private sector workers have the right to strike; however, the huge group of foreigners working as domestic servants are not protected. Women are legally disadvantaged in matters of personal status and inheritance. Stateless people (*bedoon*), though often longtime residents, are denied full civil rights.

ECONOMY

The constitution guarantees the right to private property. The national economy's stated goal is social justice. Natural resources and their revenues are state property.

RELIGIOUS COMMUNITIES

Islam is the state religion. Sunnis and Shiites worship freely, though the latter complain of insufficient government funding for mosques. Christians are allowed to practice without interference, but Hindus, Sikhs, Baháis, and Buddhists can worship only in private. All inhabitants of Kuwait have the duty to observe and respect public morals.

MILITARY DEFENSE AND STATE OF EMERGENCY

The *amir* is the supreme commander of the armed forces and can declare defensive war; offensive war is forbidden.

He can also proclaim martial law, but only with the approval of the majority of the National Assembly.

AMENDMENTS TO THE CONSTITUTION

An amendment may be proposed by either the *amir* or one-third of the National Assembly. A two-thirds vote in the assembly is needed for passage. Even then the *amir* has the final decision—he may refuse to promulgate it. The monarchical system and the principles of liberty and equality are not subject to amendment, although the "title of the emirate" may be changed, and guarantees of liberty and equality may be increased.

PRIMARY SOURCES

Constitution in English. Available online. URL: http://www.kuwait-info.com/sidepages/cont.asp. Accessed on September 13, 2005.

Constitution in Arabic. Available online. URL: http://208.21.175.109/RelatedArticlesGvnSPName.asp?SPName=CHRN&StructuredIndeCode=0&LawBookID=021020011648202&Year1=&Year2=&YearGorH. Accessed on June 21, 2006.

SECONDARY SOURCES

Michael Herb, "Princes and Parliaments in the Arab World." In *Middle East Journal* 58, no. 3 (summer 2004): 367–384.

Mary Ann Tétreault, *Stories of Democracy: Politics and Society in Contemporary Kuwait.* New York: Columbia University Press, 2000.

Katja Niethammer

KYRGYZSTAN

At-a-Glance

OFFICIAL NAME
Kyrgyz Republic

CAPITAL
Bishkek

POPULATION
5,081,429 (July 2004 est.)

SIZE
76,641 sq. mi. (198,500 sq. km)

LANGUAGES
Kyrgyz and Russian (official languages)

RELIGIONS
Muslim 75%, Russian Orthodox 20%, other 5%

NATIONAL OR ETHNIC COMPOSITION
Kyrgyz 64.9%, Uzbek 13.8%, Russian 12.5%, Dungan 1.1%, Ukrainian 1%, Ungur 1%, other 5.7% (1999 census)

DATE OF INDEPENDENCE OR CREATION
August 31, 1991

TYPE OF GOVERNMENT
Authoritarian presidential regime

TYPE OF STATE
Centralist state

TYPE OF LEGISLATURE
Bicameral parliament

DATE OF CONSTITUTION
May 5, 1993

DATE OF LAST AMENDMENT
February 2, 2003

Kyrgyzstan is a presidential autocracy with a strong president exercising control over executive, legislative, and judicial powers. The president appoints and dismisses the administration, the judges, and the governors. Free, equal, direct, fair, and transparent elections are guaranteed by the constitution.

Kyrgyzstan is made up of seven provinces and of the cities of Bishkek and Osh. The constitution provides fundamental human rights; individuals as well as selected government institutions may appeal to the Constitutional Court to protect these rights. Religious freedom and state noninterference in religious matters are guaranteed. Nontraditional religious groups may act relatively freely, although the Islamist Party Hizb ut-Tahrir has been designated by the Constitutional Court as "extremist." It is charged with inciting interethnic hatred and seeking to overthrow constitutional order.

CONSTITUTIONAL HISTORY

Around the year 1000 C.E., members of 40 Central Asian Turkic tribes began to identify themselves collectively as Kyrgyz or forty tribes; they established the Great Kyrgyz Khanate in the Yenisei River basin, in today's southern Siberia and western Mongolia. After the khanate was destroyed by the Mongolian invasion of the 13th century, the Kyrgyz tribes moved west to the territory currently known as Kyrgyzstan, where they continued to develop a distinct language and identity and a culture mainly characterized by a nomadic lifestyle.

At the beginning of the 19th century, the rulers of the khanate of Kokand gradually captured vast territories of today's Kyrgyz Republic. In 1876, the epoch of the Kokand Khanate came to an end, and territories were incorporated into the Russian Empire, under the czar's

Turkistan governor-generals. After the Russian Revolution of 1917, the Bolsheviks consolidated their control of the region in 1918. With the establishment of the Soviet Union in 1926, the Kyrgyz Autonomous Soviet Socialist Republic was founded, renamed the Kyrgyz Soviet Socialist Republic in 1939. After the collapse of communism in Russia and the failure of the hardliners' coup in Moscow, Kyrgyzstan reluctantly declared its independence on August 31, 1991. On May 5, 1993, a new constitution was introduced, replacing the 1978 constitution of the Kyrgyz SSR and the 1977 constitution of the Soviet Union. The post-Soviet constitution was amended several times by means of national referenda, most recently on February 2, 2003.

FORM AND IMPACT OF THE CONSTITUTION

Kyrgyzstan has a written constitution, codified in a single document that takes precedence over all other national law. International law must be in accordance with the constitution to take precedence over Kyrgyz law.

BASIC ORGANIZATIONAL STRUCTURE

Kyrgyzstan is a centralistic state. It is made up of seven provinces (*oblasttar*) and the cities of Bishkek and Osh. The provinces differ considerably in geographical area, population size, and economic strength.

The provinces are governed by *akims* (governors), appointed and dismissed by the president upon recommendation of the prime minister and after approval of the corresponding local *kenesh* (council). The *akims* of towns and villages are directly elected.

According to the constitution, the *akims* coordinate the activity of the local offices of the central ministries, administrative agencies, and other executive bodies. They are accountable to the president and the prime minister.

LEADING CONSTITUTIONAL PRINCIPLES

The Kyrgyz system of government is dominated by the president, who controls executive, legislative, and judicial power. The judiciary is not fully independent. The constitutional system is defined by a number of leading principles: state sovereignty, centralism, democracy, and secularity.

Political participation is restricted, as major key positions—such as governors—are appointed by the president. However, the Parliament and the councils of the regions, districts, and towns are directly elected. Rule of law is an important principle; all state bodies, public associations, and citizens are obligated to act according to the constitution and the law. State and religion are separated.

CONSTITUTIONAL BODIES

The predominant bodies provided for in the constitution are the president; the administration; the Parliament, called Jogorku Kenesh; and the judiciary, including the Constitutional Court.

The President

The president is the head of state and the highest official of Kyrgyzstan, defined as the "symbol of the unity of the people and state power, the guarantor of the Constitution of Kyrgyzstan, and of rights and freedoms of the person and citizen." The president defines the fundamental directions of internal and external state policy, adopts measures to protect the sovereignty and the territorial integrity of the republic, ensures the unity and continuity of state power, and coordinates the functions and interactions of state bodies in line with their responsibility to the people. The president is directly elected for a five-year term and can be reelected only once.

The president appoints the prime minister with the approval of the Jogorku Kenesh. The president also appoints—in consultation with the prime minister and with the consent of the respective Parliament—the members of the administration and the *akims* (governors) of the provinces. The president also appoints and dismisses other key governmental figures such as prosecutors and judges.

The Administration

The administration consists of the prime minister, the ministers, and the state committees. Jointly with the administrative agencies and local state administration, the national administration implements the executive power. The prime minister and the ministers he or she recommends are appointed by the president with the consent of the Jogorku Kenesh. The Jogorku Kenesh may recall the administration in a motion of no confidence.

The administration ensures enforcement of the constitution and all legislative acts; ensures pursuance of state policy in major policy fields, including foreign policy; develops and carries out nationwide development programs; takes measures to secure state sovereignty, the defense of the country, and national security; and ensures interaction with the civil society.

The Jogorku Kenesh (Parliament)

The Jogorku Kenesh is the main representative body. It consists of 75 deputies, elected for a term of five years. The Jogorku Kenesh introduces amendments and supplements to the constitution, adopts laws, and approves the national budget. It approves the administration on the recommendation of the president and can dismiss it by a vote of no confidence. Also, it elects and removes the ombudsperson and the members of the Constitutional Court and the Supreme Court, all on the recommendation of the president.

The Lawmaking Process

The right of legislative initiative belongs to the president, the Jogorku Kenesh, the administration, and any 30,000 voters by means of a popular initiative. A law goes into effect after it has been adopted by the Parliament, signed by the president, and published in the media. The president has the right to return the law with objections to the Jogorku Kenesh but lacks the right to a final veto.

The Judiciary

The judicial system in Kyrgyzstan comprises the Constitutional Court, the Supreme Court, the Supreme Arbitration Court, and local courts. All high-ranking judges as well as the procurator are elected by the Jogorku Kenesh upon the suggestion of the president; all judges of local courts are directly appointed and dismissed by the president with the consent of the Jogorku Kenesh.

The Constitutional Court consists of eight judges elected for 10-year terms. It has exclusive jurisdiction over constitutional disputes, which can be submitted by government agencies and individuals. It validates presidential elections and has the power to dismiss the president. It judges the constitutionality of the actions of political parties and social and religious organizations.

The Supreme Court of Kyrgyzstan consists of 24 judges. It is the highest body of judicial power in the sphere of civil, criminal, and administrative legal proceedings.

The constitution also provides for courts of elders who consider property and family disputes and any other matters submitted to them with the aim of reaching reconciliation among the disputing parties. The decisions made by the courts of elders may not contradict the law and may be appealed.

THE ELECTION PROCESS

All Kyrgyz citizens over the age of 18 have the right to vote in elections. Citizens who have reached the age of 25 by election day and have been permanent residents in Kyrgyzstan not less than five years have the right to stand for parliamentary elections. To be registered as a candidate in presidential elections, one has to have reached the age of 35 and not exceeded 65; be able to speak fluently the state language, Kyrgyz; and have lived no less than 15 years on Kyrgyz territory.

Citizens who have been judicially certified as insane, as well as those sentenced to prison, may not take part in the elections. Citizens whose verdict is outstanding or who have previous convictions may vote; however, they are not eligible to stand for elections.

During a state of emergency or martial law, referenda and elections are not permitted.

POLITICAL PARTIES

The constitutional right to form political parties is limited by provisions banning organizations that violate fundamental constitutional principles, aim at changing the constitution, endanger national security, or are established on religious grounds. The participation of political parties in state affairs is restricted to the nomination of candidates for election to the Jogorku Kenesh and bodies of local self-governance, and the formation of factions in representative bodies.

Very few political parties are known to the population. More than 40 political parties reflecting local interests have been registered; they are centered around charismatic figures and lack broad membership. The role they play in public life is limited by the overall presence of the strong civil society.

CITIZENSHIP

All people who were living on the territory of Kyrgyzstan on December 15, 1990, are entitled to acquire Kyrgyz citizenship. A person can acquire Kyrgyz citizenship if at least one of his or her parents holds Kyrgyz citizenship, or if the person has lived on Kyrgyz territory for more than five years.

FUNDAMENTAL RIGHTS

The constitution defines fundamental rights in its second chapter. The first part, which relates to "human rights and freedoms," emphasizes the traditional set of individual, political, economic, and social rights. The second part explains the "citizen's rights and duties." The dignity of an individual is absolute and inviolable.

Impact and Functions of Fundamental Rights

According to the constitution, every person is entitled from birth to basic human rights and freedoms that are absolute, inalienable, and protected by law and guaranteed by the judiciary. Human rights and freedoms determine the meaning, content, and application of laws in Kyrgyzstan. Kyrgyz customs and traditions that do not contradict human rights and freedoms (such as respect for the elderly and caring for relatives and friends) are supported by the state. Control over the observance of human and civil rights and freedoms in Kyrgyzstan is exercised by the ombudsperson, who is elected by Parliament.

Limitations to Fundamental Rights

According to the constitution, restrictions on the exercise of rights and freedoms may be imposed only on the basis of a law reviewable by a court decision, and only for the purpose of protecting the rights and freedoms of other persons, public safety and order, territorial integrity, or the constitutional structure.

ECONOMY

The constitution does not specify the economic system of Kyrgyzstan. However, it provides certain rights that have economic implications. Among them is the legal protection of all forms of ownership (private, state, communal, and others). According to the constitution, no person can be deprived of his or her property arbitrarily; confiscation against the will of the owner is allowed only by decision of a court. The constitution also defines social rights, such as the right to work, to the free use of one's abilities and free choice of profession and occupation; to free education; and to free use of the network of state and municipal public health institutions.

RELIGIOUS COMMUNITIES

Freedom of religion or belief is guaranteed as a basic human right. According to the constitution, religious organizations and associations must be separate from the state and equal before the law. Religious organizations are not allowed to pursue political goals and tasks. The Constitutional Court may decide upon the constitutionality of the activity of religious organizations. In November 2003, the Constitutional Court designated the moderate Islamist Party Hizb ut-Tahrir as "extremist" for their role in inciting interethnic hatred and seeking to overthrow the constitutional order.

MILITARY DEFENSE AND STATE OF EMERGENCY

The president is the chief commander of the armed forces and appoints and dismisses its commanders. The president has the power to declare a universal or partial mobilization and announces—in close cooperation with Jogorku Kenesh—a state of war.

The armed forces may be used in case of external aggression or upon the request of another state within a collective defense system. The use of the armed forces to resolve internal state political issues is prohibited. The armed forces may be used to assist in the aftermath of natural disasters.

In Kyrgyzstan, general conscription requires all men over the age of 20 to do basic military service of 18 months (from 2006, 12 months). In addition, there are professional soldiers who serve for fixed periods. Women are not required to serve but may serve as professional soldiers. There is an alternative nonmilitary service option for conscientious objectors, which lasts 24 months.

According to the constitution, Kyrgyzstan strives for universal and just peace, mutually beneficial cooperation, and resolution of global and regional problems by peaceful means. It has obliged itself by international treaties not to produce atomic, biological, or chemical weapons.

AMENDMENTS TO THE CONSTITUTION

Amendments and supplements to the constitution may be introduced by referendum or by Jogorku Kenesh by a two-thirds majority of all deputies. No amendments or supplements to the constitution are allowed during states of emergency.

PRIMARY SOURCES
Constitution of Kyrgyzstan, adopted on May 5, 1993, including amendments of February 2, 2003, in English. Available online. URL: http://www.cis-legal-reform.org/constitution/kyrgyz-constitution.htm. Accessed on September 29, 2005.

SECONDARY SOURCES
Draft Constitution of the Republic of Kyrgyzstan. Strasbourg: Council of Europe, European Commission for Democracy through Law, 1992.
John T. Ishiyama and Ryan Kennedy, "Superpresidentialism and Political Party Development in Russia, Ukraine, Armenia and Kyrgyzstan." *Europe Asia Studies* 53, no. 8 (2001): 1177–1191.
Kyrgyz Respublikasynyn Konstitutsiiasy, Konstitutsiia Kyrgyzskoi Respubliki—Constitution of the Republic of Kyrgyzstan, adopted at the Session of the Supreme Soviet of the Kyrgyz Republic, the Constitution as of February 18, 2003, in Russian and Kyrgyz. Bishkek: Arkhi, 2003.
"Organization for Security and Co-operation in Europe (OSCE), Centre in Bishkek." Available online. URL: http://www.osce.org/. Accessed on September 22, 2005.

Marie-Carin von Gumppenberg

LAOS

At-a-Glance

OFFICIAL NAME
Lao People's Democratic Republic

CAPITAL
Vientiane

POPULATION
6,368,481 (July 2006 est.)

SIZE
91,429 sq. mi. (236,800 sq. km)

LANGUAGES
Lao

RELIGIONS
Theravada Buddhist 60%, other 40%

NATIONAL OR ETHNIC COMPOSITION
Lao Lum 66%, Lao Thoeng 24%, Lao Sung 10%

DATE OF INDEPENDENCE OR CREATION
July 19, 1949 (from France); full sovereignty 1954

TYPE OF GOVERNMENT
Socialist People's Republic

TYPE OF STATE
Unitary state

TYPE OF LEGISLATURE
Unicameral parliament

DATE OF CONSTITUTION
August 14, 1991

DATE OF LAST AMENDMENT
May 6, 2003

Laos is a single-party socialist state, which in the 1990s experienced the transition to a free market economy model but retains a political structure typical of communist states in the 20th century. The "leading nucleus" of the political process is the Lao People's Revolutionary (Communist) Party (Article 3 of the Lao constitution). Since the beginning of the 1990s, a gradual strengthening of the rule of law can be observed; the constitution, first adopted in 1991, was significantly amended in 2003. An increasing amount of legislation has been adopted since the early 1990s, but the implementation of genuine rule of law is still considered to be deficient, and pluralist political democracy is absent.

CONSTITUTIONAL HISTORY

The birth year of Laos as a state is commonly considered to be 1353, when King Fa Ngoum founded the Kingdom of Lane Xang with the northern city of Luang Prabang as capital. During the 18th century, the state broke into three separate kingdoms, which eventually all were under Siamese (Thai) control. Laos was recreated as a French protectorate, but a significant part of the Lao ethnic and formerly Lao-ruled territory remained under Thai control. After a short period of independence during the turmoil of the final phase of World War II in 1945, the modern Laos, as it was territorially shaped by France, finally gained full sovereignty in 1954.

Laos traditionally was a monarchy, and French colonial rule did not change this system in principle. With the first constitution, passed May 11, 1947, under the French, Laos became a parliamentary monarchy. The constitution was suspended for a short period in 1960–61 but basically remained in force until the communist takeover in 1975. In that year the monarchy was abolished. The communist leadership did not at first issue a constitution; it ruled the country for more than 15 years on the basis of government decrees. The legal basis of government was reduced to a minimum, with no constitutional framework and little legislation.

In the era of profound transformation of communist countries that began in the late 1980s, Laos retained its political structure but transformed economically. Some progress was made toward the rule of law; a constitution was adopted in 1991, and subsequent attempts were made to regulate the most important fields of law by parliamentary legislation. A potentially significant leap forward was taken with the constitutional amendments in 2003.

FORM AND IMPACT OF THE CONSTITUTION

The constitution is a single document, adopted in 1991 and amended in 2003. After its adoption, for the first time since the communist takeover a parliamentary lawmaking process became routine. The amendment of the constitution in 2003 demonstrates an attempt to strengthen this impact, as the new Article 96 provides: "The Constitution of the Lao P.D.R. is a fundamental law of the nation. All laws must comply with the constitution."

However, questions of interpretation of the constitution are still within the competence of the Standing Committee of the National Assembly rather than any kind of independent judicial power. As a further sign of the constitution's limited impact, the precise content of the 2003 amendments was not published within Laos for more than six months.

BASIC ORGANIZATIONAL STRUCTURE

Laos is a unitary state. For administration purposes, the country is organized into 16 provinces plus a "special zone," which is administered by the military, and the independent prefecture of the capital, Vientiane. Further administrative entities are districts and villages. The strengthening of local powers has been on the legislative agenda recently, but democratic centralism remains a primary constitutional principle (Article 5).

LEADING CONSTITUTIONAL PRINCIPLES

Although the Lao political structure is clearly of socialist origin, the constitution does not use the word *socialism*. However, Article 3 provides for the role of the Lao People's Revolutionary Party, which it calls the "leading nucleus," and Article 5 states that "democratic centralism" must guide the creation and functioning of all state organizations.

CONSTITUTIONAL BODIES

The predominant constitutional body is the National Assembly, with its powerful standing committee. Other constitutional bodies are the president and the executive administration. The constitution also mentions the leading role of the Lao People's Revolutionary Party, and the importance of certain other political organizations such as the Lao People's Revolutionary Youth Union and the Lao Women's Union, but no details about their powers and competences are defined.

The National Assembly

The National Assembly is supposed to represent the people of Laos. It has the typical duties of a National Assembly, such as adopting laws and choosing members of the administration. In reality, the formal authority of the National Assembly is largely constrained by the informal powers of the Lao People's Revolutionary Party. The members of the National Assembly are elected in general elections for a term of five years.

The Lawmaking Process

Legislation is typically prepared by the administration, adopted by the National Assembly, and promulgated by the head of state.

The President

The president is the head of state and is elected by a two-thirds majority of the National Assembly. Reelection is allowed. The president is not the head of the administration, but rather represents the country abroad; promulgates laws; officially appoints the prime minister, the ministers, and other officials; is head of the armed forces; and exercises the right to pardon. In general, these functions can be described as the typical competencies of presidents in parliamentary democracies or kings in parliamentary monarchies. However, some of the provisions are vague, so that a more political presidency could emerge. In practice, the office of the president was at first merely ceremonial; however, because more recently the most powerful person in Laotian political life, Khmatay Siphandone, holds the presidential office, it now has much more political relevance.

The Executive Administration

The executive administration consists of the prime minister, deputy prime ministers, cabinet ministers, and chairs of organizations with ministry status. The prime minister is appointed by the president after the approval of the National Assembly. The prime minister is the head of the executive administration and responsible for its policies and for the appointment of a range of officials. The National Assembly can force the resignation of the executive administration or any of its members by a vote of no confidence.

The Judiciary

The judicial branch consists of the People's Supreme Court, the Courts of Appeal, the People's Provincial and Municipality Courts, District Courts, and the Military

Court. Some internationally assisted reform projects have tried to strengthen the independence and efficiency of the courts and helped inspire the constitutional amendments of 2003. However, the standing committee of the National Assembly still has the authority "to interpret and explain the provisions of the Constitution and laws."

THE ELECTION PROCESS

The constitution leaves most elements of the election process to be detailed by respective laws. It does set the age of suffrage at 18 and the age of eligibility at 21.

POLITICAL PARTIES

The constitution mentions only one political party, the Lao People's Revolutionary Party (LPRP), which is called the leading nucleus of the political system (Article 3). The constitution does not mention the possibility of other political parties, and there are no laws providing for them. In reality, since 1975 Laos has been a one-party system, in the tradition of Soviet-style democratic centralism (Article 5). Demands for a multiparty system have been rejected as unlawful in court rulings.

CITIZENSHIP

According to the constitution, Lao citizens are persons who hold Lao nationality as prescribed by law. A new nationality law, combining features of both *ius sanguinis* and *ius soli,* was adopted in 2004.

FUNDAMENTAL RIGHTS AND DUTIES

The constitution provides for human rights, including social and economic rights. The classic liberal rights are guaranteed within a framework of laws, which define the scope of the freedoms in detail. However, the practical importance of human rights has been limited so far; for example, the use of political rights is under strict scrutiny for conformity to the system. Effective remedies to enforce the rights guaranteed by the constitution are not yet available. The Criminal Code of 1989 imposes repressive criminal sanctions on "infractions against the Nation's stability and social order." It has been used as an instrument to silence even modest activism on behalf of political reform, despite the fact that Article 31, now Article 44, has officially protected freedom of speech, press, and assembly since the constitution was first promulgated.

Laos is party to some international human rights treaties. The International Covenant on Civil and Political Rights and the International Covenant on Economic, Social and Cultural Rights were signed in 2000, but ratification has not yet been undertaken. In general, national laws are not well harmonized with international treaty obligations.

ECONOMY

In the aftermath of the 1975 revolution, Laos adopted a socialist model command economy based on state planning. As have other countries in the region, since the late 1980s it has moved toward a market economy within a classic socialist political framework. In contrast to that in Vietnam, this shift is not clearly documented in constitutional history, because "socialist" Laos adopted a constitution very late, after the new free market policies had already been implemented. However, in comparison to the original text of 1991, the 2003 amendments provide some evidence of the new economic path; for example, they protect foreign investments and strengthen private property and ownership in general. Nevertheless, the language of Chapter 2, The Socio-Economic System, still shows a belief in the efficacy of a state-controlled economy.

RELIGIOUS COMMUNITIES

The majority of Laos's population is Buddhist, and the Buddhist religion plays a significant role in life, culture, and politics. However, the constitution does not accord Buddhism the rank of a state religion, as in neighboring Cambodia. According to Article 9, "The state respects all lawful activities of Buddhists and other religious followers" but strictly prohibits "all acts of creating division of religion and classes of people." Within the provisions on basic rights, the constitution grants the right to believe or not to believe in any religion.

MILITARY DEFENSE AND STATE OF EMERGENCY

According to its constitution, Laos pursues a foreign policy of peace, independence, friendship, and cooperation. It promotes peaceful coexistence and respects the principle of noninterference. The obligations to defend the country, to maintain security, and to perform military service are explicitly mentioned as fundamental duties of Lao citizens, but the details are to be prescribed by law. Currently, there is three-year compulsory military service for males. The 2003 constitutional amendments call on the defense and security forces to improve and strengthen themselves and call on the state to provide any support needed to ensure the physical and mental condition of these forces.

AMENDMENTS TO THE CONSTITUTION

Amendments to the constitution require approval by two-thirds of the members of the National Assembly. The 2003 amendment of the Constitution of 1991 was a substantial reform, adding 18 new provisions and changing many more.

PRIMARY SOURCES

Constitution in English. Available online. URL: http://www.bkklaoembassy.com/Lao%20laws/Constitution.pdf. Accessed on June 21, 2006.

SECONDARY SOURCES

Martin Stuart-Fox, "The Constitution of the Laos People's Democratic Republic." *Review of Socialist Law* 17 (1991): 299.

Martin Stuart-Fox, "Politics and Reform in the Lao People's Democratic Republic." In *Political Economy of Development: Working Paper No.* Williamsburg: 2004.

T. Lamb, "Outline of the Lao Legislative System." In *East Asia—Human Rights, Nation-Building, Trade,* edited by Alice Tay, 498. Baden-Baden: Nomos Verlags-Gesellschaft, 1999.

Jörg Menzel

LATVIA

At-a-Glance

OFFICIAL NAME
Republic of Latvia

CAPITAL
Riga

POPULATION
2,300,000 (2005 est.)

SIZE
24,938 sq. mi. (64,589 sq. km)

LANGUAGES
Latvian (official), Lithuanian, Russian, other

RELIGIONS
Lutheran 24.17%, Roman Catholic 18.71%, Orthodox 15.22%, Old Believer Orthodox 3.48%, Baptist 0.28%, Seventh-day Adventist 0.17%, Methodist 0.04%, Mormon 0.04%, Jewish 0.03%, Muslim 0.02%, unaffiliated or other 37.84%

NATIONAL OR ETHNIC COMPOSITION
Latvian 57.6%, Russian 29.6%, Belorussian 4.1%, Ukrainian 2.7%, Polish 2.5%, Lithuanian 1.4%, Jewish 0.4%, German 0.1%, other 1.6%

DATE OF INDEPENDENCE OR CREATION
November 18, 1918
(from Soviet Union, August 21, 1991)

TYPE OF GOVERNMENT
Parliamentary democracy

TYPE OF STATE
Unitary state

TYPE OF LEGISLATURE
Unicameral parliament (Saeima)

DATE OF CONSTITUTION
February 15, 1922

DATE OF LAST AMENDMENT
January 3, 2006

Latvia is a unitary republic based on the rule of law and the principles of proportionality, justice, and legal certainty. It is a parliamentary democracy with a pluralist system of political parties. There is a clear separation of powers with checks and balances. Fundamental rights are guaranteed and widely respected. Religious freedom is guaranteed, and state and church are separated.

CONSTITUTIONAL HISTORY

Despite the fact that the fundamental law of the state—the constitution—was adopted more than 80 years ago, it is still at the beginning of its development. One of the major reasons is that in 50 years of Soviet occupation, the state of Latvia and constitutionalism could exist only in the imagination of the people. The Republic of Latvia was established on November 18, 1918, and existed till the Soviet's occupation in 1940. The Republic of Latvia was restored on May 4, 1990.

The Republic of Latvia's first legislative institution was called the People's Council. A protoparliament was established with the agreement of eight political parties as a body of 40 members on November 17, 1918, at a time when elections could not yet be held. Mandates in the council were granted not to individuals, but to parties. Each party had a certain number of seats in the council, and these were filled by the members it authorized.

The People's Council adopted several important laws, on rural local governments and their election, on the Latvian monetary system, on educational institutions, and on citizenship. Council elaborated a political platform that can be regarded as the first provisional constitution of the Republic of Latvia. On August 19, 1919, the People's Council adopted a law calling for a constitutional assembly, which was duly elected and held its first session on May 1, 1920.

The Declaration of the State of Latvia was adopted on May 27, 1920. It proclaimed Latvia to be an independent, sovereign republic with a democratic political system vested in the people of Latvia. This declaration together with the Temporary Provisions of the State of Latvia of June 1, 1920, functioned as the country's second temporary constitution.

The Constitutional Assembly (Satversmes Sapulce) was Latvia's first elected legislative body. On February 15, 1922, it adopted the Latvian Constitution (Satversme). After that, a period commenced that may be called the period of parliament, lasting until 1934.

The political atmosphere grew favorable to authoritarianism. Latvia was surrounded by nondemocratic regimes such as Estonia, Lithuania, and Poland. In the unstable lead up to World War II (1939–45), a significant crisis of democracy and constitutionalism seized Latvia. After the recurrent resignations of Latvian administrations, Kārlis Ulmanis became prime minister. He overturned the state on May 15, 1934. Revolution followed quickly, with neither bloodshed nor resistance. On the pretext of internal riots, martial law was proclaimed for six months.

Freedom of speech was restricted, and censorship was introduced. Labor unions and hundreds of other associations were closed. More than 100 organizations of that time were closed, without any exception. Unlike other authoritarian countries of the time, Latvia did not even retain a leading party. All processions and political meetings were prohibited. Dozens of newspapers and magazines were closed, and hundreds of books were banned. Several hundred social democrats were sent to a concentration camp, although they were set free after a year of work on peat marshes. Many officials, municipal employees, teachers, and others lost their jobs for political reasons. The total number of the arrested and dismissed people was approximately 3,000. During that time, anybody could be handed over to a court martial for any crime.

President Alberts Kviesis had remained in office, but when his constitutional term was over on April 11, 1936, he handed over his powers to Ulmanis, who remained president and prime minister until the Soviet occupation. His initial authoritarianism developed into a dictatorship, as he controlled the executive, legislative, and judicial powers.

On June 16, 1940, the government of the Soviet Union issued an ultimatum that the Latvian government resign. The following day the Soviets invaded, in violation of basic principles of international law, and occupied the country. Kārlis Ulmanis signed legal documents dictated by the invaders once the country was occupied. The incorporation of Latvia into the Soviet Union was carried out under the direct supervision of Moscow.

Elections to the Parliament of occupied Latvia were conducted in July in conditions of political terror under an illegal and unconstitutional election law. The new Parliament adopted the Constitution of the Latvian Soviet Socialist Republic—a copy of Stalin's constitution. At first Soviet power lasted only a year as World War II Nazi Germany invaded and occupied Latvia. The country fell into the Soviet sphere after the war as an involuntary republic of the Soviet Union.

Taking advantage of the gathering collapse of the Soviet Union, Latvia renewed its independence as did its two Baltic neighbors. On July 28, 1989, the Supreme Council of the Latvian Soviet Socialist Republic adopted the Declaration On the Sovereignty of the Latvian State.

Elections of the Supreme Council of Latvia were held on March 18, 1990. For the first time since the Soviet occupation, candidates from various political movements were allowed to run for parliament.

On May 4, 1990, the Supreme Council adopted the Declaration on the Renewal of Independence of the Republic of Latvia. As a start toward dismantling Soviet law in the country, the declaration proclaimed that de jure the state had never ceased to exist; the principle of continuity was applied to the laws of the republic of November 18, 1918. The old 1922 constitution was thus once more in effect.

Independent Latvia has since taken its place in the community of nations. It is a member state of the European Union and a member of the North Atlantic Treaty Organization (NATO).

FORM AND IMPACT OF THE CONSTITUTION

The Constitution of the Republic of Latvia (Latvijas Republikas Satversme) is a written, codified single document. It is quite short and laconic. Because of the relative ease of amendment, it may be classified as a flexible constitution.

BASIC ORGANIZATIONAL STRUCTURE

The Republic of Latvia is a unitary republic; the country may be defined as a parliamentary republic. As far as the administrative division is concerned, the territory of the state of Latvia, within the borders established by international agreements, consists of the regions Vidzeme, Latgale, Kurzeme, and Zemgale.

LEADING CONSTITUTIONAL PRINCIPLES

According to the constitution, Latvia is an independent democratic republic. It rests on the rule of law and the principles of proportionality, justice, and legal certainty. There is a division of powers.

As a key principle of the constitution, Latvian is the official language in the Republic of Latvia. The sovereign power of the state is vested in the people of Latvia. All state authority must therefore be justifiable as the will of elected representatives of the people and thus, ultimately, of the people as the sovereign. Parliament is chosen in general, equal, and direct elections by secret ballot, using proportional representation.

Another fundamental constitutional principle, which is gaining increasing importance, is openness to European integration. It is no longer possible to understand Latvian law without taking into account the laws of the European Union.

CONSTITUTIONAL BODIES

The constitutional bodies are Parliament (Saeima), the president, the cabinet of ministers, the State Audit Office, and the courts.

Parliament (Saeima)

The Latvian Parliament consists of 100 delegates elected for a term of four years. The Parliament itself reviews the qualification of its members. It makes decisions by an absolute majority of members present, except in cases specifically set out in the constitution.

Delegates have broad immunity. They can refuse to give evidence in court and may not be called to account by any judicial, administrative, or disciplinary process in connection with their voting or their views as expressed during the execution of their duties. However, court proceedings may be brought against members of Parliament if, even in the course of performing parliamentary duties, they disseminate defamatory statements that they know to be false or any defamatory statements about anyone's private or family life. Delegates may not be arrested, their personal liberty be restricted, or their premises be searched without the consent of Parliament. Delegates may be arrested if apprehended in the act of committing a crime. Without the consent of the Parliament, a criminal prosecution may not be commenced; nor may administrative fines be levied against its members.

The President

The Latvian president is elected by secret ballot by a majority of the votes of members of Parliament, for a term of four years; he or she may be reelected once only. Any person who enjoys full rights of citizenship and who has attained the age of 40 years may run for president. The president may not hold any other office concurrently. If the person elected as president is a member of the Parliament, he or she must immediately resign from the mandate. The president is not responsible to Parliament or the administration in the fulfillment of presidential duties.

The president is the head of the army of Latvia in times of peace. He or she can declare war on the basis of a decision of Parliament. The president has the right to grant clemency to criminals against whom a judgment of the court has come into legal effect.

The head of state can propose the dissolution of Parliament, subject to the approval of a majority of votes in a national referendum. If the voters agree, Parliament is considered dissolved and new elections occur within two months. If more than half of the votes in the referendum are cast against the dissolution of Parliament, the president shall be deemed to be removed from office, and Parliament shall elect a new president to serve for the remaining term of office of the president so removed.

The Cabinet of Ministers

The cabinet of ministers is the administration and the highest executive body of the country. It consists of the prime minister and the cabinet ministers chosen by the prime minister. The cabinet is assembled by the person who has been invited by the president to do so. The cabinet of ministers starts exercising its duties only after receiving a confidence vote in Parliament. Parliament has the right to submit requests and questions to the prime minister or to an individual minister; one of them, or another responsible government official duly authorized by them, must answer.

The number of cabinet ministries and the scope of their responsibilities, as well as the relations among state institutions, are provided for by law.

The Lawmaking Process

The right to legislate is given to Parliament. Draft laws may be submitted by the president, the cabinet, Parliament committees, any five members of the Parliament, or any group that totals one-tenth of the electorate. Legislative initiatives must generally be drawn up in the form of draft laws, but the state president is entitled to submit proposals that are not in the form of draft laws.

All international agreements that might require new or changed laws need ratification by Parliament. International agreements that delegate state power to international institutions must be ratified by Parliament, with a quorum of two-thirds of all members and the approval of two-thirds of members present.

The president has the right to suspend the proclamation of a law for a period of two months; he or she must do so if requested by at least one-third of the members of Parliament. In either case, the decision must be made within seven days of the adoption of the law by Parliament. The suspended law must be submitted to a national referendum if so requested by not less than one-tenth of the electorate. If no such request is received during the two-month period, the law is proclaimed. Parliament can prevent a national referendum by voting on the law again and approving it by a three-quarters majority of all members of the Parliament.

Finally, the cabinet of ministers has the right, if there is an urgent need during the time between sessions of the Parliament, to issue regulations that have the force of law.

Such regulations may not amend the law regarding elections of the Parliament, laws governing the court system and court proceedings, the budget and rights pertaining to the budget, or laws adopted during the term of the current Parliament, and they may not pertain to amnesty, state taxes, customs duties, and loans. These regulations shall cease to be in force unless submitted to Parliament not later than three days after the next session of Parliament has been convened.

The State Audit Office (Valsts Kontrole)

The State Audit Office is an independent collegiate body that reports to the Parliament on the utilization of public funds. The tasks of the State Audit Office are to supervise the legal, effective, and accurate collection and spending of resources in line with the basic budget and special budget of the state and local governments and to moderate the use of state and local government property. The State Audit Office provides annual reports to the Parliament on actual implementation of the state budget of the previous year and issues opinions on the collection and spending of state resources and handling of state property. Auditors general shall be appointed to their office and confirmed pursuant to the same procedures as judges, but only for a fixed period, during which they may be removed from office only by a judgment of the court.

The Courts

The judiciary is composed of district (city) courts, regional courts, the Supreme Court, and the Constitutional Court. The court system is financed from the state budget. In the Republic of Latvia, only a court can administer justice. Judges in Latvia are independent and subject only to the law. Judicial appointments are confirmed by Parliament and are as a rule irrevocable. Parliament may remove judges from office only in the cases provided for by law, on the basis of a decision of the Judicial Disciplinary Board or a judgment of the court in a criminal case. The age of retirement from office for judges may be determined by law. Latvian courts work in accordance with the following principles: legality, openness, presumption of innocence, equality of parties, and collegiality.

A judge has immunity during his or her term of office. A criminal matter against a judge may be initiated only by the prosecutor general of the Republic of Latvia. A judge may not be detained or subjected to criminal liability without the consent of Parliament. A decision concerning the detention, forcible conveyance, arrest, or subjection to search of a judge shall be taken by a Supreme Court justice specially authorized for that purpose. An administrative sanction may not be applied to a judge, and a judge shall not be arrested pursuant to administrative procedures.

The Constitutional Court

The Constitutional Court is an independent institution of judicial power. It reviews cases concerning the compliance of laws with the constitution, and it has the right to declare laws or other enactments or parts thereof invalid. The Constitutional Court also reviews international treaties entered into by Latvia, to verify their compliance with the constitution; it may rule even before Parliament has confirmed the agreement. The court reviews the compliance of other normative acts with legal norms of a higher legal force (such as ordinary law vis-à-vis the constitution). It has responsibility to ensure that Parliament and the cabinet of ministers, president, chairperson of the Parliament, and prime minister all act in compliance with the law (except in their administrative acts). It also rules in cases of ministers' overruling local council regulations and checks the compliance of the national laws of Latvia with the international agreements entered into by Latvia, as long as they are not contrary to the constitution.

THE ELECTION PROCESS AND POLITICAL PARTICIPATION

All citizens of Latvia who have reached the age of 18 have the right to vote. Elections to Parliament are secret and by proportional representation.

Any legally registered political organization (party) or association of political organizations (coalition) may submit a list of candidates for Parliament. Any citizen of Latvia who has reached the age of 21 by election day may be nominated as a candidate. Only those candidates on lists that have received at least 5 percent of the total number of votes cast will be elected to Parliament. In the seventh Saeima elections of October 3, 1998, six lists of candidates received more than 5 percent of the total number of votes, in 21 candidate lists, which contained a total of 1,081 candidates.

A national referenda may be initiated if the president proposes a dismissal of the Parliament; if the president suspends the publication of a law for two months; if at least one-tenth of the electors request a referendum; if Parliament amends Articles 1, 2, 3, or 6 of the constitution; or if one-tenth of the electors present a complete draft law to the president and Parliament does not accept it.

The constitution prohibits referenda on the following topics: the state budget, loans, taxes, customs, or railroad tariffs; conscription; proclamation of war and opening of hostilities; entry into a peace treaty; proclamation or termination of a state of emergency; mobilization and demobilization; and treaties with foreign countries.

POLITICAL PARTIES

A party (a political organization) can be formed by any group of at least 200 people. The Communist Party and parties of national socialist (Nazi) disposition are outlawed. At present, there are about 40 political organizations in Latvia, of which eight parties are represented in Parliament.

CITIZENSHIP

Latvian citizens have equal rights and obligations irrespective of the manner in which they have acquired citizenship. Latvian citizens are persons who were Latvian citizens on June 17, 1940, and their descendants who have registered in accordance with the procedures set out in law and who have not acquired the citizenship of another state since May 4, 1990. Persons can acquire Latvian citizenship by naturalization or otherwise in accordance with the procedures set out by law.

A noncitizen, as defined by the "Law on the status of those former U.S.S.R. citizens who do not have the citizenship of Latvia or that of any other state," has the right to a noncitizen passport issued by the Republic of Latvia.

Dual citizenship is not allowed for those who acquire Latvian citizenship. Even if a Latvian citizen, in accordance with the laws of a foreign state, is simultaneously considered a national of that state still, in legal relations with Latvia he or she shall be considered solely a Latvian citizen.

FUNDAMENTAL RIGHTS

The state undertakes to recognize and protect fundamental human rights in accordance with the constitution, laws, and international agreements; all people in Latvia have the right to know about these rights. All are equal before the law and the courts, as human rights must know no discrimination of any kind. All people have the right to defend their rights and lawful interests in fair court proceedings. Courts shall judge trials irrespective of a person's origin, social and financial status, race or nationality, sex, education, language, attitude toward religion, type and nature of occupation, place of residence, or political or other views. All people have the right to court protection against threats to their life, health, personal freedom, honor, reputation, and property. Everyone is presumed innocent until guilt has been established in accordance with law. Everyone has a right to commensurate compensation when rights are violated without legal basis, and everyone has a right to the assistance of counsel. The right to life of everyone must be protected by the law.

According to the Latvian constitution, all citizens have the right to participate in the activities of the state and of local government and to hold a position in the civil service, as provided for by law. Local governments shall be elected by Latvian citizens. The working language of local governments is Latvian. Persons who are members of ethnic minorities have the right to preserve and develop their language and their ethnic and cultural identity. The Latvian constitution guarantees everyone the inviolability of private life, home, correspondence, free movement, and choice of residence. Everyone has the right to depart from Latvia freely. Everyone who has a Latvian passport shall be protected by the state while abroad and has the right to return to Latvia freely. A citizen of Latvia may not be extradited to a foreign country.

In the sphere of labor rights, everyone in Latvia has the right to choose employment and workplace freely according to his or her abilities and qualifications. Forced labor is prohibited; participation in the relief of disasters and work pursuant to a court order shall not be deemed forced labor. Every employed person in Latvia has the constitutional right to receive commensurate remuneration for work done, which must not be less than the minimal wage established by the state. Everyone has the right to weekly days off and a paid annual vacation. Employed persons have the right to collective labor agreements and the right to strike. The state must protect the freedom of trade unions. The Latvian state recognizes the freedom of scientific research and artistic and other creative activity and protects copyright and patent rights.

The state must generally protect human honor and dignity; as a result, torture or other cruel or degrading treatment of human beings is prohibited. Freedom of previously announced peaceful meetings, street processions, and pickets is guaranteed. The state supports marriage, the family, the rights of parents, and the rights of children. The state is obliged to provide special support to disabled children, children left without parental care, or children who have suffered from violence. Human health must be protected with a basic level of medical assistance. Everyone has the right to live in a benevolent environment; the state must provide information about environmental conditions and promote the preservation and improvement of the environment.

Everyone has the right to the liberty and security of the person. No one may be deprived of or have his or her liberty restricted, other than in accordance with law. The constitution guarantees freedom of thought, conscience, and religion, and freedom of expression, which includes the right to receive, keep, and distribute information and express views freely. Censorship is prohibited. The right to form and join associations, political parties, and other public organizations is guaranteed, as is the right to address petitions to national or local government institutions and to receive a materially responsive reply in the Latvian language. There is a right to own property, although such property may not be used contrary to the interests of the public.

Social security in old age, for work disability, for unemployment, and in other cases as provided by law is guaranteed. To guarantee the right to education, the state must ensure that everyone may acquire primary and secondary education without charge. Primary education is compulsory.

Impact and Functions of Fundamental Rights

To implement fundamental rights further in practice the Ombudsperson (Tiesibsargs) is an independent institution that promotes the observance of human rights. It is contributing to the creation of a society in which human rights are genuinely respected. The office is independent in its decisions and activities and can only make recommendations to the competent administrative authorities in order to prevent and to remedy injustices.

Limitations to Fundamental Rights

The rights of persons may be subject to restrictions in circumstances provided for by law in order to protect the rights of other people, the democratic structure of the state, or public safety, welfare, and morals.

ECONOMY

The Latvian constitution does not mention economic matters directly. It does, however, secure the right to own property. Property may not be used contrary to the interests of the public, but property rights may be restricted only in accordance with the law. The expropriation for public purposes is allowed only in exceptional cases on the basis of a specific law and in return for fair compensation.

RELIGIOUS COMMUNITIES

The separation of church and state has never implied segregation of religion from society or complete exclusion of the church from social life. This would not be possible in a democratic country, as religion and religious associations form one of the structural elements of society. The role of the church in the internal national processes in Latvia should not be underestimated. Public polls show that 70 percent of Latvian citizens and 60 percent of noncitizens trust the churches. Embracing this potential, churches have sought to influence state policy and laws. Latvia is a multiconfessional country, where the three largest denominations are the Catholics, the Lutherans, and the members of the Orthodox Church. There are about 170 different denominations and religious groups.

The Law on Religious Organizations, special agreements with the traditional denominations, and special laws for churches govern the state-church relationship in Latvia. It is based on separation, respectful neutrality, religious freedom, and the delegation of some peculiar powers. The government has delegated the right to register marriages to some denominations only; their clerics thereby assume the responsibilities of state officials, but they are not provided with any compensation from the state.

MILITARY DEFENSE AND STATE OF EMERGENCY

The Parliament determines the size of the armed forces during peacetime. If in accordance with the constitution of the Republic of Latvia (Article 62) the state is threatened by an external enemy, or if an internal insurrection anywhere in the country endangers the existing political system, the cabinet has the right to proclaim a state of emergency.

The leading institution of state administration in the defense field is the ministry of defense, which is directly subordinated to the minister of defense. The minister of defense is a civilian who has political responsibility to the Parliament and to the cabinet.

The president of state is the commander in chief of the armed forces. During wartime the president appoints a supreme commander. The president has the right to take whatever steps necessary for the military defense of the state, should another state declare war on Latvia or an enemy invade its borders. Concurrently and without delay, the president must convene Parliament, which decides as to the declaration and commencement of war.

During peacetime, military units are recruited from Latvian citizens via conscription into mandatory active military service. No one may be accepted into military service if he or she has been sentenced for a criminal offense; is a suspect, accused, or defendant in a criminal case; is unfit for service because of health; or is or has been a staff employee or a supernumerary of the security service, intelligence, or counterintelligence service of the Soviet Union; the Latvian Soviet Socialist Republic; or any foreign state.

There is an alternative service of 24 months for conscientious objectors, 18 months for those who have higher education.

AMENDMENTS TO THE CONSTITUTION

Parliament may amend the constitution. The amendments require three readings and must be approved by two-thirds of the members present (with a quorum of two-thirds of all members). Amendments that affect the form of the state, the sovereign power of the people, territorial components, the state language, the election of Parliament, or certain other basic elements must be submitted to a national referendum. Any group of one-tenth of the electorate may submit a fully elaborated draft amendment to the president, who must present it to Parliament. If Parliament does not adopt it without change, it is submitted to national referendum.

PRIMARY SOURCES

Constitution in English. Available online. URL: http://www.saeima.lv/LapasEnglish/Constitution_Visa.htm. Accessed on September 8, 2005.

Constitution in Latvian. Available online. URL: http://www.saeima.lv/Lapas/Satversme_Visa.htm. Accessed on September 6, 2005.

SECONDARY SOURCES

Ringolds Balodis, *The Constitution of Latvia,* Legal Policy Forum Series, vol. 26. Trier: Institute for Legal Policy, Trier University, 2004.

"Constitution as a Legal Base for a System and Functions of Organs of the State." In the *Fourth Baltic–Norwegian Conference on Constitutional Issues,* March 1996. Tallinn: Estonian Academy of Sciences, 1996.

Tâlavs Jundzis, ed., "First Year in the European Union: Current Legal Issues." In *Proceedings of the International Conference,* April 29–30. Riga: Poligrâfists, 2005.

Tâlavs Jundzis, ed., *Latvia in Europe: Visions of the Future.* Riga: Baltic Center for Strategic Studies, Latvian Academy of Sciences, 2004.

Tâlavs Jundzis, ed., *The Baltic States at Historical Crossroads.* Riga: Latvian Academy of Sciences, 2d edition, 2001.

Caroline Taube, *Constitutionalism in Estonia, Latvia and Lithuania.* Uppsala: Iustus Förlag, 2001.

Ringolds Balodis

LEBANON

At-a-Glance

OFFICIAL NAME
Lebanese Republic

CAPITAL
Beirut

POPULATION
3,874,050 (2006)

SIZE
4,015 sq. mi. (10,400 sq. km)

LANGUAGES
Arabic (official), French, English, Armenian

RELIGIONS
Muslim (Shia 32%, Sunni 20%, Ismailite, Alawite 54%, Christian (Maronite 23%, Greek Orthodox, Greek Catholic, Armenian Orthodox [Gregorian], Armenian Catholic, Protestant, Syrian Orthodox, Syrian Catholic, Latin [Roman Catholic], Copt, Assyrian, Chaldean Catholic) 39%, Druze, Yazidi, Jewish, and other 7%

NATIONAL OR ETHNIC COMPOSITION
Arab 95%, Armenian 4%, other 1%

DATE OF INDEPENDENCE OR CREATION
November 22, 1943 (from League of Nations mandate under French administration)

TYPE OF GOVERNMENT
Republic

TYPE OF STATE
Centralist state

TYPE OF LEGISLATURE
Unicameral national assembly

DATE OF CONSTITUTION
May 23, 1926

DATE OF LAST AMENDMENT
September 3, 2004

Lebanon's governmental system is a mix of parliamentary and presidential elements. The 1926 constitution, still in effect, provides for a republican form of government and stipulates that the people are the source of authority and sovereignty. It was complemented by the unwritten National Pact of 1943, which provided for representation by religious confession: a Maronite Christian president, a Sunni Muslim prime minister, and a Shiite Muslim speaker of parliament. The 1991 Taif Agreement led to fundamental amendments to the 1926 constitution. The abolition of political confessionalism is a basic national goal.

Checks and balances among the three branches of government are detailed. Since its independence in 1943, Lebanon has had nearly 50 cabinets and about a dozen presidents. Lebanon is a centralist state, divided into six governorates.

The president is the head of state and the prime minister is head of the administration. The president of the republic is elected by a two-thirds majority of parliament. The president appoints the prime minister in consultation with the parliament's speaker. Since 1990, a Constitutional Council rules on the constitutionality of laws and on electoral disputes. A Higher Court judges the president and the ministers.

There is a multiparty system based on multiple religious groups. The constitution stresses freedom and equality as fundamental rights. The constitution's economic system can be characterized as a social market economy.

CONSTITUTIONAL HISTORY

Lebanon is situated in what is broadly called the Middle East. Because of the territory's centralized location, it changed hands many times throughout antiquity before it was under the control of the Ottoman Turks in 1516.

When World War I (1914–18) broke out, the Ottoman Empire (centered in today's Turkey) took the side of the German Empire and Austria-Hungary. The Allies (including the United States, France, the United Kingdom, and Russia) held out the hope of postwar independence to the Arabs in order to gain support against the Ottoman Empire. At the same time, Britain, France, and Russia made the secret 1916 Sikes-Picot Agreement to divide the Middle East among them. Furthermore, the British Balfour Declaration (1917) promised the establishment of a national home to the Jewish people in Palestine.

The Ottoman Empire was defeated, and the League of Nations (founded after World War I) awarded France a mandate (a treaty between the league and the mandatory power that promised to establish an independent administration in the future) over "Greater Syria," including the territory of Lebanon. The areas that now comprise Syria and Lebanon were assigned to France, and those that now comprise Israel, including the territories of the Palestinian Authority, and Jordan were assigned to Great Britain.

The establishment of Greater Lebanon was proclaimed on September 1, 1920, by General Gouraud, who was appointed by the French to implement the mandate provisions. The country had its present boundaries. The first Lebanese constitution was promulgated in 1926; it was modeled on the 1875 French constitution. It was amended several times and remained in force until 1987.

The French high commissioner suspended the Lebanese constitution in 1932 to prevent the election of a Muslim as president. After a president was elected in 1936, he partially reestablished the 1926 constitution, which was again suspended by the French high commissioner at the outbreak of World War II. The French presence was acknowledged in the constitution, but they exercised their influence outside the constitutional structure.

In 1943 the Chamber of Deputies amended the constitution, abolishing the articles that referred to the French mandate. France arrested the leaders of this effort but released them in the face of internal and external pressure on November 22, 1943, which has been celebrated as Independence Day since.

Leaders of the nation's ethnic groups then reached a political consensus called the 1943 National Pact, which complemented the 1926 constitution. This unwritten covenant included four principles: (1) Lebanon would be a completely independent state, (2) it would not cut its spiritual and intellectual ties with the West, (3) it would cooperate with the other Arab states, and (4) public offices would be distributed proportionally among the recognized religious groups. A Maronite Christian would be president (under the most recent census, from 1932, Christians were in the majority), a Sunni Muslim would be prime minister, and a Shiite Muslim would be Speaker of parliament. The ratio of seats in parliament would be six Christian seats for every five Muslim seats; this was amended in 1990, and the ratio was changed to parity.

With the proclamation of an independent state of Israel in 1948, a series of Arab-Israeli wars started, some of which involved Lebanon.

The elimination of the Palestinian armed presence in Jordan in 1970 led to the arrival of new waves of Palestinian refugees in Lebanon. Palestinian guerrilla groups used Lebanon as a base of operations in their struggle against Israel. They also fought with the Lebanese army until a cease-fire was reached.

By 1975, the Lebanese government had been weakened so much that it could not prevent the outbreak of a civil war, which lasted until 1990. This war has often been characterized as Christian-Muslim conflict. However, the reality was far more complex and involved a shifting constellation of the Lebanese army, Maronite Christians, Sunni and Shiite Muslims, Druze, Palestinians, and other groups. Furthermore, the war also saw the involvement of the country's two neighbors, Israel and Syria.

Syria first intervened on behalf of the Maronite Christians and later switched to backing Sunni Muslim groups. Syria had previously tried to help negotiate a reform of the National Pact, known as the Constitutional Document. Syria's influence was always exercised outside the constitutional structure. In 1989 Lebanese deputies met in the city of Taif (Saudi Arabia) and adopted a document of national understanding. It established, or rather confirmed, the special relationship with the Syrian Arab Republic: Lebanon is linked to Syria by distinctive ties deriving from kinship, history, and common interests. This agreement also ended the civil war in Lebanon. In 1990, the constitution was amended to reflect the Taif Agreement.

In 1982, Israel attacked the Palestine Liberation Organization (PLO), as well as Syrian and Muslim Lebanese forces, and then occupied a band of territory in southern Lebanon. Israel withdrew some forces in 1985 and completed their withdrawal in 2000. After ongoing protests by the Lebanese people in 2005, Syria also withdrew its troops, which had been stationed there since 1976, from Lebanon.

In 2002, the Lebanese Republic was finally recognized as an independent state by Syria. Lebanon, however, does not have bilateral relations with the state of Israel. Lebanon is a founding member of the League of Arab States (LAS).

FORM AND IMPACT OF THE CONSTITUTION

Lebanon's constitution is codified in a single document consisting of 102 articles. It was complemented by the unwritten National Pact of 1943. Among its provisions, the pact provided for the sharing of power among the religious groups: A Maronite Christian would be president, a Sunni Muslim would be prime minister, and a Shiite Muslim would be speaker of parliament.

This earlier arrangement left the Christians the most powerful group politically, the Shiites the least influential. The 1989 Taif Agreement, known as the Document of National Accord, rectified this imbalance, and it too was introduced into the constitution (1990). The president's powers were limited, while the powers of the prime minister and the speaker were enhanced. The fact that ending the civil war entailed a constitutional revision demonstrates the impact that is assigned to the Lebanese constitution.

The constitution is at the top of the hierarchy of domestic norms. All legislative provisions contrary to the constitution are abrogated by Article 102. All treaties that are ratified by Lebanon have the force of law within the country.

BASIC ORGANIZATIONAL STRUCTURE

Lebanon is a unified centralist state, divided into six regional governments.

LEADING CONSTITUTIONAL PRINCIPLES

The preamble, as amended in 1991, outlines a number of constitutional principles. Lebanon subscribes to the Covenants of the League of Arab States, the United Nations Covenants, and the Universal Declaration of Human Rights. The government embodies these principles "in all fields and areas without exception."

Lebanon is a parliamentary democratic republic based on respect for public liberties. People are the source of authority and sovereignty.

The constitution contains the principles of separation of powers and balance and cooperation among the three branches of government. For instance, executive ministers are responsible before parliament, and the dissolution of parliament is a complex process.

The abolition of political confessionalism, the traditional system of allocating power according to criteria of religious affiliation, is a basic national goal. However, in practice, the Taif Agreement has perpetuated political confessionalism as a key element of Lebanese political life.

CONSTITUTIONAL BODIES

The predominant bodies provided for in the constitution are the president, the prime minister, and the Council of Ministers or cabinet; and the unicameral parliament (National Assembly or chamber of deputies). A Constitutional Council and a Higher Court, rather than a Constitutional Court, review the constitutionality of laws. A National Committee also plays a constitutional role. The senate, an earlier constitutional body, no longer exists.

The President of the Republic

The president is the head of state; the prime minister is head of the administration. The president of the republic is elected by the National Assembly or chamber of deputies in a secret ballot by a two-thirds majority. After a first ballot, an absolute majority is sufficient. The president serves a six-year term and may not be reelected until six years after the expiration of the president's last mandate. In 2004, the sitting president's term was extended to three more years by constitutional amendment. The president appoints the prime minister in consultation with the speaker of the parliament.

The president presides over the Supreme Defense Council and is the commander in chief of the armed forces. The president also negotiates international treaties in coordination with the prime minister.

The president has the right to request the Council of Ministers to reconsider its decisions. The president issues, in agreement with the prime minister, the decree appointing the cabinet and the decrees accepting the resignation of ministers. The president also may ask the cabinet to dissolve parliament.

The president's legal responsibility is generally limited. He or she is liable only in cases of violations of the constitution, high crimes, or treason. In those cases, a president may be impeached by a two-thirds majority of the Constitutional Council.

Even since the Taif Agreement, the president remains a strong and visible constitutional player. However, presidential decisions must be countersigned by cabinet ministers. The only exceptions are the decree appointing the prime minister and the decree accepting the resignation of the cabinet.

The Council of Ministers

The executive power is entrusted primarily to the cabinet or Council of Ministers, who are responsible to parliament. The council is headed by the prime minister, who is also known as the president of the council. The president of the republic also can preside over the Council of Ministers at his or her discretion but does not have a vote.

The council sets the general policy of the executive administration in all fields and prepares bills and decrees. Council meetings are called into session by the prime minister, who sets their agenda. The president may also call the Council of Ministers to an extraordinary session, but only in agreement with the prime minister.

The council may also dissolve the National Assembly at the request of the president of the republic, under certain conditions.

Instead of simple majority decisions, "basic national issues" require the approval of two-thirds of the members of the council. Such issues include amendments to the constitution; declarations of a state of emergency, war, or peace; general mobilization; international agreements; budgets; and dissolutions of parliament.

Along with the president, the prime minister is a strong constitutional figure; only the prime minister has the constitutional authority to call cabinet meetings. The prime minister may also prevent the cabinet from considering a constitutional amendment.

The Parliament

Legislative power is vested in the chamber of deputies or National Assembly. The chamber meets each year in two ordinary sessions. The National Assembly elects the president of the republic.

Any deputy may raise a motion of no confidence in the administration during ordinary and extraordinary sessions. The National Assembly has the right to impeach the prime minister and cabinet ministers for high treason or for serious neglect of duties.

If the Council of Ministers, requested by the president, dissolves the National Assembly before the expiration of its mandate, a new chamber must be elected within three months. If elections are not held in due time, the decree is void and the old parliament continues to exercise its powers.

In practice, parliament plays a significant role, especially in financial affairs, since it is competent to levy taxes and pass the budget. Its power is further enhanced by the right to hold a no confidence vote.

The Lawmaking Process

Both the National Assembly and the Council of Ministers have the right to propose laws. Laws proposed by the council are delivered to the president, who then forwards them to the assembly for consideration.

A bill indicated as "urgent" must be issued by the president within 40 days of its communication to the assembly, after it is included on the agenda of a general meeting and read aloud before the assembly and after the expiration of the time limit without action by the assembly. Any bill that has been rejected by the assembly cannot be reintroduced during the same session.

The constitution emphasizes that the president promulgates the laws only after they have been approved by the assembly. The president has the laws published; he or she may not modify them or exempt anyone from compliance with their provisions. The president must promulgate the approved law within one month of its transmission, or in cases of urgent laws, within five days.

The president has the right of veto, by requesting that a law be reconsidered, after consultation with the Council of Ministers. The National Assembly can override this veto by an absolute majority of all the members of the assembly. If the president delays action beyond the time limits, the law is considered legally operative and must be promulgated.

Constitutional Council and Council of State

The 1990 Constitutional Council rules on the constitutionality of laws and on electoral disputes. According to the law on the Constitutional Council, it is composed of 10 justices who serve for a term of six years and cannot be reelected. Five members are elected by the National Assembly and five members are elected by the Council of Ministers. The president of the republic, the president of the National Assembly, the prime minister, or any 10 members of parliament have the right to consult the Constitutional Council. Recognized heads of religious communities have the right to consult the Constitutional Council only on laws relating to personal status, the freedom of belief and religious practice, and the freedom of religious education.

The Judiciary

The constitution guarantees that judges are independent in the exercise of their duties. According to the constitution, there is an independent judiciary; however, in practice, the judiciary is often subject to political pressure. The Judicial Organization Law governs the structure and functioning of the judiciary.

The judiciary is composed of ordinary and exceptional courts. The ordinary court system is composed of the courts of first instance, the courts of appeal, and a Court of Cassation (final appeal), all of which have separate civil and criminal branches.

Sharia Courts settle matters of personal status among Muslims. Christian and Jewish ecclesiastical courts deal with matters of personal status for individuals in their respective communities. Finally, there are some courts with specialized jurisdiction, such as the labor court, the land court, the customs committee, military courts, and juvenile courts.

A Higher Court judges the president and the ministers. There is no Constitutional Court.

National Committee

The constitution provides for a National Committee, composed of the president of the republic, the president of the National Assembly, the prime minister, and "leading political, intellectual, and social figures." This National Committee must work toward the abolition of religious confessionalism by making proposals to the chamber of deputies and the cabinet ministers and supervising the execution of a transitional plan. During the transitional phase, equitable confessional representation should still prevail in the cabinet. Eventually, however, it must be abolished in accordance with the requirements of national reconciliation and should be replaced by the principles of expertise and competence.

Senate

The Senate was abolished in 1927. When the National Assembly is finally elected on a national, nonreligious basis, the Senate will be established to guarantee representation for all the religious communities. Its authority will be limited to major national issues. The 2005 draft electoral law, which calls for a nonconfessional national constituency, also revives the Senate.

THE ELECTION PROCESS

Every Lebanese citizen above the age of 21 has the constitutional right to vote. According to the 1990 Electoral Law, Lebanese citizens can stand for election as deputy to parliament when they have reached the age of 25.

Parliamentary Elections

The 1990 constitution provides that until such time as the chamber enacts new electoral laws on a nonconfessional basis the distribution of seats is according to the principles of equal representation between Christians and Muslims and proportional representation among the confessional groups within each religious community and among geographic regions. As an exception, vacant seats and newly created seats are to be filled simultaneously by a two-thirds majority of the cabinet. This provision establishes equality between Christians and Muslims as stipulated in the Taif Agreement.

The seats in the National Assembly were allocated by the 1990 electoral law as follows: 34 seats for Maronite Catholics, 27 for Sunni Muslims, 27 for Shiite Muslims, 14 for Greek Orthodox, eight for Druze, five for Armenian Orthodox, five for Greek-Melkite Catholics, two for Alawites, and one each for Armenian Catholics, Protestants, and other groups. A 2005 draft electoral law that created a single constituency for the whole of Lebanon has been heavily criticized by many Lebanese.

POLITICAL PARTIES

Lebanon has had a multiparty system since the 1920s, mostly based on religious affiliation. However, Lebanese political life has never been organized around political parties. Powerful families still play an independent role in mobilizing votes in both local and parliamentary elections, and the confessional element is even more important. The sophisticated electoral system has further contributed to the weakening of the political parties.

CITIZENSHIP

Nationality is determined by law. Citizenship is primarily acquired by descent; that is, a child acquires Lebanon citizenship when he or she is born of a Lebanese father, regardless of the child's country of birth. Dual citizenship is recognized.

FUNDAMENTAL RIGHTS

The constitution stresses freedom and equality as fundamental rights. Economic, social, and cultural rights are somewhat underrepresented in the amended constitution; however, human rights are explicitly mentioned in the preamble.

All Lebanese are equal before the law. Individual liberty is guaranteed and protected by law. There is absolute freedom of conscience. Freedom of expression and the press as well as the rights of assembly and association are guaranteed.

Impact and Functions of the Fundamental Rights

The preamble of the Lebanese constitution as amended in 1990 states in paragraph (b) that Lebanon subscribes to the United Nations Covenants and to the Universal Declaration of Human Rights. Lebanon has ratified both the International Covenant on Economic, Social and Cultural Rights and the International Covenant on Civil and Political Rights.

Human rights organizations have criticized the covert presence and activity of Syrian military intelligence personnel in Lebanon. Palestinian and Lebanese security forces have also purportedly committed numerous serious human rights abuses.

Limitations to Fundamental Rights

The fundamental rights specified in the constitution are not without limits. Some rights are guaranteed only within the "limits established by law," and others are limited by "public order and morals." On the other hand, no fundamental right can be disregarded completely.

ECONOMY

According to the preamble of the constitution, the economic system is based on a free market and ensures private initiative and the right to private property. Expropriation requires fair compensation.

RELIGIOUS COMMUNITIES

There is absolute freedom of conscience. The state, in rendering homage to the "Most High," must respect all religions and creeds. The state guarantees the free exercise of all religious rites provided that public order is not disturbed. The state also guarantees that the personal status and religious interests of the population, to whatever religious sect they belong, are respected.

Nineteen religious groups are recognized; however, no official census has been taken since 1932. It is estimated that Muslims, as a whole, make up a majority, and that Shiite Muslims, Sunnis, and Maronites are the three largest groups. The relationship of all these religious groups has been characterized as "coexistence."

The abolition of political confessionalism has been a basic national goal since 1926. According to Article 95 of the constitution, this should be achieved by means of a transitional plan.

MILITARY DEFENSE AND STATE OF EMERGENCY

The National Defense Law stipulates that military service is compulsory for all men aged 18 to 30 for a 12-month period. Exemptions are available for those whose family members have died in service or on grounds of sickness or economic need. Women are not required to serve. Voluntary participation of women is possible.

The president presides over the Supreme Defense Council and is the commander in chief of the armed forces. The deputy head is the prime minister. The constitution emphasizes that the armed forces are subject to the authority of the Council of Ministers.

Declarations of war and peace, as well as the declaration of a state of emergency, are "basic national issues" that require the approval of two-thirds of the members of the Council of Ministers. The constitution does not further explain what measures the executive is then allowed to take and which rights may then be suspended.

AMENDMENTS TO THE CONSTITUTION

The president has the right to initiate a revision to the constitution. The Council of Ministers then submits a draft law to the National Assembly. A revision of the constitution is a "basic national issue" that requires the approval of two-thirds of the members of the Council of Ministers and approval by two-thirds of all members of the National Assembly.

The assembly may also initiate a revision, at the request of at least 10 of its members and a recommendation of a two-thirds majority of all the members. If the recommendation satisfies certain material requirements, the president of the assembly transmits it to the Council of Ministers. If the latter approves the recommendation by a two-thirds majority, the amendment becomes law. Otherwise, the Council of Ministers returns the proposal to the assembly for reconsideration. If three-fourths of all the members approve the amendment, the president of the republic must either accede to the assembly's recommendation or request the dissolution of parliament.

If the assembly is dissolved, and its newly elected replacement still backs the amendment, the Council of Ministers must yield and approve the amendment within four months.

PRIMARY SOURCES
Constitution in English. Available online. URL: http://www. presidency.gov.lb/presidency/symbols/constitution/constitution.htm. Accessed on July 21, 2005.
Constitution in French and Arabic. Available online. URL: http://www.conseil-constitutionnel.gov.lb/fr/constitution.htm. Accessed on August 11, 2005.
Taif Agreement in English, French, and Arabic. Available online. URL: http://www.mideastinfo.com/documents/index.html. Accessed on September 27, 2005. Available online. URL: http://www.conseil-constitutionnel.gov.lb/fr/taef.htm. Accessed on September 27, 2005.
1990 Electoral Law. Available online. URL: http://www.arabelectionlaw.net/eleclaw_eng.php. Accessed on August 18, 2005.

SECONDARY SOURCES
Ziad K. Abdelnour, "The US and France Tip the Scale in Lebanon's Power Struggle." Available online. URL: http://www.meib.org/articles/0407_l1.htm. Accessed on August 3, 2005.
Nathan J. Brown, Constitutions in a Nonconstitutional World—Arab Basic Laws and the Prospects for Accountable Government. New York: State University of New York Press, 2002.
Bureau of Public Affairs, U.S. Department of State, "Background Note and Country Reports on Human Rights Practices and International Religious Freedom Report 2004." Available online. URL: http://www.state.gov/g/drl/rls/hrrpt/41726.htm. Accessed on June 21, 2006.
"The League of Arab States." Available online. URL: http://www.arableagueonline.org/. Accessed on September 29, 2005.
Thomas Collelo, Lebanon—a Country Study. Washington D.C., Government Printing Office, 1989. Available online. URL: http://countrystudies.us/lebanon/l.htm. Accessed on June 21, 2006.
United Nations, "Core Documents Forming Part of the Reports of the States Parties: Lebanon" (HRI/CORE/1/Add.27) October 12, 1993. Available online. URL: http://www.bayefsky.com/core/hri_core_1_add_27_1993.pdf. Accessed on February 4, 2006 and (HRI/CORE/1/Add.27/Rev.1) October 3, 1996. Available online. URL: http://www.hri.ca/fortherecord1997/documentation/coredocs/hri-core-1-add27-rev1.htm. Accessed on February 4, 2006.
United Nations Development Programme (UNDP), "Constitutions of the Arab Region." Available online. URL: http://www.pogar.org/themes/constitution.asp. Accessed on September 23, 2005.

Michael Rahe

LESOTHO

At-a-Glance

OFFICIAL NAME
Lesotho

CAPITAL
Maseru

POPULATION
2,022,331 (July 2006 est.)

SIZE
11,720 sq. mi. (30,355 sq. km)

LANGUAGES
Sesotho (native), Sesotho, English (official)

RELIGIONS
Christian (est., including Catholic, Lesotho Evangelical, Methodist, Zion, Pentecostal) 90%, African traditional, Islam, and Bahai (statistics not readily available)

NATIONAL OR ETHNIC COMPOSITION
Basotho (a conglomeration of nationalities: Sephuthi, Ndebele, Xhosa, Batlokoa, Zulu, other) 99.7%, European, Asian and other 0.3%

DATE OF INDEPENDENCE OR CREATION
October 4, 1966

TYPE OF GOVERNMENT
Parliamentary democratic monarchy

TYPE OF STATE
Unitary state

TYPE OF LEGISLATURE
Bicameral parliament

DATE OF CONSTITUTION
February 5, 1993

DATE OF LAST AMENDMENT
March 13, 2001

Lesotho is a parliamentary democracy; the first section of its 1993 constitution mandates that "Lesotho shall be a sovereign democratic kingdom." There is a clear constitutional division of the executive, legislative, and judicial powers. However, in practice, only the judiciary is independent of the other branches; members of the executive are, necessarily, members of Parliament, the legislative organ. Lesotho is a unitary state made up of 10 administrative districts. The constitution of the state entrenches "fundamental human rights and freedoms," which are, essentially, civil and political rights. Economic, social, and cultural rights are consigned to the third chapter of the constitution, Principles of State Policy, which are not enforceable by any court. However, Lesotho has ratified the United Nations Covenant on Economic, Social and Cultural Rights, 1966.

The king is a constitutional monarch and head of state, whose functions are basically ceremonial and representative. The paramount political figure is the prime minister, who is assisted by ministers and assistant ministers. However, the king has the constitutional right to be consulted by the prime minister and the other ministers on all matters relating to the government. The prime minister and the ministers, who form the cabinet, depend upon the Parliament, whose members are the peoples' representatives and are chosen through both the first-past-the-post and proportional representation electoral systems.

There is no state religion in Lesotho; the government is secular. The constitution guarantees freedom of conscience, including freedom of thought and of religion. Though privatization has accelerated of late, the economy is still predicated upon a mixture of private and public enterprises. Regardless of past unconstitutional forays into government, the military is subject to the civil government.

CONSTITUTIONAL HISTORY

Lesotho has only one neighbor, the Republic of South Africa, which entirely surrounds it. This geographical reality had a lot to do with the early constitutional history of Lesotho. After persistent imperialistic pressures from the Boers in South Africa, Lesotho, then Basutoland, sought the protection of the British Crown and became a British protectorate or colony on March 12, 1868. Between 1871 and 1884, Britain annexed Basutoland to its Cape Colony, which formed part of present-day South Africa. However, after the Gun Wars of 1880–81, Britain assumed direct control of Basutoland from the Cape colonial government in 1884 and administered the country on its behalf. The constitutional and political governance of Basutoland thus was directly under the authority of orders in council issued by the British Crown and administered by a colonial governor, who was known as a high commissioner. This constitutional arrangement remained in force until Lesotho became independent on October 4, 1966.

The Independence Constitution of 1966, which secured a pluralistic system of political parties, was seriously compromised when in 1970 the ruling Basotho National Party cancelled parliamentary elections (while vote counting was already in progress), when it appeared set to lose. They remained in power during this unconstitutional quagmire, periodically attracting military attacks by guerrilla fighters of the Basutoland Congress Party, which believed it had been cheated of its apparent electoral victory.

In 1986, the military took over the reins of government from the Basotho National Party and remained in power until 1993, when parliamentary elections based on a new constitution put a democratic administration in power. The Basutoland Congress Party, which formed this administration, felt vindicated by its massive electoral victory. The 1993 constitution, which has been amended four times, remains the constitution of Lesotho.

FORM AND IMPACT OF THE CONSTITUTION

The constitution of Lesotho is a written one; it takes precedence over all other laws as it is the supreme law of the land. Any other national law that is inconsistent with the constitution is void to the extent of its inconsistency. Likewise, international law must comply with the provisions of the constitution in order to be applicable within Lesotho. International treaties to which Lesotho is a party apply within the country only when their provisions are internalized through legislation.

Certain provisions of the constitution are entrenched and cannot be amended by the passage of ordinary legislation. These provisions deal with, inter alia, the following: the designation of the country as a sovereign democratic kingdom, the supremacy of the constitution, the protection of fundamental human rights and freedoms, the office of king, succession to the throne of Lesotho, the king's right to be consulted and informed concerning matters of government, the vesting of all land in the Basotho nation, and the vesting of the judicial power of the state in the courts of Lesotho.

BASIC ORGANIZATIONAL STRUCTURE

Lesotho is a unitary state, made up of 10 administrative districts. Through enabling acts, some legislative and executive powers may be delegated to these units. However, these powers remain largely centralized in the national government. There is no constitutional division of powers between the national government and the administrative structures in the districts.

LEADING CONSTITUTIONAL PRINCIPLES

The system of government of Lesotho is one of parliamentary democracy, largely following the British Westminster model; the major difference between the two is that Lesotho's system of government is predicated wholly upon a written constitution. The prime ministers and his or her ministers, who form the executive arm of government, are, necessarily, members of Parliament, the legislative arm of government. The cabinet (the prime minister and his or her ministers) exercises the executive authority of state on behalf of the king, who is a constitutional monarch and head of state. The independence of the judiciary is constitutionally secured; the constitution obligates the government to accord such assistance as the courts may require to enable them to protect their independence, dignity, and effectiveness.

The supremacy of the constitution is a major constitutional principle. It is this feature that gives flesh and viscera to the entrenchment of major constitutional principles as discussed earlier. The right to take part in the government of the country, either directly or indirectly through freely chosen representatives in free and fair elections, is availed to all citizens through constitutional guarantees.

The unitary nature of Lesotho, which entails the centralization of the powers of government, is no indication that arbitrariness is the order of the day in the exercise of these powers. The supremacy of the constitution facilitates challenges to the exercise of any of these powers; the rule of law is, thus, a constitutional predicate for governmental action in any form or shape.

CONSTITUTIONAL BODIES

The main constitutional bodies are the office of king, the cabinet, the Parliament, the judiciary, the Council of State, and the ombudsperson.

The King

The king, who is a constitutional monarch, is the head of state. Though the executive authority of the state is vested in the king, such authority is exercised in fact by the prime minister and his or her ministers.

Acting on the advice of the Council of State, the monarch appoints the prime minister. This power is not unfettered, as the king is obliged to choose the member of the National Assembly who appears to the Council of State to be the leader of the political party or coalition of political parties that will command the support of a majority of members of the National Assembly.

The College of Chiefs appoints the king by designating, in accordance with customary law, the person entitled to succeed to the office of king upon the death of the holder of, or the occurrence of any vacancy in, that office.

The Cabinet

The cabinet is made up of the prime minister and other ministers. These other ministers, one of whom is the deputy prime minister, must be at least seven in number. The king appoints the prime minister on the advice of the Council of State and the other ministers on the advice of the prime minister.

The cabinet is responsible for advising the king in the government of Lesotho. Its members are collectively responsible to the two houses of Parliament. The king, acting on the advice of the prime minister, may, in writing, assign any responsibility for any business of the government to any member of the cabinet.

The Parliament

The Parliament, which is the legislative arm of government, comprises the king, the National Assembly, and the Senate. The constitution of 1993 provided for 80 members of the National Assembly. By virtue of the 2001 Fourth Amendment to the Constitution Act, which added a proportional element to the National Assembly elections, there are now 120 members. These members are popularly elected through a general election that is free, direct, and secret. The period of office of the National Assembly is five years.

The Senate, the second house of Parliament, is composed of members nominated by the king acting on the advice of the Council of State and members designated by principal chiefs as senators in their place.

The Lawmaking Process

Lawmaking is effected through bills passed by both houses of Parliament, the National Assembly and the Senate, and assented to by the king. These bills may originate only in the National Assembly. The entrenched provisions of the constitution can be amended only by following a special procedure that goes beyond the passage of ordinary legislation.

The Judiciary

The judiciary is made up of a Court of Appeal, a High Court, Subordinate Courts, Courts-martial, and such tribunals exercising a judicial function as may be established by Parliament. The highest court of the land is the Court of Appeal. The courts enjoy constitutionally mandated independence and freedom from interference in the performance of their functions. They are subject only to the constitution and any other law; however, such other law should not affect their independence.

In underlying this independence, the administration is constitutionally obliged to offer the courts such assistance as they require so as to protect their independence, dignity, and effectiveness.

The Council of State

The Council of State is a body that assists the king in the discharge of the monarch's functions; it also performs other functions as are conferred on it by the constitution. The king is obliged by the constitution to call a meeting of the council to seek its advice on certain enumerated subject areas. If the king fails to do so, the prime minister must summon such a meeting. If he or she, likewise, fails to call such a meeting, any member of the council, with the support of no fewer than seven other members, may call such a meeting.

The Ombudsperson

The king appoints the ombudsperson on the advice of the prime minister. The ombudsperson is empowered to investigate actions taken by any officer or authority whenever it is alleged that a person has suffered injustice in consequence of the exercise of an administrative function.

THE ELECTION PROCESS

All citizens of Lesotho over the age of 18 years have the right to vote in elections and to stand for election. However, a citizen of Lesotho who owes allegiance to any foreign power or state or is under a sentence of death or is adjudged or otherwise declared to be of unsound mind under any law in force in Lesotho does not have the right to vote in any election. In addition to these limitations, a Lesotho citizen who is an unrehabilitated insolvent or who has an interest in a government contract in respect of which Parliament has not granted an exception does not have the right to stand for election to Parliament.

POLITICAL PARTIES

Lesotho operates a multiparty system that underpins the proportional electoral system for the election of members to the National Assembly. Political life in Lesotho is very active; currently, there are 16 political parties in the country.

CITIZENSHIP

The primary mode for the acquisition of Lesotho citizenship is birth, either in or outside Lesotho. However, at the time of a person's birth, one of the parents must be a Lesotho citizen.

FUNDAMENTAL RIGHTS

Chapter 2 of the constitution sets out "fundamental human rights and freedoms," which basically consist of the classic civil and political rights. Those rights traditionally classified as economic, social, and cultural are set out in Chapter 3 of the constitution, Principles of State Policy. Section 25 in this chapter provides that these principles are not enforceable by any court. However, in line with general international agreement on the indivisibility of all human rights, Lesotho has ratified the 1966 International Covenant on Economic, Social and Cultural Rights as well as the 1966 International Covenant on Civil and Political Rights.

The constitution provides a means for enforcing the provisions of Chapter 2: Any person who alleges that any provision of the chapter has been, is being, or is likely to be contravened to his or her prejudice may apply to the High Court for judicial redress.

Impact and Functions of Fundamental Rights

The stipulation that human dignity is the quintessence of human rights is axiomatic in current rights discourse. This idea provides the underlying momentum for the recent spate of legislation to ensure that women in Lesotho enjoy true equality in the enjoyment of the human rights provided for by the constitution. These include the 2003 Married Persons Equality Act and the 2003 Sexual Offences Act. Ironically, the constitution itself exempted customary law practices that might discriminate against some individuals from its definition of discrimination in the enjoyment of human rights. This exemption has had a negative impact on women, who are subject to such discrimination in Lesotho's patrilineal society, in which men are, by and large, the sole decision makers.

The values underpinning the human rights provisions of the constitution are being given practical effect by an independent judiciary in Lesotho. A good example is the politically charged 1999 case of *Commander of Lesotho Defense Force and Others v. Rantuba and Others*. The respondents, who were wives of soldiers of the Lesotho Defense Force who had been detained by the military authorities after a mutiny in the Force, applied to the High Court seeking an order that their detained husbands be allowed access to legal adviser and that they be either charged with an offense or released forthwith. The commander of the Lesotho Offense Force opposed the application, contending that investigations were still under way regarding a deep-rooted conspiracy within the army, which threatened the nation at large; when this situation improved, he would consider allowing the detainees access to counsel. The Court of Appeal confirmed the High Court's order that the detainees be allowed access to counsel before the said investigations were completed, thereby upholding the human right of access to counsel for legal assistance.

Limitations to Fundamental Rights

There are limitations to the human rights provided for by the constitution; however, the constitution generally requires that any such limitation or derogation must be in the interest of public safety, defense, public order, public morality, or public health. Furthermore, any action taken in the course of such derogation must be a necessary measure that a democratic society would use in dealing with the situation that warranted the limitation or derogation.

ECONOMY

There is no constitutional provision that mandates any specific economic system by Lesotho. The recent increase in the privatization of public-owned utilities and the liberalization of key economic sectors might seem to suggest that the country is heading toward a totally free market system devoid of any governmental or public control whatsoever, in which market forces operate at will. Nothing could be further from the true state of affairs in the country. Because Lesotho is a least developed country whose economy is ranked 147th of 207 and in which poverty is a major problem, most people in the country believe it can ill afford to allow market forces to drive its economy totally.

Thus, market freedom aimed at attracting much needed foreign investment is encouraged, but it is tempered with policies aimed at social responsibility and social justice. This emphasis is in line with the constitutional stipulation that Lesotho shall adopt policies aimed at achieving steady economic, social, and cultural development and full and productive employment under conditions safeguarding fundamental political and economic freedoms to the individual. The government of Lesotho has, for example, periodically stipulated statutory minimal daily wages and minimal monthly wages for specified occupations such as drivers, domestic servants, messengers, shop assistants, and waiters.

RELIGIOUS COMMUNITIES

Lesotho is a secular state; it has no state religion. The constitution provides for freedom of conscience, which includes freedom of thought and of religion and the right to propagate one's religion or belief in worship, teaching, practice, and observance. Christian religions form an overwhelming majority in terms of established religions; their adherents are estimated to number around 90 percent of the population.

There is cooperation between the state and the established religions, especially in matters of formal education, as a large number of educational institutions belong to and are largely controlled by religious organizations. For example, of the 1,300 primary schools in Lesotho in 1999, only six were government-owned, 43 were community-owned, one was privately owned, and 1,250 were owned by churches.

MILITARY DEFENSE AND STATE OF EMERGENCY

The constitution provides for a defense force vested with the power to maintain internal security and the defense of Lesotho. After the report of a commission of enquiry that investigated certain disturbances within the defense force, the 1996 First Amendment to the Constitution Act was passed. The act makes provision for the establishment and governance of the defense force, police force, and Prison Service. After that act, the 1996 Lesotho Defense Force Act, which provides for the command, control, and administration of Lesotho's defense force, was promulgated. The functions of the defense force, as set out in the act, include the maintenance of law and order, the prevention or suppression of terrorism and internal disorder, the defense of the country, and the maintenance of essential services.

The military must remain subject to the civil government. There is a general sense in recent years that the military is subordinate to the rule of law, and that law and order prevail in the country.

In 1986, the military overthrew the civilian government of the day. This was an apparently illegal act, but it was welcomed by a large segment of the society. The military coup reversed the effect of a constitutional coup d'état carried out in 1970 by the Basotho National Party administration, which had halted the counting of votes in a general election it appeared to be losing. However, popular as the military coup was at first, the military hung on to power until 1993.

A few years later in 1998, the prime minister was forced to rely on the military forces of South Africa and Botswana, acting on behalf of the Southern African Development Community, to quell disturbances that broke out when opposition parties disputed the results of that year's general election, which the governing party won with a landslide. He could not rely on the Lesotho military forces, a sizable segment of which mutinied and refused to quell the disturbances. The case *In re: Court Martial Between the King and Second Lieutenant Sekoati and 50 Others,* in which the accused were charged with the military offense of mutiny and arraigned before a court-martial, emanated from this mutiny.

AMENDMENTS TO THE CONSTITUTION

Any bill, public or private, that seeks to amend the constitution is subject to the overall supremacy of the constitution and should not be inconsistent therewith. Furthermore, whereas any ordinary bill may be passed by a majority of members of Parliament present and voting, a bill to amend the constitution must be supported at the final voting in the National Assembly by a majority of all the members.

Amending the entrenched provisions of the constitution is even harder. They fall into two categories. The first category deals with, inter alia, the designation of Lesotho as a sovereign, democratic kingdom; fundamental human rights and freedoms; and the office of king. After Parliament approves any amendment to these provisions, it must be endorsed in a national referendum.

The second set of entrenched provisions deal with citizenship, the composition of Parliament, constituencies, and the office of the ombudsperson. Any amendment to these provisions requires the votes of no less than two-thirds of the members of each house of Parliament.

PRIMARY SOURCES
1993 Constitution in English: *Constitution of Lesotho.* Maseru, Lesotho: Government Printer, 1993. Available online. URL: http://www.lesotho.gov.ls/constitute/gcconstitute.htm. Accessed on June 21, 2006.

SECONDARY SOURCES
K. A. Acheampong, "Human Rights in Lesotho." In *Human Rights Law in Africa,* edited by Christof Heyns. Vol. 2. The Hague: Kluwer Law International, 1997: 1203–1225.

S. J. Gill, *A Short History of Lesotho.* Morija, Lesotho: Morija Museums and Archives, 1993.

Government of Lesotho, *Report of the National Dialogue on the Development of a National Vision for Lesotho.* Lesotho Vision 2020, Vol. 1. Maseru, Lesotho: Government of Lesotho, January 2001.

Government of Lesotho, *Report of the National Dialogue on the Development of a National Vision for Lesotho.* Lesotho Vision 2020, Vol. 2. Maseru, Lesotho: Government of Lesotho, January 2001.

Bjorn Gustafsson and Negatu Makonnen, "Poverty and Remittances in Lesotho." *Journal of African Economics* 2, no. 1, 1993: 44–65.

International Labor Organization, *Promoting Gender Equality in Employment in Lesotho: An Agenda for Action.* Geneva: International Labour Office, 1994.

Kenneth Asamoa Acheampong

LIBERIA

At-a-Glance

OFFICIAL NAME
Republic of Liberia

CAPITAL
Monrovia

POPULATION
3,482,211 (July 2005 est.)

SIZE
43,000 sq. mi. (111,370 sq. km)

LANGUAGES
English

RELIGIONS
Christian 40%, indigenous beliefs 40%, Islam 20%

NATIONAL OR ETHNIC COMPOSITION
Indigenous tribes (including Kpelle, Bassa, Gio, Kru, Grebo, Mano, Krahn, Gola, Loma, Kissi, Vai, Dei, Bella, Mandingo, and Mende) 95%, Americo-Liberians (descendants of former U.S. slaves) 2.5%, Congo people (descendents of former Caribbean slaves) 2.5%

DATE OF INDEPENDENCE OR CREATION
July 26, 1847

TYPE OF GOVERNMENT
Republic

TYPE OF STATE
Unitary state

TYPE OF LEGISLATURE
Bicameral legislature

DATE OF CONSTITUTION
July 3, 1984

DATE OF LAST AMENDMENT
No amendment

Liberia is a republic in which power is distinctly divided among the executive, the legislature, and the judiciary, consistently with the principle of separation of power and checks and balances. As a unitary sovereign state, the central government retains all governing authority. The country is divided into counties for administrative purposes, at present numbering 15.

The elected president is the head of state and the executive and commander in chief of the armed forces. The bicameral legislature comprises a Senate and House of Representatives that pass legislation on behalf of the nation.

Liberia has a dual legal system based on Anglo-American common law and customary law. The Supreme Court is the custodian of the constitution and is the final appellate authority. Fundamental human rights are preserved throughout the constitution with high regard for the principle of equality before the law.

CONSTITUTIONAL HISTORY

With the growth of abolition sentiment in the United States, the American Colonization Society sent its first group of immigrants to present-day Liberia in 1820, with the aim of repatriating former enslaved African Americans to the African continent. Before departing they signed a constitution that in essence granted the society all powers of government and administration in Liberia.

The effort to repatriate slaves intensified, and various independent colonization societies soon founded their own colonies in Liberia, separate from those of the American Colonization Society. In 1838, all these colonies merged to form the Commonwealth of Liberia.

The constitution of 1839 redefined the administration of government in Liberia. The new constitution vested all executive and legislative powers in an appointed governor and council, the latter chosen by popular vote. On

July 26, 1847, a Declaration of Independence was signed and adopted. Liberia became Africa's first independent republic.

The 1847 constitution legitimized the status of the colony and afforded Liberia international recognition as an independent sovereign state. The constitution primarily is an assertion of rights by the former African American slaves to govern themselves. For the most part the document is closely modeled on the constitution of the United States and embraces such principles as democracy, centralism, popular sovereignty, and the rule of law.

On April 12, 1980, the 1847 constitution that had been in force continuously for 133 years was suspended after a military coup d'état. The National Constitutional Drafting Commission submitted a new draft constitution in 1983 and a constitution advisory assembly was appointed to review the draft. On July 3, 1984, the draft constitution was submitted to a national referendum and approved. It entered into force on January 6, 1986.

In December 1989, a group of insurgents entered Liberia from Côte d'Ivoire with the aim of toppling the government. A devastating civil war ensued. Oddly, a national state of emergency was never declared throughout years of bitter conflict; only parts of Nimba County were declared to be under martial law in 1990.

In August 1996, a supplemental agreement to a 1995 peace pact was signed in Abuja, Nigeria. Elections were held in July 1997. Because of the experience of successive interim governments during the civil war, one of the first official actions of the newly appointed administration was to reconfirm the supremacy of the 1984 constitution.

In August 2003, a Comprehensive Peace Agreement was signed in Accra, Ghana. The agreement officially ended the 14-year civil war in Liberia and brought about the resignation of the former president, Charles Taylor. A National Transitional Government was put in place.

FORM AND IMPACT OF THE CONSTITUTION

Liberia has a written constitution embodied in a single document. The constitution is the supreme and fundamental law. Its provisions have binding force and effect throughout the country. The Supreme Court is empowered to declare any laws inconsistent with the constitution unconstitutional.

BASIC ORGANIZATIONAL STRUCTURE

Liberia is a unitary sovereign state divided into counties for administrative purposes. The main governing authority rests with the central government seated in the capital city, Monrovia.

LEADING CONSTITUTIONAL PRINCIPLES

Liberia's system of government is a presidential republic. There are three separate and coordinate bodies of government that function on the basis of a system of checks and balances.

The Liberian constitution adheres to a variety of essential principles. Liberia is a democracy, a republic, and a unitary state that upholds the principle of limited government and accedes to the supremacy of the judiciary.

On the national level there is a strong insistence on tolerance. The constitution recognizes that all Liberian people, irrespective of history, tradition, creed, or ethnic background, are one common body politic.

CONSTITUTIONAL BODIES

The main bodies provided for in the constitution are the executive, the legislature, and the judiciary.

The Executive

The executive power of Liberia is vested in the president, who is the head of state and of the executive and the commander in chief of the armed forces. The president is elected for a term of six years with a limit of two consecutive terms. In order to be eligible for the presidency a person must be a natural-born Liberian citizen, at least 35 years old, the owner of unencumbered property valued at not less than $25,000, and a resident of Liberia for 10 years prior to election.

The president's powers are far reaching and range from such duties as appointing cabinet ministers to concluding international agreements with the concurrence of the legislature. While in office the president cannot be held accountable for actions done in accordance with the provisions of the constitution. Nonetheless, the president may be impeached on a number of grounds, including treason, bribery, and gross misconduct.

The Legislature

The bicameral legislature consists of a Senate and House of Representatives. Each house adopts its own rules of procedure, which must comply with the requirements of due process of law as stipulated in the constitution.

To be eligible to become a member of the legislature a citizen must be a taxpayer and must have been domiciled in the country and constituency to be represented at least one year prior to the time of election. The minimal age requirement is 30 years for the Senate and 25 years for the House of Representatives.

Senators are elected for a term of nine years. Each administrative county sends two members to the Senate. The vice president of Liberia is the president of the Senate and presides over its deliberations.

Members of the House of Representatives are elected for a term of six years. An elected speaker presides over deliberations.

The Lawmaking Process

Both houses of the legislature are authorized to enact laws. A simple majority constitutes a quorum.

The president must approve of all bills and resolutions before they become law. The president has the power of veto, but it can be overridden by a two-thirds majority of members voting in each house.

The Judiciary

The judicial power of Liberia is vested in the Supreme Court, which applies statutory law, based on Anglo-American common law and customary law.

Decisions of the United States Supreme Court are valid and applicable under Liberian law where the Liberian Supreme Court has not ruled on the issue, and where such a decision is not inconsistent with the constitution of Liberia.

The Supreme Court is the final arbiter of constitutional issues and exercises final appellate jurisdiction. Its judgments are final and not subject to appeal or review by any other branch of government. The court is independent.

THE ELECTION PROCESS

At the age of 18 years, all Liberian citizens have a right to be registered as voters and may vote by secret ballot in public elections.

POLITICAL PARTIES

Liberia operates under a pluralistic system of political parties. The constitution, in recognition of the essence of democracy, encourages the existence of multiple parties in order to reflect the varied political opinions of the people. Parties that seek to hinder the existence of free democratic society are denied registration.

CITIZENSHIP

Persons who are black or of African descent may qualify by birth or by naturalization to be citizens of Liberia.

FUNDAMENTAL RIGHTS

The Liberian constitution defines fundamental rights in Chapter 3. As their basis, it states that all persons are equally free and have certain natural, inherent, and inalienable rights that must be legally enforceable. It offers protection against state interference and abuse of power.

The constitution protects conventional civil rights and liberties. Freedom of thought and conscience, women's rights, and the right to privacy are among those safeguarded. The writ of habeas corpus is guaranteed at all times, even during a state of emergency.

Impact and Functions of Fundamental Rights

The intrinsic notion of human rights goes to the root of the Liberian conscience. Liberia is a nation founded on the principle of freedom and social justice, and the protection of fundamental rights is enshrined in the constitution.

Limitations to Fundamental Rights

Save for inalienable rights, such as the right to life, fundamental rights may be subject to qualifications as provided for in the constitution. In particular they may be suspended or limited by the president during a state of emergency.

ECONOMY

The Liberian constitution does not specify a chosen economic system. In developing the nation's economy, emphasis is placed on conditions of equality, the maximal participation of Liberian citizens in the market economy, and the principle of free competition. It is worth noting that only Liberian citizens have the right to own real property.

RELIGIOUS COMMUNITIES

The constitution guarantees freedom of religion. All religious denominations and groups are treated in the same way. In accordance with the principle of separation of religion and state, there is no established state religion.

MILITARY DEFENSE AND STATE OF EMERGENCY

The president is the commander in chief of the armed forces. At all times military power should be in subordination to civil authority and the constitution. The president, in consultation with members of cabinet, may declare a state of emergency when the nation is in clear and present danger.

AMENDMENTS TO THE CONSTITUTION

A proposal to amend the constitution requires a vote of two-thirds of members of both houses of the legislature. It may be initiated by a petition submitted to the legislature by at least 10,000 citizens and approved by two-thirds of the members of both houses.

If the proposal is ratified in a referendum by at least two-thirds of registered voters no sooner than one year after the legislature action, the amendment goes into effect.

PRIMARY SOURCES

Constitution in English. Available online. URL: http://www.onliberia.org/con_index.htm. Accessed on July 31, 2005.

SECONDARY SOURCES

D. Elwood Dunn, Amos J. Beyan, and Carl Patrick Burrowes, *Historical Dictionary of Liberia*. 2d ed. Lanham, Md.: Scarecrow Press, 2001.

Liberian Ministry of Information, Cultural Affairs, and Tourism, *Background to Liberia*. Monrovia, Liberia, 1979.

Amina Ibrahim

LIBYA

At-a-Glance

OFFICIAL NAME
Great Socialist People's Libyan Arab Jamahiriya

CAPITAL
Tripoli

POPULATION
5,631,585 (July 2004 est.)

SIZE
679,362 sq. mi. (1,759,540 sq. km)

LANGUAGES
Arabic, Italian, English

RELIGIONS
Sunni Muslim 97%, other 3%

NATIONAL OR ETHNIC COMPOSITION
Berber and Arab 97%, other (including Greek, Maltese, Italian, Egyptian, Pakistani, Turk, Indian, Tunisian) 3%

DATE OF INDEPENDENCE OR CREATION
December 24, 1951 (from Italy)

TYPE OF GOVERNMENT
Jamahiriya (a state of the masses) in theory, governed by the populace through local councils

TYPE OF STATE
Unitary state

TYPE OF LEGISLATURE
Unicameral General People's Congress

DATE OF CONSTITUTION
December 11, 1969

DATE OF LAST AMENDMENT
March 2, 1977

Libya is currently heading gradually toward a free market economy. The Holy Quran is called the constitution of the nation, and Islam is its religion. The theory of people's authority based on the concept of direct democracy forms the basis of political power. The system of governance is regarded to be unique in the world. In practice, the center, especially the revolutionary leader, exercises the dominant power in the state.

CONSTITUTIONAL HISTORY

Libya was declared an independent state on December 24, 1951, in accordance with a United Nations General Assembly resolution of 1949. The United Nations assisted in drafting the Libyan constitution, which was adopted on October 7, 1951, by the Libyan National Assembly. This assembly represented the three territories that constituted the Federal Kingdom of Libya at the time (Tripolitania, Cyrenaica, and Fezzan). The constitution entered into force on the day of Libyan independence.

Although the constitution did not expressly give the Supreme Court constitutional jurisdiction, a constitutional chamber within the Supreme Court was introduced by law. In fact, the first judgment issued by the Supreme Court was in a constitutional case, in which the Supreme Court issued its famous ruling that a royal decree was unconstitutional.

The 1951 constitution was amended in 1962 and again in 1963. These amendments replaced the federal system of the United Kingdom of Libya by a unitary form of state under the name of Kingdom of Libya.

On September 1, 1969, the monarchy was abolished in a revolution, and Libya was declared a republic. On the same day Colonel Muammar al-Qaddafi issued his first revolutionary decree, proclaiming the principles and main outlines of the new government. On December 11 that year the Revolutionary Committee issued its Constitutional Declaration.

The first chapter of this declaration listed the objectives of the revolution, such as socialism and social justice. The document then presented a tripartite system of government, under the supreme authority of a Revolutionary Command Council, which exercised sovereign legislative and executive powers. None of its measures, including acts of law, decisions, or decrees, would be subject to appeal. The Command Council appointed the Council of Ministers, which executes the general policy laid down by the Revolutionary Command Council and could dismiss the council. It also has the jurisdiction to conclude and ratify treaties, declare war, and proclaim a state of emergency. The constitutional declaration contained several human rights principles. Since the promulgation of the Constitutional Declaration, no permanent constitution has been adopted.

Although the Constitutional Declaration continued to be in force, a new document, the Declaration on the Establishment of the Authority of the People, was issued on March 2, 1977. This declaration completely changed the form of the state and the system of government. Article 2 of the declaration also proclaimed: "The Holy Quran is the Constitution" of the nation.

On the basis of theories developed in Qaddafi's *Green Book,* the new state was called a *jamahiriya* (state of the masses). The theory of the people's authority was based on the concept of direct democracy, exercised by the people themselves. In this unique political system, power was to start from the base and mount to the summit. This was achieved by dividing the state into governorates, containing people's congresses and people's committees. Both congresses and committees were primarily, but not exclusively, entrusted with control over local affairs. At the summit of the people's committees was the General People's Congress.

The people's power concept as briefly specified in the 1977 declaration has been elaborated by laws and practice. The current law organizing the system is law number one of 2001, as amended.

FORM AND IMPACT OF THE CONSTITUTION

Currently, Libya no longer has a single constitution, but rather several constitutional instruments, including the 1969 Constitutional Declaration and the 1977 Declaration of the Authority of the People, which proclaimed the Quran the nation's constitution. Since the declaration, Libya has issued other proclamations of a constitutional nature, such as the Green Charter for Human Rights issued by decision number 11 of 1988 of the General People's Congress, and law number 20 of 1991, Consolidation of Freedom. Both instruments contain provisions relating to the system of government as well as human rights principles.

BASIC ORGANIZATIONAL STRUCTURE

The unitary state is divided into governorates, each with a people's congress and a people's committee.

LEADING CONSTITUTIONAL PRINCIPLES

The preamble of the 1977 declaration specifies a number of basic principles. Among them are the adherence to socialism, freedom, and the commitment to spiritual values to safeguard morals and human behavior.

CONSTITUTIONAL BODIES

The 1977 declaration states that the people's direct democracy is the basis of the political system. The people exercise their authority through the People's Congresses, the People's Committees, and the Professional Unions. At the national level are the General People's Congress; its chairperson, who is head of state; its General Secretariat; and the revolutionary leader.

The Libyan people is divided into people's congresses. All citizens register themselves as members of the People's Congress in their area. Each congress chooses among its members a People's Committee to lead the congress. The committee is responsible to the congress. While the committees have executive and administrative powers, the congresses exercise legislative as well as sovereign functions.

General People's Congress

The General People's Congress is the national conference of the People's Committees and Professional Unions. It is in this forum where laws are enacted and treaties and conventions are ratified. The congress chooses and can dismiss the head and the members of the General Secretariat, the chief justice of the Supreme Court, the prosecutor general, and other high-level state officials.

The General People's Congress chooses a chairperson to preside over its sessions and to accept the credentials of the representatives of foreign countries. This chairperson is also known as the secretary general of the General People's Congress. The first secretary general of the General People's Congress was, since March 2, 1977, the revolutionary leader Muammar al-Qaddafi, who held this position until 1979, but continues to exercise the most important and vital role in the state.

The General Secretariat of the General People's Congress

The General Secretariat (or General People's Committee) of the General People's Congress performs the function of a council of ministers. The secretary general (prime minister) and the secretaries (cabinet ministers) are chosen and dismissed by the General People's Congress. The secretary general and the secretaries are jointly responsible to the congress; each secretary is responsible for the sector the secretary supervises.

Lawmaking Process

Laws are enacted by the General People's Congress.

The Judiciary

The Supreme Court has competence to adjudicate claims submitted by any person with a personal and direct interest that legislation is in contradiction with the constitution. In addition, the Supreme Court has competence over any substantial legal matter related to the constitution or its interpretation that may arise during the proceedings of any case before any court.

THE ELECTION PROCESS

The Basic People's Congresses, as the local bodies that comprise all Libyan citizens, choose their leadership committees. All Libyans over the age of 18 have the right and the duty to vote in the election. The election process continues until the General People's Congress chooses the General People's Committee at the apex of the hierarchy.

POLITICAL PARTIES

The people's power theory is based on the concept of direct democracy, which is exercised by the people themselves. All political parties are banned by the 1972 law related to the criminalization of political parties.

CITIZENSHIP

Libyan citizenship is primarily acquired by birth. This means that a child acquires Libyan citizenship if his or her father is a Libyan citizen. It is of no relevance where a child is born.

FUNDAMENTAL RIGHTS

The 1969 Constitutional Declaration, the 1988 Green Charter for Human Rights, and the 1991 Consolidation of Freedom law all contain fundamental rights provisions. The 1969 declaration states that all citizens are equal before the law. It also states that work is a right and a duty, and an honor for every ablebodied citizen. The home is said to be inviolable and cannot be entered or searched except under circumstances and conditions defined by law. Freedom of opinion is guaranteed within the limits of public interest and the principles of the revolution. Education and health are rights, and education is also a duty for all Libyans.

ECONOMY

The 1969 constitutional declaration calls socialism the aim of the state. The state endeavors through building a socialist community to achieve self-sufficiency in production and equity in distribution. The state endeavors to liberate the national economy from dependence and foreign influence, and to turn it into a productive national economy, based on public ownership by the Libyan people and private ownership by individual citizens. Private ownership, if it is nonexploitative, is protected. Inheritance is a right that is governed by the Islamic Sharia. The state has a system of national planning covering economic, social, and cultural aspects. Libya is heading to a free market economy and to encourage foreign investment.

RELIGIOUS COMMUNITIES

Islam is the religion of the state.

MILITARY DEFENSE AND STATE OF EMERGENCY

Defending the country is the responsibility of every citizen.

AMENDMENTS TO THE CONSTITUTION

Since the promulgation of the 1969 Constitutional Declaration, no permanent constitution has been issued, although additional constitutional instruments have been issued from time to time.

PRIMARY SOURCES
Constitution in English. Available online. URL: http://www.oefre.unibe.ch/law/icl/ly00000_.html. Accessed on July 28, 2005.

SECONDARY SOURCES
General People's Congress, "The Great Green Charter of Human Rights in the Jamahiriyan Era (1988)."

Available online. URL: http://www.qadhafi.org/ THE_GREAT_GREEN_CHARTER.html. Accessed on September 12, 2005.

Christof Heyns, ed., *Human Rights Law in Africa*. Vol. 2. Leiden: Martinus Nijhoff, 2004.

"Libya." *Wikipedia Encyclopedia*. Available online. URL: http://en.wikipedia.org/wiki/Libya. Accessed on September 12, 2005.

Mu'ammar al-Qadhafi. *The Green Book*. Available online. URL: http://www.qadhafi.org/the_green_book.html. Accessed on September 12, 2005.

Azza Maghur

LIECHTENSTEIN

At-a-Glance

OFFICIAL NAME
Principality of Liechtenstein

CAPITAL
Vaduz

POPULATION
33,987 (July 2006 est.) of whom 34% are foreigners, mainly Swiss, Austrian, Germans, Italians, Turks, Portuguese, Yugoslavs

SIZE
62 sq. mi. (160 sq. km)

LANGUAGES
German (official), Alemannic dialect (spoken)

RELIGIONS
Roman Catholic 80.4%, Protestant 7.1%, other 12.5%

NATIONAL OR ETHNIC COMPOSITION
Alemannic 86%, Italian, Turkish, and other 14%

DATE OF INDEPENDENCE OR CREATION
January 23, 1719: Imperial Principality of Liechtenstein
July 12, 1806: Independence

TYPE OF GOVERNMENT
Constitutional, hereditary monarchy on a democratic and parliamentary basis

TYPE OF STATE
Unitary state

TYPE OF LEGISLATURE
Unicameral parliament

DATE OF CONSTITUTION
October 5, 1921

DATE OF LAST AMENDMENT
September 15, 2003

Liechtenstein is a constitutional hereditary monarchy with a democratic and parliamentary basis; the power of the state is embodied in the reigning prince and the people. The principle of monarchy and the principle of democracy are of equal importance. Legislative, executive, and judicial powers are separated.

Fundamental rights are guaranteed and freedom of religion is respected. The Catholic Church is the national church. Freedom of religion is respected.

CONSTITUTIONAL HISTORY

Prince Johann Adam Andreas of Liechtenstein was able to purchase the Lordship of Schellenberg in 1699 and the County of Vaduz in 1712. Both dominions were elevated to the Imperial Principality of Liechtenstein in 1719. Meanwhile the rulers continued to reside in Vienna, and governors administered the principality on their behalf.

In 1806, Napoléon abolished the old German Empire and established the Rhine Confederation. Liechtenstein was accepted into the Rhine Confederation as a sovereign state.

In 1852, Liechtenstein and the Austria-Hungarian Empire concluded a customs agreement and several reforms were initiated, finally leading to the constitution of 1862. Power remained with the prince, but parliament could no longer be ignored in the legislative process.

Although Liechtenstein remained neutral in World War I (1914–18), it was affected by the economic sanctions against Austria. After the collapse of the Austrian monarchy, Liechtenstein turned toward Switzerland. The 1923 customs treaty, which to this day forms the basis for the close partnership, was concluded by the two neighboring states. Liechtenstein has used the Swiss franc as its official currency since 1921, although a Currency Treaty was only concluded in 1980.

After negotiations between the reigning prince and parliament a new constitution was adopted in 1921. In

2003, after 10 years of discussions, a long-standing constitutional dispute was settled and the constitution was amended.

FORM AND IMPACT OF THE CONSTITUTION

Liechtenstein has a written constitution consisting of 12 chapters containing 115 articles. It prevails over all other national laws.

BASIC ORGANIZATIONAL STRUCTURE

The Principality of Liechtenstein is a union of two regions, the Upper Country (Oberland) and the Lower Country (Unterland). It contains 11 municipalities. Vaduz is the capital and seat of parliament and government.

LEADING CONSTITUTIONAL PRINCIPLES

The principality is a constitutional hereditary monarchy that has a democratic and parliamentary basis; the power of the state is embodied in the reigning prince and the people. The principle of monarchy and the principle of democracy are of equal importance. Legislative, executive, and judicial powers are separated.

CONSTITUTIONAL BODIES

The main constitutional bodies are the reigning prince, parliament, the administration, and the judiciary.

The Reigning Prince

The reigning prince is the head of state and exercises the monarchical rights in accordance with the provisions of the constitution and other laws. The reigning prince represents the state in its relations with foreign states. International treaties by which territory of the state is ceded, state property alienated, sovereign rights affected, rights of citizens limited, or new burdens imposed on the country require the assent of parliament and approval by the head of state and the administration.

The reigning prince contributes to the legislative process through his right to initiative in the form of proposals of the administration and through his right to veto legislation within six months of passage.

The reigning prince has the right to open parliament at the beginning of the year and to adjourn it at the end of the year. Traditionally, the reigning prince opens parliament with a ceremonial speech from the throne. The reigning prince may suspend parliament for three months at most or dissolve it on grounds of considerable importance. The authority of the reigning prince also includes the right of pardon, of mitigating or commuting legally adjudicated sentences, and of quashing initiated investigations.

On August 15, 2004, Reigning Prince of Liechtenstein H.S.H. Prince Hans-Adam II entrusted Hereditary Prince Alois, pursuant to the constitution, to exercise his sovereign powers as his representative in preparation for the succession. The representation is comprehensive and of unlimited duration.

Parliament (Landtag)

The Diet, called Landtag, is the legal organ representing all Liechtenstein citizens and is therefore called upon to ensure their rights and interests. The Diet consists of 25 members who are elected by the people by universal, equal, secret, and direct suffrage according to the system of proportional representation. Of the 25 members of parliament, 15 are elected by the Upper Country and 10 by the Lower Country. Alternate members of parliament are elected in each voting district, in order to ensure the party balance in parliament, if a member is unable to attend parliamentary sessions.

The constitution requires a minimal threshold of 8% of the valid votes cast in the entire country in order for a party to gain seats in parliament. Members of the administration and the courts may not be members of the Diet at the same time. The term of office is four years; reelection is permissible. Voter turnout in Liechtenstein is traditionally very high. It was 86.5% in the 2005 parliamentary elections. At its first meeting, the Landtag elects a president and a vice president from its ranks to direct its affairs for the current year.

Among the main duties of the Diet is legislation. Without the participation of parliament, no law can be adopted or amended. Parliament also participates in the conclusion of international treaties. Any international treaty that affects state sovereignty, imposes a new burden on the state, or affects the rights of Liechtenstein citizens must be presented to the Landtag, which may not amend a treaty signed by the government, but may only adopt or reject it in its entirety.

Other duties of parliament are the establishment of the annual budget and the authorization of taxes and other public dues. The state budget is prepared by the administration and adopted by parliament. Parliament has the right to amend individual budget items. If the administration requires additional appropriations over the course of the year for new mandates or if individual budget appropriations are exceeded, the administration must obtain a supplementary credit from parliament. Without the approval of parliament, no direct or indirect taxes or other national dues or general levies may be imposed or collected.

The administration submits an accountability report to parliament covering the entire state administration annually. Parliament supervises the state administration and receives requests and complaints about it. It can impeach cabinet ministers before the constitutional court for violations of the constitution or of other laws. Also, parliament can vote no confidence against the administration or any of its ministers.

The Lawmaking Process

Parliament, the reigning prince, and the people (by petition) have the right of constitutional and legislative initiative. In practice, most legislative proposals are drafted by the administration or its experts. Parliament can send legislative proposals back to the administration or form its own committees to revise them. Each legislative proposal is first subject to an initial debate, followed by two readings and a final vote.

During the initial debate, parliament decides whether to consider the proposal. Suggestions can be made that will be evaluated by the government. In the second reading, each individual article is voted on. A valid decision of parliament requires the presence of at least two-thirds of all members of parliament; the bill can then be approved by the majority of the members present. In order for a law to become valid, the sanction of the reigning prince, the countersignature of the head of administration, and publication in the *Liechtenstein Legal Gazette* are all required.

The Administration

The administration is a collegial body consisting of five ministers including the head and the deputy head of the executive administration. All cabinet ministers are appointed by the reigning prince on the recommendation of parliament. The ministers must be citizens of Liechtenstein and eligible for election to parliament. Each of the two regions of Liechtenstein is entitled to at least two ministers. The term of office is four years.

A valid decision of the administration requires the presence of at least four cabinet ministers and the support of the majority of those present. In the event of a tie, the chairman has the deciding vote. Voting is compulsory. The head of the administration chairs its meetings. The reigning prince can assign duties directly to the head of administration, who is also responsible for countersigning laws and any decrees or ordinances issued by the reigning prince or the regent. The head of administration informs the reigning prince about its ongoing business.

The administration is responsible for the execution of all laws and of all legally permissible mandates by the reigning prince or parliament.

The Judiciary

The entire jurisdiction is carried out in the name of the reigning prince and the people by legally bound judges appointed by the reigning prince. Jurisdiction in civil and criminal matters is exercised in the first instance by the Court of Justice, in the second instance by the Court of Appeal, and in the third and last instance by the Supreme Court. Courts of public law are the Administrative Court and the Constitutional Court.

The reigning prince and Landtag jointly select all judges. If parliament elects a candidate approved by the reigning prince, he or she is appointed. If parliament rejects the candidate and no agreement can be reached on a new candidate, the judge is elected by the people.

THE ELECTION PROCESS AND POLITICAL PARTICIPATION

All citizens above the age of 18 who reside in Liechtenstein have both the right to stand for election and the right to vote. This right was extended to women in 1984 (in the third attempt); thanks to a 1976 constitutional amendment, they could already vote on the commune level.

One thousand voters can force parliament to convene. One thousand five hundred voters can call for a popular vote on its dissolution.

The right of referendum gives voters the opportunity to subject parliamentary decisions to a popular vote. One thousand voters are needed to call a referendum on legislative and financial decisions; 1,500 are needed in the case of constitutional amendments and international treaties. However, parliament has the option of declaring amendments and financial decisions as urgent, thereby excluding the possibility of a referendum.

A total of 1,000 voters have the right of initiative with regard to legislation; 1,500 are required in the case of an initiative concerning the constitution. A total of not less than 1,500 Liechtenstein citizens have the right to submit a reasoned motion of nonconfidence against the reigning prince or to submit an initiative to abolish the monarchy.

POLITICAL PARTIES

Political parties emerged for the fist time in 1918. Until 1933, the Progressive Citizens' Party (Fortschrittliche Bürgerpartei [FBP]) and the Patriotic Union (Vaterländische Union [VU]) were the only parties in parliament. They formed a long series of coalitions. In 1993, the Free List (Freie Liste [FL]) was the third party to jump over the strong 8% hurdle into parliament. Since March 2005, the FBP and the VU have formed a coalition.

CITIZENSHIP

Liechtenstein citizenship may be transferred from either the father or the mother to their mutual child. The acquisition of Liechtenstein citizenship on the basis of birth in Liechtenstein (*ius soli*) is not possible.

FUNDAMENTAL RIGHTS

Chapter 4 of the constitution relates to the fundamental rights and duties of the citizens. These include the right to reside freely in any location within the territory of the state and to acquire all forms of property. They also include personal liberty, the immunity of the home, and the inviolability of letters and documents. Private property is inviolable and free commerce and free trade are guaranteed. There are freedom of religion and conscience, freedom of expression, and freedom of association and assembly. Equal protection is guaranteed. Liechtenstein has—among other international treaties—ratified the European Convention on Human Rights and the United Nations (UN) Pact on Civil and Political Rights.

ECONOMY

Liechtenstein is a modern industrialized and service-oriented state with ties to countries all over the world. It owes its economic success over recent decades to the favorable overall conditions created by a liberal economic legislative framework.

RELIGIOUS COMMUNITIES

Freedom of belief and conscience is guaranteed. According to the constitution, the Roman Catholic Church is the national church and as such enjoys the full protection of the state. Other denominations are entitled to practice their creeds and to hold religious services within the limits of morality and public order.

MILITARY DEFENSE AND STATE OF EMERGENCY

All men fit to bear arms are required to do so until the age of 60, to serve in the defense of the country in the event of emergency.

In urgent cases, the reigning prince has the authority to take necessary measures for the security and welfare of the state. However, emergency decrees are limited in time and content.

AMENDMENTS TO THE CONSTITUTION

Amendments to the constitution may be proposed by the administration, by parliament, or by way of a public initiative. Any amendment requires unanimity of the members of parliament present or a majority of three-quarters of the members present at two consecutive meetings. A popular vote is necessary if called for by public initiative. In any event, any amendment needs the subsequent assent of the reigning prince.

PRIMARY SOURCES

1921 Constitution in English. Available online. URL: http://www.geocities.com/Athens/Crete/2122/lieconst19211005.html. Accessed on July 30, 2005.
Constitution in German. Available online. URL: http://www.liechtenstein.li/pdf-fl-staat-verfassung-sept2003.pdf. Accessed on September 5, 2005.

SECONDARY SOURCES

Günther Winkler, *Verfassungsrecht in Liechtenstein*. Vienna: Springer-Verlag, 2001.
———, *Die Verfassungsreform in Liechtenstein* Vienna: Springer-Verlag, 2003.
Available online. URL: www.llv.li. Accessed on July 31, 2005.

Gregor Obenaus

LITHUANIA

At-a-Glance

OFFICIAL NAME
Lithuania

CAPITAL
Vilnius

POPULATION
3,607,899 (2005 est.)

SIZE
25,212 sq. mi. (65,300 sq. km)

LANGUAGES
Lithuanian (official)

RELIGIONS
Roman Catholic 79%, Greek Catholic 0.01%, Orthodox Church 4.07%, Old Believers 0.78%, Evangelical Reformers 0.2%, Evangelical Lutheran 0.56%, Jewish 0.04%, Sunni Muslim 0.08%, Baptist 0.04%, Jehovah's Witnesses 0.1%, other 15.12%

NATIONAL OR ETHNIC COMPOSITION
Lithuanian 80.6%, Russian 8.7%, Polish 7%, Belarusian 1.6%, other 2.1%

DATE OF INDEPENDENCE OR CREATION
February 16, 1918 (from Soviet Union March 11, 1990)

TYPE OF GOVERNMENT
Parliamentary democracy

TYPE OF STATE
Unitary state

TYPE OF LEGISLATURE
Unicameral parliament

DATE OF CONSTITUTION
October 25, 1992

DATE OF LAST AMENDMENT
July 13, 2004

Preceded by the provisions on human rights, the first 17 articles of the Lithuanian constitution deal with the fundamental principles of statehood. The constitution affirms that Lithuania is an independent and democratic republic. It asserts the right of defense against attempts to encroach upon or overthrow state independence or the constitutional system by force. The constitution also disallows division of the territory into any state derivatives. This constitutional structure is an expression of the fact that state independence is understood by Lithuanians as the greatest nation-state value.

The powers of the state in Lithuania are exercised by the Parliament (Seimas), the president, the administration, and the judiciary. The president deals with broadscale questions of national and international politics. In practice, the influence of the president is defined first by the moral authority of the officeholder. The Seimas is not only involved in legislation; it also has significant authority over the implementation of laws. Political observers sometimes characterize Lithuania as a semiparliamentary republic in which the Seimas, the president, and the government seek consensus through a continuous process of consultation.

According to the constitution, state and religion are separated. The military is under the power of civil government. Currently, Lithuanian law is in the process of harmonization with European Union law.

CONSTITUTIONAL HISTORY

The deepest roots of Lithuanian constitutional law reach down to the three Statutes of the Grand Duchy of Lithuania (1529, 1566, 1588). These statutes divided power and defined the rights and relationships among the grand duke, Seimas (Parliament), and the court. They defined human rights in the event of delinquency and punishment, and they stated explicitly that they applied to all citizens, state institutions, and the grand duke himself.

A further important document was the Constitution of the Lithuanian-Polish Commonwealth of May 3, 1791. It was largely based on the system created by the French Revolution, though it preceded the French constitution by a few months. In fact, it was the first written document of such a kind in Europe. However, Russia, Prussia, and Austria partitioned the Lithuanian-Polish state in 1795, after which it disappeared from the political map of Europe. Lithuania was annexed by Russia.

The fact that Lithuania managed to reestablish its statehood in 1918 owes much to the memory of the constitution of May 3, 1791. Nevertheless, parliamentary democracy, which was losing ground throughout Europe at the time, did not survive in Lithuania either. The authoritarian regime of President Antanas Smetona was, however, relatively mild in comparison to the regimes in Germany and Italy, or to the totalitarian rule in the Union of Soviet Socialist Republics (USSR). Lithuania was occupied by the USSR in 1940.

The Lithuanian constitutions adopted during the period of 1918–40, especially that of 1922, which complied with the fundamental requirements of democratic constitutions, had great influence on the drafters of the new constitutional order after the declaration of independence of Lithuania in 1990. Lithuania is a member state of the European Union and the North Atlantic Treaty Organization (NATO).

FORM AND IMPACT OF THE CONSTITUTION

Lithuania has a written codified constitution. It is composed of three documents: the Constitution of Lithuania, the constitutional law On the State of Lithuania, and the constitutional act On the Non-Alignment of the Republic of Lithuania with post-Soviet Eastern Alliances. The constitution is an integral, stable, and directly applicable statute. Constitutional norms are of the highest juridical power. Any law or international agreement that contradicts the constitution is invalid in Lithuania.

BASIC ORGANIZATIONAL STRUCTURE

Lithuania is a unitary state, composed of administrative-territorial units that have some right of self-government. The self-governing institutions and local governments act independently within the limits established by the constitution and the law.

LEADING CONSTITUTIONAL PRINCIPLES

The constitution declares that Lithuania is an independent and democratic republic. It strives for an open, just,

and harmonious civil society and state under the rule of law. Other principles such as the separation of state and church and the geopolitical orientation are included in the Lithuania constitution as well.

The power to govern is divided among the legislative, executive, and judicial branches. The judiciary is independent of the other two branches.

CONSTITUTIONAL BODIES

The constitutional bodies are the president, the administration or Council of Ministers (comprising the prime minister and the cabinet), the Seimas (Parliament), and the judiciary.

The President

The president of the Republic of Lithuania is the head of state. The president is elected directly by the people for a term of five years and can be reelected only once for a consecutive term. The candidate must be a citizen of the Republic of Lithuania by birth who has lived in Lithuania for at least the past three years and has reached 40 years of age prior to the day of election.

The president rules on the major issues of foreign policy and appoints and recalls diplomatic representatives to foreign states and international organizations, on the recommendation of the government. The president appoints and dismisses the prime minister and cabinet ministers with the approval of the Seimas. The president appoints and dismisses the head of the armed forces and the head of the security service and signs and promulgates the laws enacted by the Seimas.

The president has the right to nominate and the Seimas has the right to approve the nomination of the chief justice, three other justices of the Constitutional Court, and all justices of the Supreme Court. The president also appoints, with legislative approval, judges of the Court of Appeals.

The Administration

The newly approved administration is empowered to act after the Seimas has approved its program. The administration, which is accountable to the Seimas, must resign if the Seimas rejects its program. When more than half of the cabinet is changed, the administration must be reinvested with authority by the Seimas. In that event, the president empowers the administration to act until it receives renewed powers from the Seimas or a new administration is formed. A minister must resign if more than half the Seimas expresses, in a secret ballot vote, a lack of confidence in him or her.

Seimas (Parliament)

The Seimas consists of 141 members, who are elected for a four-year term. Any citizen who is not bound by an oath or pledge to a foreign state and who, on the day of the election, is 25 years of age or over and resides permanently in Lithuania may be elected to the Seimas. The Seimas is the key institution of legislation of the state. However, the president may veto its legislation. The president's veto can be overridden only by an absolute majority of the Seimas membership. The president can also dissolve the Seimas if it refuses to approve the administration's budget within 60 days or if it expresses lack of confidence in the government.

The Lawmaking Process

The laws enacted by the Seimas are enforced after signing and official promulgation by the president. The president must either sign and promulgate the law or refer it to the Seimas for reconsideration. After reconsideration, the law is enacted if the amendments submitted by the president are adopted or if more than half of all the Seimas members vote in favor. For constitutional laws, the quorum is three-fifths of the members. Laws may also be adopted by referendum.

The Judiciary

The judicial system in Lithuania is independent of the legislative and executive branches. The following courts operate in Lithuania: the Constitutional Court, the Supreme Court, the Court of Appeals, and county, district, and administrative courts.

The right to appeal to the Constitutional Court is held by the president, one-fifth of the members of the Seimas, the administration, and ordinary courts. Judges of the Constitutional Court are nominated for nine years each, for a single term only. Every three years, one-third of the court is appointed. The decisions of the Constitutional Court are final and are not subject to appeal.

THE ELECTION PROCESS

All Lithuanians who are 18 years old or over on election day have the right to vote. Anyone whom the court declares legally incapable cannot vote.

POLITICAL PARTIES

The founding, functioning, and banning of political parties are regulated by law. Although the pluralist system of political parties in Lithuania has already been developed, individual political parties as well as the entire multiparty system are still in a state of flux. Some sociologists assert that institutionalization of the party system is still a matter to be achieved in the future.

CITIZENSHIP

Lithuanian citizenship is acquired by birth or according to the law. A child acquires citizenship if he or she is born in Lithuania, regardless of the citizenship of the parents. However, if one of the parents is a Lithuanian citizen, a child acquires citizenship independently of the place of birth.

A person may not be a citizen of Lithuania and another state at the same time, except in certain cases established by law.

FUNDAMENTAL RIGHTS

The conception of fundamental rights in Lithuanian law is based on the constitutional provision that human rights and freedoms are innate. Human rights are at the top of the hierarchy of all law values. As part of those constitutional norms that are applicable directly, human rights have great influence on the functioning of all branches of state power.

Impact and Functions of Fundamental Rights

Personal, civic, political, economic, cultural, and social rights are defined in Chapters 2, 3, and 4 of the Lithuanian constitution. The constitutional catalog of human rights, as well as the guarantees of their protection, are in accordance with generally accepted standards of the protection of human rights. Any person whose constitutional rights are violated has the right to appeal to the courts.

Limitations to Fundamental Rights

Limitations to fundamental rights are inscribed in the constitution. The exercise of rights and freedoms must not impair the rights and interest of other people, and it must not cause damage to the morals, public order, or safety of society, or to a person's health. In the case of martial law or a state of emergency, fundamental rights are also limited.

ECONOMY

According to the constitution, Lithuania's economy is based on the right of private ownership and freedom of individual economic activity. However, the state regulates economic activity so that it serves the general welfare of the people.

RELIGIOUS COMMUNITIES

The constitution guarantees freedom to express convictions, to choose religion or faith freely, and to manifest one's religion or faith in worship, practice, or teaching. There is no state religion in Lithuania. According to the ruling of the Constitutional Court, this primarily denotes separation of state and church: Religious organizations do not interfere in the state's activities and the state does not interfere in the internal affairs of religious communities. The state's and the religious areas' activities and functions are delimited. However, the term *separation* stresses the importance of both state and church in the social life of Lithuania rather than absence of any contact between them.

MILITARY DEFENSE AND STATE OF EMERGENCY

In Lithuania all men over 18 years must serve in the national defense service. Conscientious objectors must perform alternative service.

The president is the chief commander of the armed forces. The imposition of martial law, the declaration of a state of emergency, the announcement of mobilization or demobilization, and the decision to use the armed forces in the defense of the homeland are all prerogatives of the Seimas. In the event of an armed attack, martial law may be imposed by the president. However, the Seimas has the right to approve or to overturn the decision.

AMENDMENTS TO THE CONSTITUTION

The provisions of Chapter 1 and Chapter 14, which concern the state of Lithuania and amendments to the constitution, may be amended only by referendum. A proposal to amend or to append the constitution must be submitted to the Seimas by no less than one-fourth of the members of the Seimas or by at least 300,000 voters. Amendments must be voted upon in the Seimas twice and must be approved both times by two-thirds of all the members.

PRIMARY SOURCES
Constitution in English. Available online. URL: http://www3.lrs.lt/c-bin/eng/preps2?Condition1=239805. Accessed on August 14, 2005.
Constitution in Lithuanian: *Lietuvos Respublikos Konstitucija*. Vilnius: Teisines informacijos centras prie Teisingumo ministerijos, 1994. Available online. URL: http://www3.lrs.lt/cgi-bin/preps2?Condition1=237975. Accessed on August 7, 2005.

SECONDARY SOURCES
Aivars Endzinš, "The Constitutional Courts of the Republic of Latvia and the Republic of Lithuania—Similarities and Differences." *In Constitutional justice: the present and the future.* Vilnius: Lietuvos Respublikos Konstitucine Teianas, 1998.
Egidijus Jarašiunas, *Constitutional Justice in Lithuania.* Vilnius: Constitutional Court of the Republic of Lithuania, 2003.
Estonia, Latvia, and Lithuania: Country Studies. Washington, D.C.: United States Government Printing Office, 1996.

Jolanta Kuznecoviene

LUXEMBOURG

At-a-Glance

OFFICIAL NAME
Grand Duchy of Luxembourg

CAPITAL
Luxembourg

POPULATION
448,300 (2005 est.)

SIZE
999 sq. mi. (2,586 sq. km)

LANGUAGES
Luxembourgish, French, and German

RELIGIONS
Catholic 65.9%, Protestant 1.2%, Muslim 0.7%, Jewish 0.5%, Christian Orthodox 0.4%, unaffiliated or other 31.3%

NATIONAL OR ETHNIC COMPOSITION
Luxembourgish 63.1%, Portuguese 13.1%, French 4.5%, Italian 4.3%, Belgian 3.4%, German 2.3%, other 9.3%

DATE OF INDEPENDENCE OR CREATION
April 19, 1839

TYPE OF GOVERNMENT
Parliamentary democratic monarchy

TYPE OF STATE
Central state

TYPE OF LEGISLATURE
Unicameral parliament

DATE OF CONSTITUTION
October 17, 1868

DATE OF LAST AMENDMENT
November 19, 2004

The Grand Duchy of Luxembourg is a parliamentary democracy in the form of a constitutional monarchy based on the principle of separation of powers. It is organized as a central state with no federal or regional governments.

The nominal head of state is the grand duke, whose function is, however, mostly representative and whose powers are strictly limited by the constitution. The actual executive power resides with the cabinet, headed by a prime minister and currently including 14 ministers or state secretaries.

The legislative power belongs to the parliament, called the Chamber of Deputies. The chamber is composed of 60 deputies who are elected for five years.

Fundamental human rights are guaranteed by the constitution. Their application is assured by the judiciary, especially the Constitutional Court, which determines the conformity of the laws with the constitution.

Religious freedom is guaranteed. The chief religious communities receive financial aid from the state on the basis of conventions approved by the Chamber of Deputies. The economic system can be described as a social market economy. The public force, comprising the military, the police, and the civil guard are regulated by the law and subject to the civil government.

CONSTITUTIONAL HISTORY

On June 9, 1815, the Congress of Vienna established Luxembourg as a grand duchy governed by the king of Holland and a state of the German Confederation. Luxembourg gained formal political independence through the Treaty of London of April 19, 1839, which was concluded between the dominant European nations of the time along with Belgium and the Netherlands. The treaty fixed the borders of Belgium, the Netherlands, and Luxembourg.

The first democratic constitution of the country emerged in 1848, largely inspired by the Belgium constitution. After the Treaty of London of May 1, 1867, which recognized the absolute independence of the Grand Duchy of Luxembourg, the constituent assembly elaborated and amended a new constitution that is still in force. It has been modified several times, for example, in 1919 to provide universal suffrage, and in 1956 to allow the Grand Duchy of Luxembourg to adhere to international institutions, such as those of the European Union, of which Luxembourg is a founding member state.

FORM AND IMPACT OF THE CONSTITUTION

The constitution of Luxembourg is a single written document. The Chamber of Deputies needs a majority of two-thirds of the votes to modify it. The constitution takes precedence over all other national law. In case of a conflict between the national law, including the constitution, and an international law that has a direct effect within the legal system of Luxembourg, the latter takes precedence. Therefore, European Union law overrides national law.

BASIC ORGANIZATIONAL STRUCTURE

Luxembourg is a central state. All powers remain with the national institutions. However, the constitution specifies that the communes created by law form autonomous authorities, possessing legal personality and administering their own affairs under the supervision of the national authorities.

LEADING CONSTITUTIONAL PRINCIPLES

Luxembourg is a representative parliamentary democracy. There is a strong division of the executive, legislative, and judicial powers. The constitutional system of Luxembourg is defined by the leading principles of democracy and constitutional monarchy and by the guarantee of individual freedom and equality before the law.

CONSTITUTIONAL BODIES

The predominant bodies provided for in the constitution are the grand duke, the administration, the parliament (called the Chamber of Deputies), the Council of State, the civil and administrative courts, and the Constitutional Court.

The Grand Duke

The grand duke is the head of state. The Crown of the Grand Duchy is hereditary in the Nassau family. The grand duke appoints and dismisses the members of the cabinet, who need the support of the Chamber of Deputies. The grand duke takes part in the legislative power by sanctioning and promulgating the laws. The grand duke also enacts the regulations and orders necessary for carrying laws into effect. Justice is rendered in the name of the grand duke, but the monarch has no right to interfere in the exercise of the judicial power. All acts of the grand duke require the countersignature of a member of the cabinet.

The Administration

The administration (the cabinet) exercises de facto executive power and has in addition the right to initiate legislation by presenting draft laws to the Chamber of Deputies. It consists of a prime minister and several ministers and state secretaries. The prime minister is the leader of the political party or coalition of parties that has most seats in the Chamber of Deputies. The Council of Ministers is submitted by the prime minister to the grand duke, who then appoints the ministers. The administration thus named presents its political program to the Chamber of Deputies, who, by positive vote, express confidence.

The Chamber of Deputies

The Chamber of Deputies represents the people. It is elected by straightforward universal suffrage on the party list system, in accordance with the rules of proportional representation. It exercises the legislative power together with the head of state, the grand duke, and controls the administration. The principal function of the Chamber of Deputies is to vote on proposed laws.

The Council of State

In the absence of a second chamber or a senate, the Council of State is required to advise the Chamber of Deputies in drafting legislation. It is composed of 21 members appointed by the grand duke on the advice of the Chamber of Deputies, the cabinet, or the Council of State itself.

The Lawmaking Process

Legislation is the prerogative of the Chamber of Deputies. The process of making laws is fixed by the constitution, special laws, and the internal regulations of the chamber. It requires the participation of several constitutional bodies. All bills are submitted to a first and a second vote, with an interval of at least three months between the two, unless the Chamber of Deputies in agreement with the Council of State decides otherwise.

The Judiciary

The judiciary is an independent power. The Grand Duchy of Luxembourg has a civil law system, so that the judges have only to apply the law to individual cases without being obliged to follow judicial precedent. There are two jurisdictions: the judicial and the administrative. All judges are appointed for life by the grand duke. The Constitutional Court, created in 1995, determines the conformity of the laws with the constitution.

THE ELECTION PROCESS

Every citizen of Luxembourg over the age of 18 has both the right to stand for election and the obligation to vote. National elections to select members of the Chamber of Deputies and European elections to elect the Luxembourgish members of the European Parliament are held every five years. Municipal elections to choose the mayors and councils of the 117 communes are held every six years.

POLITICAL PARTIES

Luxembourg has a pluralistic system of political parties. After national elections in June 2004, five parties were represented in the Chamber of Deputies.

CITIZENSHIP

Citizenship of Luxembourg is acquired by birth, by option, or by naturalization. Every child, even born outside the country, becomes Luxembourger if one of his or her parents is a citizen of Luxembourg. Foreigners who are born in Luxembourg or who marry a citizen of Luxembourg can also choose citizenship of Luxembourg. Every other foreigner of age can become Luxembourger if he or she fulfils the conditions fixed by the law, in particular living in Luxembourg for at least 5 years.

FUNDAMENTAL RIGHTS

The constitution defines and guarantees the fundamental rights, such as equality before the law, the natural rights of the individual and of the family, individual freedom, the right to private property, freedom of religion, the inviolable secrecy of correspondence, and the legality of penal prosecution. The constitution also guarantees the right to work and social rights.

Impact and Functions of Fundamental Rights

Since the fundamental rights are enshrined in the constitution, they rank above all other national legislation. All other laws must be compliant to the constitution.

Limitations to Fundamental Rights

The fundamental rights are not without limits, and the constitution foresees the regulation of some rights by the law. For most of the fundamental rights, the constitution foresees explicitly that they can be exercised only in respect of other legal rights. The fundamental rights can be subject to restrictions in case of a criminal offense committed in the exercise of such a right.

ECONOMY

The Luxembourg constitution does not specify any economic system. However, it guarantees freedom of trade and industry and the exercise of the professions and of agricultural labor apart from any restrictions imposed by the legislature. Moreover, the constitution guarantees freedom of private property and association. It also mandates laws to organize social security and guarantees the freedom of trade unions. Combining all these elements, the economic system of Luxembourg can be described as a social market economy.

RELIGIOUS COMMUNITIES

Freedom of religion and of public worship, as well as freedom to express one's religious opinions, is guaranteed. There is no established state church. Nevertheless, the constitution specifies that the state can conclude conventions with religious communities in order to establish the church's relation to the state and to provide financial aid from the state. Such conventions have been made with the Catholic Church, the Protestant Church, the Jewish Community, the Anglican Church, and several Christian Orthodox churches.

MILITARY DEFENSE AND STATE OF EMERGENCY

The constitution requires that every matter that concerns the public force be regulated by law. The armed forces are subject to the civil government. The grand duke is officially the chief of the army, but command is exercised by military officers under the responsibility of the minister in charge. There is no compulsory military service; the army has been an all-volunteer force since 1967, composed of citizens of Luxembourg and, since 2002, of citizens of the European Union. In a state of emergency, the grand duke can take exceptional measures for a period of three months.

AMENDMENTS TO THE CONSTITUTION

Any constitutional provision can be amended by a vote of at least two-thirds of the members of the Chamber of

Deputies. Every amendment is subject to two votes with an interval of at least three months between them. During this period, either one-quarter of the members of the Chamber of Deputies or 25,000 electors can demand that the amendment be voted on by referendum, which then must take place.

PRIMARY SOURCES

Constitution in English (as amended in 1998). Available online. URL: http://www.oefre.unibe.ch/law/icl/lu00000_.html. Accessed on July 20, 2005.

Basic Law in Luxembourgish: *Constitution et Droits de l'Homme.* Luxembourg: Service Central de Législation, 2003. Available online. URL: http://www.legilux.public. lu/leg/textescoordonnes/recueils/constitution_droits_de_lhomme/CONST1.pdf. Accessed on June 21, 2006.

SECONDARY SOURCES

Bureau of Public Affairs, U.S. Department of State, "Background Note and Country Reports on Human Rights Practices and International Religious Freedom Report 2004." Available online. URL: http://www.state.gov/r/pa/ei/bgn/3182.htm. Accessed on June 21, 2006.

Pierre Majerus, *L'Etat Luxembourgeois.* Esch-sur-Alzette: Imprimerie Editpress S. A., 1990.

Paul Henri Meyers

MACEDONIA

At-a-Glance

OFFICIAL NAME
Republic of Macedonia

CAPITAL
Skopje

POPULATION
2,022,547 (2005 est.)

SIZE
9,781 sq. mi. (25,333 sq. km)

LANGUAGES
Macedonian, Albanian

RELIGIONS
Orthodox Christian 64.78%, Muslim 33.32%,
Catholic 0.35%, Protestant 0.03%, other 1.52%

NATIONAL OR ETHNIC COMPOSITION
Macedonian 64.18%, Albanian 25.17%, Turkish 3.8%,
Roma 2.66%, Serbian 1.77%, Vlach 0.47%, Bosniac
0.84%, other 1.04%

DATE OF INDEPENDENCE OR CREATION
November 17, 1991

TYPE OF GOVERNMENT
Parliamentary democracy

TYPE OF STATE
Unitary state

TYPE OF LEGISLATURE
Unicameral parliament

DATE OF CONSTITUTION
November 17, 1991

DATE OF LAST AMENDMENT
December 26, 2003

The constitution of the Republic of Macedonia was adopted in November 1991, as the country gained its independence during the dissolution of the former Socialist Federal Republic of Yugoslavia. It has been a key factor in promoting democratic values and providing a framework for the activities of the emerging political forces in the country.

Macedonia is a parliamentary democracy based on separation of powers, the rule of law, and the protection of fundamental freedoms and rights. The legislative power rests in a unicameral parliament elected in free and direct elections. Parliament in turn chooses and politically controls the administration. The president of the republic is elected directly by the people but has a primarily representative role, except in foreign affairs and defense. The freedoms and rights of individuals are protected by ordinary courts and, in certain instances, by the Constitutional Court. The Constitutional Court plays an important role in protecting constitutionality and legality, and it is highly respected by the public. Every citizen may challenge a law or other normative act before the Constitutional Court.

The Republic of Macedonia is a unitary state with a system of local self-government. Since Macedonian society is multiethnic, many provisions have been made for the protection of the rights and interests of national minorities, especially the Albanian minority, including double-majority vote in Parliament in certain matters. In those cases, ethnic communities act as political entities. Religious freedom is guaranteed. Religious communities are equal before the law and are separate from the state. The market economy and freedom of enterprise are among the basic values of the constitutional order, but the social character of the state is also emphasized in the constitution.

CONSTITUTIONAL HISTORY

The constitutional history of the Republic of Macedonia goes back to December 31, 1946, when the first constitution of the then People's Republic of Macedonia was adopted. The Macedonian state had been created in 1944 at the Antifascist Assembly of National Liberation of Macedonia (ASNOM), a body of elected representatives of the people.

ASNOM not only was important in the creation of the Macedonian state as a political entity but served as an interim institutional structure of executive and legislative power until a permanent government could be created. ASNOM's Presidium adopted various measures on the territorial and administrative organization of the country, on the police, and on other matters. A human rights act was passed, an official language introduced, and a national holiday proclaimed. Until 1991, Macedonia remained a federated state within the former Socialist Federal Republic of Yugoslavia. New constitutions were implemented in 1953, 1963, and 1974 in line with structural reforms at the federal level and changing concepts of socialism.

The Republic of Macedonia became an independent state in 1991, and the constitution of November 17 of the same year marked the conclusion of that process. It is the first constitution of Macedonia that introduced a democratic political regime. In 2001, Parliament adopted 15 amendments to the constitution aimed at the improvement of the position of national minorities.

FORM AND IMPACT OF THE CONSTITUTION

The Republic of Macedonia has a written constitution, codified in a single document. It is the highest legal act within the hierarchy of norms, and all laws and other regulations must accord with its provisions. Ratified international treaties are part of the internal legal order and must not contradict the constitution. The Constitutional Court decides on constitutionality and legality of normative acts. Few laws have been found unconstitutional as a whole, but every year the Constitutional Court repeals about a dozen detailed articles within laws.

BASIC ORGANIZATIONAL STRUCTURE

The Republic of Macedonia is a unitary state with a parliamentary system of government. The direct election of the president of the republic by the people implies some elements of a presidential system, but not enough to classify the government as semipresidential. The central government is very strong in terms of both legislative and executive competencies. However, there is an ongoing process of decentralization in education, social policy, and other fields, so that the system of local self-government is gradually becoming more meaningful.

LEADING CONSTITUTIONAL PRINCIPLES

The Republic of Macedonia is a parliamentary republic. The constitution defines the country as a democratic and social state. It also lists several other key principles such as the separation of powers into legislative, executive, and judicial; the rule of law; political pluralism and free, direct, and democratic elections; equitable representation of persons belonging to all ethnic communities in public bodies; and separation of the state and religious communities. The principle of constitutionality and legality of state action is of paramount importance for the legal order and for the protection of freedoms and rights of individuals.

CONSTITUTIONAL BODIES

The most important constitutional bodies are the Parliament, the president of the republic, the administration, the Constitutional Court, and the ordinary courts.

The Parliament

The Parliament is a unicameral representative body of the people and the sole bearer of the legislative power. It is called the Sobranje. It chooses the government and exercises political control over it. Parliament is composed of 120 members elected in general, direct, and free elections by secret ballot for a term of four years. It decides on war and peace, calls for referenda, elects judges of the ordinary courts and of the Constitutional Court, adopts the state budget, and elects an ombudsperson, among other duties. The Parliament may be dissolved only by a majority vote of its members.

The President

The president of the republic is head of state and is elected directly by the people. Any person over the age of 40 is eligible to run for president. The president nominates a mandator (who can then be elected prime minister) to assemble new administrations but does not directly appoint the ministers. He or she does appoint various high-level public officials, including ambassadors and generals. The president serves as commander in chief of the army, concludes international treaties, presides over the Security Council, promulgates laws, and can exercise a suspensive veto on pending legislation.

The Administration

The administration (cabinet) is the bearer of the executive power. It consists of the prime minister and the cabinet ministers. Ministers are proposed by the mandator, and the cabinet is elected by the Sobranje as a body. A cabinet minister may be dismissed by Parliament on the recommendation of the prime minister. The cabinet must have the confidence of the Parliament.

The cabinet sets policy and uses its legislative initiative to obtain necessary laws. In addition, its wide range of executive competencies and instruments makes the administration the most powerful among the political branches.

The Lawmaking Process

Laws are adopted by Parliament. Legislative initiative rests with the cabinet, any member of Parliament, and any group of 10,000 voters. Laws are adopted in two or three readings at a plenary session, in which committees report on their findings. In general, laws are adopted by simple majority, but there are instances when an absolute or qualified majority is required. A majority vote of the major ethnic communities in addition to an overall majority is required for certain laws. Amendments to the text of a bill are allowed up to 48 hours before the final reading.

The Constitutional Court

The Constitutional Court is not part of the judiciary, but rather represents a separate constitutional body of the state, responsible for the protection of the constitutionality and legality. Although the vast majority of cases pertain to review of normative acts, the court also protects certain freedoms and individual rights by way of constitutional complaints in individual cases.

The court's decisions have had great legal and political impact. It has decided important issues concerning the separation of powers, freedom of religion and belief, and denationalization of property. For example, it decided that a law that sets deadlines for submission of a conscientious objection by a conscript was unconstitutional, since a person might change his or her belief at any time, including during military service. The need of the military authorities for exact numbers of troops in planning its activities was deemed irrelevant.

The Judiciary

The judiciary is composed of courts of first instance, three appellate courts, and the Supreme Court. A special department within the Supreme Court decides administrative disputes.

The leading principle of the judiciary is its independence of the political branches of government. Judges are nominated by the Judicial Council of the republic and chosen by the Sobranje for a permanent term until retirement. The fact that Parliament has the last word in the election of judges has led to some public doubts about the full independence of judges.

THE ELECTION PROCESS AND POLITICAL PARTICIPATION

All citizens of Macedonia over the age of 18 have the right to vote and to run in parliamentary and local elections.

Citizens over the age of 40 have the right to run in presidential elections.

The constitution provides for some forms of direct democracy, at both the national and local levels. The Parliament may call for a referendum concerning matters within its sphere of competence. It must call a referendum if requested by 150,000 voters and if any law would change the borders of the state or associate the republic in a union or community with other states.

POLITICAL PARTIES

The Republic of Macedonia has a pluralistic system of political parties. The constitution does not regulate their status and role, except in the context of freedom of association and in the selection of candidates for president of the republic. Nevertheless, the parties play a crucial role in the democratic life of the country, which is regulated by electoral law and the law on political parties.

The Constitutional Court may decide on the unconstitutionality of a statute or a program of a political party, but the decision to ban its activity rests with ordinary courts.

CITIZENSHIP

Citizenship is acquired by origin, by birth, and by naturalization. Citizenship affects participation in state institutions.

FUNDAMENTAL RIGHTS

According to the constitution, the basic freedoms and rights of the individual and citizen, recognized in international law and set down in the constitution, represent a fundamental value of the constitutional order of the republic. The second chapter of the constitution, about one-third of the entire text, sets out classical political and civil rights and liberties, as well as numerous social, economic, and cultural rights. Given their constitutional status, these rights are binding for all state organs. One section in the constitution focuses on the means through which these freedoms and rights are guaranteed; it invokes judicial protection, including the protection of the Constitutional Court, publicity of laws, ban on retroactivity of laws, and the role of the bar.

Impact and Functions of Fundamental Rights

The constitution is based on a liberal-democratic concept of human rights that gives those rights primacy over state authority. Human rights are crucial for a life of dignity and represent a limit on the exercise of public powers.

Limitations to Fundamental Rights

Freedoms and rights of the individual and citizen can be restricted only for purposes prescribed in the constitution, which usually involve combatting crime, protecting public health, or defending the republic. The principle of proportionality must be invoked in balancing conflicting rights and interests.

ECONOMY

The constitution considers market freedom and entrepreneurship as among the basic values of the constitutional order and as foundations for economic relations. The equal legal standing of all parties in the marketplace is guaranteed. The owner's property and the worker's labor form the basis for management, and workers have a right to share in decision making. Free transfer of capital and profits by foreign investors is also guaranteed. However, there is a constitutional obligation for the republic to provide for more balanced regional development and for the more rapid development of economically underdeveloped regions. In addition, the constitution defines the republic of Macedonia as a social state.

RELIGIOUS COMMUNITIES

Freedom of religion is guaranteed. Religious communities and groups are separate from the state and equal before the law. There is no state religion. The separation of church and state bars religious activities in public institutions, including public schools. There is mutual respect between the state and the religious communities and among themselves. Religious communities and groups are free to administer their own affairs and to establish schools and other social and charitable institutions.

MILITARY DEFENSE AND STATE OF EMERGENCY

The military is governed by civil authorities in peacetime and wartime. The president of the republic is the commander in chief of the armed forces; the minister of defense must have been a civilian for at least three years before being elected to that office. The decision about the use of the armed forces is made by the president of the republic, but Parliament decides on deploying military personnel for peacekeeping operations abroad. The armed forces can be used for the defense of the country, as well as in humanitarian actions in cases of natural disasters or epidemics.

A state of emergency or a state of war is declared by the Sobranje or, if it cannot meet, by the president of the republic. A state of emergency exists when major natural disasters or epidemics take place. In both states of emergency and states of war, the administration may issue decrees with the force of law. In a state of war, if Parliament cannot meet, the president of the republic may appoint and discharge the administration, as well as appoint or dismiss officials whose election is normally within the sphere of competence of Parliament.

Military service is compulsory for men over the age of 18 for a term of six months. There are also professional soldiers under contract. Conscientious objection is not specifically provided for in the constitution, but it derives from the freedom of conscience and is regulated by law. Conscientious objectors perform alternative service in social institutions for a term of nine months.

AMENDMENTS TO THE CONSTITUTION

The constitution can be changed by amendments adopted by a two-thirds vote of the total number of representatives. Any amendment to the preamble of the constitution or to provisions relating to the rights of members of ethnic communities requires the same two-thirds majority vote and must be approved by a majority of the votes of those members who belong to nonmajority ethnic communities. Constitutional amendments are adopted after they have been submitted to public debate.

PRIMARY SOURCES
Constitution in English. Available online. URL: www. usud.gov.mk. Accessed on August 27, 2005.
Constitution in Macedonian: *Ustav na Republika Makedonija.* Available online. URL: www.usud.gov. mk. Accessed on September 11, 2005.

SECONDARY SOURCES
Dimitar Mircev, *Constitution of the Republic of Macedonia,* translated by Dimitar Mircev. Skopje: Nova Makedonija, 1994.
Organization for Security and Co-operation in Europe, "Spillover Monitor Mission to Skopje." Available online. URL: http://www.osce.org/skopje. Accessed on June 21, 2006.
United Nations, "Core Document Forming Part of the Reports of State Parties: Macedonia" (HRI/CORE1/Add.83) June 25, 1998. Available online. URL: http://www.unhchr. ch/tbs/doc.nsf. Accessed on August 8, 2005.

Igor Spirovski

MADAGASCAR

At-a-Glance

OFFICIAL NAME
Republic of Madagascar

CAPITAL
Antananarivo

POPULATION
17,501,871 (2005 est.)

SIZE
226,657 sq. mi. (587,040 sq. km)

LANGUAGES
Malagasy (official), French

RELIGIONS
Indigenous beliefs 52%, Christian 41%, Muslim 7%

NATIONAL OR ETHNIC COMPOSITION
18 ethnic groups (mainly Malayo-Indonesian and mixed African, Malayo-Indonesian, and Arab), French, Indian, Creole, and Comoran

DATE OF INDEPENDENCE OR CREATION
June 26, 1960

TYPE OF GOVERNMENT
Semipresidential republic

TYPE OF STATE
Unitary state

TYPE OF LEGISLATURE
Bicameral parliament

DATE OF CONSTITUTION
August 19, 1992

DATE OF LAST AMENDMENT
April 8, 1998

Madagascar is a unitary state decentralized at the level of six autonomous provinces and 22 regions. The current constitution provides for a semipresidential system of government with a clear division of executive, legislative, and judicial powers and a system of checks and balances.

A wide range of civil and political, social, economic, and cultural rights are granted, and the state is the main guarantor of the respect and realization of these rights. The constitution is the supreme law of the land. Its provisions prevail over international laws, national laws, and provincial laws. Everyone has to abide by the provisions of the constitution.

CONSTITUTIONAL HISTORY

Early forms of state organization existed in Madagascar in the 17th century C.E. The country was organized into two main kingdoms, the Kingdom of the Boina and the Kingdom of the Imerina. There were no formal constitutions, but the will of the kings became constitutional practice, and the assembly of the people adopted laws related to general concerns.

The first written constitution of Madagascar was adopted on April 29, 1959, in preparation for independence from France. It took inspiration from the constitution of the French Fourth Republic, but the drafters were also influenced by the ideas of Ravoahangy and Raseta, two pro-independence activists who championed the traditional concept of *fihavanana:* brotherhood, peaceful settlement of conflicts, and solidarity.

After three years of social and political instability, a military *directoire* composed of 18 members from all corps of the army took the reins of the country in 1975, after the president, Colonel Ratsimandrava, was assassinated. By a secret vote, the military *directoire* nominated Ratsiraka, also an army man, president of Madagascar. Four months later, on December 31, a new constitution was adopted by public referendum and Ratsiraka was elected president of the second republic of Madagascar.

This second constitution of Madagascar instituted a socialist regime and gave more power to the president and the ruling party in order to strengthen the hold of the centralist state on public affairs. The state functioned on the basis of decentralized localities, which in fact had minimal powers. In 1989, the constitution was amended to allow political parties to emerge and function freely.

In 1991, an economic and social crisis, combined with the fall of the Soviet Union, provoked massive demonstrations all over the country in favor of abrogating the socialist constitution of 1975 and forcing President Ratsiraka to resign. These demonstrations turned into generalized strikes that immobilized the country for nearly a year, after which a state of emergency was instituted and a government of transition put in place.

On August 19, 1992, a new constitution was adopted and a new president elected. This third constitution was amended by referendum on September 17, 1995, to allow the president to choose and nominate the prime minister. On March 5, 1998, the constitution was amended once more, to include a system of provincial autonomy.

FORM AND IMPACT OF THE CONSTITUTION

Madagascar has a written constitution, codified in a single document. It is the fundamental law of the land and enjoys supremacy over all other international and national laws. International law has precedence over all national laws, but it must comply with the constitution in order to be applied. Further, the law of the state prevails over that of the provinces.

BASIC ORGANIZATIONAL STRUCTURE

Madagascar is a unitary state organized in six different provinces with independent financial and administrative management, and further decentralized into 21 regions. The provinces have their own executive, legislative, and judicial organs, whose powers are limited to the concerns of their own province. The state is represented in each province by a general delegate of the central administration, whose duty is to make sure that the division of authority between state and province is respected, and that provincial authorities comply with the laws of the state.

LEADING CONSTITUTIONAL PRINCIPLES

The Malagasy constitutional system rests on a number of leading principles: Madagascar is an indivisible and united democratic republic based on popular sovereignty and the rule of law. It is a sovereign and secular state that grants civil and political, economic, social, and cultural rights to all but also assigns duties to all citizens.

The current Malagasy constitution establishes a semi-presidential regime with a clear division of the executive, legislative, and judicial powers, with a system of checks and balances among the three. The administration, which is in charge of the implementation of state policy and plans, is accountable to Parliament. The latter can dissolve the administration by a motion of censure. The judiciary is independent.

CONSTITUTIONAL BODIES

The predominant bodies provided for in the constitution are the president of the republic, the administration headed by the prime minister, the Parliament composed of the National Assembly and the Senate, and the judiciary including the High Constitutional Court.

The President

The president of the republic is elected by universal suffrage for a five-year term; he or she can be reelected only once. The president can be removed from office by a vote of impeachment, passed by a two-thirds vote of each chamber of Parliament, and only for a physical or mental incapacity to perform the presidential duties. The president is liable for his or her actions in the exercise of office only in cases of high treason or serious and repeated violations of the provisions of the constitution.

The president is the main figure of the country's political life. The office has great powers, including the nomination of the prime minister, the nomination of one-third of the members of the Senate, and the nomination of three of the nine members of the High Constitutional Court. The president also has the power to dissolve the National Assembly.

The Administration

The administration is in charge of implementing government policy. The prime minister is appointed by the president, who appoints and dismisses the cabinet ministers on the proposal of the prime minister.

The Parliament

The Parliament is made of two chambers: the National Assembly and the Senate. The members of the National Assembly are elected by universal suffrage for a five-year term. They are the representatives of the people and enjoy immunities in the exercise of their function.

One-third of the members of the Senate are nominated by the president of the republic; two-thirds are elected by representatives of each autonomous province for a six-year term—although once in office they exercise their functions independently of the province where they were elected.

The Lawmaking Process

One of the main duties of Parliament is the passing of legislation. The executive can issue ordinances, but certain domains listed in the constitution are strictly reserved to Parliament. A bill can be initiated in either chamber or by the administration.

The Judiciary

The judiciary is independent of the administration, and all judges enjoy immunities in the exercise of their duties. For constitutional disputes, the High Constitutional Court is the supreme jurisdiction. It is composed of nine judges who serve for a seven-year term. In all other matters, the Supreme Court is the highest jurisdiction.

THE ELECTION PROCESS

All Malagasy citizens over the age of 18 have both the right to stand for election and the right to vote in the elections. National Assembly candidates must be at least 21 years old, and presidential candidates must be at least 40. One can lose the right to vote only by a court decision, for reasons of conviction for criminal, economic, or financial offenses; for offenses such as negligence, bankruptcy, or guardianship; or for insanity. Voting is regarded as a civic duty but is not compulsory.

The president is elected by a direct and universal vote. The candidate who receives the absolute majority of votes is elected. If none of the candidates reaches this majority, there is a second round between the two leading candidates; the winner of this round is elected president.

Members of the National Assembly are elected by a mixed system: simple majority voting in 82 single-member constituencies and party list proportional representation voting in 34 two-member constituencies, using the rule of highest average. The "next-in-line" candidate on the party list fills that party's vacancies that arise between general elections.

POLITICAL PARTIES

The constitution of Madagascar establishes a multiparty system but forbids the creation of racist and secessionist political parties that might endanger the unity and indivisibility of the state. There are more than 130 political parties, about a dozen of them major parties, including the ruling party, I Love Madagascar (TIM); Pillar and Podium for the Development of Madagascar (AREMA); Militants for the Development of Madagascar (MFM); Be Judged by Your Work (AVI); Work, Truth and Harmonized Development (AFFA); National Union for Development and Democracy (UNDD); Social Democrat Party (PSD); Reflection and Action Group for Development in Madagascar (GRAD-Iloafo); Rally for Social Democracy (RPSD); Economic Liberalism and Democratic Action for Reconstruction Party (LEADER-Fanilo); and Independence and Renewal Party of Madagascar (AKFM-Fanavoazana).

CITIZENSHIP

Malagasy citizenship is regulated by a law, as the constitution does not have any related provision. It is primarily acquired by birth. A child acquires Malagasy citizenship if one of his or her parents is a Malagasy citizen; the place where the child is born is of no relevance. Malagasy citizenship can also be acquired by naturalization. One can lose Malagasy citizenship if he or she acquires another nationality.

FUNDAMENTAL RIGHTS

The constitution of Madagascar defines the fundamental rights and duties of citizens immediately after its general principles. In two different subchapters, it guarantees civil and political rights as well as economic, social, and cultural rights, on both the individual and the group level. The rights to opinion, expression, and information are considered to be the most important rights and receive first mention in the Malagasy constitution.

The constitution does not provide an explicit philosophical foundation for individual rights. It defines human dignity and integrity as an aim rather than the source of human rights.

Impact and Functions of Fundamental Rights

The state is the main guarantor of the respect and implementation of the enumerated individual rights. However, for certain rights such as the right to nondiscrimination and work-related rights, private persons are bound as well.

Limitations to Fundamental Rights

The exercise of each right is regulated by the law and is limited by the respect for others' rights and the respect for public order.

ECONOMY

The Malagasy constitution does not specify an economic system according to which the country must function. However, certain provisions of the constitution tacitly impose a model of a free market economy and free enterprise system. These include the right to individual property, the freedom of occupation or profession, and the right to form and join associations. Further, the constitution guarantees the exercise of free enterprise and the security of capital and investments.

RELIGIOUS COMMUNITIES

Freedom of religion is guaranteed as a human right, and religion is listed as prohibited grounds for discrimination. The constitution does not explicitly mention any religious communities, since religious conflict has never been a problem in Madagascar. There is no established state church; the constitution expressly specifies that the state is secular and therefore establishes a clear division between church and the state.

The Christian church is the strongest civil institution of the country. It has intervened in public affairs, but only in times of national crisis.

MILITARY DEFENSE AND STATE OF EMERGENCY

Military service is compulsory for all men over the age of 18, and it is widely considered to be a duty of honor. Conscientious objection is possible, and no alternative to serving in the armed forces is imposed on conscientious objectors.

The army is not considered independent; it is a prerogative granted to the prime minister to assist in ensuring public security and order. No provision of the constitution specifically deals with the army. However, apart from defending the country against a military attack, the armed forces may intervene in the event of a national insurrection, a natural disaster or a major accident, when the *gendarmerie* is unable to cope successfully with the situation.

The president of the republic and the administration may declare a state emergency after consulting the chairpersons of the National Assembly, the Senate, and the High Constitutional Court. The constitution grants the president special powers at such a time, including that of issuing laws. An organic law regulates the duration and extent of these powers.

AMENDMENTS TO THE CONSTITUTION

The constitution can be amended at the initiative of the president and the administration, or of either of the two chambers of Parliament. The amendment is adopted either by a vote of three-fourths of the members of Parliament or by popular referendum. However, the integrity of the national territory as well as the republican form of the state cannot be changed.

PRIMARY SOURCES
Constitution in English. Available online. URL: http://www.oefre.unibe.ch/law/icl/ma00000_.html. Accessed on September 13, 2005.
Constitution in Malagasy. Available online. URL: http://www.justice.gov.mg/txtfond.htm. Accessed on September 18, 2005.

SECONDARY SOURCES
Charles Cadoux, "La constitution de la Troisième République malgache." Available online. URL: http://www.politique-africaine.com/numeros/pdf/052058.pdf. Accessed on February 1, 2006.
Xavier Philippe, "Les nouvelles constitutions malgache et mauricienne—un renouveau du constitutionnalisme dans l'Océan Indien?" *Annuaire des pays de l'Océan Indien* 14 (1995–96): 115–149.
United Nations, "Core Document Forming Part of the Reports of States Parties: Madagascar" (HRI/CORE/1/Add.31/Rev.1), 18 May 2004. Available online. URL: http://www.unhchr.ch/tbs/doc.nsf. Accessed on August 30, 2005.

Mianko Ramaroson

MALAWI

At-a-Glance

OFFICIAL NAME
Republic of Malawi

CAPITAL
Lilongwe

POPULATION
13,013,926 (July 2006 est.)

SIZE
45,747 sq. mi. (118,484 sq. km)

LANGUAGES
English (official), Chichewa (official), Chilomwe, Chingonde, Chinyanja, Chisena, Chitonga, Chitumbuka and Chiyao

RELIGIONS
Protestant 55%, Roman Catholic 20%, Muslim 20%, indigenous beliefs 3%, other 2%

NATIONAL OR ETHNIC COMPOSITION
Maravi (including the Chewa, Nyanja, Tonga, and Tumbuka) 58.3%, Lomwe 18.4%, Yao 13.2%, Ngoni 6.7%, other 3.4%

DATE OF INDEPENDENCE OR CREATION
July 6, 1964

TYPE OF GOVERNMENT
Multiparty democracy

TYPE OF STATE
Centralist state

TYPE OF LEGISLATURE
Unicameral parliament

DATE OF CONSTITUTION
May 18, 1994

DATE OF LAST AMENDMENT
November 30, 2001

The Malawian constitution was adopted in 1994 to mark the end of a 30-year one-party dictatorship. It is one of the most progressive constitutions adopted after the end of the cold war. In addition to recognizing the key principles of separation of powers, judicial independence, and the rule of law, it entrenches a bill of rights that transcends the traditional divide between civil and political rights and economic, social, and cultural rights. The bill of rights binds both state and nonstate actors. Any rights recognized under it can be enforced through a court of law, the Human Rights Commission, and the ombudsperson.

The consolidation of democracy and the development of constitutionalism have been a slow and testing process for the poverty-stricken country. However, unlike its predecessors, the current constitution in its first decade enhanced respect for individual rights, sowed a culture of tolerance, promoted competitive politics, and widened the horizons for challenging the exercise of state power.

The president is the head of state and head of the administration. Malawi has a unicameral parliament. Any act of the administration and any law passed by parliament may be declared invalid to the extent that it is inconsistent with the constitution.

The Malawian economic system is largely a market economy. Freedom of religion is respected. The military is enjoined to operate under the direction of civil authorities at all times.

CONSTITUTIONAL HISTORY

Before colonization, Malawi was inhabited by Bantu speakers who organized themselves under kingdoms. The era of kingdoms ended in 1891 when Britain declared the country a British protectorate. From then on English law applied. Customary law was applicable only to the extent that it was not repugnant to the law and justice received from Britain.

Colonialism displayed little regard for the human rights of the colonized people, and the violent rebellion led by the Reverend John Chilembwe in 1915 signified a growing resistance to colonialism. However, it was not until the African National Congress (later renamed Malawi Congress Party [MCP]) was formed in 1944 that a more organized struggle against colonial rule emerged. In 1953, the British government formed the Federation of Rhodesia and Nyasaland, consisting of Northern Rhodesia (Zambia), Southern Rhodesia (Zimbabwe), and Nyasaland (Malawi). This development strengthened the fight for independence, led by Hastings Kamuzu Banda. Success was achieved in 1963 when the federation was finally dissolved and constitutional talks in preparation for self-rule were arranged in Lancaster House in London.

On July 6, 1964, Nyasaland became the first country in the federation to gain independence from Britain under the new name, Malawi. The constitution adopted that year enshrined a range of civil and political rights, and the principles of judicial independence and separation of powers. However, on July 6, 1966, Malawi became a republic under a new constitution. While it recognized the Universal Declaration of Human Rights (UDHR), the 1966 constitution, unlike its predecessor, did not have a bill of rights. It also declared the country to be a single-party state and concentrated great power in the president, in violation of the doctrine of separation of powers. In 1971, the constitution was amended to make Banda the president for life.

The Banda regime lasted for 30 years and was marked by oppression and lack of respect for the rule of law and constitutionalism. A successful resistance to the regime crystallized in 1992 and culminated in a national referendum held in 1993 to decide whether the country wanted to proceed as a multiparty state. The regime took a resounding defeat. It also lost the presidential and parliamentary elections held in 1994. A new constitution was adopted provisionally on May 18, 1994, after a four-month period of negotiation and national debate. It became fully operational on May 18, 1995. Modeled after the 1993 interim constitution of South Africa, the new constitution represents the most progressive constitution the country has ever had.

FORM AND IMPACT OF THE CONSTITUTION

Malawi's constitution is written and embodied in a single document comprising 215 sections. Any law or act of the administration that is inconsistent with the constitution is invalid to the extent of the inconsistency. Courts are obliged to consider current norms of public international law where applicable in interpreting constitutional provisions.

While international treaties require an act of parliament to be enforced by domestic courts, customary international law automatically forms a part of the law of Malawi. The Law Commission has undertaken wide-ranging law reforms since 1994 in many areas, including labor and employment law, criminal law and procedure, children's rights, and environmental protection, to align the laws with the constitution. The Malawian government generally abides by the constitution. However, poverty, insufficiency of human and other resources in the administration of justice, frequent constitutional amendments, and occasional political violence and intolerance have helped slow the development of constitutionalism and the consolidation of democracy.

BASIC ORGANIZATIONAL STRUCTURE

Malawi is divided into three regions: Northern, Central, and Southern. While these divisions have significant political implications, the constitution does not create any state structures based on them. As a centralist state, Malawi is neither parliamentary nor presidential; perhaps it can best be described as a constitutional state since both presidential and parliamentary actions and omissions are subject to constitutional scrutiny. The constitution also makes provision for the establishment of local government authorities, whose officers are elected every five years.

LEADING CONSTITUTIONAL PRINCIPLES

Malawi practices constitutional democracy. The executive, legislature, and judiciary have separate functions and are all bound by the constitution. Article 6 of the constitution entrenches the principle of democracy. It states that the authority to govern "derives from the people of Malawi as expressed through universal and equal suffrage" in periodic elections. The principles of judicial independence and respect for the rule of law are given express recognition. Religious freedom is also guaranteed and respected in practice.

CONSTITUTIONAL BODIES

The key constitutional bodies are the executive, the legislature, the judiciary, the Human Rights Commission, and the ombudsperson.

The Executive

The president is the head of state and of the administration. The president (together with the vice president) is elected directly by a majority of the electorate in elections held every five years. A person can serve a maximum of two consecutive terms in the presidency. An attempt to amend this provision by the former president Bakili Muluzi in 2002–3 to extend the maximal number of terms was widely criticized and failed. The president has powers to appoint and dismiss ministers and deputy ministers.

The Legislature

All legislative powers are vested in parliament, which consists of the president and the National Assembly. A widely criticized constitutional amendment made by parliament in 2001 removed the possibility of establishing a senate. Members of the National Assembly are elected directly by the electorate in single-member districts under the first-past-the post electoral system every five years. An act of parliament has primacy over other forms of law except the constitution.

The Lawmaking Process

The drafting section, based at the ministry of justice, is generally responsible for the drafting of principal and subsidiary legislation on behalf of the government. After a draft has been produced it is sent to the cabinet for approval. It is thereafter sent to parliament for enactment. If the president withholds assent to a bill, the bill is returned to parliament. When a bill is again presented to the president for assent the president shall assent to the bill within 21 days of its presentation. The law goes into force when it is published in the official gazette.

The Judiciary

The judiciary has played a central role in enforcing democratic norms and constitutional principles. In particular, it has assisted immeasurably in ensuring that elections are fair by judging controversial electoral disputes in a manner that has earned it considerable public confidence. While the constitution does not provide for a separate constitutional court, a legislative amendment made in 2004 required that any constitutional issue must be heard by at least three judges of the High Court chosen randomly on a case-by-case basis.

However, blatant interference with the independence of the judiciary occurred in 2001–2, when the government tried to impeach four judges who had rendered judgments unfavorable to it. International and local pressure worked together to render the proposed impeachment unsuccessful.

THE ELECTION PROCESS

Any person above the age of 18 years has the right to vote in presidential, parliamentary, and local government elections. To contest a parliamentary seat, one must be at least 21 years old. In the case of presidential elections, the minimal age requirement is 35 years. The Electoral Commission has the mandate to conduct elections. The High Court can review appeals against the electoral decisions of the Commission.

POLITICAL PARTIES

Malawi is a multiparty state. A political party must be registered under the Political Parties (Registration) Act to be recognized as such.

CITIZENSHIP

Citizenship can be acquired by birth, descent, marriage, registration, and naturalization.

FUNDAMENTAL RIGHTS

The Malawian constitution subscribes to the view that all human rights are universal, interdependent, and interrelated. It recognizes a range of civil and political rights and such economic, social, and cultural rights as the rights to education; to family protection, culture, and language; to economic activity; and to fair labor practices. It also guarantees the right to development. Furthermore, Section 13 of the constitution stipulates a range of principles of state policy concerning gender equality, nutrition, health, the environment, and education.

The human rights recognized under the constitution bind all organs of government and all natural and legal persons in Malawi. Any person who claims that any of these rights has been infringed or threatened is entitled to apply to the High Court, the ombudsperson, or the Human Rights Commission for a remedy.

Impact and Functions of Fundamental Rights

Malawi has improved considerably in its human rights record since the end of the one-party regime. However, the deepening poverty in the country has hindered the full enjoyment by the majority of the population of their socioeconomic rights. Human rights violations still occur in prisons, and state- and party-sponsored violence happens during elections. Furthermore, the country rarely fulfills its reporting obligations under international and regional human rights treaties.

Limitations to Fundamental Rights

Certain rights, such as the right to life, are not open to any limitation or derogation. However, most rights can be limited by law provided that the limitation does not negate the essential content of the right and that it is reasonable, recognized by international human rights standards, and necessary in an open and democratic society. Derogations may be permitted only during a state of emergency.

ECONOMY

Section 13 of the constitution enjoins the state to take measures aimed at a sensible balance between the creation and the distribution of wealth through the nurturing of a market economy, on the one hand, and long-term investment in health, education, economic, and social development, on the other. This provision suggests that the state has an obligation to strike a balance between developing a market economy and fulfilling its welfare obligations to its citizens. In practice, Malawi's economic system is disproportionately market-oriented as dictated by its donors and the conditions of its debt.

RELIGIOUS COMMUNITIES

Malawi is a secular state. Unlike many other African countries, it has not experienced any major conflict arising from religious differences. Freedom of religion and conscience is a fundamentally protected right. However, the church has historically played an important role in fighting oppressive regimes in Malawi.

MILITARY DEFENSE AND STATE OF EMERGENCY

Malawi does not have a history of military rule. The constitution provides that the Defense Forces of Malawi shall operate under the direction of civil authorities at all times. The responsibilities of the Defense Forces include defending the sovereignty and territorial integrity of the country, upholding and protecting the constitutional order, and assisting authorities in the maintenance of essential services in emergencies. They may also perform other functions outside the country pursuant to the country's international obligations.

Recruitment into the Defense Forces is voluntary. The president may declare a state of emergency only with the approval of the Defense and Security Committee of the National Assembly in times of war, threat of war, or natural disasters. The rights that may be suspended during a state of emergency are specifically mentioned in the constitution. Even then, the derogation of any right must be consistent with the country's international obligations.

AMENDMENTS TO THE CONSTITUTION

Certain constitutional provisions, including the bill of rights, principles of national policy, principles on the interpretation and application of the constitution, and provisions on judicial independence and separation of powers, require a referendum prior to their amendment. Parliament also has amendment powers. With respect to those provisions that require an amendment by a referendum, parliament may amend them if two-thirds of the members of the National Assembly support the amendment. However, the amendment must not affect the substance or purpose of the constitution.

Other constitutional provisions may be amended by a two-thirds majority of the members of the National Assembly. That too many amendments affecting these provisions have occurred since 1994 indicates that this method of amendment is not difficult enough to ensure the development of constitutionalism.

PRIMARY SOURCES
Constitution in English. Available online. URL: http://www.sdnp.org.mw/constitut/intro.html. Accessed on August 19, 2005.

SECONDARY SOURCES
Danwood Chirwa, "Democratisation in Malawi 1994–2002: Completing the Vicious Circle?" *South African Journal on Human Rights* 19, no. 2 (2003): 316–338.

Danwood Chirwa, "A Full Loaf Is Better than Half: The Constitutional Protection of Economic, Social and Cultural Rights in Malawi." *Journal of African Law* 49, no. 2 (2005): 207–241.

Thomas Handsen, "Implementation of International Human Rights Standards through the National Courts of Malawi." *African Journal of Law* 46 (2002): 31–42.

John Hatchard, "Statute Note: The Human Rights Commission Act, 1998 (Malawi)." *Journal of African Law* 43 (1998): 253–257.

Fidelis Kanyongolo, "The Limits of Liberal Democratic Constitutionalism in Malawi." In *Democratisation in Malawi: A Stocktaking,* edited by K. M. Phiri and K. R. Ross, 353–375. Blantyre: CLAIM, 1995.

Lone Lindholt, *Questioning the Universality of Human Rights: The African Charter on Human and Peoples' Rights in Botswana, Malawi and Mozambique.* Aldershot, England: Ashgate, 1997.

"Malawi Government Website." Available online. URL: http://www.sdnp.org.mw/. Accessed on July 26, 2005.

Tiyanjana Maluwa, "The Role of International Law in the Protection of Human Rights under the Malawian Constitution of 1995." *African Yearbook of International Law* 3 (1995): 53–79.

Peter Mutharika, "The 1995 Democratic Constitution of Malawi." *Journal of African Law* 40 (1996): 205–220.

B. P. Wanda, "The Rights of Detained and Accused Persons in Post-Banda Malawi." *Journal of African Law* 40 (1996): 221–233.

Danwood Chirwa

MALAYSIA

At-a-Glance

OFFICIAL NAME
Malaysia

CAPITAL
Kuala Lumpur

POPULATION
25,580,000 (2005 est.)

SIZE
127,317 sq. mi. (329,750 sq. km)

LANGUAGES
Malay, English, and other ethnic languages

RELIGIONS
Muslim 60.4%, Buddhist 19.2%, Christian 9.1%, Hindu 6.3%, Confucian/Taoist/other traditional Chinese religion 2.6%, other 2.4%

NATIONAL OR ETHNIC COMPOSITION
Bumiputera (Malays and other indigenous groups) 65.1%, Chinese 26.0%, Indian 7.7%, other 1.2%

DATE OF INDEPENDENCE OR CREATION
August 31, 1957 (Malaya), September 16, 1963 (Malaysia)

TYPE OF GOVERNMENT
Parliamentary democracy

TYPE OF STATE
Federal state

TYPE OF LEGISLATURE
Bicameral parliament

DATE OF CONSTITUTION
August 31, 1957

DATE OF LAST AMENDMENT
February 10, 2005

Malaysia is a parliamentary democracy with a constitutional monarchy, based on the rule of law and constitutional supremacy. Joined in a federation, Malaysia is made up of 13 federal states and a strong central government. Each of the states has a state constitution, and the whole federation is governed by a federal constitution. The federal constitution is the supreme law of the nation and provides for the institutions of government, the relationships among them, their rights and duties, and the rights and duties of citizens. In particular, the constitution provides for guarantees of human rights, subject to some qualifications. The rights and duties prescribed by the constitution are enforced by a judiciary independent of the other two arms of government, namely, the legislature and the executive body.

The Yang di-Pertuan Agong is the head of state, but his function is mostly in accordance with advice from the executive body. The central political figure is the prime minister, who is the head of the executive body and leads the administration of the country. The prime minister depends on Parliament, a representative body of the people, of which the prime minister is also a member, for legitimacy in running the country. Free, equal, periodic, and direct elections of the members of the lower house of Parliament are guaranteed.

The upper house or Senate is an appointed and specially elected house. A pluralistic system of political parties is in existence, but the ruling government party dominates and the opposition parties have limited impact on the political scene.

Malaysia is multiracial and multireligious, and religious freedom is guaranteed. Although Islam is declared as the official religion, Malaysia is essentially a secular state. The economic system can be described as a market economy. The constitution provides for the preservation of traditions that are regarded as important in ensuring the stability of the multiracial society and the nation as a whole.

CONSTITUTIONAL HISTORY

The Malay Peninsula was under British rule by the late 19th century, although British forces had the island of Penang ceded to them as early as 1786. Various agreements between local Malay rulers and the British government resulted in a strong British influence over the laws and in particular the constitutional structures that developed.

After World War II (1939–45), the first formal constitution governing the whole of the peninsula was proposed by the British government. Named the Malayan Union in 1946, this political entity, however, was rejected by the Malay people. Hence, the Federation of Malaya was formed in 1948 and became the basis of the present day constitutional structure. In 1955, the first elections in Malayan history were held to choose members of the Federal Legislative Council. This paved the way for independence through an agreement with the British government, and a constitutional commission was formed to propose a constitution for the nation. The commission, consisting of foreign jurists, drafted a constitution based on the terms of reference given to it and existing models. This constitution was accepted by the people, and Malaya was born in August 1957. Malayan independence had implications for the destiny of the other British territories in the region, which consisted of Sabah, Sarawak, and Singapore. The three territories merged with the Malayan states in 1963, forming the Federation of Malaysia. Singapore left the federation soon after in 1965.

FORM AND IMPACT OF THE CONSTITUTION

Malaysia has a written federal constitution codified in a single document that takes precedence over all other laws. International law must be in accordance with the constitution to be applicable within Malaysia.

BASIC ORGANIZATIONAL STRUCTURE

Malaysia is a federation made up of 13 states. All of them have identical autonomous rights specified in the constitution; their powers are not as great as those of the central government. The federal constitution takes precedence over the state constitutions, which have to be adapted to fit into the working of the federal constitution, as no inconsistencies in the organizational structure and working of government are allowed.

The doctrine of the supremacy of the constitution is in operation, as opposed to parliamentary sovereignty.

LEADING CONSTITUTIONAL PRINCIPLES

Malaysia's system of government is a parliamentary democracy with a constitutional monarchy. There is a fusion of powers between the executive and the legislature just as in any government that follows the Westminster model. The judiciary, however, is separate, and there is a system of checks and balances.

The rule of law is implicit in all the provisions of the constitution and the law. However, Parliament has authority from the constitution to pass laws to counter subversive or terrorist activities that may derogate from the principles of rule of law.

Although Islam is declared to be the official religion, the constitution and the law are essentially secular.

CONSTITUTIONAL BODIES

The predominant bodies provided for in the constitution are the Yang di-Pertuan Agong, the prime minister, and the cabinet ministers; the Parliament, consisting of the Dewan Rakyat (House of Representatives) and Dewan Negara (Senate); the Conference of Rulers; and the judiciary, including Superior Courts.

The Yang di-Pertuan Agong (King)

The Yang di-Pertuan Agong is the head of state. He is a constitutional monarch elected for a five-year term by the Conference of Rulers.

The head of state has the discretionary power to appoint the prime minister, who is the head of the executive body, but very few other discretionary powers. Most of his powers are to be exercised in accordance with the advice—in essence, instructions—of the prime minister or anybody else specified by the constitution.

The Prime Minister

The executive body conducts the day-to-day running of government affairs. It is headed by the prime minister and assisted by the federal ministers. The constitution provides a great deal of power to the prime minister, who is thus a dominant figure in the administration and Malaysian political life.

Dewan Rakyat (House of Representatives)

The Dewan Rakyat is the lower chamber of Parliament. The members are elected for a five-year term in a direct, free, equal, and secret balloting process. The support of the majority of the Dewan Rakyat is required in order for a member to be appointed prime minister by the Yang di-Pertuan Agong.

Besides legislative functions, the Dewan Rakyat monitors the administration, which is responsible to it. The session of the Dewan Rakyat is five years.

Dewan Negara (Senate)

The Dewan Negara is the upper chamber of Parliament. Some of its members are elected by the state legislative assemblies to represent the interest of the federal states; the others are appointed by the Yang di-Pertuan Agong on the advice of the administration. The term of the Senate is three years.

The Dewan Negara acts as a political monitor to the Dewan Rakyat.

The Lawmaking Process

The main role of Parliament is the passing of legislation. Most of the laws passed are initiated by the administration. The draft law is debated and passed by each house of Parliament and receives the formal royal assent of the Yang di-Pertuan Agong before it becomes law. Some laws require the consent of other bodies such as the Conference of Rulers.

The Conference of Rulers

The Conference of Rulers consists of the hereditary rulers of the nine Malay states of the federation. Besides choosing the Yang di-Pertuan Agong from among themselves, this body is responsible for special functions relating to traditional elements of the constitution.

The Judiciary

The judiciary is established by the constitution as a body independent of other branches of the government. It interprets and enforces the law and the constitution and resolves disputes between them.

The highest Malaysian court is the Federal Court, which also serves as the constitutional court. The Federal Court has ruled several times on the supreme authority of the constitution and on its interpretation according to its general aims and principles.

Malaysia practices a two-tier appeal system; below the Federal Court are the Court of Appeal and the High Courts. These courts deal with all matters except those that are the exclusive province of Sharia (Islamic law), such as family matters. Sharia matters are within the jurisdiction of the federal states and are administered by the state sharia courts, which are not part of the federal judiciary.

THE ELECTION PROCESS

All Malaysians over the age of 21 are eligible to stand for and vote in an election. Elections are held periodically (usually about every five years), and seats for both state legislative assemblies and the federal Parliament are contested.

POLITICAL PARTIES

Malaysia allows for a pluralistic system of political parties. Federal laws govern their activities. One of the main parties of the ruling coalition was at one time declared unlawful by a high court under an ordinary federal law.

CITIZENSHIP

Malaysian citizenship is primarily acquired by birth. A child acquires citizenship if one of his or her parents is a citizen.

FUNDAMENTAL RIGHTS

The federal constitution provides for the protection of human rights and fundamental freedoms. The provisions protect basic fundamental rights including the right to life, equality, free speech, religion, and property.

Impact and Functions of Fundamental Rights

Fundamental rights are subject to qualifications found in the provisions of the federal constitution and in the interpretation of the courts. It is normally the function of the courts to protect fundamental rights, and the interpretations of the courts form the main body of law.

Limitations to Fundamental Rights

Constitutional amendments and exceptions, restrictive judicial decisions, and legislative interventions have played an important role in limiting and restricting fundamental rights.

ECONOMY

The Malaysian constitution does not specify any particular economic system but provides for conditions such as property rights and the right to form associations that encourage a market economy. However, there are provisions for affirmative action to balance certain inequalities.

RELIGIOUS COMMUNITIES

Freedom of religion is guaranteed by the constitution, although it declares Islam to be the official religion of the country. The highest court has declared that the status of

Islam does not alter the secular nature of the laws of the country.

MILITARY DEFENSE AND STATE OF EMERGENCY

The military defense consists of professional soldiers who serve for fixed periods. There is also a volunteer force. The military is under the direction of the executive body.

During civil chaos or natural disasters, a state of emergency can be declared by the Yang di-Pertuan Agong on the advice of the prime minister and cabinet. During a state of emergency, provisions of the constitution may be suspended, and the executive body may take over and issue laws that are inconsistent with the constitution. During this time, the police and military may be directed by the executive body to take certain measures to restore order.

AMENDMENTS TO THE CONSTITUTION

In general, the constitution can be amended by a two-thirds majority in both the Dewan Rakyat and Dewan Negara. However, certain amendments may require the consent of the Conference of Rulers or the consent of certain state governments whenever their interests are affected.

The courts have so far not recognized any basic provisions of the constitution that cannot be amended. Since the ruling administration has usually commanded a two-thirds majority in Parliament, there do not appear to be any limitations as to the extent to which the constitution can be amended.

PRIMARY SOURCES

Federal Constitution in English: *Federal Constitution.* Kuala Lumpur: Malayan Law Journal, 2002. Available online. URL: http://www.helplinelaw.com/law/malaysia/constitution/malaysia01c.php. Accessed on June 21, 2006.

SECONDARY SOURCES

Abdul Aziz Bari, *Malaysian Constitution: A Critical Introduction.* Kuala Lumpur: The Other Press, 2003.
Andrew Harding, *Law, Government, and the Constitution in Malaysia.* London: Kluwer Law International, 1996.

Johan S. Sabaruddin

MALDIVES

At-a-Glance

OFFICIAL NAME
Republic of Maldives

CAPITAL
Male

POPULATION
349,100 (July 2005 est.)

SIZE
115 sq. mi. (298 sq. km)

LANGUAGES
Dhivehi

RELIGION
Islam (Sunni, state religion)

NATIONAL OR ETHNIC COMPOSITION
Sinhalese, Dravidian, Arab, Australasian, and African
ethnicities

DATE OF INDEPENDENCE OR CREATION
July 26, 1965

TYPE OF GOVERNMENT
Republic

TYPE OF STATE
Unitary state

TYPE OF LEGISLATURE
Unicameral People's Council (Majlis)

DATE OF CONSTITUTION
January 1, 1998

DATE OF LAST AMENDMENT
No amendment

The Republic of Maldives is a unitary state with a strong president. The country is governed centrally from its capital, Male. The president has vast powers in making policy and appointing and dismissing public officials. The president is head of state, head of the executive, and commander in chief.

The constitution provides that the Republic of Maldives is a state founded on Islamic principles and that the state religion is Islam. Together with Islamic law (the Sharia), the constitution is the fundamental law of the country. No law or act shall violate the constitution or Islamic law.

The constitution establishes an executive and legislative branch of government. The administration of justice is in the authority of the president, thus making the judiciary subordinate to the executive. The president appoints and dismisses judges at his discretion. The constitution contains a number of fundamental rights, which are subject to limitations based on principles of Islamic law.

CONSTITUTIONAL HISTORY

Maldivian constitutional history begins with the conversion from the Buddhist religion to Sunni Islam in the mid-12th century C.E. By 1153, an independent Islamic sultanate was established. This sultanate, with short interruptions, ruled until 1968, when it was abolished and replaced by the current Republic of Maldives.

From 1558 to 1573, the Maldives were under Portuguese rule but returned to independence after citizen uprisings. By 1645, the sultanate of the Maldives was under the protection of the Dutch in Ceylon, who were replaced by the British in 1796. In 1887, the Maldives were accorded the status of a protected state included in the administrative unit of Ceylon, without becoming a formal protectorate. The inner structures of the sultanate were not affected.

The first written constitution was adopted in 1932, making the formerly hereditary sultanate elective and providing for a parliament and a prime minister. Several constitutions followed. After the independence of Ceylon in 1948, the Maldives gained self-government status from the British. In 1953, a republic was proclaimed, but the sultanate was reimposed shortly afterward.

On July 26, 1965, Great Britain and the Maldives, by agreement, ended the British status of protector, and the sultanate of Maldives gained official independence. On November 11, 1968, a constitution establishing the Republic of Maldives and eventually abolishing the sultanate was adopted by referendum. The 1968 constitution was replaced by the current constitution on January 1, 1998, in a referendum.

On June 9, 2004, the president announced his plans to democratize the Maldives. A constituent assembly (People's Special Majlis) was convened the same year. It is currently finalizing its deliberations.

On February 14, 2005, the president presented a list with 31 proposals for amendments of the constitution. They mark a significant step toward more democracy and a clearer separation of powers and change many aspects of the constitutional order of the Maldives. Whether all proposed amendments will be passed could not be assessed at the date of writing this article. If they are passed, the president's role will shrink decisively: The president will be allowed to serve for only two terms of five years and need no longer be male. Presidential elections will be direct. A prime minister will be head of government with broad powers, reducing the president's role. Parliament will be bicameral and have stronger influence on the selection of government officials. The judiciary will be completely separated from the president's office with a newly established Supreme Court and the office of a chief justice as administrator of all judicial affairs. Several extensions of fundamental rights are foreseen, among them gender equality.

FORM AND IMPACT OF THE CONSTITUTION

The Republic of Maldives has a written constitution in a single document that, together with Islamic law, is the supreme law of the country. According to Article 148 (1), no law shall be made in contravention of the constitution. All laws passed before the constitution took force must be in accordance with it.

BASIC ORGANIZATIONAL STRUCTURE

The Republic of Maldives consists of 26 natural atolls with approximately 2,000 islands. The country is centrally governed from its capital. The atolls are grouped into 19 administrative units; the capital forms a separate unit. The administrative units are of only marginal importance. The atolls are governed by atoll chiefs, appointed by and under the direction of the president and the cabinet.

LEADING CONSTITUTIONAL PRINCIPLES

According to Article 1, the Republic of Maldives is a republic based on the principles of Islam. Islam is the state religion of the Maldives (Article 7), but the president, rather than religious authorities (Article 38), has the supreme authority to propagate the principles of Islam. Therefore, Islamic law plays a major part in civil and criminal matters.

The constitutional framework makes the judiciary a branch of government dependent on the president. The president has the right to appoint and dismiss all judges. A judge of the High Court can be dismissed if "in the opinion of the president, . . . [he] fails to satisfactorily discharge his duties and responsibilities." Any other judge can be dismissed at the discretion of the president.

Maldives is a presidential democratic republic, with elections of president and parliament every five years.

CONSTITUTIONAL BODIES

The constitution provides for a president, cabinet of ministers, parliament (People's Majlis) atoll chiefs, and a judiciary, including a High Court.

The President

The presidency is the strongest constitutional institution in the Maldives. The president's election follows a special procedure; from among all persons seeking the office, one person is chosen through a secret ballot by parliament. This person is put to a general public vote. The president must be a male Sunni Muslim and must not be married to a foreign national.

The president is head of state, head of the executive, and commander in chief. He appoints and dismisses the vice president, the cabinet ministers, major public officials, the heads of the lower administrative units, and all judges. He presides over the cabinet of ministers and promulgates decrees, directives, and regulations. The president exercises duties subject to Sharia law and the constitution. The president can take over the responsibilities of all ministries and the office of the attorney-general.

The president is the representative of the state in dealing with foreign governments and discharges all acts and functions under international law.

The Lawmaking Process

Parliament can pass bills with a simple majority vote, except those bills that constitutionally require a two-thirds majority. A bill is forwarded to the president for assent within seven days. The president can take 30 days to assent or resubmit the bill to parliament with alterations or recommendations. If the president does not react within the 30 days, the bill is deemed to have his assent. Parliament can override presidential changes in a bill by a two-thirds majority. To become law, the bill has to be published in the *Government Gazette*.

The Cabinet of Ministers

The cabinet of ministers is appointed by the president without the need for approval by parliament, although parliament can force a cabinet minister to resign by passing a no confidence vote. The cabinet consists of the president, the vice president, cabinet ministers, and the attorney-general.

The cabinet ministers support the president in formulating and executing policy and in governing the republic. All cabinet ministers are accountable to the president. The constitution provides that if a cabinet minister's negligence causes loss or damage to the state, the minister is personally responsible.

The People's Majlis

Parliament consists of 50 members, who serve for a five-year-term. Two members are elected from each of the 20 atolls and two from the capital, Male, in direct elections. The president appoints eight additional members.

The speaker of parliament is appointed and can be dismissed by the president. The speaker is not a member of parliament.

Parliament sits in three sessions each year, as stipulated by the constitution. The president can convene extraordinary sessions.

Parliament passes legislation in all areas. The annual budget, as well as all tax-related matters, must be approved by parliament. The president can object to bills passed by parliament, but his objection can be overridden by a two-thirds majority. Decisions by parliament cannot be questioned by courts, except claims of unconstitutionality.

Atoll Chiefs

The 20 atolls are administered by atoll chiefs, appointed by the president. The president and cabinet ministers can issue directions to the atoll chiefs.

The Judiciary

The judiciary in the Maldives does not constitute an independent branch of government. The president, as the highest authority administering justice in the Maldives, has the right to appoint all judges, as well as to dismiss them at his discretion. The courts are administered by a cabinet minister whom the president assigns. The presi-

dent also determines the number of courts in the Maldives. Judges must be Muslims. The Sharia is the source for the administration of civil and criminal law and is interpreted by the courts.

Each inhabited island of the Maldives has a judge or magistrate. Serious cases are regularly referred to the capital, Male. Male has eight lower courts dealing with theft, debt, and property cases. There are approximately 200 general courts in the Maldives.

The High Court

The High Court hears appeals cases from lower courts and all such cases that the president assigns to it by regulation, especially politically sensitive cases. The High Court consists of the chief justice and a variable number of judges, at the discretion of the president.

THE ELECTION PROCESS

The constitution provides that all Maldivian citizens (who must be Muslims) of at least 21 years of age are allowed to vote in elections and public referendums. Candidates for the presidency must be at least 35 years old and must never have been convicted of an offense under Islamic or criminal law. Candidates for parliament must be at least 25 years old and may not have been convicted of offenses under Islamic or criminal law in the past five years. All candidates must be Muslims.

POLITICAL PARTIES

Until mid-2005 there were no organized political parties allowed in the Maldives. Candidates were running on the basis of personal qualifications and merit in each of the atolls. In the first significant action on the president's proposals for constitutional reform in the Maldives, parliament on June 2, 2005, unanimously supported a bill to allow the formation of political parties.

CITIZENSHIP

A citizen of the Republic of Maldives is one who had citizenship at the enactment of the 1998 constitution, or is a child born to a citizen of the Maldives, or is a foreigner who becomes a citizen in accordance with the law. As, according to Article 7, Islam is the state religion of the Maldives, the government interprets the provision to impose a requirement that citizens be Muslims.

FUNDAMENTAL RIGHTS

Chapter 2 of the constitution devotes its 19 articles to the fundamental rights and duties of the citizens. The constitution guarantees equality before the law, the inviolability of the private sphere, freedom of education and expression, property rights, a right to work and to a pension, as well as the freedom of assembly and association. The presumption of innocence in criminal matters is contained in the constitution. A Human Rights Commission was created in 2005 to support the protection of fundamental rights.

Impact and Functions of Fundamental Rights

Citizens owe loyalty to the state and to the constitution. Restrictions to fundamental rights stem from the strong position of the president and his ability to influence all offices in the Republic of Maldives.

Limitations to Fundamental Rights

Individual rights are restricted in areas that potentially conflict with Islamic law, namely, in the fields of education and freedom of expression. Freedom of belief is rendered impossible, as Islam is the state religion.

ECONOMY

The Maldives are among the poorest countries in the world. Economic activities focus on tourism and fishing.

The constitution does not provide for a specific economic system. Nominally, all land, sea, and natural resources are vested with the state, according to the constitution. However, the fundamental rights chapter contains provisions on the right to acquire and hold property, as well as the protection of property.

RELIGIOUS COMMUNITIES

As the constitution proclaims Islam to be the state religion, no other religious communities are recognized. Foreigners can practice their religion, if they do so privately. The president's role as supreme authority to propagate the tenets of Islam and the use of Islamic law in civil and criminal cases is evidence of the mingling of state and religion in the Maldives.

MILITARY DEFENSE AND STATE OF EMERGENCY

The constitution stipulates that the president is commander in chief. Since the Maldives have historically experienced few external threats, a military was never established. However, a National Security Service consisting of army, naval, and air forces was created in the early 1980s; it is composed of about 2,000 voluntary members.

The constitution provides for a state of emergency. The president can proclaim such a state for three months if the security of the Maldives is threatened by war, foreign aggression, or civil unrest. The president takes over all legislative power, and fundamental rights may be suspended for the time of emergency. If the period is to be extended, parliament must assent.

AMENDMENTS TO THE CONSTITUTION

The constitution can only be amended by a constitutional assembly (The People's Special Majlis). It consists of all members of the cabinet, members of parliament, an equal number of specially elected members from the atolls and the capital, as well as eight members appointed by the president.

The assembly decides on amendments of the constitution by simple majority. The president has the right to object but can be overridden by a two-thirds majority in the assembly.

PRIMARY SOURCES
Constitution in English. Available online. URL: http://www.presidencymaldives.gov.mv/publications/constitution.pdf. Accessed on February 2, 2006.
2005 Amendments proposed by the president. Available online. URL: http://www.presidencymaldives.gov.mv/publications/DemocracyHumanRightsReformAgenda.pdf. Accessed on June 21, 2006.

SECONDARY SOURCES
Library of Congress, "Country Studies—Maldives." Available online. URL: http://lcweb2.loc.gov/frd/cs/mvtoc.html. Accessed on September 26, 2005.

Oliver Windgätter

MALI

At-a-Glance

OFFICIAL NAME
Republic of Mali

CAPITAL
Bamako

POPULATION
12,291,529 (July 2005 est.)

SIZE
478,780 sq. mi, (1,240,036 sq. km)

LANGUAGES
French (official language), Bambare, spoken by 80% of the population

RELIGIONS
Muslim 90%, animist 6%, Christian 4%

NATIONAL OR ETHNIC COMPOSITION
Manding (Bambara or Bamana, Malinke) 52%, Fulani 11%, Saracolé 7%, Mianka 4%, Songhai 7%, Tuareg and Maur 5%, other 14%

DATE OF INDEPENDENCE OR CREATION
September 22, 1960

TYPE OF GOVERNMENT
Presidential democracy

TYPE OF STATE
Unitary state

TYPE OF LEGISLATURE
Unicameral parliament

DATE OF CONSTITUTION
January 12, 1992

DATE OF LAST AMENDMENT
No amendment

Despite being one of the poorest countries in the world, Mali has reached a respectable level of constitutional development. Some 10 years after the introduction of multiparty rule, the democratic process allowed a free and peaceful election of a second president. Democratic structures such as political parties and independent media are growing, and their rights are respected to a considerable extent—but not completely. Human rights are still threatened by the lack of full independence of the judiciary and excessive use of force by security forces.

CONSTITUTIONAL HISTORY

Sitting astride ancient trading routes, great kingdoms developed the first statelike structures in Africa within the territory today known as Mali, after the eighth century C.E. As an integral part of an international Arab-Muslim culture, society was richly developed in the 14th through 16th centuries. The arrival of the Europeans in the 15th century along the coastal shores of Africa dramatically changed the trading patterns in Africa and, together with the slave trade, severely disrupted the political organization of the area. The territory eventually became part of the French colonial empire as French Sudan in 1895. The French colonial power developed infrastructure, railroads, and agriculture in the arable portions of the Niger and Senegal River valleys.

French Sudan acquired independence in a federation with Senegal on June 20, 1960. The federation rapidly fell apart, and on September 22 of the same year, Mali was proclaimed a sovereign republic.

Under its first president, Modibo Keita, a Soviet-style political and economic system was introduced. After eight years in office, Keita was ousted in a military coup and replaced by a one-party system of military rule that lasted until 1991. With the arrival of the multiparty democracy movement to Africa, the then military ruler, Moussa

Traore, was deposed by his own forces after he ordered troops to shoot at demonstrators. A new constitution was framed in a national conference in 1991, and new institutions were elected in 1992. The current, second president of what is now called the Third Republic was a leader in the anti-Traore coup, who subsequently presided over the democratic transition process.

FORM AND IMPACT OF THE CONSTITUTION

Mali is one of the more successful African countries with regard to the introduction of multiparty democracy. While the elections of the National Assembly and the president of the republic in 1997 were characterized by grave administrative problems, and later by opposition boycotts, the election in 2002 went smoothly. It produced a peaceful handover of the office of the president, after the incumbent was barred from running for another term by constitutional provisions. The outgoing president, Alpha Oumar Konare, became chairman of the African Union.

During the 1997 electoral crisis, basic liberties were threatened by the excessive use of force by police. The judiciary did not provide adequate remedies for those ill treated. However, overall the constitution has contributed much to the dramatic change of Malian society toward pluralism and democracy.

BASIC ORGANIZATIONAL STRUCTURE

Mali is an indivisible republic and a unitary state. It is a presidential democracy based on the French model. The constitution provides for a certain amount of decentralization by giving responsibility to substate entities, in particular to municipalities. These decentralized entities are represented on the national level in a High Council for Decentralized Entities.

LEADING CONSTITUTIONAL PRINCIPLES

Modeled on the French example, Mali is a laicist (secular) social republic, one and indivisible. It is founded on the principles of democracy, the rule of law, and justice.

Mali's government is a presidential republic with separation of powers. The position of the president of the republic is strong. Unlike in the French model, the parliament, the National Assembly, is unicameral.

Fundamental rights are complemented by the affirmation of civic duties. The constitution allows for the transfer of sovereign powers to organizations of African unity.

CONSTITUTIONAL BODIES

The institutional provisions follow, to a great extent, the French model. The main constitutional bodies are the president of the republic, the cabinet, the National Assembly, the Constitutional Council, the High Court of Justice, the High Council for Decentralized Entities, and the Economic and Social Committee.

The President of the Republic

In Mali, the president is the most powerful figure under the constitution. He or she not only enjoys vast powers in the governmental process but is also the guardian of the constitution and of the integrity and the sovereignty of the nation. The president assures the continuity of the state.

The president is directly elected for five years and may be reelected only once. In order to be eligible, candidates must have Malian nationality. If no candidate wins more than 50 percent of the votes counted in a first round, the two best-placed candidates compete in a second, final round.

The president may not hold any other office. Specific provisions were included in the constitution to prevent improper enrichment.

The president is replaced by the prime minister in cases of temporary incapacity. In the event of vacancy or permanent incapacity the president is replaced by the president of the National Assembly.

The president appoints the prime minister and cabinet ministers and can demand the resignation of the prime minister at any time. The president also fills high posts in the civil administration and military.

The constitution allows the president to dissolve the National Assembly after consultation with the prime minister and the president of the National Assembly. The president may only dissolve the subsequent National Assembly one year after its election.

The Lawmaking Process

The National Assembly disposes of the power of lawmaking. The division between parliamentary lawmaking power and regulatory power of the executive branch of government is determined by a catalog in the constitution.

Laws may be initiated either by the cabinet or by members of parliament. They require a simple majority of votes in the National Assembly. Organizational laws, that is, those related to the functioning and the organization of the institutions of the republic, require a favorable vote of the majority of the members of the National Assembly. The constitution determines the areas to be regulated by organizational laws.

The Cabinet

The cabinet is composed by the prime minister and the cabinet ministers. It is appointed by the president and is responsible to the assembly. It directs the administration and security forces in the exercise of their functions. Some functions of the president of the republic can be delegated to the prime minister.

Membership in the cabinet is incompatible with holding of any other office in public and private institutions.

The cabinet has extensive regulatory power to issue ordinances.

The National Assembly

Deputies are elected by universal suffrage for four-year terms with the possibility of reelection. The constitution affirms the principle of representation of the whole nation, not of constituencies.

The size of the assembly is determined by organic law. It currently has 147 members. Parliamentary activity is limited to two biannual sessions with a maximum of 75 days. The constitution provides for parliamentary immunity of members.

The National Assembly has the power to make law. The division between parliamentary lawmaking power and the cabinet's regulatory power is determined by a catalog in the constitution. Laws may be initiated by either the cabinet or members of parliament.

Parliament has the usual means of controlling the executive. The National Assembly can challenge the authority of the cabinet by a motion of censure at the demand of one-tenth of its members.

The Constitutional Council

As in France, the control of constitutionality of laws and international treaties is assured by a Constitutional Council. The council is composed of nine members. The president of the republic, the president of the National Assembly, and the president of the Supreme Council of the Judiciary appoint three members each. The term of office is seven years with one possible renewal. Only lawyers who have at least 15 years of professional practice experience are eligible.

The council is responsible for determining the constitutionality of laws, especially new laws not yet in force, which may be presented to the council by the president of the republic, the prime minister, the president of the National Assembly, the president of the High Council for Decentralized Entities, the president of the Supreme Court, or one-tenth of the members of either the National Assembly or the High Council for Decentralized Entities. It also has the authority to resolve disputes among the different institutions of the republic and disputes over elections. The Constitutional Council also rules on the permanent incapacity of the president of the republic.

The High Court of Justice

The High Court of Justice is responsible for judging charges of high treason against the president of the republic and members of the cabinet. It is made up of deputies from the National Assembly. The charges are raised by the National Assembly by a vote of two-thirds of its members.

High Council for Decentralized Entities

The High Council for Decentralized Entities is responsible for all issues of local and regional development. It is part of an effort to promote local self-government and has to be seen within an as-yet-incomplete larger effort to restructure the organization of local municipalities. Members of the High Council have some rights of parliamentary immunity.

The cabinet must submit a draft law within 15 days after a request by the High Council on matters concerning improvement in the environment and the quality of life within the decentralized entities.

The Economic and Social Committee

The Economic and Social Committee is to be consulted about all economic, social, and budgetary issues. It is composed of representatives of labor organizations and of professional and employer associations.

The Judiciary

There is a single jurisdiction for civil, criminal, and administrative affairs. It is formally independent, and the independence of individual judges is constitutionally protected. The Supreme Court is at the apex of the judiciary. The judiciary has the task of ensuring respect for fundamental rights.

The president of the republic is the guarantor of the independence of the judiciary. The president chairs the Council of the Judiciary, which is responsible for all career-related questions within the judiciary and for its independence.

Judicial independence is still not sufficiently developed. The important role of the president in the selection of judges has led to the appearance of partiality in important judgments against opposition leaders; these cases have displayed a flagrant disregard of constitutional provisions and domestic law.

THE ELECTION PROCESS

Every Malian citizen at least 18 years of age may participate in elections, which are universal, direct, equal, and secret.

An Independent National Elections Commission, composed of members chosen by the cabinet, the majority and opposition parties in the National Assembly, and associations of civil society, watches over the procedures. Serious administrative difficulties plagued the organization of the first democratic elections for president and National Assembly under the new constitution in 1997. In reaction, the Constitutional Council annulled the National Assembly elections, and major parties boycotted the presidential elections.

The 2002 elections were also characterized by allegations of corruption, and voter turnout remained low. Once more, a quarter of the votes in the presidential election were ruled invalid by the Constitutional Council because of fraud and other irregularities.

Referenda can be held on any draft law or international agreement affecting the organization of state institutions.

POLITICAL PARTIES

Mali has become a multiparty system. Political parties are regulated by a law that prohibits parties that have only an ethnic, linguistic, or religious basis. Parties founded on programs aiming to destroy national territorial integrity or the republican form of government are also banned. Political parties benefit from financial aid from government revenue.

The right of a party to oppose the administration is explicitly recognized by law.

CITIZENSHIP

Citizenship is acquired by descent from a Malian parent regardless of the country of birth. Naturalization is possible after five years of residence and renunciation of former citizenship. Citizenship can be revoked within the first 10 years after naturalization on the grounds of criminal or other actions not in the interest of the country.

FUNDAMENTAL RIGHTS

Unlike its French model, the constitution includes a catalogue of rights and civic duties. Fundamental rights include those of the first and second generation (civil liberties and social rights) as well as rights of the third generation (rights to culture and a safe environment).

Impact and Functions of Fundamental Rights

The general human rights record is good. Still, excessive violence by the security forces puts basic liberties at risk. The constitution explicitly provides for the punishment of individuals and state agents who commit torture. Nonetheless, torture has been used, especially during the 1997 electoral crisis, when administration officials refused to recognize convincing reports on this issue.

Time limits on police detention are frequently disregarded. Female genital mutilation remains legal and is commonly practiced. Libel suits are a threat to one of Africa's most open presses, but independent newspapers and radio stations do exist, and even state-run radio and TV outlets present a diversity of views.

The judiciary has not provided sufficient protection and appears biased toward the executive. A Democratic Questioning Area is organized annually in which the executive submits itself to a one-day hearing on human rights violations. It is designed as a forum of mediation.

The death penalty, while not formally abolished, is never carried out.

Limitations to Fundamental Rights

Some of the fundamental rights guaranteed in the constitution can be limited or defined by law, such as freedom of the press or freedom of cultural activity.

ECONOMY

The constitution does not favor any economic system over another. Private property is protected and the liberty to join a labor organization is recognized.

RELIGIOUS COMMUNITIES

Although predominantly Muslim, Mali is a secular republic. Freedom of religion is assured. No one may be treated discriminatorily on the basis of his or her religious beliefs. A law that provides for the registration of religious communities is not applied.

MILITARY DEFENSE AND STATE OF EMERGENCY

The president of the republic is the commander in chief of the armed forces. The military submits to civil rule, and the armed forces are not political.

Declarations of war need parliamentary approval. In a state of emergency the president may take necessary measures, although the president may not dissolve the National Assembly once it is convened.

AMENDMENTS TO THE CONSTITUTION

Amendments to the constitution may be initiated by either the president or members of parliament. An amendment proposal needs a two-thirds majority in the National Assembly and approval in a popular referendum. Excluded from amendment are the republican form of government, the laicist (secular) character of the state, and political pluralism.

PRIMARY SOURCES
Constitution in English. Available online. URL: http://confinder.richmond.edu/admin/docs/Mali.pdf. Accessed on June 21, 2006.

SECONDARY SOURCES
United Nations, "Core Document Forming Part of the Reports of States Parties: Mali" (HRI/CORE/1/Add.87), 17 February 1998. Available online. URL: http://www.unhchr.ch/tbs/doc.nsf. Accessed on August 9, 2005.

Christof Heyns, ed., *Human Rights Law in Africa*. Vol. 2. Leiden: Martinus Nijhoff, 2004.

Malte Beyer

MALTA

At-a-Glance

OFFICIAL NAME
The Republic of Malta

CAPITAL
Valletta

POPULATION
400,214 (July 2006 est.)

SIZE
122 sq. mi. (316 sq. km)

LANGUAGES
Maltese (national language), Maltese and English (official)

RELIGION
Catholic

NATIONAL OR ETHNIC COMPOSITION
Maltese

DATE OF INDEPENDENCE OR CREATION
September 21, 1964

TYPE OF GOVERNMENT
Parliamentary democracy

TYPE OF STATE
Unitary state

TYPE OF LEGISLATURE
Unicameral parliament

DATE OF CONSTITUTION
September 21, 1964

DATE OF LAST AMENDMENT
Act V of 2003 amendment for accession to European Union; treaty signed April 16, 2003

Malta is an island republic with a long history of development within a small territory not far from the European and African landmasses. Though frequently occupied and used by major foreign powers, it has retained a separate identity while absorbing the influences of its occupiers. Its independence of spirit, as well as a long tradition of self-administration regardless of occupation, has produced a nation that is intensely participatory and democratic and has the usual features of a member state of the European Union and the Council of Europe.

CONSTITUTIONAL HISTORY

Malta has a long history and traces of an important prehistory in a number of Neolithic hypogea and temples. Malta and its neighboring island Gozo were Phoenician colonies, but became part of the Roman Empire after the Punic Wars (264–41 B.C.E. and 218–02 B.C.E.). The Christian faith was introduced to the island by Saint Paul, as attested to by the narrative in the Acts of the Apostles.

When the Roman Empire was divided, Malta was assigned to the Byzantine East. The Arabs conquered the Islands in 800 C.E. and the Normans under Count Roger of Hauteville reconquered them in 1090. Thereafter, Malta and Gozo shared the ups and downs of political life in Sicily, ruled by the Norman kings and their Swabian, Angevin, Aragonese, and Castilian successors in title. During most of the Middle Ages, the islands were governed internally by two Università chambers, one for each island, that were administered by elected *jurats*.

In 1530, Emperor Charles V granted Malta to the knights of Saint John, who were to respect the rights and privileges conceded by his forebears to the Maltese inhabitants. The order not only assumed the defense of the island, as was the intent of the grant, but also encroached on the government of the islands. The order did defend the island successfully during the Great Siege of 1565 and preserved the islands, with the concurring heroic resistance of the Maltese, from Ottoman attack. In 1798, the order was dissolved by Napoléon, then a general of the French Republic, who later became the French emperor.

By that time the order had effectively been, for almost 268 years, the government of an independent country. They provided Malta with codes of municipal law, with an administration, some social services, forts and fortifications, and urban centers complete with palaces and churches. A *collegium melitense* founded by the Jesuits in 1584 was made a state public university in 1775. Although the order's government was absolutist, there was considerable collegiality in its internal management. Most public officials were Maltese; the status of the knights as a religious order, subject to the authority of the pope, tempered the harsh tone of sovereignty.

When Napoléon Bonaparte, commanding a large fleet of 118 ships bound for Egypt, took over the islands, he tried in six momentous days in June 1798 to change the nation's structure completely. He disbanded the university and substituted a central technical school, and he centralized the administration, dividing the islands into two municipalities. He also abolished slavery and granted Jews and Muslims equal rights. However, the government he left behind also began to sell the churches' gold, silver, and precious objects; enforced a decree limiting each religious order to one monastery; and trampled on other well-established rights and customs.

The Maltese organized a rebellion and managed to regain possession of the islands, except for the capital, Valletta, and three port cities guarded by high fortifications. The Maltese insurgents asked for, and obtained, the assistance of the admiral Lord Nelson's British fleet and their Portuguese allies. Eventually, after a two-year siege maintained by the Maltese assisted by the British, the French capitulated.

The British entered to assist, but then took possession, supposedly at the request of the Maltese Congress of Representatives. The congress issued a Declaration of Rights in 1802, stating that Malta had not been acquired by conquest but by compact. It was sent to London to form the basis of the relationship between Britain and Malta; nevertheless, for most of the period of British rule Malta was treated as a crown colony, administered by a governor responsible to London.

Initially, the governor was not even assisted by a council. After several years of protest meetings, petitions, and incessant criticism of the colonial administration, the British imperial government conceded some degree of self-government in 1887, enacting the Mizzi-Strickland Constitution, which provided for an elected majority in the Council of Government and for elected representatives in the Executive Council. However, partial self-government proved short-lived. When the elected majority rejected the education budget, in opposition to the imperial government's policy of supplanting the Italian language with English in the schools, the constitution was amended in 1889 and the education budget was approved by the appointed councilors.

Decades of political agitation in favor of genuine self-government ensued. Between 1890 and 1919, elected councilors would routinely resign en masse, or alternatively, eccentric individuals would be elected in mockery of the constitution. During World War I (1914–18) one of the more prominent nationalist politicians was court-martialed for allegedly inciting Britain's Italian allies against Britain over the language issue.

In 1918, Filippo Sceberras, a public-spirited and respected physician, called upon all the voluntary societies of Malta to appoint two delegates to a national assembly to draft a new constitution, with the goal of a Maltese government responsible to an elected parliament. The social-economic situation in the country had deteriorated, with demobilization, unemployment, and high inflation, and in June 1919, riots broke out in Valletta. In response, the governor was replaced, and the bishop was asked to help restore calm. The new governor promised changes, and in the ensuing months the draft constitution was substantially approved by the British government.

The constitution functioned smoothly during the first two elected legislatures (1921–24, 1924–27), during which an administration was formed and supported by a majority formed of the moderate Nationalist and the Labour Party, the first all Nationalist and some dissident Labour members in the second. After 1927, however, the constitution was strained by conflicts between the pro-British Constitutional Party and the Catholic Church. It was suspended in 1930, restored in 1932, but suspended again in 1933 as a result of political problems, as the Nationalist government was suspected by Britain of harboring pro-Italian tendencies. In 1939 a new constitution was promulgated with a provision for a Council of Government with 10 elected members, but with substantially reduced powers and functions. In 1947, after World War II (1939–45), the self-governing constitution was restored, but with the former senate suppressed. In 1958 self-government was suspended, then reinstated in 1962.

In May 1964, a referendum approved an independence constitution drafted under the Nationalist prime minister Borg Olivier. With some minor amendments, it was approved by the British Parliament at Westminster and entered into force on September 21 that year. Malta retained the British monarch as head of state and was admitted as an independent member to the Commonwealth. Malta's constitution was amended, and the islands became a republic on December 13, 1974. Malta became a member of the European Union on May 1, 2004.

FORM AND IMPACT OF THE CONSTITUTION

Malta has a written constitution that prevails over all other laws. Laws that do not conform to the constitution can be declared unconstitutional by the constitutional and other courts; parliament is then called upon to abrogate or amend them, if need be, with other provisions.

BASIC ORGANIZATIONAL STRUCTURE

Malta is a unitary state. The 67 local councils, one for each city and sizable village, enjoy a considerable delegation of powers.

LEADING CONSTITUTIONAL PRINCIPLES

Article 1 of the constitution of Malta describes the country as (1) "a democratic republic founded on work and on respect for the fundamental rights and freedoms of the individual." Subarticle (3) further states that "Malta is a neutral state actively pursuing peace, security and social progress among all nations by adhering to a policy of non-alignment and refusing to participate in any military alliance."

The republic is a parliamentary democracy, and the principles and provisions of the constitution follow the pattern of the unwritten constitution of Great Britain and its conventions. The rule of law, the separation of powers, and the supremacy of parliament, within the bounds of a written constitution, provide the implicit and explicit premises of the constitutional regimen.

CONSTITUTIONAL BODIES

The organs of the state are the president; the House of Representatives, which has the exclusive power of legislation; the cabinet or administration, which is responsible to parliament for the good government of the country; the judiciary; and the Local Councils.

The President

The president of the republic is elected for five years by the parliament, cannot be reelected, and has, in general terms, the same powers as those of the monarch in Great Britain.

The president as head of state has primarily a representative function but can, on occasion, exercise a unifying role of moderation and appeal to fundamentals. A senior, experienced and highly respected political leader is usually elected as president, and although the prime minister is supposed to "advise" the president according to the letter of the constitution, in actuality, the president gives unpublicized advice to the prime minister.

The Parliament

According to the constitution, parliament consists of a single chamber of 65 members elected by proportional representation and by a single vote, together with the president. It has only one chamber: the House of Representatives.

The leader of the opposition holds an official position and is appointed by the president as the member who enjoys the confidence of the majority of opposition members. Cabinet ministers and parliamentary secretaries (junior ministers) have to be members of the house; cabinet ministers reply to members' questions at the beginning of each sitting.

Malta is a member of the British Commonwealth and inherits most of the traditions, procedures, and style of British political life. The country also acquired the ethos of the British civil service during the long colonial period (1800–1964), and the Maltese bureaucracy continues to follow these patterns.

An ombudsperson is elected by, and is responsible to, parliament but can directly address the administration as well. Though not binding, the report of the ombudsperson to parliament is made public and has considerable political impact. The auditor general is also chosen by and is responsible to parliament. The audit, which is concerned with finances as well as the efficiency of government, is given great weight by public opinion and at times hotly debated in parliament.

The Administration

The executive power is vested formally in the president but is exercised by the prime minister and the cabinet, who are collectively responsible to parliament. The prime minister is appointed by the president, who chooses the person who would have the trust of the majority of parliament, in practice the leader of the largest party in the house. The other ministers are designated by the prime minister after taking office and then appointed by the president. The president acts, in all matters, on the advice of the prime minister except in those cases specified by the constitution. These include the decision to dissolve parliament and hold new elections, the replacement of the prime minister when the prime minister no longer enjoys the trust of the majority of the house, and the choice of the leader of the opposition. It is the prime minister and the cabinet ministers who are subjected to criticism for all the acts of the executive.

There is no formal investiture of the prime minister and the cabinet through a vote of confidence in the House of Representatives. The appointment by the president confers on the prime minister and then the cabinet ministers all legal executive powers as soon as they take the oath or solemn affirmation of office. At the start of every legislative session, the president delivers to parliament from the throne a speech, which is handed to the president by the prime minister in open house and lists the measures and general policy line of the administration's program. A debate follows with a vote on the motion of reply to the speech. On the strength of the majority expressed on this motion, the house is deemed to have shown its confidence or lack of it.

The Lawmaking Process

Parliament is exclusively vested with the legislative power. Any member can introduce a draft bill, but in practice most legislation is proposed by the cabinet through its ministers. When a draft bill is proposed, it is put on the agenda for a first reading, after which it is distributed to the members. The debate on the second reading is limited to the principles that inspire the bill. A division (vote) is frequently called on the second reading, if the opposition does not agree with the bill in principle. If passed on second reading, the bill is referred either to the house sitting in committee or to one of the permanent committees. Any member can propose amendments in this stage, and bills are frequently amended.

The bill is then proposed for a final, third reading. In the case of bills that according to the constitution require a qualified majority, this majority is needed on the final, third reading. The bill as passed in the third reading is then sent by the clerk of parliament to the president for his or her assent.

The Judiciary

The judiciary is independent of the legislative and executive organs of government. While the executive appoints the judges and magistrates, the assignment of judges to the various courts follows the recommendations of the chief justice in consultation with the other members of the bench and countersigned by the minister of justice.

The Constitutional Court is formed through the automatic machinery ordained in the constitution and does not rely on the Ministry of Justice. Judges can be dismissed only by parliament, on impeachment by two-thirds of the members, at the recommendation of the Commission for the Administration of Justice. This commission is presided over by the president and includes cabinet members, judges, and other leading public figures.

THE ELECTION PROCESS AND POLITICAL PARTICIPATION

Elections to the House of Representatives are determined by proportional representation through the single transferable vote. Each of the 13 electoral divisions elects five deputies.

Malta has a very active civil society. During the long period of colonial rule, a panoply of social and cultural groups as well as labor, trade, patriotic, and political unions voiced the aspirations and grievances of the Maltese people. Even with the provision of more formal constitutional institutions, these societies have continued to contribute to the richness and diffusion of Maltese political and sociocultural discussion.

POLITICAL PARTIES

The period of self-rule that began in 1921 offered the opportunity for the development of the political system and of parliamentary conventions and customs. Notwithstanding the initial multiplicity of political parties, Malta has evolved into a substantially stable two-party system, with alteration in power between the parties. Since independence in 1964, the Nationalist (originally proindependence, now Christian Democrat) Party has been in power from 1964 to 1971, from 1987 to 1996, and from 1998 to date, and the Labour Party from 1971 to 1987 and from 1996 to 1998.

CITIZENSHIP

The acquisition, possession, and loss of Maltese citizenship are regulated by the constitution and a special citizenship law. Dual or multiple citizenship is permitted in accordance with law.

FUNDAMENTAL RIGHTS

The constitution guarantees the classical fundamental rights and freedoms of the individual such as the right to life, protection from arbitrary arrest or detention, freedom of expression, and freedom of movement. There is also protection from forced labor and inhuman treatment. Respect of private and family life is guaranteed. As general principles of government policy, the constitution also enumerates certain social rights such as the right to work and the equal right of men and women to enjoy all economic, social, cultural, civil, and political rights.

Impact and Functions of Fundamental Rights

Fundamental rights are well protected in Malta. If, in an individual case, state authorities infringe upon an individual's rights there are effective court remedies. Malta subscribed to the 1950 European Convention on Human Rights together with its Protocol with the right of individual petition to the Human Rights Court at Strasbourg.

Limitations to Fundamental Rights

The rights and freedoms guaranteed by the constitution are subject only to limitations designed to ensure that they do not prejudice the rights and freedoms of others or the public interest.

ECONOMY

The constitution does not explicitly decide on a specific economic system. However, Article 37 states that private property cannot be taken by force except on the basis of a law and for the payment of adequate compensation. The constitution also explicitly encourages private economic enterprise. Taking into account the social principles guaranteed by the constitution, such as the right to work, the economic system can be described as a social market economy.

RELIGIOUS COMMUNITIES

Malta enjoys constitutional guarantees of freedom of religion, belief, and opinion. Even though Malta is a predominantly Catholic country, there has been a tradition of religious tolerance, strengthened by long centuries of the existence of mostly smaller non-Catholic religious communities. There are Anglican churches, Methodist and Greek Orthodox chapels, Baptist churches, a mosque, and a synagogue. In the law courts, confirmation on oath according to one's belief can be substituted with a simple solemn affirmation. The crucifix as a traditional Catholic symbol is found in the parliamentary chamber, without any ostentation, as well as in hospitals and schools. Parents can, and a few do, ask that their children should not be made to attend religious classes in the state or private schools, and there is no direct or indirect pressure on the children to conform to any kind of religious practice. Article 2 of the constitution states, "The religion of Malta is the Roman Catholic Apostolic Religion."

MILITARY AND STATE OF EMERGENCY

The military in Malta is always subject to the civil government. The president can proclaim a period of public emergency if Malta is engaged in war or faces exceptional circumstances. The House of Representatives then decides on the continuance of that period of emergency.

AMENDMENTS TO THE CONSTITUTION

Bills to amend the constitution need to be supported by the votes of a majority of all the members of the House of Representatives. Certain amendments, such as those concerning the basic principles contained in Article 1, require a majority of two-thirds of all the members of the house. Furthermore, a referendum is required in certain cases, such as a change in the ordinary term of parliament.

PRIMARY SOURCES

Constitution in English. Available online. URL: http://docs.justice.gov.mt/lom/legislation/english/leg/vol_1/chapt0.pdf. Accessed on September 9, 2005.
Constitution in Maltese. Available online. URL: http://www.constitution.org/cons/malta/kap0.pdf. Accessed on September 10, 2005.

SECONDARY SOURCES

"The Constitution of Malta." *The Malta Government Gazette,* September 18, 1964.
Consuelo Pilar Herrera, "A Historical Development of Constitutional Law in Malta, 1921–1988." Ph.D. University of Malta, 1988.
The Malta Independence Order 1964. London: H.M.S.O., 1964.
Joseph M. Pirotta, *Fortress Colony: The Final Act 1945–64.* Malta: Studia Editions, 1987.

Ugo Mifsud Bonnici

MARSHALL ISLANDS

At-a-Glance

OFFICIAL NAME
Republic of the Marshall Islands

CAPITAL
Majuro

POPULATION
59,788 (2004 est.)

SIZE
Land area 70 sq. mi. (181 sq. km) Ocean 301,160 sq. mi. (780,000 sq. km)

LANGUAGES
English and Marshallese (both official), two other Marshallese dialects, Japanese

RELIGIONS
Christian (mainly Protestant), Bahá'í

NATIONAL OR ETHNIC COMPOSITION
Micronesian

DATE OF INDEPENDENCE OR CREATION
October 21, 1986 (from United States–administered United Nations trusteeship)

TYPE OF GOVERNMENT
Parliamentary democracy

TYPE OF STATE
Unitary state

TYPE OF LEGISLATURE
Unicameral parliament

DATE OF CONSTITUTION
May 1, 1979

DATE OF LAST AMENDMENT
No amendment

The Marshall Islands is a unitary state with a republican and parliamentary democratic form of government. It is based on the rule of law and a clear separation between the judicial branch of the state and the executive and legislative branches.

The written constitution of the country contains provisions protecting fundamental rights and freedoms that are enforceable by the courts. The Marshall Islands has entered into a Compact of Free Association with the United States and has been host to the U.S. Army base on Kwajelein atoll since 1964.

CONSTITUTIONAL HISTORY

The two archipelagic chains of atolls that are now known as the Marshall Islands first attracted the attention of Europeans when Spanish explorers were groping their way across the Pacific Ocean in the early 16th century, and they were claimed by Spain. Later the islands were called the Marshall Islands after a British sea captain who sighted and named a number of them on his voyages from Botany Bay in Australia to China. In the mid-19th century, American missionaries were sent to the islands. About the same time, several large German trading companies set up stations for coconut products in some of the islands. The Spanish claim to ownership of the islands was contested by Germany, and in 1885 the pope, to whom the dispute had been referred, held that Spain was entitled to exert its sovereignty, but Germany was entitled to continue to occupy the islands for trading purposes.

The following year Germany annexed the islands outright and held them until defeated in World War I (1914–18). The islands then were placed by the League of Nations as a mandate under the administration of Japan. After World War II (1939–45), the islands were included in the Trust Territory of the Pacific Islands, which was placed by the United Nations under the administration of the United States.

In 1967, negotiations for future independence of the Trust Territories began with the United States. In 1979, Marshall Islands promulgated its own constitution. In 1982, it signed a Compact of Free Association with the United States, which was approved by the United States Congress in 1985. The following year, 1986, Marshall Islands was recognized as a separate independent state by the United States. It was not, however, until 1990 that the United Nations formally dissolved the Trust Territories, and Marshall Islands was recognized internationally as an independent country.

The legal system of Marshall Islands includes not only the constitution, which is the supreme law, but also provisions of the Trust Territory code applicable to Marshall Islands. It furthermore includes legislation and executive instruments, originating both before the 1979 constitution and since that date. It also includes treaties that have been ratified by the legislature, including in particular the Compact of Free Association. American common law, which was stated by the Trust Territory Code to be part of the law of the Trust Territory, has been carried forward by the constitution of the Marshall Islands as part of the existing law of the country. This is subject to the terms of the constitution and any legislation enacted by the legislature. Customary law relating to land tenure is preserved by the constitution, and the legislature is authorized to recognize the customary law in any part of Marshall Islands.

FORM AND IMPACT OF THE CONSTITUTION

The constitution of Marshall Islands, which took effect on May 1, 1979, is one of the few constitutions of a former dependent country in the Pacific that do not adopt the constitutional system of the former controlling country. Instead of establishing an executive president elected by the people, as in the United States, the constitution of Marshall Islands establishes a parliamentary executive along the lines adopted in England.

The constitution is expressly stated to be the supreme law of the country, and any law that is inconsistent with it is void to the extent of the inconsistency. Furthermore, any action taken by any person or body that is inconsistent with the constitution is, to the extent of the inconsistency, unlawful.

BASIC ORGANIZATIONAL STRUCTURE

Marshall Islands is a unitary state. There are some 33 municipalities or local government bodies, but the national legislature and executive established by the constitution have power to exercise control over these.

LEADING CONSTITUTIONAL PRINCIPLES

Marshall Islands is a republic based upon a national parliamentary democracy. The legislature is elected by popular vote.

The executive is drawn from, and ultimately controllable by, the legislature. The administration of government is carried out by a politically neutral public service appointed by, and disciplined by, a politically neutral Public Service Commission. The head of the executive, the president, is also the head of state.

The judicial power is vested in courts that are required to be independent of the executive and the legislature, and the judiciary is appointed by, and disciplined by, a politically neutral Judicial Service Commission. A Traditional Rights Court is authorized to give opinions on matters of titles or land rights or other matters that depend wholly or partly upon custom, but those opinions are not binding.

Fundamental human rights are spelled out in some detail in the constitution and can be enforced by the courts.

CONSTITUTIONAL BODIES

The predominant constitutional bodies are the parliament, called Nitijela, the president, the Council of Chiefs, and the judiciary.

The Legislative

The unicameral legislature, called Nitijela, a Marshallese word that means "council of wise or powerful people," consists of 33 members elected by popular vote from 24 constituencies. Elections for the Nitijela are held every four years.

The President

The president, who is the head of the executive, as well as head of state, is elected by the members of the Nitijela from among their number at the first meeting of the Nitijela after a general election. The president then nominates six to 10 members of the Nitijela to form the cabinet, which is chaired by the president. The cabinet is responsible to the Nitijela, and four or more members of the Nitijela may at any time move a motion of no confidence in the cabinet. If this is carried by a majority of the total membership of the Nitijela, the president is deemed to have resigned along with the other members of the cabinet.

The Council of Chiefs

The Council of Iroij, or council of paramount chiefs, consists of 12 paramount chiefs drawn from 12 districts who hold office for one year. In those districts where there is more than one paramount chief, the paramount chief who is to be the member of the council is either selected by his or her peers or, if there is no agreement, appointed by the Nitijela.

The Lawmaking Process

The council receives copies of all bills approved by the Nitijela, and if in its view the bill relates to customary law, traditional practice or land tenure, or a related matter, it can request that the bill be reconsidered by the Nitijela. The approval of the council is not, however, required for any bill.

The Judiciary

The judicial power of Marshall Islands is stated by the constitution to be vested in the Supreme Court, the High Court, a Traditional Rights Court, and such District Courts, Community Courts, and other subordinate courts as are established by law. The High Court is established as the principal court with general jurisdiction at first instance with regard to criminal offenses and civil claims. It enjoys powers of judicial review over decisions of government agencies, and appellate jurisdiction to hear appeals from decisions of subordinate courts as is provided by legislation. Decisions by the High Court about the interpretation of the constitution are required to be made by a bench of three judges. Appeals from the High Court are heard by the Supreme Court, which is the final court in Marshall Islands.

The Judiciary Act enacted by the Nitijela has established a District Court that has minor civil and criminal jurisdiction and a Community Court with very minor civil and criminal jurisdiction in each local government area.

The Traditional Rights Court established by the constitution is authorized to express opinions on questions relating to titles or land rights or to other interests that depend partly or wholly on customary law referred to it by a court. The opinions of this court are to be given substantial weight by the court that consulted it, but they are not binding on that court. The court's members consist of panels of three or more judges who are representative of all classes of land rights as determined by the High Court.

THE ELECTION PROCESS

Persons over the age of 18 years, unless certified insane or serving a prison sentence, are entitled to vote in the constituency in which they reside or have land rights. There are 24 constituencies, most with one member each, but the five more populous constituencies provide more than one member. In these constituencies each voter is able to cast a vote for as many candidates as there are seats to be filled. The candidates who receive the greatest number of votes are elected even if they do not have an absolute majority. Persons over the age of 21 years who are entitled to vote are entitled to stand for election.

POLITICAL PARTIES

There are no legal restrictions on the existence of political parties. As in many Pacific countries, political parties did not form initially, but in more recent years political groupings have tended to emerge, particularly the United Democratic Party.

CITIZENSHIP

Persons who were citizens of the Trust Territory when the constitution went into effect in 1979 automatically became citizens of Marshall Islands if they or their parents had land rights in the country. Persons born after the constitution took effect are automatically citizens if at the time of their birth one of their parents is a citizen or they are born in the Marshall Islands and not entitled to citizenship of any other country.

Persons are also entitled to be registered as citizens upon application to the High Court. Citizenship is granted if the court is satisfied that they have land rights or they have been resident within the country for not less than three years and have a child who is a citizen. Persons can also become citizens if they are of Marshallese descent and it is in the interests of justice that they be granted citizenship.

Citizenship may be acquired by naturalization by persons who have been resident in the country for five years, are of good character, are able to speak Marshallese, have an understanding and respect for the customs and traditions of the country, have the means to support themselves, and are not citizens of another country.

FUNDAMENTAL RIGHTS

The constitution recognizes the normal civic rights to liberty and due process, and to freedom from cruel and unusual punishment, from compulsory search and seizure, from seizure of property without compensation, and from discrimination. Freedoms of thought, speech, press, religion, assembly, association, and petition are also recognized.

In addition, the constitution recognizes the right of every person to access to the judicial and electoral processes; to health care, education, and legal services; to ethical and responsible government; and to freedom from quartering of soldiers, imprisonment for debt, conscription, and interference with personal privacy. The constitution expressly states that the enumeration of rights and freedoms in the constitution does not deny or disparage other rights and freedoms that are not so enumerated.

ECONOMY

The constitution recognizes the customary land rights of chiefs in Article 10(1), notwithstanding the fundamental rights recognized in Article 2, and it specifically empowers the Traditional Rights Court to give opinions as to land rights, which opinions are to be given "substantial weight" by any court that has sought its opinion.

Agriculture is basically subsistence, and there is only a limited amount of small-scale industry. Tourism provides some contribution to the national economy, but the largest contribution is from the United States government under the terms of the Compact of Free Association. It is estimated that over $1 billion U.S. in aid has been provided since 1986.

RELIGIOUS COMMUNITIES

The constitution recognizes freedom of belief and religion but allows for government funding of religious institutions to reimburse them for the costs of providing educational, medical, or other services, provided that there is no favoring of one religious group or belief over another. The main religious bodies are Christian, mainly Protestant churches, but in recent years there has been an increase in Bahá'í groupings.

MILITARY DEFENSE AND STATE OF EMERGENCY

Marshall Islands has a police force, but no army. Defense of the country is the responsibility of the United States under the terms of the Compact of Free Association with the United States.

AMENDMENTS TO THE CONSTITUTION

Many of the provisions of the constitution can be amended by a two-thirds majority of the members of the Nitijela, followed by endorsement by a majority of qualified voters at a referendum. Crucial provisions of the constitution, however, can be amended only by proposals submitted to a referendum by a constitutional convention. A convention can be called by the Nitijela on its own initiative or upon the request of at least 25 percent of the voters. In those cases, the amendment must be approved by a two-thirds majority of voters at that referendum.

PRIMARY SOURCES
Constitution in English. Available online. URL: http://www.paclii.org/mh/legis/consul_act/cotmi363/. Accessed on June 21, 2006.

SECONDARY SOURCES
Jean G. Zorn, "The Republic of the Marshall Islands." In *South Pacific Island Legal Systems,* edited by Michael A. Ntumy. Honolulu: University of Hawaii Press, (1993): 100.

Don Paterson

MAURITANIA

At-a-Glance

OFFICIAL NAME
Islamic Republic of Mauritania

CAPITAL
Nouakchott

POPULATION
3,086,859 (July 2005)

SIZE
397,955 sq. mi. (1,030,700 sq. km)

LANGUAGES
Arabic (official), Poular, Soninke, French, Hassaniya, Wolof

RELIGION
Islam (Sunni) 99%, other 1%

NATIONAL OR ETHNIC COMPOSITION
Moor (black) 33%, Moor (white) 33%, other (Tukulor, Fulani, Soninke, Wolof) 33%

DATE OF INDEPENDENCE OR CREATION
November 28, 1960

TYPE OF GOVERNMENT
Republic

TYPE OF STATE
Unitary state

TYPE OF LEGISLATURE
Bicameral parliament

DATE OF CONSTITUTION
July 11, 1991

DATE OF LAST AMENDMENT
June 25, 2006

The Islamic Republic of Mauritania is a unitary state with a strong presidency. The country is governed centrally from the capital; municipalities have elected councils. The executive is by far the strongest power in the constitutional framework.

The constitution states that Islam is the religion of the state and of its citizens. It is the main factor in uniting the country, which has a very diverse population. In the past, tensions existed among Arabs, black Africans, and Berbers, but they have diminished in recent years.

The constitution establishes three branches of government: an executive, a legislative, and an independent judiciary. The legislative branch is rather weak in comparison with the presidential powers, as is the judiciary. The constitution contains a number of fundamental rights, which, however, can be limited by ordinary laws.

CONSTITUTIONAL HISTORY

The area of what is now Mauritania was settled by Berber tribes in the first millennium B.C.E. Migration from north-ern to southern regions led to the displacement first of native black tribes and then of the Berber tribes by Arabs. The region formed the center of the first of the centralized black kingdoms in western Africa, the Ghana Empire (700–1200 C.E.), and was part of subsequent African empires.

European settlements began around 1440, when the Portuguese established an outpost on Mauritanian shores. The French opened trading posts in 1659; by the early 19th century they had gained control over the region, and they had established colonies by the mid-19th century. They governed Mauritania from Senegal. In 1903, Mauritania became a protectorate of the French, and in 1920, it was declared a separate colony in French West Africa.

After World War II (1939–45), in which the African colonies participated, a continentwide struggle for independence developed that finally led to Mauritania's independence from France in 1960. A constitution enacted in 1961 resembled the constitution of the Fifth French Republic. The country was under one-party rule as early as 1965. Civil unrest and ethnic tensions followed, further aggravated by droughts that lasted from 1969 to 1974.

In 1975, Spain bequeathed its colonial territory of Western Sahara jointly to Morocco and Mauritania, with Mauritania receiving the southern third of the territory. Morocco had only relinquished its claims to Mauritanian territory in 1969, and tensions had arisen immediately. Moroccan guerrilla troops attacked the Mauritanian occupying forces in Western Sahara and a war ensued. A military coup toppled the Mauritanian government in 1978. In 1979, Mauritania relinquished its claims to Western Sahara and ended its engagement in the region.

Military governments ruled the country and abolished the 1961 constitution. After another military coup in 1984, Colonel Maouiya Ould Sidi Ahmed Taya gained power, and a Constitutional Charter was enacted in 1985.

Taya undertook modest steps toward democracy, although retaining a strong presidency. In 1991, he introduced a new constitution. General elections were held, and the transition to slightly more democratic structures took place peacefully, although conditions never completely settled.

On August 3, 2005, a military coup ousted President Taya, and a Military Council for Justice and Democracy under the guidance of Colonel Ely Ould Mohamed Vall was established. On August 6, 2005, the council published a Constitutional Charter suspending parts of the existing constitution. Parliament was dissolved, and the council as well as the military forces took over legislative and executive powers. The courts continued their duties. A constitutional referendum was scheduled for June 24, 2006. It took place on June 25, 2006, and was supported by virtually all political parties now registered in Mauritania. With a 97 percent approval rate, the referendum reestablishes the constitution of 1991, but significantly reduces the president's role. According to Article 4 of the Constitutional Law, the amendments will enter into force at the end of the transitional period, which the Constitutional Charter of August 6, 2005, limits to a maximum of two years. The preamble, all articles on Islam, and individual and collective liberties and rights are sustained.

FORM AND IMPACT OF THE CONSTITUTION

The Islamic Republic of Mauritania has a written constitution in a single document. The constitution is the supreme law of the country.

BASIC ORGANIZATIONAL STRUCTURE

Mauritania is divided into 13 regions, including the capital district, which form the judicial and administrative units of the state. However, the government is still rather centralized. The government aims to further decentralization of the country, and laws on decentralization exist;

however, in many areas the division of responsibilities between the central government and local government has not been clarified. Since 1990, municipal elections have strengthened the position of the lower entities.

LEADING CONSTITUTIONAL PRINCIPLES

Article 1 of the constitution establishes Mauritania as a social Islamic republic, and Article 5 proclaims Islam as the religion of the state and the citizens. Because of Mauritania's ethnic diversity, it is a common faith rather than a cohesive national identity that unites the country. Islamic law was introduced in 1980, and in accordance with the provisions in the constitution, it plays a major part in civil and criminal matters. Islamic courts exist beside Western-style law courts.

The balance of power of the three branches is tilted toward the presidency. The constitution guarantees the judiciary's independence, but the president, the strongest political factor in Mauritania's constitutional framework, is its guarantor. The judiciary therefore is subject to pressure from the executive branch.

The Islamic Republic of Mauritania is a democratic republic, with regular elections of president, both chambers of parliament, and municipal councils.

CONSTITUTIONAL BODIES

The constitution provides for a president; a prime minister and council of ministers; a bicameral Parliament, composed of a National Assembly and a Senate; a judiciary; a Constitutional Council; and an advisory body called the High Islamic Council.

The President

The presidency is the strongest constitutional institution in Mauritania. The president is head of state, head of the executive branch, and commander in chief. The president is the guardian of the constitution. All executive power is vested in the president. The president also represents the country in dealings with foreign governments and ratifies international treaties.

According to the constitutional amendment of June 25, 2006, the president is elected every five years by universal suffrage and can stand for one single reelection. Candidates must be born Mauritanians of 40 years up to a maximum of 75 years of age. The limitations pertaining to age and number of reelections, according to the new Article 99, cannot be altered.

The president appoints and dismisses the prime minister and the cabinet ministers, and he or she may delegate presidential powers to them. The president has statutory powers and can dissolve the National Assembly at his or her discretion. The president appoints civil servants and military personnel. On any question of national importance, the president can ask for a referendum.

Until the end of the transitional period in 2007, presidential duties and rights are exercised by the president of the Military Council for Justice and Democracy as well as the council itself. Presidential elections and, with them, the end of the transitional period have been scheduled for March 11, 2007.

The Prime Minister and the Council of Ministers

The prime minister and the council of ministers are appointed by the president and are responsible to the president and the National Assembly.

The prime minister defines the policy of the executive administration only by authority of the president. The council of ministers implements this policy. The National Assembly can force the prime minister to resign by a vote of censure or no confidence.

The office of prime minister continues to exist in the new system of the Constitutional Charter.

Parliament

Mauritania has a bicameral parliament. The two chambers sit in two sessions per year, each session limited to a maximum of two months. The short sessions strengthen the executive power by limiting the direct possibility of checks and balances. Extraordinary sessions may be held for specific reasons at the request of 50 percent of the members or of the president. Extraordinary sessions may not exceed one month.

The two chambers share legislative power and do not differ in political importance. In exceptional cases, Parliament can authorize the executive government to issue ordinances in areas that are nominally restricted to formal laws.

Both chambers of Parliament have been dissolved in the wake of the military coup of August 3, 2005. Its powers are exercised by the Military Power for Justice and Democracy.

National Assembly

The National Assembly consists of 81 members who serve for a five-year term, elected by direct suffrage. The National Assembly has the right to take a vote of no confidence in the prime minister and force the prime minister to resign.

Senate

The Senate consists of 56 senators. Its members are elected by indirect suffrage; that is, they are nominated by municipal councils. They represent the districts of Mauritania as well as Mauritanians living abroad. The term of office is six years; one-third of the members are renewed every two years.

The Lawmaking Process

Bills can be introduced in either chamber of Parliament by members themselves or by the executive administration. Finance bills must be submitted to the National Assembly first. After bills are accepted in both houses, the president can propose amendments to the National Assembly, which can accept them by simple majority.

The Judiciary

According to the constitution, the judiciary is an independent branch of government; in reality, the central executive government interferes heavily with judicial proceedings. The highest court in the country is the Supreme Court, which has jurisdiction in appeals and administrative matters. The main source of law is the Sharia; only in commercial and some criminal matters does a Western-style legal code apply.

The judiciary so far has not been affected by the military coup.

Constitutional Council

The Constitutional Council is a central institution in Mauritanian constitutional law. It reviews every law as to its constitutionality before its promulgation. If the council declares a law to be unconstitutional, it cannot enter into force. Additionally, the Constitutional Council evaluates the legality of presidential elections and referenda. The council's decisions cannot be appealed.

Three of the council's six members are appointed by the president, two by the president of the National Assembly, and one by the president of the Senate. The president of the republic also appoints the head of the council. The term for members is nine years and is nonrenewable. One-third of the council is replaced every three years. The minimal age is 35, and members must not belong to the leadership of a political party.

The Constitutional Council continues its functions under the new leadership advising the Military Council on Justice and Democracy.

High Islamic Council

The High Islamic Council is an advisory body to the president and is composed of five members appointed by the president. It issues opinions in all matters that the president refers to it.

The High Islamic Council is not affected by the military coup.

THE ELECTION PROCESS

The constitution provides that all Mauritanians at least 18 years of age are allowed to vote in elections and public referenda. Candidates for the presidency have to be born Mauritanians, 40 years of age or above. Candidates for the National Assembly must be 25 years of age or above. Candidates for the Senate must be at least 35 years old. Since 1992, more candidates have competed in elections, and safeguards against fraud and manipulation were introduced in 2001.

POLITICAL PARTIES

Under military rule, political parties were banned, and only with the new constitution of 1991 were they legalized. The constitution provides for a pluralistic party system, which can be abolished only by a constitutional revision. Since the Military Council for Democracy and Justice took over in 2005, the number of political parties has increased. Under the old rule, the political scene was dominated by the presidential party, which occupied almost every seat in parliament. Political opposition parties claimed irregularities in every election. It will have to be seen what the parliamentary elections of 2006 and 2007 and the presidential election in 2007 will bring.

CITIZENSHIP

The constitution does not contain any provisions regarding citizenship. Mauritanian citizenship is acquired mainly by birth to a Mauritanian parent. Noncitizens can apply for citizenship after five years of residence in Mauritania. Dual citizenship is recognized only in very few cases, mainly if a Mauritanian female marries a noncitizen and has to assume his citizenship. In that case she can retain her Mauritanian citizenship as well.

FUNDAMENTAL RIGHTS

Article 10 of the constitution is the most important to fundamental rights. It names the following as citizen rights: freedom of movement and settlement; freedom of thought, opinion, and expression; freedom of assembly and association; and freedom of the arts and sciences. Citizens can participate in political parties, and the presumption of innocence in criminal matters forms part of the constitution. The right to strike is guaranteed.

The Constitutional Charter upholds the fundamental rights of the constitution.

Impact and Functions of Fundamental Rights

The citizens are obliged to fulfill their duties to the welfare of the state and must protect the country. In practice, fundamental rights are restricted in many areas by the strong position of the executive and the rather weak judicial system.

Limitations to Fundamental Rights

All fundamental rights can be restricted by laws or provisions in the constitution itself. The human rights record of the Mauritanian government remains weak; fundamental rights abuses are reported continuously. The principles of Islam interfere with fundamental rights in many aspects, inhibiting especially the freedom of the press.

ECONOMY

Mauritania has a market-driven economy, and its constitution protects private property. The economy is focused on iron mining and agriculture. Mauritania ranks among the poorest countries in the world with a per capita income of $340 per year.

RELIGIOUS COMMUNITIES

A full 99 percent of the population are Muslims. Islam is the state religion. Other religions are tolerated, and non-Muslim citizens, as well as non-Muslim expatriates, can practice their faith freely and openly. Religious groups are not registered with the government. Religious groups, along with nongovernmental organizations, are not subject to taxation. Under a 2003 law, the use of mosques for political purposes is prohibited.

MILITARY DEFENSE AND STATE OF EMERGENCY

The constitution stipulates the president as commander in chief. Two-year military service is obligatory for every male at the age of 18. The military consists of army, navy, and air force, as well as police forces and the presidential guard. Several attempts at military coups since 1992 have been suppressed.

The president may declare a state of emergency or martial law by presidential decree for a maximum of 30 days without specified reasons. Parliament can change this duration in regular session.

AMENDMENTS TO THE CONSTITUTION

There are two ways to amend the constitution. By initiative of the president or one third of the members of one chamber of Parliament, the constitution can be amended through a simple majority vote in a referendum. Prior to the referendum, the National Assembly and the Senate must each vote in favor of the bill with a two-thirds majority.

Another way to amend the constitution is the presentation of the bill to Parliament convened jointly as "Congress." Then, a three-fifths majority in Congress is necessary for the amendment without the need for a referendum.

The president has discretion on which method of amendment to follow.

PRIMARY SOURCES

Mauritanian constitution in English. Available online. URL: http://www.oefre.unibe.ch/law/icl/mr00000_.html. Accessed on August 30, 2005.

Mauritanian Constitution in French original. Available online. URL: http://droit.francophonie.org/doc/html/mr/con/fr/1991/1991dfmrcofr1.html. Accessed on June 21, 2006.

Constitutional Charter of August 6, 2005, in French original. Available online. URL: http://www.mauritania-today.com/francais/news131.htm. Accessed on August 31, 2005.

Amendments to the constitution through the constitutional referendum of June 25, 2006, in French original. Available online. URL: http://www.un.mr/revuepresse/avril06/semaine4/HOR%204209_Projet%20de%20la%20loi%20constitutionnelle%20190406.pdf. Accessed on June 27, 2006.

SECONDARY SOURCES

Library of Congress, "Country Studies—Mauritania." Available online. URL: http://lcweb2.loc.gov/frd/cs/mrtoc.html. Accessed on August 27, 2005.

Anthony G. Pazzanita, "The Origins and Evolution of Mauritania's Second Republic." *Journal of Modern African Studies* 34, no. 4 (1996): 575–596.

University of Bordeaux, Department of Political Sciences, *Institutional Situation—Mauritania.* Available online. URL: http://www.etat.sciencespobordeaux.fr/_anglais/institutionnel/mauritania.html. Accessed on September 28, 2005.

Oliver Windgätter

MAURITIUS

At-a-Glance

OFFICIAL NAME
Republic of Mauritius

CAPITAL
Port Louis

POPULATION
1,240,827 (July 2006 est.)

SIZE
788 sq. mi. (2,040 sq. km)

LANGUAGES
English (language of administration), French (language of business), Creole and Asian languages (Bhojpuri, Hindi, Urdu, Tamil, Hakka, and Mandarin)

RELIGIONS
Hindu 49.6%, Catholic 29.9%, Muslim 16.6%, Buddhist 0.7%, Protestant 0.3%, other 2.9%

NATIONAL OR ETHNIC COMPOSITION
Indo-Mauritian 68%, Creole 27%, Sino-Mauritian 3%, Franco-Mauritian 2%

DATE OF INDEPENDENCE OR CREATION
March 12, 1968

TYPE OF GOVERNMENT
Parliamentary democracy

TYPE OF STATE
Unitary state

TYPE OF LEGISLATURE
Unicameral parliament

DATE OF CONSTITUTION
March 12, 1968

DATE OF LAST AMENDMENT
August 15, 2003

Mauritius, found just below the equator in the middle of the Indian Ocean off the coast of Madagascar, is a parliamentary democracy with an impressively elaborate written constitution modeled on the British or Westminster system of government. A unitary state administered from Port Louis, the chief city of the main island of Mauritius, it encompasses other smaller islands of varying sizes and population: Rodrigues, Agalega, Tromelin, Cargados Carajos, and Chagos Archipelago, including Diego Garcia. Its constitution formally guarantees the fundamental freedoms and liberties of the citizen similar to those found in the European Charter of Human Rights. It became a republic in 1992.

CONSTITUTIONAL HISTORY

The island was discovered in the middle of the 16th century by Arab traders. However, it was first occupied by the Dutch, who named it after Prince Maurice de Nassau. The Dutch used it as a convenient stop and for exploitation of timber for two short periods: 1638–58 and 1664–1710.

The French took over from 1715 to 1810, when it was captured by the British. Mauritius attained independence from British rule on March 12, 1968.

FORM AND IMPACT OF THE CONSTITUTION

Mauritius boasts a third-generation constitution in that it states explicitly all the principles, powers, and responsibilities of government. The charter takes precedence over all other laws. International law is not directly applicable. Any legal obligation taken at international level by the executive needs to be incorporated in national legislation to become the law of the land.

BASIC ORGANIZATIONAL STRUCTURE

Unlike in the British system, the parliament of Mauritius is unicameral. Rodrigues alone among the islands that make up the country has its own local legislature, the Regional Assembly. It differs considerably in geographical area, population size, and economic strength from the others. The powers and responsibilities of its legislature are specified in the Rodrigues Regional Assembly Act 2002 and are limited to the island's own administration.

LEADING CONSTITUTIONAL PRINCIPLES

The following leading constitutional principles are enshrined in the Mauritian Charter and influence the growth of its parliamentary democracy: (1) a sharp division of powers among the executive, the legislature, and the judiciary; (2) adherence to the rule of law; (3) guarantee of constitutional protections to citizens as regards their fundamental freedoms and liberties; (4) the periodic holding of free and fair elections; and (5) a multiparty system. The civil service is by tradition and convention politically neutral. Because the constitution is secular, government is also religion-neutral.

As regards foreign affairs, Mauritius adopts a policy of openness and takes an active part in world and regional politics. It is a member of the Commonwealth of Nations. Regionally, it plays a leading role in African integration through such organizations as the South African Development Community, the New Economic Program for African Development, and the African Union.

CONSTITUTIONAL BODIES

The predominant constitutional figures are the president, the prime minister, the deputy prime minister, and the cabinet ministers. These figures decide policy. The chief justice, the judges, and the magistrates represent the judicial authority, by interpreting and administering the law. The National Assembly is the legislative body and representative organ of the people, which enacts the nation's laws. There is also an ombudsperson, the parliamentary commissioner to whom complaints may be made by a citizen aggrieved by maladministration.

The President

Executive authority is vested in the president. The president appoints the prime minister and may remove the prime minister from office. The prime minister is the political head presiding over the cabinet and also the leader in the National Assembly.

The president is appointed by the National Assembly for a term of five years. There is no restriction as to the number of terms a president may serve.

Cabinet Government

The cabinet is the political nerve center of government affairs. It comprises the prime minister and the ministers. The powers of the prime minister largely derive from his or her role as the dominant figure in the National Assembly.

The National Assembly

The National Assembly is the central representative organ of the people and the supreme legislative body. Its members are elected for a period of five years in direct, free, equal, and secret balloting in general elections. The island of Mauritius is divided into 20 constituencies, each electing three candidates. The island of Rodrigues constitutes a separate constituency, electing two candidates. Since 2000, the island of Agalega has participated in the general elections as an attachment of one of the urban constituencies.

The Lawmaking Process

The main function of the National Assembly and the Regional Assembly of Rodrigues is to enact legislation, the former for the whole country and the latter for Rodrigues. A draft law or bill becomes law only after the president has given assent. The president may withhold assent once; once the National Assembly has resubmitted the bill it must be signed.

The Judiciary

The judiciary is independent of the executive and the legislature. It is regarded by the public with trust and confidence as a guarantor of their rights. The legal professions comprise barristers, attorneys, and notaries.

The highest court in the Mauritian judicial system is the judicial committee of the Privy Council, based in London. In Mauritius itself, the local apex court remains the Supreme Court. The Supreme Court comprises an appellate division and an original division with unlimited jurisdiction to deal with all matters of a civil, criminal, administrative, labor, or financial nature. It also has a constitutional division that deals exclusively with constitutional disputes. Many of the court's decisions have had the highest legal and political impact.

THE ELECTION PROCESS AND POLITICAL PARTICIPATION

All Mauritians over the age of 18 have both the right to stand for election and the right to vote in the election.

POLITICAL PARTIES

The Mauritian electoral process is based on the multiparty system. Subject to its compliance with the laws, no party may be banned from participation in an election. However, all parties are required to register before the electoral commission, which manages the elections. The work of the electoral commission, which is itself an independent body under the constitution, is further supervised by the electoral supervisory commission.

CITIZENSHIP

Mauritian citizenship is primarily acquired by birth. A child acquires Mauritian citizenship if one of his or her parents is a Mauritian citizen, wherever the child is born. However, in case of birth abroad, soon after the minor attains adulthood he or she must apply for citizenship.

FUNDAMENTAL RIGHTS

The fundamental rights and freedoms enshrined in the Mauritian constitution are specified as follows: right to life, right to personal liberty, protection from slavery and forced labor, protection from inhuman treatment, protection from the deprivation of property, protection of the law, protection of freedom of conscience, protection of freedom of expression, protection of freedom of assembly and association, protection of freedom to establish schools, protection of freedom of movement, and protection from discrimination on account of race, caste, place of origin, political opinions, color, creed, or sex.

Impact and Functions of Fundamental Rights

These fundamental rights have generally been respected in Mauritius. Over and above the protection of the courts in cases of breach, Mauritians can seek the assistance of the Human Rights Commission, a recent institution set up to handle rights complaints in a less formal manner on a case-to-case basis.

Limitations to Fundamental Rights

Those fundamental rights are not, however, absolute. Each basic right is subject to a certain number of specified limitations that in turn are not themselves absolute. For instance, Article 12 guarantees the freedom of expression and at the same time legitimizes any law restricting that right in the interest of defense, public safety, public order, public morality, or public health. However, the limitation must be "reasonably justifiable in a democratic society." Thus, the European principle of "limitation limits" based on proportionality is basically followed in Mauritius.

ECONOMY

The Mauritian constitution does not impose any specific choice of economic system. However, insisting as it does on the fundamental freedoms and liberties of a liberal democracy, it has an economy that has grown and developed as a free market economy. Market freedom in Mauritius, however, is not interpreted as license; it is subjected to a degree of control in the interest of social responsibility.

RELIGIOUS COMMUNITIES

Freedom of religion or belief is constitutionally protected as part of freedom of conscience. It goes hand in hand with freedom of assembly and association. There is no established state church or religion.

All public authorities are bound to remain strictly neutral in their relations with religious communities, and no one religion may be given any preferential treatment to another without violating antidiscrimination provisions.

The fact that Mauritius is a secular state does not prevent government from encouraging religious and sociocultural organizations to proliferate. They operate as autonomous organizations subject to the laws of the land and compliance with a number of statutory requirements for registration, annual returns, and audit and the supervision of the Registrar of Association.

MILITARY DEFENSE AND STATE OF EMERGENCY

Mauritius does not possess any armed forces. It does have forces for the maintenance of law and order called the Disciplined Forces, which include a section specially trained to deal with situations of national emergencies and natural disaster such as cyclones, floods, riots, or major accidents. Defense and security are the responsibility of the prime minister, who decides how best the country may be protected internally and from outside threats.

When the need for military intervention arises, the prime minister may have recourse to assistance from friendly nations. In 1967, for instance, British troops from Aden were called to quell rioting in the country on the apprehension that it might develop into a major pre-independence civil disturbance. There is a present pact for military assistance between Mauritius and India. The likelihood of its use is quite remote, however.

Accordingly, there is no general conscription. The Disciplined Forces are always under the control of civil government. Mauritius also belongs to the group of non-allied countries as regards its international politics.

AMENDMENTS TO THE CONSTITUTION

The constitution sets different requirements for amending different sections. In many cases, it can be changed by a two-thirds vote of the members of the National Assembly. Other provisions, such as Chapter 2 (fundamental rights and freedoms), require a three-quarters vote of all the members of the National Assembly for amendment. In a few cases, such as the postponement of elections beyond the five-year mandate, it may be altered only by a unanimous vote in the assembly after a national referendum.

PRIMARY SOURCES

The Constitution of the Republic of Mauritius. Vol. 1. Best Graphics, 2000. Available online. URL: http://www.gov.mu/portal/site/AssemblySite/menuitem. ee3d58b2c32c60451251701065c521ca/. Accessed on September 1, 2005.

SECONDARY SOURCES

Satyabooshum B. Domah, *Constitutionae Africae, the Mauritian Constitution.* Antwerp: Antwerp University, 1994.
"The Laws of Mauritius in English." Available online. URL: http://supremecourt.intnet.mu/Entry/legislation. htm. Accessed on July 28, 2005.
Dheerujlall B. Seetulsingh, *Mauritius, Country Report.* Port Louis: Human Rights Commission, Attorney-General's Office 28 March 2005. Available online. URL: http://www.gov.mu/portal/goc/nhrc/file/annrep04.pdf.
For bibliography on human rights in Mauritius. Available online: URL: http://www.up.ac.za/chr. Accessed on September 27, 2005.

Satyabooshum B. Domah

MEXICO

At-a-Glance

OFFICIAL NAME
Estados Unidos Mexicanos

CAPITAL
Ciudad de México, D.F.

POPULATION
105,000,000 (2005 est.)

SIZE
761,606 sq. mi. (1,972,550 sq. km)

LANGUAGES
Spanish

RELIGIONS
Catholic 88%, Protestant 5.20%, biblical not evangelical 2.07%, Jewish 0.05%, other 1.16%, without any religion 3.52%

NATIONAL OR ETHNIC COMPOSITION
Mestizo (Amerindian-Spanish) 60%, Amerindian or predominantly Amerindian 30%, white 9%, other 1%

DATE OF INDEPENDENCE OR CREATION
September 27, 1821

TYPE OF GOVERNMENT
Presidential system, representative democracy

TYPE OF STATE
Federal state

TYPE OF LEGISLATURE
Bicameral parliament

DATE OF CONSTITUTION
February 5, 1917

DATE OF AMENDMENT
April 7, 2006

Mexico is organized as a democratic, representative, and federal republic that comprises 31 federal states and one federal district. Its constitutional system is based on two fundamental principles: the division of legislative, executive, and judicial powers and the recognition and guarantee of fundamental human rights. While a reasonable balance exists among the three federal powers, the central figure of public life, according to the presidential model, continues to be the president of the republic, who is both head of state and head of the executive.

The current constitution was enacted on February 4, 1917, and became effective on May 1 of the same year. It contains 136 articles, of which only 27 have escaped reform during their nine decades of existence. It was the first constitution in the world to recognize and guarantee the social rights of workers and peasants.

A politically pluralist system has emerged as a result of a gradual, delayed process toward a democratic transition, which culminated in the year 2000 with the election of a president from the opposition. Political parties compete on a level ground protected by an electoral organization that guarantees free and respected elections at both federal and local levels.

The state and religious communities are separated. The state respects the right to religious freedom, although some restrictions do apply. The economic system can be described as a social market economy. The army has a strong popular component and is subject to the civil government both in law and, in recent decades, in fact.

CONSTITUTIONAL HISTORY

Mexico began to emerge as a political entity in 1821, after the independence of the Viceroyalty of New Spain from Spain. This new political entity was populated by a people—the Mexican people—of mixed heritage, a blend of Spaniards from the Iberian Peninsula of Europe who entered to conquer and colonize the newly discovered lands and the Amerindian peoples who inhabited the territory of what would become New Spain.

The Great Tenochtitlan, capital of the Aztec Empire (and site of today's Mexico City), fell on August 13, 1521, after a 75-day siege. Although the Aztecs resisted, the Spanish conquerors led by Hernán Cortés finally took the main square. For three centuries, from 1521 to 1821, the country was subject to the Spanish Crown. It was granted the rank of kingdom and known as the Viceroyalty of New Spain.

The discovery, conquest, and colonization of America took place with the financial backing of Spain. Although a special legal system known as the Indian Rights was drafted for the Indies, as America was initially called, Spanish language and law were imposed on New Spain.

The revolution for independence began in 1810, led by Don Miguel Hidalgo. It ended in 1821, after a victorious movement led by Don Agustín de Iturbide.

On May 19, 1822, Iturbide was proclaimed emperor of Mexico. During the time of the empire, the provinces of the old Captaincy of Guatemala, known today as the countries of Guatemala, Honduras, El Salvador, Nicaragua, and Costa Rica, were annexed by Mexico. The Captaincy of Yucatán, which had not belonged to New Spain, was also annexed. In the north, the sparsely populated Mexican territories of Texas, New Mexico, and Alta California extended their borders north of the 40th parallel. During this early stage of the Mexican state, its territorial extension could be calculated at approximately 1,737,460 square miles. On March 19, 1823, Iturbide abdicated. After the empire dissolved, the Central American provinces, with the exception of Chiapas, separated.

The next portion of territory to be lost was the prosperous province of Texas. On March 2, 1836, over 50 representatives and colonists proclaimed the "independence" of Texas in Washington, D.C. On July 5, 1845, the United States Senate approved the annexation of Texas. As a consequence of the ensuing war between Mexico and the United States, and by virtue of the 1848 Treaty of Guadalupe Hidalgo, Mexico lost over half of its territory.

In 1864, for the second time in independent Mexico's history, a monarchy was established. Emperor Maximilian of Habsburg was crowned by the Conservative Party. On June 19, 1867, Maximilian's execution ended his short-lived empire. This date also marks the final triumph of a liberal faction over the conservatives. For years, their power struggle had caused turmoil in the Mexican territory.

From 1808 until 1867, Mexico saw many constituent assemblies and proposed constitutions, as well as plans for change. Several constitution projects were drafted but never prospered.

The Mexican Revolution of 1910, resumed in 1913, is the historical event that led to the current constitution, which was enacted on February 5, 1917. In its initial stages, the revolutionary movement brandished the slogan of political democracy, "Effective Suffrage. No Re-election." Economic, social, and cultural demands were added later. Another antecedent of the revolution was the regime of Porfirio Díaz, who remained in power for 31 years through seven elections.

On November 20, 1910, an armed movement led by Francisco I. Madero emerged. On May 25, 1911, President Diaz stepped down. Madero was chosen president of the republic in the first democratic elections in Mexican history. Jose María Pino Suárez was elected as vice president.

On February 18, 1913, Victoriano Huerta usurped the presidential seat—a usurpation that he veiled with constitutional formalities—and had Madero and Pino Suárez murdered. On March 26, 1913, the governor of Coahuila, Venustiano Carranza, launched a long military campaign, managing to defeat the army first, and later Huerta's disaffected revolutionaries themselves, until he was finally able to convene a Constituent Congress in September 1916. The constitution it drew up, enacted on February 5, 1917, and effective in May 1917, has remained in effect to the present day.

FORM AND IMPACT OF THE CONSTITUTION

The Mexican constitution is a rigid, written document that cannot be reformed by ordinary constitutional powers except under those rare exceptions that the document itself justifies. It plays a central role in the national judicial order. The constitution is based on the recognition of two fundamental principles: the principle of supremacy and the principle of inviolability. The principle of supremacy is consecrated expressly in Article 133, which establishes that the constitution is the supreme law of the union. The principle of inviolability, which is found in Article 136, states that the "constitution will not lose force or vigor even if and when a rebellion interrupts its observance."

The principle of supremacy in Article 133 contains the hierarchical order of the laws, as follows: (1) constitutional laws, (2) laws of the congress of the union that emanate from the constitution and international treaties, and (3) federal and local laws.

Traditionally the Supreme Court of Justice of the Nation has granted the same constitutional rank to laws that emanate from the Congress and those pursuant to international treaties. However, in an interpretative declaration in 1999, the Supreme Federal Tribunal abandoned this criterion, sustaining the jurisprudential thesis that places international treaties first, above federal laws, but second to those of the federal constitution.

BASIC ORGANIZATIONAL STRUCTURE

Mexico is a federation made up of 31 federal states and one federal district. The Mexican Federation was not a union of preexisting states that had already acquired sovereignty and independence; such states did not exist in Mexico. After it became independent of Spain and attained its sovereignty, federalism and centralism were the two major proposals for the organization of a Mexican state. Mexico chose the federalist option at its first constituent congress in 1824. The federal system was maintained in the 1824 constitution, in the Constitutive Act, in the 1847 reforms and constitution, and in the current 1917 constitution. Yet federalism has remained a central issue in Mexico's constitutional history ever since, often dividing the nation.

Though federalism eventually prevailed in theory, it was mostly as a theoretical expression of an ideal that could never crystallize into a political reality in the face of the existing reality of centralism. It was not until recent years that firm steps were taken to establish a cooperative federalism that gives reality to the constitutional norm.

In the Mexican constitutional model, federalism signifies a dual system of authority distributed between the federal government and the local governments. The shared authority can be legislative, executive, or judicial in nature. Authority that is not explicitly granted to federal organs is understood to be reserved for the member states. Next to the explicit and reserved powers are the so-called concurrent faculties, which are powers exercised simultaneously by the federation and by the states.

As the utmost expression of their autonomy, each state in the Mexican Federal Republic drafts its own constitution, thereby creating its own local government bodies and granting them authority. There are 31 constitutions that correspond to 31 state entities. The content of these local constitutions is in part determined by the federal constitution, which imposes a series of obligations and prohibitions with which they must abide.

Generally speaking, the constitution stipulates that the states are obliged to accept a republican, representative, and democratic form of government, and to have as the basis of their political and administrative organizations free municipalities. It also stipulates that the public power of each state must be divided for its exercise into executive, legislative, and judiciary powers.

Each state entity has its own local executive power, led by the governor of the state, a legislative branch in the form of a unicameral congress, and a judiciary, the highest organ of which is a superior tribunal of justice. Local constitutions, for the most part, have lacked originality and followed the federal model instead of accepting local customs and adapting to them. It has only been in recent years that they have shown a tendency to move toward the exercise of their autonomy by introducing amendments to their constitution more consonant with the particular circumstances of each state.

Along with the state entities or members, there exists another unique entity called the federal district, where both the federal powers and the capital of Mexico are located. Mexico City and the federal district occupy the same geographic district. The constitution merges Mexico City and the federal district into a single entity.

Unlike the state entities, the federal district does not have a constitution of its own. Its organizational roots are found in the federal constitution.

LEADING CONSTITUTIONAL PRINCIPLES

Mexico can be described as a democratic, republican, federal, and nonreligious state, with a clear division of powers and a system of protection for human rights.

The Mexican system is democratic; part of the leading principle found in Article 39 of the constitution states: "National sovereignty resides essentially and originally in the people" and "All public power originates in the people and is instituted for their benefit."

However, the people, who are sovereign and by definition maintain this attribute of sovereignty forever, do not exercise power directly, but instead through their representatives. Popular participation in the renewal of the legislative and executive powers is carried out through free and periodic elections.

The classic tripartite principle of the division of powers is defined in Article 49 of the constitution, which establishes that "the Supreme Power of the Federation is divided, for its exercise, into legislative, executive and judicial branches." This principle of the separation of powers extends to the states in their internal regimes. Historically, however, and despite the tripartite principle, power has been concentrated in the executive branch, to the detriment of the remaining two branches. With the 1917 constitution, the power of the president of the republic was so excessive that a historian justifiably called it an "Imperial Presidency."

In recent decades, this reality has gradually changed into a government of separation, a balance of powers, and free and respected elections. On July 2, 2000, Mexico's process of democratic transition culminated in the first election since 1917 of a candidate from the opposition to the presidency of the republic. A system of absolute political democracy was established.

The Mexican constitutional system is organized under the rule of law (Estado de Derecho). The authorities are subject to the law. There is an extensive catalog of recognized and constitutionally protected human rights.

The 1917 Mexican constitution was the first in the world to guarantee the social rights of workers and peasants. It can be affirmed that social constitutionalism, or the social democratic rule of law, was modeled by this constitution. Article 3 considers democracy not solely as a legal structure and a political regime but also as a system of life founded on constant economic, social, and cultural improvement for the people. However, and despite recent serious efforts, an enormous gap continues to exist today between the recently attained political democracy and a social democracy that still looms in the distance.

Mexico is a republic. The executive position is periodically renewed with the participation of the people through elections. It is a secular state, with the separation of the state and religious communities. It recognizes and guarantees the human right to religious freedom.

According to the constitution, the municipality is the foundation of territorial division and of the political organization of the states. A council (*ayuntamiento*) is chosen by direct popular election to govern each municipality. The council is composed of a municipal president, who chairs the council, and the councilors (*regidores* and *síndicos*). The councilors are chosen through direct popular elections, hold the post for a three-year term, and may not be reelected for the term that immediately follows.

CONSTITUTIONAL BODIES

Historically and until recently, the predominance of the executive power over the other two branches blurred the principle of the separation of powers. With the exception of brief periods, the subjection of the judicial and legislative powers to the executive has been the historical norm, to such a degree that for a long time the legislative organ was no more than a type of registration office under the orders of the president of the republic. The president practically monopolized the power to introduce bills before a congress that approved them automatically.

Fortunately, this situation has changed substantially through a series of amendments to the constitution that began in 1977. A system of proportional representation was introduced into the election of deputies, without abandoning the election method of relative majority, establishing a mixed electoral system that set the renewal of the country's political life in motion.

As do most democratic constitutions, Mexico's constitution adopts the theory of the division of powers with the consideration that the separation should not be mechanical, but rather organic. Through the balance and cooperation of the powers they can better satisfy the purposes of the state.

Accordingly, the predominant bodies established in the constitution are the president of the republic, with the aid of the public administration apparatus, the Congress of the union, composed of the Chamber of Deputies and the Chamber of Senators, and the judiciary, made up of diverse federal tribunals and headed by the Supreme Court of Justice of the Nation.

The President of the Republic

The president of the republic exercises the federal executive power and is simultaneously the head of state and the head of the administration. To be president, a person must be a Mexican citizen by birth and a child of a Mexican mother or father. The candidate must also have reached the age of 35 at the time of the election. No one can be candidate for president who is in active service in the army, is a secretary of state (minister), holds any high position in the national government, or is governor of a federal state, unless the candidate resigns from the post six months prior to the day of the election. A candidate also must not be a member of a religious order or a minister of any cult.

The election of the president is direct. The president assumes the duties of office for a period of six years, cannot be reelected, and cannot occupy the position, under any circumstances, for a second term. During the six-year period in office the president can be impeached only for treason and serious crimes. The president may resign from the post only under very grave circumstances, which are specified by the Congress of the union, and before whom the resignation must be presented.

The president of the republic is the representative of the Mexican state and commander in chief of the military forces. Among the president's duties are the promulgation and execution of laws enacted by the Congress of the union. The president also has the power to introduce bills or decrees before the congress and to veto laws adopted by the congress. The purpose of the veto, which can be total or partial, is to return the bill, with any observations deemed pertinent, to the Congress of the union so that they may discuss it again. If and when the congress accepts it with two-thirds of the votes, the bill then becomes law and is returned to the executive for its enactment. If it does not obtain this majority, the bill is defeated.

The president holds the power to direct foreign policy and sign international treaties after submitting them to the approval of the Senate. The president declares war in the name of the Mexican state pursuant to a previous congressional law to that effect. The president can also grant pardons to criminals according to the law.

The president is supported by the federal public administration, whose main components are the secretaries of state. They are the most immediate collaborators and closest in rank within the executive to the president, who has the power to designate and remove them freely. The secretaries of state lack their own authority since they exercise power in their respective fields by delegation and as representatives of the president. The acts of the secretaries are by law presidential acts. However, the constitution demands that all regulations, decrees, agreements, and orders of the president be countersigned by the secretary of state covering the matter and stipulates that they must not be obeyed if lacking this prerequisite.

The Legislature

The legislative power is entrusted to the Congress of the union, which comprises two chambers: the Chamber of Deputies and the Chamber of Senators. Both hold the same constitutional rank and are essentially endowed with the same powers. Senators and deputies alike represent the nation and are chosen directly by the people.

The Chamber of Deputies is renewed in its entirety every three years. It comprises 500 deputies. Of these, 300 are elected according to the principle of relative majority voting, and 200 are elected according to the principle of proportional representation, through a system of regional lists. For each proprietary deputy, an alternate is elected as a replacement in case of special leave, resignation, or an absence from sessions of 10 consecutive days without justifiable cause.

A deputy must be a Mexican citizen by birth and have reached 21 years of age by the day of the election. Deputies are representatives of the nation. Each represents the totality of the people and not only the district or region in which he or she was chosen.

The Chamber of Senators is renewed in its entirety every six years. It is composed of 128 senators. In each state and in the federal district, 96 senators are elected by majority vote. The remaining 32 senators are elected according to the principle of proportional representation, according to lists presented by the political parties for each election.

A senator must be a Mexican citizen and must be 35 years of age by the date of the election. As in the case of the deputies, for each proprietary senator an alternate is also elected.

Senators and deputies cannot be reelected for the term that immediately follows their term. The constitution also states that proprietary deputies and senators may not hold any other commission or employment of the federation or of the states for which they receive a salary during their term of office.

To preserve the independence of the parliamentary function, members of both chambers are granted parliamentary immunity. Deputies and senators cannot be legally prosecuted during their term of office, until the chamber previously approves a bill, similar to impeachment, that entails the removal of the representative from office. No legal action whatsoever may be taken against them for expressing their opinions in the exercise of their duties.

The general quorum rule is that for the chambers to open their sessions, more than half of all the members must be present. Once quorum has been reached, the chambers can act. Decisions are generally made by a majority of the members present.

For the opening of the ordinary sessions of the first period of Congress of the union, the president of the republic must be in attendance and present a written report on the general state of the country's public administration.

Neither the Chamber of Deputies nor the Chamber of Senators on its own has the formal power to expedite laws. Their joint action is necessary to draft laws. The congress can perform some functions that are administrative and jurisdictional in nature.

The Lawmaking Process

The right to introduce bills or decrees before the Congress of the union is granted to the president of the republic, the deputies and senators of the Congress of the union, the local chambers of deputies of the states, and the Legislative Assembly of the federal district, for issues concerning the federal district itself. Most bills can be presented in either of the two chambers. Bills concerning loans, contributions or revenues, or the recruitment of troops, however, must be introduced first in the Chamber of Deputies.

Once the bill or decree is submitted, a period of discussion begins, and it is eventually either approved or rejected. If both chambers approve it, the law is remitted to the president. The president either vetoes the bill or promulgates it and publishes it immediately. A veto can be total or partial; in either case, congress can override the veto with two-thirds of the votes, and the executive must enact it.

The Judiciary

The judiciary in Mexico is independent of the other two federal powers. The judicial power of the federation is vested in a Supreme Court of Justice, an Electoral Tribunal, Collegiate Tribunals, Circuit Courts, and District Courts.

The Federal Judicature Council also plays an important role in the judiciary. It is a predominantly administrative body that oversees the administration of the federal judiciary and monitors and disciplines it—with the exception of the Supreme Court. The Federal Judicature Council has contributed much to the establishment of a judicial career path and, consequently, to the professionalization of the judicial system.

Other jurisdictional organs also exist but are not considered to form part of the federal judicial power. These include military tribunals, misdemeanor councils, agrarian tribunals, the Tribunal of Fiscal and Administrative Justice, the Board of Conciliation and Arbitration, and the Federal Tribunal of Conciliation and Arbitration.

The Supreme Court of Justice of the Nation is the highest organ of the federal judiciary. It can be considered a constitutional tribunal on which the protection of the constitutional order has been conferred.

The Supreme Court is composed of 11 judges. The president of the republic nominates the judges, who are then submitted for approval to the Chamber of Senators. After hearing the proposed candidates, the Senate elects them.

Over the last decade, and particularly since the democratic transition of 2000, the Supreme Court of Justice has played a crucial role in resolving conflicts between federal and local powers in the country and in defending the fundamental values found in the constitution. In a paradigmatic case, in January 2002 the court issued an interpretive ruling, expanding on a fundamental law: "The constitution protects the product of the conception as a manifestation of human life, independently of the biological process in which it is found." The recognition and protection of the human right to life are not explicitly expressed in the text of the constitution.

THE ELECTION PROCESS AND POLITICAL PARTICIPATION

The right to vote is acquired at the age of 18 years, both for Mexicans by birth and for those who have acquired citizenship by naturalization. However, in order to be voted into public office, one must be a Mexican citizen by birth and have reached a higher age, which varies with the office.

Federal elections are organized by an autonomous public organ called the Federal Electoral Institute (IFE), which has a judicial character and its own resources. This institute is independent in its decisions. Its guiding principles are certainty, legality, independence, impartiality, and objectivity.

Another key instrument in the process of democratic transition and in the current consolidation of the democratic system is the Federal Electoral Tribunal, created in 1996. It is the leading jurisdictional authority in electoral matters and a specialized organ of the federation's judiciary with far-reaching autonomy. It can be defined as a court of constitutionality in electoral matters.

Mexico is a representative democracy. The federal constitution does not recognize any so-called direct or semidirect democratic instruments, such as referenda, plebiscites, popular initiatives, or repeals. However, in recent years, some of these instruments have been introduced in several local constitutions, though, in practice, they have not been used.

POLITICAL PARTIES

The constitution considers political parties to be entities of public interest, the purpose of which is to promote the participation of the people in democratic life. They provide citizens with access to public power; enable them to express their views through the programs, principles, and ideas that the parties proclaim; and present candidates for election. Only citizens can be full members of political parties, and only as individuals. Collective bodies, unions, or political groups cannot join political parties.

A pluralistic system of political parties is currently established and consolidated in Mexico. There are three large parties that have the most electoral force within the multiparty regime, alongside three smaller parties that, on occasion, can determine an election through strategic alliances.

The constitution guarantees that national political parties be granted equal shares of subsidies in order to perform their activities. Therefore, they have the right to public financing, with funds from the state to support both their ordinary permanent activities and their electoral campaigns. Political parties have the right to continual access to the mass media, according to procedures established by law.

CITIZENSHIP

The Mexican constitutional system distinguishes between nationality and citizenship. Mexican nationality is acquired by birth or by naturalization.

Mexicans by birth are those born in the territory of the republic, regardless of the nationality of their parents; those born in a foreign country of a Mexican-born or naturalized mother or father; and those born on board a Mexican vessel or airplane. Foreigners may acquire Mexican nationality, provided they are domiciled on national territory and fulfill additional requirements established by law.

The constitution states that no Mexican by birth may be denied his or her nationality. This implies that a Mexican may have dual nationality.

Foreigners, in general, enjoy the same rights as Mexicans. However, they have no right to participate in the political life of the country. They are not allowed any active or passive vote in elections; nor do they have the rights of petition or association in any political matters. They are also not permitted direct ownership of lands or waters within a zone of 100 kilometers along the frontiers and of 50 kilometers along the shores of the country. There are further restrictions in matters of employment and participation in military forces. It should be noted that the federal executive has the exclusive power to compel any foreigner whose presence it may deem inexpedient, without previous legal action, to leave the national territory immediately.

Nationality is a prerequisite for Mexican citizenship. Citizens of the republic are those Mexicans—by birth or by naturalization—who have reached 18 years of age and live an honest life.

Citizenship can be lost by the acceptance or use of titles of nobility, by rendering of voluntary official services to a foreign government without permission of the Congress of the union, and in several other cases stated in the constitution. Citizenship may be suspended if the person is subject to criminal prosecution, serves a term of imprisonment, or has committed an electoral crime as determined by electoral law.

FUNDAMENTAL RIGHTS

The traditional human rights of equality, liberty, and judicial protection were affirmed in the Mexican constitutions of the 19th century. The current 1917 constitution also recognized social and economic rights. In recent years, so-called third-generation rights have also been incorporated.

A number of amendments to the constitution in recent years have added new fundamental rights and broadened and perfected several existing rights. For example, changes to Article 1 in 2001 added the right of all persons not to be discriminated against by reason of ethnic or national origin, gender, age, different capacities, social conditions, health conditions, religion, opinions, preferences, marital status, or any other reason contrary to human dignity. The principle of the fundamental dignity of the human being, while implicit in the original text, had not been explicitly included until the 2001 amendment.

The recognition and protection of the rights and cultures of the indigenous peoples were given constitutional status. In penal matters, the guarantees of the penal process have broadened, both for the accused and for the victim.

Concerning family matters, amendments have established the legal equality of the sexes and added statutes for family protection and responsible parenthood. The right to health care and the right to housing were also introduced into the constitution.

The majority of these fundamental rights are found in Chapter 1 of the constitution, ambiguously and inappropriately titled Individual Guarantees, outlined in Articles 1 through 29.

Article 123 enumerates the social rights and guarantees of the working class, which were elevated to constitutional rank in 1917 for the first time in the history of Western constitutionalism. They include such stipulations as the maximal duration of the working day, wages, the weekly rest, the prohibition of the employment of minors, the participation of the workers in the profits of the company, the principle of equal salary for equal work, the protection of women during pregnancy, the right of the workers to form unions, stability in employment, and the right to strike.

The human rights recognized in the International Covenant on Civil and Political Rights (ICCPR) and the International Covenant on Economic, Social and Cultural Rights (ICESCR) of 1966 also form a part of national law, as do those of the 1969 American Convention on Human Rights.

Impact and Functions of Fundamental Rights

The constitution not only considers fundamental rights to be of utmost importance and relevance for the democratic rule of law, but establishes a far-reaching system for their protection. The ruling principle is that recognition of a right is not sufficient without the effective judicial protection of the state.

The trial of *amparo* constitutes the most important constitutional guarantee of human rights. The structure and breadth of this procedural institution are considered an important contribution of Mexican legal philosophy to universal legal culture. It is incorporated into Article 8 of the 1948 Universal Declaration of Human Rights of the United Nations.

By now, Mexicans have developed a complex legal structure of *amparo* that encompasses several procedural instruments. Depending on the situation, an *amparo* can be used for the protection of personal freedom, in contesting of unconstitutional laws, as a form of appeal against judicial sentences, as a protest against the acts and the resolutions of the administration, and as protection of the social rights of the peasants.

In 1990 Mexico established the National Human Rights Committee (CNDH), equivalent to the ombudsperson in other countries and to similar committees in the federal states. It is a national system for the nonjurisdictional protection of human rights, which responds quickly and in a simple way to the complaints of citizens that their fundamental rights have been violated. This committee is headed by a president, nominated by the federal executive with the approval of the Senate for a term of five years. The term can be extended only once. This organ has complete autonomy over its functions and its budget and is judicial in nature.

Limitations to Fundamental Rights

The constitution asserts that fundamental rights can be limited or restricted only in particular cases that it enumerates. Thus, for example, the freedom of thought and freedom of the press are limited by the rights of others and by the respect for private life and public peace. Foreigners are restricted in their rights in political matters, including the right to active and passive voting and the right of association. The rights to associate and assemble are limited by the conditions that associations and assemblies must be legal, that the participants in a gathering may not be armed, that no insults be proffered against authorities, and that there be no violence or threats. The right to freedom of work, industry, and commerce is subject to the limiting condition that the activity be legal. Limitations or restrictions that are not found expressly established in the text of the constitution cannot be added by law, either by the Congress of the union or a Local Congress.

The constitution anticipates extreme conditions when fundamental rights may not only be limited, but also temporarily suspended, as in the case of invasion, serious disturbance of public peace, or any other event that may place society in great danger or in conflict. Under these conditions, constitutional rights can be suspended through rigorous proceedings established by the constitution. Such measures can be implemented by the president of the republic with the consent of the secretaries of state and the attorney general of the republic and with the approval of the Congress of the union. Even then, not all individual rights can be suspended—only those that may act as obstacles to the rapid resolution of the event; the restrictions must be for a limited time, whether throughout the country or in a specific place. Along with the power to suspend constitutional guarantees, the Congress of the union can grant the executive extraordinary powers to legislate on certain matters for the duration of the state of emergency.

ECONOMY

The Mexican constitutions of the 19th century were strongly influenced by economic liberalism. The norms that ruled the economy were those related to freedom of commerce, industry, and labor: the right to property without any major limitations, and freedom in economic activities in which the state participates to assure free competition and to prohibit monopolies.

The current 1917 constitution introduced social constitutionalism, which set the foundation for a state of social democratic rights, although the reality differs greatly from the constitutional model. The constitution allowed greater powers of intervention to public authorities on issues of importance concerning the economy, land, free competition and monopolies, labor issues, and foreign commerce.

In later amendments, other important principles of an economic character were incorporated into the constitution, such as the leadership of the state. The state was given the leading role in national development to guarantee that it be integral, that it strengthen the sovereignty of the nation and its democratic regime. The state should aim, through economic growth, employment, and a more just distribution of wealth, to allow the full exercise of the liberty and dignity of the people, groups, and social classes.

Another principle found in the constitution is that of a mixed economy, which is understood as the concurrence with social responsibility of the public, social, and private sectors for national economic development; this must not affect other forms of economic activity that contribute to the development of the nation. The constitution establishes the process of democratic planning, which aims to ascertain, through the participation of the diverse social sectors, the needs of society in order to incorporate them into the plan of national development and other programs.

RELIGIOUS COMMUNITIES

The human right to religious freedom for individuals and groups is guaranteed in the constitution. However, there are some restrictions that evoke historical conflicts between the state and the Catholic Church.

The original text of the current constitution contained several provisions that constituted serious violations to this fundamental right. While, on one hand, it recognized the freedom of religious beliefs and worship, on the other, churches were denied legal personality. Religious instruction in public and private schools was banned. Ministers of worship were denied political rights—active or passive—and were even denied the right to criticize the fundamental laws of the country, not only in public meetings but in private ones as well.

In 1992, the constitutional provisions on religious matters were reformed, and a more open regime was established to recognize and protect the rights of religious freedom. Along with individual rights, which already existed in the original document, churches and religious groups were now allowed to acquire legal personality under the generic name of *religious association* by registration with the Secretariat of Government.

The law determines the requirements that a church or religious group must fulfill in order to register as a religious association. The observance, practice, propagation, or instruction of a religious doctrine must have been exercised for a minimum of five years. It must also have been recognized and taken root among the population, it must have statutes, and it must have sufficient means to fulfill its objectives. Religious associations and their ministers still cannot own or administer licenses for radio and television stations or acquire, possess, or administer any other form of mass media. Religious instruction is authorized for private schools but not for public schools. Ministers have the right to vote but may not hold elective office.

According to the constitution, the leading principle that guides all laws relating to religious issues is that of the separation of the church and state. Mexico is a secular state. The constitution grants the Congress of the union the exclusive power to legislate on religious matters. It also establishes the principle of equality for all religious associations, whereby the state cannot establish any form of preference or privilege in favor of any religion.

MILITARY DEFENSE AND STATE OF EMERGENCY

The army is organized and regulated by the Congress of the union and the president of the republic. The president is the supreme commander and may freely deploy armed forces for purposes of internal security and the exterior defense of the federation.

The president of the republic is also in charge of appointing the higher commanders of the army, with the ratification of the Senate. The remaining officers are appointed and promoted by following strict regulations determined by the constitution.

The Mexican army has achieved a high grade of professionalism and depoliticization. Its submission to civil political power is entrenched as well.

In May 1942, as a consequence of the sinking of Mexican ships by Nazi German submarines, Mexico declared war on Germany, Italy, and Japan. While its participation in World War II (1938–45) was mostly symbolic, the merit of the members of Squadron 201, who completed several missions in the Pacific in which five Mexican pilots died, cannot be denied. In World War I (1914–18), Mexico remained neutral.

Given the emergency provoked by the world wars, compulsory military service was introduced and continues to this day. Service is required for male citizens who are 18 years of age. In reality, such military service is often restricted to brief, light outdoor instruction on Sundays.

With respect to the participation of the military forces in public security, the Supreme Court of Justice of the Nation has determined that the armed forces can participate in civil activities that promote public security in situations that do not require the suspension of guarantees. In doing so, they must strictly abide by the constitution and the laws and respect the fundamental rights guaranteed by the constitution.

Conscientious objectors are not considered exempt from military service in defense of the republic under the terms stated by the law.

AMENDMENTS TO THE CONSTITUTION

The constitution is relatively rigid and in theory is difficult to change. It can be amended only by a positive vote of two-thirds of the members of the Congress of the union. In addition, amendments and additions require the approval of the majority of the state legislatures.

The constitution does not explicitly foresee the possibility that it could be completely revised, but neither does it forbid it. There would be no constitutional obstacle to a thoroughgoing reform, if it were done according to the established constitutional procedure.

A new constitution could not be issued by an assembly or congress convoked expressly for this purpose, since the constitutional text does not provide for such an eventuality. It is also not possible to replace the present constitution with one imposed by revolutionary groups, since it is expressly stated that the constitution will not lose force or vigor even when a rebellion interrupts its observance.

In contrast to the 19th-century constitutions, the 1917 constitution has had hundreds of amendments. For several decades a system of authoritarian presidentialism existed in the country, in which the federal and local legislatures lacked independence. The president only had to send a project of constitutional reform for it to be automatically approved by the Congress of the union and the local congresses, whose members belonged almost entirely to the Institutional Revolutionary Party (PRI), the official party.

This situation changed after 1988, when the PRI lost its majority in the Chamber of Deputies, and the process of transition to a democracy began, culminating on July 2, 2000, with the election of a president of the republic nominated by the opposition.

PRIMARY SOURCES

Constitution in English. Available online. URLs: http://www.ilstu.edu/class/hist263/docs/1917const.html; http://historicaltextarchive.com/sections.php?op=viewarticle&artid=93. Accessed on September 2, 2005.

Constitution in Spanish. Available online. URL: http://www.cddhcu.gob.mx/leyinfo/pdf/1.pdf. Accessed on September 16, 2005.

SECONDARY SOURCES

Francisco Avalos, *The Mexican Legal System.* 2d ed. Littleton, Colo.: F. B. Rothman, 2000.

Tim L. Merrill, *Mexico—a Country Study.* Washington, D.C.: United States Government Printing Office, 1996.

United Nations, "Core Document Forming Part of the Reports of States Parties: Mexico" (HRI/CORE/1/Add.12/Rev.1) 2 February 1995 and (HRI/GEN/2/Rev.1/Add.1), 18 March 2002. Available online. URL: http://www.unhchr.ch/tbs/doc.nsf. Accessed on August 23, 2005.

Raúl González Schmal
Assisted by Jaqueline Robinson

FEDERATED STATES OF MICRONESIA

At-a-Glance

OFFICIAL NAME
Federated States of Micronesia

CAPITAL
Palikir, Pohnpei

POPULATION
110,000 (2005 est.)

SIZE
271 sq. mi. (702 sq. km), islands sprinkled over
1,000,000 sq. mi. of ocean

LANGUAGES
Chuukese, Pohnpeian, Yapese, Kosraean, Woleaian,
Kapingingamarangi, Ulithian, and Nukuoran, English
(common language)

RELIGIONS
Roman Catholic, Protestant

NATIONAL OR ETHNIC COMPOSITION
Chuukese, Pohnpeian, Yapese, Kosraean, Woleaian,
Kapingingamarangi, Ulithian, and Nukuoran
(sometimes generically referred to as Micronesian)

DATE OF INDEPENDENCE OR CREATION
Constitutional government May 10, 1979; Trust
Territory dissolved November 3, 1986

TYPE OF GOVERNMENT
Hybrid executive, parliamentary democracy

TYPE OF STATE
Federal state

TYPE OF LEGISLATURE
Unicameral legislature

DATE OF CONSTITUTION
Ratified in plebiscite July 12, 1978; constitutional
government initiated May 10, 1979

DATE OF LAST AMENDMENT
July 2, 1991 (ratified by referendum)

The Federated States of Micronesia is a hybrid executive and parliamentary democracy based on the rule of law. There are clear operating divisions of executive, legislative, and judicial powers within the national government, but the president and vice president are selected from and by the legislative branch, known as the Congress. The president is head of state, ceremonial leader, and head of the administration. Organized as a federal system, the Federated States of Micronesia comprises four states—Chuuk, Kosrae, Pohnpei, and Yap—and a central government.

The constitution is the supreme law of the land and the primary guide for this young Pacific Island nation. It provides broad guarantees of human rights, which are respected by all public authorities. If a violation occurs in individual cases, remedies are enforceable by independent state and federal judiciaries, subject to review and final decision by the Federated States Supreme Court. Religious freedom is guaranteed.

The Federated States of Micronesia has no military, having delegated defense matters to the United States under a Compact of Free Association, which spells out a special working relationship between the two countries.

The developing economy is a market economy.

CONSTITUTIONAL HISTORY

The Federated States of Micronesia (FSM) is a tropical Pacific Island nation located north of the equator in the Caroline Islands, extending west over some 2,000 miles in the area between Hawaii and the Philippines. About 110,000 people live on approximately 600 islands, most of which are coral atolls sprinkled across 1,000,000 square miles of ocean. All told, the FSM comprises a land area of approximately 270 square miles. About half of the population resides on the four high volcanic island state capitals of Kosrae, Pohnpei, Chuuk, and Yap. At least six different indigenous languages and numerous dialects are spoken by FSM citizens, but English is the commonly used language.

Spain laid claim to the area during the 19th century. In 1898, the Spanish American War led to dissolution of most of what then remained of the former Spanish Empire. Germany "purchased" Micronesia from the Spanish and continued to claim control of the area until displaced by Japan during World War I (1914–18). In 1919, Japan received authority to govern the area as part of a League of Nations mandate. Japan withdrew from the League of Nations in the mid-1930s, but Japanese hegemony over the islands continued until World War II (1938–45).

Micronesia was an area of considerable conflict in that war. It was ultimately placed under the control of the United States and its allies. From 1947 through 1986, the area now known as the FSM remained part of the Trust Territory of the Pacific Islands, a United Nations Trusteeship administered by the United States.

On July 12, 1978, the Trust Territory districts of Truk (now called Chuuk), Ponape (now Pohnpei), Kusaie (now Kosrae), and Yap voted in a plebiscite to join under the new FSM constitution. The constitution went into effect on May 10, 1979. The new national government became fully functional when the national judiciary was certified on May 5, 1981. The Trust Territory of the Pacific Islands, with approval of the United Nations, was formally dissolved in 1986. The FSM is now an independent, self-governing nation, and a member of the United Nations, with a relatively new form of working arrangement with the United States known as free association. Traditional systems continue to play a significant role in the daily life of people in substantial parts of the Federated States of Micronesia.

FORM AND IMPACT OF THE CONSTITUTION

The Federated States of Micronesia have a written constitution, modeled upon that of the United States but with numerous modifications. The constitution is the supreme law. International law, including the Compact of Free Association with the United States, must be in accordance with the constitution.

BASIC ORGANIZATIONAL STRUCTURE

The four states differ considerably in geographical area, population size, and economic strength. All have identical rights in legislative, administrative, and judicial competencies. The constitution endows the national gov-

ernment with a broad range of powers, primarily relating to foreign affairs, defense, maritime, and commercial matters. Except other powers of indisputably national character, powers not expressly delegated to the national government or prohibited to the states are state powers.

LEADING CONSTITUTIONAL PRINCIPLES

The national government is a hybrid form of executive and parliamentary democracy. Except that the president and vice president are selected from and by the Congress, there is a strong division of the executive, legislative, and judicial powers, based on checks and balances. The judiciary is independent.

The constitutional system is defined by a number of leading principles: The Federated States of Micronesia is a democracy, a federation, and a republic, based on the rule of law. On the federal level, political participation is shaped as an indirect, representative democracy.

Religious freedom is guaranteed. The constitution states, "No law may be passed respecting the free exercise of religion, except that assistance may be provided to parochial schools for non-religious purposes."

CONSTITUTIONAL BODIES

The predominant bodies provided for in the constitution are the president, the Congress, and the judiciary. A public auditor is appointed by the president, with the advice and consent of the Congress. Within three of the states, Yap, Pohnpei, and Chuuk, traditional leaders play a significant role as well.

The President

The president, the head of state, is both a ceremonial leader and head of the administration of the national government. Elected by the Congress, the president serves a four-year term and can be reelected for a second term. The president must be a member of Congress, elected by one of the four states to serve as that state's at-large senator. As a practical matter, this power of the Congress to elect and reelect the president affects the balance of powers, weakening the presidency and making it difficult for a president to advocate a strong position contrary to the will of the Congress.

The president appoints the cabinet with the advice and consent of Congress. The president and the cabinet have authority to set government policy and to administer the national government. The weakness in the presidency is exacerbated by the fact that the president runs for popular election only in one state, when vying to become an "at-large" member of the Congress. The absence of formal political parties and lack of effective nongovernmental media further diminish the capacity of the president to establish a true national political base and serve as an effective balance to the national Congress.

The Congress

The Congress is unicameral, the central representative organ of the people in the national government, and the sole legislative body in the FSM empowered to enact the statutes that constitute the primary body of national law.

The Congress has 14 members, chosen in free, general, and direct elections. Each of the four states, on the basis of state equality, elects one at-large member. To be eligible for election to serve as president or vice president of the national government, a candidate must be elected for one of these four at-large positions. The other 10 members are elected from congressional districts apportioned by population. Each state is permitted at least one proportionate senate member, and the larger states have additional members.

The Lawmaking Process

Congress is the sole body empowered to enact the statutes that constitute the primary body of national law. To become law, a bill must pass two readings on separate days. To pass first reading, an affirmative two-thirds of all members is required. On final reading, each state delegation casts one vote, and an affirmative two-thirds vote of the states is required.

A bill passed by Congress is presented to the president for approval. The president may return the bill with relevant objections. If the president does not return a bill within the appropriate period, it becomes law. If the president vetoes the bill, Congress may override the veto through repeating the original voting process.

The Judiciary

If a violation of the constitution occurs, there are effective remedies enforceable by independent state and federal judiciaries, with courts in each state. Their decisions regarding national constitutional violations and remedies are subject to modification and overruling by the Federated States of Micronesia Supreme Court.

Although the constitution authorizes additional courts, there is presently only one national court, the Supreme Court, which consists of a trial division and an appellate division. Cases at the trial level are heard by one justice. The remaining justices are available to hear an appeal from the case, as the appellate division.

The Supreme Court has jurisdiction over cases that involve issues of national law; cases in which opposing parties are diverse, that is, are from different states of the Federated States of Micronesia; and cases in which one party is from another nation. Justices are appointed by the president, subject to advice and consent of Congress, and enjoy lifetime appointments, subject to impeachment powers of Congress.

Traditional Leaders

Within three of the states, Yap, Pohnpei, and Chuuk, traditional leaders play a significant role; by custom they can affect certain rights of people within the respective traditional systems. The constitution recognizes the existence of traditional leaders but does not vest them with formal governmental powers. It states, "Nothing in this Constitution takes away a role or function of a traditional leader as recognized by custom and tradition"; provides for statutory protection of "traditions of the people of the Federated States of Micronesia"; and requires court decisions to be "consistent with this Constitution, Micronesian customs and traditions, and the social and geographical configuration of Micronesia."

THE ELECTION PROCESS

Citizens 18 years or older are entitled to vote in national elections. No candidate runs nationwide. Only members of the Congress are elected during national elections, and each is elected from within the borders of his or her own state.

POLITICAL PARTIES

There are no formal political parties.

CITIZENSHIP

Citizenship of the Federated States is primarily acquired by birth; a child acquires citizenship if one of his or her parents is a citizen.

FUNDAMENTAL RIGHTS

The constitution guarantees human rights in the Declaration of Rights article, which is patterned closely on the Bill of Rights in the United States Constitution, except that the Declaration of Rights prohibits capital punishment and does not support a right to bear arms. Rights in the Declaration of Rights are binding for all public authorities in any circumstances.

ECONOMY

Although many areas, especially the outer islands, operate on a subsistence economy built on fishing and farming, the economic system contemplated by the constitution is a free enterprise market economy, subject to certain adjustments aimed at protecting the small indigenous population from being overrun by outside forces. For example, the constitution prohibits landownership by noncitizens and noncitizen corporations, including corporations partially owned by noncitizens.

RELIGIOUS COMMUNITIES

The constitution provides, "No law may be passed respecting the free exercise of religion, except that assistance may be provided to parochial schools for non-religious purposes."

MILITARY DEFENSE AND STATE OF EMERGENCY

The constitution delegates to Congress power to provide for the national defense, and that power has been delegated to the United States in the Compact of Free Association.

AMENDMENTS TO THE CONSTITUTION

Amendments to the constitution may be proposed by a constitutional convention, popular initiative, or Congress. Every 10 years, Congress must submit to the voters the question, Shall there be a convention to revise or amend the constitution? If the majority says yes, a convention must be convened. Proposed amendments become part of the constitution when approved by three-fourths of the votes cast on the amendment in each of three-fourths of the states.

PRIMARY SOURCES

Constitution in English. Available online. URL: http://www.paclii.org/fm/legis/consol_act/cotfsom468/. Accessed on June 21, 2006.

SECONDARY SOURCES

Alan Burdick, "The Constitution of the Federated States of Micronesia." *University of Hawaii Law Review* 8 (1986); 419.

Edward C. King, "Custom and Constitutionalism in the Federated States of Micronesia." *Asian-Pacific Law & Policy Journal* 3, no. 1 (July 2002): 249 Available online. URL: http://www.hawaii.edu/aplpj/pdfs/v3-10-King.pdf. Accessed on June 21, 2006.

Norman Meller, *Constitutionalism in Micronesia*. Honolulu: Institute for Polynesian Studies, 1985.

Brian Tamanaha, *Understanding Law in Micronesia: An Interpretive Approach to Transplanted Law*. Leiden: E. J. Brill, 1993.

Edward C. King

MOLDOVA

At-a-Glance

OFFICIAL NAME
Republic of Moldova

CAPITAL
Chisinau

POPULATION
3,388,071 (2004 census) and 739,700 residents in
Transnistrian region (1989 census)

SIZE
13,067 sq. mi. (33,843 sq. km)

LANGUAGES
Moldovan (official), Russian, Gagauz

RELIGIONS
Eastern Orthodox 98%, Jewish 1.5%, Baptist (about
1,000 members), Catholic, and other 0.5% (2000)

NATIONAL OR ETHNIC COMPOSITION
Moldovan 76.1%, Ukrainian 8.4%, Russian 5.8%,
Gagauz 4.4%, Romanian 2.1%, Bulgarian 1.9%, other
1.3% (2004 census); in Transnistrian region (1989

census) Moldovan 38.0%, Ukrainian 26.4%, Russian
28.5%, Gagauz 0.6%, Bulgarian 2.0%, other 4.4%

DATE OF INDEPENDENCE OR CREATION
August 27, 1991 (from the Soviet Union)

TYPE OF GOVERNMENT
Parliamentary republic

TYPE OF STATE
Unitary state

TYPE OF LEGISLATURE
Unicameral parliament

DATE OF CONSTITUTION
July 29, 1994

DATE OF LAST AMENDMENT
July 15, 2004

Moldova is a parliamentary republic based on the rule of law with a clear division of executive, legislative, and judicial powers. It is a unitary state, made up of 32 districts, four municipalities, and the autonomous territorial unit of Gagauzia. The constitution guarantees the principle of decentralization of public services; it is, however, not much observed in practice, because of the small size of the districts and their dependence on the central government. The constitution includes the traditional set of human rights and civil freedoms. Although there is a well-described system of legal remedies available for redressing human rights violations, the implementation of this system and the independence of the relevant public authorities have been widely questioned.

The president is the head of state. According to the constitution, Parliament plays the central political role; however, when the president is supported by the major-

ity of Parliament members, he or she in fact becomes the central political figure. The president therefore directly depends on the Parliament, which is the representative body of the people. Free, equal, general, and direct elections of the members of Parliament are guaranteed. Moldova has a pluralistic system of political parties, which all contribute to the definition and expression of public political will.

Religious freedom is guaranteed, and state and religious communities are separated. By constitution, Moldova has a socially oriented market economy.

CONSTITUTIONAL HISTORY

The Republic of Moldova presently occupies most of the territory of what was historically known as Bessarabia. An independent Moldovan state emerged briefly in the

14th century C.E., but the region subsequently fell under Ottoman Turkish rule in the 16th century. After the Russo-Turkish War (1806–12), the eastern half of Moldova, between the Prut and Dniester Rivers (Bessarabia), was ceded to Russia, while Romanian Moldova (west of the Prut) remained under Turkish rule. Romania, which gained independence in 1878, regained control of the eastern half of Moldova in 1918.

As a result of reunification, the constitution of Romania of 1866 became applicable on the territory of Moldova. The 1866 constitution was one of the most liberal constitutions in Europe and was inspired by the ideas of the French Revolution, but it no longer corresponded to the reality of a new, enlarged state. In 1923, a new constitution, drafted by the National Liberal Party, was adopted. The next constitution of 1938, in force only two years, introduced a royal dictatorship.

After the Molotov-Ribbentrop pact of 1940, Romania was forced to cede eastern Moldova to the Soviet Union, which established the Moldovan Soviet Socialist Republic by merging the annexed Bessarabian portion and the autonomous Moldovan republic east of the Dniester, created by the Soviet Union in 1924. The first constitution of the Moldovan Soviet Socialist Republic was adopted in 1941; in the spirit of all the other Soviet constitutions, its main goal was the consolidation of the proletarian dictatorship. The system of soviets of popular deputies as well as the socialist economic system was introduced. In the context of Soviet reforms that followed the breakdown of the Stalinist regime, a new constitution of the Moldovan Soviet Socialist Republic, the so-called Constitution of Developed Socialism, was adopted in 1978. This constitution confirmed the principles of state property, economic planning, and strict centralization. The constitutional provisions on the independence of Moldova had no real force.

Moldova declared its independence from the Soviet Union in August 1991, the start of its transition toward democratic principles. The opposition's drive for immediate reunification with Romania led to a separatist movement of the Gagauz (Christian Turk) minority in the south, which was defused by the granting of local autonomy in 1994. However, unrest in the majority Slavic Transdnistrian region on the east bank of the Dniester River, where in 1992 the government negotiated a cease-fire with Russian and Transdnistrian officials, led to the rise of a separatist movement, which shortly proclaimed itself as the "Transdnistrian Moldovan Republic."

The need for political and economic reform led to constitutional reform. Moldova became a democratic, sovereign, independent, and unitary state, based on the principles of the rule of law. The new constitution was adopted on July 29, 1994, and entered into force on August 27, 1994. Since then, Moldova has actively sought Western recognition. It ratified the main international human rights instruments and became a member state in the main regional and international institutions.

FORM AND IMPACT OF THE CONSTITUTION

Moldova has a written constitution, codified in a single document. The Moldovan constitution is the supreme law of the country and takes precedence over all other national laws. If an international treaty contains provisions contrary to the constitution, it cannot enter into force unless the latter is revised. In general, the law in Moldova does comply with the constitution, whose principles follow international standards.

BASIC ORGANIZATIONAL STRUCTURE

Moldova is a unitary state made up of 32 districts (*raions*), four municipalities, and the autonomous territorial unit of Gagauzia governed by a special statute. Gagauzia has significant autonomy in political, economic, and cultural affairs, within the limits of its authority and pursuant to provisions of the Moldovan constitution. The territory on the east bank of the Dniester River, the self-proclaimed Transdnistrian Moldovan Republic, may be assigned special forms and conditions of autonomy.

Public administration is based on the principles of local autonomy and decentralization of public services. The local public authorities are assigned the task of solving local public affairs. District councils coordinate the activities of the local public authorities and are responsible before the national government.

LEADING CONSTITUTIONAL PRINCIPLES

Moldova is a republic. There is a division of the executive, legislative, and judicial powers, based on the constitutional principle of separation and cooperation of powers.

The Moldovan constitutional system is defined by a number of general principles: Moldova is a sovereign, unitary, and democratic republic, governed by the rule of law, incompatible with dictatorship or totalitarianism, in which the rights and freedoms of people, justice, and political pluralism represent supreme state values. Political participation is shaped as a direct and representative democracy. Any state action impairing the rights of the people must have a basis in organic laws adopted by the Parliament. In the context of the multiethnic composition of Moldova, its national unity constitutes the foundation of the state. The constitution implicitly contains a number of rights and freedoms guaranteed to its citizens, which are to be implemented in accordance with the Universal Declaration of Human Rights and other conventions and treaties endorsed by Moldova.

CONSTITUTIONAL BODIES

The main bodies enshrined in the constitution are the president, the prime minister and administration, the Parliament, the judiciary, and the Constitutional Court.

The President

The president of Moldova is the head of state, its representative in international relations, and the guarantor of national sovereignty and territorial integrity. The president has the prerogative to dissolve Parliament before the end of its term; he or she designates a candidate for the office of prime minister and appoints the administration on the basis of a vote of confidence by Parliament. The president promulgates laws adopted by the Parliament, issues decrees, concludes international treaties in the name of the state, appoints judges, and is the commander in chief of the armed forces.

After the constitutional amendment of 2000, Moldova became a parliamentary republic; the president was now chosen not by the people, but by a secret vote in Parliament. The president is elected for a four-year term and can be reelected only once. The role of the president depends on the political affiliation of the majority in Parliament. When supported by the majority, the president becomes the central political figure in the state.

The Administration and Prime Minister

It is the role of the administration to carry out the domestic and foreign policy of the state and to exert general control over the work of the executive. The administration is responsible to the Parliament and requires its approval of its programs.

The administration consists of a prime minister, ministers, and their cabinets. The prime minister exercises the leadership of the administration and coordinates the activity of its members.

The Parliament

The Parliament is the supreme representative body of the people and the sole legislative authority of the state. It consists of 101 members, who are elected in a general, direct, free, equal, and secret balloting process for a four-year-term. The Constitutional Court validates the election of members of Parliament. The speaker of the Parliament is elected by the majority of votes cast by the members in a secret ballot.

While the main competence of the Parliament is passing laws and ratifying international treaties, it is also empowered to declare referenda, provide legislative interpretations, approve the main directions of the state's internal and external policy, and approve the national budget. Under the conditions prescribed by law, the Parliament has the prerogative to carry a motion of no confidence in the administration.

The Lawmaking Process

The Parliament is endowed with the competence to pass constitutional, organic, and ordinary laws. This is done in cooperation with various other constitutional bodies. The right to legislative initiative belongs to members of Parliament, the president of Moldova, the administration, and the People's Assembly of the autonomous territorial unit of Gagauzia. Before entering into force, the laws must be promulgated by the president. In case objections raised by the president are rejected by Parliament, the president must then promulgate the law.

The Judiciary

According to the constitution, the judiciary is independent of the legislative and executive powers. Since the 2003 judicial reform, justice in Moldova is administered by the Supreme Court of Justice, five Courts of Appeal, three specialized courts (military and economic), and Courts of Law. According to the constitution, judges are to be independent, impartial and irremovable under the law. However, the procedure of their appointment raises concerns. Judges and the presidents of the courts are nominated by the Superior Council of Magistrates and appointed by the president of Moldova. The president and judges of the Supreme Court of Justice are proposed by the Superior Council of Magistrates and are appointed by Parliament.

The Constitutional Court

The Constitutional Court is not a judiciary body. It deals exclusively with constitutional disputes, with the aim of guaranteeing the supremacy of the constitution. It is composed of six judges, appointed by Parliament, the administration, and the Superior Council of Magistrates. Many of its decisions have had the highest legal and political impact. In a major precedent, the Constitutional Court ruled in 1997 that the institution of the *propiska* (the residence permit) violated the constitutional right to freedom of movement; it was therefore abolished. The mechanism for implementing this decision, however, is still lacking.

THE ELECTION PROCESS

Elections in Moldova are based on universal, equal, direct, and free suffrage. All citizens who have attained the age of 18 have the right to stand for office and to vote in the election. Candidates for the president of the country should be over 40 years old, have lived permanently in the country for at least 10 years, and speak Moldovan, the official language. The elections are organized and undertaken by the Central Electoral Commission, which is a permanent body. The mandates are validated by the Constitutional

Court. Regional elections in Gagauzia are organized by the ad hoc Gagauz Election Commission.

POLITICAL PARTIES

Moldova has a pluralistic system of political parties and ensures the right to free association to all its citizens. All parties are equal before the law and contribute to the definition and expression of public political will. Political parties need to register with the Ministry of Justice. They are required to have local branches in at least half of the administrative units. The number of their adherents must be annually confirmed by the Ministry of Justice. Parties can be dissolved by a decision of the Supreme Court of Justice. The Constitutional Court has the competence to decide the constitutionality of a party.

CITIZENSHIP

A person acquires citizenship if one of his or her parents is a Moldovan citizen, regardless of the place of birth, or if the child is born on the territory of Moldova and the parents are stateless or foreign persons. Moldova allows its citizens to hold dual citizenship. No citizen of the Republic of Moldova may be extradited or expelled from the country. Any request to acquire or renounce Moldovan citizenship must be addressed to the president of the republic. The president's decree can be appealed to the Supreme Court of Justice.

FUNDAMENTAL RIGHTS

In its constitution, the Republic of Moldova guarantees respect for the traditional set of human rights and civil freedoms to all its citizens and pledges equal treatment as guaranteed by the main international rights documents. The dignity of individuals and their potential to develop their personality are supreme values of the state. Constitutional provisions for human rights and freedoms must be implemented in accordance with the Universal Declaration of Human Rights and other conventions endorsed by the Republic of Moldova. The basic rights set out in the constitution have binding force for the legislature, executive, and judiciary in any circumstances.

Impact and Functions of Fundamental Rights

According to the constitution, human rights represent the supreme value of the state and should have priority over all other areas of law. This is a novelty for Moldovan society, which had a strong socialist emphasis for 45 years and an unstable rights system. All persons are expected to exercise their constitutional rights and freedoms in good faith, without violating the rights of others.

Limitations to Fundamental Rights

No laws suppressing fundamental human rights and freedoms can be adopted in Moldova. The exercise of certain rights or freedoms may be restricted only by law and only for a specific period. The restriction must be proportionate to the conditions that prompted it and must not affect the ultimate existence of the right.

ECONOMY

According to the constitution, Moldova has a socially oriented market economy based on the coexistence of freely competing private and public properties, the interaction of market forces, free enterprise, and fair competition. It ensures freedom of association and assembly and the right to establish and join trade unions.

Assistance from international financial organizations has been crucial for repaying large government debts and reducing poverty. Privatization of important state-owned industries is under way.

RELIGIOUS COMMUNITIES

Considering the multiethnic composition of its population, the constitution recognizes and guarantees to all its citizens the right to preserve, develop, and express their religious identity in the spirit of tolerance and mutual respect. No one shall be discriminated against on the basis of religion either by the public authorities or by other individuals.

Religious communities are autonomous vis-à-vis the state, and all enjoy equal state support. There is no established state church; however, there are many areas where the authorities and religious organizations cooperate. Religious communities are free to organize themselves and administer their affairs independently. The state ensures both lay and religious education.

MILITARY DEFENSE AND STATE OF EMERGENCY

The Republic of Moldova has proclaimed its permanent neutrality. The national armed forces constitute the framework for performing military services, ensuring national defense, guarding the borders, and maintaining public order. The president of the Republic of Moldova is the commander in chief of the armed forces. The president exercises general leadership of the national defense system and coordinates the activities of administration authorities in national defense issues. The president declares a state of war and with prior approval from the Parliament declares partial or general mobilization. It is the competence of the Parliament to approve the state's military doctrine. The military always remains subject to civil government.

Performance of military service is binding for all male citizens of the Republic of Moldova over the age of 18 and is voluntary for women. The basic military service is 12 months. A citizen can be released from the military service as a conscientious objector but must perform alternative civil service.

AMENDMENTS TO THE CONSTITUTION

The revision of the constitution may be initiated either by the administration, one-third of the members of Parliament, or at least 200,000 voting citizens of the Republic of Moldova in at least half of the administrative-territorial units. Before their submission to Parliament for adoption, constitutional law drafts must obtain a written opinion (recommendation) from the Constitutional Court, supported by at least four judges. The amendment is then passed by a two-thirds majority.

Certain provisions relating to sovereignty, independence, and the unity of the state as well as its permanent neutrality may be revised only by referendum with a majority vote of the voting citizens. No revision suppressing the fundamental rights and freedoms of citizens is allowed. The constitution may not be revised during a state of emergency or war.

PRIMARY SOURCES
Constitution in English. Available online. URL: http://confinder.richmond.edu/admin/docs/moldova3.pdf. Accessed on June 21, 2006.

SECONDARY SOURCES
Alexandru Arseni, *Drept Constitutional si Institutii Politice, Teoria Constitutiei.* Chisinau: Editia a II-a, 1997.
Ion Guceac, *Curs Elementar de Drept Constitutional: Conf. Univ.* Chisinau: Ministerul Afacerilor Interne/ Academia de Politie Stefan cel Mare, 2001.
Mariana Harjevschi and Svetlana Andritchi, "An Overview of the Legal System of the Republic of Moldova." Available online. URL: http://www.llrx.com/features/moldova.htm.
Organization for Security and Co-operation in Europe, "Mission to Moldova." Available online. URL: http://www.osce.org/. Accessed on September 1, 2005.
United Nations, "Core Document Forming Part of the Reports of States Parties: Moldova" (HRI/CORE/1/Add.114), 14 May 2001. Available online. URL: http://www.unhchr.ch/tbs/doc.nsf. Accessed on August 14, 2005.

Ludmila Shargov

MONACO

At-a-Glance

OFFICIAL NAME
Principality of Monaco

CAPITAL
Monaco

POPULATION
35,000, including 6,000 Monegasques (2005 est.)

SIZE
0.75 sq. mi. (1.95 sq. km)

LANGUAGE
French (official)

RELIGIONS
Roman Catholic 90%, other 10%

NATIONAL OR ETHNIC COMPOSITION
Monegasque 16%, Italian 16%, French 47%, other 21%

DATE OF INDEPENDENCE OR CREATION
1641, 1814, 1861

TYPE OF GOVERNMENT
Constitutional monarchy

TYPE OF STATE
Unitary state

TYPE OF LEGISLATURE
Unicameral parliament

DATE OF CONSTITUTION
December 17, 1962

DATE OF LAST AMENDMENT
April 2, 2002

The Principality of Monaco is a sovereign and independent state, constituted as a hereditary and constitutional monarchy, with respect for fundamental rights and freedoms and the rule of law. Monaco is unusual for its small dimensions and its privileged relationship with France.

Monaco is a "microstate." It has but a single municipality, also called Monaco but legally distinct from the state, although its territory corresponds to that of the state. The character of an independent and sovereign state gives the principality an international status, expressed in its diplomatic relations with other states and by its admission to the United Nations Organization in 1993 and to the Council of Europe in 2004. The accession of Monaco to the Council of Europe has been a decisive element in the confirmation of its international status and the development of its constitutional status.

The links with France are underlined by the constitution itself, which cites the "particular treaties signed with France." The Treaty of July 17, 1918, establishes "a friendship," which, being "protective," is confining. On October 24, 2004, a treaty "destined to adopt and to confirm relations of friendship and cooperation between the Principality of Monaco and the French Republic" that takes better account of the independence and sovereignty of the principality was concluded. The Convention of July 28, 1930, under which France nominates the highest officials of the cabinet (the minister of state), judiciary, and administration, is currently under renegotiation.

The political and economic system is characterized by its liberties; Monacan residents also enjoy economic and social rights. The prince is the fundamental political figure within the state, but separation of executive, legislative, and judicial functions is guaranteed. There is a free market economy. Catholicism is the religion of the state, but freedom of religion or belief is guaranteed.

CONSTITUTIONAL HISTORY

Monaco, once ruled by the Italian city of Genoa, became a possession of the Grimaldi family in 1297. It has seen periods of "protection" by Spain (1524–1641) and annexation by France (1793–1814), but it became completely independent in 1861.

The first constitution was promulgated on January 5, 1911. It was characterized notably by the proclamation of rights and freedoms, whose guarantee was entrusted to a Supreme Tribunal, which is one of the oldest bodies of constitutional jurisdiction in the world.

A new constitution was promulgated on December 17, 1962. Its drafting, performed with the assistance of very high-ranking jurists, was marked by a crisis in relations with France. It gave the Monacan state the essential constitutional structures that are still in force today.

The constitutional revision of April 2, 2002, was passed to ensure entry into the Council of Europe. The reports submitted by representatives of the council had suggested certain amendments. The modifications reinforce the rule of law and democracy.

FORM AND IMPACT OF THE CONSTITUTION

The constitution is made up of one single and permanent document, at the apex of the legal system. The Supreme Tribunal can punish any infringements of rights and liberties by a law, regulation, or other administrative act.

According to Article 1, the principality is a sovereign and independent state within the framework of general principles of law and particular treaties with France. The wording can be interpreted as placing general principles of international law and the particular treaties with France above the constitution. However, one can also say that those general principles and particular treaties draw their authority in Monaco from their very recognition by this constitutional provision, which does not position them above it. In fact, observers have questioned whether it gives them constitutional rank at all.

BASIC ORGANIZATIONAL STRUCTURE

The Principality of Monaco is a unitary state. Its territory forms one single municipality, which has its own administration and authorities (municipal council, mayor).

LEADING CONSTITUTIONAL PRINCIPLES

The constitutional principles are expressed in the first articles of the constitution: "The principle of government is the hereditary and constitutional monarchy. The principality is a state of law attached to the respect of fundamental freedoms and rights."

The prince reigns and governs. The executive power lies in the prince's high authority, the legislative power is exercised by the prince and the National Council, and the judicial power is exercised by courts and tribunals. The separation of executive, legislative, and judicial functions is guaranteed.

CONSTITUTIONAL BODIES

The fundamental institution is the prince. Other bodies are the executive government, the National Council, and the judicial bodies.

The Prince

The position of the prince is determined by the constitution and by a sovereign regulation adopted in 1882 and modified in 2002 at the same time the constitution was amended. The sovereignty of the Principality of Monaco is hereditary in the direct and legitimate descent of the princes of Monaco of the Grimaldi dynasty. The succession is reserved to the direct and legitimate descendant of the reigning prince by order of first born with priority to the male descendant.

The prince exercises sovereign authority in conformity with the provisions of the constitution and the law. In the international field, the prince represents the principality in its relations with foreign powers. The prince signs and ratifies treaties, in some cases after they have been approved by law, which applies to treaties that affect the constitutional organization or create budgetary burdens.

In domestic matters, the executive government is exercised under the high authority of the prince. The prince signs sovereign decrees, which without exception have already been discussed in the Council of Government. The prince makes the necessary decrees for the execution of laws and for the application of international treaties and appoints high officials in the executive and the judiciary. The prince also can veto the decisions of the minister of state.

The prince signs bills of laws that are presented to the prince by the executive government. Such bills cannot be submitted to the National Council without the prince's consent.

The Executive Government

The executive government is administered by a minister of state, assisted by the Council of Government, the members of which are appointed by the prince and the minister of state. According to conventions that link Monaco with France, the appointment of the minister of state is subject to recommendations by the French government. It is by tradition a French high civil servant, and most often a diplomat. However, once appointed minister of state, he or she becomes exclusively an official of the principality.

The minister of state represents the prince and directs the activities of the executive, administers the public forces, and presides over the Council of Government.

The minister of state and the Council of Government are responsible for the administration of the principality to the prince, who can terminate their functions at any moment.

National Council (Conseil National)

The National Council constitutes the "parliament" of the principality. It consists of 24 members who are elected for a term of five years. The prince can dissolve the National Council.

The National Council has two sessions per year, neither of which may exceed three months. The minister of state and the Council of Government have access to the National Council and must be heard by it whenever they demand.

The Lawmaking Process

The passing of a law requires the consent of the prince and the National Council. Initiative for a bill belongs to the prince; it is then presented to the National Council with the prince's consent by the minister of state. The National Council discusses and votes on bills and can amend them.

The National Council can also propose new laws, but they become bills only by an explicit decision of the minister of state, or implicitly, if the minister of state does not react to the proposition within a period of six months. The minister of state can also interrupt the legislative procedure by a declaration to the National Council on which debate follows.

The National Council votes the budget. Only a law can establish direct or indirect taxes and duties.

The Judiciary

The judicial power is vested in theory in the prince, who, however, delegates full exercise to the courts and tribunals. The independence of the judges is guaranteed. The director of the judicial services is directly affiliated to the prince and does not form part of the Council of Government.

The Supreme Tribunal is composed of five ordinary and two supplementary members appointed for four years by the prince on the recommendation of different bodies. The Supreme Tribunal has constitutional jurisdiction to decide on internal regulations of the National Council and on the laws insofar as they infringe upon the freedoms and rights enshrined in the constitution. The Supreme Tribunal has administrative jurisdiction to decide on the validity, interpretation, or annulment of administrative decisions and of sovereign decrees made for the execution of laws.

Jurisdiction in all other matters is entrusted to a number of other judicial bodies: the Tribunal of First Instance, the Court of Appeal, the Criminal Tribunal, and the Court of Revision.

THE ELECTION PROCESS

The National Council and the Municipal Council are elected by universal and direct suffrage in a combined system of majority and proportional representation.

All Monacan citizens regardless of gender who are at least 18 years of age have the right to vote. Those over 25 years old are eligible to be elected to the National Council and those 21 years of age to the Municipal Council.

POLITICAL PARTIES

There are no political parties in a traditional sense. However, different groupings assemble lists for the elections. In 2003 elections to the National Council the majority was won by the list that had presented itself as the opposition to the outgoing majority. There is high participation in the elections.

CITIZENSHIP

Monacan citizenship is acquired by birth according to the *ius sanguinis* principle. Foreigners can be naturalized by sovereign decree.

Those foreigners who have been residents in Monaco for a long period are called "children of the country" and enjoy the same benefits as do the Monacans themselves. All foreigners enjoy rights and freedoms that are not formally reserved for nationals.

FUNDAMENTAL RIGHTS

Monaco is a state based on the rule of law and respect for the fundamental freedoms and rights, which are guaranteed in Title 3 of the constitution. Equality before the law is guaranteed as well as individual freedom and safety, the inviolability of domicile, the right to privacy and family life and to privacy of correspondence, freedom of belief, freedom of assembly, freedom of association, and freedom to submit petitions.

In economic and social matters, the inviolability of private property is guaranteed as well as the freedom to work; the right to strike and to form trade unions; the right of Monacans to state aid in case of poverty, unemployment, illness, invalidism, old age, and maternity; and the right to free primary and secondary education.

Since Monaco is a signatory state to the United Nations Pact on Civil and Political Rights and the United Nations Pact on Economic and Social Rights, as well as to the European Convention for the Protection of Human Rights and Fundamental Freedoms, the rights and freedoms proclaimed by these international instruments form part of Monacan law.

ECONOMY

The Monacan economy is a free market economy.

RELIGIOUS COMMUNITIES

The Catholic religion is the religion of the state. The majority of the Monacan population is Catholic. However, freedom of religion and belief and their public exercise are guaranteed.

MILITARY DEFENSE AND STATE OF EMERGENCY

There are no armed forces; nor is there a specific military law. The defense of the Monacan state is guaranteed by the convention concluded with France.

AMENDMENTS TO THE CONSTITUTION

The total or partial revision of the constitution is subject to mutual consent of the prince and the National Council. The initiative for a revision can be taken only by the National Council with a majority of two-thirds of its members (16 of 24).

PRIMARY SOURCES

Constitution in English. Available online. URL: http://www. uni-trier.de/~ievr/constitutions/worldconstitutions. htm. Accessed on September 12, 2005.

Constitution in French. Available online. URL: http:// www.monaco.gouv.mc/. Accessed on August 16, 2005.

Constitution in English: A. P. Blaustein and G. H. Flanz eds., *Constitutions of the Countries of the World.* Dobbs Ferry, N.Y.: Oceana, 1971.

SECONDARY SOURCES

L. Aurélia, *Contribution à l'histoire constitutionnelle de Monaco.* 2d ed. 1961.

M. Bettati, "Monaco." In *International Encyclopedia of Comparative Law.* Vol. 1, *National Reports,* edited by K. Zweigert and K. Drobnig. Tübingen, Germany: Mohr, 1974.

Norbert François, *Introduction au droit monégasque.* Baden-Baden: NomosVelagsgesellschaft,1998.

Revue de droit monégasque, 5, 2003, consacrée à *Droit public et institutions monégasques,* p. 13 (159).

J. P. Gallois, *Le régime international de la Principauté de Monaco.* Paris: Pédone, 1964.

G. Grinda, *Les institutions de la Principauté de Monaco.* Monte Carlo: Editions du Conseil National Monaco, 1999.

A. F. Hancock, "The Legal System of Monaco." In *Modern Legal Systems Cyclopedia,* edited by Redden. Buffalo, N.Y.: Hein, 1990.

V. Margossian-Cotta, "La Principauté de Monaco: Un Etat protégé?" Ph.D. diss., Nice: Institut du Droit de la paix et du développement, 1999.

United Nations, "Core Document Forming Part of the Reports of States Parties: Monaco" (HRI/CORE/1/Add.118), 25 April 2002 and (HRI/GEN/2/Rev.1/Add.1), 18 April 2002. Available online. URL: http://www.unhchr.ch/ tbs/doc.nsf. Accessed on September 2, 2005.

Pierre Delvolvé

MONGOLIA

At-a-Glance

OFFICIAL NAME
Mongolia

CAPITAL
Ulaanbaatar

POPULATION
2,791,272 (2005)

SIZE
603,909 sq. mi. (1,564,116 sq. km)

LANGUAGES
Khalkha Mongol 90%, Turkic, Russian (1999)

RELIGIONS
Buddhist Lamaist 50%, none 40%, shamanist and Christian 6%, Muslim 4% (2004)

NATIONAL OR ETHNIC COMPOSITION
Mongol (mostly Khalkha) 94.9%, Turkic (mostly Kazakh) 5%, other (including Chinese and Russian) 0.1% (2000)

DATE OF INDEPENDENCE OR CREATION
July 11, 1921 (from China)

TYPE OF GOVERNMENT
Parliamentary-presidential system

TYPE OF STATE
Unitary state

TYPE OF LEGISLATURE
Unicameral parliament

DATE OF CONSTITUTION
February 12, 1992, at 12:00 hours

DATE OF LAST AMENDMENT
December 14, 2000

Mongolia has a mixed parliamentary and presidential system of government with a division of executive, legislative, and judicial powers. Organized as a unitary state, Mongolia is made up of 18 provinces and three autonomous cities. The constitution of the post-Soviet state provides for liberal and social human rights and a Constitutional Court.

The powerful president is the head of state and the prime minister is the chief executive. Both the president and the cabinet are responsible to the strong Parliament, the highest organ of state power. Free, general, equal, and direct elections of the members of Parliament are guaranteed. There is a pluralistic system of political parties.

Religious freedom is guaranteed and state and religious communities are separate. The economic system can be described as a social market economy. The military is subject to the civil government in terms of law and fact. Mongolia is constitutionally obliged to pursue a peaceful foreign policy.

CONSTITUTIONAL HISTORY

In 1203 C.E., a single Mongolian state was formed. It was based on nomadic tribal groupings under the leadership of Genghis Khan, who became khan of all Mongols in 1206, when the Great Mongol Empire was established. The Mongols sent conquering armies to nearly all of Asia and European Russia, even to central Europe and Southeast Asia. Kublai Khan, Genghis Khan's grandson, conquered China and established the Yuan dynasty (1279–1368 C.E.). When the Mongol dynasty in China was overthrown, the empire began to decline. In 1640, the Grand Code (Ikh Tsaaz) was written.

The Manchus, after they had conquered China in 1644 and formed the Qing dynasty, added parts of Mongolia to their control in 1691, when Khalkha Mongol nobles swore an oath of allegiance. These nobles enjoyed considerable autonomy. In 1727, Russia and Manchu China concluded the Treaty of Khiakta. The treaty delimited the borderline between China and Mongolia, which still exists in large part today.

The northern part of the territory, also called Outer Mongolia, was a Chinese province (1691–1911), an autonomous state under Russian protection (1912–19), and again a Chinese province (1919–21). In 1921, Mongolia declared its independence from China on the basis that its allegiance had been to the Manchus, not to China. The formalization of Mongolian-Soviet relations then was accelerated, whereas China did not recognize the autonomous theocratic government (led by a holy ruler). The Mongolian People's Republic, based on the first Mongolian constitution, was proclaimed in November 1924, under Soviet Russian auspices. The constitution abolished the system of monarchial theocracy, provided for a legislative consolidation of state power, proclaimed a basic statement of socioeconomic and political rights, and included a national plan to establish socialism.

During World War II (1939–45), Japanese forces invaded eastern Mongolia and were finally defeated by a Soviet-Mongolian army. The constitutions in the following years continued to demonstrate Soviet influence. In 1940, the second Mongolian constitution was adopted, modeled on the Soviet constitution of 1936. In 1960, the third Mongolian constitution was adopted. It included a commitment to a socialist society and culture and the aim of establishing a communist society.

The decline of the Soviet Union in the 1990s was mirrored by political changes in Mongolia. The Politburo of the Communist Party, the Mongolian People's Revolutionary Party (MPRP), resigned in 1990, and Mongolia's first multiparty elections were held. In 1992, the fourth Mongolian constitution was adopted and a Constitutional Court was established.

FORM AND IMPACT OF THE CONSTITUTION

Mongolia has a written constitution, codified in a single document. The constitution consists of 70 articles and takes precedence over all other national law. International law must be in accordance with the constitution to be applicable within Mongolia.

BASIC ORGANIZATIONAL STRUCTURE

Mongolia is a unitary state made up of 18 provinces (*aimags*) and the three autonomous cities of Ulaanbaatar, Darhan, and Erdenet.

LEADING CONSTITUTIONAL PRINCIPLES

Mongolia has a mixed parliamentary-presidential system of government. There is a division of the executive, legislative, and judicial powers, based on checks and balances. The judiciary is independent.

The fundamental purpose of state activity is characterized by a number of leading principles: The Mongolian state ensures democracy, justice, freedom, equality, national unity, and respect for law.

CONSTITUTIONAL BODIES

The predominant bodies provided for in the constitution are the president, the prime minister and cabinet of ministers, the parliament, and the judiciary, including the Constitutional Court.

The President

The president is the head of state. The president nominates the prime minister, who is the head of the administration, in consultation with the majority parties in Parliament. The prime minister is elected or deposed by Parliament.

The president is popularly elected for a four-year term and can be reelected only once. Candidates are nominated by each of the political parties that are represented in Parliament.

The president enjoys some more prerogative rights such as the rights to initiate and veto laws and to issue decrees. However, the president is responsible to Parliament and can be removed from office on the basis of a finding of the Constitutional Court, if an overwhelming majority of members of Parliament agrees.

The Executive Administration

The executive administration comprises the prime minister and other members of the cabinet, who are chosen by Parliament on the basis of the prime minister's recommendation in consultation with the president. The term of the cabinet is four years; it starts at the moment the prime minister is appointed by Parliament.

The cabinet is responsible for the implementation of state laws and is accountable for its work to the Parliament. If one-fourth of the members of Parliament propose the dissolution of the cabinet, Parliament must vote on the matter within 15 days. The president may also propose a no confidence vote, and the cabinet itself may submit a draft resolution requesting a vote of confidence.

The State Great Hural (Parliament)

The State Great Hural, the national Parliament, is the supreme legislative power. The constitution stresses the importance of Parliament and underlines in Article 21 that it is the highest organ of state power. Besides ordinary legislation, it is competent to define a number of policies, such as the basic domestic and foreign policies of the state.

The State Great Hural consists of a single chamber with 76 members. Its term is four years. However, if "extraordinary circumstances arising from sudden calamities," martial law, or the outbreak of public disorder prevents regular elections, the Parliament retains its mandate until these circumstances cease to exist and the new Parliament is sworn in.

The Lawmaking Process

The president, members of the Parliament, and the cabinet have the right to initiate legislation. Citizens and organizations can forward suggestions on draft laws as well.

The president may veto any law or decision of Parliament, but Parliament can override the veto by a two-thirds majority of members present. Parliament then promulgates national laws through publication, and, if not specified otherwise, they are effective within 10 days from the day of publication.

The Judiciary

The judiciary is independent of the administration. A General Council of Courts is constitutionally empowered to nominate judges, who are then confirmed by Parliament and the president.

The judicial system consists of the Supreme Court, *aimag* (provincial) and capital city courts, *soum* and *intersoum* (subdivisions) courts, and district courts. The Supreme Court is the highest judicial body, constitutionally empowered to review all lower court decisions.

The Constitutional Court of Mongolia is known as the Constitution Tsets. Its jurisdiction extends solely to the interpretation of the constitution. If it decides that an act is unconstitutional, the act is considered invalid.

According to Article 50, a Supreme Court decision is final. However, some people believe that the Constitutional Court has the power to review a Supreme Court's decision if the decision breaches the constitutional rights of a citizen.

THE ELECTION PROCESS

All Mongolians over the age of 18 have the right to vote in elections.

Presidential Elections

The president is elected on the basis of universal, free, and direct suffrage by secret ballot. There is a two-round system; the second round is held if no candidate receives a majority of the votes cast in the first round. The second round involves only the two candidates who have obtained the largest number of votes. All Mongolians are eligible to run if they are 45 years of age and have resided in the country for five years.

Parliamentary Elections

Members of Parliament are elected on the basis of universal, free, and direct suffrage by secret ballot. Mongolians who have reached the age of 25 years have the right to stand for elections.

There have been significant changes to the electoral system in the past. Under the current system, the winning candidate is the one who gains more votes than any other candidate (first-past-the-post system).

POLITICAL PARTIES

Since the MPRP, which had governed from 1921 until 1996, yielded its monopoly on power, a pluralistic system of political parties has evolved. Discrimination against and persecution of a person for joining a political party are constitutionally prohibited.

CITIZENSHIP

Mongolian citizenship is primarily acquired by birth: A child acquires Mongolian citizenship if one of his or her parents is a Mongolian citizen. It is of no relevance where a child is born.

FUNDAMENTAL RIGHTS

The 1992 Constitution of Mongolia provides a wide range of human rights and freedoms. Starting with the general equal treatment clause in Article 14, the constitution guarantees that all persons are equal before the law.

Article 16 enumerates the traditional set of liberal human rights and civil liberties as well as some social human rights, such as a right to a basic general education free of charge.

Impact and Functions of Fundamental Rights

The constitution acknowledges the importance of human rights in the preamble. To strengthen their protection further, a National Human Rights Commission was established by Parliament in 2001. According to its reports, the most serious human rights challenges are in the areas of law enforcement and criminal prosecution. Political opponents of the government have suffered human rights violations, including arbitrary detention and ill treatment.

Limitations to Fundamental Rights

The fundamental rights are not without limits, but no fundamental right may be disregarded completely. Some rights may not be suspended even in a state of emergency, such as the right to life and freedom of thought, conscience, and religion.

Article 19 contains a general limitation clause. In exercising rights and freedoms one shall not infringe on national security, the rights and freedoms of others, or public order.

ECONOMY

Mongolia has an economy based on public and private forms of property. The state regulates the economy with a view to ensuring the nation's economic security, the development of all modes of production, and the social development of the population. Taken as a whole, the Mongolian economic system can be described as a social market economy.

RELIGIOUS COMMUNITIES

Buddhist monasteries were dissolved, their property was seized, and monks were secularized under the communist regime in 1938. Today, freedom of conscience or religion is guaranteed as a fundamental right. The separation of church and state is constitutionally recognized, and their relationship is regulated by law.

MILITARY DEFENSE AND STATE OF EMERGENCY

It is a constitutional duty in Mongolia to defend the motherland and to serve in the army. Conscription for men is at 18 to 25 years of age and is compulsory for a minimal term of one year. Conscientious objection is recognized. The president is the commander in chief of the armed forces and head of the National Security Council.

The constitution distinguishes among a state of emergency, martial law, and the state of war. The president declares a state of emergency or a state of war in an emergency. Parliament must approve or disapprove the presidential decree within seven days; otherwise it is deemed void.

Parliament itself can declare a state of emergency, if there are unforeseen dangers, or if state authorities are "not able to cope with public disorders." The Parliament may also declare martial law if public disorders create a real threat of an armed conflict. Furthermore, Parliament can declare a state of war if the sovereignty and independence of Mongolia are threatened.

In case of a state of emergency or war, human rights and freedoms may be subject to limitations, but only by law. Such a law must not affect the right to life; the freedom of thought, conscience, and religion; or the right not to be subjected to torture or inhuman and cruel treatment.

AMENDMENTS TO THE CONSTITUTION

Amendments may be initiated by the president, members of Parliament, the cabinet, or the Constitutional Court. If two-thirds of the members of Parliament so decide, a national referendum on the amendment is held.

The amendment itself is adopted by a majority of three-fourths of all members of Parliament. If an amendment fails twice, it may not be reconsidered before a new Parliament convenes. The first constitutional amendment was made in 2001.

PRIMARY SOURCES

Constitution in English. Available online. URL: http://www.mongolianembassy.us/eng_foreign_policy/the_constitution_of_mongolia.php. Accessed on July 18, 2005.

Constitution in Mongolian. Available online. http://www.mongolia-foreign-policy.net/uh.doc. Accessed on June 21, 2006.

SECONDARY SOURCES

Bureau of Public Affairs, U.S. Department of State, "Background Note and Country Reports on Human Rights Practices and International Religious Freedom Report 2004." Available online. URL: http://www.state.gov/r/pa/ei/bgn/2779.htm. Accessed on June 21, 2005.

"Database of Laws." Available online. URL: http://www.parl.gov.mn/law_english.php. Accessed on September 21, 2005.

Tom Ginsburg, *Judicial Review in New Democracies: Constitutional Courts in Asian Cases*. New York: Cambridge University Press, 2003.

Transition to Democracy—Constitutions of the New Independent States and Mongolia. Strasbourg: Council of Europe Publishing, 1997.

United Nations Development Program, "Electoral Reforms for Mongolia." Available online. URL: http://www.undp.mn/. Accessed on July 25, 2005.

Michael Rahe

MOROCCO

At-a-Glance

OFFICIAL NAME
Kingdom of Morocco

CAPITAL
Rabat

POPULATION
30,088,000 (2005 est.)

SIZE
275,117 sq. mi. (712,550 sq. km)

LANGUAGES
Arabic (official), Amazigh (Berber), French

RELIGIONS
Islam (state religion) 99%, Judaism about 3,000 members

NATIONAL OR ETHNIC COMPOSITION
Arabs, Berbers, Jews

DATE OF INDEPENDENCE OR CREATION
March 2, 1956

TYPE OF GOVERNMENT
Constitutional monarchy; semiparliamentarian regime

TYPE OF STATE
Unitary decentralized state

TYPE OF LEGISLATURE
Bicameral parliament

DATE OF CONSTITUTION
December 7, 1962

DATE OF LAST AMENDMENT
October 10, 1996

Morocco is a constitutional, democratic, and social monarchy. The system recognizes the legitimacy, permanency, and priority of the monarchy and at the same time recognizes the need of the people for representation. This compromise serves as a basis for a certain form of rule of law.

There is a separation of powers. Morocco is a unitary state that is experiencing more and more decentralization. The constitution enshrines and guarantees fundamental rights by an independent judiciary.

The king is the head of state. He reigns, governs, and constitutes the center of the Moroccan constitutional system. He is the secular and spiritual head of the country, whose historical, religious, and national legitimacy places him over all other powers.

The prime minister, coordinator of ministerial activities, is responsible before the king and the bicameral Parliament. Elections are free, equal, and general. Multipartism is enshrined in the constitution and in fact.

Freedom of religion is guaranteed, although Islam is the state religion. The economic system is liberal. The military depends on the civil government.

According to its constitution, Morocco is bound by the principles of the United Nations Charter. The constitution affirms the country's determination to work for the maintenance of peace and "for its attachment to the universally accepted human rights."

CONSTITUTIONAL HISTORY

Situated in the extreme west of Africa, broadly opening into the Mediterranean, Morocco, formerly called the Extreme Maghrib (West), saw successive occupations of which only one left permanent traces: Islam. The Arab Muslims conquered territory and society. However, at the start of historical times, Morocco was inhabited by the Berbers, a population whose origin remains a mystery. They have since maintained the uniqueness of their society.

The Extreme Maghrib was occupied by Phoenicians, Carthaginians, Romans, Visigoths, and Byzantines. The 2,000-year Jewish presence is also worth mentioning. It dates back to antiquity but was invigorated by the Jewish expulsion from Spain in 1492, still a determining element in the Jewish Maghrebian memory. Spanish Jews had considerable impact and contributed in forming Moroccan culture in many fields (costume, arts, jewelry, music, food, other). Better treated than in Europe, Jews lived in harmony with Muslims ("the Moroccan exception") with the exception of some painful episodes in times of troubles (political tensions and droughts). After the independence of Morocco a considerable number of Moroccan Jews emigrated, mostly to Israel and France, where they retain a sense of Moroccan identity.

The Arab Muslim conquest was achieved by the Arab chief Oqba Ibnou Nafi'i, founder of the city of Kairouan in Tunisia, who extended Muslim domination over all of the local population. Succeeding Arabic and Berber dynasties created a state that annexed all of the Maghrib (North Africa), a great part of Spain, and regions south of the Sahara. It even succeeded in resisting the otherwise triumphant advances of Portugal and Spain in the 15th and 16th centuries. The dynasties had to reckon with powerful religious brotherhoods and great tribes. Its climax of cultural and spiritual strength is represented by the Quaraouyine, built in Fes under the Idrissides, considered to be the first university and mosque of the world created by a woman, the educated Fatima El Fihrya.

In 791 C.E., the state of Morocco was founded by Idriss I, a descendent of Ali, son-in-law of the Prophet Muhammad. He founded the first dynasty of the Idrissides with the city of Fes as its capital. Later, in the 11th century, the Berber dynasty of the Almoravides under Yusuf Ibn Tashfine took power and made Marrakech its capital. His project was the political unification of Morocco and Muslim Spain. At that time, the Andalusian civilization in Spain extended to the Maghrib. Under the next Berber dynasty of the Almohades in the 12th century, headed by Ibn Tumart, Marrakech remained the capital, with the mosque of Koutoubia as its landmark. In times of decline, the Berber dynasty of the Marinids (13th-14th centuries) reached out to Fes, conquered the cities of Tlemcen and Tunis, but did not succeed in retaining Spain.

Later on, the Arab dynasty of the Sa'dis (1548–1659) made itself famous by the victories of Sultan Ahmad Al-Mansur in the battle of the three kings (including the king of Portugal and a dethroned Moroccan sultan) in 1578 and by the conquest of the city of Timbuktu.

In 1666, the Arab dynasty of the Alawis under Mawlay ar-Rashid tried to reunify Morocco by way of a coherent economic and military strategy. From 1672 to 1727 Mawlay Ismail reigned as absolute monarch, subdued the local powers, and founded the Sharif Empire. His power stretched to Senegal. He founded a professional army and maintained fruitful diplomatic relations, especially with France and England. Mohammed III (1757–90) lowered the high taxes, issued a stable currency, and reconstituted the army. He also reinforced the numerous diplomatic relations. There are more than 40 international treaties from his reign, and Morocco was the first country to recognize the independence of the United States of America after its Declaration of Independence.

The government of Mohammed III is remembered for the construction of the city of Mogador by the French architect Gournot. Moulay Abd ar-Rahman (1822–59) reconquered Oujda from the Turkish Ottoman Empire and extended his powers to the Algerian coast. When he supported the emir Abdelkader of Algeria, Morocco experienced intense political tensions with France and Spain.

Moulay al-Hassan I (1873–94) faced the challenge of consolidating his power by gathering the tribes around him and modernizing the state. Morocco faced difficult economic, political, social, administrative, and military conditions at the beginning of the 20th century, when it found itself caught in Western aspirations. The "Moroccan crisis" was the product of competition among the European powers such as France, Spain, England, and Germany. Military defeats (Isly 1844, Tetouan 1860), the imposition of unequal treaties (Madrid 1880, Algeciras 1906), the high national debt of the country (especially under the reign of Moulay Abd al-Aziz, 1894–1904), and the secret accord between European powers to divide Morocco (French-Spanish convention of October 3, 1904) contributed to the loss of sovereignty of the kingdom in the Convention of Fes on March 30, 1912, which established the French protectorate. The protectorate developed quickly into direct administration. The French tried to divide the ethnicities of the country with the promulgation of the famous Berber Dahir (decree) of 1930, which is considered an attempt to break up the unity of the Moroccan people.

The administration of the protectorate radicalized the demands of the national movement, led by a number of great personalities (el-Fasi, el-Quazzani, Balafrej, Bouabid, Ben Barka, el-Khateb, Torres, Nacirri, and others), which created the Committee of Moroccan Action in 1934. The signing of the Manifesto of Independence (1944) and the armed resistance (el-Khattabi) increased tension between the parties and underlined the mutual ideological influence between the national movement and the monarchy.

The precarious situation of France after World War II (1939–45) and the growing intensity of revolts and rebellions in Morocco led to negotiations between the national movement and the French government, which culminated in the conference of Aix-les-Bains and the treaties of Celle-Saint-Cloud of October 31, 1955. These treaties marked the end of the protectorate. The treaties provided for the return of the deposed king, Mohammed V, and established the option of a Moroccan government formed on the basis of negotiations among different Moroccan interests and an evolution toward a constitutional monarchy.

The constitutional ideas of the organization and limitation of powers, division of responsibilities, and consultation were not unfamiliar to Morocco even before the protectorate. Governed by Muslim and customary law, Morocco was familiar with institutions such as *shoura* (consultation), *jemaas* (local assemblies), and ulemas (religious legislators). Immediately before the protectorate, the

1908 constitution, inspired by Ottoman ideas, established a regime of rights and freedoms, separation of powers, and a bicameral parliamentary system. During the protectorate, the Democratic Constitutional Party was created. The constitutional idea did not contradict the idea of nationalism. Both contributed to focusing Moroccan power and action in practice to regain sovereignty.

From independence in 1956 until 1962, the date of the promulgation of the first Moroccan constitution, Morocco saw a parliamentarism without parliament, under a customary constitutional regime, the *bey'a*. A code of public freedoms was adopted—the Charter of 1958—and a fundamental law was promulgated on June 2, 1961, as a precondition for a constitutional regime. Elections were held for a consultative assembly.

Moroccan parliamentarism has always been the joint project of the monarchy and the national movement, though they have aimed at different structures and procedures. For the monarchy, democratization had to develop in several steps, taking account of the Moroccan social situation of that time, whereas the parties of the national movement demanded immediate democracy.

Although the monarchy failed in its first attempt to create a constitutional council, it decided to draft the constitution itself. The national movement, however, called for a constitutional assembly. The dispute stayed alive for 38 years, until the 1996 constitution was drafted. All constitutional developments in Morocco before that date were discredited by the nonparticipation of the progressive minority of the national movement, who refused to participate in the government.

The first Moroccan constitution was thus the fruit of a silent pact between the royal will and popular consent. The 1962 constitution was considered progressive at its time; contrary to those in other states that had recently regained their independence, it guaranteed a multiparty system in its text as well as in political practice.

The decisive year 1975 rallied all political forces around the issue of territory, that is, the retrieval of the Sahara provinces, formerly under a Spanish protectorate. Before that date, the regime could have been considered authoritarian, as it struggled against military rebellions and the rise of the Left, of which one party was republican. After 1975, a consensus was reached that held for a while despite many challenges (cancelled elections, periods of hunger, others).

By the 1990s, an inflexible policy was facing democratic demands from the opposition and civil society. The country faced World Bank demands for urgent social evolution, the unresolved territorial issue, and the worldwide pressure for democracy that followed the fall of the Berlin wall. At the end of the reign of Hassan II, clear signs of an opening were visible: constitutional amendments, more guarantees of fundamental rights, the creation of administrative courts, the founding of the Ministry for Human Rights, the ratification of international instruments on human rights, the release of political prisoners, and the founding of a Consultative Council for Human Rights.

The succession to the throne of King Mohammed VI in 1999 maintained these trends, although some signs of tensions have appeared, notably after the terrorist acts of May 16, 2003. While Mohammed V could be described as the liberator and Hassan II as the builder of the modern state, Mohammed VI seems to be positioning himself as the constructor of the rule of law, despite the opposition of radical Islamists, who question his religious status and want to introduce Quranic law, and reactionary monarchists, who consider the division of powers to be *siba* (anarchy).

FORM AND IMPACT OF THE CONSTITUTION

The constitution of Morocco is one single document with 108 articles. Islam has an important place in two non-secularized contexts: in constitutional law (particularly concerning the status of the head of state) and in family law. These are always open to progressive interpretation, as recently occurred in the amendment of the family code leading to more equality and better protection of the rights and freedoms of women and the family.

Alongside the written constitution are customary constitutional law and constitutional practice.

Ratified international treaties form part of the hierarchy of norms that have status at least equal to that of law. The constitution does not say anything about the role of international treaties, but law, jurisprudence, and royal interventions seem to head in the direction of the superiority of international conventions to law.

The hierarchy of norms is difficult to determine; nevertheless it is possible to infer a normative system.

The "constitutional bloc" comprises Islam, the constitution, and custom. The organic laws follow, then the ordinary laws (international treaties are at least equal to laws), the regulations, and jurisprudence. Royal acts called *dahirs* are outside the hierarchy of norms and are not open to judicial recourse.

BASIC ORGANIZATIONAL STRUCTURE

Morocco is a decentralized unitary state that grants some autonomy to local entities, which include regions, prefectures, provinces, and urban and rural communities.

There are 16 regions. They are placed over the prefectures and the provinces. The rural communities have financial autonomy. Local representatives are elected for six-year terms by universal and direct suffrage.

LEADING CONSTITUTIONAL PRINCIPLES

Morocco is a Muslim state. The king is "commander of the faithful." Human rights as universally recognized are guaranteed. Morocco is a democracy and a constitutional monarchy that has national sovereignty.

CONSTITUTIONAL BODIES

The main constitutional bodies are the king, the bicameral Parliament, the executive administration, and the judiciary, including the Constitutional Court.

The King

The Crown of Morocco is hereditary and passes from the father to the male descendants in direct line and by order of primogeniture, unless the king while alive designates a successor other than his son. The king is a minor until he reaches the age of 16 years, and in this case a regency council exercises the constitutional rights of the Crown.

The person of the king is inviolable and sacred: "The King is the commander of the believers, supreme representative of the nation, symbol of its unity, guarantor of the perpetuity and continuity of the state, guardian of the respect of Islam and the constitution. He is the protector of the rights and freedoms of the citizens, social groups, and collectivities" (Article 19).

The king appoints the prime minister and on the suggestion of the latter appoints the other members of the executive administration. He chairs the Council of Ministers, promulgates the laws within 30 days, can dissolve either or both chambers of Parliament, and can address messages to the nation and to Parliament, but the latter cannot be the object of any debate.

The king exercises his powers by *dahir* (decree), often countersigned by the prime minister. He accredits the ambassadors before foreign powers and signs and ratifies the treaties; only those treaties that entail public financing need the prior approval of Parliament.

The king presides over the Superior Council of Magistrates, the Supreme Council of Education, and the Supreme Council of National Development and Planning. He appoints the judges and exercises the right of pardon. The king can ask Parliament for a new reading of a bill of law; if the bill is not accepted, the king can submit it to a referendum.

In case of a threat to territorial integrity or circumstances that endanger the proper functioning of constitutional institutions, the king can, after consultation with the presidents of the chambers and the president of the Constitutional Court, declare a state of exception, which does not involve the dissolution of Parliament. Morocco experienced a state of exception regime between 1965 and 1970 after the failure of the first parliamentary experience.

The king must inform Parliament before issuing a declaration of war.

The Parliament

The Parliament is bicameral. The House of Representatives is composed of 325 elected members (since 2002, 30 seats are reserved for women). It is elected from a national list for five years by universal and direct suffrage. The House of Counselors has 270 members elected for nine years, one-third renewed every three years by universal indirect suffrage. Three-fifths of the members of the House of Counselors are representatives of local communities, and two-fifths are representatives of professional organizations and of employees.

The Parliament sits for two sessions a year; an extraordinary session can also be summoned. Members of Parliament are protected by parliamentary immunity except if they are caught in the act of committing a serious crime. Members of Parliament can be members of the executive government.

Parliament has powers to create laws in the fields determined by the constitution and to control the executive administration by using questions, investigative committees, and the threat of censure. In order to dismiss the executive government by a vote of no confidence, the House of Representatives needs an absolute majority, and the House of Counselors needs a majority of two-thirds. The latter can also address a motion of admonition to the executive administration or call to order any act or policy it finds unsuitable.

The Lawmaking Process

The initiative for bills rests with the prime minister and with Parliament. They are sent for examination to the relevant committees.

The two chambers must adopt identical texts. If they do not, the executive administration can call for a joint committee; if that fails, the House of Representatives has the last word, by an absolute majority.

Organic laws, as well as parliamentary rules, cannot enter into force until they have been declared to be in conformity with the constitution by the Constitutional Council.

The Executive Administration

The executive administration is made up of the prime minister and the cabinet ministers. It is responsible before the king and before Parliament. After the appointment of the executive government the prime minister presents his or her program before Parliament. In the House of Representatives there are a debate and vote; in the House of Counselors there is only a debate. The prime minister needs the confidence of the House of Representatives.

The prime minister is responsible for the execution of laws, administers the country, and issues ordinances by decree. The prime minister does not determine the policy of the nation and is more of a "supercoordinator" below the king.

The Judiciary

The judicial power is independent of the legislative and executive powers. Decisions are made in the name of the king. The judges are appointed by *dahir* on the recommendation of the Superior Council of the Magistrate. The judges cannot be removed.

The current organization of the judiciary reflects the French model and functions along the same principles: independence of the judges, pyramidal and hierarchical organization, headed by a centralized jurisdiction charged with watching over the good application of the law. There are homogeneous jurisprudence and diversity of means of recourse. Administrative courts were created in 1990 and courts of commerce in 1997.

The Constitutional Council (Conseil Constitutionnel)

The Constitutional Council was created by the amendment of 1992 to strengthen the rule of law by controlling the constitutionality of laws. It is composed of 12 members who are appointed for nine years and cannot be reappointed. Six judges are nominated by the king, three by the president of the House of Representatives, and three by the president of the House of Counselors after consultation with the parliamentary groupings. One-third of each category is renewed every three years. Currently it is composed in its majority by jurists (academics, judges, or advocates). One of the judges is a woman.

The Constitutional Council can be addressed by the king, the prime minister, the presidents of the chambers, or one-quarter of the members of each chamber. The call is performed before promulgation of a law; it thus is a preventive control.

The Constitutional Council decides on the conformity with the constitution of organic laws (important laws specified in the constitution), ordinary laws, and parliamentary rules; it decides on jurisdiction to make ordinances and legislation and verifies the status of members of Parliament (ineligibility and incompatibility). It can judge disputes about elections to the legislature and referendums. The Constitutional Council is consulted by the king prior to the declaration of a state of exception or the dissolution of Parliament.

The decisions of the Constitutional Council are binding on all public powers and all administrative and judicial authorities. It makes its decisions within one month except in cases of urgency.

Recently the Constitutional Council has been especially active in controlling elections for the legislature. It has also made decisions that protect fundamental rights such as access to employment and offices, the exercise of parliamentary mandates, freedom of communication, the right to join or not to join a political formation, and the independence of the judiciary.

Audit Office (La Cour des Comptes)

The Audit Office is charged with administration of the budget and finance laws. It assists Parliament and the executive administration and reports to the king. The regional audit offices control the expenses and management of local communities and associations.

The High Court

The High Court is composed in equal parts of members elected from each chamber of Parliament and is chaired by a member nominated by the king. The High Court judges the members of the executive administration who are charged with crimes and offenses committed in exercising their functions. The accusation requires one-quarter of the members of one of the chambers and then the consent of two-thirds of its members.

THE ELECTION PROCESS

On the eve of the legislative elections of September 2002, the rules for election were amended in order to obtain more representative results and a more legally and ethically proper campaign. The changes included greater penalties for electoral fraud, introduction of minimal female representation, lowering of the voting age to 18 years, and inclusion of nonparty candidates who obtain a minimal number of voter signatures. The elections are secret, personal, optional, and individual. There is no voting by proxy or absentee voting.

Moroccan citizens resident abroad can vote only in referenda. Some of them formed a nongovernmental organization to campaign for their right to vote; however, they lost their case before the Supreme Court.

A number of officials, such as military personnel, judges, or governors, are ineligible to vote.

Elections take place by proportional representation.

POLITICAL PARTIES

Article 3 of the constitution enshrines pluralism and prohibits a single-party system. In 1959, the Moroccan courts dissolved the Moroccan Communist Party (PCM) on the basis of a royal discourse that declared the Marxist-Leninist doctrine incompatible with the principles of Islam. However, the party survived under a different name. The only current criterion for banning a party is that its program is considered to contradict the principles of the constitution.

The freedom to found a political party is guaranteed to all Moroccans without any discrimination based on race, gender, belief, or region of origin.

CITIZENSHIP

Moroccan citizenship is primarily acquired by birth. The child of a Moroccan father, regardless of the child's country of birth, acquires Moroccan citizenship. The child of a Moroccan mother and an unknown or stateless father also acquires Moroccan citizenship. It is of no relevance where a child is born.

FUNDAMENTAL RIGHTS

From the first constitution on, a whole title has been dedicated to fundamental rights. The 1992 amendments add to the preamble an affirmation that Morocco is committed to human rights as they are universally recognized. This change places Morocco under the rein of the international conventions that it has ratified.

The 1996 revision added freedom of enterprise, in line with the current conception of a slim, disengaged state, removing itself from the sectors of production and distribution in order to encourage the system of competition.

The accent is placed on civil and political rights, although economic and social rights are present as well. The following are guaranteed: equality before the law in access to public offices, in education, and in the exercise of civil rights of the two genders; freedom of opinion, expression, assembly, association, and movement; safety; inviolability of domicile and communication; the right to strike; the right of property; and freedom of exercise of religion.

Impact and Functions of Fundamental Rights

Various institutions have been founded for the protection of fundamental rights: the Ministry of Human Rights; the Consultative Council for Human Rights; the Constitutional Council, and the Administrative Courts; the mediator called Diwan al Madhalim, which receives and pursues citizens' complaints about decisions or acts of a public authority; the Courts of Commerce; the Institution of Equity and Reconciliation (IER), which works for the collective memory and reconciliation of the state and the victims of injustices under previous regimes.

Several changes to existing laws have strengthened fundamental rights. The code of criminal procedure includes stronger limits on police custody and preventive confinement, and a new labor code has strengthened workers' rights.

The family code was made more egalitarian. The family is now considered the common responsibility of both spouses; the notion of obedience of the wife has disappeared; the minimal marriage age is 18 years for both men and women; the father's consent to marriage is no longer obligatory; verbal repudiation has disappeared in favor of divorce by mutual consent, which is guaranteed; polygamy has been placed under more severe restrictive conditions; and the rights of the child have been strengthened. These changes were supported by royal intervention and by the work of nongovernmental women's groups.

The creation of the High Authority of Communication and Audiovisual Media on August 31, 2002, put an end to the state monopoly in radio and television broadcasting. It is mandated to fight for a pluralist and diversified broadcast sector.

The new press code promulgated in 2002 strengthened freedom of the press and entrusted the judicial authorities with powers to suspend or dissolve newspapers. Sometimes the press oversteps boundaries, which causes censorship and endangers freedom of speech. These exceptions, however, are rather few for this geographical region.

Pluralism also applies to the recognition of the Berber culture. Thus, the Royal Institute of the Amazigh Culture (IRCAM) was founded by the king on October 17, 2001, to work for the recognition, promotion, and teaching of the Berber culture and language. Some members of this institution resigned recently, in protest that demands for constitutional recognition of the Berber language had not yet been taken into account.

Limitations to Fundamental Rights

An antiterrorist law imposed after the attack of May 16, 2003, in Casablanca included a prolongation of police custody and limitations to the secrecy of communication. The organic law on the right to strike limits this right. The equality guaranteed in the constitution for the political rights of both genders raises the question of equality in other fields. Another important limitation to fundamental rights is individual citizens' lack of access to the Constitutional Council.

ECONOMY

The right to property is guaranteed, as are freedom of enterprise and freedom for trade unions. Privatization and nationalization require a law. The administration's development plans concern strategy, objectives, and means of action rather than traditional detailed planning. The goal is sustainable human development. The constitution provides for an Economic and Social Council, representing economic interests and civil society; however, this has not yet been instituted.

RELIGIOUS COMMUNITIES

There is freedom of religion but not freedom of conscience. For the latter, the constitution is silent. Morocco, though having ratified the International Pact on Civil and Political Rights, does not adhere to the universal concept of freedom of religion. Islam is the religion of the state.

Jewish citizens are considered to be nationals and thus are not banned from any function, mandate, or activity. They have been counselors to the king, members of the executive administration, members of Parliament, judges, members of the opposition, active in civil society, and cherished writers.

It is worth mentioning the strong moral and courageous attitude of the late Mohammed V when he refused during the Nazi period to collaborate with the French government of Vichy, which ordered him to extradite his subjects of Jewish religion, declaring, "I do not have Jews; I have but Moroccan citizens!"

MILITARY DEFENSE AND STATE OF EMERGENCY

In principle, the armed forces are subordinate to the civil powers. The king is commander in chief of the royal armed forces; he appoints the civil and military officers and can delegate this right. There is a minister of national defense.

A state of emergency can be declared by the king together with the Council of Ministers for a period of 30 days; it can be prolonged by law.

There is no military conscription.

AMENDMENTS TO THE CONSTITUTION

The initiative for an amendment to the constitution rests with the king and with Parliament. In case of a royal initiative, it can be adopted directly by referendum. In case of a parliamentary initiative, a majority of two-thirds is needed in each chamber before passing it to a referendum.

All the amendments that have passed to the present originated as royal initiatives. This is the settled constitutional practice.

There are untouchable provisions or "eternity clauses" that cannot be amended: the provisions relating to Islam and to the monarchical form of the state.

The parties of the national movement have addressed a memorandum to the king that lists demands such as a more balanced division of powers, a more effective role for the prime minister, and a better guarantee of fundamental rights. The memorandum marks a breach with the past, when the national movement demanded that a constituent assembly be summoned. By the addressing of a memorandum to the king, an old demand has been dropped, and a culture of systematic opposition has been replaced by a culture of participation.

Some in the opposition have reconciled themselves with the current constitution and merely deplore its incomplete implementation, concluding that the time for major revision has not yet arrived.

PRIMARY SOURCES

Constitution in English. Available online. URL: http://www.mincom.gov.ma/english/generalities/state_st/constitution.htm. Accessed on August 29, 2005.

SECONDARY SOURCES

Bureau of Public Affairs, U.S. Department of State, "Background Note and Country Reports on Human Rights Practices and International Religious Freedom Report 2004." Available online. URL: http://www.state.gov/r/pa/ei/bgn/5431.htm. Accessed on June 21, 2006.

Ahmed Mahiou, Rapport introductif. *L'Etat de droit dans le monde arabe*. Paris: CNRS ÈDITIONS. Iremam, 1997.

Michel Rousset, *Le Royaume du Maroc IIAP*. Paris: Edition Berger levrault, Paris, 1978.

Nadia Bernoussi

MOZAMBIQUE

At-a-Glance

OFFICIAL NAME
Republic of Mozambique

CAPITAL
Maputo

POPULATION
18,811,731 (July 2004 est.)

SIZE
308,646 sq. mi. (799,390 sq. km)

LANGUAGES
Portuguese (official), Makua-Lomwe, Cishona, Xitsonga, Swahili, Ciyao, Cisena, Chenwa-Nyanja, Echuawabo, Shimaconde, Cicopi, Bitonga, English

RELIGIONS
Christian (Catholic, Protestant) 30%, Muslim 10%, Hindu and traditional African 60%

NATIONAL OR ETHNIC COMPOSITION
Makua, Makonde (northern region), Sena (central region), Shangan (southern region) 99%, other 1%

DATE OF INDEPENDENCE OR CREATION
June 25, 1975

TYPE OF GOVERNMENT
Presidential state

TYPE OF STATE
Unitary state

TYPE OF LEGISLATURE
Unicameral parliament

DATE OF CONSTITUTION
November 16, 2004

DATE OF LAST AMENDMENT
No amendment

Mozambique is a presidential democracy based on the rule of law with a clear division of executive, legislative, and judicial powers. It is organized territorially into 11 provinces, including Maputo City which recently gained the status of a province, and many districts, administrative centers, localities, and villages. It has a strong central government. The constitution of Mozambique contains a bill of rights ensuring fundamental rights. In the event of violations, the constitution also contains remedies enforceable by an independent judiciary, which includes courts and the Constitutional Council.

The president of the Republic of Mozambique is the head of state, the head of the executive administration, the guardian of the constitution, and the commander in chief of the armed forces: however, the latter two functions are mostly representative. The president, a prime minister who is not head of the executive administration, ministers, provincial governors, and administrators compose the executive government structure.

Free, equal, general, and direct elections of the president and members of parliament are guaranteed. A plu-ralistic system of political parties has intense political impact.

Religious freedom is constitutionally guaranteed, and state and religious communities are separated. The economic system can be described as a market economy. The military is subject to the civil government in both law and fact.

CONSTITUTIONAL HISTORY

Mozambique, a former Portuguese colony, was discovered for Portugal in 1489 by Vasco da Gama on his way to India. During the 1884–85 Berlin Conference on Colonization, the geographical area now called the Republic of Mozambique was "officially" allocated to Portugal.

In the 1960s, the first liberation movements to fight against Portuguese colonization emerged as the Frente de Libertação de Moçambique (Front for the Liberation of Mozambique [FRELIMO]). The struggle led to independence from Portugal in 1975.

After independence in 1975, a civil war emerged in Mozambique between the ruling party (FRELIMO) and the rebel movement called Resistência Nacional de Moçambique (RENAMO). The civil war continued for about 16 years. In October 1992, RENAMO and FRELIMO signed a General Peace Agreement. Since independence in 1975, three new constitutions have been adopted in succession, in 1975, 1990, and 2004.

FORM AND IMPACT OF THE CONSTITUTION

Mozambique has a written constitution, codified in a single document, that takes precedence over all other national law. International law must be in accordance with the constitution to be applicable within Mozambique. The African Charter and the United Nations Charter apply directly in the country without transformation into ordinary law; other international treaties and agreements must be transformed into ordinary law to be applied within Mozambique.

BASIC ORGANIZATIONAL STRUCTURE

Mozambique is a unitary state made up of 11 provinces. The provinces are subdivided into districts, administrative centers, localities, and villages. These subprovincial municipalities are decentralized from the central government with limited autonomy in dealing with some matters, although they are still very dependent on state funds.

LEADING CONSTITUTIONAL PRINCIPLES

Mozambique's system of government is a presidential democracy. The constitution provides for the separation of the executive, legislative, and judicial powers; the independence of the judiciary is constitutionally guaranteed.

In the Mozambican constitution, the following principles are enshrined: Mozambique is a unitary republic based on the rule of law and legal pluralism; it is secular, social, sovereign, and respectful of human rights.

CONSTITUTIONAL BODIES

The constitution provides for three branches of government: the executive, legislative, and judicial. The main constitutional bodies are the executive administration, including the president, ministers, and vice ministers; the Assembly of the Republic; the Council of State; the Constitutional Council; and tribunals and courts.

The Executive Administration

The executive branch includes the president and the cabinet ministers and vice ministers. The president of the Republic of Mozambique is the head of state, the head of the executive administration, the guardian of the constitution, and the commander in chief of the armed forces. The president is elected for a five-year term and can be reelected only once. Any further reelection is possible only when five years has elapsed since the last mandate.

The president has the authority to appoint and dismiss the prime minister, cabinet ministers, vice ministers, governors, rectors and vice rectors of public universities, and the attorney general. The president also has the power to dissolve the Assembly of the Republic.

The Legislature

The legislative branch of government comprises the Assembly of the Republic, which is the central representative organ of the people. There are 250 members representing several political parties in the assembly. Its period of office is five years. The members of the assembly are elected in a general, direct, free, equal, and secret balloting process.

The Council of State

The Council of State was introduced in 2005 when the new constitution was implemented; it serves as the political consultation organ for the president of the republic. Members include the president of the Assembly of the Republic, the president of the Constitutional Council, and former heads of state and prime ministers.

The Constitutional Council

The Constitutional Council is a new organ in the Mozambican constitution. It is charged with the administration of justice in constitutional matters and matters related to elections.

The Judiciary (Courts and Tribunals)

The courts and tribunals administer justice in the name of the people. A special law determines their respective subject matters and geographic jurisdictions. The Supreme Court of Justice is the highest court in Mozambique.

The Lawmaking Process

The main function of the Assembly of the Republic is to pass laws. Deliberations can begin only when more than half of the members are present. After the assembly passes a law, the president of the republic must sign it and publish it in the official gazette in order for it to become the law in Mozambique.

THE ELECTION PROCESS

All Mozambican citizens over the age of 35 years have the right to stand for presidential elections. They may vote in both presidential and parliamentary elections when they are over the age of 18 years.

POLITICAL PARTIES

The Mozambican constitution provides for the right of association. Mozambique has a pluralistic system of political parties, with two major political parties: FRELIMO and RENAMO. The multiparty system is a basic structure of the constitutional order, and the political parties are a fundamental element of public life. The creation of political parties is regulated by ordinary law and guaranteed by the constitution.

CITIZENSHIP

A child acquires citizenship if one of his or her parents is a Mozambican citizen, regardless of where the child is born. Citizenship also can be acquired by naturalization.

FUNDAMENTAL RIGHTS

The constitution provides for a bill of fundamental rights, and it accepts and applies directly in Mozambican law the United Nations Charter and the African Charter. The constitution also states that the interpretation of fundamental rights should be in accordance with the African Charter on Human Rights and the United Nations Universal Declaration of Human Rights. Application of international instruments protecting fundamental rights by the local courts in Mozambique is very rare, partly because of the lack of appropriate knowledge of such instruments by the judges.

Chapters 3 and 4 of the Mozambican constitution provide for traditional civil and political rights as well as economic, social, and cultural rights. These chapters also contain provisions that guarantee the rights of women, the disabled, and elderly people.

Impact and Functions of Fundamental Rights

The constitution provides for a set of traditional human rights and their enforcement mechanisms. The foundations for democracy are enshrined in the Mozambique constitution. In Mozambique there is no special legal, independent entity apart from the tribunals to hear and decide cases related to human rights violations.

Limitations to Fundamental Rights

The fundamental rights in the Mozambican constitution can be limited or suspended only in very limited cases, such as a state of emergency, state of war, public disorder, or severe, widespread moral lapses. Such limitations must be applied to all citizens equally, and any decree limiting rights must specify the legal basis for the limitation.

ECONOMY

Mozambique has an open market economy, although the constitution does not specify any particular economic system. The constitution does provide for some rights related to the economy, such as freedom of association, the right to property, and the prohibition of expropriation of private property, except for the public interest and by law.

RELIGIOUS COMMUNITIES

The Mozambican constitution in Article 54 guarantees freedom of religion or belief. Religious associations are regulated by ordinary law. The constitution provides for separation of state and church; there is no state religion.

MILITARY DEFENSE AND STATE OF EMERGENCY

In Mozambique the executive administration is responsible for creating and maintaining the armed and security forces, namely, the police, the army, and the intelligence service. The army also can be used for civil purposes in some special cases.

Basic military service in Mozambique is compulsory for a period of two years for both women and men over the age of 18 years. After the two-year period, recruits may become professional soldiers serving for fixed periods or for life. Civil service may be performed by those who cannot perform basic military service. The military always remains subject to civil government.

AMENDMENTS TO THE CONSTITUTION

Amendments to the Mozambican constitution can be proposed by the president of the republic or by one-third of the members of the Assembly of the Republic. Approval requires two-thirds of the members of the assembly. The following provisions can be amended only by referendum: fundamental rights, the system of government, the autonomy of the municipalities, and the constitutionally guaranteed independence of judges.

PRIMARY SOURCES
2005 Mozambican Constitution in Portuguese (and English). Available online. URL: http://www.mozlegal.com/

content/download/256/1521/file/Constitution%20_in %20force%2021%2001%2005__English_pdf. Accessed on June 28, 2006.

SECONDARY SOURCES

"History of Mozambique." Available online. URL: http:// www.answers.com/topic/history-of-mozambique. Accessed on September 15, 2005.

"Official Website of the Republic of Mozambique." Available online. URL: www.mozambique.mz. Accessed on August 24, 2005.

Christof Heyns, ed., *Human Rights Law in Africa.* Vol. 2. Leiden: Martinus Nijhoff, 2004.

João Miguel Fernandes

MYANMAR

At-a-Glance

OFFICIAL NAME
Union of Myanmar

CAPITAL
Pyinmana

POPULATION
52,000,000 (July 2004 est.)

SIZE
261,970 sq. mi. (678,500 sq. km)

LANGUAGES
Burmese, ethnic minority languages

RELIGIONS
Buddhist 89%, Christian (Baptist 3%, Roman Catholic 1%) 4%, Muslim 4%, animist 1%, other 2%

NATIONAL OR ETHNIC COMPOSITION
Burman 68%, Shan 9%, Karen 7%, Rakhine 4%, Chinese 3%, Indian 2%, Mon 2%, other 5%

DATE OF INDEPENDENCE OR CREATION
January 4, 1948

TYPE OF GOVERNMENT
Military regime

TYPE OF STATE
Unitary state

TYPE OF LEGISLATURE
No legislature; laws issued by military decree of ruling State Peace and Development Council (SPDC)

DATE OF CONSTITUTION
January 3, 1974 (defunct)

DATE OF LAST AMENDMENT
1974 constitution no longer in force since September 18, 1988

Burma, today officially called Union of Myanmar, has had three official names since independence from Great Britain: the Union of Burma (January 1948 to March 1974), the Socialist Republic of the Union of Burma (March 1974 to September 1988), (again) the Union of Burma from September 1988 to May 1989, and the Union of Myanmar (the last two name changes were made by order of the ruling State Law and Order Restoration Council, May 1989). It has had two constitutions.

The 1947 constitution established a parliamentary form of government, whereby political parties operated freely, a prime minister chosen by the lower house of the legislature held executive power, and a ceremonial president acted as the formal head of state. The supreme court enforced citizens' rights and the judiciary was independent.

With the military coup of March 1962, the liberal parliamentary constitution of 1947 effectively ended. The group of army officers who took power at that time ruled by military decree for 12 years. In January 1974, a new

constitution entered into force; in effect, it legalized and perpetuated one-party rule under the Burma Socialist Programme Party (BSPP).

Massive protests against one-party rule resulted in another military takeover, by the State Law and Order Restoration Council (SLORC), on September 18, 1988. The protests, known as the 1988 Uprising, were crushed, but at the same time the one-party system ended. After the SLORC takeover, political parties were allowed to operate, albeit under severe restrictions, and some were allowed to contest the May 1990 elections.

However, more than 15 years after these elections the political parties—the National League for Democracy (NLD) and its allies—have still not gained political power or nominally share it with the ruling SLORC or with the State Peace and Development Council (SPDC). They continue to operate under severe restrictions. Since January 1993, a military-run National Convention has been meeting periodically to draft basic principles for a promised new constitution. There is no timetable for this drafting process; nor is there any indication as to how such a constitution is to be adopted. The country remains under military rule, as the State Peace and Development Council rules by decree.

This article presents and briefly compares selected provisions of the defunct 1947 liberal and 1974 one-party constitutions, as well as some of the principles or provisions agreed upon by the National Convention. Since September 1988, Burma does not have a constitution in force. Therefore, the agreed upon principles adopted so far in the National Convention must be seen as highly contingent.

CONSTITUTIONAL HISTORY

The Union of Burma gained independence from Britain on January 4, 1948. During the 19th century, the British and the Burmese fought three wars (1824–26, 1852, 1885). After the third Anglo-Burmese war in November 1885, the whole country was annexed into the British Indian Empire on January 1, 1886.

Prior to the regaining of independence in January 1948, a 111-member Constituent Assembly met from June to September 1947 and adopted the constitution on September 24, 1947. The constitution was fully in force with independence in January 1948.

The 1947 constitution can be described as based on the British Westminster parliamentary form of government. It established a two-chamber parliament. The lower chamber, the Pyithu Hluttaw (Chamber of Deputies in the official English translation), was elected nationwide on the basis of universal adult suffrage, while the upper chamber, the Lumyosu Hluttaw (Chamber of Nationalities), was elected or appointed on the basis of ethnicity, with designated numbers of representatives from the various indigenous ethnic groups. Political parties operated freely; the leader of the political party that received most votes in the Chamber of Deputies (also known generally as parliament, even in Burmese) became the prime minister, who was also the head of the administration. The president was the head of state, but this was largely a ceremonial post. The constitutional system that was practiced during the time of the 1947 constitution can be generally described as prime ministerial or parliamentary rather than presidential.

The 1947 constitution lasted until the military coup of March 2, 1962. On that day a group of army officers led by the late General Ne Win (1910?–2002) took power. On the day of the coup the president, the chief justice of the union, the prime minister, and the cabinet ministers were arrested. Parliament was abolished by a decree of the Revolutionary Council on March 3. The Supreme and High Courts of Burma were abolished by another decree, on March 30. A 17-member Revolutionary Council (RC) was formed. Later, a revolutionary administration was also formed, consisting mainly of active duty military officers. The RC, which issued laws by decree during its 12-year existence, can be considered the legislature and the revolutionary government can be considered the cabinet of that era. Membership in the RC and the revolutionary government overlapped, especially in the early days.

The 1947 constitution was never formally abolished either by decree or by military announcement. But it can be safely said that it ceased to function sometime after March 1962. On July 4, 1962, the Revolutionary Council formed a new political party, the Burma Socialist Programme Party (BSPP). The system of multiple political parties competing for elections also ended when the RC issued the Law Protecting National Unity on March 23, 1964. All political parties except the BSPP were banned and their assets confiscated.

From 1962 to 1974, when the new constitution took force, no formal constitution operated in the country. In December 1973, a referendum was held to adopt a new constitution, which is now known as the 1974 constitution. The referendum presented an illusory choice. If the people rejected the draft constitution, then the RC would continue to rule by decree. If the constitution was adopted, then power would be transferred to the Pyithu Hluttaw, a unicameral legislature almost all of whose members were members of the single and ruling BSPP. The chairman of the Revolutionary Council was U Ne Win. The chairman of the Burma Socialist Programme Party was also U Ne Win. Not surprisingly, the official tally showed that 90.19 percent of the voting populace had endorsed the new constitution.

After the adoption of the 1974 constitution, U Ne Win became the first president of the Socialist Republic of the Union of Burma, on March 4, 1974. The preamble of the 1974 constitution pledged that "we the people will faithfully follow the leadership of the Burma Socialist Programme Party." Article 11 stated: "The State shall adopt a single-party system. The Burma Socialist Programme Party is the single political party and it shall lead the state."

The 1974 constitution itself effectively ended as a result of a coup, on September 18, 1988. For several months there had been widespread demonstrations against the ruling BSPP government. On September 11, 1988, an emergency session of the Pyithu Hluttaw passed a resolution to hold multiparty elections "not earlier than 45 days and not later than 90 days" from that date. Just a week later on September 18, 1988, another group of army officers took over power and formed a military junta called the State Law and Order Restoration Council (SLORC). The SLORC abolished all organs of state power that were formed under the 1974 constitution. The SLORC changed its name to State Peace and Development Council (SPDC) on November 15, 1997. Each group in turn declared that they were not bound by any of the provisions of either the 1947 or the 1974 constitution.

Within 10 days of SLORC takeover on September 18, 1988, the main opposition party, National League for Democracy (NLD), was formed under its general secretary, Daw Aung San Suu Kyi (Nobel peace prize laureate for 1991). The former BSPP renamed itself the National Unity Party

(NUP). Multiparty elections took place on May 27, 1990. Ninety-one political parties contested in the elections. The NLD won nearly 60 percent of the votes and 81 percent of the seats—392 of the 485 seats contested. But the new National Assembly was never allowed to convene. After the election the SLORC, in violation of its promises before the election, issued an announcement (Order 1/1990) on July 27, 1990, that the role of elected delegates was not to act as a legislature but to draft a new constitution.

Since 1990, many elected members of parliament have been arrested. Some managed to flee the country. Some resigned or were forced to resign.

On January 9, 1993, a National Convention to draft the principles of a new constitution was convened, only to be adjourned the next day. Of the 702 delegates, only 86 were from the NLD. Even before the convention began, the SLORC had already stipulated six objectives that had to be followed. They were (and still are) (1) nondisintegration of the union; (2) nondisintegration of national solidarity; (3) perpetuation of sovereignty; (4) flourishing of a genuine multiparty system; (5) further flourishing of the noblest and worthiest of world values, namely justice, liberty, and equality; and (6) participation of the Tatmadaw (the armed forces) in the national political leadership of the future state.

Between January 9, 1993, and March 30, 1996, the National Convention was convened and adjourned a few times. In November 1995, the NLD delegates boycotted to protest restrictions and the predetermined agenda. As a result of the boycott, the NLD delegates were expelled from the convention. Since 1996, the convention has met only twice, in 2004 and 2005. It was adjourned on March 30, 1996, to be reconvened only after eight years on May 17, 2004, and it was again adjourned in July 2004. It was convened again in February 2005 and was yet again adjourned in March 2005.

As of mid-2005 only certain "basic principles" have been "agreed upon" by the National Convention which has been held periodically since 1993. As of the time of writing (February 2006) not even a partially completed draft of a future constitution exists. It is not known when the constitution might be completed or how it might be adopted.

FORM AND IMPACT OF THE CONSTITUTION

From September 18, 1988, until the beginning of 2006, the country did not have a constitution.

BASIC ORGANIZATIONAL STRUCTURES

Under the current de facto arrangement, at the top of the state hierarchy is the State Peace and Development Council (SPDC), which is the supreme body of the state. Among other functions it issues laws, which are usually signed by the chairman of the State Peace and Development Council, Senior General Than Shwe, who is referred to in the official media as head of state. He has held those posts since April 1992. He is also the commander in chief of the armed forces.

There is an administration, which since October 1994 has been headed by Prime Minister Lieutenant General Soe Win. (Until August 2003, Senior General Than Shwe was also the prime minister; at that time he relinquished that post in favor of General Khin Nyunt, who was put under house arrest on corruption charges in October 2004.)

The SLORC established a Supreme Court, which originally consisted of five members. The current Supreme Court consists of 15 judges, all appointed by the ruling SLORC or SPDC. There are a chief justice and two deputy chief justices. The SLORC and SPDC can remove justices as well. For example, on November 13, 1998, five of the then-six judges of the Supreme Court were "permitted to retire."

LEADING CONSTITUTIONAL PRINCIPLES

The principles agreed upon by the National Convention can be described as a military-presidential system or a praetorian-presidential system.

CONSTITUTIONAL BODIES

The organs of state power under the 1974 constitution were the unicameral (one-party) Pyithu Hluttaw, the Council of State, the Council of Ministers, the Council of People's Justices, and the Council of People's Attorneys. All the members of these bodies were also members of the Pyithu Hluttaw and reported to it.

Since September 1988, the main organs of state power are the State Peace and Development Council (SPDC), which can be regarded as a legislature, headed by its chairman, who is also officially designated as the head of state; the cabinet appointed by the SPDC; and the Supreme Court, whose members are also appointed by the SPDC.

The President

According to the agreed upon principles of the National Convention, the president would be both head of state and head of the administration. He or she would have to be at least 45 years old and would have to have political, military, and administrative experience. The president's parents, spouse, and children could not be the subjects of any foreign power, and the person must have resided in the country continuously for at least 20 years.

The president would be elected by an electoral college consisting of representatives of the Pyithu Hluttaw (House of Representatives), of the Amyotha Hluttaw (House of Nationalities), and of the Tatmadaw (army). Since there would at least be a few members of the Tatmadaw in the first two electoral groups, and considering the qualifications required for the presidency, it is all but certain that only a military man or a former military man would be likely to become president. Each of the three groups would nominate a candidate. The whole Pyidaungsu Hluttaw (Union Parliament, a joint session of the two chambers) would vote on the three candidates; the candidate who received most votes would become president, and the two other candidates would become vice presidents.

The Parliament

According to the principles agreed upon in the National Convention, there will be two chambers in parliament: the Pyithu Hluttaw, filled largely by nationwide elections, and the Amyotha Hluttaw, elected on the basis of state divisions. In both chambers, one-fourth the members would be appointed by the commander in chief of the armed forces.

The Lawmaking Process

Currently, the SPDC issues new laws, makes amendments to preexisting laws, and repeals laws. There are no formal or conventional rules to this process.

The Judiciary

Currently, under the Supreme Court are Divisional Courts, District Courts, and Township Courts. The judges in these courts are generally appointed by the Supreme Court with the approval of the SPDC.

In the 1947 constitution, the top courts were totally separate from and independent of both the executive and the legislature. In the 1974 constitution, the members of the top judicial body, the Council of People's Justices, were all members of the unicameral one-party legislature, the Pyithu Hluttaw, and they were responsible to it.

According to the principles agreed upon in the National Convention, the Supreme Court judges must not concurrently be members of the legislature. The president would appoint the chief justice of the union and other Supreme Court judges on the approval of the Pyidaungsu Hluttaw or Union Parliament. However, the Union Parliament "shall not have the right to reject the person nominated by the president for appointment of the chief justice of the Union unless it can clearly prove that the person does not meet the qualifications for the post of the chief justice of the Union (or as Supreme Court judges) as prescribed by the constitution." Similar provisions have also been agreed upon for the appointment of ministers by the president.

THE ELECTION PROCESS

Multiparty elections were held under the 1947 constitution in 1951, 1956, and 1960. Elections in which candidates from the ruling Burma Socialist Programme Party (BSPP) ran unopposed were held under the provisions of the 1974 constitution in 1974, 1978, 1981, and 1985.

What were officially designated as "multiparty democratic general elections" were held on May 27, 1990. The leading opposition party, NLD, overwhelmingly won the elections.

The Nobel peace prize laureate Aung San Suu Kyi was disqualified from standing in the 1990 elections because her husband was a British national. Another top NLD official, the former general Tin U, was also barred from the election on the grounds of his conviction in what was seen as a politically motivated prosecution.

POLITICAL PARTIES

There were single-party elections in 1974, 1978, 1981, and 1985, in which voters could vote only for the BSPP candidate. These elections were similar to those held in the former Soviet Union and other countries where only one ruling party is allowed.

In the 1990 elections, by contrast, 91 political parties participated. Since then, many political parties have been deregistered by the Election Commission. The main opposition party, NLD, operates under extremely harsh conditions. Many NLD offices have been closed, and the top two NLD leaders, Aung San Suu Kyi and the former general Tin U, have been under house arrest since May 30, 2003. Quite a few of the middle-ranking NLD officials are also in jail under various charges.

CITIZENSHIP

The 1982 citizenship law provides for three types of citizenship: full, associate, and naturalized citizens.

FUNDAMENTAL RIGHTS

Under the 1947 constitution, certain fundamental rights, mainly of a civil and political nature, were enforceable in courts. They were protected by the Supreme and High Courts.

Under the 1974 one-party constitution, the courts were also supposed to enforce certain enumerated rights. But the judiciary was controlled by the ruling party and failed to fulfill that responsibility. The current Burmese judiciary is also under the control of the military authorities.

Impact and Functions of Fundamental Rights

The provisions of both the 1947 and 1974 constitutions are not applicable in the country since September 1988. Hence the "rights" mentioned in these two defunct charters have no role, impact, or function.

Limitations to Fundamental Rights

Both the 1947 and 1974 constitutions contained some provisions limiting civil and political rights under certain conditions. Although violations of fundamental civil and political rights could be challenged before the nation's courts under the 1947 constitution, since 1962 no litigation has successfully challenged violations of fundamental rights.

ECONOMY

During the Revolutionary Council period (1962–74) and the 1974 constitution period Burma's economic system was officially described as a "socialist economic system." It was characterized by large-scale nationalizations, state ownership of most industries and enterprises, and central economic planning. In 1963, the Revolutionary Council promulgated the Law Protecting the Socialist Economy, which remained in force until 1988, when it was repealed by the SLORC.

Since 1988, both the SLORC and the SPDC have followed a more market-oriented economic system, and laws have been issued on foreign investment. Since then, business dealings and transactions operate under an informal system of corruption and patronage of both domestic and foreign businesspersons.

RELIGIOUS COMMUNITIES

The majority (about 85 percent) of Burmese are Buddhists. There are also Christians, Muslims, Hindus, animists, and others. Nevertheless, except for a brief period in 1961 when the 1947 constitution was amended to accord Buddhism the "recognition that it was a religion of an overwhelming majority of its citizens," Buddhism has never obtained official recognition. Even then, the status of Buddhism did not prevent non-Buddhists from freely practicing their own religion; freedom of worship was guaranteed under the same 1961 constitutional amendment. The "status" of Buddhism as a "state religion" did not survive the military takeover of March 1962. Although the 1947 constitution was not formally abolished after the takeover, its designation of Buddhism as the state or official religion died together with the entire constitution.

The 1974 one-party constitution mentioned freedom of religion but also stipulated that "religion could not be used for political purposes. Laws will be made to implement this provision." The principles adopted by the National Convention so far do not mention Buddhism.

There have been many charges that the SLORC and SPDC persecute some Christians and Muslims. Though there could be some truth in those allegations, those who bear the main brunt of SLORC and SPDC violations of human rights are Buddhists.

MILITARY DEFENSE AND STATE OF EMERGENCY

For most of the time since independence Burma has been under various forms of military rule. Such rule has been direct and openly exercised since 1988. It is believed that between 40 and 50 percent of the national budget is spent for the military. Since 1988, the armed forces have doubled their number of soldiers and their fire power. There are currently about 350,000 to 500,000 soldiers in the armed forces of the country.

Under the provisions agreed upon by the National Convention, when the commander in chief of the armed forces (whose post is different from that of the president) is of the view that there is a national emergency, then he has the right to take over the reins of power. In addition, the Tatmadaw (armed forces) may administer their own affairs free of legislative or parliamentary supervision.

AMENDMENTS TO THE CONSTITUTION

The now-defunct 1974 one-party constitution stated that certain key provisions could be amended only if three-fourths of the members of the legislature approved, along with a majority of all eligible voters in a national referendum. Among such entrenched provisions is Article 11, which stated, "The state shall adopt a single party system. The Burma Socialist Programme Party is the sole political party and it shall lead the state."

On September 11, 1988, in the wake of massive demonstrations against the BSPP government and demands for multiparty elections, the Pyithu Hluttaw passed a resolution "overcoming the constitution," in effect setting aside the one-party provision of the 1974 constitution by scheduling multiparty elections without going to the people via referendum. In any case, a week later the State Law and Order Restoration Council seized power.

PRIMARY SOURCES
Copies of the defunct 1947 and 1974 Constitutions in English. Available online. URLs: http://jurist.law.pitt.edu/world/myanmar.htm. Accessed on September 28, 2005; http://mishpat.net/law/Countries/Myanmar_-_Burma/constituion/index.shtml. Accessed on September 28, 2005.

SECONDARY SOURCES
A. P. Blaustein and G. H. Flanz, *Constitutions of the World.* Dobbs Ferry, N.Y.: Oceana, 1990 (an English translation of the 1974 constitution can be found under the heading Union of Myanmar, formerly Union of Burma).
Burma's Constitution. Rev. ed. The Hague: Martinus Nijhoff, 1961 (a copy of the 1947 Constitution can be found in the appendix of each edition of the book).

Albert D. Moscotti, *Burma (Union), Burma's Constitution and Elections of 1974: A Source Book*. Singapore: ISEAS, 1977.

The Basic Principles and Detailed Principles Laid Down by the National Convention Plenary Sessions Up to March 30, 1996. Yangon: Union of Myanmar, 1996.

Myint Zan, "Law and Legal Culture, Constitutions and Constitutionalism in Burma." In *East Asia—Human Rights, Nation-Building, Trade,* edited by Alice Tay, 204–281. Baden-Baden: Nomos Verlags-Gesellschaft, 1999.

Myint Zan

NAMIBIA

At-a-Glance

OFFICIAL NAME
Republic of Namibia

CAPITAL
Windhoek

POPULATION
2,044,147 (July 2006 est.)

SIZE
318,252 sq. mi. (824, 268 sq. km)

LANGUAGES
English (official); other spoken languages, including Oshiwambo dialects, Oshiherero, Khokoe (Nama/Damara), Kavango and Lozi dialects; Afrikaans, German

RELIGIONS
Christian (Lutheran 50–60%, Catholic, Anglican, independent African churches, pentecostals) 90%, traditional African religion 10%

NATIONAL OR ETHNIC COMPOSITION
Ethnicity not reflected in national census; estimates based on census language statistics: Wambo (consists of five smaller tribes) 43%, Herero 7%, Damara 7%, Nama 5%, Kavango 9%, Caprivian 4%, Rehoboth Baster 4%, Colored 4%, Tswans 5%, two Nomadic groups (San 3% in the east, Himba 0.5% in the northwest); white (Afrikaner, German, Portuguese, and English-speaking whites) 4%; other 4.5%

DATE OF INDEPENDENCE OR CREATION
March 21, 1990

TYPE OF GOVERNMENT
Presidential democracy with parliamentary features

TYPE OF STATE
Unitary state

TYPE OF LEGISLATURE
Bicameral parliament

DATE OF CONSTITUTION
March 21, 1990

DATE OF LAST AMENDMENT
December 24, 1998

Namibia is a presidential democracy with a directly elected president. The president appoints the cabinet, which consists of the prime minister, deputy prime minister, and other ministers. The constitution provides for a clear division of the legislative, executive, and judicial powers of the state. Namibia is a unitary state. The country is divided into 13 regions, but the political power of the regions is limited. The legal system provides for an independent judiciary and a prosecutorial authority independent of any political influence or intervention. The constitution includes an entrenched Bill of Rights. In terms of the entrenchment clauses, no existing rights can be taken away. The individual can defend his or her right against both the state and other individuals and institutions. Namibia sees itself as a Rechtsstaat based on the rule of law.

The directly elected president is the head of state. General elections for Parliament and the presidency are conducted every five years. Namibia is a multiparty democracy.

The constitution guarantees religious freedom and protection of minorities. The Bill of Rights also includes an antidiscrimination clause.

Namibia has a mixed economy with a constitutional guarantee of property rights. While the economy has some centralized elements, it also adheres to basic trade and economic freedom and other market economy trends.

The defense force is mandated by the constitution to defend the territory and national interest of Namibia. The Namibian defense force has been involved in peacekeeping operations in Africa.

CONSTITUTIONAL HISTORY

The boundaries of Namibia were, as were those of most African countries, drawn by the European colonial powers at the end of the 19th century. Before the arrival of the German occupation forces, Namibia was populated by some 12 tribes who had very different customs and vaguely demarcated areas over which the tribal kings had jurisdiction.

From 1890, German forces in Namibia subjugated the native tribes. This policy resulted in the death of 75 percent of the Herero population and 50 percent of the Nama and Damara populations.

After World War I (1914–18), South Africa received a mandate to govern Namibia under the guidance of the League of Nations. The South African authorities governed Namibia as a fifth province rather than as a league mandate.

After a popular uprising against the forced removals of indigenous people from the city of Windhoek to a township on the outskirts in 1921–22, many young Namibians left the country. The two major liberation movements, South West African National Union (SWANU) and South West Africa People's Organization (SWAPO), started working for the independence of Namibia. In 1966, the People's Liberation Army of Namibia (the military wing of SWAPO) clashed with South African forces at Omgulubashe in the north of the country. This was the beginning of a long and bitter armed struggle.

In 1978, the internal pro–South African political parties accepted in principle a United Nations resolution demanding the independence of Namibia. They were, however, unwilling to talk to SWAPO, by then the only significant liberation movement.

The next important initiative was the drafting of the constitutional principles by the Western Contact Group or the Eminent Persons Group, consisting of Canada, France, Germany, Great Britain, and the United States, in 1984. The principles were eventually accepted by both South Africa and SWAPO.

In 1988, South Africa agreed to United Nations–supervised elections. Elections for a Constituent Assembly were held in November 1989, and the Assembly met for the first time on November 21. A draft was distributed on January 25, 1990. On February 9, 1990, the constitution was accepted unanimously. Namibia became independent the following month, on March 21.

FORM AND IMPACT OF THE CONSTITUTION

Namibia has a written constitution, which takes precedence over common law and statutory law. The High and Supreme Courts have the authority to review the common law and statutory law in the light of the constitution.

BASIC ORGANIZATIONAL STRUCTURE

Namibia is a unitary state. All laws of parliament are applicable in the entire country. The High Court, with its seat in Windhoek, has jurisdiction over all the country.

The country is divided into 13 regions, governed by elected Regional Councils. The Regional Councils have limited legislative and governmental powers.

LEADING CONSTITUTIONAL PRINCIPLES

Namibia is a presidential constitutional democracy. The president is directly elected by the people. The president appoints the cabinet from sitting members of Parliament. There are several checks and balances built into the system. The High and Supreme Courts of Namibia have review powers over the laws of the country. The decisions of the Supreme Court are binding on Parliament. The judiciary and the prosecutorial authority are independent.

The leading principles in the Namibian constitutional system can be defined as constitutional democracy with a directly elected president, who with a cabinet appointed by the president fulfills the executive functions of government. Namibia is a secular state and consequently neutral on the religion of its people. The government is compelled by the constitution to uphold the rule of law.

CONSTITUTIONAL BODIES

The most important constitutional bodies are the directly elected president; the cabinet ministers; Parliament, consisting of the National Assembly and the National Council; and the judiciary. The offices of the ombudsperson and prosecutor-general are independent constitutional offices.

The President

The president is the political and ceremonial head of state, directly elected by the people for five years. The president can serve only two terms. The constitution was amended in 1999 to provide that the founding president, Sam Nujoma, would be allowed to serve a third term because he was not elected directly by the people in 1989, when the Constituent Assembly was transformed into the National Assembly and the National Assembly elected the president.

The president appoints and dismisses members of cabinet and is the commander in chief of the national defense force.

The Cabinet

The president, the prime minister, and the other presidentially appointed ministers form the cabinet, which functions as the executive branch of government. The prime minister is the leader of government business in Parliament. The fact that the president is directly elected and is the dominant figure in the cabinet makes the cabinet the dominant office in Namibian political and public life.

Parliament

Parliament consists of two chambers, the National Assembly and the National Council. The National Council is chosen by the elected regional councils, each electing two members.

The legislative power of Namibia is vested in the National Assembly subject to the review powers of the National Council. The National Assembly has 72 members, directly elected for five years from party lists. The National Assembly approves the budgets of government ministries and directorates, agrees to the ratification of international agreements, and ensures that apartheid, tribalism, and colonialism do not manifest themselves in Namibia.

The National Council reviews all legislation of the National Assembly.

The Lawmaking Process

The legislative power of Namibia is vested in the National Assembly subject to the review powers of the National Council. The National Council can either approve legislation or send it back with recommendations. After the National Assembly has reconsidered the bill, it does not send it back to the council. If the National Council objects to the principle of a bill, and the National Assembly does not reaffirm the bill with a two-thirds majority, the bill lapses. Once the National Council gives final approval, the bill is sent to the speaker, who sends it to the president. The president signs the act into law.

The Judiciary

Namibia has an independent judiciary, subject only to the constitution and the law. It consists of community courts, magistrate courts (lower courts), the High Court, and the Supreme Court.

The community courts exercise customary law in the traditional communities. Appeals lie with the magistrate courts. The magistrate courts are lower courts with limited jurisdictions. Appeals from the magistrate courts lie with the High Court. The High Court and the Supreme Court have review jurisdiction over the constitutionality of legislation. Supreme Court decisions are binding on all courts in Namibia, and High Court decisions on all lower courts.

The prosecutorial authority is vested in an independent prosecutor-general.

THE ELECTION PROCESS

All Namibians over the age of 18 have both the right to stand for election and the right to vote in elections. Elections are by secret ballot on party lists, except in the case of regional councils, in which elections take place in constituencies. The members of the National Council are elected by the regional councils.

POLITICAL PARTIES

Namibia is a multiparty democracy. The party system is an integral part of the Namibian political system. The election of members of Parliament is on party lists in accordance with proportional representation.

CITIZENSHIP

Namibian citizenship is primarily based on birth in Namibia. Both children of Namibian citizens and those of ordinary residents obtain citizenship by birth. A child born elsewhere whose father or mother was a Namibian citizen at his or her birth can apply for citizenship by descent. Ordinary residents who have been in the country for at least five years can apply for citizenship by registration.

FUNDAMENTAL RIGHTS

An enshrined Bill of Fundamental Human Rights and Freedoms forms part of the Namibian constitution (Chapter 3). Chapter 3 protects the right to life, liberty, and dignity (especially in judicial proceedings). It protects persons against torture, slavery, forced labor, and arbitrary detention and against discrimination on the grounds of sex, race, color, ethnic origin, religion, creed, or social or economic status.

The constitution guarantees equality before the law, a fair trial, privacy, and the right to marry and found a family. It protects property rights, the rights of children, and the right to political activity, culture, and education.

The constitution also protects fundamental freedoms, such as freedom of speech, conscience, religion, peaceful assembly, association, and movement.

No rights can be taken away by means of constitutional change.

Impact and Functions of Fundamental Rights

Human rights are generally respected in Namibia. The independent courts jealously guard over the rights and freedoms protected by the constitution. When citizens allege violations of their rights and freedoms, the courts give the broadest meaning possible to their rights.

Limitations to Fundamental Rights

The fundamental rights and freedoms are not without limits, but limitations must be reasonable, of general application, and not aimed against individuals.

ECONOMY

The Namibian constitution describes economic order in Namibia as a "mixed economy with the objective of securing economic growth, prosperity and a life of human dignity." The Bill of Rights guarantees the right to freedom of occupation, association, and property and the rights of workers. The constitution makes membership in the International Labor Organization (ILO) and adherence to the international conventions and recommendations of the ILO objectives of the state.

RELIGIOUS COMMUNITIES

The constitution defines Namibia as a secular state. However, religious freedom is guaranteed as well as the right not to be discriminated against on the grounds of religious belief. Consequently, there is no state church, and no specific religion is taught in state schools. Religious instruction in state schools is informative and neutral.

Religious communities do not receive church taxes or any other form of financial assistance from the state. The religious communities are free to administer their own affairs and to express their religious liturgy in terms of their own history and customs.

MILITARY DEFENSE AND STATE OF EMERGENCY

Namibia has a permanent defense force, staffed by full-time professional soldiers. There is no conscription. The defense force is subject to civil government.

The president can declare a state of emergency at times of national disaster, national defense, or public emergency. The National Assembly may at any time revoke such a declaration. The president may make regulations and suspend the operation of any rule of common law or statute during a state of emergency for the protection of national security and public safety. If these regulations lead to detention without trial, an advisory board shall review the detention on a regular basis.

AMENDMENTS TO THE CONSTITUTION

Only a two-thirds majority in the National Assembly can amend the constitution. No rights in the enshrined Bill of Rights can be taken away by an amendment of the constitution. In 1999, the constitution was amended to make provision for the founding president, Sam Nujoma, to serve a third term, whereas the constitution allows only two terms. There have been no other amendments made to the constitution.

PRIMARY SOURCES
Constitution in English. Available online. URL: http://www.grnnet.gov.na/Nav_frames/Nutshell_launch.htm. Accessed on July 25, 2005.

SECONDARY SOURCES
Suffian H. Bukurura, *Essays on Constitutionalism and the Administration of Justice in Namibia 1990–2002.* Windhoek: Out of Africa, 2002.

Manfred O. Hinz, Sam K. Amoo, and David van Wyk, eds., *The Constitution at Work: Ten Years of Namibian Nationhood.* Windhoek: University of Namibia Press 2002, and Verloren van Themaat Centre, Pretoria: University of South Africa, 2000.

Gino J. Naldi, *Constitutional Rights in Namibia.* Kelwyn: Juta & Company, 1995.

Nico Horn

NAURU

At-a-Glance

OFFICIAL NAME
Republic of Nauru

CAPITAL
Yaren

POPULATION
12,320 (2005 est.)

SIZE
Land 8 sq. mi. (21 sq. km) Ocean 123,552 sq. mi. (320,000 sq. km)

LANGUAGES
Nauruan, English

NATIONAL OR ETHNIC COMPOSITION
Nauruan 58%, other Pacific Islander 26%, Chinese 8%, European 8%

RELIGIONS
Protestant (approximately 66%), Roman Catholic (approximately 34%)

DATE OF INDEPENDENCE OR CREATION
January 31, 1968

TYPE OF GOVERNMENT
Parliamentary democracy

TYPE OF STATE
Unitary state

TYPE OF LEGISLATURE
Unicameral parliament

DATE OF CONSTITUTION
January 31, 1968

DATE OF LAST AMENDMENT
May 17, 1968

Nauru is a republic that has a parliamentary democratic form of government, based on the rule of law and a clear separation between the legislative and executive branches of government and the judicial branch. It is a unitary state, but the Nauru Island Council has substantial power as a local government body.

There is a written constitution, which contains provisions that recognize fundamental human rights and freedoms, which are enforceable by the Supreme Court. The country is a republic, with a parliamentary system on the British model.

CONSTITUTIONAL HISTORY

Nauru, which was settled by people of Micronesian descent, first attracted the attention of Europeans in 1798, when it was discovered by Captain John Fearn of the British ship *Hunter,* who named it Pleasant Island, because of its attractive appearance. Whaling ships started to call for water and supplies in the 1830s, and some beachcombers, dropped off from ships of various countries, started to live with the indigenous clans, contributing to the almost incessant clan warfare that developed. In the 1870s, several German trading companies established themselves and pressed their home government for protection. In 1888, the island was subsumed within the protectorate that Germany established over the Marshall Islands.

The island stayed under German control until after World War I (1914–18), when it was placed by the League of Nations as a mandate under Britain. The British government made an agreement with Australia and New Zealand to provide joint administration of the island; Australia took the dominant role. During World War II (1939–45), the island was occupied by the Japanese, who deported many of the inhabitants to work on Truk in the Caroline Islands. The island was returned by the United Nations to Australian administration after World War II as a trusteeship territory. The United Nations insisted that the island quickly gain independence, and this was achieved on January 31, 1968.

The legal system of Nauru comprises the constitution and legislation enacted by Parliament since independence, as well as preindependence ordinances made by the Australian administrator. Certain Australian and English legislation, adopted by the Customs and Adopted Laws Act of 1971, is also part of the legal system, as well as subsidiary legislation made under that law. Moreover, principles of common law and equity apply, so far as is appropriate to the circumstances of Nauru. Nauruan custom is also part of the legal system. It regulates land titles, disposition of real and personal property among living people and by will, succession to the property of Nauruans who die intestate, and any matters affecting Nauruans only. The Nauruan customs that allowed certain persons to deal with the property of others without their consent or to take custody or control of a child without the consent of the parents were abolished.

FORM AND IMPACT OF THE CONSTITUTION

A Constitutional Convention prepared the constitution that entered into force on the day of independence, January 31, 1968. The convention remained in session and issued amendments a few months later. The constitution states that it is the supreme law of Nauru, and that any inconsistent law must be held void to the extent of the inconsistency.

BASIC ORGANIZATIONAL STRUCTURE

Nauru is a unitary state. However, local government, known as the Nauru Island Council, has important powers and a substantial income, which have resulted in effect in a two-tier system of government.

LEADING CONSTITUTIONAL PRINCIPLES

Nauru is a republic. As are many other republics in the South and Central Pacific, it is based upon the English model of parliamentary democracy, rather than the American or French model of a presidential republic.

Fundamental human rights and freedoms are recognized by the constitution, and the Supreme Court has been given power to grant redress for any infringements.

CONSTITUTIONAL BODIES

The main bodies established by the constitution, in order of their appearance in the constitution, are the president, the legislature, the Supreme Court, and the public service.

The President

The president, who must be a member of Parliament, is elected by Parliament and may be removed by a vote of no confidence passed by at least half of the members. The president is authorized to appoint four or five members of Parliament as ministers. The president and the ministers form the cabinet, in whom the executive power of the country is vested. The cabinet is collectively responsible to Parliament and may be removed by a vote of no confidence by at least half the members of Parliament.

The Legislature

The legislature, called Parliament, is a unicameral body comprising 18 members. Members of Parliament are directly elected by electors on a common roll under a preferential voting system devised by an Australian administrator, known as the Dowdall system. Voters express preferences for each of the candidates running in their districts. There are eight districts, each of which elects more than one member of Parliament.

Parliament has a life of three years. It can be dissolved earlier by the speaker of Parliament, acting on the advice of the president, if it fails to act on a motion to remove the president and cabinet.

The Lawmaking Process

Proposed laws must be approved by a majority of the members of Parliament present and voting, with the Speaker having a casting vote if votes are equally divided. A proposed law which has been passed by Parliament becomes a law when the Speaker certifies that it has been passed by Parliament.

The Supreme Court

The Supreme Court of Nauru has, in addition to the normal civil and criminal jurisdiction of a superior court, jurisdiction to enforce the constitution and to determine the right of a person to be, or to remain, a member of Parliament. Appeals from decisions of the Supreme Court lie with the High Court of Australia. There are two subordinate courts—the District Court, composed of the resident magistrate and at least three lay magistrates, which has jurisdiction in minor civil matters, and the family court, presided over by the resident magistrate, which has jurisdiction in matters of divorce and maintenance and custody of children. Judges of the Supreme Court are appointed by the president and may be removed on the ground of proved incapacity or misconduct by a resolution passed by at least two-thirds of the members of Parliament. The resident magistrate and lay magistrates are also appointed by the president.

The Public Service

The public service is appointed, disciplined, and removed by the chief secretary. This chief secretary is appointed by, and can be removed by, the cabinet.

THE ELECTION PROCESS

Nauruan citizens 20 years or older are entitled to vote and to stand for election for Parliament unless they are disqualified from so doing. The constitution does not specify the electoral system. However, the country has adopted a system similar to that devised by the French scientist Jean-Charles de Borda in the 17th century, whereby voters express preferences in diminishing order for as many candidates as are standing for election; the candidates who receive the highest total of votes are elected. In Nauru the method is referred to as the Dowdall system, after its inventor, Desmond Dowdall, an Australian who was secretary for justice in Nauru in the early 1970s. Whether Dowdall was aware of the Borda system is not known.

POLITICAL PARTIES

There are no restrictions on the formation of political parties. However, as in many South Pacific island countries, political parties have not been significant and political groupings have been mainly based on personalities.

CITIZENSHIP

Persons born before independence automatically became citizens of Nauru if they were members of the Nauruan community as defined in the Nauruan Community Ordinance 1956–66. Persons born after independence automatically become citizens of Nauru if at the time of their birth they had parents who were both Nauru citizens or one parent who was a Nauruan citizen and another who was a Pacific Islander; or if they were born in Nauru and do not have citizenship of another country. Women married to Nauruan citizens are entitled to receive Nauruan citizenship upon application.

FUNDAMENTAL RIGHTS AND DUTIES

The constitution recognizes the fundamental human rights to life, liberty, and security of the person; enjoyment of property; protection of the law; protection from forced labor, torture, and inhuman and degrading treatment; and freedom of conscience, expression, assembly, and association. These rights and freedoms are enforceable by the Supreme Court.

ECONOMY

The economy of Nauru has been based almost entirely on large deposits of phosphate, as is recognized by Article 93 of the constitution, which maintains an agreement made between the government of Nauru and the governments of Australia, New Zealand, and the United Kingdom. At one time, Nauru was one of the most productive countries of the Pacific island countries, but the phosphate supplies are now almost exhausted. Investment of the phosphate royalties was seriously mismanaged, so that the country is currently going through a painful economic downturn. Australian officials have been involved in trying to rectify the situation.

RELIGIOUS COMMUNITIES

The right to freedom of worship and assembly is recognized and protected by Articles 11 and 13 of the constitution. The people of Nauru are Christian, about two-thirds members of Protestant churches, especially the Nauru Congregational Church and the Nauru Independent Church, and one-third members of the Roman Catholic Church.

MILITARY DEFENSE AND STATE OF EMERGENCY

Nauru has no army. The president may declare a state of emergency if satisfied that a grave emergency that threatens the security or economy of the country exists. Such a declaration lapses after seven days if Parliament is sitting, or, in any other case, after 21 days, unless it has been approved by a majority of the members of Parliament. While a state of emergency is in effect, the president may make such orders as appear to the president to be reasonably required for securing public safety, maintaining public order, or safeguarding the interests or maintaining the welfare of the community; such orders are to have effect notwithstanding the fundamental human rights and freedoms recognized by the constitution and notwithstanding any inconsistency with any law.

AMENDMENTS TO THE CONSTITUTION

Most provisions of the constitution can be amended by a law enacted by Parliament with the support of at least two-thirds of the total members of Parliament. Certain provisions can be amended only by a bill enacted by two-thirds of the total members of Parliament, as well as two-thirds of the voters at a national referendum.

PRIMARY SOURCES
Constitution in English. Available online. URL: http://www.paclii.org./nr/legis/num_act/con256/. Accessed on June 21, 2006.

SECONDARY SOURCES
T. Deklin, "Nauru." In *South Islands Legal Systems,* edited by M. Ntumy, 142–157. Honolulu: University of Hawaii Press, 1993.

Don Paterson

NEPAL

At-a-Glance

OFFICIAL NAME
Kingdom of Nepal

CAPITAL
Kathmandu

POPULATION
27,676,547 (July 2005 est.)

SIZE
56,757 sq. mi. (147,000 sq. km)

LANGUAGES
Nepali 58%, Newari 3%, Tibeto-Burman languages 20%, Indian languages 19%

RELIGIONS
Hinduism 90%, Buddhism 8%, Muslim, Christian, and other 2%

NATIONAL OR ETHNIC COMPOSITION
Tamang, Gurung, Newar, Rai, Sherpa, Tharu, others (tribal groups); Brahman and Chhetri (major caste groups); Indians, Tibetans

DATE OF INDEPENDENCE OR CREATION
1768

TYPE OF GOVERNMENT
Constitutional monarchy

TYPE OF STATE
Unitary state

TYPE OF LEGISLATURE
Bicameral parliament

DATE OF CONSTITUTION
November 9, 1990

DATE OF LAST AMENDMENT
No amendment

Nepal is a landlocked country lying between China to the north and India to the south. It is a constitutional monarchy. The current constitution was promulgated on November 9, 1990, after a period of major political unrest that forced King Birendra to relinquish royal powers and agree to a new democratic constitution. Nepal was an emerging parliamentary democracy until October 2002, when the head of state, King Gyanendra (2001 to date), dissolved Parliament. He was facing political opposition and an ongoing insurgency by Maoist guerrilla forces that now operate throughout Nepal. In February 2005, he announced a state of emergency, which has seriously escalated the political conflict in Nepal. On May 18, 2006, parliament passed a resolution containing far-reaching changes in the constitutional system.

CONSTITUTIONAL HISTORY

Modern Nepal emerged in the 18th century after the process of unification and conquest started by King Prithivi Narayan Shah (1722–75). This process was completed during the reign of Bahadur Shah (1775–95). However, Nepal was defeated in the Anglo-Gurkha war (1814–16); after the signing of the Treaty of Sugauli the concept of a greater Nepal faded. By the mid-19th century, the Rana family had seized de facto control and the monarchy was unable to counter the growth in Rana power.

In the 1930s, the first political parties emerged in Nepal, notably the Nepal Praja Parishad in 1938. As opposition to Rana rule mounted, the Nepal National Congress Party was established in 1946 by Nepali students in India. This party joined the Nepali Democratic Congress in April

1950 to form the Nepali Congress Party with the aim of ousting the Rana regime.

However, the flight of King Tribhuvan to New Delhi in November 1950 added a new twist to the process of political change. The king gave moral backing to the opponents of the Rana regime and a compromise was reached in January 1951 among the king, the Rana regime, and the political parties supporting an armed struggle in Nepal. After a period of political uncertainty, a constitution was announced by royal proclamation in February 1959.

This new constitution was not to last long. In December 1960, King Mahendra dissolved the first elected government and suspended the constitution. During the next 30 years, the monarchy governed on the basis of a second amendment to the constitution issued in 1962, vesting all powers in the king. In the years to follow, the *panchayat* system was developed. The system, based on the Five Man Village Council, provided for locally elected, nonparty representative government at the ward, village, district, and zone levels, as well as a National Council appointed by the king. A third amendment to the constitution, which sought to refine the *panchayat* system by allowing direct elections by universal suffrage to the National Assembly, was issued in 1980.

The amendments in 1962 and in 1980 could not prevent the tensions that mounted among the ordinary people, which increased in the Kathmandu valley in early 1990, leading to the widespread arrest of opposition leaders, who were either held under house arrest or imprisoned. A major general strike was held in April 1990, forcing King Birendra to compromise, and in November 1990 a new constitution was promulgated for Nepal. In the mid-1990s, Maoist opponents of the monarchy began an armed insurgency that continues. The massacre of King Birendra and the immediate royal family in June 2001 by Crown Prince Dipendra had a major impact on Nepali politics. His successor, King Gyanendra, dissolved Parliament and appointed a transitional government on October 11, 2002, under Article 127 of the Nepalese constitution. King Gyanendra took extraordinary steps in February 2005 when he assumed direct control of government. His actions have seriously damaged the democratic system in Nepal and may prevent a peaceful solution to the Maoist insurgency. The resolution passed by the parliament on May 18, 2006, may lead to far-reaching changes in the constitutional system

FORM AND IMPACT OF THE CONSTITUTION

The current constitution, promulgated in 1990, is the result of a process of constitutional evolution over the 30-year period that followed the overthrow of the Rana regime. It emphasizes the rule of law in Nepal and seeks to establish human rights.

BASIC ORGANIZATIONAL STRUCTURE

Nepal is divided into 14 zones and 75 districts that are grouped into five development zones. After the prodemocracy movement in 1990, the former village *panchayat* was renamed the Village Development Committee. The town *panchayat* was renamed the Municipal Development Committee. Each district is under a chief district office that is responsible for law and order and coordination of the work of the various government agencies.

LEADING CONSTITUTIONAL PRINCIPLES

The 1990 constitution sought to establish a democratic parliamentary system with universal suffrage and free elections. It marked a move away from royal authority and toward popular political participation. The constitution recognizes the ethnic, linguistic, and religious diversity in Nepal and the importance of the rule of law. However, the insurgency by Maoist guerrillas and the dissolution of Parliament by the king have undermined the emerging, if unstable, parliamentary democracy.

CONSTITUTIONAL BODIES

The main bodies are the king, the State Council, the Council of Ministers, the House of Representatives, the National Assembly and the judiciary. Below these are the zonal and district levels of government.

The King

Article 27 describes the king as a descendent of King Prithvi Narayan Shah and an adherent to the Hindu religion. This article highlights the importance of descent and continuity in succession to the throne. In the constitutional monarchy the power of the Crown is vested in the executive; however, recent events have seen the king's resumption of executive control.

The king is advised by a State Council (Raj Parishad) that is also responsible for designating a regent in the event of the king's incapacitation. The State Council consists of members of the royal family, the Council of Ministers, and leading national figures. It holds fewer powers than it did in the past.

The Council of Ministers

Article 36 provides that the king will appoint as prime minister the leader of the party that commands the majority in the House of Representatives. The prime minister will act as a chairman of the Council of Ministers, which is appointed on his recommendation by the king. Under Article 35, executive power is vested in the Council of Ministers and the king. The Council of Ministers is, under the constitution, the effective administration of Nepal.

The Legislature

There are two elements that together with the king form the legislature. The House of Representatives (Pratinidhi Sabha) is composed of 205 members, each elected from a district constituency for a five-year fixed term. The National Assembly (Rashtriya Sabha) consists of 60 members—10 royal nominees, 35 (including at least three women) elected by the House of Representatives, and a further 15 elected by an electoral college.

The Lawmaking Process

Parliament is empowered to enact any law, unless otherwise provided for by the constitution. A bill passed by one house of Parliament is transmitted to the other house; if it is passed by the receiving house as well, it is presented to the king for royal assent. This royal assent makes the bill an act. The king can, however, send the bill back for further deliberation. If the bill is then presented to the king, he has to give his assent within 30 days. When a bill is rejected by the National Assembly, the House of Representatives has the authority to override the decision.

The Judiciary

The constitution provides for a three-tier judiciary—a Supreme Court, appellate courts, and district courts. The chief justice is to be appointed on the recommendation of a constitutional council, and other justices of the Supreme Court on the recommendation of a judicial council. In theory, the courts are independent and free of outside influence, with the Supreme Court having the power to declare any law contrary to the constitution.

THE ELECTION PROCESS AND POLITICAL PARTICIPATION

Each Nepali citizen of age 18 is entitled to vote or stand for election. Political parties are free to canvass for votes, and elections are subject to investigation by an Election Court. The term of the House of Representatives is five years, and if a vacancy arises, a by-election is held.

POLITICAL PARTIES

Article 112 of the constitution provides for the organization of political parties and for the freedom of political participation. Currently, the main political parties in Nepal are the Nepal Congress, the Communist Party of Nepal/United Marxist-Leninist, the National Democratic Party, and the National People's Front. Political parties may not be based on religion, caste, community, tribe, or region. There are various smaller political groups, mainly antimonarchist groups, and student groups in the capital.

CITIZENSHIP

Under Article 8, a person is deemed to be a citizen if he or she is domiciled in Nepal, born in Nepal, or has a father who has Nepalese citizenship or is a naturalized citizen. Dual nationality is not recognized under Article 9. Citizenship may be terminated for naturalized citizens only after due legal process.

FUNDAMENTAL RIGHTS

Part 3 of the 1990 constitution sets out the fundamental rights to which the Nepalese are entitled. These include equality irrespective of caste, religion, race, and gender. Fair trials, the right to bail, due process of law, and freedom from cruel and unusual punishment are established as part of the fundamental rights of all Nepalese citizens.

Impact and Functions of Fundamental Rights

The constitution recognizes vulnerable groups, notably women, children, and the physically and mentally handicapped, who must be protected from exploitation. Article 11(4) specifically prohibits discrimination against untouchables, members of Hindu society who are perceived as socially unclean and are highly stigmatized.

Limitations to Fundamental Rights

Fundamental rights are, in varying degrees, subject to laws that impose reasonable restrictions based on interests such as the sovereignty and integrity of Nepal; harmonious relations among the people of various castes, tribes, or communities; or public morality.

ECONOMY

There are no articles in the constitution, directly dealing with the economy. However, trade is regulated by the government and there are prohibitions against trafficking in people and slavery. The prohibition against exploitation in Article 20 applies to the use of child labor in factories or mines.

RELIGIOUS COMMUNITIES

Nepal is officially a Hindu kingdom. During the process of preparing the current constitution, there were fierce debates over whether or not to enshrine Hinduism in the constitution. Article 4 of the 1990 constitution describes Nepal as a "multiethnic, multilingual, democratic, independent, indivisible, sovereign, Hindu and Constitutional Monarchical Kingdom." However, although Hinduism is the official religion of Nepal, Article 19 provides for the freedom of religion, subject to a prohibition against proselytization.

MILITARY DEFENSE AND STATE OF EMERGENCY

The king is the supreme commander in chief. The king appoints a commander in chief on the prime minister's recommendation. The prime minister heads the National Security Council.

There is a current state of emergency due to the ongoing Maoist insurrection against the monarchy. The insurgency began in the mid-1990s and has claimed thousands of lives. In 2000, five platoons of the Royal Nepalese Army were deployed in districts where there had been no previous army presence. This action was followed by the creation of the armed police force in 2001. A cease-fire was declared in July 2001 but has since broken down. King Gyanendra has used the emergency powers under Articles 115 and 127 to assume power, just as King Mahendra, his father, did in 1960.

AMENDMENTS TO THE CONSTITUTION

The 1990 constitution represents a modification of the earlier constitutions promulgated after the collapse of the Rana regime. It marks a major move toward establishment of the rule of law.

Article 116 addresses the amendment process. Two-thirds of both the House of Representatives and the National Assembly are required to pass an amendment. The king has 30 days to assent or return the proposed amendment with comments. The king has to assent to the amendment if it is presented to the king again.

PRIMARY SOURCES

Constitution in English. Available online. URL: http://www.oefre.unibe.ch/law/icl/np00000_.html. Accessed on June 21, 2005.

SECONDARY SOURCES

Hem Narayan Agrawal, *Nepal—a Country Study in Constitutional Change.* New Delhi: Oxford & IBH, 1980.

M. Hutt, ed., *Himalayan "People's War": Nepal's Maoist Rebellion.* London: C. Hurst, 2004.

M. Hutt, ed., *Nepal in the Nineties.* Oxford: Oxford University Press, 1994.

Andrea Matles Savada, *Nepal and Bhutan—Country Studies.* Washington, D.C.: United States Government Printing Office, 1993.

National Research, "Website on Nepal and Himalayan Studies." Available online. URL: http://nepalresearch.org/politics/inclusion.htm. Accessed on August 18, 2005.

Francis Robinson, *The Cambridge Encyclopedia of India, Pakistan, Bangladesh, Sri Lanka, Nepal, Bhutan and the Maldives.* Cambridge: Cambridge University Press, 1989.

United Nations, "Core Document Forming Part of the Reports of States Parties: Nepal" (HRI/CORE/1/Add.42), 14 June 1994. Available online. URL: http://www.unhchr.ch/tbs/doc.nsf. Accessed on September 25, 2005.

Richard Whitecross

THE NETHERLANDS

At-a-Glance

OFFICIAL NAME
Kingdom of the Netherlands

CAPITAL
Amsterdam

POPULATION
16,193,000 (2005 est.)

SIZE
16,033 sq. mi. (41,526 sq. km)

LANGUAGES
Dutch

RELIGIONS
Roman Catholic 31%, Protestant 21%, other (Muslim 5.7% and Hindu 0.6%) 8%, none 40%

NATIONAL OR ETHNIC COMPOSITION
Dutch 81%, Western nonnatives 8.7%, non-Western nonnatives (Turkish background 2.1%, Moroccan background 1.8%) 10%

DATE OF INDEPENDENCE OR CREATION
November 1813

TYPE OF GOVERNMENT
Parliamentary monarchy

TYPE OF STATE
Decentralized unitary state

TYPE OF LEGISLATURE
Bicameral parliament

DATE OF CONSTITUTION
March 30, 1814

DATE OF LAST AMENDMENT
April 9, 2002

The Kingdom of the Netherlands is a parliamentary democracy, based on the rule of law. It is a decentralized unitary state. The constitution focuses on establishing the basic organizational structure of the state rather than providing substantive guidance on laws. Courts are not allowed to review the constitutionality of acts of parliament; judgment is left to the parliamentary legislature itself.

The government consists of the monarch and the ministers. The monarch (currently a queen) is head of state. The monarch acts under ministerial responsibility. Ministers are answerable to both houses of parliament; they are not members of parliament. Lack of confidence obliges ministers individually, or collectively, to offer their resignation. The lower house of parliament is directly elected; the upper house is elected by the States Provincial, the legislatures of the provinces. The party system is pluralistic. Elections are organized on the basis of proportional representation, with free and secret ballots.

The constitution contains a catalog of fundamental rights and includes social rights. Freedom of religion or belief is guaranteed. Church and state are separated. The economic system is a social market system. The military is under the supreme command of the government. The constitution states that the government shall promote the development of the international legal order.

CONSTITUTIONAL HISTORY

The starting point of the Netherlands as an independent political entity is usually held as 1579, when the Union of Utrecht was concluded by the seven sovereign provinces of the Northern Netherlands, declaring their autonomy against the Spanish rule of King Philip II. Internationally, the Republic of the United Netherlands was fully recognized at the Peace of Münster in 1648.

The focus of the confederate republic was on common defense and foreign affairs. At the head of the republic was the *stadhouder,* the highest civil servant of the State General, the body consisting of the delegates of the sovereign provinces; he combined civil duties with leadership of the fleet and army of the union. In 1747, the position became hereditary, the prerogative of the descendants of a brother of William of Orange. The old republic was replaced in 1795 by the Batavian Republic under the guidance of revolutionary France.

The period between 1795 and 1814 saw several constitutions: the modern republican constitution of 1798, the more traditional constitutions of 1801 and 1805, and the constitution of the Kingdom of Holland of 1806, under which a brother of Napoléon was made king. In 1810, France annexed the Netherlands outright, but independence was regained in 1813. The son of the last *stadhouder* returned to the country and was crowned on December 2. He later became King William I. The constitution of 1814 established a decentralized unitary state.

In 1815, after the Congress of Vienna, Belgium became part of the Netherlands, and the constitution was revised accordingly. After Belgium became independent in 1830, a revised constitution was issued in 1840.

The revision of 1848 was of paramount importance. It introduced many fundamental rights and laid the groundwork for the parliamentary system of government. It also determined the organizational structure of the provinces and municipalities. From then until the general revision of 1983, 11 partial revisions took place. Of these, the revision of 1917 stands out. It introduced proportional representation to the electoral system and universal suffrage for men and women, independently of social or economic status. It also introduced public funding for private denominational elementary schools on a par with that for nondenominational public schools. Ordinary legislation later extended this principle to other school levels and types, including universities.

Shortly after World War II (1939–45), a process was set in motion to consider a general revision of the constitution. Concrete proposals were introduced in parliament in the mid-1970s. These led to the general revision of 1983. Five partial revisions have taken place since then.

The changing relationships between the Netherlands and the overseas territories after World War II led to the establishment of the Charter of the Kingdom of the Netherlands in 1954. In its present version, it regulates the constitutional structure of the Netherlands, the Netherlands Antilles, and Aruba. The constitution must comply with the charter.

The Netherlands has an open and positive attitude toward international law and the international legal order. From the start, the Netherlands has been a member of international organizations such as the Council of Europe, the North Atlantic Treaty Organization (NATO), the predecessors of the European Union, and global institutions such as the United Nations.

The capital city is Amsterdam. However, the seat of government is (and has always been) in The Hague.

FORM AND IMPACT OF THE CONSTITUTION

The Dutch constitution is a single, normative document containing 142 articles. The constitution is stable, despite frequent alterations. The most notable change, introduced by the general revision of 1983, concerns the protection of fundamental rights.

The constitution reflects an open attitude toward international law. So-called self-executing provisions of treaties and of resolutions by international organizations are binding after they have been published. Courts cannot apply any statutory regulations that, in the court's judgment, conflict with these provisions. European Union law takes precedence over Dutch law.

The Dutch constitution provides the basic outlines for the organization of the state, determines what happens at important moments, and prescribes important procedures. It has a more modest impact on the broader legal and political life of the country.

One reason is that the constitution itself prohibits the courts from reviewing the constitutionality of acts of parliament. The parliamentary legislative body itself determines the constitutionality of its own acts.

Another reason is that even when dealing with the basics of the organization of the state, the constitution is not exhaustive, leaving various areas of constitutional law unmentioned. The most prominent rule of the parliamentary system, the so-called no confidence rule in the relation of ministers to parliament, is unwritten. The process of the formation of a cabinet is also not discussed.

The constitution provides guarantees for the independence and impartiality of the judiciary, but most of the actual organization of the judiciary is determined by act of parliament. Processes such as the dynamic between the administration and parliament, or between the administration and parliament on the one side and the courts on the other, escape the wording of the constitution. The same is true for processes of centralization and decentralization (only the basic organization of provinces and municipalities is defined), or for the dynamics between state and society. Although the constitution provides the legal framework for attribution of powers to supranational authorities, the actual and growing impact of European law is obviously not reflected in it.

The constitution does not contain an explicit statement on the hierarchy of national norms. The hierarchy between norms created at the national, provincial, and municipal levels is largely a matter of custom. Courts test the validity of legal norms vis-à-vis higher norms—for example, regulations against laws passed by parliament—but they are not allowed to test acts of parliament against the constitution.

The Dutch constitution does not contain a preamble or create a value system, as the German constitution does. There is no hierarchy in the fundamental rights contained in the constitution. The leading constitutional principles, those of a social and liberal democracy, are reflected in the guarantees of fundamental rights and implicitly expressed further through a set of mechanisms and procedures. The constitution does not contain an expression of the source of authority.

BASIC ORGANIZATIONAL STRUCTURE

The Netherlands is a decentralized unitary state. Absolute monarchy and strong centralization have never taken root in the Netherlands. In the course of the last century, however, there has been a creeping, but distinct tendency toward centralization. This concerns legislation rather than administration.

The Netherlands has three territorially organized tiers of government. There are 12 provinces and currently between 450 and 500 municipalities.

Municipalities are headed by a council and administered by an executive including the mayor. The mayor is appointed by royal decree. The executive and the mayor are responsible to their councils and can be dismissed or forced to resign.

Provinces are organized on a similar basis, with minor differences; for example, the appointed commissioner of the monarch chairs the executive without actually being a member of it. Furthermore, the commissioner of the monarch also fulfils certain national functions. Over the course of time, the position has evolved from being the "eyes and ears" of The Hague in the province to a promoter of the interests of the province in The Hague. The provincial council is called the States Provincial.

Municipalities are active in fields such as housing, education, culture, recreation, welfare, public health, and public order. Provinces are active in fields such as water regulation, road maintenance, environment and nature protection, and environmental hygiene. Furthermore, provinces fulfil a crucial role as a middle tier in planning law and execute many coordinating activities.

Both municipalities and provinces implement higher law. They have autonomous legislative and administrative powers only insofar as the "higher" tiers of government leave room for them and the subject matter falls in their sphere of concern.

LEADING CONSTITUTIONAL PRINCIPLES

The Netherlands is a parliamentary democracy, based on the rule of law. The judiciary is independent. Ministers and secretaries of state who lose the confidence of either house of parliament are obliged to offer their resignation. This is called the no confidence rule.

The Netherlands is a constitutional monarchy. The monarch is inviolable. The "title to the Throne shall be hereditary and shall vest in the legitimate descendants of King William I, Prince of Orange-Nassau." The rules of succession are contained in the constitution. The actions of the monarch are subject to ministerial responsibility. Only in very limited areas, notably in setting in motion the formation of a new cabinet, does the monarch have decisive influence.

The Netherlands is a decentralized unitary state. It is a social and liberal democracy. Freedom of religion and belief is guaranteed. The state is neutral with respect to religion and belief. Church and state are separated. The Netherlands has a tradition of an open and positive attitude toward the international legal order.

CONSTITUTIONAL BODIES

The main bodies at the central level of government designated in the constitution are the monarch, the administration (composed of the prime minister, the ministers, and state secretaries), the lower house of parliament, and the upper house of parliament. The judiciary is independent. Other bodies explicitly mentioned in the constitution are the Council of State, the Court of Audit, and the national ombudsperson. The Council of State has its origin in the Conseil d'Etat established in the Netherlands in 1531 by the emperor Charles V. It advises the administration and parliament on draft legislation; one division of the council functions as the highest independent administrative court in cases in which no special administrative court procedure exists.

The Monarch

The monarch is the head of state and, together with the ministers, part of the administration. An act of parliament regulates membership of the royal house, but the rules of succession are determined by the constitution. The constitution provides for the occasions in which the royal prerogative is not, or cannot be, exercised by the monarch.

The monarch acts under ministerial responsibility. Royal signature is required for an act of parliament to be promulgated. Royal decrees are countersigned by a minister.

In the process leading to the formation of a new cabinet, the monarch usually appoints one or more "informers" after consulting various officials, and a "former" of a cabinet, usually the designated prime minister. This occurs without countersignature. The prime minister of the cabinet that results, however, is responsible to parliament for its establishment.

The monarch is president of the Council of State. Usually the Council of State is presided over by its vice president.

The Administration

Article 42 of the constitution states that the administration consists of the king and the ministers. The constitution mentions concrete tasks of the administration in various places. In general, it states that the Council of Ministers shall consider and decide upon overall administration policy and shall promote the coherence thereof. One responsibility of the administration is to promote the development of the international legal order.

Prime Minister

The prime minister presides over the Council of Ministers (or cabinet), and certain appointments to high offices need his or her signature. The prime minister is "first among equals"; no hierarchical relationship exists among ministers.

A number of modern developments have made the office of prime minister more crucial. The prime minister speaks to the public on behalf of the Council of Ministers after its meetings; the coordinating role of the office has become more important; and its importance has increased at the international—notably the European—level.

Ministers

Ministers are appointed by royal decree. Some, but not all, are heads of department. Cabinet ministers are collectively and individually responsible to both chambers of parliament; the most important political relation is with the lower house. Ministerial responsibility entails responsibility of ministers for their own conduct and for that of their state secretaries, their civil servants, and the monarch (and other members of the royal house). Lack of confidence obliges ministers individually or collectively to offer their resignation. If a cabinet minister offers his or her resignation for political reasons, the secretary of state does likewise; however, the converse does not follow. Cabinet ministers and state secretaries enjoy immunity and privilege as parliamentarians do.

In case of dissolution of a house of parliament, custom requires ministers to offer their resignation. Dissolution for other than political reasons is, in certain instances, prescribed by the constitution.

While neither a minister nor a state secretary of state can be a member of parliament, an exception is made when a resignation has been offered; pending a decision on the matter, the minister can become a member of parliament.

Parliament

The States General represents the entire Dutch people. It consists of a lower house and an upper house.

Lower House of Parliament

The lower house is directly elected for a four-year term on the basis of proportional representation. It consists of 150 members.

The lower house is the center of political activity. Although ministers and state secretaries are fully answerable to and need the confidence of both houses and must provide requested information to members of either house, the political significance of the lower house is greater. This is also true with respect to the right to inquiry. In addition, the lower house has the right to introduce and amend a bill.

Members of both houses enjoy parliamentary privilege. In the formulation of the constitution, they "may not be prosecuted or otherwise held liable in law for anything they say during the sittings of the States-General or of its committees or for anything they submit to them in writing." The Supreme Court tries present and former members of both houses for offenses committed while in office. A royal decree or resolution of the lower house sets this in motion.

The system of proportional representation has included a wide variety of parties in parliament, reflecting the pluralistic nature of the electorate, which leads to coalition governments. These are usually based on detailed agreements negotiated between the coalition partners in the lower house. Thus, a tight connection is established between the administration and its political base of support in the lower house, which does not always allow the cabinet room for maneuver.

Upper House

The upper house is elected by the 12 States Provincial on the basis of proportional representation. It consists of 75 members.

The upper house is a more deliberative body, as reflected in its constitutional position. The house is part of the legislature, but it has no right to introduce a bill; neither does it have the right to amend a bill. The house has the right of inquiry and its members have the right to request information from ministers and state secretaries.

As the relationship between administration and the lower house has become closer over the years, making it less likely for the house to challenge the administration, the upper house has gained a higher political profile. In addition, the 1983 constitution reduced its term from six years to four years and replaced the system of alternating elections with one single election for the entire house.

Thus, at times the upper house may be more representative of the mood of the nation than the lower house. In addition, the upper house is less likely to be dissolved; after all, if the 12 States Provincial that chose them are still sitting, dissolution will accomplish no change. Of course, it depends on the issues at hand, on political constellations, and on the personalities of the politicians involved.

Although the upper house is more aloof from day-to-day politics, ministers and state secretaries are fully responsible to it. The no confidence rule also functions with regard to the upper house.

The Lawmaking Process

The Cabinet and the State General enact an act of parliament jointly. The right to introduce a bill resides with the cabinet and the lower house. The upper house does not have this right. A minister's proposal (which constitutes the overwhelming majority) needs prior approval of the Council of Ministers and prior consultation with the Council of State. The proposal, accompanied by explanatory memorandum, by the advisory opinion of the Council of State, and by the Cabinet's reaction to this advisory opinion, is then introduced as a bill to the lower house. The lower house has the right to amend the bill. After adoption by the lower house, the bill is introduced in the upper house.

The upper house does not have the right to amend the bill; it can either adopt it or reject it. There is no mediation committee between the houses. However, if the upper house makes clear that it does not agree with the bill on some point, through the threat of rejecting the bill it can pressure the cabinet or the lower house to introduce a revised bill and in the meantime adjourn further treatment of the bill. When a bill is passed through both houses, it needs the signature of the king and the countersignature of a minister. To take effect, the act must be promulgated.

A bill that is introduced by the lower house proceeds to the upper house and is then submitted to the cabinet. In such a case, the lower house consults the Council of State.

In some cases, mostly concerning the Crown, extraordinary situations, or the constitution itself, a strengthened majority is needed. For such occasions, the constitution requires both houses to meet in joint session.

The Judiciary

The constitution provides only basic outlines and conditions for the judiciary. The actual system is determined by act of parliament. The general court system (for civil and criminal cases) is organized on a national level and made up of one Supreme Court, five courts of appeal, 19 district courts, and 61 subdistrict courts.

The organization of recourse in administrative cases is profoundly characterized by the 19th- and 20th-century ambivalence toward dealing with complaints against the administration. The key question was, Should such complaints be dealt with by an independent court or by a higher branch of the executive itself? As no principled decision was made, a patchwork of recourses emerged using both approaches, through the executive body—with the highest recourse to the Crown—or through the various specialized and independent administrative courts. These courts existed alongside the general independent court system for civil and criminal cases.

The European Court on Human Rights has ruled that the appeal to the Crown as the ultimate recourse in administrative cases, to determine an individual's civil rights or obligations or to decide on a criminal charge against him or her, is contrary to Article 6 of the European Convention on Human Rights, because it does not meet the standards of independence. As a result, the appeal to the Crown was replaced by an appeal to a branch of the Council of State serving as an independent administrative court.

In recent years, an effort has been made to integrate the administrative courts in the general system. Thus, for most administrative cases, initial appeals can be made to an administrative section of the general courts. The integration process is continuing.

THE ELECTION PROCESS

All persons of Dutch nationality have both the right to stand for election and the right to vote in elections of general representative bodies. This is guaranteed as a fundamental right and further specified in the constitution with respect to both houses of parliament and the decentralized councils. The right is subject to restrictions and exceptions by act of parliament. The age threshold is 18 years.

Dutch nationality is no longer a requirement to vote in, or to stand for, municipal elections.

POLITICAL PARTIES

Political parties are not mentioned in the constitution; nevertheless, they play an important role in the political process. The Netherlands has a multiparty system, stimulated by the electoral system of proportional representation and a low threshold of entrance—one seat is sufficient for representation in parliament.

Candidature takes place through political parties. However, members of parliament are obliged to represent not their party, but the people. They are not legally bound by any political instructions or party discipline. However, their behavior may have repercussions for their functioning within the party or for their future candidature.

Political parties are required to have the legal form of an association. They receive only limited subsidies of public funds.

Political parties can be banned only by a court decision. Banned parties cannot register to take part in elections. The criteria for banning a political party are the same as those for any forbidden legal entity in conjunction with Article 140 of the Criminal Code.

Although a political party has been banned, such an event is highly exceptional and the general attitude is in favor of a free democratic process.

CITIZENSHIP

The leading principle for acquiring Dutch citizenship is that of *ius sanguinis*. Therefore, Dutch citizenship is primarily acquired by birth. A child acquires Dutch citizenship if one of his or her parents is a Dutch citizen, regardless of where the child is born. The law provides for the possibility of naturalization in a number of cases, such as long and legal residence in the country.

FUNDAMENTAL RIGHTS

Fundamental rights are guaranteed in the first chapter of the Dutch constitution. This is to express their importance to the legal order.

Prior to the 1983 revision, fundamental rights were found in several different parts of the constitution. The 1983 revision reformulated rights that were already explicit, such as freedom of religion; extended other rights, such as freedom of opinion; and added new rights, such as the right to privacy. For the first time, a systematic catalog of social rights was added to the constitution. Changes regarding rights were made outside the first chapter as well, including a few rights that may be seen as fundamental, such as public access to information, independence of the judiciary, the ban on the death penalty, and conscientious objection to military service.

Most classic rights are guaranteed to everyone without respect to nationality; a few rights are specifically addressed to Dutch nationals, such as the right to be equally eligible for appointment to public service or electoral rights. Insofar as relevant and not explicitly stated otherwise, minors also enjoy fundamental rights. It is also acknowledged that insofar as relevant, fundamental rights protect groups and organizations.

The sequence of fundamental rights in the first chapter does not imply any hierarchy. Thus, Article 1 on equal treatment and nondiscrimination does not, by definition, take preference over other rights.

Impact and Functions of Fundamental Rights

Fundamental rights have many functions, such as defensive, participatory, and entitlement. Generally speaking, fundamental rights in the Netherlands share in all these functions, to the extent recognized in modern Western constitutional thought.

Traditionally, classic rights protect the individual from state interference, whereas social rights oblige the state to act. This difference between classic rights and social rights is not as clear-cut as it seems. With regard to classic rights, the constitution implies, or even explicitly requires, public authority action. For instance, the right to access a court requires a legal infrastructure with a solid judicial system; the constitution explicitly requires "rules to protect privacy." Courts carefully explore the "active component" in classic rights, such as a public obligation to provide billboard space for expression of one's opinion through the press. Social rights are usually formulated as a concern of the government instead of a right for the citizen, but ex-

ceptions exist. Generally speaking, classic rights are legally enforceable; this is different for social rights. In line with the preceding, courts carefully explore this field too.

Fundamental rights, both classic and social rights, primarily address the relationship between the state and private individuals. In that sense, they are equally important to all branches of government. Even in instances when they are not enforceable through a court (whether through the ban on judicial review of parliamentary legislation in accordance with the constitution, or in cases concerning social rights), the legislature and the administration are under an obligation to respect these rights.

Fundamental rights are also relevant to the relationships of private individuals. Their relevance may be specified and solidified through legislation (e.g., equal treatment legislation) or given shape in court decisions, through direct reference to the constitution, or through interpretation of open legal norms.

The impact of international law in the Dutch legal system is clearly visible in the field of fundamental rights. Moreover, Dutch courts are under an obligation to apply international fundamental rights, giving preference to them above Dutch law. This is significant, especially given that courts are not allowed to review acts of parliament regarding their conformity to the Dutch constitution. The European Union's fundamental rights law is also gaining increasing importance.

Limitations to Fundamental Rights

Fundamental rights are subject to limitation. The constitution specifies which body has the authority to limit fundamental rights, defines purposes to be met by the restriction, and/or introduces a specific procedure to be followed. In practically all cases, the competent authority for limiting fundamental rights is the parliamentary legislature. It may or may not be allowed to delegate this authority, depending on the formulation used by the constitution. Thus, the main guarantee for the protection of fundamental rights is found in the legislative process.

The notion of a "limitation" of a right is far-reaching: Not only are deliberate limitations regarded as such, so are those measures that are not aimed at explicitly limiting rights but may limit a fundamental right as a side effect. The combination of this broad notion of a "limitation" and the strict, centralizing system of competent authority is meant to provide a maximum of freedom to the citizen. The 1983 revision has led to a systematic effort to make legislation conform to the new constitutional standards. The courts have slightly mitigated this strict dogma in a sensible way, thus adjusting personal freedom to the requirements of everyday life.

ECONOMY

The Dutch system can be characterized as a liberal democracy, with a free market and social rights, therefore, a mixed economy or a social market economy. The general mood of society, alternating political preferences, and major economic trends and fluctuations influence the flavor and balance of the mix at any particular time.

The constitution makes no explicit statement on the economic system. It provides underpinnings in the chapter on fundamental rights. Fundamental rights protect the freedom of property, choice of profession, and freedom of assembly and association; the latter includes freedom of economic organization and freedom to establish trade unions. The constitution also mandates that parliament establish rules "concerning the legal status and protection of working persons and concerning codetermination."

The constitution also defines it as a concern of the authorities to ensure sufficient employment opportunities. Similarly, it mentions the security of the means of subsistence of the population and the distribution of wealth. It requires parliament to legislate "rules concerning entitlement to social security" and guarantees "Dutch nationals resident in the Netherlands who are unable to provide for themselves" the right to financial benefits from the state.

RELIGIOUS COMMUNITIES

The Dutch constitution contains no explicit statement on the institutional arrangements with religious communities, nor on the relationship between church and state. The principles implied by the constitution, and generally acknowledged, are separation of church and state neutrality with regard to religion or belief. Churches as organizations are not mentioned in the constitution.

The constitutional basis for the position of religious communities and their relation to public authorities are the fundamental rights guaranteed by the constitution. Article 6 of the constitution guarantees everyone freedom of religion and belief, individually and in community with others, notwithstanding everyone's responsibility under the law. It applies to groups and organizations as well.

Other fundamental rights are also important. Article 1, for example, guarantees equal treatment and nondiscrimination on the grounds of religion and belief. Article 23 guarantees respect for religion and belief in the public school system and lays the foundation for a dual school system of public (neutral) education and private (confessional) education, funded on equal footing by public funds.

The legal relationship between church and state is further shaped through ordinary legislation. This includes diverse fields of law such as the law on legal entities, mass media, tax law, labor law, privacy law, education law, or the law on ancient monuments.

The Civil Code gives churches as organizations a status as legal entity sui generis: Churches, their independent units, and structures in which they are united have legal personality, and they are "governed by their own statute, in so far as this does not conflict with the law." Religious organizations are, nevertheless, free to opt for a more regulated, predetermined structure, such as an association or a foundation.

MILITARY DEFENSE AND STATE OF EMERGENCY

The armed forces are under the supreme command of the administration. Their task is the defense and protection of the interests of the kingdom, and of the maintenance and promotion of the international legal order. The armed forces are currently professional forces and may also consist of conscripts. Conscription and conscientious objection are regulated by an act of parliament.

A declaration of war or end of a war requires permission of the States General meeting in joint session. In declaring war, the requirement is waived if prior permission is impossible because of an actual state of war.

Prior informing of the States General is required to employ the armed forces for the maintenance and promotion of the international legal order. This includes humanitarian aid in case of armed conflict, unless urgent reasons make this impossible, in which case, the States General must be informed soon afterward.

Civil defense is regulated by an act of parliament. In such a case, Dutch residents without Dutch nationality can also be mobilized.

The constitution mandates parliament to define the exceptional circumstances in which, for the internal or external safety of the kingdom, a royal decree can declare a state of emergency. The relevant law may even depart from a number of explicit constitutional guarantees. Immediately after the declaration of an exceptional circumstance by royal decree and for its duration, the States General decides on its continuation in joint session.

AMENDMENTS TO THE CONSTITUTION

The Dutch constitution is a rigid constitution. This means that the procedure to change the constitution is more elaborate than that of an ordinary act of parliament. The purpose is to prevent lighthearted changes to the constitution.

The first stage follows the ordinary procedure for any bill. Then, the lower house is dissolved and new elections take place. The election is usually made to coincide with the ordinary end of the house's term. In the second stage, the proposal goes through the identical procedure as in the previous parliament, but without the right of amendment. This time both houses can adopt the proposal only with a majority of two-thirds of the votes cast.

Existing legal norms need to be adjusted by parliament to changes in the constitution. Until this is done, they remain in force. For adjusting the constitution itself to the Charter of the Kingdom, a less demanding procedure exists. Changes to the constitution can in effect also emerge through political events, through court interpretation, or through interpretative legislation.

A two-thirds majority of both houses is needed to approve a treaty that conflicts with the constitution.

PRIMARY SOURCES

Constitution in English. Available online. URL: http://www.minbzk.nl/uk/constitution_and/publications/the_constitution_of. Accessed on September 17, 2005.

Constitution in Dutch. Available online. URL: http://www.minbzk.nl/grondwet_en/grondwet/publicaties/de_grondwet. Accessed on August 20, 2005.

SECONDARY SOURCES

Sophie van Bijsterveld, "The Constitution in the Legal Order of the Netherlands." In *Netherlands Report to the Fifteenth International Congress of Comparative Law, Bristol 1998,* edited by E. H. Hondius, 347–364. Antwerp/Groningen: Intersentia Rechtswetenschappen, 1998.

Sophie van Bijsterveld, *The Empty Throne: Democracy and the Rule of Law in Transition.* Utrecht: Lemma, 2002.

J. M. J. Chorus et al., *Introduction to Dutch Law.* The Hague: Kluwer Law International, 1999.

C. A. J. M. Kortmann and P. P. T. Bovend'Eert, *Dutch Constitutional Law.* The Hague: Kluwer Law International, 2000.

S. Taekema, ed., *Understanding Dutch Law.* The Hague: Boom Juridische Uitgevers, 2004.

Sophie van Bijsterveld

NEW ZEALAND

At-a-Glance

OFFICIAL NAME
New Zealand

CAPITAL
Wellington

POPULATION
4,035,461 (July 2005 est.)

SIZE
103,738 sq. mi. (268,680 sq. km)

RELIGIONS
Anglican 14.9%, Roman Catholic 12.4%, Presbyterian 10.9%, Methodist 2.9%, Pentecostal 1.7%, Baptist 1.3%, other Christian 9.4%, unspecified 17.2%, none 26%, other 3.3%

LANGUAGES
English and New Zealand Maori

NATIONAL OR ETHNIC COMPOSITION
European 69.8%, Maori 7.9%, Asian 5.7%, Pacific Islander 4.4%, mixed 7.8%, unspecified 3.8%, other 0.5%

DATE OF INDEPENDENCE OR CREATION
November 25, 1947

TYPE OF GOVERNMENT
Constitutional monarchy

TYPE OF STATE
Unitary state

TYPE OF LEGISLATURE
Unicameral parliament

DATE OF CONSTITUTION
No single date

DATE OF LAST AMENDMENT
No single date

New Zealand is an island state made up of two main islands, the North Island and the South Island, and several smaller islands. It is an independent state of the Commonwealth. It has inherited the English Westminster system of government and has no single written constitutional document. New Zealand's constitution can be found in a number of written and unwritten materials such as legislation, decisions of the courts, and constitutional practices.

The system of government is that of a democratic constitutional monarchy within a unitary state. The government has three branches, following the principle of the separation of powers: the parliament, which has full power to make law; the executive, which is responsible for the administration of the country; and the judiciary, which has power to interpret and to enforce the law. Although the branches have different roles, they are not totally separate. For example, ministers of government are also members of parliament.

The head of state is the sovereign of New Zealand. The sovereign is currently Queen Elizabeth II, who is also the sovereign of the United Kingdom. She is represented in day-to-day matters in New Zealand by a governor-general. Although the monarch remains symbolically and legally important, all political powers are exercised by the ministers of government. The governor-general as a matter of general practice follows the advice of the ministers.

New Zealand is a secular state, with a free enterprise economy.

CONSTITUTIONAL HISTORY

New Zealand was first inhabited by the Maori people of Polynesia about 1,000 years ago. It was discovered by Europeans in 1642, when the Dutch navigator Abel Tasman saw the West Coast of New Zealand but did not land. In 1769, New Zealand was rediscovered, by the British naval captain

James Cook. He was the first European to lay claim to New Zealand and did so on behalf of the British Crown.

Cook's claim did not have the effect of annexing New Zealand to the British Empire because the territory was not officially settled. However, some Europeans had in fact settled in the islands and tensions between them and the Maori were frequent. Britain was reluctant to intervene in these affairs for a long time, but in 1832 a British resident was appointed. This was the first signal of British willingness to become involved with New Zealand affairs.

In 1839, however, New Zealand was annexed to the Colony of New South Wales in Australia. Britain considered it necessary to reach an agreement with the Maori inhabitants, and Captain William Hobson was commissioned to sign a treaty with the Maori by which they would cede sovereignty to the British.

On February 6, 1840, a formal agreement, the Treaty of Waitangi, was signed between the Maori chiefs present at the meeting and the British Crown. The treaty was then circulated around New Zealand for further signatures, and in all 500 chiefs signed it. As a consequence, Hobson issued proclamations of British sovereignty on May 21, 1840. The proclamation asserted sovereignty over the North Island by way of cession pursuant to the treaty and over the South Island by way of discovery.

The British then set up a colonial system of government. A legislative council was created, but its lawmaking power was restricted and subordinate to that of the British Parliament. Hobson was officially declared governor. In 1846, the United Kingdom Parliament passed the New Zealand Constitution Act, an attempt to introduce elections and to give New Zealand self-governance. However, the country was not ready and the act was never implemented.

The New Zealand Constitution Act 1852 can be described as the first effective constitutional act. It established a provincial system of government consisting of six provinces, each having its own elected Provincial Council and superintendent. The provincial system was abolished in 1875, but the 1852 act also provided for a more lasting bicameral General Assembly that included the governor, an appointed Legislative Council, and an elected House of Representatives. The General Assembly was clearly subordinate to the Parliament of the United Kingdom until 1947, when New Zealand acquired full power to make its own laws. That meant formal legal autonomy from England. Since 1950, the New Zealand parliament has been unicameral and consists of an elected House of Representatives plus the head of state.

By the 1980s, many constitutional laws, particularly the New Zealand Constitution Act 1852, had lost significance. A far-reaching amendment was necessary to reflect the needs of the modern government. The Constitution Act 1986 was passed by the New Zealand parliament to effect the necessary reforms.

The act does not purport to be a written constitution or a supreme law. It is an ordinary act and can be amended as any other act. Despite its name, it does not deal with many matters of constitutional significance such as the role of the cabinet.

The majority voting system was inherited from England, but it was amended to account for New Zealand's special circumstances, and it was finally replaced in 1993 by a system of proportional representation. In 1867, Maori were given guaranteed representation in parliament by the creation of Maori seats. In 1893, women were granted the right to vote, and New Zealand became the first country to recognize this right for women.

FORM AND IMPACT OF THE CONSTITUTION

New Zealand's constitution can be found in a number of primary sources:

1. Acts of parliament.   These are ordinary statutes and not supreme law in any sense.
2. Common law.   The common law can be defined as "judge-made law." The decisions of courts play an important role in the development of constitutional principle. Many of the most fundamental rules of New Zealand constitutional law are found in the classic decisions of the English courts of centuries ago. The New Zealand courts have in recent times been particularly active in relation to the rights of individuals and local matters of importance, such as the Treaty of Waitangi of 1840.
3. Letters patent.   These are orders issued by the monarch to regulate the office of the governor-general. They spell out the relation of the sovereign as the head of state to the government and, in particular, establish the Executive Council, which consists of the ministers of government and the governor-general. This is the senior administrative organ of government and the source of regulations that are the main type of delegated legislation.
4. Constitutional conventions.   These are unwritten rules that are regularly followed and reflect widely held expectations about constitutional behavior. They are not legal rules and cannot be directly enforced through the courts. Constitutional conventions arise from precedent or agreement. They represent practices that are respected because their breach would cause adverse consequences for the system. Important constitutional conventions are those related to the operation of the cabinet and to the appointment of ministers. A key convention is that the governor-general will always act on the advice of ministers. The appointment of ministers is by the governor-general on the recommendation of the prime minister.
5. The Treaty of Waitangi.   The status of the Treaty of Waitangi within the domestic law and its validity as an international treaty are still issues of debate. The treaty has not been incorporated into domestic law, but its principles are referred to in many enactments.

The courts have recognized the treaty as having a quasi-constitutional status.

The government has recognized the following treaty principles:

Principle of government (Kawanatanga)—this principle emphasizes the right of the government to govern and make law.
The principle of self-management (Rangatiratanga)—the right of Maori to control and enjoy their resources.
The principle of equality—partnership of government and the Maori.
The principle of reasonable cooperation—consultation and cooperation to share understandings and objectives.
The principle of redress—commitment of the government to redress grievances.

In 1975, the Tribunal of Waitangi was created to investigate grievances of Maori caused by government breaches of the treaty. The tribunal can recommend that the Crown compensate Maori or take other remedial action. Although the tribunal's recommendations have only political and moral force and in theory the Crown could ignore them, in practice they have formed the basis for negotiations between Maori petitioners and the government for the settlement of the grievances.

BASIC ORGANIZATIONAL STRUCTURE

New Zealand is a unitary state with a strongly centralized system of government. It is one state and the most important one in what is known as the Realm of New Zealand. The Realm of New Zealand, described in the letters patent of the governor-general, comprises the state of New Zealand, the associated state of the Cook Islands, the associated state of Niue, the territory of Tokelau, and the Ross Dependency. The link among the countries in the realm is allegiance to a common sovereign and common nationality.

The Cook Islands is a small nation in the South Pacific with a number of islands spread over a large ocean expanse. The current population is about 15,000. The Cook Islands is, as New Zealand, a constitutional monarchy governed by a unicameral parliament elected by universal suffrage.

Niue is a single island state in the South Pacific. It has a population of 1,500. It is a constitutional democracy with a cabinet system of government and a legislative assembly elected by universal suffrage.

Tokelau has a population of 1,500 people spread over three atolls just south of the equator in the Pacific. It is listed as a New Zealand colony by the United Nations. It has a high level of internal autonomy based on traditional government structures at the village level.

Tokelau is being prepared to exercise its right to self-determination.

The Ross Dependency is a small section of Antarctica under New Zealand authority. A base for extensive scientific investigation, it has no resident population and no internal government structure.

LEADING CONSTITUTIONAL PRINCIPLES

New Zealand is a constitutional monarchy, whose monarch must, except under very special circumstances, follow the advice of the responsible ministers. It is also a democracy with an elected House of Representatives and ministers and systems that provide for transparency and governmental accountability.

Leading constitutional principles are the rule of law, the separation of powers, and parliamentary sovereignty. The rule of law entails that no individual should be beyond the control of the law, that all individuals should be treated equally by the law, and that all should have equal access to the law.

The separation of powers principle derives from the thinking of Montesquieu: Freedom is best protected when the powers to make law, administer the law, and make judgments on the law are exercised by different bodies—the legislature, the executive, and the judiciary. In New Zealand the principle is respected, but in practice there is a high level of interaction among the three areas of government. For instance, it is in the nature of the cabinet system of government that the members of the executive usually control the legislature by virtue of a government majority in the parliament. It is also the case that formally, at least, the governor-general (the head of state) appoints the ministers and the judiciary.

The parliamentary sovereignty doctrine is part of the ordinary law inherited from England. In New Zealand, there is no supreme law in the sense of a constitution that overrides inconsistent legislation or enables the judiciary to declare invalid laws made by parliament. Therefore, there is no judicial supremacy. The New Zealand parliament is the sovereign lawmaking body and, as such, alone has the power to make or unmake any law. Thus, if a new law is inconsistent with an earlier law, the latter is by implication repealed. A supreme constitutional law that could not be repealed by future law would amount to a restriction on the sovereign power of a future parliament.

CONSTITUTIONAL BODIES

The main constitutional bodies are the governor-general, the cabinet, the prime minister, the parliament, and the judiciary.

The Governor-General

The sovereign of New Zealand is the head of state, and the governor-general appointed by the sovereign on the advice of the prime minister is the representative of the sovereign. The sovereign has, in practice, no political power but a significant ceremonial role. The prime importance of the office is that it represents the unity of the nation.

The Cabinet

The cabinet is the main decision-making body of government. Its members are members of parliament who are appointed as ministers by the governor-general on recommendation of the prime minister. The ministers belong to the political party that has the majority in the House of Representatives. The prime minister is the leader of that majority. In cabinet, the ministers formulate government policies and legislative programs and are collectively responsible for the decisions taken.

The Prime Minister

The prime minister is the head of government. Although the office has great political powers, the duties of the prime minister are not described in any law.

The prime minister's key function is to lead the government. This is done by chairing cabinet meetings, allocating cabinet portfolios, and exercising some discipline over the government. Another important function of the prime minister is to be the public face of the government. This entails representing the government at political functions in New Zealand and abroad.

The prime minister has the power to instruct the governor-general to dissolve parliament and to hold an early election. The prime minister also advises the sovereign to appoint or remove the governor-general.

The Parliament

Parliament, the House of Representatives plus the head of state, is the supreme lawmaking body and its laws cannot be challenged or declared invalid by any court or government institution. The ordinary laws of parliament are the highest source of law. Parliament can delegate its lawmaking powers to other bodies. The delegated legislation has the same effect as ordinary legislation as long as it does not exceed the powers listed in the delegation.

Parliament raises government money and approves the expenditure of money; it checks on the operations of government by questioning ministers or conducting investigations. It provides a forum for the discussion of grievances. Petitions can be made to parliament by members of the public for redress of grievances on any matter of public importance.

The Lawmaking Process

A bill is generally debated in the House of Representatives three times. After the first reading it is sent to a select committee for examination. The bill is reported back to the House of Representatives with any recommended changes from the Select Committee. It then receives its second reading, at which stage the house decides whether it wishes the bill to proceed. The Committee of the Whole House stage then follows, when the bill is debated in detail, clause by clause. Finally the bill receives its third reading. If the House of Representatives votes to pass the bill, it receives the royal assent from the governor-general and becomes an act.

The Judiciary

The judiciary interprets and applies parliament's law and creates its own case law. It is a body independent of the political branches of government. Its function is to resolve disputes of facts and law between individuals and between the state and individuals.

In New Zealand, the system of courts is, in descending order, the Supreme Court, the Court of Appeal, the High Court, and the District Courts. There are also specialist courts, such as the Youth and Family Court, which are branches of the District Court.

There are two other judicial bodies, the Waitangi Tribunal and the Maori Land Court, which were created by statute. Although they are part of the judiciary, they do not settle claims. They follow an inquisitorial process aimed at determining whether a claim is well founded, and they make nonbinding recommendations to the government. Claims are eventually settled by negotiation with the government.

THE ELECTION PROCESS

Any New Zealand citizen over the age of 18 who is qualified to be on the electoral roll or any person who has resided in New Zealand for at least a year is entitled to vote in elections to the House of Representatives. There is a three-year electoral term.

All New Zealand citizens who are registered electors and are not public servants have the right to stand for elections.

Parliamentary Elections

Members of parliament are elected under the mixed member proportional (MMP) system, which was introduced into New Zealand in 1993 to replace the "first-past-the-post" (FPP) electoral system. The MMP system was adopted to increase the number of political parties represented in parliament and to make the executive less dominant. Under the FPP system the House of Representatives was dominated by two major parties, and political power was concentrated in the governing party. Under a pure proportional system, the number of parliamentary seats is proportionate to the number of votes. In New Zealand there is a threshold requirement:

A party must win 5 percent of the national votes in order to be allocated any seats.

The 1993 system, by giving every voter two votes, added a proportional feature to the FPP system. The country remained divided into geographical constituencies of approximate equal population. A voter casts one vote for his or her preferred candidate in the area, and another for one of the political parties. There are 120 seats in the House of Representatives, seven of which are reserved for Maori.

Political Participation

Democracy at a local level is exercised through elections to local government bodies. New Zealand local government consists of 12 regional councils. Each region is divided into territorial authorities, which can be districts or cities, each of which has a council of its own. There are 74 territorial authorities within the 12 regional districts.

Regional councils are responsible for functions such as resource management, biosecurity, civil defense, and land transport. City and district councils are responsible for community well-being and development, infrastructure (roads, sewers), recreation, and culture.

Local governments are subordinate to central government and controlled by legislation passed by parliament. Local governments have power to make their own laws, called by-laws, but only in matters that are strictly defined by parliament. A by-law cannot contradict a law passed by parliament.

POLITICAL PARTIES

Political parties in New Zealand have evolved as part of the political process. The first party to have an extraparliamentary support structure was the Labour Party, founded in 1916. The example was followed by liberal parties that officially organized themselves as the National Party in 1936. The Labour Party and the National Party are the two main political parties in New Zealand.

The Labour Party follows traditional socialist policies, while the National Party supports individualism in the economic, social, and political spheres. Other smaller parties have been formed from time to time and have had representation in parliament. Some of these parties have been the Alliance Party, New Zealand First, the Greens, United Future, Social Credit, and the Act Party. Political parties are generally unincorporated societies that regulate their own procedures and structure. They are subject to very little regulation.

Until 1993, the two main parties dominated New Zealand's political scene. The party in power exercised a virtual monopoly within parliament. The MMP system introduced in 1993 helped to change the political situation. Elections under MMP have resulted in the representation in parliament of a number of other parties, leading to coalition governments. For example, after the 2002 election, the Labour Party entered into a coalition with the Progressive Coalition and had a confidence vote agreement with the United Future Party.

CITIZENSHIP

Every person born in New Zealand is a New Zealand citizen by birth. A child acquires New Zealand citizenship if at least one parent is a New Zealand citizen. Permanent residents can, under certain circumstances, acquire citizenship. Grant of citizenship may be made in special cases and for humanitarian reasons.

FUNDAMENTAL RIGHTS

In 1978, the New Zealand government ratified the International Covenant on Civil and Political Rights. As a belated sequel, parliament passed the New Zealand Bill of Rights Act 1990, which is concerned with the protection of individual human rights against abuses by the state. The act is not supreme law and can be amended by ordinary means.

The 1990 act protects four sets of rights: rights pertaining to life and security of the person, democratic and civil rights, nondiscrimination and minority rights, and rights pertaining to search, arrest, and detention. The list of rights is not exhaustive, and rights and freedoms not enumerated but within the ambit of the act are preserved.

The act applies to the relationship between the state and individuals. Therefore, individuals can invoke the act only for breaches committed by one of the three branches of government—executive, legislative, and judiciary.

The act makes it clear that the courts have no authority to declare any statute invalid or refuse to apply any statute on the grounds that it is inconsistent with the rights and freedoms protected in the act. When interpreting an enactment, courts are required only to prefer a meaning consistent with these rights and freedoms, if such an interpretation is possible. If no consistent meaning is possible, courts must apply the statute in question anyway. Furthermore, the rights and freedoms protected in the act "are subject to such reasonable limits prescribed by law as can be demonstrably justified in a free and democratic society."

All the same, courts have interpreted the act broadly, so as to give full effective protection to individual fundamental rights. For example, though the act does not have a remedy provision, courts have ruled that damages and other effective remedies should be available for its breaches. This expansive interpretation has conferred on the act a quasi-constitutional status.

The Human Rights Act 1993 extends the protection of human rights by prohibiting discrimination by private persons. The act applies to discrimination on many grounds, such as sex, religion, race, disability, and political opinion in the ambit of education, employment, provision of goods and services, access to public places, and provision of accommodation.

Other laws affecting human rights are the Official Information Act 1982 and the Privacy Act 1993. These laws provide individuals access to official information (information held by the government) relating to them. Such information must be made available unless there is good reason for withholding it; the preservation of personal privacy is a good reason and is protected to the extent consistent with the public interest. The Privacy Act established principles for the protection of privacy to be applied in the collection, use, and disclosure of information held by the government and by private agencies.

New Zealand was one of the first countries outside Scandinavia to adopt the idea of the ombudsperson. The first ombudsperson was appointed in 1962. The office has the important constitutional role of investigating complaints from citizens related to government action affecting them.

ECONOMY

The modern New Zealand economy operates on free market principles. There are sizable manufacturing and service sectors complementing a highly efficient agricultural sector. Exports of wool, meat, and dairy products are very important in the economy, as is tourism, which contributes almost 10 percent of the gross domestic product (GDP).

The economy is strongly trade-oriented, with exports of goods and services accounting for around 33 percent of total output. New Zealand is the world's largest exporter of dairy products and second only to Australia in wool exports. Trade is mainly with Europe, the United States of America, Australia, and Japan.

RELIGIOUS COMMUNITIES

New Zealand is predominantly Christian, including the Anglican (14.9 percent), Roman Catholic (12.4 percent), and Presbyterian (10.9 percent) Churches. Nonreligious people account for 21 percent, and other minorities, including Jews, Buddhists, Muslims, and members of other Christian denominations, account for the rest.

Churches are common all over the country; mosques, temples, and synagogues are also found.

MILITARY DEFENSE AND STATE OF EMERGENCY

The military is organized on traditional British patterns. It has in recent years participated actively in the United Nations and other international peacekeeping endeavors, both regionally (for example, in East Timor and the Solomon Islands) and internationally (for example, in Bosnia and Herzegovina, Afghanistan, and Iraq). New Zealand also has a formal civil defense system to deal with natural disasters such as floods and earthquakes.

AMENDMENTS TO THE CONSTITUTION

Since there is no one written constitution, changes to the political system can be made at liberty by way of ordinary legislative process.

PRIMARY SOURCES
"New Zealand Legislation." Available online. URL: http://www.oefre.unibe.ch/law/icl/nz_indx.html.   Accessed on June 21, 2006.
"Treaty of Waitangi Principles." Available online. URL: http://www.waitangi-tribunal.govt.nz/treaty/principles.asp. Accessed on June 21, 2006.

SECONDARY SOURCES
Philip A. Joseph, *Constitutional and Administrative Law.* 2d ed. Wellington: Brookers, 2001.
Morag McDowell and Duncan Alexander Webb, *The New Zealand Legal System: Structures, Process and Legal Theory.* 3d ed. Wellington: LexisNexis Butterworths, 2002.
Geoffrey Palmer and Matthew Palmer, *Bridled Power: New Zealand's Constitution and Government.* 5th ed. Auckland: Oxford University Press, 2004.

Anthony Angelo

NICARAGUA

At-a-Glance

OFFICIAL NAME
Republic of Nicaragua

CAPITAL
Managua

POPULATION
5,465,100 (July 2005 est.)

SIZE
49,998 sq. mi. (129,494 sq. km)

LANGUAGES
Spanish (official), English and indigenous languages on Caribbean coast

RELIGIONS
Catholic 73%, Evangelical 15%, Moravian Church 1.5%, unaffiliated or other 10.5%

NATIONAL OR ETHNIC COMPOSITION
Mestizo (mixed Amerindian and white) 69%, white 17%, black 9%, Amerindian 5%

DATE OF INDEPENDENCE OR CREATION
September 15, 1821

TYPE OF GOVERNMENT
Mixed presidential-parliamentary government system

TYPE OF STATE
Centralist state

TYPE OF LEGISLATURE
Unicameral parliament

DATE OF CONSTITUTION
January 9, 1987

DATE OF LAST AMENDMENT
October 20, 2005

Nicaragua is a democratic republic with a government system that is a mixture of presidentialism and parliamentarism. The 1987 constitution, from the social-revolutionary Sandinista era, gave excessive power to the president; it was amended in 1995 to provide for a more even distribution of power among the four branches of government. The predominant constitutional bodies are the president (executive), the National Assembly (legislative), the Supreme Court of Justice (judicial), and the Supreme Electoral Council (electoral). Another constitutional reform in 2000 increased the number of justices of the Supreme Court and made changes to the electoral laws. Further constitutional reforms adopted by the National Assembly in January 2005, which intended to limit many presidential powers, have been postponed until January 2007.

The constitution provides for individual rights, political rights, social rights, family rights, and labor rights. It also gives standing to several international and regional human rights treaties. Every citizen may present writs of unconstitutionality (*amparo*) or writs of habeas corpus. Nicaraguan citizenship may be acquired either by birth or by naturalization; in the latter case, nationals of other Central American states face fewer obstacles.

CONSTITUTIONAL HISTORY

The name *Nicaragua* is derived from *Nicarao,* the chief of the indigenous tribe who lived near present-day Lake Nicaragua around 1500. In 1524, Hernandez de Cordoba founded the first Spanish permanent settlements in the region. Nicaragua gained independence from Spain in 1821, briefly becoming a part of the Mexican Empire and then a member of the Central American Federation. When this federation was dissolved in 1838, Nicaragua became a fully independent republic.

Between 1838 and 1974, Nicaragua had 10 constitutions. The U.S. adventurer William Walker and his "filibusters" seized the presidency in 1856, but they were overthrown a year later. From 1893, General Jose Santos Zelaya established a dictatorship until he was driven from office after a United States–backed coup in 1909. After the coup, Nicaragua allowed the United States to run its customs and excise, the national bank, and the railway. Guerrillas led by Augusto Cesar Sandino campaigned against the U.S. military presence, which had been established in 1912. Sandino was assassinated in 1934 by National Guard officers; three years later, Anastasio Somoza Garcia took over the presidency.

The Somoza dynasty ended in 1979 with a massive uprising led by the social-revolutionary Sandinista National Liberation Front (FSLN). The United States broke off diplomatic links with Nicaragua in 1981 and subsequently supported the rebel contra forces. Nicaragua instituted international proceedings concerning responsibility for military and paramilitary activities against the United States. In 1986, the International Court of Justice (ICJ) in The Hague found that the United States had violated a number of principles of customary international law and ordered reparations.

A new Nicaraguan constitution was promulgated in 1987. The opposition presidential candidate, Violeta Chamorro, won the presidential election in February 1990. Chamorro refused to sign a revised constitution in February 1995. The conflict was resolved by the "Political Pact" of June 15, 1995, which stipulated that the constitution would be enacted together with a law concerning its interpretation and reforms. A package of amendments, including a reduction in the presidential term, was eventually agreed. The new Supreme Electoral Council prepared for parliamentary and presidential elections, which were held in October 1996. The first transfer of power in recent Nicaraguan history from one democratically elected president to another took place in January 1997, when the administration of Arnoldo Aleman was inaugurated. However, Aleman became the first Central American former president to be imprisoned for crimes in office after a trial on charges of corruption and money laundering. The constitution was amended again in 2000 to increase the powers of the Supreme Court of Justice and to make changes to the electoral laws.

Additional constitutional reforms, which seek to limit many of the presidential powers and increase those of the legislature, were ratified by the opposition-dominated National Assembly in January 2005, sparking a political crisis in the country. In March 2005, the Central American Court of Justice (CCJ), a regional court based in Managua, declared the constitutional reforms to be "inapplicable," arguing that they violated Central American treaties and Nicaragua's constitution. However, the opposition parties FSLN and PLC have rejected that ruling, and they are supported by the Supreme Court, which held that the CCJ acted beyond its powers. This essentially left Nicaragua with two constitutional frameworks: the unamended constitution accepted by the executive and the amended text promoted by the majority of the legislature. In October 2005, however, the parties agreed to postpone the constitutional reforms until the next president's term begins in January 2007.

FORM AND IMPACT OF THE CONSTITUTION

Nicaragua has a written constitution, codified in a single document, Constitución Política de la Republica de Nicaragua. The Electoral Law, the Emergency Law, and the Law of *Amparo* are considered constitutional laws.

All persons in Nicaragua enjoy state protection and recognition of their inherent rights as human beings. The constitution gives explicit standing to the Universal Declaration of Human Rights (1948), the American Declaration of the Rights and Duties of Man (1948), the International Covenant on Economic, Social and Cultural Rights (1966), the International Covenant on Civil and Political Rights (1966), and the American Convention on Human Rights (1969). In the Nicaraguan constitutional reforms of 1995, the Convention on the Rights of the Child (1990) was raised to constitutional status.

BASIC ORGANIZATIONAL STRUCTURE

Nicaragua is divided into 15 departments and two autonomous regions on the Atlantic coast. The 1995 constitutional reform guaranteed the integrity of those regions' several unique cultures and gave the inhabitants a say in the use of the area's natural resources.

LEADING CONSTITUTIONAL PRINCIPLES

Nicaragua is a constitutional democracy with executive, legislative, judicial, and electoral branches of government. The leading constitutional principles are liberty; justice; respect for human dignity; political, social, and ethnic pluralism; acknowledgment of different forms of property; free international cooperation; and respect for the free self-determination of peoples. According to Article 9 of the constitution, Nicaragua advocates Central American unity and supports political and economic integration and cooperation as well as establishment and preservation of peace in the region.

CONSTITUTIONAL BODIES

The predominant bodies provided for in the constitution are the president, the National Assembly, the Supreme Electoral Council, and the judiciary. The president and the members of the National Assembly are elected to concurrent terms of five years.

The President

The president is chief of state, head of government, and commander in chief of the army. The president and vice president are elected on the same ticket by popular vote for a five-year term. The constitutional reforms of January 2000 provide outgoing presidents and vice presidents with a lifelong seat in the legislature. Under the contested 2005 constitutional amendments, the government would submit the appointment of ministers, vice ministers, and top diplomats to ratification by the National Assembly.

The National Assembly

The unicameral National Assembly consists of 90 deputies. In addition, former presidents and vice presidents hold a seat for life and occupied three seats after the 2001 elections. Members of the National Assembly are elected by proportional representation and party lists to serve five-year terms. In 1995, the executive and legislative branches negotiated a reform of the 1987 Sandinista constitution that gave important new powers and independence to the legislature. As a result, the National Assembly is able to override a presidential veto with a simple majority vote.

The Supreme Electoral Council

The Supreme Electoral Council is responsible for organizing and conducting elections, plebiscites, and referenda. It is led by a council of seven magistrates, who are elected to five-year terms by the National Assembly. Constitutional changes in 2000 gave the two leading political parties, the Liberal Constitutional Party (PLC) and the Sandinista National Liberation Front (FSLN) more power to name party activists to the council. These changes prompted allegations that both parties were politicizing electoral institutions and processes and excluding smaller parties.

The Lawmaking Process

The initiative to propose laws can be taken by members of the National Assembly or by the president. In addition, the Supreme Electoral Council, the Supreme Court of Justice, and the autonomous regional and municipal councils may initiate laws concerning subject matters within their authority. Finally, citizens may petition for a referendum on a proposed law, excluding certain subject areas such as taxes, amnesty, or international affairs. Once the bill has been approved by the National Assembly, it is sent to the president for approval, promulgation, and publication. The president may veto the bill as a whole or in part, but the National Assembly can reject the presidential veto. The 2005 constitutional reforms, however, seek to outlaw partial and total presidential vetoes.

The Judiciary

The Supreme Court supervises the functioning of the judicial system and appoints all appellate and lower court judges. Organization and judicial career of the courts of appeal, district, and local judges are regulated by law. In Nicaragua, justice is free of court costs according to the constitution.

The Supreme Court is divided into specialized administrative, criminal, constitutional, and civil chambers. Supreme Court justices are elected to five-year terms by the National Assembly. As part of the 2000 constitutional reforms, the number of justices was increased to 16 justices. According to the constitution, the judiciary must receive no less than 4 percent of Nicaragua's general budget.

THE ELECTION PROCESS

The minimal voting age is 16 years. The president is directly elected by universal suffrage. Under the 2000 constitutional reforms, a presidential candidate needs to win only 35 percent of the vote to preclude a second-round runoff. He or she may not serve two consecutive terms but may stand for reelection in a later election. Close relatives of the incumbent president may not stand for presidential elections.

POLITICAL PARTIES

Some 35 political parties participated in the 1996 elections. However, more restrictive electoral laws were passed in 2000, and only three parties participated in the 2001 national elections: the Liberal Alliance (including the PLC), the Sandinista National Liberation Front (FSLN), and the Conservative Party of Nicaragua (PCN).

CITIZENSHIP

Nicaraguan citizenship may be acquired either by birth or by naturalization. Nationals of other Central American states who reside in Nicaragua may opt for dual citizenship. In turn, a Nicaraguan national does not lose citizenship when he or she is naturalized in another Central American state. Other foreigners, however, must give up their previous nationality upon naturalization in Nicaragua.

FUNDAMENTAL RIGHTS

The constitution provides for individual, political, social, family, and labor rights. It prohibits discrimination based on birth, nationality, political belief, race, gender, language, religion, opinion, national origin, and economic or social condition. Nicaraguans have the right to be protected against hunger as well as the right to decent, comfortable, and safe housing that guarantees familial privacy. All public and private sector workers, except the military and the police, are entitled to form and join unions of their own choosing. Nearly half of Nicaragua's workforce, including agricultural workers, is unionized.

Impact and Functions of Fundamental Rights

Citizens whose constitutional rights have been violated or are in danger of violation have the right to present writs of habeas corpus or *amparo* (writ of unconstitutionality).

Limitations to Fundamental Rights

The rights of each person are limited by the rights of others, collective security, and the just requirements of the common good. According to Article 24 of the constitution, all persons also have duties to their family, the community, the homeland, and humanity.

ECONOMY

Nicaragua remains the second-poorest nation in the Western Hemisphere and faces economic problems such as low per capita income, massive unemployment, and huge external debt. Also, thousands of property confiscation cases from the Sandinista era must be resolved. In the 2001 judgment of *Mayagna Awas Tingni v. Nicaragua,* the Inter-American Court of Human Rights (IACHR) upheld the rights of an indigenous community to its traditional lands and resource tenure; the IACHR further ordered Nicaragua to establish an adequate mechanism to secure the land rights of all indigenous communities of the country.

RELIGIOUS COMMUNITIES

The constitution provides for freedom of religion and prohibits discrimination on the basis of religion. It also states that no one shall be obligated by coercive measures to declare his or her ideology or beliefs. However, nobody may disobey the law or prevent others from exercising their rights and fulfilling their duties by invoking religious beliefs.

The requirements for legal recognition of a religious group are similar to those for other nongovernmental organizations. After approval of the National Assembly, a religious group must register with the Ministry of Government as an association or a foundation. A recognized church may be granted tax-exempt status; this exemption is a contentious issue because of perceived unequal treat-

ment of different religious groups. However, missionaries do not face special entry requirements other than obtaining religious worker visas.

MILITARY DEFENSE AND STATE OF EMERGENCY

The president and the Council of Ministers may order the intervention of the army only in exceptional circumstances when national stability is threatened by internal disorder, calamity, or natural disaster. The establishment of foreign military bases on national territory is prohibited by the constitution.

AMENDMENTS TO THE CONSTITUTION

The National Assembly may partially or totally reform the constitution. Upon the initiative of one-third of its members or of the president, a partial constitutional reform is transmitted to a special commission and must be discussed in two congressional terms. A general reform of the constitution requires the election of a National Constituent Assembly, two-thirds of whose members must approve the draft.

PRIMARY SOURCES
Constitution in English: Gisbert H. Flanz, *Constitutions of the Countries of the World.* Dobbs Ferry, N.Y.: Oceana, 2004.
Constitution in Spanish. Available online. URL: http://www.asamblea.gob.ni/constitu.htm. Accessed on August 21, 2005.

SECONDARY SOURCES
S. James Anaya and Claudio Grossman, "The Case of *Awas Tingni v. Nicaragua:* A New Step in the International Law of Indigenous Peoples." *Arizona Journal of International and Comparative Law* 19, no. 1 (2002): 1–15.
Inter-American Court of Human Rights, "Case of *The Mayagna (Sumo) Awas Tingni Community vs. Nicaragua* (Judgment of August 31, 2001)." Available online. URL: http://www.corteidh.or.cr/seriecpdf_ing/seriec_79_ing.pdf. Accessed on September 14, 2005.
International Court of Justice, "Case Concerning Military and Paramilitary Activities in and against Nicaragua. Judgment of June 27, 1986. *I. C. J. Reports* (1986): 14–150.
Kenneth J. Mijeski, *The Nicaragua Constitution of 1987: English Translation and Commentary.* Athens: Ohio University Center for International Studies, 1991.

Michael Wiener

NIGER

At-a-Glance

OFFICIAL NAME
Republic of Niger

CAPITAL
Niamey

POPULATION
11,360,000 (2005 est.)

SIZE
490,000 sq. mi. (1,267,000 sq. km)

LANGUAGES
French (official), Hausa, Zarma, Fulfulde, Tamajak, Kanuri, Toubou, Gurmance, Arabic

RELIGIONS
Sunni Muslim 95%, other (Christian, pagan) 5%

NATIONAL OR ETHNIC COMPOSITION
Hausa 56%, Zarma 22%, Fulani 8.5%, Tuareg 8%, Kanuri 4.3%, other (Arab, Toubou, Gurma) 1.2%

DATE OF INDEPENDENCE OR CREATION
August 3, 1960

TYPE OF GOVERNMENT
Semipresidential

TYPE OF STATE
Unitary state

TYPE OF LEGISLATURE
Unicameral parliament

DATE OF CONSTITUTION
July 18, 1999

DATE OF LAST AMENDMENT
July 9, 2004

Niger is a democracy based on the rule of law, with a clear division of executive, legislative, and judicial powers. It is a unitary state comprising eight administrative regions. The constitution provides for guarantees of human rights. There are remedies for violation of the constitution, enforceable by an independent judiciary including a constitutional court. The constitution has been modified several times in recent years in response to political turmoil that occurred in the country.

The president is the head of state and has extensive power according to the constitution. Appointed by the president, the prime minister is the head of the administration. The administration determines and conducts the policy of the nation. As representatives of the nation, the members of parliament are elected by popular vote. A multiparty system of government allows safe competition for power.

Religious freedom is guaranteed, and state and religious communities are officially separated. However, the main religion, namely, Islam, has an important impact on social and political life. The economic system can be described as a developing market economy. By law, the military is subject to the civil government; in practice, the military has several times taken a dominant role in the political scene.

CONSTITUTIONAL HISTORY

Niger emerged as an administrative and political entity under French colonial rule at the end of the 19th century. The Cercle du Moyen-Niger, created in 1898, was initially a simple administrative structure. It became the Military Territory of Niger in 1904, and then the Territory of Niger in 1922, with the status of a French colony, part of French West Africa.

In 1946, the constitution of the Fourth Republic in France officially put an end to the French colonial empire. The Territory of Niger became an overseas territory and member of the French Union. From this period, multiple institutional changes that encouraged the development of political life took place in Niger.

After the French referendum of September 28, 1958, the territory of Niger gained membership in the French Community. The Republic of Niger was proclaimed on December 18, when its first administration and assembly took office.

A constitution, based on a model common to the member states of the community, was adopted on February 25, 1959. The new state acceded to independence on August 3, 1960. The first constitution of the newly independent republic of Niger was adopted on November 8, 1960. It provides for a presidential system of government.

In 1974, a military coup overthrew the civil government. The military junta, known as the Supreme Military Council, immediately suspended the constitution and political party activities and dissolved the assembly.

The constitution of September 24, 1989, which inaugurated the Second Republic, had the main objectives of restoring democracy and preserving public order. In 1991, vigorous popular claims for democracy from civil society organizations led to the organization of a National Conference. The popular forum abolished the institutionalized single-party regime and paved the way for a more liberal regime in the country. A new constitution, adopted in 1992, inaugurated the Third Republic.

After serious institutional gridlock stemming from rivalries at the top of the administration, the military once again took over the political scene. The constitution of the Fourth Republic was adopted in 1996. Repeated social and political unrest and contested elections led to a new military coup in 1999. The adoption of a new constitution the same year and the handover of power to a civil government marked the beginning of the Fifth Republic.

Niger is a member of the African Union, the former Organization of African Unity.

FORM AND IMPACT OF THE CONSTITUTION

Niger has a written constitution, codified in a single document that takes precedence over all other national laws. Duly ratified international treaties and conventions have precedence over national laws, but compliance with the constitution is required. The Constitutional Court controls the conformity of national laws to the constitution.

BASIC ORGANIZATIONAL STRUCTURE

Niger comprises eight regions, which have relative autonomy from the central government. A wide decentralization program is currently under way, with the objective of giving more self-governing powers to local communities.

LEADING CONSTITUTIONAL PRINCIPLES

Niger's system of government is a pluralistic democracy, with a clear division of the executive, legislative, and judicial powers, based on checks and balances. By constitutional law, the judiciary is independent of the executive and the legislative, but in practice this independence is not effective.

A number of essential principles characterize the Nigerian constitutional system: Niger is an independent, sovereign, united, democratic, and social republic and is governed by the rule of law. Political participation is guaranteed through a mixture of direct and indirect representation. The constitutional system shows a strong commitment to democracy and rule of law. The separation of state and religion is explicitly affirmed in the constitution.

CONSTITUTIONAL BODIES

The main bodies provided for in the constitution are the president; the administration, which includes the prime minister and the cabinet ministers; the National Assembly; and the Constitutional Court. Other constitutional organs include the High Court of Justice and the Economic, Social, and Cultural Council.

The President of the Republic

The president of the republic is the head of state. The president appoints the prime minister from a list of three prominent figures proposed by the party or coalition of parties holding a majority in the National Assembly. The president appoints and dismisses the cabinet ministers upon the advice of the prime minister and dismisses the prime minister when the administration resigns.

The president of the republic is elected by universal suffrage for a five-year term and can be reelected once.

The Administration

Directed and coordinated by the prime minister, the administration determines and conducts the policy of the nation. Under the authority of the president, the administration exercises some power over the civil service, the police forces, and the armed forces. During the Third Republic (1993–96), a lack of clear delimitation of powers between the president and the prime minister led to institutional gridlock that led to a military coup.

The National Assembly

A unicameral parliament, the National Assembly, exercises the legislative power. Its members are elected for five-year terms by universal suffrage. The constitution prescribes free, direct, equal, and secret election of the members of the National Assembly.

The Lawmaking Process

The National Assembly has the task of passing legislation. In exercising this power, cooperation with the executive is required. The constitution defines clearly and explicitly the fields in which the National Assembly has lawmaking power. Other fields are left to the competence of the executive. The National Assembly and the administration have concurrent roles in drafting bills. Bills become law only if the National Assembly assents. The president promulgates the law. However, the president can send back a law for a second deliberation. In cases in which the National Assembly insists on the law with an absolute majority, it goes into force without the president's approval.

The Judiciary

As a matter of principle, the judiciary is independent of the legislative and the executive. The Constitutional Court, formerly one of the chambers of the Supreme Court, is now an autonomous institution with general and exclusive competence on constitutional and electoral matters. It comprises seven members.

THE ELECTION PROCESS

All Nigerians who either are over the age of 18 or have attained majority have the right to vote in elections.

POLITICAL PARTIES

Niger has a pluralistic system of political parties. Adopted recently, the multiparty system is now an essential element of the constitutional order. All recognized political parties have the right to compete through elections. However, political parties constituted on ethnic, regionalist, or religious grounds are banned.

CITIZENSHIP

Nigerian citizenship is acquired by birth, by descent, or by naturalization.

FUNDAMENTAL RIGHTS

Fundamental rights have an important place in the legal order in Niger. These rights are defined in the second title of the constitution.

The constitution first proclaims the sanctity of the human being and then enumerates numerous specific fundamental rights that are guaranteed. Basic rights are binding upon public authorities, whether executive, legislative, or judiciary. The exercise of rights and liberties must be in accordance with the law.

Article 8 of the constitution provides for equal treatment of all persons, without any distinction based on gender or social, racial, ethnic, political, or religious origin. Apart from the recognition of rights, the constitution sets out a number of duties for citizens, among them the duty to respect the constitution and the legal order of the republic.

Impact and Functions of Fundamental Rights

In Niger, the full recognition of fundamental rights is closely linked to the advent of democracy and the rule of law. There is an increasing awareness among citizens that basic rights are integrated into the legal order of the state and that they are binding upon public authorities.

Limitations to Fundamental Rights

According to the constitution, the exercise of fundamental rights and liberties should be in accordance with laws and executive orders in force.

ECONOMY

The constitution of Niger does not provide for a specific economic system. However, there are a number of prescriptions contained in the fundamental law that can be regarded as the foundation of the economic system. Among them are the recognition and protection of property right, the recognition of the right to work and the duty imposed on the state to set the conditions that will make that right effective, and freedom of association. In general, the Nigerian economic system can be described as a market economy, with the features of a developing economy.

RELIGIOUS COMMUNITIES

As a human right, freedom of religion or belief is guaranteed. Certain rights are afforded to religious communities, namely, freedom of association and assembly. As a matter of principle, all religions and religious communities must be treated on an equal basis.

The constitution affirms the separation of religion and state. However, this separation is not absolute since some interactions exist between them. In Niger, Muslims constitute the most important religious community. Despite the separation set forth in the constitution, Islam has a great impact on political and social life.

MILITARY DEFENSE AND STATE OF EMERGENCY

According to the constitution, the president of the republic is the supreme chief of the armies. The armed forces are at the disposal of the administration under conditions determined by law.

The president can take exceptional measures in certain circumstances specified in the constitution, namely, when the institutions of the republic, the independence of the nation, the integrity of the national territory, or the implementation of international commitments is threatened in a grave and immediate manner and the functioning of the constitutional power is interrupted. However, strict conditions limit the exercise of this power by the president.

The president also has the power to declare a state of emergency within certain conditions determined by law.

AMENDMENTS TO THE CONSTITUTION

The president and the members of the parliament have concurrent powers to initiative amendments to the constitution. A favorable vote of three-quarters of the members of the National Assembly is required for the change to be considered. A four-fifths vote is required to pass the measure. If it fails, the amendment is submitted to popular vote, by means of a referendum.

In any case, the constitution cannot be revised to violate the integrity of the national territory. Certain fundamental provisions are excluded from revision, namely, the republican form of the state, the pluralistic system of parties, the principle of the separation of state and religion, and some special provisions specified in Articles 36 and 141 of the constitution.

PRIMARY SOURCES

Constitution in French: *Constitution du 18 juillet 1999.* Niamey: Commission Nationale des Droits de l'Homme et des Libertés Fondamentales, 2004.

Constitution in English (extracts). Available online. URL: http://www.chr.up.ac.za/hr_docs/constitutions/docs/Niger(english%20summary)(rev).doc. Accessed on July 29, 2005.

Boubacar Hassane

NIGERIA

At-a-Glance

OFFICIAL NAME
Federal Republic of Nigeria

CAPITAL
Abuja

POPULATION
137,253,133 (July 2004 est.)

SIZE
356,669 sq. mi. (923,768 sq. km)

LANGUAGES
English (official), Yoruba, Hausa, Igbo (Ibo), Fulani, Efik

RELIGIONS
Muslim 50%, Christian 40%, indigenous beliefs 10%

NATIONAL OR ETHNIC COMPOSITION
Over 250 ethnic groups identified; largest and most politically influential: Hausa and Fulani 29%, Yoruba 21%, Igbo (Ibo) 18%, Ijaw 10%, Kanuri 4%, Ibihio 3.5%, Tiv 2.5%, other 12%

DATE OF INDEPENDENCE OR CREATION
Colonial protectorates amalgamated in 1914; independence on October 1, 1960

TYPE OF GOVERNMENT
Democracy

TYPE OF STATE
Federal state

TYPE OF LEGISLATURE
Bicameral legislature

DATE OF CONSTITUTION
May 1, 1999

DATE OF LAST AMENDMENT
No amendment

Nigeria operates a three-tier federal system made up of federal, state, and local governments. The national president has far-reaching executive powers, controlled to a degree by parliament. Fundamental rights are guaranteed by the constitution. Muslim Sharia law has widespread influence in some parts of the country. The constitution prohibits the introduction of a state religion.

CONSTITUTIONAL HISTORY

Nigeria's constitutional history dates back to the encounter of the different sections and peoples of the territory with British colonial rule. British rule began with the ceding of Lagos as a colony to the Crown in 1861 and the establishment of a Legislative Council for the Colony of Lagos in 1862. In 1885, Britain proclaimed the Oil River Protectorate in Eastern Nigeria to protect its economic interests in the area. In 1886, it granted the charter to the Royal Niger Company (RNC) over the area. In 1893, the Niger Coast Protectorate was established. In 1900, Britain revoked the Charter of the Royal Niger Company and proclaimed a northern and a southern protectorate of Nigeria under the control of the British government. No constitution was specifically adopted for the colony and protectorates; there is evidence that the unwritten British constitution was applied, especially in the colony of Lagos.

Nigeria, as one country, was created in 1914 with the amalgamation of the Colony of Lagos and the northern and southern protectorates by Governor-General Lord Lugard (1900–21). The constitutional instruments created under the British constitution vested all executive powers in the governor; there were also an Executive Council and an Advisory Deliberative Council, which had the power to legislate for the whole country.

Both councils were dominated by British officials. The presence of six Africans in the Advisory Council did not impress the emerging Nigerian nationalists. Nationalism was mainly concentrated in the southern part of the country, evidently influenced by the democratic principles and structures of the British state.

The first written constitution for the country emerged in 1922 as the Clifford Constitution. The name was derived from the incumbent governor-general, Sir Hugh Clifford. It abolished the two existing councils for the Colony of Lagos, created a single executive for the whole country, and introduced a Legislative Council made up of 10 Africans, four of whom were elected, and 36 Europeans, with powers to legislate for the southern portion of the country. It reserved the legislative power for the northern protectorate in the governor.

From 1922, political associations began to emerge with the formation of Nigeria National Democratic Party (NNDP) by Herbert Macaulay. In the elections of September 1923 carried out under the Clifford Constitution, the NNDP won three seats in the Legislative Council. The activists Vaughan, Ikoli, and Akinsanya formed the Lagos Youth Movement (LYM) in 1933, which became the National Youth Movement (NYM) in 1936. The *West African Pilot* newspaper was established in 1937. Under its founding editor, Nnamdi Azikwe, it provided a platform for nationalist resistance.

With increasing political awareness, pressures intensified on the colonial administration for constitutional reforms to allow for more participation of Nigerians in their governance. This movement led to the Richards Constitution of 1946 and the replacement of the Legislative Council for the south with the Central Legislative Council, composed of the governor, 16 officials (13 ex officio and three nominated), and 28 members who were either freely elected or selected through processes listed in the constitution. This council had authority to legislate for the whole country; in practice, laws were made by the governor with the consent of the council. The 1946 constitution also set up regional Houses of Assembly in the east, west, and north and a House of Chiefs in the north.

These constitutional reforms proved inadequate to satisfy the growing nationalism. In 1947, Nnamdi Azikwe led a delegation of seven representatives of the National Council of Nigeria and the Cameroons (NCNC), a political party formed in 1944, to demand constitutional reforms. At the 1950 Ibadan General Conference, nationalist political leaders agreed that only a federal system of government, which would allow each region to progress at its own pace, would be acceptable.

In 1951, the Macpherson Constitution went into effect. It provided for a lieutenant-governor and House of Assembly in each region and a federal House of Representatives with legislative powers, subject to the veto of the secretary of state for the colonies. The House of Representatives had veto power over the Regional Houses. The system's model was the British Westminster style, although the executive governor or lieutenant governor shared legislative power with the respective houses. Legislation in the areas of public revenue and public service was reserved to the executive.

The majority of the members of the houses were elected Nigerians, although the constitution continued to provide for ex officio members, as well as appointed members to represent interests and communities that had inadequate representation in the houses. The emerging political parties, including the National Council of Nigeria and the Cameroons (NCNC), Action Group (AG), and Northern People's Congress (NPC), participated in the elections to the houses. In the face of further agitation for independence and self-rule, the Macpherson Constitution was subjected to a number of revisions in the London Constitutional Conference of 1953 and the Lagos Conference of 1954.

In 1954, the Lyttleton Constitution went into effect. It divided Nigeria into five parts: the northern, western, and eastern regions; southern Cameroon; and the Federal Capital Territory of Lagos. Legislative powers were transferred to the regions with few exclusive powers reserved for the center. The constitution allocated areas of competence into three legislative lists: the Exclusive Legislative List, specifying the items on which the House of Representatives had the power to make laws; the Concurrent Legislative List, with items on which both the House of Representatives and the regional Houses of Assembly had the power to make laws; and the Residual Legislative List, with items on which only the Regional Houses had the power to make laws. This has become a constant feature in subsequent constitutions designed to foster the division of power between the federal and state tiers of government.

Under the Lyttleton Constitution, the House of Representatives had its own Speaker, a departure from the Macpherson Constitution, under which the governor presided over the house. Under the Lyttleton Constitution, the eastern and western regions achieved self-government in 1957 and the north on March 15, 1959. As agitation for self-rule intensified, further talks were held to fashion acceptable constitutional arrangements for the entire country. In May 1957, the London Constitutional Conference proposed independence for the country in 1959 but not later than April 2, 1960. The conference resumed in 1958 and chose October 1, 1960, as the date for the country's independence. Final constitutional talks were held in May 1960.

Human rights played a very important role in the early development of Nigeria's constitutional history. The agitation for decolonization and self-rule was largely premised on the right of all human beings to nondiscrimination and equality, regardless of race or color, and the right of individuals and people to participate in their own government either personally or through their elected representatives. The importance of constitutional safeguards of individual rights to secure citizens against state repression became apparent in light of the colonial government's resistance to the nationalists' call for independence. In 1958, the Willinks Commission was established to address the fears of minority groups in an independent Nigeria. It proposed the inclusion of a constitutional Bill of Rights, which was in fact adopted.

On October 1, 1960, Nigeria gained independence, and the 1960 Independence Constitution took force. The queen of England remained the country's head of state, represented by the governor-general, Sir Nnamdi Azikwe. The governor-general exercised power and authority on the advice of the Council of Ministers presided over by the prime minister, Sir Abubakar Tafawa Balewa. A bicameral legislature, the National Assembly, was made up of the upper house (the Senate) and the lower house (the House of Representatives). Nigeria remained a federal state made up of three regions—northern, western, and eastern—each led by a regional premier. Each region had its own constitution and its own House of Assembly. The new constitution was the culmination of the progressive introduction of the Westminster parliamentary system of government in Nigeria.

Nigeria's postindependence constitutional crisis commenced almost immediately. By May 29, 1962, a state of emergency had been declared over the western region. Between November 1962 and September 1963, prominent nationalist politicians from the western region stood trial for treason. The crisis in the western region also impacted the legal system and led to a constitutional amendment to remove the Privy Council as the highest court of appeal.

In 1963, Nigeria became a republic. The Republican Constitution of 1963 provided for a president as the head of state, a prime minister as head of the administration, and governors for the regions. The 1963 constitution collapsed as a result of a bloody coup d'état of January 15, 1966, which put in power General J. T. U. Aguiyi-Ironsi. The general tried to impose constitutional changes to put the country under unitary rule. General Aguiyi-Ironsi was killed in another military coup on July 29, 1966, and it is widely believed that opposition to a unitary form of government contributed greatly to the July 1966 coup. The July 1966 coup put in power Major-General Yakubu Gowon.

The Hausa and Fulani of the north saw ethnic overtones in the January 1966 coup, as they had lost a larger proportion of their leaders in the violence than had other groups. As the main leaders of the coup had been from among the Igbo, ethnic violence broke out against Igbo living in the north. As an act of self-preservation, the Igbo declared the secession of the eastern region, where they were the predominant ethnic group. They proclaimed the Republic of Biafra; a punishing civil war ensued from May 30, 1967, to January 12, 1970.

From 1966 to 1979 the military remained in power in Nigeria. By 1975 there were serious disenchantment with military rule and clamor for return to civil rule; it was widely believed that General Gowon's resistance to any transfer of power sparked the coup d'état of July 29, 1975, which ousted him in favor of General Murtala Mohammed. General Mohammed was killed in an unsuccessful coup of February 13, 1976; he was succeeded by his next in command, General Olusegun Obansanjo.

On October 18, 1975, the regime set up a Constitution Drafting Committee (CDC), comprising 50 people under the leadership of Chief F. R. A. Williams. However, Chief Awolowo Obafemi refused to serve as a member of that committee, reducing membership to 49. On September 14, 1976, the CDC submitted its report to General Obasanjo's government, which later established an elected Constituent Assembly led by Justice Udo Udoma. The assembly consisted of 230 members; it was mandated to consider the report and propose an acceptable constitution for Nigeria, to take effect with the return to civilian rule. On the basis of the report submitted to the federal military government by the Constituent Assembly on September 20, 1978, the military government promulgated the Constitution of the Federal Republic of Nigeria, to go into effect October 1, 1979.

The CDC's view was that the overarching objective of the Nigerian constitution should be to foster "an effective leadership that expresses aspirations for national unity without at the same time building up a Leviathan whose powers may be difficult to curb; . . . the need to balance the stakes of politics so that each section . . . will come to feel a sense of belonging to a great nation; the need to develop an approach of consensus to politics and finally the need to accentuate our national inclination towards a bargaining approach to decision-making rather than regarding politics as a game of winner-takes-all." The CDC considered that these goals could not be realized through the Westminster parliamentary system of government. It therefore recommended a departure in favor of the American presidential system of government, which provided for an executive president at the federal level and an executive governor at the state level. The 1979 constitution retained the federal arrangement of three levels of government, the bicameral legislature at the federal level, and the unicameral legislature at the state level. The constitution also retained other features, such as the Exclusive and Concurrent Legislative Lists, which facilitated the sharing of powers among the federal, state, and local governments.

Another military coup in December 1983 ended the democratic rule that had begun on October 1, 1979. The 1983 coup put in power General Muhammadu Buhari, who was himself ousted in August 1984 by another military coup, that of General Babangida. By 1987, General Babangida established the Constitution Review Committee (CRC) to examine the suitability of the 1979 constitution and propose other options. The CRC recommended the retention of the 1979 constitution with some slight modifications. The 1989 constitution entered into force in piecemeal fashion but was finally abandoned with the political crisis that resulted from the annulment of the June 12, 1993, presidential elections by General Babangida. General Sani Abacha succeeded General Babangida in August 1994 and in response to the popular clamor for an immediate return to civil rule inaugurated yet another Constitutional Conference.

The conference produced what is commonly referred to as the 1995 draft constitution. That constitution was, however, neither promulgated nor adopted before the death of General Abacha in July 1998 and the emergence of the military administration of General Abdulsalami Abubakar that year. The latter, mindful of the widespread dissatisfaction with the 1995 draft constitution, considered it necessary to provide a new constitution for the new democratic dispensation and set up the Constitution Debate Coordinating Committee (CDCC), led by Justice Niki Tobi. The CDCC was tasked with organizing nationwide consultations and indigenous constitution-making efforts and making recommendations for a constitution to "enthrone a true constitutional and democratic system of government in Nigeria." The CDCC divided the country into zones, called for memoranda, organized debates, held special hearings, and traveled to selected sites to listen to views from a wide array of groups. The General Abubakar government, through Decree No. 24 of May 5, 1999, promulgated the Constitution of the Federal Republic of Nigeria in 1999.

The 1999 constitution is Nigeria's fifth since independence and the ninth since the creation of the country by the British colonial government in 1914. The multiplicity of constitutions that have emerged over time cannot be divorced from the fact that the creation of one country out of the many groups found in the territory known today as Nigeria was imposed from the outside. It reflects the challenge of working out acceptable arrangements to address the diversity, aspirations, and fears of the different peoples.

Each effort at constitution making since the 1951 Macpherson Constitution has been a response to the dissatisfactions expressed by the constituent groups and their fear of marginalization within the national polity. The failure to mediate the balance of power of the tiers of government, especially the federal and state levels, effectively has also been a constant source of concern and call for constitutional rearrangements. The penchant of each military government to leave the legacy of a new constitution for the successive democratic government also cannot be ignored. It was believed that the constitution-making process was generally nondemocratic, even when a small number of formal structures for participation were put in place. In more recent times, the failure of governments to realize the aspirations of the people for a country where all citizens are equal and where the welfare of the majority of citizens is adequately ensured has been critical.

FORM AND IMPACT OF THE CONSTITUTION

The constitution of Nigeria is contained in a single document known as the Constitution of the Federal Republic of Nigeria, 1999. It is not a transitional document, although there is clamor from some quarters for the convocation of a national conference to engage in constitutional talks. The 1999 constitution remains a stable document, despite its current review in two parallel initiatives of the executive and legislative arms of government in response to popularly expressed dissatisfaction. These reviews are, however, preliminary critiques and are not part of the constitutionally recognized process for constitutional amendment.

The 1999 constitution is the supreme law and establishes Nigeria as a country under constitutional supremacy. All branches of the government (the executive, legislature, and judiciary) as well as all tiers of government (federal, state, and local) derive their powers from the constitution, which delineates the scope of the powers of each branch and tier.

All laws, including international laws, derive their validity from the constitution, and any law that is inconsistent with the constitution is void to the extent of its inconsistency. No treaty between the federation and any other country has the force of law except to the extent that it has been enacted into law by the National Assembly. When, however, the National Assembly enacts the treaty into law in line with the constitutional prescription, the treaty becomes enforceable, and Nigerian courts must give effect to it in the same fashion as all other laws falling within the judicial powers of the courts. A good example is the African Charter on Human and Peoples' Rights (Ratification and Enforcement) Act, which enacts that document as part of Nigerian municipal law.

An international treaty that has been domesticated (enacted locally in line with the constitution) is not necessarily superior to other statutes, although the courts must be mindful of the international nature of obligations created under it. However, an international treaty cannot override the constitution even if it has been domesticated.

BASIC ORGANIZATIONAL STRUCTURE

The 1999 constitution establishes a federal state. Governmental powers are shared by the federal government, the 36 state governments, and 774 local governments. The National Assembly at the federal level is allotted exclusive power to legislate matters in the Exclusive Legislative List, such as defense, citizenship, foreign affairs, banking, currency, and the police. The federal and state legislatures share legislative power over matters contained in the Concurrent Legislative List, which includes collection of taxes; electoral laws relating to the local government; electric power supply; industrial, commercial, and agricultural development; and university, technological, and postprimary education. States have a constitutional duty to make laws to provide for the establishment, structure, composition, finance, and functions of local government councils to implement the local government system. The state legislatures are also deemed to retain the residual powers, that is, powers over matters not stated in either of the two legislative lists.

The functions of the local government as the third tier include participation in the planning and development of their area; collection of rates; establishment and maintenance of cemeteries; licensing of trucks; registration of births, deaths, and marriages; and provision and maintenance of health services.

The constitution provides, in broad terms, the basis of revenue sharing from the Consolidated Revenue Fund between the federal and state levels. It establishes a Revenue Allocation Mobilization and Fiscal Commission, which has the power to review, from time to time, the revenue allocation formulas and operations to ensure conformity with changing realities.

At the state level, each state is headed by an executive governor, who has the power to appoint commissioners, subject to the approval of the State House of Assembly, to assist in running the state. The tenure of the governor is four years, renewable once for another four years through reelection.

The local governments are headed by chairpersons.

LEADING CONSTITUTIONAL PRINCIPLES

The leading constitutional principles are democracy, republicanism, secularism, the rule of law, and separation of powers among three branches of government.

The constitution entrenches representative democracy through periodic elections to the executive and legislative arms of government at all tiers of the federal state. The president, vice president, governors, deputy governors, members of the National Assembly and State Houses of Assembly, local government chairs, and councilors are elected by a simple majority of voters.

Nigeria became a republic on October 1, 1963. This status has been retained in all constitutions to date. The 1999 constitution states that Nigeria is one indivisible and indissoluble sovereign state to be known by the name of the Federal Republic of Nigeria and vests sovereignty in the people of Nigeria.

Section 10 of the constitution prohibits the adoption of any religion as the state religion. This applies to the government of the federation or of a state.

Principles of the rule of law such as the supremacy of the constitution, equality of all persons before the law, and equal access to justice are entrenched in the 1999 constitution. The Constitution of the Federal Republic of Nigeria, 1999, is the supreme law, and all its provisions have binding force on all authorities and persons throughout the Federal Republic of Nigeria. All citizens are equal before the law, although the constitution grants the president, vice president, governors, and deputy governors immunity from criminal prosecutions while in office.

The powers of government are shared by the three arms of government, to wit, the executive, legislature, and judiciary. These arms check and balance one another's powers in line with the constitutional safeguards.

CONSTITUTIONAL BODIES

The predominant constitutional bodies are the president, the National Assembly, and the courts.

The President

At the federal level, the constitution makes the president the head of state, chief executive of the federation, and commander in chief of the armed forces of the federation. It is the responsibility of the president to execute and implement the policies and programs of the federal administration in line with legislation. The president appoints cabinet ministers and special advisers who assist with running the administration. The president also has the power to appoint the judges of the different courts, exercise the prerogative of mercy, or declare a state of emergency. The president can initiate bills or enter into a treaty on behalf of the country.

The 1999 constitution provides for a presidential system of government at the federal level. Under the constitution, the vast constitutional powers of the president are nonetheless subject to checks through the exercise of the oversight powers of the National Assembly and the judiciary. The tenure of the president is four years, renewable once for another four years through reelection.

A person is qualified for election to the office of the president if that person is a citizen of Nigeria by birth, has attained the age of 40 years, is a member of a political party and is sponsored by that political party, and has been educated up to at least school certificate level or its equivalent. A person is not qualified for election to the office of president if that person has voluntarily acquired the citizenship of a country other than Nigeria or, except in such cases as may be prescribed by the National Assembly, has made a declaration of allegiance to such other country. A person is also not qualified to be a candidate for president who has been elected to such office at any two previous elections under the law in any part of Nigeria or is adjudged to be of unsound mind. Several other disqualifications are stated in the constitution.

Federal Legislature

The highest lawmaking body in Nigeria is the National Assembly, made up of the Senate and the House of Representatives. There are 109 senators and 360 members of the House of Representatives. All states have an equal number of Senate seats and the federal capital territory has one seat. The number of seats a state has in the House of Representatives, however, varies. Other offices that have been established outside the constitution are the majority leader, minority leader, party whip, and sergeant-at-arms.

A person is qualified to run for the Senate if that person is a citizen of Nigeria and has attained the age of 35 years. A candidate for the House of Representatives must be a citizen of Nigeria and must have attained the age of 30 years. In either case, the candidate must have been educated up to at least school certificate level or its equivalent, be a member of a political party, and be sponsored by that party.

The Lawmaking Process

There are four stages in the making of legislation. At the first stage, the law is prepared in a draft form called the bill. The bill is then forwarded to either the speaker of the House of Representatives, the Senate president, or the speaker of the state House of Assembly, depending on the house from which it originates. At the second stage, the bill is read to members of the house for the first time by the clerk. The bill is thereafter read to the house a second time and the bill becomes open to debate by members of the house. The bill is then passed to one of the standing committees of the house tasked with deliberating further on the interests and issues on the bill. The committee presents its report to the house and moves as to whether or not there should be a third reading of the bill. During the third reading, the bill is corrected, amended or modified, and then passed.

At the third stage, a printed copy of the passed bill is produced and signed by the clerk of the house. From there it is passed to the other house for assent and then to the president for assent, the fourth stage. The president has 30 days to sign the bill, which becomes law immediately after it is signed. If the president refuses or fails to sign the bill on the expiration of the 30 days, it is recalled by the National Assembly and a joint meeting of the National Assembly shall be convened. If the bill is passed by two-thirds majority of members of both houses at the joint meeting, it becomes law and the assent of the president is required.

The Senate or the House of Representatives at the federal level, and the House of Assembly at the state level, may appoint a committee of its members for such special or general purpose as in its opinion would be better regulated and managed by means of such a committee and may by resolution, regulation, or otherwise, as it thinks fit, delegate any functions exercisable by it to any such committee. The house, however, may not delegate to a committee the power to decide whether a bill shall be passed into law.

Courts

The 1999 constitution provides for the establishment of courts of different categories with varying degree of powers to hear and determine cases. The courts that are constitutionally provided for are the Supreme Court, the Court of Appeal, the Federal and States' High Courts, the Sharia Court of Appeal, and Election Tribunals. Although not constitutionally provided for, courts martial, magistrate courts, customary courts, and area courts created under other legislation are constitutionally recognized.

The Supreme Court is the highest court in Nigeria. It is composed of 20 justices presided over by the chief justice of the federation. There is only one Supreme Court in Nigeria, and it is located in the federal capital territory of Abuja. It is generally an appellate court, although it has original jurisdiction in disputes between the federal government and state governments and between state governments. The decisions of this court are final.

The Supreme Court is duly constituted when it consists of at least five judges. However, the court considers an appeal with seven justices in a number of cases, such as criminal proceedings in which any person has been sentenced to death and decisions on any question as to whether any person has been validly elected to the office of president or vice president, whether the term of office of president or vice president has ceased, and whether the office of president or vice president has become vacant.

Just below the Supreme Court is the Court of Appeal. The court has the power to hear appeals from the Federal and State High Courts, Sharia Court of Appeal, and Customary Court of Appeal. It can also hear fresh disputes relating to the election of a person to the office of the president or vice president. The Court of Appeal presently sits in 10 zones of the federation. The court may sit with either three or five judges, depending on the matter before it. The Court of Appeal is headed by the president of the Court of Appeal.

There is only one Federal High Court, although the court has different divisions in the states of the Federation; it is headed by the chief judge. The court is duly constituted when it sits with one judge. The court has original and exclusive jurisdiction only in matters relating to government revenue, banking and financial institutions, and taxation, among others.

Every state in Nigeria has a State High Court. The State High Court has very wide powers and has original as well as appellate powers to entertain both civil and criminal matters.

The Sharia Court of Appeal is more commonly found in the northern parts of Nigeria. It is headed by a person called a grand khadi. The court has jurisdiction to determine issues relating to Islamic personal law, for example, disputes relating to inheritance, succession, and marriage contracted under Islamic law. The Customary Court, as have the Sharia courts, has jurisdiction over personal law governed by customary law, such as dissolution of marriages contracted under customary law and intestate succession and inheritance under customary law. The head of the Customary Court is known as the president. Customary courts are more commonly found in the southern parts of the country.

THE ELECTION PROCESS AND POLITICAL PARTICIPATION

An eligible voter must be a Nigerian citizen who has attained the age of 18 years and whose name is in the voters' register made under the electoral laws. To run in elections for any political post in Nigeria, the candidate must be a Nigerian citizen; he or she must have attained the age of 35 years, or in the case of the president or vice president, must have attained 40 years of age; he or she must be a member of a political party and be sponsored by that party; and he or she must be educated up to at least school leaving certificate level or its equivalent. The elections to the different posts are conducted by the Independent National Electoral Commission.

Election Tribunals

The National Assembly Election Tribunal has, to the exclusion of any other tribunal, original jurisdiction to hear and determine petitions as to whether any person has been validly elected as a member of the National Assembly, the term of office of any person under the constitution has ceased, or the seat of a member of the Senate or a member of the House of Representatives has become vacant. The constitution similarly provides for the establishment in each state of the federation one or more election tribunals to be known as the governorship and legislative house's election tribunals that have original jurisdiction to hear and determine petitions as to whether any person has been validly elected to the office of governor or deputy governor or as a member of any legislative house.

POLITICAL PARTIES

The constitution provides for a multiparty political system. At present, there are 30 political parties in Nigeria. The Supreme Court has ruled that it is unconstitutional to impose registration qualifications on political parties, thus ending a practice that was introduced by the national electoral bodies in 1979. Political parties are banned from retaining, organizing, training, or equipping any quasi-military group.

CITIZENSHIP

The constitution provides that every person born in Nigeria before the date of independence either of whose parents or any of whose grandparents belongs or belonged to a community indigenous to Nigeria and at least one of such parents or grandparents was born in Nigeria; every person born in Nigeria after the date of independence either of whose parents or any of whose grandparents is a citizen of Nigeria; and every person born outside Nigeria either of whose parents is a citizen of Nigeria is a citizen of Nigeria by birth. Persons who are not citizens by birth may acquire citizenship by registration or naturalization. Both male and female Nigerians can confer citizenship by birth on their children, but only female spouses of Nigerian citizens can acquire citizenship by registration. Nigerian citizens by birth may hold dual citizenship. A person can forfeit his or her Nigerian citizenship by either renouncing citizenship or in the case of a citizen by registration acquiring another citizenship.

The duties of a citizen include abiding by the constitution; respecting its ideals; helping to enhance the power, prestige, and good name of Nigeria; respecting the rights and dignity of other citizens; and helping to maintain law and order.

FUNDAMENTAL RIGHTS

The constitution distinguishes between civil and political rights, on the one hand, and economic, social, and cultural rights, on the other hand. Economic, social, and cultural rights are included in Chapter 2 of the constitution as Fundamental Objectives and Directive Principles for State Policy. In other words, they are presented as state obligations that are not enforceable through the courts. Civil and political rights are provided in Chapter 4 of the constitution and include the following: right to life; right to the dignity of the human person; right to personal liberty; right to a fair hearing; right to private and family life; right to freedom of thought, conscience, and religion; right to freedom of expression and the press; right to peaceful assembly and association; right to freedom of movement; right to freedom from discrimination; and right to acquire and own immovable property anywhere in Nigeria.

Impact and Functions of Fundamental Rights

The constitution protects, guarantees, and preserves these human rights and makes all citizens aware of their existence. If any of these rights is violated, a person can seek redress in a court of law.

Limitations to Fundamental Rights

A number of fundamental rights provisions such as the freedom of expression have specific limitation clauses usually referring to limitations that are reasonably justifiable in a democratic society for certain legitimate purposes.

The enforcement of fundamental human rights is limited during the period of a state of emergency.

ECONOMY

The 1999 constitution prescribes economic objectives for the Nigerian state under the Fundamental Objectives and Directive Principles of State Policy. Section 16 prescribes that the state shall harness the resources of the nation and promote national prosperity and an efficient, dynamic, and self-reliant economy; control the national economy in such manner as to secure the maximal welfare, freedom, and happiness of every citizen on the basis of social justice, equality of status, and opportunity; manage and operate the major sectors of the economy (and retain the right to participate in nonmajor areas); protect the right of every citizen to engage in any economic activities outside the major sectors of the economy (and participate in the major areas as well). In addition, the state is required to direct its policy to ensuring that planned and balanced economic development is promoted, that material resources of the nation are harnessed and distributed as optimally as possible to serve the common good, that the economic system is not operated in such a manner as to permit the concentration of wealth or the means of production and exchange in the hands of a few individuals or of a group, and that suitable and adequate shelter, suitable and adequate food, a reasonable national minimal living wage, old age care and pensions, unemployment and sick benefits, and welfare for the disabled are provided for all citizens.

RELIGIOUS COMMUNITIES

The constitution prohibits the adoption of a state religion and allows citizens the freedom of belief and the freedom to choose and practice any religion of their choice. This extends to the right not to be subject to religious education, ceremony, or observance of a religion other than one's own, or, in the case of a child, a religion not approved by one's parent or guardian. It also includes the right not to choose a belief. Religious communities can be established and exist in exercise of religious freedom.

There is, however, no requirement of separation of the state and religion. The constitution itself facilitates the exercise of religious freedom, for example, by the Muslim population. It recognizes Islamic personal law and provides for its enforcement, including the establishment of relevant institutions under the legal system up to the Supreme Court level. Official support for religion is evidenced by the introduction of religious education in public schools and state sponsorship of religious pilgrimages.

While no state has directly adopted any religion as an official or compulsory state religion, a number of states in the northern part of the country have expanded the scope of applicable Islamic law beyond the personal sphere with the adoption of Sharia criminal codes and the introduction of Sharia public law since October 1999. With the pervasive influence of Sharia in the public sphere, including the administration of government, Islam, though not proclaimed as such, becomes effectively a de facto state religion.

MILITARY DEFENSE AND STATE OF EMERGENCY

The military in Nigeria consists of the army, the navy, and the air force, all under the president as the commander in chief of the armed forces. The functions of the military are to defend the country from external aggression; main-

tain its territorial integrity and secure its borders from violation on land, sea, or air; and suppress insurrection and act in aid of civil authorities to restore order when called upon to do so by the president. The military has no constitutional power to take over government in a state of emergency or war and remains subject to the president at all times. However, in spite of identical provisions in previous constitutions, the military has taken over on a number of occasions and has, in fact, ruled the country for 31 of its 44 postindependence years. Their usual approach has been to suspend, by means of decrees, aspects of the constitution that prohibit the military takeover of government.

The constitution itself does not mandate compulsory military service but allows for such compulsory service in the armed forces of the federation to be prescribed by an act of the National Assembly.

The president may declare a state of emergency in the federation or any part of it when the country is at war; the federation is in imminent danger of invasion or involvement in a state of war; there is actual breakdown of public order and public safety in the federation or any part thereof to such extent as to require extraordinary measures to restore peace and security; there is a clear and present danger of an actual breakdown of public order and public safety in the federation or any part thereof requiring extraordinary measures to avert such danger; there is an occurrence of imminent danger, or the occurrence of any disaster or natural calamity, affecting the community or a section of the community in the federation; there is any other public danger that clearly constitutes a threat to the existence of the federation; or the president receives a request from the governor of a state, with the sanction of a resolution supported by a two-thirds majority of the House of Assembly, to issue a proclamation of a state of emergency in the state when there is in existence within the state any of the situations specified earlier and such situation does not extend beyond the boundaries of the state.

During such a state of emergency, the governor and the legislators are suspended and the president appoints an administrator for the area. In May 2004, President Obasanjo exercised, for the first time, the power under Section 305 of the 1999 constitution when he declared a state of emergency in Plateau State and appointed a sole administrator.

AMENDMENTS TO THE CONSTITUTION

The constitution can be amended by the National Assembly, although the prescribed process is difficult. The constitution prescribes, generally, that before an act of the National Assembly for the alteration of the constitution is passed in either house of the National Assembly, the proposal for such amendment must be supported by the votes of not less than a two-thirds majority of all members of that house and approved by resolution of the Houses of Assembly of not less than two-thirds of all the states. However, when the proposal attempts to alter the provisions relating to amending the constitution or the fundamental rights provisions, it shall not be passed by either house of the National Assembly unless the proposal is approved by the votes of not less than a four-fifths majority of all the members of each house, and approved by resolution of the Houses of Assembly of not less than two-thirds of all the states.

PRIMARY SOURCES

Constitution in English. Available online. URL: http://www.nigeria-law.org/ConstitutionOfThe FederalRepublicOfNigeria.htm. Accessed on August 1, 2005.

SECONDARY SOURCES

Constitution of the Federal Republic of Nigeria, 1999. Lagos: Citizens' Forum for Constitutional Reform, 1999.

Otive Igbuzor, *A Critique of the 1999 Constitution Making and Review Process in Nigeria.* CFCR Monograph Series no. 1. Lagos: Citizens' Forum for Constitutional Reform, 2002.

Nigeria—a Country Study. Washington, D.C.: United States Government Printing Office, 1992.

Ayodele Atsenuwa

NORWAY

At-a-Glance

OFFICIAL NAME
Kingdom of Norway

CAPITAL
Oslo

POPULATION
4,525,000 (2005 est.)

SIZE
149,405 sq. mi. (386,958 sq. km)

LANGUAGES
Norwegian (two written forms: Bokmål and Nynorsk).
Sámi also official language in some districts in the
north

RELIGIONS
Protestant 85%, other Christians 3.5%, Muslim 1.7%,
secular humanist 1.5%, other 2.3%, unaffiliated 6%

NATIONAL OR ETHNIC COMPOSITION
Norwegian, immigrants (Swedes, Danes, Iraqi, British,
Somali, Bosnian, German, Vietnamese, American,

Pakistani 4.5%) 7.6%, Sami population and national
minorities (Roma, Kvens, Skogfinns, and others, all
Norwegian citizens) 1%

DATE OF INDEPENDENCE OR CREATION
May 17, 1814

TYPE OF GOVERNMENT
Constitutional monarchy

TYPE OF STATE
Centralist state

TYPE OF LEGISLATURE
Modified unicameral parliament

DATE OF CONSTITUTION
May 17, 1814

DATE OF LAST AMENDMENT
June 27, 2003

Norway is a constitutional monarchy with a parliamentary system of governance, based on the constitution of 1814 as amended and reinterpreted several times since. The principle of division of powers is not explicitly proclaimed in the constitution, although the text is structured into chapters referring to the Executive Power, the Legislative Power, and the Judicial Power.

According to the written constitution, the administration derives its authority from the executive power vested in the monarch. The political power and competence of the monarch in person have decreased gradually since 1814, leading to a different reading of the basic constitutional paragraphs on the monarch's role. Today, the office has a mainly symbolic and unifying function, although some formal powers remain.

Parliamentarianism was introduced in practice from 1884 onward, when it was made clear that the administration, the executive power, cannot govern if it loses the

confidence of parliament (called Storting), the legislative power. Today, the administration gains its democratic legitimacy from the Parliament, although this relationship does not follow from the written constitution.

The role of the judiciary has also changed since 1814, to a large extent thanks to new interpretations of the constitution. For example, it is now widely accepted that the Supreme Court has the formal power to invalidate laws that are not in compliance with the constitution, and it has done so on some occasions.

The 1814 constitution cited certain principles of human rights and the rule of law, but freedom of religion was not included until 1964. The original provisions giving the state church system a constitutional basis remain in force, although the interpretation of these provisions has changed. In 1994, a new paragraph stating that the basic human rights are to be respected was included.

CONSTITUTIONAL HISTORY

Norway as a political entity emerged after the struggle of the Norwegian kings (especially Harald I and Olav II) from the ninth and 10 century C.E. to unify the country, which until then had been divided among several chiefs. During the union with Denmark (1381–1814 C.E.), Norway was under the rule of the Danish king and seemed little more than a Danish province. However, it was agreed from the beginning that Norway should be respected as its own legal and political entity.

It is a common understanding in Norwegian constitutional law and legal history that the country upheld its status as a separate state or kingdom despite its actual dependence on Denmark. This self-understanding grew stronger during the 18th century and the Napoleonic wars that followed (1807–14). When the Danish king agreed, at the Treaty of Kiel in 1814, to give Norway to the Swedish king in compensation for his sacrifices, the deal was not accepted by the leading Norwegian public officials. They decided first to devise a constitution for the Kingdom of Norway and then to decide—as an independent country—on the relationship with Sweden.

The constitution was drafted by a committee headed by Christian Magnus Falsen at Eidsvoll. Some of the drafters had been strongly influenced by Enlightenment ideas during their studies at the University of Copenhagen at the end of the 18th century. The elements of human rights, the principle of separation of powers, and the democratic ideals that are to be found in the original 1814 constitution can be understood against this background. The French, English, and American constitutions all influenced the makers of the constitution, which is today the oldest written European constitution still in use.

Although the monarchy was retained, the constitution established a national assembly (Storting) directly elected by the citizens. The national assembly was given legislative power and the authority to decide on taxation and the state budget. The establishment of the Storting was the clearest break with absolute monarchy, which had been introduced in Denmark and Norway in 1661. This new body was inspired by the idea of the sovereignty of the people, which spurred the very process of drafting a constitution.

During the union with Sweden, from 1814–1905, the power balance of the different constitutional bodies changed, thanks to continuous political tension between Swedish rulers and Norwegian politicians and public officials. The personal power and legal competence of the king were largely reduced, while more power accrued to the prime minister and the administration. The introduction of parliamentarianism during the last decades of the 19th century reduced the powers of the administration, making it dependent for legitimacy on the elected Storting instead of the king.

In 1905, the Norwegian parliament prime minister, and government broke with the Swedish king, refusing to accept his decision not to promulgate an important law passed by the Storting. This "quiet revolution," which effectively ended the union with Sweden, was supported by the Norwegian citizens in a referendum by an overwhelming vote of 370,000 to 187. In another referendum the same year, the Norwegian people decided (260,000 to 70,000) to welcome the Danish Prince Carl (who later took the name Haakon VII) as king of the independent Kingdom of Norway, instead of changing to a republican system.

Parliament remained the most powerful political and constitutional body throughout the 20th century, although this situation has not been reflected by changes in the written constitution. The role of the judiciary has also departed from the explicit wording of the constitution, to a large extent because of new interpretations of the constitution and the division of power. For example, it has been widely accepted since the late 19th century that the Supreme Court has the formal power to set aside laws that are not in compliance with the constitution. In practice, Supreme Court has been reluctant to use its powers of judicial review, preferring to harmonize questionable laws with the constitution by means of interpretation.

FORM AND IMPACT OF THE CONSTITUTION

Norway has a written constitution. It is codified in one single document, the Constitution of 1814. The 1814 constitution has been changed by amendments, by new interpretation of existing provisions, and by the development of customary constitutional law and other unwritten conventions and norms. All changes in the written constitution are made in a language resembling that of the original text of 1814, making it difficult for the public to distinguish between the original and new articles.

In addition to the written text, there exists a set of unwritten rules of constitutional order, so-called customary constitutional law. Many fundamental rights guarantees derive from this unwritten tradition, including the principle of legality (the rule of law) and freedom of association of political parties. Parliamentarism, the obligation of the administration to leave office if it loses the confidence of the parliament, is also found as a rule of customary constitutional law.

The unwillingness to make major revision in the written constitution or to make a new constitution might, on the one hand, have contributed to the strong position of the constitution in the legal and political fields, as well as in the mind of the citizens, as a national symbol. On the other hand, the increasing gap between the written constitution and the material constitution (taking all established conventions and customs into consideration) might in the long run also threaten the legitimacy of the written constitution. For example, the role of the monarch has changed in the same period to such an extent that several of the paragraphs in the constitution are quite misleading. Many references to "the king" are now taken to refer to the administration.

The Norwegian legal system is dualistic. This means that the national legal system and the system of international law have been seen as separate systems, so that international law has no direct impact on national law. International law has to be implemented explicitly into national law to have a more direct impact.

The international treaty with the most extensive direct legal impact on Norway was the 1992 agreement signed, together with other members of the European Free Trade Association (EFTA), with the European Union (EU) to create the European Economic Area (EEA). Under the treaty, as it has been interpreted and implemented, much of EU legislation has entered into Norwegian national legislation, even though Norway is not an EU member state and hence has little influence in shaping the many new laws and directives that are to be implemented as a consequence of the EEA treaty. Norway is a member of the North Atlantic Treaty Organization (NATO).

BASIC ORGANIZATIONAL STRUCTURE

The Norwegian state is centralistic, but with a rather developed system of local and regional self-governance. As of 2004, there were 434 municipalities in Norway, each with an elected municipal council and a local administration. The ideal stated in the Municipality Act is that the municipalities should enjoy a large degree of independence from the state administration, limited only by their law-given duties. The practical freedom of action of the municipalities is also manifested by their budgets, which are decided by the state. In addition to the municipalities, there are 19 regional counties with their own administration. The powers of the county and municipal councils for self-government have been delegated from the state and are set out in legislation, not in the constitution. The principle of local self-governance has been, however, deeply rooted in the political tradition, since the Municipality Act was first introduced in 1837.

LEADING CONSTITUTIONAL PRINCIPLES

According to the constitution (Article 112), no changes to the constitution can be made if they conflict with its "spirit and principles." This provision has been interpreted to refer, for example, to Article 1, which states that Norway is a free, independent, indivisible state, with a hereditary monarchy. Although the constitution normally speaks of the "king," it also provides that the monarch can be a queen.

However, even if monarchy is a principle, there are many other leading principles of the (written or unwritten) constitution that have undermined the power of the monarch. The very character of the monarchy has changed. Today, the monarch has mainly symbolic functions.

Norway is a democratic constitutional monarchy with a parliamentarian system of governance; the source of legitimacy for both law and governance is the will of the people, expressed mainly in parliamentary elections. The constitutional system, as expressed in the written constitution and by customary constitutional law, is also built upon the principle of division of power among the legislative, the executive, and the judiciary.

The state is also generally bound by the principles of the rule of law. This concept is partly expressed in the constitution and underlined by other legislation, for example, concerning the practices of the different levels of state administration.

In addition to these democratic values and principles, some argue that the constitutional provisions on the status of the Evangelical-Lutheran religion as the "official religion of the state" (Article 2, 2) gives the constitution—and hence the state—a foundation in Christian values. This may be true at a historical or symbolic level, but the Supreme Court has underlined that the religious foundation of the state does not put any legal boundaries on the freedom of the Parliament or other constitutional bodies in their general decision making. It is only in decisions concerning the activities of the state church itself ("the church of Norway") that the norms of this church must be taken into account.

CONSTITUTIONAL BODIES

The main constitutional bodies are the Parliament (Storting); the Council of State, which is the administration including the prime minister; the king; and the judiciary.

The Parliament (Storting)

The Norwegian national assembly has served as the highest political body in Norway since the introduction of parliamentarianism in 1884. Elections to the Storting are held every four years, and mandates are distributed according to a system of proportional representation. The Storting comprises 165 elected deputies, all representing a party. It is a modified unicameral parliament: When it is exercising legislative functions, it is divided into two chambers, the Odelsting (three-fourths) and the Lagting (one-fourth), with relatively equal powers. The Storting nominates the members of the Odelsting and the Lagting at its first session after general elections.

The Administration and the King

According to the constitution, the king has the executive power, but in practice the prime minister on behalf of the Council of State, the administration, serves as the executive power. The administration's most important functions are to submit bills and budget proposals to the Storting and to implement decisions through the ministries. The administration has its democratic basis in the Storting and is headed by the prime minister. Formally speaking, it is the monarch who asks the head of the party that can get majority support in Parliament to form the administration. Decisions of the administration are formally made by the monarch in council (that is, jointly approved by the monarch and the Council of State, which is the administration) every Friday. All royal decrees must be signed by the monarch and countersigned by the prime minister.

The Lawmaking Process

Bills introduced by the administration are submitted first to the Odelsting and thereafter to the Lagting. Members of Parliament can also present suggestions for new laws or legal revision. State budgets and amendments to the constitution are dealt with in the plenary assembly. Amendments to the constitution require a two-thirds majority vote, but otherwise a simple majority is sufficient.

The Judiciary

The ordinary courts of law in Norway consist of the Supreme Court of Justice (Høyesterett), the Interlocutory Appeals Committee of the Supreme Court (Høyesteretts kjöremålsutvalg), the courts of appeal (lagmannsrettene), the district courts (tingrett), and the conciliation courts (forliksrådet), as well as several special courts.

Norway is divided into six territorial jurisdictions and 15 judicial districts. There is no constitutional court. However, the Supreme Court is able to declare void a statute passed by the Storting if it is found to be in contradiction of the constitution. The judiciary is an independent branch of government. This status is underlined by the way judges are appointed and by the tasks and competence of the judiciary. For example, the constitution was amended in 2003 to ensure the independence of the Supreme Court by prohibiting judges of this court to serve simultaneously as elected members of Parliament. All judges are public servants who cannot be fired, a provision that also helps secure their independence.

THE ELECTION PROCESS AND POLITICAL PARTICIPATION

The participation of the people in the political sphere takes place both through direct elections and through their membership in organizations. Election turnout is usually in the vicinity of 80 percent. General suffrage for men was introduced in 1898 and for women in 1913. The age of majority to be entitled to vote was originally 25 but has been reduced step by step and is currently 18.

POLITICAL PARTIES

Norway has a multiparty system with more than 30 registered parties, of which about one-third are currently represented in the Parliament. Only the Supreme Court can ban a political party, according to certain established criteria.

CITIZENSHIP

Citizenship can be acquired by birth or upon application. A child whose mother is a Norwegian citizen has the right to Norwegian citizenship. Foreigners can apply for Norwegian citizenship according to rules given by law. Citizenship can also be lost according to rules given by law.

FUNDAMENTAL RIGHTS

Among the few basic human rights that were referred to in the original 1814 constitution were freedom of expression, property rights, freedom from torture, and the principle of rule of law in criminal matters. The right to religious freedom was included in 1964, at the 150th anniversary of the constitution. Later, the right to work and the rights of the Sami people were included in a new Article 110.

Since Norway's accession in 1956 to the 1950 European Convention on Human Rights and Fundamental Freedoms, international law in general, and human rights case law from the European Court of Human Rights in particular, has gained an increasingly important role both in constitutional law and in other fields of national law. Norway has ratified all the major United Nations (UN) Human Rights Conventions; in 1994, a new provision that calls on the state to respect and ensure human rights was added to the constitution (in new paragraph 110 c). That article requires that the main human rights treaties be implemented into national legislation by a new law. Such a "human rights law" went into force in 1999. By this law, the 1950 European Human Rights Convention (ECHR) and the two major UN Human Rights conventions of 1966 were incorporated into national legislation. This Human Rights Act did not officially give these conventions a constitutional status. It did, however, state that the conventions should prevail over other legislation if conflicts arise.

Some argue that the human rights conventions have a status between the constitution and other national legislation. Other legal experts have claimed that it is neither possible—nor desirable—to give human rights laws superior status to other legislation without making them part of the constitution. The fact that the Human Rights Act can be changed by Parliament with a regular majority vote (and not a two-thirds majority, as for constitutional changes) clearly shows that it does not have constitutional status.

Impact and Functions of Fundamental Rights

Despite the lack of constitutional status of the human rights conventions, the Supreme Court has in several decisions referred to international human rights provisions, in particular those of the ECHR. In some recent decisions, Norwegian legal provisions have been interpreted so that they are in compliance with the relevant articles of the ECHR. In several Supreme Court decisions, especially after 1999 when the new Human Rights Act came into force, the court referred also to the case law of the European Court of Human Rights, stating that this was a legal source that the court had to take into account.

Limitations to Fundamental Rights

Limitations to fundamental rights in Norway are themselves based on the provisions of the international human rights conventions that Norway has ratified and incorporated in national legislation. Any limitations are based on the need to protect other people's fundamental rights or to protect public morals, order, or health. They must be in accord with the practices of any democratic society. The principle of proportionality must be taken into consideration.

National legislation includes specific limitation provisions. For example, parents' rights are limited in certain areas by provisions that aim to protect the child. This can be relevant if parents refuse to accept medical treatment for a child who is seriously ill. Legislation and court rulings have also dealt with conflicts of rights, for example, in relation to women's rights, on the one hand, and the right to freedom of religion or belief, on the other.

ECONOMY

Apart from stating the budgetary and taxation powers of the parliament, as well as the right to property and the right to work for citizens, the constitution does not give any guidelines for the economic system of Norway. The comprehensive welfare state system that has been developed in Norway, in particular since World War II (1939–45), has no clear constitutional basis, but rather depends on the political will of the majority in each new Parliament. Numerous state regulations and an active welfare policy through legislation and other political decisions, combined with a market economy, make it reasonable to describe the actual Norwegian economic system as a social market economy.

RELIGIOUS COMMUNITIES

According to the constitution, the king is the formal head of the state church, the Church of Norway, and is bound to protect and support this church. The monarch must ensure that the religious leaders of the church are teaching according to the Evangelical-Lutheran religion. The monarch, as well as (at least) half of the cabinet ministers, is obliged to "confess" the Evangelical-Lutheran religion. This is interpreted as a duty to be a member of the Church of Norway (the state church). The monarch, together with those cabinet ministers who are members of the church, makes decisions in certain important matters of church doctrine. One might say that this function is performed by the monarch and ministers as head of the church, and not as head of state.

Legal and political developments in recent decades have increased the independence of the elected church bodies of the Church of Norway at national, regional, and local levels, granting the state church a certain degree of autonomy in practice. On the national level, the church still does not have the status of an independent legal person, although the Church Act of 1996 gave that status to the local parishes. Much of the power that lies formally with the monarch as head of the church has been delegated to the elected church bodies. However, it is still "the king" (the monarch together with the church-member ministers) who appoints bishops and deans in the state church. Appointments are based on nominations from the church bodies, but the politicians are not bound to appoint the person who receives the most votes in the church nomination process. Controversial appointments of bishops who did not receive the most church votes have helped intensify the debate on the changed relations between church and state.

Although Norway still has a constitutionally based state church system, the constitution and other legislation clearly state that freedom of religion for all shall be respected. This right is interpreted to include the right both to have and not to have a religious belief, and the right both for individuals and for faith communities to practice according to their belief as long as the rights of others and the laws applying to all are respected.

Despite the priority given to the Church of Norway in the constitution and in certain fields of practice, the Norwegian religiopolitical system is also based on the principle of equal treatment. For example, the Faith Communities Act of 1969 states that all religious communities have the right to receive the same financial support per member per year as the state church receives from the state and municipal budget per member per year. From 1981, this right has also been applied by law to nonreligious "life stance" communities, in practice mainly the Secular Humanist Association.

While the state church is seen as a public law institution, all other faith and life stance communities have a nonpublic status. They can choose whether they want to be registered or not.

MILITARY DEFENSE AND STATE OF EMERGENCY

The constitution declares that the king is the head of the Norwegian military and hence makes decisions concerning the defense forces. The minister of defense, rather than the prime minister, countersigns the monarch's decisions in matters concerning the military.

In states of emergency such as war or similar situations, constitutional provisions can be set aside. The constitutional emergency provisions were further developed in the Emergency Act of 1950.

AMENDMENTS TO THE CONSTITUTION

According to Article 112 of the constitution, the constitution itself can be changed only by a qualified majority vote of two-thirds of Parliament. It also declares that constitutional changes never must undermine the "spirit and principles" of the constitution. This provision has been interpreted to refer, for example, to Article 1 of the constitution, which states that Norway is a free, independent, indivisible state.

PRIMARY SOURCES

Constitution in English. Available online. URL: http://odin.dep.no/odin/engelsk/norway/system/032005-990424/index-dok000-b-f-a.html. Accessed on August 28, 2005.

Constitution in Norwegian. Available online. URL: http://www.lovdata.no/all/nl-18140517-000.html. Accessed on August 15, 2005.

SECONDARY SOURCES

Johs Andenæs, *Statsforfatningen i Norge [The Norwegian Constitution].* Oslo: Universitetsforlaget, 2004.

Mads T. Andenæs and Ingeborg Wilberg, *The Constitution of Norway: A Commentary.* Oslo: Universitetsforlaget, 1987.

Jan Helgesen, "The Constitution of the Kingdom of Norway." In *Constitutional and Administrative Law,* edited by Eivind Smith. Oslo: University of Oslo, The Faculty of Law, 1996.

Per Helset and Bjørn Stordrange: *Norsk statsforfatningsrett [Norwegian Constitutional Law].* Oslo: Ad Notam Gyldendal AS, 1998.

Eivind Smith, *Stat og rett: Artikler i utvalg 1980–2001 [State and Law: Selected articles 1980–2001].* Oslo: Universitetsforlaget, 2002.

Ingvill Thorson Plesner